AN AIRMAN'S STORY

Dr. Rene H. Contreras

PublishAmerica
Baltimore

Softcover 9781462669677
PUBLISHED BY PUBLISHAMERICA, LLLP
www.publishamerica.com
Baltimore

Printed in the United States of America

Dedication

I dedicate this book to my wife that at an early age joined me through my military journey. Like me without knowing the true sacrifice that, it would take for our small family during three decades of service to our nation. Second to my mother and both of my grandmothers that helped me become the adult and family man. Where Darlene's strong love for life and her family made all of Hubert's dreams come true after a humble start and being raised by a single mother.

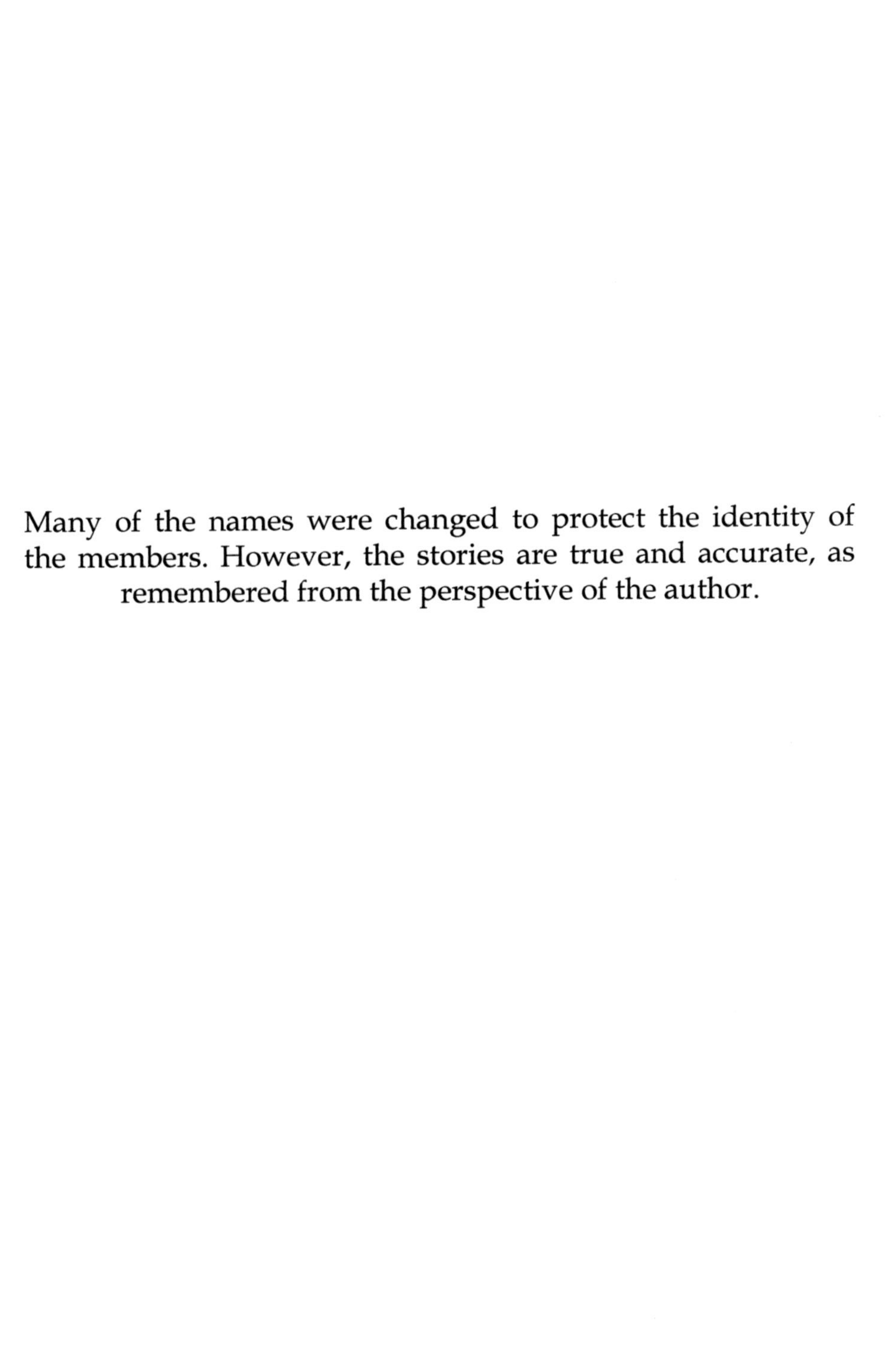
Many of the names were changed to protect the identity of the members. However, the stories are true and accurate, as remembered from the perspective of the author.

PROLOGUE

This book reveals the life of a young man, Hubert Contreras and his life once he enlisted in the United States Air Force (USAF), and how he worked his way through the ranks eventually becoming a Lieutenant Colonel. Towards the end of his military career, Hubert could have taken the jobs that would have given his Colonel but instead decided to pursue a doctoral degree. He declined the offers due to family considerations in order to pursue his doctoral degree. It was towards the end of the Vietnam War and the draft was still ongoing when Hubert as a senior in High School signed up in the United States (US) Air Force under the Delayed Entry Program.

Hubert would enlist in 1972 in the USAF under the Delayed Entry Program in a year after he graduated from High School in order to avoid the draft and not to enter the US Army. Under the agreement, Hubert would report on active duty a year later to Basic Training after taking the oath two mouth's prior in Phoenix, Arizona. Hubert had known too many of his friends in High School that he gone and returned from Vietnam that were no longer the same individuals or had returned in coffins to a nations that called them "baby killers".

Raised by a legal Mexican immigrant that knew more about America than anyone he ever met to be a proud America, he believed that it was his duty was to serve his country. Hubert's post-Vietnam experiences would serve him well once the US entered hostile environments in Latin America, Korea, Panama, Haiti, the Balkans, throughout the Middle-East including Saudi Arabia, Bahrain, Kuwait, Iraq, Afghanistan, and many other areas. Raised in Tucson, Arizona,Hubert would enter a new world as a naïve young man and would soon be referred as a "baby killer" for having the privilege of wearing the US Air Force uniform.

"Do you mind serving as the President for the youth activities?" asked the Ward President", which is a leadership role in the Mormon church. Hubert had grown up in the 1970s while in High School growing up as a young man who had gone to church nearly daily until the events of a young man led to his decision to join the Air Force. This story starts during High School and the events that led to early 1974 when he enlisted as an airman basic, the early life as a newlywed, and the early days in uniform. This sacrifice eventually led to commissioning as an Air Force Officer and higher ranks.

"Now I know what love at first sight is," thought Hubert to himself as he stared at Darlene, his new wife that he married after seeing her at his friends wedding then waiting for her to graduating from High School and knowing her for 72-hours. Like many young men, he was lucky to meet a woman who would allow him to mature as his ego many times affected his actions. Hubert's friends had taken bets that this marriage would not last for six months. Although Hubert was four years older, with both having strong, his young wife allowed Hubert to grow up over time as he made many vain mistakes that only age and maturity could change.

There is nothing fare about serving in the US Air Force (USAF) when it pertains to its political climate. During Hubert's military career, he experienced the Black, Gender, and the beginning of the Gay movements where each group used their base as a political weapon. On the other hand, as a Mexican American serving in the Air Force, Hubert had to work twice as hard to receive the same treatment than the average Air Force member as an officer. As an enlisted member, the promotion culture is different because an individual is promoted mainly through testing while in the officer ranks, promotions are based on politics.

Time was passing so fast they both thought by the time Hubert completed his final deployment to the Middle East. During this deployment, Hubert traveled from Qatar to Kuwait, Bahrain, Iraq, Cairo, and Afghanistan fixing countless wartime operational problems. This young couple had to live on a small Air Force salary that took a lot of sacrifice and love. With time, each rank meant the life would in some ways easier, but in other ways, more difficult.

TABLE OF CONTENTS

CHAPTER 1

STAFF SERGEANT

As a good student at Amphitheater High School in Tucson, Arizona, Hubert played football, and ran on the track team. Although Hubert fitted well with the rest of the jocks, he typically chose to stand-up for anyone who lacked physical talents or protect students that others picked on. He never forgot the days in elementary school when bullies picked on him because he stayed to himself.

Since Hubert fitted well with the High School,geeks and he loved learning and much as he loved sports, he regularly found himself protecting the schools geeks who were all his friends. One such friend would become a weight lifter because of Hubert even though he lacked coordination. Nevertheless, Hubert gave 'Hotrock' all the support and protection that he needed to excel in gym.

Being born the forth of six children to Jose and Olga Contreras would allow Hubert an early opportunity to grow in a large family. At the same time, being the fourth child meant that although loved, no one paid him much attention since he was not the oldest or the youngest child. His mother Olga would be the primary person in his life who would influence the man Hubert grew up believing that his mother was more of a man than his father would ever be, as he saw her worked day and night to provide for her family. For Olga served as the mother and father in his family and was always there when needed. Even though Olga was born to an affluent Mexican family, she refused to go back to her family in Mexico for help at any time in her adult life. Olga met Jose when her father sent her off to Nogales, which was a border town in Southern Arizona.

Olga grew up in the family ranch in Obregon, Mexico and finished college at the early age of fifteen and as the oldest of 12th children. Unfortunately, a female meant in the Spanish culture meant that although she was the oldest child and the smartest child, she was not male and would not inherit the family ranch. Instead, she the expectation was that she marries the man that her father selected for her without question. However, her father raised her to run the business from an early age, took her with him to America on all his trips to Texas, and met her United States (US) cousins. That made her strong willed and opinionated and not the typical woman of her era.

Her mother Marie was the first of seven Mormon wives and her family genealogy tree was full of Mexican history. Her father would travel between Houston, Texas and Obregon to visit his family that had moved to the US in the 1800s as Swedish immigrants. Since Marie was the first wife and a Mexican native, this did not go well with Olga's father family. Except for Olga, none of her brothers and sisters would every meet their American cousins since they were Mexicans. Olga like her father was white skinned with green eyes and looked like her American Great Grandmother, which was why her father took her to Texas. Olga would travel with her father to Texas and California to meet her American family. Later, she would travel to Michigan to a family reunion to meet her entire American family who all accepted her.

It did not matter that like Olga's father Narciso Smith-Parra, his mother had married the local ranch hand in Texas against her father's orders. In the Spanish culture, the children take the mothers surname. Grandmother Marie's father was a Spanish Army Officer assigned in Mexico, which gave Olga dual citizenship in Spain and Mexico. During that era, three brothers were Generals in the Spanish Army and the Spanish military deployed two to Mexico and one to Colombia. Olga also had dual citizenship when her father sent her to live with his sister in Nogales, Mexico. Years later, Olga would always say that this is why Hubert joined the military especially when she found a picture of her great grandfather in the Mexican history book and Hubert looked just like him.

Olga had taken her American grandmothers clear freckled skin color, her green eyes, and bright red hair. Even when Olga crossed the border in Nogales, Arizona, no one would have thought that she not a 'Gringa' unless someone asked her to speak since she did not speak any English. However, since she was a radiant beauty, her smile was her only requirement in getting across the border each time she went shopping in the American side even though she had a passport. She had a passport since the age of five when she first started traveling to Texas with her father. She missed receiving the passport stamps as they did when she was a small girl in her passport book.

As a young eighteen-year-old woman with a strong will like her father, her father had already selected her mate and she refused to marry him. As an embarrassment to her family, she had to live with an aunt in Nogales, Mexico after refusing to marry the man her father picked for her to marry. In Nogales while living with her aunt, she met Jose who had just returned from Germany and World War II (WW-II). Olga instantly fell in love with the US Army uniform and the dark haired man that wore the clothing. While shopping with her American female cousin in the US side of the border, they reminisced about his recent WW-II experiences.

"Hey brother, what the heck are you doing here?" asked Jose. His brother Jesus like him received a two-week R&R (rest and relaxation) from WW-II. Jesus received a field commission to second lieutenant but on this RR trip, he would lose his commission when a senior Officer stopped with his young brother Jose over his shoulder. Alcohol had a lot to do with his judgment but after four invasion tours; Jesus was a veteran with little tolerance for Senior Officers that wanted to make a name as a war hero.

As a young teen, Hubert had heard from his father Jose stories of when he was in WW-II and stationed in Germany. Especially when he was near the Rhine River and his division was camped on one side and a second division was camped on the opposite side. During the night, a fellow soldier and Jose took off for a local German village to drink and upon returning were too drunk so they decided to sleep it off under the bridge. During the night, German snipers cut the throats of most division soldiers except the two drunken soldiers, saving their lives. Later in the month, an enemy howitzer blast almost killed Hubert's father. After six months, the US Army put him in the new Tucson Veterans Administration (VA) that was still under construction. At the time, Jose received notice that he would never walk again. Upon Jesus' separation from the Army, went to the VA and told his brother to get his butt off the bed and stop feeling sorry for himself. He reminded Jose how before the war he dreamed on running in the Olympics. Within a month, he slowly started walking again. Jose never claimed disability like millions of WW-II veterans.

"He is so handsome," mentioned Olga to first cousin. Later her cousin would marry a politician who would become a state senator. Olga would help him while trying to go to Washington. Jose had just returned from WW-II where he served in Germany. Jose was still in his US Army uniform and to Olga looked like a model. Her knight in shinny Armor took her in her arms, as her dark haired Latin lover quickly swept her off her feet. Within a week, Olga and Jose eloped. For years, Olga and Jose lived close to his family in the west side of Tucson. The entire family moved to Tucson after living in Bisbee most of their lives. Jose purchased a business, drove the bus to the mine, and then worked a shift at the mine as a miner so was providing well for his family.

For years, they lived the American dream until one day Jose come home and told Olga that he needed to find himself. At this point, as a couple, they had purchased a home and had a successful business together. However, after having six children, Jose left Olga and never paid one cent in child support. Although the court ordered Jose to pay child support, he never paid a cent and Olga never went to court to force him to pay. Within ten years and the time Jose left his family, Olga would be the mother of six young children. She never stopped loving Jose and did not give him a divorce until her children were all grown up. Olga was too proud to go back home to her father's ranch and instead raised her children while she worked two jobs for the rest of her life. Along the way, Olga had many friends that were in politics and during Hubert's senior year in High School, she proudly served at the Democratic Convention as an Arizona Delegate.

Within week's they wed without any family present. It would be years before Olga's father would welcome him to his family. After all, although he was an American, he not a "Gringo" since his skin not while as his. Years later, Hubert would not understand why she did not accept his bride when he brought Darlene home to meet his family. Olga had wanted her son to marry a Mexican woman and not a "Grinda." Maybe the way her Texas family treated her impacted how she felt but it still did not made sense to him.

Like many towns that were in the verge of growing into a small city, Tucson in the late 1960s or early 1970s was a combination of the old southwest and changing its surroundings to one of the north as more retirees moved into the city limits. Yet, Tucson was still a friendly place where most individuals would say good morning or make small talk as they passed each other on the downtown sidewalks. Downtown was still thriving as Woolworth and the clothing stores had their mannequins with the latest fashions. Congress had two theaters across from each other named Fox and the Paramount theaters.

Another important street was Fourth Street, which ran from north to south. Fourth street had mainly small stores that all started in the early 1940s and 1950s or earlier. Here too was the Baptist Church that Hubert and his brother Timmy would go on Sundays. The Baptist Minister gave them each a bag of cookies for attending Bible Study. This was the first time that Hubert learned something different that was not Roman Catholic where Olga took her children. The Baptist service was later in the afternoon so Hubert and Timmy were able to go to their regular Catholic service in the morning, as Olga demanded.

Here is where Hubert first went to bible study and started learning many Bible stories of the Old Testament. Years later, the City of Tucson tore down Fourth Street to build the Tucson Convention Center and its large parking lot. A large part of Tucson's history lost forever during an era when life in Tucson was simple. Where an entire neighborhood that stood a hundred year of Tucson history, received emphasis by the new young elected city council and changed it to a large parking lot that remained empty most of the time in the name of progress.

After Hubert's mother separated from her husband, she would refuse help from her family. Hubert's father Jose left Tucson so that he did not have to pay child support. Olga refused to take welfare and worked two jobs so that she could raise her family of six children without any help from the state, her husband, and her family. Then after working her second job, Olga would make burritos and sell them at the local bars in an effort to make extra gas and lunch money for her young family. Hubert would always help Olga prepare the burritos especially at times when Olga was running late from work. Hubert would start cooking the meat and start preparing the burritos for his mother. It never entered his mind why his two older sisters and older brother never helped but they were always ready to ask for money from her burro's profits.

In the early 1960s, Hubert's father left his family to find himself without providing any financial assistance. However,

Hubert's mother Olga would not divorce her husband for another twenty-eight years for her children would have a father even if solely in name. Since Olga grew up in Mexico to a privileged family, she believed that one's family was everything important. When it came to marrying, the man that her father had chosen for her, as was the custom, Olga rebelled and her refusal meant she would leave her home and life in Nogales, Mexico with an aunt. It was during one of her trips to go dancing that she met Jose in Nogales. Twenty-eight years later when all of Olga's children were finally grown up and out of the house, she finally filed for a divorce.

Throughout those years, Jose would visit his children and take them out to the park on the drive-in. Nevertheless, Hubert would never forget each school event that he had to make excuses for a missing father. Olga never spoke badly of her husband and remained friends with him for the sake of her children. Jose would pick up his children for a day and take them for a ride in his car. Many times, go riding on back roads where the small roads had many hills and the children felt like they were on roller coasters. Eating bags of candy, that Jose purchased his children prior to their ride on the back roads. Returning the children home, where they knew that they would not see daddy for months or maybe years.

Every memory that Hubert had of his mother consisted of Olga waking up in the dark to go to work and coming home in the dark after a long day of work. Hubert also remembered that his mother always had a smile on her face and told her children that if they worked hard, that they would have the American dream. She kept telling her children that they could achieve anything as long as they were willing to work for their dreams. Olga was full of life and passionate for the life that America offered.

Even though she lost a life of luxury, that she was accustomed to in Mexico at an early age to work for everything that her family had in America, she loved her new adopted country.

Because she was too proud to return to Mexico when left penniless. Like many divorcees, the court gave her the house with the mortgage that she could not afford and eventually lost. In a few months, Olga would start renting for the next two decades when she would finally be able to purchase her own first house. Like all true immigrants, she worked for everything that she received in America and refused to take any welfare from the US government. She would tell her children stories of America that the US history books failed to cover. As an avid reader, Olga loved reading and even though she worked two jobs per day, she still made time for reading American history, economics, and US political books.

Family was always important to Hubert since every child memory consisted of a family event of his mother or mothers parent where he lived in Mexico for a year prior to starting school. Hubert returned to the US prior to start kindergarten school at the Saint Augustine School in downtown Tucson, Arizona. Years later Saint Augustine would move to east Tucson and become a High School but in the 1960s, classes consisted of kindergarten to 12th grade. At that time Hubert's Grandpa (mother's father) had a local grocery story in Obregon, Sonora in Mexico where Hubert spent every summer. It was there where Hubert first learned to work from his grandfather.

Hubert's family beliefs are mainly due on how who raised him, which were the women in his life. Experts suggest that within the child's first six years, what they learn in this short period affects their future development. All Grandparents love their grandchildren and spend time with them. The most important individuals that affected Hubert's future development during those years were Hubert's mother, and both Grandparents. Regularly holding picnics making sure all family members stayed together as a single-family entity. Until Hubert joined the Air Force, he was with family members and influenced by a grandmother or his mother.

In Tucson, Nana (grandmother) Maria lived near where Hubert and all his brothers and sisters were born at the Saint Mary's Hospital. Nana Maria was the typical grandmother who was a short woman who was always in the kitchen cooking for her grandchildren. Just down the road on Silver Bill Road, was their first house where their German Shepard dog would escort them to school and back until he passed away. Olga would keep the house when Jose divorced her but she would not be able to keep it because she could not afford the mortgage payment. That is when she found the house on Linda Street so that her children could continue going to Menlo Park Elementary School. Nana Maria was always in her grandchildren's lives making sure Grandpa Joaquin brought them to her for a visit on weekends. She also made sure Grandpa Joaquin (father's father) purchase her babies anything they wanted.

She would be the center of her family keeping all her children of three boys and three boys together. With regular family outings or families taking turns visiting their momma in her tiny house as she cooked their favorite meal. For Nana Maria was always cooking for someone with a smile and always hugging her family. Telling them stories of the old days of when Grandpa Joaquin had his ranch before he lost it because he was too stubborn to pay taxes when he became an American. Grandpa Joaquin was always at work and sometime Hubert would go with him. As a lumberjack, he sold wood throughout the city and did odd jobs. Even though he was in his sixties at the time, one would think that he was much younger physically.

Once the US purchased Southern Arizona the Gadsden Purchase where Grandpa Joaquin and Nana Maria's ranch fell, they became Americans and were no longer Mexican citizens. Hubert Heard stories of how by the US Senate on April 25, 1854 and signed by President Franklin Pierce, with final approval action taken by Mexico on June 8, 1854. Nana Maria would tell them stories of how Grandpa Joaquin inherited his ranch from his father. Nana Maria told stories of how the family ranch had been in the family for over a hundred years and before the Mexican Civil War. Grandpa Joaquin's father fought in the Mexican Civil War and knew Pancho Villa as a friend.

However, as the tax collectors kept coming to collect the taxes each year, he refused to pay the taxes as they kept increasing saying that he was never asked to be part of America. Besides, his sons were both overseas fighting for the America, now a US citizen paying taxes in a country forced to be a citizen. It was World War II (WWII) and his oldest son was in Europe after serving in Africa. Jose his youngest son forged his birth certificate to joint his brother so Joaquin thought that he had already given his adopted country enough. Later Maria (Nana) and Joaquin had a son Edward and the family moved to Tucson.

During that time, it was the last major territorial acquisition in the contiguous United States adding a large area to the United States, and Maria and Joaquin became Americans. The purchase included lands south of the Gila River and west of the Rio Grande. The Gadsden Purchase was for the purpose of the America's construction of a transcontinental railroad along a deep southern route. Grandpa's and Nana's ranch fell in the town of Bisbee, which was in the Gadsden area. This is where Hubert's father Jose grew up until he entered the Air Force and moved to Tucson once he married Olga. Once Grandpa Joaquin and Nana Maria lost their ranch, they too, moved to Tucson where Grandpa Joaquin worked selling wood and doing odd jobs. They moved near two of their children, one of their daughter who live a block away and Jose who live two miles south on Silver Bell Road.

After Nana Maria passed away, Hubert would live with his for a few months. Each day, Grandpa Joaquin would go through his coins and put the old coins in one jar and the newer coins in a different jar. This would be how Hubert would become a lifetime coin collector. Although Grandpa Joaquin's coins would go to someone else because Hubert was in Mexico when he passed away and not to him as he promised, in time Hubert continued Grandpa Joaquin's coin collecting tradition. Since only he was the only grandchild that would spend time with his grandpa going over the coins for hours and talk about their age and their quality as they explored for coins.

In Mexico, Grandma Marie's house consisted of the main house, which was typical of most homes of the day. Then there was a large garden willed with fruit trees and a second house where Grandpa Parra also had a work area. At one end of the workspace was a large window that opened to the fields. It was there that Grandpa Parra's rocker was located and where Hubert would take his bottle collection for payment. Hubert's first paying job occurred when Grandpa Parra suggested that he go around the neighborhood collecting empty bottles, clean them, and them bring them to him for payment. Since Grandpa Parra owned a grocery store, he would purchase the empty bottles from Hubert.

This gave Hubert His first vacation spending money that he earned on his own. He would also go with his younger brother and cousins and pick cotton. As a cotton picker, once the bag was full of cotton, the cotton picker took the bag, weighed and payment received. Sometimes, the boys would put tiny rocks in the bags so that the bags would weigh more. However, Hubert would be one of the boys that would decline on doing this type of behavior. Therefore, he tended to earn less money when they went cotton picking. Normally, after a few hours when the boys had earned the amount of monies that they wanted to earn, they would walk back or try to get a ride back into city since the cotton fields were miles out of the city. Many times the boys would get a ride in one of the flatbed trucks used by the farmers to sell the vegetables or watermelons when they took them to market.

"Momma, can we go to the movies, this week?" asked Hubert. When times were good, Hubert's mother would drop all her six children each Saturday at one of the theaters with enough to get a candy or small popcorn and a small coke for everyone. The Beatle's movie titled "Help" was showing at the Fox and the line of excited fans had lined up for over a half mile. At the Paramount, Hubert had seen the sound of music during a school field trip as he experienced his first crush on Julie Andrews. During a class field trip, Hubert and his class saw the "The Sound of Music" at the Paramount Theater for the first time.

"I like the tractor," yelled Hubert. As was the annual custom, Olga's landlord on Linda Street each year just before Christmas brought his children's old toys for the Contreras family. This year was special with the three-wheeled green tractor that each of the Contreras family took turns riding. Olga asked Hubert not to help her with the tractor in the garden since he was killing her vegetables. Another year, Hubert received a rifleman's rifle that he used during one of his cowboy's and Indian wars at the local San Xavier River after a heavy rain. Hubert would never forget the day when they almost drowned. While walking by the riverbank, the sides gave and both fell into the river until Hubert and Timmy were able to grab the roots of a tree. At that point, their older sister pulled both of them out of the river saving their lives.

"Mom, is this our car?" yelled all the Contreras children. The month prior, Olga had purchased a new car with a touch button on the column, which was an automatic transmission. Although the new green car was over a decade old, to the Contreras' it was a new family car. The entire family felt that they were rich since they had a new vehicle. Now Olga did not have to take the bus every day to work. The family was still using the iron stove for cooking, which required wood. There were plenty of dry tree branches around to put into the iron stove. After going for over six months without electricity, the year would end well thanks to kind friends and neighbors.

Strangely, in the late 1960s, downtown Tucson had seen an inch of snow that lasted for a few minutes as the hot desert temperatures quickly melted the snow away. Tucson in the early 1970s was a great place for anyone to grow up in and get along with their neighbors. No matter where he walked, everyone was friendly and said good morning to each other as they walked on the sidewalks. Money was always tight for the Contreras family since his parents had divorce when he was only four years old. Somehow, Olga would make extra monies after work by making burritos and selling them at the local bars so that her children would have lunch money and be able to go to the movies on weekends. As a small boy, Hubert would learn how to cook and help his mom cook the meat and make the burritos before his mom arrived from her second job. He never quite understood why his older brothers and sisters were always too busy to help but never asked momma for spending money.

"I think that I'll go home," thought Hubert. It was during recess at Saint Augustine that Hubert saw the back gate open and decided to go home. Unfortunately for him, by the time he arrived home even though the walk was only about a fifteen minute walk, Father Carrillo was waiting with Olga at the front door of his house. Father Carrillo would become Bishop Carrillo and Olga's lifetime friends. After a proper spanking and an hour of kneeling where Hubert had time to think about what he had done, Olga took him to the local 'Conchinta' or Burger Bar. The Conchinta was fashioned in the typical 1950s style burger bar where customers could sit by the bar and the server would bring them their burgers, shakes, or other types of drinks. At the rear was the local pharmacy with a mixture of table and chairs where customers could sit for their meals. The Conchinta also had tacos and a few other Mexican foods.

Hubert's mother Olga was still working two jobs, refusing to take welfare over the years. Olga would always say it is distasteful to take unearned money. At this point, the Contreras family lived on the east side of Congress and although the house wired for electricity, when money was tight they had to go without light for months. Never lacking was Olga's love filled with music and happy memories. Understanding true love during hard times and good times showing Hubert and his siblings what family truly meant. Even on trips to Mexico, Olga would get a Mariachi Band for Grandma Marie each mother's day. It did not matter how tight she was on money, somehow she saved enough money to pay for the Mariachi's for her mother each year on mother's day.

For a while, Olga was the manager of some apartments in the south side of Tucson near the Rodeo Grounds. This allowed Hubert and her other children to help Olga manage the apartments while she worked her other jobs. Eventually a close friend was selling a house in the north side of town and sold it to Olga at a price mainly because he wanted to help her. He also wanted her family start a better life and felt that she deserved a break. Olga had always been blessed with good friends her entire life. Eventually, Olga would pay off her home and sell her home to her youngest son Timmy.

Hubert was attending Ajo Elementary School when his school caught fire. The students attended class split days with half starting early in the morning and half-ending late at night. The school put on a half-day school period when one of Olga's friends asked Olga if Hubert could babysit for her while, she worked in the evenings. Olga left it up to Hubert to decide and Hubert volunteered to help Olga's friend who had a young son who was six years old. For a young boy, Hubert was learning to take on real responsibility.

Eventually, Olga was able to purchase a home on Kelso Street in northern Tucson, which was in a good neighborhood that had one of the best school districts in town. Tucson had less than 300,000 citizens and growing. Olga had met a good property owner who knew she was a struggling single mother of six and allowed her to make affordable house payments when he told Olga that the rent payments were actually house payments. Olga also believed that good things happen to good people who try to be good citizens. Although she was supposed to get alimony payments, she never saw a penny from her ex-husband who was too busy going after women and not worrying about his children.

Hubert was still had his newspaper route and each morning he had to walk half a mile to his friend's house to pick up his papers and start his delivery. Since Hubert did not have a bike since he had just started the route, he would put the newspapers in his sack and walk from house to house until he completed his route and then walked to school. At this point Hubert was only fourteen and took a job on Speedway at the Lion's Grocery store by saying that he was older than he actually was. Since he did not have a car or a bike, he would run to work, which normally took him around two hours as part of his route one way. Hubert would treat this part of his daily workout until he purchased a ten-speed bicycle, stolen and then replace a second time.

Once he arrived at the store, he would go into the store bathroom, wash up with a washrag, and change into his work cloths. Hubert took this job mainly to help Olga until hired at the Pioneer Hotel as a 'busboy', which was much closer to walk. Once he purchased a ten-speed, bicycle, but stolen while Hubert was in class. Even though he had put a chain on his ten-speed, someone cut the chain and stole Hubert's bike. During that era, it was normal for individuals to put identification numbers on their ten-speed bicycles. However, this did not mean that they would eventually receive they bicycles back from the Police if found. If anything, it made them feel, as it was a preventive measure.

At the Lion's Grocery, that Hubert saw many stars that were at the local Old-Tucson Studios. Lee Marvin and his childrenentered the store where he worked. Hubert had already met John Wayne who was a friend of Olga who makes many movies at the Old Tucson Studios.

Hubert only worked at the Lion's Grocery store for only four months until he received a job at the Pioneer Hotel, which was much closer to his home. By the time Hubert started working at the Pioneer Hotel, Hubert had just turned fifteen. Eventually he was able to get his younger brother Timmy a job as a kitchen helper but initially, Hubert adapted well as a kitchen helper mainly because he was a hard worker. When given a task by Betty the Banquet Superintendent, Hubert did any task well and completed the task in minimal time. Betty was already in her seventies but did not want to retire. He had mentioned to Hubert that when her husband died that she decided to continue to work because she did not have any children and wanted to stay active.

Hubert's first Mentor was Betty and showed him how to be a structured and dependable employee. Hubert's work ethics eventually earned him the position as the 'busboy' manager ahead of individuals much older by his senior year in High School. Throughout this time, Hubert had two jobs, had seminary at church in the morning before going to school, played sports in school, and still maintained good grades in school. During Hubert's senior year football season when the team went seven and three, on weeks that the team won their games, the team would meet at the Dairy Queen to get their free ice cream cones. Saturday morning was normally the only time that Hubert had time to take time off to rest each week.

Each day, Betty would give Hubert the day's schedule of the requirements for the conference rooms setups for the following day. Then Hubert would divvy up the duties with all the "busboy's" who accomplished the work in the conference rooms of all sizes. Hubert made sure that overall, he maintained a fair schedule so that each 'busboy' eventually worked at the same level when working on the same types of conference rooms each week. Each 'busboy' would first clear a room and then reset a conference room to the new requirement for the following day needs with the table and seating needs. Then the table settings would be set and Betty would return and verify each room.

In addition, all the 'busboy's had to work on the large ballroom that normally used at least two or three times per week, especially on holidays. For a teen, Hubert learned to take on responsibility at an early age, thanks to Betty. This did not mean that as a teen that Hubert did not have experiences that could have gotten him in trouble. While working at the Pioneer hotel, while setting up one of the conference rooms for a small conference, unexcitingly a waitress walked in and started grabbing at him and kissing him after she closed the door. Weeks later Hubert found out that the server was married when he saw her husband that was also a Police Officer. What Hubert never forgot was the Officer's thirty-eight pistol that seemed much larger than it actually was. To a young and in experienced teen, the thirty-eight pistol looked like a two-barrel cannon. The server never told him that she was married and Hubert was too inexperienced to know better.

"I hope someday I grow up to be a better father than my dad," thought Hubert to himself. He had seen his mother work two jobs at a time in an effort to provide for her family. On occasion when Jose visited his children, he would take them out to eat and buy them candy. However, not once had he paid on cent on child support. In a way, Olga had been too proud to ask for any support. Nevertheless, Hubert had thought that his father, Jose should have still made an effort to help raise the children that he brought into the world. This is why he had little respect for his father who he felt earned the title 'father' only in title.

"I wonder how anyone can call himself a man?" thought Hubert. A real man would help his children by helping feed them and providing clothing for his children. Instead, Hubert and his brothers had worked odd jobs to help their momma. Nevertheless, at an early age, any help they provided was more symbolic than of substance. Olga had always brought happiness within her home but working two jobs and selling her burritos on weekends at the local bars to make extra money had made her age faster than normal. In the meantime, Jose was still the handsome ladies' man that he had been accustomed to as the standard that he had set for himself.

"How about if we stay here and play soldiers all day," mention Hubert to his younger brother. On the way to Menlo Park Elementary School, they purposely walked slowly to stay in the rear of the pact walking to school. Since all the children were born within twelve to eighteen month apart, all six were in Menlo Park Elementary School from Kindergarten to sixth grade. For this year, all six of the Contreras children were walking to school together since each were in grades one through six. After a long day of playing soldiers, Hubert and his brother returned home to see the truant Officer and his mom that called her at work. Once the boys entered the house, the truant Officer simply mentioned that they were to meet the principle in the morning and left.

Decades before time-out would become the American fad, Olga had her sons kneel on the corner of the dining room wall. That would be the last time that these two young brothers would think of staying at the rear to play versus going to school. At that point, Hubert saw Olga going for her belt so he ran under the bed. At first, she grabbed a broom to get Hubert out from under the bed. Olga asked what he was doing with a smile and Hubert crying replied that he did not want a spanking. Olga overtaken by the event did not spank the boys and as she normally did, took the boys for a hamburger meal at the local A&W after their time-out prayer. Hubert knew that anytime he got in trouble that momma would take him somewhere to eat after she punished them. After all, momma loved her boys too much to yell at them without telling them that she was sorry. Nevertheless, what Hubert Hated the most was her non-stop lecturing, even during their A&W meal where he and Timmy had to promise that they would be good boys forever and ever.

"Are you ready," asked Olga as the Contreras family packed their car in preparation for a trip to Cuidad Obregon, Mexico. Each summer Olga would collect boxes of clothing to take to the Indian villages. In addition, each summer Olga and her brothers paid a mariachi band to play for Marie, Olga's mother. It was during one of these trips when Hubert's grandmother Maria (in Spanish) passed away back in Tucson. Hubert's aunt made sure that they did not contact Olga about this family event. Hubert's would also be in Cuidad Obregon when his grandfather Joaquin Contreras passed away. His aunt Francis would make sure that they would not receive the notification of their passing in time to return to see their grandparents buried. That would also allow her to take the promised items that she wanted that she knew her parents promised Hubert and his siblings. Especially the family picture hand painted with his father after WW-II that Nana Maria promised his sister Lupe.

Nana Maria would have grandfather Joaquin bring US boxes of potato chips or watermelons or anything her grandchildren wished for in his 1949 Ford pickup. She had been the center of the family that kept the family together until she passed away when the family no longer came together. Nana Maria had always treated Hubert, his brothers, and sisters kinder than all her other grandchildren. Perhaps because Jose, her son had been the only family member to leave his family to find himself. Moreover, Jose not once paid a single cent in support as the court ordered him to pay for his children, with Olga never taking him to court. Perhaps Olga was too much in love to take her former husband to court or too proud to ask for assistance from anyone. In the end, she aged sooner than she should have while Jose stayed young and lived longer as a carefree bachelor.

Jose visited his children occasionally and then dropped them off once he spent his token time with them. Leaving all the responsibility to Olga to raise his children and pay for all their needs including emotional needs. While Jose knew that, he could come or go without having any responsibilities for his children or having to pay for anything that his children required in life. While Jose disappeared for months or a year at a time from his children's lives, before returning with a new partner in his life, expecting his children to accept his new woman in his life each time. Still, his young children would love their father whenever he gave them anytime that he spared or took the time with them. Finally, Jose would find a woman with young children that he would raise as his own. Finally, he would expect his own children to accept them as their sisters and brothers now that he was in his fifties.

"This is a bargain book," mentioned the salesperson. As an avid reader, Olga always made sure that her children read books their entire life. On this day, Olga purchased an encyclopedia book volume that consisted of one large book. Hubert would use this book in college, as would his daughter Tawny when she went to the University of Arizona decades later. Learning had been an important part of their lives where she insisted that going to school and earning good grades was a top priority. Even when Hubert received a high 'A-', Olga would ask why he did not do better. Many times, Olga expected Hubert to earn 'A+' since she knew that when he applied himself that he had the ability to earn such grades in school. Years later, Hubert would teach his daughter to be an avid reader because the family was avid readers. Tawny would become an avid reader not because of Hubert but because of Hubert's wife, Darlene who was also an avid reader similar to Olga.

When alive, once a month, Nana Maria would hold a picnic at Randolph; renamed to Reed Park or Sabino Canyon in the Rincon mountains, or in the lake south of Tucson, at a museum, or at a family member house. Each month a family caravan would form with Nana Maria's Ford pickup leading the way with the pickup bed full of food and drinks. At Sabino Canyon, all the children would jump into the freezing canyon windy river waters all at once and all that the children could hear was their screams and laughter. At Randolph Park, all the children hoping to catch the first fish formed the long lines of fishing poles. Hamburgers, hotdogs, and ribs cooked for everyone at every picnic as Nana Maria hugged and kissed her grandchildren. Nana Maria made it a point that her grandchildren would visit all the lakes in Arizona with family during her lifetime.

During a visit in Mexico, Hubert asked, "Grandpa is all that land yours?" His earliest memory had been visiting his grandfather in Obregon and sitting on his lap talking with Grandpa. Grandpa Parra grew up in Texas where his father a Mexican American married the rancher's daughter. His mother, Olga was half-Swedish since her mother was born in Europe but immigrated to the US and Texas as a young girl. Although Grandpa had blue eyes, he had his father's dark hair but his mother's clear white skin. At the age of fourteen, Grandpa Parra inherited $10 million from his Grandparents. It would take him his lifetime to spend his inheritance after living a grand life between Mexico and Texas. Many times, Grandpa Parra would call home and ask Nana Maria for money after some woman stole all his money after a night of partying.

"Grandpa, I washed the bottles for you," said Hubert. Grandpa Parra would pay him a centavo (cent) for each bottle that he washed at Grandpa's General store. Hubert was too young to understand why he had such a large family. His grandfather was a LDS (Latter Day Saints) Mormon and held dual citizenship as a Mexican and an American. Having seven wives, Grandpa Parra had decided to live in Mexico since the LDS church in the US was changing and outlawed multiple wives. On this day, Hubert was in the servant's quarters that had two large bay windows that overlooked the ranch farmlands. For days at a time, Hubert and Grandpa Parra would sit at the two large bay windows where Hubert would listen to Grandpa's stories about his family or about ranching, growing crops, his business, or his store.

In between the main home and the servant's quarters, their courtyard was full of fruit trees including bananas and lemons. A few years later, Grandpa Parra would lose his wealth when after stocking his store for the year; a fire took away the family's wealth. This was the early eighteenth century and insurance was still in the future in Mexico. For businesspersons who experience financial problems as his grandfather did. This meant that if they invested their entire fortune in inventory and lost it in a fire, they loss of their life's future. The only thing that Grandpa Parra had left was his property, his ranch, and farmland. However, for someone that had always lived as a rich person, Grandpa Parra would have difficulties adjusting to his knew life as an average citizen.

"Why is everyone crying," asked Hubert. It was recess at Menlo Park Elementary when all the teachers came out crying from the building yelling that President John F. Kennedy (JFK) of his assassination. After leaving school for the rest of the day, the children instead of playing, they were all watching television day after day even after the killing of JFKs killer on television. It would be another 20 years before the 24/7 cable and television programs. For now, at mid-night or 1:00 AM in the morning you could expect the National Anthem played on television as the programming of the day ended. It was also a simpler time for Americans for it was a period for Americans before the liberals would make the victims secondary to criminals.

"What's wrong?" asked Hubert. Olga had just had a dream of her mother, Grandma Marie struck by lightning. After calling to Obregon, her sister mentioned that the ambulance was on its way. The lightning event had just happened a few minutes ago and Olga was already packing her bags to drive to Obregon. Over the years, Olga known for her abilities to read cards scared Hubert. Even when Hubert had his own family, he did not like having a wiggy board in his home. Hubert had seen his mother Olga read cards too many times and have many dreams that came true that scared him. He too had many strange feelings that kept him out of trouble many times that at times scared him.

"Is this your brother's car," asked the detective. As the middle child and the second eldest male, it was just before Christmas in 1973 and Hubert's senior year in High School that a Mexican couple killed his oldest brother. He worked two jobs in order to afford the car and insurance and still be able to help his mother. Hubert's father side of the family had believed that his brother was into drugs, when in fact he died in the line of duty as an undercover narcotics officer. His older brother had been an undercover narcotics officer for over five years and did not tell anyone including Olga. It would be after his death that the family received notice that he was a Police officer.

"Do you need anything to eat sweetie," asked Olga. At that point, years where as the middle child meant no one cared and he ignored, now it changed for now Hubert because he was the eldest male in the family. Hubert earliest family memories always led to his strong mother and two loving grandmothers. Hubert's grandmother had passed away when he was in kindergarten. Hubert's grandmother Marie died after he married and had his daughter. By then, Hubert's daughter was almost four years old when Marie passed away of old age. She always recalled that Hubert as a small boy said he would marry a blond blue eyed girl like Darlene.

PREPARING TO ENTER USAF

"Bob, what are you doing?" asked Hubert. Bob, Hubert's friend, had just returned from Vietnam and was driving on Congress Street when the regular siren goes off each day at noon. Bob had just returned from Vietnam and instantly slammed his brakes, put his nova on park, and within seconds was under his car sweating as vehicles were swerving all around him trying not to hit him from behind. It all happened so fast that Hubert not sure what happened. A minute later, Hubert opened the driver door, looked under the car, and asked Bob what was wrong. By now bob was also shaking when he said that he was having a war flashback. This would be an event that Hubert would never forget as a warfighter and one that few American's would never understand. This would be also being another memory added to all the memories of the friends that never returned from Vietnam or many killed in action (KIA).

"What is she doing?" thought Hubert to himself. Hubert was driving his 1969 Chevy north on stone avenue on the right lane driving thirty miles per hour on a forty miles limit when a girl on a bike without warning ran in front of his car. By then Hubert had slowed down further and swerved to the right in an effort to miss the girl riding her bike, which minimized hurting her. What amazed Hubert was that two witnesses told Police that he was speeding and that he intentionally hit her. Hubert was lucky that the girl told the truth and told the Police that she ran into Hubert and that Hubert was driving slowly. The Police also verified from the tire marks that Hubert was driving extremely slowly since there were no tire marks since Hubert had L60 tires, which were wide tired that would have left wide tire marks on the road. Even though Hubert knew the witnesses, they never apologized for not telling the truth to the Police. Nevertheless, it seems no never knows what one sees during a real accident.

"Timmy, are you ready for seminary," mentioned Hubert. Raymond his younger brother and he would get up at five each morning and drive to the local Latter Day Saints (LDS) for two hours of seminary before school each day. At that point, Hubert was the Ward President and served as the teen leader for his church. In this role, Hubert was involved in nearly every aspect of the church activities, which consumed his live outside school and work. Hubert found the LDS seminary as an opportunity to learn the bible and having good discussions before each day of High School. It was a good opportunity to learn stories of the bible that would be useful later in life once he married.

Like many young men during the Vietnam era, Hubert was eager to grow too fast. Hubertheard many Vietnam stories from friends that returned from war. Most that returned with different personalities even though they tried as best they could to be the same old friends. However, they all had one thing in common, they drank too much, they never talked about their war experiences, all were quiet, and strange in different ways. Instead of enjoying his summers, Hubert took summer school classes and worked part-time at his High School, Amphitheater (Amphi) High School. This allowed him to graduate during his junior year. Instead, he decided to go an extra year and stay for his senior year to play football.

It was during Hubert's junior year at Amphi that he decided to sign-up for the Delayed Entry Program in the US Air Force (USAF). As Hubert turns eighteen, he signed up for the draft, knowing that he did not want the US Army to draft him. The USAF Delayed Entry Program offered him six years of service, starting him as an Airman First Class (A1C) once he completed Basic Training. Hubert did not understand what that meant but he signed up for the six years. Since going into the Air Force would give him the GI Bill that would allow him to go to college. At that point, not sure, if he would earn a college scholarship Hubert decided to enlist in the Air Force. It would be years later before Hubert would understand how this commitment would affect his life and take him away from home for decades.

Nevertheless, for now, Hubert continued with his normal High School life not fully understanding what this commitment would mean to his life in the near future. Then either Hubert would go to school and one of his classes, to the track, or football practice. Each Wednesday, Saturday and Sunday each had a different LDS church activity. During Hubert's senior year, he had a job at City Hall Data Automation for four hours followed by his job at the Pioneer Hotel until ten or eleven each night. Each morning prior to school on Monday through Friday, Hubert attended an LDS seminary class for an hour. Every Saturday consisted of a church dance and every Sunday Hubert was at Church all day.

As part of the Co-Operative (Co-Op) Education Class in High School, Hubert took a two-credit class during his senior year where he worked part-time job at City Hall Data Automation for four hours Monday through Friday. During the year, Hubert learned how to operate all the Data Automation systems of the day for hard frame computers used by the City of Tucson as part of an on-the-job training program. Hubert learned how to use decollators, detachers, disk drives, tape drives, and many other systems including running payroll for the city that assisted him once he entered the US Air Force. Once Hubert completed his work at the City of Tucson, he drove to the Pioneer Hotel, which was one block from where he worked and worked until midnight or later. Sometimes he would park at the Pioneer Parking Lot since it was only a block across the road from City Hall. This way he did not have to worry about finding a parking space later on. Employees that worked at the Pioneer Hotel received free parking.

"Mijo can you help me this weekend with Senator Goldwater fund raiser," asked Olga. Hubert's mother Olga had always been an active helping Arizona politician with their election and reelection campaigns. He routinely helped his mom cooking for one political campaign or another. From an early age, having a good work ethic was part of Hubert's character. His mother had introduced him to many politicians that as a young man he had taken for granted. As Hubert grew older, he would understand some of the benefits that knowing a US Senator or a Governor offered an individual. By simply mentioning, a name of an individual and not asking for specific assistance.

"Come on Raymond, let's get our red wagon and go look for bottles," mentioned Hubert. His first job was collecting empty bottles and taking them to the store to collect their deposits. These monies would provide the candy money for his younger brother and three sisters. Years later, this work option for young children would go away as the bottles became plastics and the deposits went away. Hubert's second job was delivering the daily newspaper during Junior High School. This job kept Hubert busy until he turned sixteen and started working at the Pioneer hotel as a 'busboy'. Now Hubert could legally work anywhere without having to fib about his true age. Hubert worked for Betty his entire four years that he was in High School, which allowed him to mature each year as a manager even though he was young.

"I need you to set up the rooms for tomorrow's conferences," said Betty. Betty was the banquet conference manager and over the years, Hubert would quit and return whenever he wanted a job. Betty was in her late seventies and refused to stop working as long as she was able. She was a good mentor and boss and with time, Hubert gained more responsibility and work knowledge under her oversight. Betty would give Hubert conference room layouts with table settings normally given to older employees. She knew that Hubert was responsible and an efficient worker. Looking back, perhaps, Betty knew that Hubert was actually younger than he was but allowed him to work because he made it clear that he would work hard from his initial interview.

"Are you working late," asked Olga? Other than work, church activities took most of Hubert time six of seven days each week. Hubert's full-time job turned out to be at the Pioneer Hotel where he was by then the senior bus boy. In addition to High School sports playing football and running on the track team, Hubert was the President of the Church Sunday School, and played on his church's basketball team, Los Chapureros. Tony was the coach and Hubert had met him in his part-time job in the City of Tucson, Data Automation as a data automation specialist. It seemed that every day was a busy day for Hubert.

Even on days when he thought he had time to relax, it was common for the Ward President to call him and ask if he was available to help in a short notice project or help another group. He knew Hubert would always say yes and always make time for his church activities.

Hubert received three semester class credits for this part-time job working at City Hall in the Data Automation Section. He worked well with all his fellow employees but he knew that he needed tasks that are more challenging. In academics, Hubert had always been a good student making the Honor roll each semester but not feeling challenged and was a member of the Honor Society. He loved learning and kept focused on his education. He had just signed up for the Vietnam draft since war was still going strong. Olga raised her children to be proud Americans and would always talk about America as the land of opportunity. For a young man, knowing that he earned all his spending money that helped his mother as a young man would make him feel as if he was a good person. Yet, Hubert had to grow up too fast and wished for a life of with little responsibility.

"Did you get a scholarship," asked a classmate as they walked to receive their High School diploma. His grades had earned him an opportunity to go to college and an appointment to the Air Force academy. Olga had known Senator Goldwater who was a close friend and easily got Hubert an appointment to the academy. However, at this point, Hubert did not want to enter the military for he truly did not know what he wanted from life. Thinking that he would go to college, he signed up to start college the next semester. However, Hubert and two friends would first take a planned short vacation to Guadalajara, Mexico. His short three-week vacation would turn into a three-month vacation with the group returning once they ran out of money.

"I guess we better go back to Tucson," mentioned Hubert. Three months later, the three young men returned after spending all the money they had. By this time, college had started and Hubert told that he would have to reapply. He did not regret going to Mexico since he had a great time going to graduation parties. The Hilton head teller had gained them access to all the hotel graduation parties. Initially, they had stayed at a cheap hotel until one day they walked by the Hilton and decided to share a room. This would be the first time that the group would visit the Lago Chapala or Lake Chapala, which is the largest lake in Mexico. From the beaches in on the lake, one would think that it is an ocean due to its magnificent size. Complete with all the tourist stands on the beaches selling colorful Mexican artifacts from the nearby pyramids.

Upon his return, Hubert decided to go work at a copper mine since the pay was good. This would allow Hubert to work in one job instead of working two jobs. It would also mean that instead of working seven days a week and nearly twelve to fourteen hours per day, he would only work five days a week, and only eight hours per day. Initially, Betty offered him his old job as the Banquet room manager at a higher pay hoping that he would return as a permanent employee. Hubert received an offered as a permanent employee by the City of Tucson to work in the Data Automation fulltime that he considered prior on going on vacation. The City of Tucson offered tuition assistance and other benefits that made that job offer more appealing.

Everything seemed to go well for Hubert but he knew that he was committed to the US Air Force and had to report effective 25 July 1974 under the Delayed Entry Program. He enlisted during the draft in 1972 to avoid receiving a draft notification into the US Army, which allowed him to finish High School. Since his birthday fell in February, his mother started him in school late so he would graduate High School at an older age. This was why he had taken summer classes every year to finish High School early. At the last moment, Hubert decided not to graduate to play an extra year of football. In his senior year, he took one required class that he could have taken during the summer. Hubert took two classed of Physical Education (PE) and the Co-Operative (Co-Op) Education class during his final year in High School.

"Mom I just got a job at the mine," mentioned Hubert. After High School while waiting to enter the Air Force, Hubert took a job in San Manuel initially in the copper mine. Like his father and older brother, he would be the third family member that would work for Magma Copper mine for a short while. Hubert would work as a miner but not because it was a family tradition. After High School, Hubert applied for a job at Magma Copper Mine and accepted. Although he was in the worst shape of his life after months of not working out, he had passed his physical without any problem. After seeing two of his co-workers killed deep in the mine, he transferred to the smelter. At the time, he thought that it would be a good job to return to after a hitch in the Air Force. His co-workers mentioned that the company was required to hire him back once he returned from the military by law.

After all, in High School, he had a full scholarship and during the summer he and two of his Mormon friends had taken what was to be a three-week vacation to Guadalajara that turned out to be all summer. Instead, he lost his scholarship when he did not return in time to start classes at the University of Arizona. He had planned to take a year of college before joining the Air Force. At Magma Copper Mine, Hubert would earn more pay in one job than he had working two jobs for the last four years. Hubert did not realize that at Magma he started a trend that would follow him throughout his professional career. During his six months at Magma, Hubert worked in six different positions each holding more responsibility and each paying more money.

Nearly every month, he was able to transfer to a different position in part because of his physical ability and mainly because of his mental capacities. Magma would also be a work culture where other immigrant Mexicans would try to get him in trouble because of his ability to receive promotions so easily. One-on-one the same individuals would be friendly but behind his back, the same immigrant Mexicans would be unethical and say or do things in an effort to get Hubert in trouble. However, the same individuals did not cross the line and do anything dangerous to put his life in danger, which easily anyone could do in the work environment. At the same time, Hubert went out of his way to help all employees including the same immigrant Mexicans in any way that he could including serving as their translator and translating formal union documents posted in work common boards.

By this time, Hubert was working at a Copper Mine and Huber asked, "Mom can you fill Hubert's car with gas today while I take the car pool to work,". The Middle East embargo was ongoing and the gas lines were everywhere in Tucson. Since he was in a car pool, the days that he did not have to drive, Olga would fill his car with gasoline. Nevertheless, six months later Hubert knew that the life as a miner not what he wanted from life. Life of a miner of a young nineteen year old is like a young man going to his grave each day he goes to work. The main difference is that each day, Hubert took an elevator miles down, and lights was what everyone saw. Hubert knew at an early age that each time walking in darkness it was like losing life.

By the time, Hubert had seen the second miner killed deep in the mine and he knew that he would either quit or transfer to the mill, so he applied for and received a transfer to the smeller. He was surprised that his transfer to the smelter received approved. This meant that he would not have to go down the mineshaft anymore. He was truly surprised that his transferred received approval so fast. Hubert's first job consisted of driving the large vacuum cleaner around the smelter. However, this job would be short lived and he would take a better paying job of tapper that would also be much more dangerous. At the smelter, Hubert would see his supervisors that were in their early forty's but all looked twenty years older.

"I just can't work in this environment and age like them," said Hubert to a coworker. The sulfur in the air would get into his pores and take over an hour each day to brush off with a toothbrush. Although he brushed his teeth three of four times a day, within weeks his teeth had a layer of green sulfur buildup. Hubert knew that this type of life would shorten his lifespan and knew that he needed a new job that turned out to be the USAF. It would take him ten years in the Air Force before he would make the same salary that he earned as a nineteen year old mine employee. It was at this point that he realized that he would never return to Magma or any type of mining employment.

Hubert worked at Magma for six months and after seeing two more accidental deaths in the smelter, he knew that he needed to change jobs. Since working at the mine called for shift work, after the graveyard shift that ended early in the morning, Hubert would go play nine holes of golf in an effort to get tired. One he was tired enough to get some sleep before starting what became a normal routine. He knew that working in a copper mine and seeing two workers killed that the mine not his lifetime profession. Coming to work tired could be deadly in this work environment. Many individuals took sleeping pills butHubert did not believe in taking drugs or any type of medications.

Upon returning to work at the Smelter, Hubert would learn his first lesson about union bosses. For months, the union steward had been trying to get Hubert to join the union and each time Hubert declined. After working a night shift, the following shift he was surprised to see his co-workers that had worked the day shift with picket signs striking. At that point, the co-workers were striking because of the dangerous conditions and the lack of mine leaders to take corrective action in making the work area safer. One of the individuals on the strike line was a worker that had trained Hubert that was two years older and had two young children, a boy and a newborn daughter. Aaron was in his twenties, grew up in Kentucky, and now lived in San Manuel with his small family. He and his wife had asked Hubert over for dinner more than once over the months so they had become good friends. A few times, Hubert had baby sit for them so that they could have a night out together.

It was 1974 the year of the oil embargo when gas was only thirty-one cents for regular and thirty-three cents for premium days before embargo. However, soon gas could not be purchase at first and then sparely found by car pools used by miners driving from Tucson to San Manuel. During this period, Hubert's mom Olga was working the night shift and after she woke up in the afternoon, she would take Hubert's car and get in line to fill his car up. This would allow Hubert to drive when it was his turn to drive to San Manuel. Many times Hubert would drive out of cycle mainly because his car had fuel while the other vehicles did not. All because Olga took the time to fill up his car during the embargo when gas went from thirty cents to over a dollar for not reason only because Washington politicians refused to do anything for its citizens.

On this week, it was Hubert's turn to drive to work. At the end of the week, the group decided to eat at the local restaurant in San Manuel. When the group of miners entered the small Café diner, Hubert noticed two senior union leaders and two company Officers joking as they had diner at the diner. The group of miners could not help over hearing the union leaders and company men discuss the firing of their fellow employees. Hubert was shocked that the union leaders would be so unethical when so many of his friend's livelihoods were on the line. This social union gathering would cause not only Aarons job but also over a hundred other fellow employees' jobs as the union representatives laughed and publically stated that they did their best to represent their interests.

While his carpool members were finishing their diner and having a few more beers, Hubert returned to the smelter, cleared his locker, and told the timekeeper that he quit. The timekeeper's office was in a small building just off the main smelter building so it did not take too much time. On the way to the timekeepers building, Hubert saw Aaron in the picket line just outside the gate. As he drove past the striking employees, he told his friend what he had just overheard and mentioned that he would not be returning to San Manuel since he too was no longer an employee. He returned to the dinner to pick-up his passengers to return to Tucson. In a way, this event only convinced Hubert to quit early since he was going to quit working at the mine to go into the Air Force anyway. After this experience, Hubert lost all respect for any union and union leaders. It would not be the last opportunity that he would see similar situations with similar outcomes.

"I think that I will take the Administration job," said Hubert. He thought that he wanted to be in Administration since the job description sounded good. Olga's friend who was an Air Force recruiter talked him out and told him that he wanted to go into personnel. As always, Olga had a friend that knew the right information that her children needed. If she did not have a friend right away, each time she would find a friend that would find a friend with the right information that she needed in minimal time. He said, in personnel or the Consolidated Base Personnel Office (CBPO), you work Monday through Friday and have every weekend off. Based on the recruiters recommended, Hubert sign-up as a personnel specialist.

"If I pass my physical in Phoenix, then I will be sworn into the Air Force," thought Hubert. It was a hot summer day in Phoenix when Hubert drove to recruiting office, took his physical, and enlisted in the Air Force. At the end of a graveyard shift, which ended at 8 AM, Hubert scheduled himself to take the Air Force entry examination on May 7. Later on, he would know why his Air Force Pay Date would be 7 May 1974 and what that meant.

A few days later, the Air Force Recruiter called Hubert and gave him his report date to Basic Training of 25 July 1974. In just over two-months, he would start a life style that would be second nature to him without realizing that his life had changed forever. Once he arrived in Tucson, after breakfast, he took a bus to Phoenix Harbor International Airport for a flight to San Antonio, Texas. Once there, he would start learning the Air Force way of talking that consisted of an endless list of acronyms associated with their meaning.

1ST COMBAT SUPPORT GROUP (CSG), MACDILL, AFB, FL. (USAF)

"Do you want a window seat," asked the American Airlines (AA) flight attendant. Although the Vietnam War had ended, the airlines still treated service members with kindness. Over the next three decades, Hubert would fly in every US carrier and receive different levels of treatment that would always remind Hubert of his first AA flight and his first fight in a jet aircraft. At this point, Hubert did not realize that once he arrived to his first unit that he would deploy overseas and help close countless units that had fought in support of the Vietnam War. Then he would deploy to bases throughout the US to process the wings that he closed overseas to help process personnel into the US bases from the overseas bases. Nevertheless, first, Hubert had to learn about the US Air Force (USAF) by first completing the USAF Basic Training program.

As Hubert enters the American Airlines aircraft and takes his first flight on a jet, he never thought this would be a job that he would last over thirty-one years. He would report to the US Air Force when his first Commander-in-Chief (CINC) would be Richard N. Nixon. A few months later while still in Basic Training Hubert would hear that Nixon was in the process of impeachment. On 9 August and Gerald R. Ford, Jr.

would become his new CINC. He also did not know that he would meet his dream girl, Darlene Dixon that would come into his life when least expected. Hubert had just returned from Phoenix where he took his entrance physical and sworn into the military. Everything seemed to be moving fast and before long he would experience three moves in less than six months and not the year plus that his recruiter had mentioned.

Mainly because each location had the option where the Air Force trainee could control some portions of how fast he or she could complete each portion of the course. Therefore, he had control of the testing and course completion and was able to move through each course and the technical training program in minimal time. Since Hubert had been a Dorm Chief in Basic Training, he received the notice to be a Rope as a student leader in Technical Training School (TTS), which he declined. After serving as the senior class leader in Basic Training, Hubert would decide to serve as a student at the TTS level.

"OK girls get your butts out of the bus and line up in formation," yelled the Technical Instructor (TI). Basic Training reminded Hubert of football since the TIs called everyone 'girls' just like the coaches called the football players 'girls'. Both cultures were extremely similar to Hubert in many ways. Trainee's names called out at random and told to line up in front of a TI. The Basic TrainingTIs all seemed to have one trait in common, they loved to yell and call the male trainees "girls. " Boot camp started in Building 3701stand the 3701st Basic Military Training Squadron (BMTS) and physically it was a breeze. Building 3701stwas part of the 3701st BMTS and a number that most trainees would never forget.

When Hubert entered the Air Force, women and men were lived in separate buildings and other than seeing each other during social activities on weekends, during basic training both sexes existed as separate entities. The term Women Air Force "WAF," once in everyday use in the Air Force, faded away once society in America started changing in the late 1970s. In 1976, the office of the Director of the WAF officially discontinued as no longer necessary. By the twenty-first century, women account for 19. 5 percent of the Air Force's active duty strength and have no unique terminology that would set them apart. During World War II, some 400,000 women served in the armed forces, but that was a wartime exception. Other than nurses, women could not join the regular forces in peacetime. In the 1970s, that would change and that trend continued as the percentages only climbed each decade.

The training started when Hubert arrived in San Antonio around 2:00 AM in the morning. Later, Hubert figured that the program designed to have trainees arrive early in the morning. This way the trainees would remain up all day so that the first day would be a long day on purpose. The entire training was all about controlling the trainees. It was a short drive from the airport to Lackland Air Force Base (AFB), Texas where the trainees would be a guest for ten weeks of the Training Command. Each training Flight had two Technical Instructor's (TIs), assigned to each flight which took turns with the flight. Once Hubert arrived at Lackland AFB, he received notice that he wasa member of F-Flight as soon as he got off the bus. The majority of the training in the Air Force consisted of academics with twenty percent consisting of physical activities.

It was during the daily physical training that Hubert thought to himself, "I just wish that they would run on the outside lanes," thought Hubert to himself. Having been a lifetime runner, Hubert proudly knew that few fellow soldiers could outrun him. His flight would normally be one of the final flights to start running around the track and he easily caught up and passed all the runners from his and other flights. He quickly decided to himself that Air Force boot camp not physical but mental. His had started with soldiers but within two weeks would quickly get much smaller in size as the young soldier self-eliminated themselves or were washout because of medical reasons. His first job in his flight was as the House Mouse where all he had to do was sign in his flight into the Chow Hall whenever they went for a meal. At first, he received this position because he was a fast runner.

"I hope that I do not faint," thought Hubert to himself. Having always enjoyed learning, the academics were simple and mostly about the new life style and the military way of life that he had chosen. The normal training day for Hubert and his flight started when they all marched to the hospital to get what would be a series of injections (shots). Up to that point, his training had gone great until this day where he and his fellow military members received a long list of preventive shots. Like all soldiers, Hubert received an empty short record and joined the line where medics would soon start injecting the new pistol type injections into his arms.

As F-Flight lined up, each military member quickly followed in line and went from one medical specialist who with an injection gunshot some type of medicine into their arms. Like robots, each soldier quickly received a shot in the arm and quickly moved to the next medic for the next shot. There was no need to worry about any blood flowing from their arms before they arrived in front of the next medical specialist to receive another injection. The commotion was high with the TIs yelling some type of orders and the scared trainees following their orders. Besides, no one knew why the TIs were yelling since everyone was in line as ordered with empty faces or trying not to laugh.

"The Red Flag is out. Are the TI idiots," thought the trainees to themselves. All the trainees noticed that the Red Flag was out which meant that trainees were not to be put at attention when the Red Flag was out. However, the TI had other ideas. He kept the entire flight at attention for over an hour after the flight of trainees had received their injections. Later on, when the flight marched back to the squadron, one trainee had taken his injections and kept walking out the door and off Lackland Air Force Base AFB. It seems that he did not like the US Air

Force or the Basic Training program. Unfortunately, it would have been better for him to receive a physically discharge than receiving a dishonorable discharge.

Having had his entire haircut off, it was not hard for the civilian and military Police to see that he was a trainee who had gone AWOL. The GI haircut was another colorful event. The entire flight remained outside the barbershop and entered from one door while departing from the opposite door. Once each soldier entered the barbershop, the barber would take the time to ask what kind of haircut the member like and then in an instant the cutter went in the center of each member taking off the main portion of his or her hair. Nevertheless, Hubert and three other soldiers would get mild heat strokes from being out in the hot heat of 114 degrees and standing at attention. During this era, TIs legally physically harm soldiers as long as they did not kill them during training. In modern times, TIs yell at trainees using only certain phases by regulation.

"Sir Airman Contreras reporting F-Flight for breakfast," yelled Hubert. He was happy being the House Mouse, which would be his flight job until the end of week two of training. Hubert always had a proactive personality mainly because raised as a Mormon where he served leadership roles. Subconsciously, under any situation, Hubert always took the lead instead of being a follower. During this phase of the training, trainees kept busy and with minimum sleep going from one classroom to another. Hubert quickly learned that the best way to stay awake was to take salt pills in an effort to stay awake. Teamwork was the best rule in Basic Training and once Hubert became the Dorm Chief, his only rule was 'getting everyone to graduation'.

It was after going to the Finance Office and receiving a $50 advance to purchase the list of required items at the base Shoppet that the TI had a surprise for Hubert. Most of the items received special attention during the daily inspections in the dorm room. Every item had a specific location within every door or every locker properly spaced and measured by the trainee and the TIs. Then there were the no-notice inspections held by other inspectors. During the first week in Basic Training, the TI called him out of formation to let him know that he had just volunteered to be the Dorm Chief. Within a Flight, the Dorm Chief is responsible for the success of failure of the flight of fifty men. The Dorm Chief is the primary leader within each Flight responsible for molding the flight into a team and getting them to graduation.

Each Flight had four Squad Leaders with twelve men in each squad. During this era, the Air Force was in a draw down but still needed critical specialties. It was no surprise that the list of required items took the entire Air Force $50 advance. The Technical Instructor (TI) made it clear that if Hubert did not want to be the Dorm Chief, that he could be the House Mouse in another training flight. Knowing two weeks of the training was complete Hubert knew that he did not want to start at the beginning of the training since each day at boot camp seemed much longer. ThisBasic Training class would be the last class where the military allowed TIs to harm trainees. In one case, an airman put into a large trashcan and the TI slammed the lid repeatedly. Unfortunately, the airman's eardrums burst in the process.

Basic Training consisted of many specialized training items including firing the M-16 rifle. Here Hubert would excel and qualify as an expert and receive his second Air Force ribbon once he arrived at his first permanent base. During that era, graduates also received the National Defense Ribbon so now Hubert would receive the Small Arms Expert Ribbon since he qualified as an expert on the M-16 riffle on his first attempt. It was on a cloudy day that Hubert shot nearly a perfect score to receive this ribbon while shooting from various sitting and standing positions. Other training requirements consisted of running in the track that Hubert easily was the top runner. In most cases, since his flight was normally the second flight to start running in sequence, by the time he finished the mile run he normally outran all the first flight runners.

Being the Dorm Chief had some benefits but Hubert's TI made it clear that it was his responsibility to make sure that all his fellow Flight members made it through training. Given the choice of picking his Squad Leaders, he chose the four largest and strongest airman's as Squad Leaders. Over the remaining training period, Hubert's Squad Leaders would all hate him, but the remaining Flight like him. Any time he saw a fellow Flight member that needed help or did something that not within military standards, this issue was between the Dorm Chief and the Squad Leader. It seemed each time Hubert had to deal with one of his Squad Leaders; they had problems related to race. Two of Hubert's Squad Leaders were Black and the flight had many Italians. For some reason, one of the Black Squad Leaders had problems dealing with Italians and Hubert had to intervene with that Squad Leader often in defense of the Italian flight members.

As a Mexican American, Hubert had to work twice as hard to the same treatment as other employees. The term Hispanic was still not used the 1970 US census even though Olga taught Hubert to be proud of his Spanish and Mexican heritage equally. However, it would be another decade or so before the term would become popular within the Latin American and Iberian Peninsula. The illegal allies from Mexico and Latin America would soon be an issue that would soon force many Hispanics to hide their heritage.

In the 1970s, the US Air Force was an era where Blacks received preferential treatment. Soon Hubert would learn that Blacks in the US Air Force used their race as a political weapon and white supervisors were scared of disciplining any Black Air Force member for fear of receiving a false discrimination charge in their military record. Blacks in the Air Force used their race as a political weapon as females would use their gender as a political weapon starting in the 1980s. Caucasians were afraid to say or do anything to Blacks who would bring them up on racism charges just because they could for no reason. For now, this was a new experience for Hubert never raised with racism. During Hubert's military career, he would experience Blacks, Gender, and the beginning of the Gay revolution in the military.

As the Dorm Chief, Hubert had to deal with many issues. Many related to personnel issues even though he himself was a trainee, which made it more difficult for Hubert. In one case, a trainee wanted to 'self-eliminate' himself from Basic Training. The self-elimination condition implied a mental condition, which the individual proved to be a good actor. One of the symptoms that he claimed was his shaking hands. Unfortunately, he was a smoker and when he lit up his cigarette; his hand was steady as could be and gave him away. Eventually, while marching, the individual kept marching off the base and the local Police found him on interstate ten. He received an administrative discharge from the military. Hubert had no input on the discharge that the individual received.

"Are you going to the Rec Center," asked a fellow trainee. Other than training, there was little social time left for the trainees. Trainees received only partial payments during their Basic Training. On weekends, one of the base clubs or Recreation Centers would hold a dance and the theater was always a good option. At the Rec Center, Trainees had a two-beer limit in order to ensure that no one drank too much. It seemed that someone controlled the entire Basic Training environment. Eventually as it would turn out to be one of many training events in Hubert military career, graduation quickly came around. He had enlisted for six years, which meant that on graduation day he was had two stripes as part of the six-year contract. Except for six-year enlistees, all fellow soldiers had no stripes since they were airman basic (E-1)enlisted-one members.

Six-year enlisted members were airman first class and would become E-2s or Airmen First Class (A1C). Not knowing better, they thought that they were special since they had two stripes on their sleeves. After waiting for an additional two weeks on hold status, Hubert and many of his fellow classmates went to Keesler Air Force Base (AFB) in Biloxi, Mississippi. Since there was a large group that fell in this category, a bus drove them to Keesler AFB. However, Hubert first stayed at Lackland AFB for approximately two weeks as a trainee general on hold-status. It was during this period while walking out of the barracks that a Senior Non-Commissioned Officer (SNCO) first saluted Hubert by mistake even though he had the AIC stripes on his sleeves.

"Airman, you are going to Personnel School," said the administrative sergeant. Growing up in Tucson, Hubert had not seen much racism. Biloxi in the early 1970s was still a racist since it was in the middle of the Deep South. Vietnam had just ended and many Americans regularly called fellow soldiers"baby killers". In the Deep South, there were still license plates that had colorful wording like "kill an airman". Unlike Basic Training where they had not officially entered the military rank structure, they were now soldiers. Whenever the Technical Training School trainees were out of class, they had free time to go off base. Nevertheless, Biloxi during that period was still a place where one had to be careful.

On their first trip off the base, he and a fellow soldier thought they would have their first cold beer. Unfortunately, for both of the new soldiers, one was a Black airman. When they entered the bar, the entire room went silent and all the customers stared at both of them. They knew that drinking a cold beer at this bar was probably not a good idea. Therefore, they returned to the base and went to the club for the cold beer. Hubert would soon find out that in the Deep South, going for a beer with a Black airman was a mistake.

"Boys, what are you doing?" asked the fat muscular while bar customer as Hubert and Joe a fellow Technical Training School classmate entered the local Biloxi bar. On their first trip off the base, he and a fellow soldier thought they would have their first cold beer. Hubert was used to seeing locals with car plates with colorful phrases as "Kill an Airman" since many locals were against the Vietnam War. Unfortunately, for both of the new airman, Joe was a black airman. When they entered the bar, the entire room went silent and all the customers stared at both of them. They knew that drinking a cold beer at this bar was probably not a good idea. Before walking out of the bar, the bar tender mentioned that Hubert was welcomed to say but the 'Colored Boy' using a different word had to leave.

Therefore, Hubert and Joe returned to the base and went to the base enlisted club for the cold beer. This event would be one of many reasons that Hubert finished his three-month self-paced training in three weeks. Academically, Hubert had always been an area that he excelled. As it turned out, personnel specialist training likes Basic Training not too difficult. Since this course was a self-phased course, instead of staying in Biloxi for the scheduled three months, Hubert quickly made it through all the academics in three weeks. He had already been told that after graduation that that he would be assigned to MacDill AFB in Tampa, Florida. This time after graduation, he did not have to wait before going to his first permanent assignment.

From 5 December 1974 to 20 July 1979, Hubert would work at the 1st Combat Support Group (CSG), Consolidated Personnel Office (CBPO) located in MacDill Air Force Base (AFB) in Tampa, Florida. The 1st CSG was under the 1st Fighter Wing later redesignated to the 56th Fighter Wing, which received an official transfer to Luke AFB when the F-16 Falcons became permanent aircraft in Arizona as a training unit. As a six-year enlistee, he would automatically receive two stripes once he graduated Basic Training and become an Airman First

Class (AIC). At MacDill AFB, Florida,Hubert would receive a promotion to E-4, Senior Airman (SrA), which was a new rank in the Air Force in 1976.

Then a year later after completing a mandatory new Professional Military Education (PME) class, and he received a promotionto E-4,Buck Sergeant (Sgt). Six months prior to going to Officer Training School (OTS), he received a promotion to Staff Sargent (SSgt). A decade later, the Buck Sergeant grade would go away and the new Senior Airman (Sra) grade would become the norm. During this era, Hubert would continue his normal trend of always moving from one job to another more important job based on his achievements. It was at this point that President Jimmy Carter became the new President and Hubert's new Commander-in-Chief (CINC).

At first, the US military had hope great things from their new CINC; after all, he was an Annapolis graduate and knew about the military first hand. Unfortunately, it would not take long before Hubert and his fellow Air Force members would find out that President Carter intended on destroying the US military in the name of 'peace' and idealism. Even as a young airman, Hubert was not naïve and knew enough to understand in the short time that he had traveled overseas that there were evil humans that hated Americans. Soon, Hubert would have to purchase his own pens and pencils to be able to do his own Air Force work thanks to President Carter military cuts.

NCO OF THE QUARTER PICTURE

He would initially report to the Records Section, which would teach him how the CBPO seven-functions worked. Then he would transfer to Customer Service and the Pass and Identifications Section that would teach him a different perspective of the CBPO. Due to his technical knowledge gained while working in the Data Automation at City Hall as a civilian, next Hubert worked in the Manning Control Section and the Data Captures Section. Once promoted to Sra, Hubert became the first airman to run the In-Processing Branch and selected as a Personnel Systems Manager over senior Non-Commissioned Officers (NCOs). During this period, Hubert received the award NCO of the Quarter honors more than once, selected by the Headquarters Air Force Military Personnel Center (AFMPC) to serve as a test center, and tasked to travel to different bases in the Southwest to fix their systems issues.

"So how did you get Florida?" asked a fellow classmate? In his dream sheet, Hubert had asked for all the bases on the west coast and instead received a most east based located air force base. The dream sheet or Air Force Form 90 was the Air Force assignment Form where Air Force members put their assignment preferences. As it turned out, personnel specialists training, like Basic Training is not too difficult. Hubert's classmates were surprised that he had finished the class requirements in such a short time-period. He already knew that after graduation that he would go to MacDill AFB in Tampa, Florida. This time after graduation, he did not have to wait before going to his first permanent assignment.

"Airman Contreras, you're going to MacDill," yelled the personnel specialist. Having moved three times in just under five months seemed like a great adventure. Each time Hubert moved, he kept moving farther away from Tucson as he hoped when he entered the Air Force. During Basic Training and Technical Training School, Hubert received partial pay every two weeks. His first paycheck at MacDill AFB, Florida had all of his back pay from Basic Training and Technical Training School. When he received his first paycheck at MacDill AFB, he was impressed with what he thought was his normal paycheck. Two week later when he received his first regular paycheck and saw that actual pay amount, he thought that the finance office had made a mistake.

He promptly marched over to finance and spoke with a sergeant who laughing told him to get out of his office. His monthly paycheck reflected his regular pay that in the past had been what he used to getting each week at the mine. He could not believe that anyone could live on such a small salary. Hubert's Air Force monthly salary was not half of what he earned in one week as a miner in Arizona. Once he paid his car insurance, he did not have much money left over to purchase anything much less for entertainment or traveling. It would be another ten years in the Air Force before his income would match his mine pay again that he made when he was nineteen years old. The only difference was that now he was proudly serving his country in uniform.

"I can't believe that the Air Force thinks that anyone can live on this pay," thought Hubert to himself. Nevertheless, as the finance sergeant mentioned, he had a meal card and a dorm room to sleep in that was part of his pay. In the Air Force's view, he did not need anything else. The sergeant stated, "Airman, get the hell out of here" as he and his fellow coworkers laughed. That same week Hubert started looking for a part-time work and found a job at the Officer's Club. After working all day at the Consolidated Base Personnel Office (CBPO), he worked at the Officers Club until mid-night until he started taking college classes.

At that point, he was able to work a deal with the club manager to clean the club after his classes. Hubert would arrive at the club around 10:30 PM, work until 1:00 AM and the go back to the barracks, and go to bed. After sleeping for a few hours, he would get up, take a shower and to into the CBPO to work to his fulltime work. Here he was lucky that he had good bosses that would allow him to study once he finished his primary tasks. At the same time, his bosses tended to hold him at a higher standard. Nevertheless, they would let him study in the conference room so that when they needed him they knew where to find him.

A decade later, the Air Force would pay airmen to move out. However, in the 1970s, single enlisted members received a tiny room with a roommate and had to eat in the Chow Hall. Hubert would quickly learn that the Chow Hall was always an experience. He never quite figured out how anyone could not cook eggs or give food some taste. If he wanted to have any type of social life, it looked like getting a part time job was going to be a necessary. Nevertheless, at least, four meals of cereal that was always Excellent and so were the peanut butter and jelly sandwiches. In addition, living in the dorms was also quite an experience. It seemed that every six months Hubert received a new roommate.

"What the heck, that idiot has been smoking pot," said Hubert. His room was five feet wide by eight feet long with a bunk bed and a refrigerator in the room. The center coffee table that he purchased only fit at the end of the bed. As for his roommates, each seemed to be different.

After SSGT Clark received an assignment to Langley AFB, Virginia, other roommates were chain smokers, others were alcoholics, and a few were the pot smokers. By this time, Hubert lost a close friend. Since many soldiers came back from Vietnam with drug addictions, the Air Force like other military Services was trying to deal with its drug problems. The Air Force forced military members to go to the Social Actions course taught mainly by Black instructors. Most were clearly racist in Hubert's view. During this era, this would be the first time that Hubert would hear that officially, "Black" was the preferred name that Americans would use when referring to individuals with dark colored skin. An individual in class made the mistake of calling the instructor 'African American' only to receive a hostile reply by the profession Social Actions Instructor.

The MacDill AFB Social ActionsInstructors would purposely ask class participants to each mention words used against them during their lives. By the end of each class, each student left with an excellent list of racists' words to use against any race. In an effort to minimize his time at MacDill AFB, since Hubert was single and he joined the Air Force to see the world, he volunteered to go on any Temporary Duty (TDY) that required a personnel specialist anywhere in the world. During Hubert's first two years in the Air Force, he deployed to Taiwan, Korea, and Okinawa on staffing assistance to process a wing closure post-Vietnam. At that point, thousands of military members and their aircraft were re-deploying back to the United States. During on TDY, Hubert received a task to Hill AFB, Utah to process a new wing that he closed in Korea and now processing into Utah.

This training would be invaluable once Hubert would go through the ranks and become an Officer. Many of Hubert closes friends and co-workers had been ex-combat fighter pilots that had been part of the post-Vietnam draw down. During that era, the Air Force forced Air Force Officer to become Buck Sergeants, which gave Captains and Majors three stripes and allow them to retire once they had twenty years on active duty. At retirement, they would retire at the highest rank held on active duty. Many of these Officers became Technical Sergeants (TSgts) quickly mainly because of the many medals and seniority, which both gave them extra promotion points as enlisted members. One such TSgt gave Hubert His first military Air Force Military Mess Dress.

At that time, the Mess Dress received the title as the waiters Mess Dress due to the winter coat being a short black coat and the summer coat being a short white coat. The Officers that became NCOs would serve as Hubert's best mentors during his enlisted career. In addition to the NCOs that he worked for during this period, Hubert would never work for another good mentor in his military career. Once he became an officer, it seemed that those above him always takeHubert's accomplishments to advance their careers but never went out of their way to help Hubert advance his career. At the same time, they never hurt Hubert's career, which in the militaryofficer culture is a plus. At the same time, as a Senior Officer, Hubert became a good mentor, a good commander, and a good boss never forgetting where he came from as he worked his way through the ranks.

Even some of the lucky Officers that made Major but forced to become Squadron Commanders for units where airman lived like Hubert became bitter. After all, they felt that they deserved flying squadrons and not baby-sitting airman. Therefore, their new mission in life became making everything difficult for every airman in their squadron including Sra Hubert Contreras. Hubert's Squadron Commander received the title of 'chilly willy' because he was so cold and did not care anything about the men that he commander. That would be the first time that Hubert would understand that Officers in the USAF only care about their promotions or their next promotion. Hubert knew at that point that if he became an Officer that promotion "would never a motivation for him during his military career".

"If you do not move you'll force me to turn you into the Commander," mentioned Hubert. One of his roommates shared a room for a very short time when during the weekly security Police inspection where dogs when they walked into the dorm smelled the aftereffects of the marijuana (pot). Hubert told his roommate that if he went to jail because of him that he would turn him in to the Squadron Commander. Hubert knew that he would not turn his roommate into the Unit Commander but he only wanted to scare him. It not that he was the type of individual to start trouble, but he did not join the military to get into trouble because of drugs or any unfavorable reason. His roommate quickly moved out the following week.

"You need to return to the Security Police (SP) Squadron for another 179 days," mentioned Master Sergeant (MSgt) Miller. As an SP augmentee, members sent back to their home stations for a week and then members would start as an SP augmentee again. During this tour, Hubert allowed to work the base gates and the annual MacDill AFB Open House in Tampa, Florida. During the MacDill AFB Open House, numerous Air Force aircraft deployed to MacDill AFB in addition to the aircraft assigned to the base. Hubert received the task as the traffic control in the center of the flight line. Each day would end with Hubert Having many pieces of paper with phone numbers from girls that he threw away although flattered. Even though Hubert was a young airman, he did not feel that this was a proper manner to meet someone.

"Would you like to come home for the weekend with me?" asked David (Dave). Like any healthy young man, entertainment was always important to Hubert. Going out of the base was much better than sitting around the dorms. Florida was a great place for a young bachelor with countless beaches to show off his dark tan. Having 52-inch shoulders, a 28-inch waist, and somewhat good looks helped a bit. Having grown up as a Mormon, Hubert went to his church dances and continued that practice once he arrived in Tampa. Nevertheless, he had yet to find anyone special in his life. He was lucky since one of his coworkers lived nearby in Bradenton, which was about forty miles from MacDill AFB, Florida. His name was Dave and he lived in at his mother's home in Bradenton.

"Do you want to go home to Bradenton this weekend," asked Dave. He would take Hubert Home to Bradenton on weekends and he quickly fell in love with his family. Dave's mom, Mary was from the Maryland and had married Buddy before moving to Bradenton. Bill worked in construction and did the laid the sheet rock boards in new homes. Dave had a sister Dizy who was a senior in High School. Since Dizy was Dave's sister, Hubert became good friends but he never thought of her in any other manner than a friend. Dizy was an attractive blonde-haired person but Hubert felt that in a way that she was like his sister. In his view, dating Dizy was never an option out of respect to Dave's mother. Hubert quickly became a member of the family and visited often on weekends.

"Who is that?" Hubert asked David. As he entered Dave's house, to the left all he could see was someone bending over the corner couch where Dizy was laying down. Dizy had invited her best friend Darlene to the wedding. Darlene was wearing a short striped blue and white muscled shirt and shorts. She had been at the Bradenton Beach all week and her long blonde-haired person hear shined as it hit her waist. She walked over to Dave as they walked into the Florida Room and Darlene asked him if he could take her to the prom but Dave had to work. Dave then said that he would ask Hubert to see if he could take Darlene to the prom. On this day, Dave was getting married for the first time to Janet.

Hubert would often see Darlene's long blonde-hair wearing her short striped blue and white muscled shirt in shorts in slow motion in his dreams. Hubert's fairy tale romance started on that muggy sunny day in Bradenton, Florida in his mind when he saw Darlene Dixon walked out of the crowded Florida Room to the kitchen. Hubert saw the young girl who was too young to talk too other than say hi too because she was only seventeen years old and he was twenty-three. However, for the next year Hubert could not get her off his mind, her blue eyes, her beautiful smile, and the way she helped Mary in the kitchen. He would also remember how Darlene displayed concern for Dizy who on that day did not feel well and laid on the couch in the living room. With Darlene's dark tan and her long blond hair down to her waist always shining in his mind.

Dizy had grown up with Darlene and until recent, she had been her next-door neighbor. Darlene's father, Alfred and his brother had purchase ten acres together just down the road about two miles and built a new home on a five acre lot. Alfred's construction company had finally done well locally after years where he traveled throughout the US building bridges and gas stations. Hubert first noticed Darlene as they both were putting the dirty dishes in the kitchen sink in the kitchen. He immediately knew that he liked Darlene's looks and although he tried, he could not help himself sneaking a quick look at her. Nevertheless, what he like best was how Darlene treated everyone and how everyone reacted to her when she walked around the living room. She was just a kindhearted person that did not expect anything back for her efforts that Hubert found attractive and refreshing from someone so young.

"So Dave, how old is Darlene," asked Hubert. After asking Dave who she was, he learned that she was still too young. Although his mind went wild, the muggy Florida temperature brought reality back into his life and all he could think was, "hands off, she's jail bate". That did not stop Hubert from thinking of Darlene for he knew that when she turned eighteen that he would return to Darlene's house to meet her officially. Dave had warned Hubert that Darlene's father was a strict father. Dave had also mentioned to Hubert that Darlene would never leave Florida and her family. She would never leave Florida mainly because she was too close to her family. Since Hubert was in the Air Force, it was only a matter of time before he would receive another assignment to another location and would have to leave Tampa.

In time, he would know much more about Darlene from Dave. Up to this point, even though Hubert had gone to Bradenton for over a year, he never met Darlene. However, he never stopped asking Dave, Dizy, Buddy, and Mary questions about Darlene and knew her well even though he never met her in person. She normally came for a visit during the weekdays when he was in Tampa working. Hubert would remember Dave wedding events except seeing Darlene in the Florida Room and in the kitchen. For that first memory, he knew that he was instantly in love forever. As he sneaked one quick look after another, he knew that he not being able to stop staring at her. For at that moment Darlene stole his heart and dreams for now.

"Hey buddy, she's only seventeen," Dave said to Hubert. He knew he was twenty-two and in the Air Force, which meant trouble. Except for a quick hello, he did not say much to Darlene. As they, both kept the coffee tables in the living room and Florida Room cleared, this excuse gave them both an opportunity to be close to one another. For many months to follow his recurring dream would be of this first memory of Darlene at Dave's wedding reception as they both helped Mary. Each time they met in the kitchen all he could do was stare and smile. It would be months before Dave unexpectedly asked him if he would take Darlene to her High School prom.

"Would you mind asking Hubert to take me to the prom since you have to work that night," asked Darlene. She had asked Dave if he would ask Hubert if he would be willing to take her to her senior prom. As an excuse to talk about the prom events, the following week Hubert asked Darlene to go out to dinner. They went to the local Red Lobster just off Highway 41. Since Hubert did not make much pay from the Air Force, he had to use a coupon. It would also be a first memory for this young couple since he had to use a coupon where if you purchase one meal, the second meal was free. As they spoke about the Prom, it did not matter to him what Darlene want for her prom date, which he would give her. In a trance, all he could do was look at her smile and beautiful face. Knowing that he was falling in love with someone that he knew he could not. It would be a few months before Darlene turned eighteen.

"I'm going to Hubert's Prom in that car? Maybe he won't mind taking Hubert's car," Darlene thought to herself. The night of the Prom,Darlene seemed to want to say something to Hubert when he picked her up in his 1969 Chevy. It would be months later that he would learn that she did not like his hotrod. He was proud of the L-60 series mags and the chrome side pipes. The month prior, he painted white stripes on the lower part of the main body of his 1969 Chevy. While painting the stripes a car full of girls had stopped and asked for directions.

Hubert not wearing a shirt and with his dark tan and normal smile had charmed all the girls. Yet, he behaved and only offered directions although a few of the girls made it clear that they were interested in being more than just friends are. Years' later car stripes would be the fashion for sports cars using paste-on stripes. Off course, in his case it was cheaper buying the cans of paint. Unknown to him, Darlene thought of asking that they take her car to the Prom. Nevertheless, in the end, she said nothing and they drove Hubert's hotrod to her Prom.

"Thank you for the beautiful flowers," mentioned Darlene. Hubert went all out for the Prom. He rented a white tuxedo and Darlene purchased her Prom dress, which was white in Jacksonville, Florida. The week prior Hubert looked in the phone book and found a restaurant near the Sarasota convention center. As they drove up to the valet, Hubert was proud of his rumbling hotrod with fur on the dashboard to keep the dashboard from cracking from the hot sun. As the valet opened Darlene's door, with a big smile he got into the Chevy and quickly drove out to the valet parking lot. At that point, the door attendant already had the double doors open for the couple.

"Is this the first time that you have been at this restaurant," asked the waiter. When they entered the restaurant, they were quickly seated since Hubert had made reservations at this fancy restaurant. The waiter asked if we wanted wine and Hubert quickly said yes, a white wine off course. This had been the first time that he had ordered wine in any restaurant. It was during Technical Training School that he had drunk his first alcoholic drink but after this night, he, and Darlene, over time, they would drink white wine at it would become their favorite drink. Nevertheless, on this night, after dinner when the waiter asked if we wanted our leftover wine taken to their room, Darlene thought he had other ideas in mind. The waiter thought that they had just gotten married since both were dressed in white.

"Wow, who is that," asked many of Darlene's classmates. At the Prom,Darlene proudly walked into the ballroom with an older man holding her arm. Hubert proudly held her arm as he entered the ballroom. It seemed that the entire room became quite as all her classmates looked at Darlene and Hubert as they walked into the ballroom in slow motion. Hubert was wearing his white tuxedo and Darlene wearing her beautiful white silk dress that looked like a wedding dress. She and her mother had driven to Jacksonville in northern Florida to pick this one of a kind dress as her prom dress. After all, she had to be dressed just perfect, looked beautiful in her prom dress, would have the perfect date, and all her High School boys wondered why they had not asked her out on a date.

This would be the first time that Darlene and Hubert would truly make a stunning couple. Even at dinner, everyone thought that it was their wedding night for they looked like the perfect magical couple meant to be together. Nevertheless, for now, Hubert had just turned twenty-one, Darlene was still seventeen, and Hubert was only escorting Darlene to her Prom. Without asking, Hubertwithout knowing rented a white tuxedo that matched Darlene's dress perfectly. At the prom, they would take a prom picture that would have to replace their wedding picture since they would elope after only dating for seventy-two hours.

As Hubert looked at her radiant smile and her beautiful blue eyes, he knew that, her male classmates finally realized how beautiful she was. He had seen that beauty from the first second he saw her. He knew that only a real man would know the beauty of a woman even though he knew that Darlene was still only seventeen. Knowing that he had to behave for she was a woman that deserved nothing but respect. Even if Darlene's classmates were too foolish or too young to realize what they had missed for the last four years in High School, Hubert knew better. Yet he could see Darlene's coaches looking at him with contempt as he marched in with Darlene to her table.

"Darlene mentioned that you are in the Air Force," asked one of her classmates. Throughout the night, they dance some, but Darlene had asked if she could dance with some of her classmates. All of a sudden, all the High School "boys" who had not seen what Hubert had seen in her, all wanted to dance with her. At first, Hubert thought of giving out numbers to "all the foolish boys" but he was not sure how they would take his humor.

AsDarlene danced, Hubert could see he classmates line up and argue on who would be the next one to dance next. He was proud that Darlene was having the night that she deserved after what he could only imagine how they treated her in school. He hoped that in the end when she departed the dance that she would feel happy, as she was the queen of the ball for she was in his eyes truly beautiful. Hoping that on this night that all her dreams had truly come true as she hoped.

At the same time, all her girlfriends wanted to know all they could about Darlene's older handsome Air Force date. Actually, Darlene mentioned that she only had a few girlfriends that she could count in one hand. She had always said that she liked her man dark and handsome. Since it was her night, Hubert said yes, as he saw her dance the night away. It is not to say that it did not bother him a bit to see Darlene dancing without him. Hubert knew that in a way she was getting even with all the boys that had ignored her over the years. Even though he could see that other young girls wanted to dance with him, he did not since the other girls were not Darlene. A few times, Hubert went to the men's room to make the time pass by.

Nevertheless, he knew that for this night, he wanted everyone to know that she was special until he could make her spend the rest of his or her life together. All Hubert knew was that Darlene had asked him to take her to her Prom and that he was her date. She could to do anything she wished on this night for it was her Prom night. Hubert could see from her face that she finally was getting even with all the girls that thought that they were too good or too pretty than she was. Many who had picked on her over the years since she was in elementary school were now jealous.

"I better take you home before it gets too late," said Hubert. They ended the night when Hubert dropped Darlene at her front door. Later on, she would tell him that there were many Prom parties that she was invited to go and she decided not to attend would out Hubert. The next time he saw her was on Dizy's birthday when they went out to the Wreck. The Wreck was a bar by Leto Beach that had dancing music. Dizy had asked her and another girl friend Lorna to go with David and Hubert to celebrate her eighteenth birth date. Darlene was sure that Hubert would dance with Lorna or Dizy and surprised when he continued to ask her to dance all night. After all, considering Darlene thought that Lorna and Dizy were beautiful compared to her. Especially since, she did not consider herself to be good looking.

Darlene did not know about Hubert's dream as a little boy about marrying a girl just like Darlene. She would have blue eyes like her and blond hair like Darlene. She would exactly the right size and height as Darlene and has the same beliefs about family that Hubert felt was the most important factors in life. Overall, Darlene was Hubert's dream come true as his dream when he was a five-year-old boy in Mexico at his Grandmother Maria's house. He just never expected that he would have to travel to Florida to meet her and that she would be so young. He just was not sure how he would ask her to marry him, yet, but knew that Darlene was the love of his life. Although Dave would cause a problem for Hubert when he asked him for a favor later on, Hubert used bad judgment and did not go to work as he told Darlene earlier that day.

"Te amo mi amor!" (I love you, my love) Hubert whispered in her ear in Spanish. This time things were different; he knew that Darlene had just turned eighteen. Now Hubert knew that he would ask her to marry him but was not sure how since she had only gone out with him once and that date was to the prom.

As they danced all night, he held her close to him. Darlene was too young to understand that Hubert knew without a doubt that he wanted her. She still had the dark tan that he saw at David's wedding but she had cut her hair shorter. However, her beautiful blue eyes and sweat smile drove him crazy as he dreamed of her each night. In time, the one thing that he would love about Darlene was her ability to change hairstyles freely making her seem as another person.

"I just can't take my eyes off you," mentioned Hubert as he kept sneaking a smile at Darlene. Dizy and her friend Lorie had always thought that they were much better looking than Darlene was, but to Hubert, they were not. Lorna was Miss South East High School and Dizy was the most popular girl in school where Darlene grew up in Bradenton. He made sure that he sat in the back seat of the car with Darlene after leaving the wreck. As he spoke to her in Spanish and translated to her, what he was saying. This had been the first that he had spoken Spanish to a woman. Even though Darlene was only eighteen, and Hubert was twenty-one, he knew that he wanted her.

She might have thought it was strange but he knew that it was time for her to know that he wanted her and no other woman. Since Darlene had never dated, was still innocent and did not understand the dating ways. She kept telling him to hush as he kept talking to her in Spanish and English. He told her of her beautiful smile and her beautiful eyes. Hubert made sure that he got as close as he could to her to smell her scent that he would know forever. He knew that Darlene liked him as well but it was too early in their relationship. Hubert did not realize at this point that within seventy-two hours that he would be a married man.

"How about taking a drive to Bradenton beach," asked Hubert. It was the end of summer in Florida but even in late August and early September meant that the beach weather would be around for a while. After Dizy's birthday celebration, the next Saturday he purchased Darlene a dress although he had not indented the dress to be of such thin and revealing material. Darlene's father Alfred told Darlene the dress was "too revealing" telling her that he knew what that boy wanted. After all, Alfred was a strict and old fashion father that new what men wanted. Darlene wore the dress but with a condition. However, she had to wear a heavy cream-colored sweater over the dress. Otherwise, Darlene would not be able to go of her house with her new dress.

Hubert went by a flower shop, purchased yellow roses, and drove to Darlene's house and spoke to her parents. Darlenestayed in her room until Hubert had her parent's gave her permission to formally date her and Alfred said she could come out of her room. Darlene's dad Alfred and Hubert spoke for about two hours where Hubert made his intentions known that he was serious about his relationship with Darlene. After passing Alfred' interrogation, Darlene's mom Marie went to her room to get her and allowed to go out on a date. This had been Darlene's second date alone without her brother. Her first date had been on her Prom date. Even then, Hubert had done well when he walked straight into the dining room and sat with Alfred. From the start, Hubert shook his hand, had coffee with him, and spoke with him for over an hour before taking Darlene to diner.

"How about going to Disney World this weekend," asked Hubert? This would be their first official date; however, Darlene would have to pay for most of the entertainment. Hubert had enough for the two tickets to enter, and for food and drinks. As a Senior Airman (SrA), he did not make enough monies to purchase any gifts. Darlene would purchase matching sterling silver torques rings that unknown to both of them would be their wedding rings. Nevertheless, for this day, these rings were friendship rings that reflected their feelings for one another. Over time, Hubert would never remove his ring and the small torques rocks would fall out because of the construction work that he did working for Alfred.

"I think that we better leave," mentioned Hubert. They drove to Dave's house because Hubert knew that no one was at home. As they kissed tenderly, he knew that they could not stay there for too long. For he knew that, they would both not be able to control their lust for each other. Even though the lights in the house were turned off, the moonlight was coming through the windows still provided enough light to see that like me, she was losing control of herself. As they sat on the couch, the room turned bright as they kissed. On that night, he knew that it was time to take Darlene home before he did something wrong. As instructed by Alfred, he was to have Darlene home by mid-night and he delivered Darlene home fifteen minutes early.

"I need to return to Tampa since I have to work in the Officer's Club on Sunday," said Hubert. Since he worked in Tampa, the weekends were the only time that he had to spend time with Darlene. The following Saturday he spend the entire day with Darlene because he had a part-time job at the Officers Club cleaning the bar areas and had to return to the base. However, Dave asked him go out with him on a date since he wanted to take an old High School girlfriend, Jane to out and go to bed with her. Although he thought it was wrong since Dave was married, he eventually agreed even though he felt guilty that he did not mention anything to Dave's wife. Jane would not go out with Dave unless her girlfriend Barbie had a date. It seemed that Hubert was that stand-in blind date.

"I think we better leave," mentioned Dizy. Unfortunately, the dance place where they went was also the place that Darlene and her girlfriends was a safe place that they went to on weekends when they did not have to work. When Darlene walked into the dance area, she saw a girl on his lap being very friendly. When Darlene saw Barbie on Hubert's lap, she walked out. Although Hubert made it clear to Barbie that he was there for Dave, she did not care. The following morning Hubert went to Darlene's house.

Darlene was mad at Hubert because she saw him at the dance place the night before but Hubert did not know this and she would not tell him why. Nevertheless, with allot of begging she forgave him. The following day he asked her to marry him. By then, we had formally dated 72-hours and Hubert was afraid to wait until the end of the year to marry Darlene after the stunt he had just pulled. Their third date was to take their blood test and then they eloped the following Saturday. Even on their wedding day, Hubert dropped Darlene before midnight as he normally did.

Darlene like Hubert had been the fourth child with a younger sister Starlette. She had learned to standup for herself if she would receive any attention from her family. This would teach her to serve as a negotiator who worked hard to make everyone in her family to get along. As a freckled girl, teased often make her strong. She tried to be the one who stayed positive but she kept her feelings to herself. In High School, she would be a cheerleader primarily because she wanted to be close to her brother Dick who was the star athlete. Hubert would see this beautiful young woman in the Florida Room knowing that she would only get more beautiful with age.

During the week Darlene and Hubert had gone to take their blood tests and that following Saturday, Hubert picked Darlene up under the premise that they were going to the beach. At the time that Darlene and Hubert took the blood tests, they planned to get married in a year. During the week, Hubert went and traded in his hotrod Chevy for a Mazda station wagon because he knew that Darlene did not like his hotrod. The car payment was low and the insurance cost went down since it was an economical car and due to his new marital status. Hubert would miss his hotrod but he knew that Darlene would be happy with a family car. Since it was a five-speed manual vehicle, he took Darlene and her sister to side roads in Bradenton and taught them both how to drive the new car. Darlene would soon love her new five-speed on the floor Mazda station wagon.

"Babe I think that I am going to faint" said Darlene as her knees gave way and Hubert grabbed for her as she almost hit the floor. Later as a young married couple, they both believed that she could not get pregnant. Yet, three months later, she was expecting as he worked two jobs and went to college full time in hopes of making a better life for his young family. At one point, he would tell Darlene that he would make it with her or without her help. Time was passing so fast they both thought. Now they had a little baby girl named Tawny to think about over any hard times. Darlene knew that he was right but for a young newly turned nineteen-year-old girl who had just finished High School, eloped, and got married, life had quickly turned hard. Unknown at the time, Darlene was going through Post Traumatic symptoms due to a hard pregnancy. This young couple had to live on a small Air Force salary that took a lot of sacrifice and love that had just lived what seemed like a dream. .

"Are you sure you want to get married?" Darlene asked Hubert as they walked into the Baptist pastor's house to get married. While driving, Hubert pulled over and called the Baptist pastor and a retired Navy Admiral. He agreed to have US come to his house to marry US so Hubert called his friend and his wife Manny and Bunny to serve as their witness who met them at the Admiral's house. After the Baptist pastor married the couple, he used his Polaroid Camera and took the only picture that Darlene and Hubert had of their marriage that also included Bonny and Manny. Over time, Bonny and Manny would become good friends of Darlene as they had been for Hubert.

"Will you take this woman to be your wife?" as Hubert gladly replied yes. Manny and Bonny who were his friends stood in as our witnesses. Manny who was also one of his coworkers would be the stand in friend for Darlene. Later he would have to hold two jobs and go to college during the evenings in an effort to make a better life for his new bride. Bonny would also be a true friend as she invited them regularly free meals. After going to a movie, Hubert took Darlene home by mid-night as instructed by Alfred. The group walked out of the movie after finding out that it was not a family movie based on the title, "Cinderella". The movie was actually 'XXX' rated but no one noticed the small rating markings when the group entered the movie theater. This would be the end of their first day of marriage.

"What are we going to do? My dad is going to kill us!" Darlene told Hubert. That evening, Hubert dropped Darlene at her house. Darlene and Hubert did not have a wedding night because both were scared to death. Even though Hubert was twenty-three, that did not mean that, he was not afraid of Darlene's father. The following morning Hubert and Darlene went out for breakfast to decide what they were going to do about telling her parents that they were married. They knew that they loved each other dearly but also knew Alfred would be hurt dearly and disappointed with Darlene. Actually, at that point, Darlene was in lust and Hubert was in love. Darlene just wanted Hubert to give her a baby because she knew he would make beautiful children.

Hubert and Darlene while eating breakfast read in the Bradenton newspaper that they had applied for marriage license. Thinking that the newspaper said that they were married, they contemplated driving off the Skyway Bridge in Saint Petersburg, Florida, ha!, ha! By lunchtime, they knew that they had to tell her parents. Alfred made it clear that he was hurt and disappointed but said, "Son you wanted a wife, she's yours now, she's out by Wednesday". Not having much money, he found an apartment near the bowling alley in Tampa that he could afford. Now Hubert would be able to meet Alfred's instructions and make sure that Darlene was out of his house by Wednesday. Hubert would make sure that Darlene would never be a burden on Alfred for he would take care of her needs for her entire life.

"What did I do?" Darlene thought to herself when she walked into the new apartment. Although they had planned to keep their marriage a secret until the end of the year when they officially married, this change of plan made both of their lives quickly spin. A few days prior, she had lived in a 6,000 square foot home with a pool, a car, spending money, and a few rules that she had to follow. Now she lived in an apartment the size of her bedroom that had nothing but old furniture.

"Do you want me to submit the food stamp application for you?" said the Food and Nutrition technician from the United States (US) Department of Agriculture office. Hubert's pride did not allow him to take charity to feed his new family although he qualified. Instead, he took a part-time job that paid him more than the Air Force. The rent for the one bedroom apartment was $150 per month. Since the Air Force paid him twice a month around $180, one paycheck covered the rent and the following paycheck covered the car payment. The furnished apartment was good since the young couple had no furniture. All he had in the barracks was a small black and white television, a stereo, his military clothing, and his some civilian clothing that all fit in two small suit cases.

On Monday, Hubert went to finance and received an advance to the housing and rations allowance, which gave him the first month's rent and the required deposit. It seemed as if time was moving slowly for the new newlyweds. By Wednesday, they moved into their tiny new apartment. Although Darlene was used to living in a 6,000 square feet home, our apartment the size of her bedroom would be our new home for six months until the newlyweds could afford something nicer. Each time Darlene and Hubert got on the bed, it fell through the rails, which did not seem to bother them. It would be memories such as this that would make the new couple stronger or make them not stay together. In this case, Darlene and Hubert would grow as a married couple with each year.

"We need to go on base and get your ID card," mentioned Hubert to Darlene. Once Darlene was in Tampa, Hubert took her to MacDill AFB and the Consolidated Base Personnel Office (CBPO) where he worked to get Darlene's military dependent identification card. Manny worked in Customer Service and took care of Darlene's identification card. This meant that Darlene was now loaded in the Air Force Air Force Military Personnel Center (AFMPC) system. This would also allow Darlene to go to the base hospital when she got sick or go to the Base Exchange to go shopping or Base Commissary for groceries. However, since Darlene and Hubert only had one car since Alfred made Darlene return her car this required planning as a couple once Hubert started college. He took lunch and night classes that took most of his off time.

"We need a bookshelf," Hubert told Darlene. The following weekend after working with her father, he surprised her with a bright blue book shelf. Hubert had taken woodshop in junior high and did his best making a bookshelf out of left over pieces from the woodpile. He scraped the concrete off and cut the pieces to the length he needed for his new shelf. He also found two cans of spray blue paint and painted the shelf. Except for a few corners that were not quite level and being too heavy, it was their first shelf that they would use in two apartments. In addition, since Hubert only found a florescent blue paint in shed that Alfred had, the color at first went with the first apartment décor mainly because the couple did not have much.

Hubert did not have the correct tools to cut the wood. Besides, the wood came from the woodpiles from concrete jobs during recent driveway jobs. Hubert simply cleaned the wood as best he could, took out the nails, and hammered the wood into a three level bookshelf. The two cans of bright blue paint that he found in the shack was a plus since it was free. It took two strong men to lift the new bookshelf because weight well over two-hundred pounds mainly because Hubert not able to remove all the concrete from the wood. Later, once Darlene started purchasing furniture slowly, the shelf was place in the spare room.

"I'm going to pay you for your work," mentioned Alfred. For months, Hubert's pride would not allow himself to accept pay from Alfred. Instead, Hubert would accept some money to take Darlene out on weekends to a movie or diner after a long day at work with Alfred doing construction. Otherwise, Hubert could afford to take Darlene out on a date. Eventually, Alfred forgave Hubert and Darlene for eloping even though he had been deeply hurt. Alfred had always liked Hubert from day one and had selected Hubert for Darlene. Alfred was just hurt by Darlene since he had always wanted to walk her down the-alter and give her away in marriage. Darlene had been the sickly child that had almost died and only slept if her daddy held her until she was well.

During that period, of all the workers, on weekends because of Hubert more jobs were done on weekends that during the week with two full crews. Alfred would pay him per porch block, step-treads laid out, the number of jobs that he laid out, or the number of jobs that he cleaned at construction sites. During the same time, Hubert was going to college trying to earn a college degree so that he could become a military Officer in the US Air Force. Darlene had just told him that she was pregnant although the young couple had planned to wait five years before having children.

Darlene had planned on going to the MacDill AFB Credit Union and applying for a job. After all, she had been a bookkeeper at her last job earning three times as much than Hubert when they were dating. Once Darlene told him that she was pregnant, he was happy but knew that as a Non-Commissioned Officer (NCO) that he could not afford to give his family what it needed financially. After declining food stamps, Hubert decided that if he did not received a selection to Officers Training School (OTS) on his first attempt that he would separate from the Air Force.

When Hubert worked, Alfred's construction crew laid out more jobs than the two or three driveway jobs of concrete poured during the early part of the week. There were other ways that Alfred and Marie would help their children. Marie would regularly over purchase food and then tell Darlene to take home the food she liked. Darlene and Hubert would only take food from her mom Marie initially instead of taking any pay for working with Alfred.

Marie knew that the young couple would not take money unless they earned the monies unless it was an emergency. Even then, Darlene and Hubert would make sure that they paid back any monies borrowed during an emergency from Alfred and Marie. Hubert was never worried of working for whatever he wanted for his family. After all, since he was fourteen, most of his life, he had held two jobs and he was already twenty-four yearsold.

In time, Hubert and Darlene would receive their first income tax money that was just enough to purchase a bright red velvet living room set that was on sale. It was the only living room set that they could afford with the monies that the Internal Revenue Service (IRS) had refunded them. It would also do until Alfred would give them Darlene's bedroom set. By this time, the young couple was ready to move into their new apartment at the Teracia Apartments. Finally, the young couple had a nice apartment, a nice bedroom set, a new living room set, and the same old bright blue book rack. Hubert was still working fulltime in the Air Force, on weekends working with Alfred in construction, and going to college during the night, or during lunchtime.

"You did not think that I that I could cook like this, didn't you," asked Darlene. She had just baked fried chicken and country biscuits, white rise and green peas, and all the food that she had grown up eating. As each empty space took up the limited counter and table space, she wanted Hubert to know that she knew a little bit about cooking. As was the case for this unexpected meal, Dave and other friends would come home with him to eat his bride's country fixings. Hubert knew what it meant to have a cooked hot meal in the MacDill AFB, Florida Chow Hall. Soon he went from a twenty-eight in waist to thirty-eight inches that did not seem to matter to Darlene. Nevertheless, her cooking melted in his mouth and those of his single coworkers that came for lunch.

"What a beautiful night it is!" thought Hubert to himself as he asked Darlene to go to the beach. Their new dates as a married couple were now going to the beach with something that Darlene cooked and a bottle of seven up as our cocktail. Alfred had forced Darlene to sell her car so we were a one-car family. Initially, although Hubert worked for Alfred on weekends, he would not take any monies for the work until a few months later when Alfred insisted that he pay him since he was his best worker. In a way, Hubert was equally as proud as Alfred was or equally as stubborn. Alfred saw himself in Hubert as a young man and knew that he would make a good husband for Darlene but was hurt when they eloped.

Because of Hubert's work ethics, it seemed that the other employees worked as hard as he did when he was around. Alfred mentioned many times that his workers normally did the same number of jobs each weekend when Hubert worked that they normally did during the week. For some reason, whenever Hubert worked he always worked hard and those around him did the same. Perhaps out of pride but the result always led to more jobs accomplished during the end of each weekday. Alfred's employees behaved better whenever Hubert worked on weekends.

Alfred at first was more hurt at Darlene because of all his girls he expected more from her since she had always been the most responsible daughter of all her girls. Nevertheless, when Darlene eloped with Hubert Alfred was hurt. Alfred had instructed Hubert that he wanted Darlene out of his house by Wednesday when the previous Sunday Darlene and Hubert told him that they were married. It would not take long for Alfred and Hubert to be like father and son or long for Alfred to offer Hubert to take over his construction business.

"Babe when we go to Tucson we have an invitation to Senator Denis DeConcinni's, D-Arizona, victory part," said Hubert. It had been six months since first visiting Tucson. His mother had been part of the volunteers on his election quest to the Senate and invited to the victory party at the downtown Marriott. As Darlene and Hubert walked into the basement banquet ballroom, the first thing that all visitors saw was cake of the Senate. The following morning, both invited to the Hilton on Miracle Mile for DeConcinni's first press conference and a morning breakfast. Months later when Hubert finished college, DeConcinni's would also write a letter of recommendation for Hubert to attend Officers Training School (OTS) once he finished college.

"Sir, what would you like to eat?" As they waited in line to get something to eat, Darlene fainted as Hubert reached out to catch her. By this time, although Darlene believed all her life that she would never have children because of a serious illness that she had as a young babe, five months after we eloped, she was pregnant. At this point, Hubert knew that he could not afford to serve as a Non-Commissioned Officer (NCO) due to the low pay. Before taking the weekend job and Alfred paying for his weekend work, Hubert recalled that he had qualified for food stamps that he refused out of pride. Like so many thousands of military members that qualified for food stamps, Hubert's family joined the long list of military families that served the nation and did not receive a decent wage for serving and defending their country.

"How about buying a house" said Hubert. At the Teracia apartments, Hubert had gotten in the habit of taking Tawny in her stroller on long walks up the sidewalk in the waterfront on Gandy Boulevard. From an early age, he had always taken his baby girl out in her stroller for walks. Nevertheless, after a year at the Teracia apartments, Hubert decided that it was time to purchase their first home close to the base in an effort to help Darlene. The house was on Adams Street, which was about half a mile from the side gate near the water to MacDill AFB, Florida. Now, Darlene and Hubert had a small two bedroom home, which gave them and Tawny each a bedroom. The living room and dining room was an open area next to the kitchen with a small washroom.

In the back of the house, the owner had started an extra bedroom or playroom that Hubert added windows with Alfred's help and completed the roof. Hubert also added white planters around the front and sides of the house around each plant making the house look much prettier. Overall, although the house was in Tampa, it could easily been a country house. For Hubert, it seemed that every hour of the day received a commitment of some kind. This allowed him to jog part of theway and not allowed him to stay in shape since with two jobs, going to school full-time, and spend time with Tawny.

As Tawny got older, she looked forward to daddy coming home and taking her out. She knew that he would talk to her and sing to her the songs that he created for her when she was a baby. This way he could talk or sing to her as he walked or sang down Gandy Boulevard, which was nearly ten miles roundtrip. Once Hubert and Darlene moved into their house on Adams Street, Gandy Boulevard was too far to take their regular walk. Instead, Hubert took Baby Tawny to the base in her stroller and spent time with her as he had on Gandy Boulevard. As he had done on Gandy Boulevard, Hubert always made sure that he took plenty of water for Baby Tawny and never went when it was too hot.

Baby Tawny loved going with daddy on her regular walks even though she was still a little baby. In addition, just down the road from Adams Street, a small park had a running track that Hubert would take his baby girl in her stroller often. Since they were the only two in the park, he would sing her favorite songs that he created for her and other songs like frosty the snowman. Stopping often to give her water since it was humid and Hubert wanted to make sure that little Tawny did not get too hot as he washed her down with a wet rag.

During that time, Tawny was having medical problems. Although Darlene and Hubert had purchased a baby crib, Tawny had never slept in the crib since she always cried. Eventually, Hubert purchased a double bed to replace the crib and put a two-by-four board on one side and slept with Tawny once he arrived from school around ten thirty each night. He would get two or three bottles ready each night and a pile of diapers and go to bed with her. This was the only way that Tawny would not cry and sleep.

Hubert wrote songs for Tawny that he would sign to her every night that over the years she would ask for each time she would ask daddy for her songs before going to bed. It would not be long before Hubert would have to sleep with Tawny every night in order for everyone to be able to get any sleep. Unknown to Darlene and Hubert, the MacDill AFB doctor had given her the wrong medications for a child that should have been for someone ten years older and not an infant. This mistake made her sick for years until she grew out of the side effects.

"Mental work will make you age faster" said Alfred. Darlene laughed as her daddy told her that working in an office was harder than working construction work. Her father would tell her that Hubert would age faster using his mind than working using his body over time. They were talking of how Hubert was such a hard worker each time he worked for him on weekends. Each morning Darlene would see a pile of diapers in the corner as she got up to get Tawny. Hubert had to go to work each morning at five in the morning since he had to study before he started work. He was taking lunch classes, nighttime college classes, and working on weekends in construction in addition to his fulltime daytime Air Force job.

While working at a construction site, Hubert was able to purchase a table and six chairs for $75 from a senior couple at one of the trailer parks that he was working at. The couple sold dining room set to him at a bargain when he explained it to them that it was all he could afford. Besides, that is the only money he had left until next payday, which was still another week. Since the set was an off colored green, Hubert had to paint the dining and living room to match the table set. Although Darlene and Hubert planned to wait five years before having children, Darlene was pregnant. During her time at home, she painted the kitchen and small washroom areas.

"At that point, he knew that he needed to make a better life for his family than the Non-Commissioned Officer (NCO) pay allowed. If he was to stay in the military, he had decided to give applying to Officer Training School (OTS) one attempt. He had decided that if not selected to OTS that he would have separated from the Air Force. Before he got married, he was too busy partying since this had been the first time that he did not have any responsibility other than himself.

For almost three years, he had planned to take college courses but each time he came up with one excuse or another. Now he had twenty-six months left in his Air Force contract and graduated from college twenty-two-months later. Hubert had always been goals oriented and knew that once he applied himself that he would let nothing stop him. This time, he had a little girl that would give him the extra motivation that would force him to stop at nothing until graduation in minimum time even if it killed him physically.

"Babe I have a TDY to Keesler and I want you to come with me," said Hubert. He had to attend an Advance Personnel Systems Manager course although he had been on the job for over two years. Darlene had just found out that she was pregnant and not sure if she should go on a trip from Tampa, Florida to Biloxi, Mississippi. Once he found out that Darlene was pregnant, he did not want to leave her in Florida alone and knew that he had to attend this mandatory class in Mississippi.

Therefore, Darlene would have to go with him no matter what and he would find a way somehow. In the end, she agreed after Hubert kept assuring her that she could see a doctor at the Keesler AFB, Hospital. After the long drive, Hubert had problems getting a room on base since he was only a Senior Airman (SrA). Nevertheless, Hubert knew that he could not afford a hotel off base. At the time, Hubert did not have a credit card and only had limited cash available to pay for a hotel room.

Serving as a SrA paid very little in the late 1970s and after a while, Hubert and Darlene were down to a bucket of Kentucky Fried chicken and a bag Oreo cookies that would have to last for a week. After a lot of begging at the base billeting office, Hubert was able to get a room with two single beds. The young couple quickly pushed the beds together and made it into what seemed as a double bed. After all, Darlene and Hubert were still newlyweds.

In between class, Hubert took Darlene to the hospital that made it difficult for her to see a doctor since he not permanent party even though he was on active duty and Darlene was his dependent. Eventually the stress created by the hospital personnel caused Darlene to have a miscarriage. Luckily, the Personnel Systems Manager (PSM) course like the previous Basic Personnel course was a self-paced course, which meant that Hubert was able to make time to take Darlene to the Keesler AFB, Hospital.

Although the PSM course was a two-month course, Hubert was able to complete the course in five weeks. Mainly because of the Block Structure that put time limits on when certain subjects had to be done by. In spite of the miscarriage, Hubert and Darlene tried their best to stay busy therefore avoiding depression. Since they did not have much money, when they first arrived they had purchased a few items and decided to return them in order to be able to go to the Wing Base Theater.

Once returning the items to the Base Exchange, Hubert and Darlene were able to go to the Base Theaterafter class until payday. At the Base Theater, Darlene and Hubert were able to get popcorn and hotdogs that would be normal meal at all Base Theaters in the future. Once Hubert completed the Advance Personnel Systems Manager (PSM) course, he drove back with Darlene to Bradenton, Florida.

Since Darlene was going to a doctor in Bradenton, Florida for her pregnancy, this meant that Hubert had to drive during the last months of Darlene's pregnancy. Although Hubert could have stayed at their home in Tampa and probably should have, he drove each night after class to spend a few hours with Darlene before having to return to Tampa. On a few occasions, he almost fell asleep at the wheel but Hubert still refused to stay in Tampa since Darlene was what mattered most in his life. Even though he was working two jobs and going to college fulltime at the same time, he knew that it was also for his family.

Hubert knew that he could not afford to serve in the US Air Force (USAF) as an enlisted member because he refused to qualify for food stamps and serve in uniform. Hubert decided that if not selected for Officers Candidate School (OTS) on his first attempt, he would separate from the Air Force. During that era, it took three or four attempts for enlisted members to receive a selectionto OTS. In the early 1980, this trend would change in the Air Force for a fifteen years and then return to its former trend.

It was early in the morning of 9 January 1976 when Darlene asked Hubert to take her to Manatee Memorial Hospital. Her doctor met Darlene at the hospital and since Hubert not able to go to any of the training classes, Darlene delivered their little girl alone. At first Hubert thought, he wanted a boy until the first time he saw his little girl behind the newborns window. That was the night the his new baby girl, Tawny was crying and mad because she not able to turn her head on the crib bed because her nose was stuck on the sheet. At that point, Hubert knew that he did not want any more children and was a happy father. That same week he had to return to school to take his college finals. Like most weeks, every day had every hour committed with some important task.

"Alfred I can't work on Saturday but will be ready for work early on Sunday," mentioned Hubert. On a few occasions, Hubert had to take a class all day Saturdays that meant he could only work on Sundays. He knew that he could accomplish enough work in twelfthto fourteen hours than his fellow coworkers accomplished in days. Hubert would take turns laying patios and step treads or laying out driveways with the rest of the crews. Other times, the work consisted of cleanup the jobs once the concrete dried on the driveways or around the tailors and then cleaning the wood and taking out all the nails out of the wood. Not a popular job but a necessary part of construction work that Hubert took pride in accomplishing like all jobs that he did.

Back in the Air Force, Hubert did his normal job five days a week. Mondays through Friday at the MacDill Consolidated Base Personnel Office (CBPO), he was at work by 5:00 AM each morning and normally got off work at 4:00 PM. That gave him less than an hour to go home, which was just off one of the base gates. He would change his cloths and have dinner before going to Night College classes. It seemed that every day was a program filled with something with little free time all reserved for Tawny. Feeling guilty because Darlene needed his time as well and he did not have any at that point.

Tawny had been a healthy and energetic baby girl until the doctor in MacDill AFB gave her the wrong medication and then after Darlene's sister dog had knocked her down and smashed her front teeth. Since the Air Force did not offer dependents dental coverage and Hubert could not afford to pay for the required dental repairs, eventually Hubert would have to let his pride down and let Alfred pay for the dental repairs needed by Tawny. After this, many of Tawny's pain would go away and after years of not sleeping well, Tawny would start sleeping well once moving to Arizona after Hubert became an officer. Nevertheless, for now, Tawny lived in constant pain only because the US Air Force did not provide dental coverage for dependent other than an annual cleaning.

"Darlene, I want to make it with you because I have a baby girl and I have to make it," said Hubert. Darlene had just yelled at Hubert as he was going to school and he had turned the wheel to the car too soon and hooked the front end into the lightning rod. At first, Darlene stood by the bay window and could not help but laugh as she held her baby girl. Hubert was lucky that he was able to pull the bumper out and drive the car to school. That event would be enough to show Darlene that she had to give Hubert a break mainly because he was trying his best for her and their daughter Tawny.

Nevertheless, Hubert also knew that Darlene needed to spend some time at her mother's home while he was working two jobs and going to college fulltime. At the same time, Hubert knew that Darlene was too young and needed help with her baby girl that was always sick and did not let her get any sleep regardless to the fact that she was a super mommy and great wife. It would be memories like this that would make Hubert love her for the rest of his life. However, when one is young, one often wonders if one will ever live through it since fatigue always seems to be the winner.

"The poor baby, she's been in pain all these months and could tell us," mentioned Darlene. It would be months before Darlene and Hubert would know that Tawny was in pain since she was too young to talk. Since the military did not have a dental plan, until they could afford paying for a dentist, this only delayed knowing of Tawny's dental problem. The only way that Tawny would sleep was when Hubert purchased a king size bed and gave the baby crib to charity. Tawny would sleep the night through as long as her daddy was next to her.

He would pile a batch of dippers and bottles of milk to last him through the night. Nearly every night, Tawny slept under his armpit but at least everyone got some sleep. She would stay awake until Hubert arrived from school and wait to have her daddy hold her before going to sleep. Then once he arrived, both would go to sleep together in her bed. She would feel safe and pain free as long as she was next to her daddy.

"I have to stay awake until I get to the base," Hubert thought to himself as he drove from Bradenton to Tampa, Florida. It was an early autumn morning when he had driven to Bradenton to see Darlene and Tawny who were staying there for a few weeks. This meant that Hubert could not take Tawny on her daily walker walks each day after work before going to class. He spent as much time with his little baby Tawny in between his two jobs and fulltime college classes. Tawny knew when daddy was home since he would play with her. Weekends nights were always for Darlene since she too needed time out to relax and go out. After all, she was young and at her age, she too needed time with Hubert alone.

Many times after school or early in the morning he had scared himself as he almost fell asleep behind the wheel. Nevertheless, once Hubert came close to completing his college degree, it became clear that Darlene needed help with Tawny once her medical issues meant that Darlene and Hubert could not get any rest. At that point, Darlene moved to Bradenton and back into her bedroom for the last six months until Hubert finished college. Hubert would drive back to Tampa daily even though Alfred did not think it was a good idea and suggested that he stay in Tampa during the week.

As a Mexican American in the US Air Force, military members have to work twice as hard to get the same recognition that any other member receives. While Mexican Americans in the US Army or members of other US Services given preferential treatment, Air Force Mexican Americans have to work twice as hard as their peers do. Therefore, in normal fashion for

Hubert, it took him a year for the Air Force Military Personnel Center (AFMPC) to recognize him as a test site or a Personnel Systems Manager (PSM) Subject Matter Expert (SME), which was in record time. Partly because of his experience in gained while working at City Hall and Data Automation. As a result, Hubert assisted different bases that were experiencing systems problems such as Myrtle Beach, AFB South Carolina.

This would be the second trip that Darlene would travel with Hubert except that on this trip the couple would have more money to travel for living expenses. Unlike Officers, enlisted personnel do not receive much travel monies so the little money Hubert received to travel on, he had to spend it wisely. During the daytime, Hubert worked approximately ten hours training the base PSM office on current systems capabilities and fixing systems problems. Especially problems with the local Data Automation office and the AFMPC subject matter experts had with the routing lines. After hours, Hubert and Darlene spent together at the local Myrtle Beach and went to diner mostly on base. They would eat most meals at Myrtle AFB eating facilities mainly because the prices were less on base than off base.

Prior to returning to Tampa, the couple decided to visit Darlene's brother at Fort Bragg who was serving in the 82nd Air Borne Dick. Dick had a young wife, twin boy, and lived on post at Fort Bragg, South Carolina. When Darlene and Hubert arrived on Post, it was late so Dick was home but his wife was still working. The couple could not live in the filth that they found in Dick's apartment so the following morning when Dick and his wife left for work, Hubert and Darlene decided to clean their apartment. After two days, they decided to return to Tampa mainly because they could not live in a house like Dick and his wife ran when they saw his boys playing with kitchen knives. Therefore, the young couple drove back to Bradenton, Florida to pick up Tawny at Grandma's house and then returned to their home in Tampa.

"Babe I'll be in a little late after work," smirked Hubert. Darlene knew that something not right since he normally came home on Friday'spromptly at 4:30 PM. Hubert, Manny, and their boss Master Sergeant (MSgt) Parson were having a drink after a long week. This week they had successfully installed a new base wide software program to correct a problem that had hampered the Air Force. This small team had corrected an Air Force wide problem and deserved much phrase. However, Hubert worked on this problem on his own for weeks before determining how to fix the Air Force wide problem.

Hubert received the selection as the Team Chief to serve as a test site for the Air Force and AFMPC for this new Base Military Data Systems (BMDS) program and future BMDS programs. Unfortunately, this new task meant the he would travel throughout the southwest US to other Air Force Bases fixing their BMDS systems. Since he was going to college, this required working closely with his college professors. He was lucky that his remaining professors were not like his accounting professor. The BMDS sub-systems consisted of every program within a military installation such as finance, supply, hospital, maintenance, flying squadrons, data automation, and every aspect pertaining to MacDill AFB data systems.

"You might get away with drinking at work with your wife," yelled Darlene to MSgt Parson. MSgt Parson looked and was physically build like George Foreman but he knew that he would not argue with this small Irish girl. When Darlene yelled at him, he just smiled at her, kept saying yes mam, and kept apologizing. MSgt Parson was the best mentor, Hubert would have in his military career. Even Darlene would like him as a boss in spite of this event where she let him know that she did not like his behavior as a man.

"I am so tired and need to get some rest," said Darlene as Hubert was on his way out the door going to his college classes. This sleeping arrangement worked well until Tawny was hurt when a dog ran over her and broke her teeth. Months prior, he had agreed with Darlene that she move to Bradenton so that Tawny would help her with Tawny who was sick. This meant the he would work all day, go to school until 10:00 PM each night, and then drive to Bradenton, which was about an hour drive. Then the following morning he would get up at five in the morning and repeated this routine. At least he was able to get a few hours' sleep and Darlene had some family members who helped her with Tawny when she was too tired.

"Come on daddy," said Tawny. Each time Hubert arrived in Bradenton and entered grandma's house, Tawny would be at the door waiting for her daddy with a sheet with her two cousins Tammy and Jerry. She knew that her daddy would drag them around the house with all three on the sheet. The house in Bradenton had a wide hallway at least sixteen feet long and eight feet wide where Hubert would go to the end of the hall and turn around with all three on the sheet repeatedly. The entire house had a plush carpet so if the children rolled, it did not matter since they would not get hurt as long as they did not hit one of the walls. Hubert always made sure that he pulled the blanket with the children in the center of the hallway.

Hubert would tell Tawny to wait a minute for him to take his Air Force uniform off and then return to play with her, Tammy, and Jerry who were all under three years old. He would play with them for a few hours until it was time for dinner when Hubert would eat dinner with Tawny and study with her on his lap. Hubert would often read his college books to her as she lay in his arms until she fell asleep. Then it was time to go to bed and start the day again early in the morning to drive back to Tampa.

Hubert would drive back and forth from Bradenton, Florida that was fifty miles from Tampa so that Darlene would have some help from her mother with Tawny that was having medical problems. This would also help since the fifty miles would be sufficient distance for the Air Force to cover using the CHAMPUS option and Hubert only had to pay the deductibles.

In the end, this helped Darlene, which proved to be the best option for everyone. Especially since Darlene, was able to receive better medical care for Tawny in Bradenton, Florida.

"Sir I have to pass this class" Hubert begged his college accounting professor on the telephone. Hubert could not figure out why this professor disliked him so much. When Hubert called his professor at home, he could hear his family in the background. He could only hope that he would have a conscious as a family man and to the honorable thing and allow him to retake the class since he did not give Hubert the correct grade in the first place. Hubert was just glad that he would be able to attend Officer Training School (OTS) on time. He had worked too hard and did not want to have to file a possible discrimination suit in the school to go to OTS. It just seemed that no matter how hard he worked that something was always trying to stop him from getting ahead.

After all, he took his examination papers and compared it to a fellow classmate who had received straight "A". For nearly the same schoolwork, Hubert received an "F". When the school counselors compared both school works, they too were concerned. Later the college removed the "F" to withdrew "W" in fear that he would file a complaint. After taking his examinations and taking them to the school counselor, the school spoke with the professor who agreed to let Hubert re-take the class. The counselor noticed that Hubert's tests were within the curriculum in the textbook.

After complaining to the college administrator, the professor agreed that Hubert could re-take the class over but that he could not earn a grade higher than a "B. " Since the class tests had been the same, this time the professor gave him "B's" on all four tests even Hubert aced all four tests. Hubert was glad that he had a 4. 0 grade point average when he was single and prior to getting married when he first took college classes. He only wished that he had taken more classes when he was single and had the time to take classes without a family to worry about.

In the end, it did not matter to Hubert since it meant that he would graduate from college. Especially now that in his view he had completed what he called "mass production reading" in order to complete his college degree in only two years from the day he took his first college class. It was not the first time or the last time that Hubert had noticed discrimination no matter how much he tried to ignore it. Nevertheless, this was the first time that his family could have been hurt for no reason and without any justification. He kept remembering what his mother told him that it was up to him "not to use discrimination as a crutch but to feel sorry for those discriminated". Hubert's mother Olga would always say that no one wouldever stop ignorance.

"What happens to Hubert's grade if I do not take the final?" Hubert asked his economics professor. The professor told him that he decided not to take the final that he would receive a "B" as the final grade. Since this was his last class that he needed to graduate, he gladly took the "B" since he would be done with college. After twenty-two-months of a busy schedule, he was able to earn his first college degree. Holding two jobs and going to college had taken its toll on the Contreras family. In spite of these events, 1979 passed by quickly for the Contreras family. All Hubert could think was that he would finally have time to spend with Tawny and Darlene. They had both paid the price in loss of family time due to having Hubert being gone most of the time in spite of having him near physically.

All Hubert knew that for over two years when he got off work and school, he play a bit with his baby girl, did a little homework, and tried to go to bed by mid-night. In this time, he earned his college degree not for ego, but because as a family man, he had to in orders to improve the quality of life for his wife and child. Hubert also knew that he refused to take charity from anyone and that he earned everything he had. Now that he was going to OTS, he could be able to rest. After all, now all he had to do was hold one job. Hubert had already been holding only one job that required him to learn how to become an Officer that included learning about the Air Force. Hubert had already been living in the Air Force for the last six years. It could not be that difficult!

"I can't wait to attend OTS to get some sleep," mentioned Hubert. Hubert finished college in just over two years and accepted to Officer Training School (OTS) on his first attempt. During the late 1970s, Air Force enlisted members usually had to apply to OTS three or more times before being selected. Olga was a friend with individuals such as Congressman Barry Goldwater, the Arizona governor, and many other politicians who helped Hubert accepted to OTS. He received twenty-seven letters of recommendation. This meant that he would graduate in July from Saint Leo's College (later re-designated as Saint Leo University) and report to Medina Base in Texas in early September to start the three-month commissioning program. Most Air Force employees referred to Officer Training School (OTS) Officers as ninety-day wonder when Hubert graduated in November as a Second Lieutenant (2LT).

"Babe you have to stay in a hotel by the base," mentioned Hubert on the telephone. It was just before the Christmas holiday season when Darlene came to Texas to see Hubert become an Officer. This would be the first time that she would travel by herself. Since Hubert was required to stay at Medina Base, she would have to stay at the hotel by herself for a day. She had never been alone, much less in a large city since the only other place other than Florida that she had traveled to be to Alabama or Georgia to visit family. In the late 1970s, Medina Base was well outside the city San Antonio and close to Randolph Air Force Base (AFB). The day prior to graduation would be Darlene's first time to go to a formal function.

As a young nineteen year old, she had never experienced any formal functions in her life and had purchased a cocktail dress for the function as Hubert had mentioned on the telephone. Hubert was wearing his Mess Dress uniform with medals. He would meet Darlene once she arrived on Medina Base, near San

Antonio and Randolph AFB. With time, Darlene would become more familiar with these events but for now, Darlene was still a girl out of High School that had never gone to a formal function. After dinner a bad played with the normal dancing that is part of Air Force Military Balls, which are formal functions. Since Darlene was staying off base, she decided to leave early and Hubert agreed mainly because of the dark Texas nights so he escorted her to her car and went back to the barracks.

"It's so dark out here in Texas," said Darlene. Drivers could see the few lights from San Antonio once one leaves the base. The day before graduation, she had gone to a formal Air Force graduation party and on her way back to the hotel, she got lost. The party ended around 9:00 PM even though Darlene had departed early. By then except for the lights from the San Antonio, it was completely dark in the Texas highways. Texas in the winter is very dark unless there is a lighted sign to follow or one has clear skies so that one can see the bright stars. Darlene had missed her exit to the hotel and continued driving until she almost arrived in Houston, Texas. Since Medina Base was out miles from San Antonio, she did not realize how far she had driven. It would be years before the city of San Antonio would grow in size and grow close to Randolph AFB as its metropolitan area grew in size.

At first, the Police Officer asked Darlene if she was all right although he initially thought that she was too dressed up to be in that part of town and was in the worst side of town. "Officer, I do not know how to get to the hotel. Hubert's husband is graduating from Officers Training School(OTS) in the morning and I am lost," said Darlene crying. After she explained herself between the tears, the Police Officer directed her to follow him back to San Antonio. He could see that she was an innocent girl that was in danger and decided to protect her. By this time, it was early the following morning around 2:00 AM. Darlene was able to sleep a few hours when the Officer knocked on the door and brought her coffee. Darlene had mentioned to him that she needed to get up early the next morning to include the time and drive back to Medina Base. After the Police Officer woke Darlene up and saw that she would be all right, he drove back to Houston, Texas.

Once Darlene departed for Medina Base for Hubert's graduation, this time she did not have any problem finding the base. Initially she went inside the building where Hubert was living. Then just before the formal parade, she thought that she needed to wait for Hubert in the car. After a while when Hubert could not find Darlene, he noticed her in the car and he went over to her and told her to go to the bleachers just before the parade would start. Hubert was leading the parade formation with five formations of two hundred airmen in each formation. After the parade, the General declared the cadets were officially Air Force Officers even though each had officially received an sworn in by an military officer prior to the parade. There were no receptions after the parade but instead everyone was ready to depart Medina Base as soon as possible. Like most new Air Force Officers, Hubert would proceed to the Finance Officer, receive his pay advance, and then depart the local area.

CHAPTER 2

LIEUTENANT

"Are you sure that I do not have to pay this money back," asked Hubert as the finance sergeant replied no with a big grin. Upon receiving these monies, Hubert asked the finance sergeant if they were sure that Hubert would not have to pay any of the monies back. The Finance Officer replied that this advance was only seventy-five percent of the total entitlement. This had been the second time that Hubert had asked such a question to a finance employee. Except the last time was to ask is they had not made a mistake with his pay since it was so little. One of the benefits of being an Officer would be getting an advance for the upcoming Weapons Controller (WC) course and the $200 uniform entitlement. Now our bi-monthly paychecks were almost twice as much as the amount Hubert paid as a Staff Sergeant during the entire month.

"How about stopping in New Orleans for a honeymoon," asked Hubert? Darlene and Hubert thought they were rich when they saw the $2,000 advance that included a one-time $200 uniform payment. Hubert would receive the final payment at his final assignment in Arizona when he filed for the final payment with all the receipts for the travels on the travel days. Nevertheless, Hubert and Darlene would go on leave and take a vacation in New Orleans, Louisiana and this time have money to enjoy their vacation for their first time since being married. During their trip to Keesler AFB, Darlene and Hubert talked about taking a short trip to New Orleans but were not able to due to the limited funds at that time.

As Darlene and Hubert drove from San Antonio, Texas back to Florida, they decided to stop in New Orleans for a few days. They stopped at a Holiday Inn and rented a suite. Unlike now where one can look in the Internet, in those days the fastest way to find a hotel was using an 800-number. For the first time during their marriage, they had money to spend freely without worrying about not having enough money to pay their bills and still be able doing other things like taking a vacation. Even then, there were limitations, and the limit was $2,200 until next payday, which was all right, for now since it was the best they had been since being married.

"Do you like the earrings," asked Hubert. He purchased Darlene tiny solitaire diamond studs and a portrait from one of the local New Orleans painters. The local painter could easily see that this young couple did not have much money and nearly gave away his painting. Now the Contreras family had its first painting of value associated with a keen memory. Staying in a suite for three days and eating rich, food was a new experience for Darlene and Tawny. Since the Contreras family had driven this area many times to visit family in Dothan, Alabama, they decided to drive to Bradenton on Highway 301. On previous trips, they had seen oak clocks but could not afford to purchase one. On this trip, Darlene and Hubert knew that they could afford to purchase one for themselves and Darlene's momma, Marie.

USAF AIR DEFENSE WEAPONS CENTER (ADWC),TYNDALL AFB, FL.

"How about coming to Tyndall for a visit," asked Hubert? In early January, Hubert traveled to Panama City Florida to attend

Weapons Controller (WC)Technical Training School. Hubert felt lucky that he was able to spend time with family in Florida whileDarlene stayed in Bradenton while he attended this class. After Officer Training School (OTS), he went to Tyndall Air Force Base (AFB) for Hubert initial Weapons Control (WC)training school. The Air Force activated the 325[th]Fighter Weapons Wing at Tyndall Air Force Base (AFB), Florida, and assigned it to the USAF Air Defense Weapons Center. The tactical units assigned to the 325[th]included the 1[st]Tactical Fighter Squadron, 2[nd]Fighter Weapons (FW) Squadron, 82[nd]Tactical Aerial Target Squadron, and the 95[th]Fighter Interceptor Training (FIS) Squadron.

It was during an era when the Air Force had FISs throughout the Continental US protecting America against aerial attacks, which occurred on 9/11. When Democratic Presidents dismantled the Strategic Command and all the FISs received closure notices as a political budget initiative and not a strategic defense initiative. As a member of the USAF Air Defense Weapons Center, Hubert trained on basic aircraft intercept control procedures. Fighter aircraft from the local flying units provided the aircraft used for intercept training. At this point, the Weapons Controller (WC) Air Force Specialty Code (AFSC) career field designator was 17XX. Darlene would hear Hubert practice controlling aircraft terminology even in his sleep for years' as he became a competent fighter aircraft controller.

"Babe can you help me learn the aircraft control procedures," asked Hubert. The course criteria included flying activities based on beyond visual range (BVR)-combat techniques. Using live and simulation aircraft, the aircraft control training make it possible for the controller and pilot trainees to learn their specialty between the simulation periods and practice in live training scenarios. To digest their new knowledge, controllers had a chance to take the time to digest their Combat Management new knowledge. The first phase of training consisted of simulation training once the academic phase was completed. The second phase of training consisted of the flying phase where the Weapons Controller (WC) initially controlled two fighter aircraft conducting one versus one-bump head intercepts.

The intercept profiles were either intercepts or stern profiles that required certain rollout parameters in order for the Weapons Controller (WC) to pass each mission and progress to the next profile that each became more complex. Since Hubert like all the trainees had never worked on manual radars, it took a while to learn about the various systems, the communications systems, all the aircraft, then the weapons systems and their capabilities, followed by different types of aircraft geometry. All flying flew at each other with a closure rate of over a thousand miles per hour on a two-dimensional radar picture and with the help of two pilots talking to you as the aircraft controller.

A major reorganization occurred on July 1, 1981, with the activation of the 325[th]Fighter Weapons Wing. The wing began its mission at Tyndall AFB with F-101, F-106, and T-33 Shooting Star aircraft, while at the same time phasing out the F-101 Voodoo and F-106 Delta Dart aircraft and preparing for the arrival of the first F-15 Eagle aircraft in 1983 in Tyndall. Once Hubert arrived at his next base, since he was an active Weapons Controller (WC) and scheduler and all the Fighter Squadrons, he would have the opportunity and fly in the T-33 Shooting Star aircraft.

The McDonnell F-101 Voodoo was a supersonic military jet fighter, which served the USAF and the Royal Canadian Air Force (RCAF). Initially designed by McDonnell Aircraft as a long-range bomber escort known as a penetration fighter for the Strategic Air Command (SAC), the Voodoo was instead developed as a nuclear-armed fighter-bomber for the Tactical Air Command (TAC), and as a photo reconnaissance aircraft based on the same airframe. Extensively modified versions produced as an all-weather interceptor aircraft; serving with the Air Defense Command, later renamed the Aerospace Defense

Command (ADC), the Air National Guard (ANG), the Royal Canadian Air Force and the unified Canadian Forces after 1968. Later, Hubert worked with F-101 Voodoo while assigned to a Strategic Air Defense unit during a later assignment.

However, the majority of the live training during this period primarily used the T-33 aircraft. During that era, Hubert would control many T-33 and F-106 fighter aircraft conducting Air Defense profiles until the new F-15s Eagles and F-16s Falcons became the norm with their Dissimilar Air Combat Tactics (DACT). The T-33 aircraft was a two seat aircraft. This was an era when the F-15s Eagles and F-16s Falcons were replacing all the older fighters in the USAF inventory. In time, he would also fly in the T-33 Shooting Star aircraft.

"I'll be arriving around one in the afternoon at the Panama City airport," said Darlene. She arrived mid-day Saturday in Panama City to stay with Hubert for two weeks. He had rented a motel room close to the base that had old electric heaters. In the distance, the winds brought in the smell of the paper mill early each day and late on the evenings. The smell did not bother the young lovers since they were along and able to spend time together. During the weekdays, Hubert went to class and Darlene worked on months of lost sleep until he got off work. After a drive and a quick diner, they returned to the motel until time passed and Darlene returned to Bradenton, Florida for the remainder of this class. Unknown to the young couple, these trips to schools would be a normal part of their new life as an Officer.

"Turn right, 180, set altitude at Flight Level (FL) 240, speed 320 knots indicated," said Hubert to two F-4Fs Phantom Fighter aircraft. He was controlling four F-4Fs from one of the local flying squadrons. Learning basic aircraft control skills involves trainees learning various control techniques that allows one to default to those techniques in an effort to maintain situational awareness and accurate aircraft positioning. The air Weapons Controller (WC)School at Tyndall AFB was a manual controller course and once individuals completed the course they continued to a follow-on controller system that included Ground Tactical Air Control System (GTACS), Air Defense systems, and during this period the new E-3B/C Airborne Warning and Control System (AWACS). In Hubert case, Hubert chose the 407L GTACS system primarily because the unit was located in Phoenix, Arizona.

It was during this assignment that Hubert and his families say the new Thunderbirds using its new F-16A aircraft. From 1969 to 1973, the Thunderbirds flew the Air Force's front-line fighter, the F-4E Phantom. In 1974, the Thunderbirds converted to the T-38 Talon, the world's first supersonic trainer. The T-38 was more fuel-efficient and less costly to maintain than the larger F-4. Early in 1983, the Thunderbirds reinstituted their traditional role of demonstrating the Air Force's front-line fighter capabilities. Transition to the F-16A allowed the team to retain work force and fuel efficiency while demonstrating to spectators the latest in fighter technology. In 1986, the Thunderbirds participated in the rededication flyby of the Statue of Liberty and in September, another milestone was officially complete when the team went over the 200 million mark for total attendance.

"Babe I do not know if I'll ever become good at controlling fighter aircraft with hundreds of miles at a time closure rates," mentioned Hubert. The hardest part of learning how to become an aircraft controller included learning how to taking airborne assets from the gods view into a three dimension environment. However, the Weapons Controller (WC) had to convert the three dimensional perspective from the situational display console (SDC) and see all the aircraft flying in their minds real-time. The gods view was like seeing computer Starship game where the aircraft presented in radar blimps on top a SDC at a thousand mile plus closure rate are all maneuvering in one's mind. In the three dimensional view, with time trainees would learn to see aircraft in the vertical and horizontal dimensions as they flew in airspace if they were to become successful and safe Weapons Controller (WC).

607TH TACTICAL CONTROL TRAINING SQUADRON (TCTS), LUKE AFB, AZ.

Hubert arrived in the 607thTactical Control Training Squadron (TCTS) that recently converted from the Tactical Air Command's 407L control system Technical Training School. The first aviator to receive the Medal of Honor, Lieutenant (Lt) Frank Luke Jr. ,born in Phoenix in 1897, received the honor when Luke Air Force Base (AFB) received the name after him. Lieutenant Luke the "Arizona Balloon Buster" scored eighteen aerial victories during World War I (WW-I) in the skies over France before being killed, at age twenty-one, on September 29, 1918. Fourteen of the eighteen aerial victories were German observation balloons. In 1940, the US Army sent a representative to Arizona to choose a site for an Army Air Corps training field for advanced training in conventional fighter aircraft.

The city of Phoenix bought 1,440 acres of land, which they leased to the government at $1 a year effective March 24, 1941. On March 29, 1941, the Del. E. Webb Construction Company began excavation for the first building known then as Litchfield Park Air Base (AB). Over the years, Litchfield Park received a new partner when overtaken by the town of Glendale as the city of Phoenix and its metropolitan area kept growing. Another base known as Luke Field, in Pearl Harbor, Hawaii, released its name when the base transferred to the Navy in June 1941, and the fledgling Arizona base called Luke Field at the request of its first Commander, Lieutenant Colonel (Lieutenant Colonel) Ennis C. Whitehead. Lieutenant Colonel Whitehead went on to become a Lieutenant General as Commander of Air Defense Command in 1950.

The 607th Tactical Control Squadron (TCS) originated 12 December 1945, when the 502d Tactical Control Group (TCG) activated at Biggs Field, Texas, under the command of the Ninth Army Air Force. The 502[d]TCS, incorporating control squadrons, the 605th TCS, 606th TCS, and the 607th TCS, had as its mission to test and perfect equipment, doctrine and methods for the most effective means of early warning, spotting and tracking procedures. On 18 August 1975, the 607th TCS was designated a Replacement Training Unit (RTU) for Tactical Air Command (TAC), United States Air Forces in Europe (USAFE) and the Air National Guard (ANG). On 1 September 1980, the 607th TCS received a new designation to the 607[th]Tactical Control Training Squadron (TCTS). At the same time, its parent wing the 602nd Tactical Air Intelligence Reconnaissance Control Wing (TAIRCW) transferred from Austin, Texas to Davis-Monthan AFB, Arizona in Tucson.

The unit's primary mission became training 407L Weapons Controller (WC) and technicians for operational 407L tactical control squadrons. The mission of the unit became providing an Operationally Ready (OR), Control and Reporting Center (CRC), or Control and Reporting Post(CRP), for the Tactical Air Control System (TACS) that became the 607th's secondary mission. Decades later, the Air Force would change the Operationally Ready (OR) term to Mission Ready (MR) or Combat Ready (CR). Each CRC or CRP shelter each had twelve consoles available for control of aircraft. The first class of the weapons director/technician training course began 15 October 1975 and graduation held 11 December 1975. The first Air Combat Tactics or Dissimilar Air Combat Tactics (ACT/DACT) Course conducted at the 607 TCS 9 to 14 February 1978.

As a member of the 607th, Hubert waited six weeks before entering the 407L Weapons Controller (WC)-training program. New trainees first learned the semi-automated 407L systems and then continued the ACT/DACT training as part of the Operational Ready (OR) criteria. Controlling live airborne refueling missions was also part of the Operational Ready (OR) requirements. Initially, the training received is each student used simulated targets. On console, the students could not notice the difference between simulated or real-time aircraft except by looking at the computer symbol that told them, which type the aircraft the controller was controlling on the console. During sim-over-live exercises, if not careful, the Weapons Controller (WC) could easily make the mistake and tell pilots flying live profiles that they had live traffic when in fact the traffic was simulated traffic.

Hubert arrived at Luke AFB with two fellow Lieutenants, one a female name Terri Harland, and one a male Bob Wood. Terri was an attractive blonde-haired female and Bob was black. Black was still the proper name used prior to the African American term name being used in America. Although the Air Force's position during this era was equality, in actuality, females received special treatment. Each six months new officers received Promotion Effectiveness reports and even though Hubert and Bob had upgrade to instructor in less than the six-month period and Terri was still in training, Terri received a higher rating in controller proficiency. Hubert and Bob were both prior service, which meant they started in the Air Force as enlisted members that gave them an advantage and maturity that Terri lacked.

There were plenty of instructors with inflated egos. Terri became close to Tom the top controller, just ask him, who thought no one was better than him who would become one of the units flight evaluators, Terri's rater, and her husband. Unfortunately, for Hubert, Tom did not like officers that were competition and since Hubert worked hard at becoming a good controller and was quickly learning to be a competent aircraft controller that fighter pilots asked for regularly. Tom would try to cause problems for him as a flight evaluator but other Senior Officers would stop him. Hubert had always been aggressive and was not the typical Second Lieutenant. Unlike

Tom, a First Lieutenant that had been in the Air Force only three years, Hubert had already been in the Air Force for over seven years and well aware of the Air Force politics.

Terri received a top rating or One, while Hubert and Bob received a Two or lower rating. As a controller, Terri also had three near misses, which were all safety of flight incidents that were over looked by the unit. Any male officer would have lost their careers and one officer actually did for having one near miss. That double standard would have a long-term impact on Hubert's future military career as an officer. Nevertheless, Mexican Americans have to work twice as hard as any other officer does in the Air Force. Terri later did marry her rater that might have been a factor who wrote herpromotion effectiveness report. What was not farewas that Terri did not hold any additional duties as Hubert or Bob and a year later would become an instructor after her future husband qualified her as a Weapons Controller (WC).

In order to gain more controller experience, many times Hubert would sit on position monitoring Basic Flight Maneuver (BFM) missions that did not require any level of control other than flight following the aircraft to ensure that they stayed inside the airspace. After doing the flight follow of two F-4E Phantom, F-104 Starfighter, F-15 Eagle, or the new F-16 Falcon aircraft, Hubert would ask the fighter lead if Hubert could get a couple of intercept missions if they had fuel left. Eventually, Hubert became qualified in record time as an Instructor Weapons Controller (IWC). At the time, Hubert was also helping the local Consolidated Base Personnel Office (CBPO) with fix their data systems since he held a secondary Air Force Specialty Code (2AFSC) on his spare time. The unit and Wing Commanders were fully aware of his involvement in this area as they were in his Scheduling, Operations, and Plans Officers (OPLANS) areas.

Once the training advance to the advanced fighter aircraft, many times the closure rates were at thousand knots or greater.

This training also included learning how to accomplish simulated airborne refueling operations. The Air Traffic Controller (ATC) only had to worry about landings and takeoffs or en-route geometry, which consisted of the uni-dimensional geometry. During the PATCO strike, Hubert would deploy to New Mexico, support the Federal Aviation Administration (FAA), and see how easy it was to become an en-route controller. However, this required that he separate from the Air Force by the time he reached twenty-six years old and the same age he became an Air Force Officer. Although Hubert would enjoy his time in New Mexico, as always, his timing would not be good during his professional career.

"Babe, I passed Hubert's check ride," mentioned Hubert. He graduated on time but as a controller, Hubert felt that he only learned various manual mechanical controller techniques to follow. He also knew that at this point that he did not see the three-dimensional plain well in his mind. After graduating from the Tyndall AFBWeapons Controller (WC) School that was a manual controller program, his follow-up controller training was at the semi-automated controller school at Luke AFB, AZ. This would also be Hubert's first assignment as an Air Force Officer. Up to knew, Hubert had received every assignment that he had asked for and was surprised that he had received Arizona.

For a while, the Air Force Personnel Center (AFPC) assignments represented had tried to have Hubert volunteer of a remote assignment. This meant that he would be alone for a year in some remote location outside the United States. He begged AFPC to first give him a US assignment and that he would volunteer for a remote assignment after first serving anywhere in the US for at least two years. After a few days AFMPC agreed to let Hubert go to Arizona under the agreement that after two or three years in Arizona that he would go on a remote assignment. This meant that at the two-year point that he would have to be proactive and find a remote assignment and not wait for AFMPC to give them a remote assignment. Otherwise, he will go anywhere in the world, versus controlling the area of the world that will allow him to return to where he can visit his family and afford paying for the trip.

"Babe, we are going to Luke for Hubert's first assignment as an Officer," mentioned Hubert. Luke Air Force Base (AFB), located in Glendale, Arizona was Hubert first assignment as a new second lieutenant (2LT). However, for now, Hubert and Darlene would be able to return to Bradenton to get their baby girl Tawny and take a few weeks of vacation before driving to Glendale, Arizona. Hubert had not taken any vacation time off during the past two years that he was taking college classes and had plenty of leave time saved up. Interstate 10 had just been built just north of Panama City, which had been the normal road that Hubert took on weekends when he visited Darlene. On this trip back to Bradenton, he had Darlene fly in to Panama City to drive back with him so he decided to take Florida State Road 90, which was a scenic route. Then Hubert took the back roads that Alfred always took when they drove to Alabama or Georgia to visit family. Once just south of Tallahassee, Hubert and Darlene stopped by the roadside to purchase boiled peanuts when they notices cloaks made out of wood. Hubert purchase two clocks, one for Darlene and one for Darlene's momma, Marie.

The time spent in Bradenton went too fast and before long, Hubert, Darlene, and Tawny were on the road in their new Chevy Malibu driving on Interstate 10 to Arizona. This would be a drive that over the decades they would repeat dozens of times to visit family. Since family was always the most important factor to Darlene and Hubert. Just east of Tallahassee, the muffler fell off and Hubert tied it up with a cloth rope. Darlene would yell at him telling him how stupid he was to use cloth since it would smoke. At first, Hubert was going to argue with Darlene but knew that she was right. However, at the same time he knew that the cloth was the only item that he had to tie the muffler to start with anyway not that it mattered. Hubert would find a gas station that would fix the muffler just off the interstate and return on their long drive back to Arizona.

"We can stay here at the visiting quarters for thirty days," mentioned Hubert. After Officer Training School (OTS), Hubert would return to Florida to pick-up his family and then drive to Glendale, Arizona. Eventually, Darlene and Hubert would find an apartment in Glendale until they moved into the base housing. The hardest part of living in an apartment would be waiting for their furniture to arrive from Florida that had been in storage since Hubert went to OTS. The drive would take five days to drive from Florida to Arizona on this trip. Especially when driving with a two year old girl in a car for over 2,400 miles.

From 21 July 1980 to 20 September 1982, Hubert would receive orders to the 607th Tactical Control Training Squadron (TCTS), Luke Air Force Base (AFB), Arizona. During this period, he would serve as Instructor Weapons Controller (IWC) and Instructor Message Processing Center (MPC) Program Management lead as one of three of its primary creators of the MPC program. Mainly because of Hubert's personality, he would create all the Tactical Air Command Systems (TACS) Command and Reporting Center (CRC), and their entire related subordinate lesson plans as part of his MPC course development curriculum using Instrument Systems Development (ISD) techniques. At the same time, he earned to master degrees during the weekends.

Upon arrival in the unit, Hubert served as the Mobility Officer since his squadron was still a tactical unit until redesignated as a Technical Training School (TTS). As the Mobility Officer, Hubert was required to distribute the squadron's equipment to other Tactical Mobile units and only maintain its two radars and associated equipment required to function as a Weapons Controller (WC)Technical Training School. Although this duty would normally go to a Senior Officer, Hubert received a new task due to his prior service record in the Air Force Personnel Specialty that made him the ideal officer.

Upon completion of these duties, Hubert became the unit's Scheduling Officer responsible for scheduling flying of four Flying Wings of aircraft located at four AFB locations. At the same time, he became one of three First Lieutenants (1LTs) selected to create the new Tactical Air Command (TAC) MPC training program for the unit, the US Air Force, and the Air Force Reserves. Hubert created thirty-three percent of the MPC training program including the US Army, US Navy, and the US Marine Command and Control (C2) system portions. The ACC Major Command approved the MPC training program within three weeks instead of the normal six to twelve months earning the three 1LTs much praise. Hubert was the squadron Operations and Plans (OPLANS) Officers that received an outstanding rating during wing and Air Force inspections. Hubert received five 'outstanding' ratings during every higher headquarter inspection for programs that he was responsible for during his short time in the 607th TCTS.

Hubert's first commander would be Lieutenant Colonel Russ who would be his worst Air Force commander. After this assignment in Arizona, Hubert would work for Lieutenant Colonel Russ in Spain after going to Iceland for a year. Lieutenant Colonel Russ primary concern as an Officer was his next promotion and in this effort was in challenging each Officer to backstab each other. The Director of Operations (DO) was Lieutenant Colonel Slickee who like Lieutenant Colonel Russ had gone through the ranks following the same political style. Both Lieutenant Colonels Russ and Slickee seemed to enjoy challenging officers to go against each other in a negative manner or both used training methods seemed to make one officer seem better than another, which must have been popular during their era.

The 607th TCTS was such a political unit that once Hubert received an assignment later in his career to the Pentagon as a Lieutenant Colonel, he was well prepared. Hubert did not realize that soon he would be working for Colonel Russ in Spain for an additional year and a half whose only concern would be in using his men in making sure he received his next promotion to colonel. It time, Hubert would learn that most if not all of his Lieutenant Colonel and commanders were all the same. Few cared for their employees and he promised himself that as a commander and leader that he would never be that type of senior office, even if that meant never were promoted to the senior ranks.

For now, Hubert was early in his officer career learning new aspects of the political world that many times involved achieving tasks based on perceptions and not what was ethically right. It truly was different being an officer than being a non-commissioned officer (NCO) in the military but Hubert had no problem adjusting. After all, as an NCO he often was told that he acted as an officer. It seemed that many of the leadership theories that he was reading about in his masters courses were having an impact in his management style. Although he often wondered, what portion of his leadership-style was natural since he was told that he was a natural leader with many followers?

By the early 1980s, the Air Force culture was changing as females received higher recruitment priorities into the Air Force ranks. In the Air Force, Mexican Americans were only a minority on paper. In the Air Force, Mexican Americans still had to work twice as hard to receive the same opportunities as any military member did. Women were learning how to use their gender as a 'political weapon' for career advancement or 'political harassment' as blacks did in the 1970s. Unfortunately for Mexican Americans in the Air Force, were too proud to lower their standards to take advantage of the cultural environment to advance their careers. With each rank increase, the level of abuse also increased as Hubert continued to lose former friends. Sadly, many friends that Hubert Helped receive higher ranks seemed to forget their friendships once they attained the higher ranks. Still some remained loyal friends, which meant those were true friends.

It was an era when the Air Force Promoted after its first female General in 1971 General Jeanne Holm, the first woman to serve as Major General in the Air Force opened the door for females to become Generals and other female Generals werepromotion. She would later say, "Have you ever seen an ugly female General?"questioning the fairness of the Air Forcepromotion system. The 1980s was era when the Air Force was leading society in sexual harassment awareness. By the 1980s, the Air Force had dealt with the drug and alcohol problems of the Vietnam era. Now the Air Force was leading the charge in society in showing the world how sexual harassment was such a sensitive area, or so it thought. Nevertheless, a positive area was in the training percentage of female enlisted and officer recruitment in military forces. The Air Force Command and Control (C2) or the 17XX career field let the way with fourteen percent of all of its officers being females.

In the meantime, while waiting for their furniture to arrive from Florida, Hubert purchased an old 1967 Chevy Impala from a German F-104 Starfighter RTU Pilot that was in upgrade training in Luke AFB. He had recently graduated as a pilot and was returning home to Germany. The Impala front end needed some work, but the tires were new, the engine ran great, and the car stereo cost more than the vehicle. Since Hubert and Darlene owned a new 1980 Malibu family vehicle, Hubert thought this would be a great work car and purchased the vehicle for $150. The German pilot had taken care of the vehicle mechanically and made sure the car was in great condition even though it was an old vehicle. As for the front end, if one did not drive too fast, it drove great and had new tires. The front end only shook when driving over sixty miles per hour for a few seconds and then it was fine. Still, Hubert would not drive with his family in this vehicle except inside town and while driving within town speeds.

"That poor white girl is married to that Mexican" would say the strangers at the Glendale 7 as they saw Tawny in her shorts and matching shirt in the old Impala. Hubert drove this car each night to the Glendale Seven Drive-in. The Glendale Seven Drive-in had a new wireless speaker system that allowed members to use their car speakers. In the early 1980s, it was hi-tech and with the new Impala stereo system the Contreras, family had the best system at Glendale 7. The funny part was that families would see Hubert and Darlene with Tawny in shorts and matching shirt in the dark brown Impala and feel sorry for Darlene.

Hubert would go to the snack bar and get hot dogs, cokes, and popcorn while each night we saw different movies at the Glendale 7 until our furniture arrived with our television. After that, the Glendale 7 was still a regular family outing at least once a week. People would never understand why friends were never important to Darlene and Hubert. For being together was always what was all they wanted and needed. As long as they had Tawny with them, both were happy.

After four years of President Carter's cuts, it was almost coming into a new era of growth when President Ronald W. Reagan took office for the next eight years on 20 January 1981. President Reagan was pro-military and an excellent CINC. From day one, the US military including the US Air Force attitude changed as true improvements continued throughout all branches of the US military. During this era, anything was possible, the heavens seemed the limit, and military members did not have to worry about where funding would be coming to fight the next war that Washington politicians kept asking warfighters to fight.

"I have night classes this week," said Darlene. Since Hubert had night missions during the same period, Tawny had to go with him to work since they did not have time to find a sitter.

For a while, Darlene and Hubert both tried to go to college at the same time. However, after a while, it became clear that due to Hubert's work schedule it would be impossible for Darlene to complete her schooling. In the end, she would have to drop her education aspirations because Tawny was more important to her and she decided that Hubert career at this point was more important.

On this night, Hubert gave Tawny markers to play with on the mission boards of the Command and Reporting Center (CRC) at the 607[th]Technical Control Training School (TCTS). She also had a chance to hear her daddy control aircraft that included night air-to-air refueling missions. Tawny sat on the one of the consoles of the Operations Modules (OMs) inside the schoolhouse. Unlike the Tactical OM, the consoles were inside the 607th TCTS building where students could control aircraft in comfort. While Hubert waited for his aircraft to arrive, he taught Tawny how to use the intercom. This allowed her to talk to him while he waited for the fighters and refueling tanker aircraft aircrew-members before they checked in the control airspace. Since all conversations were recorded, she was able to hear herself on the playback during the mission debrief.

Fighter and attack aircraft represent some of the most exciting machines in the sphere of military power because of their design, speed, and weaponry in modern history. Hubert would play a crucial role in developing the US Air Force Fighter Force and the modern Command and Control Force. At the same time, Aerial refueling, also called air refueling, in-flight refueling (IFR), air-to-air refueling (AAR) or tanking, is the process of transferring fuel from one aircraft the tanker to another the receiver during flight. http://en. wikipedia. org/wiki/Aerial_refueling-cite_note-0The procedure allows the receiving aircraft to remain airborne longer, extending its range or loiter time on station.

The maximum take-off weight is loaded on the aircraft by carrying less fuel and topping up once airborne. This procedure is normally used on airfield has a short runway and the aircraft is not able to take the maximum fuel needed to complete its primary operational mission. A series of air refueling can give range limited only by crew fatigue and engineering factors such as engine oil consumption. Such factors are part of the Mission Planning (MP) process where aircrew members must plan the added fuel or how and when to add fuel to their aircraft.

Because the receiver aircraft can receive extra fuel in the air, air refueling can allow a take-off with a greater payload, which could be weapons, cargo or personnel. Air Force tanker aircraft regularly receive requests as transport aircraft anytime while flying from one location to another location between deployments. On most requests, they serve as personnel transport aircraft since both tanker aircrafts are normal airlines converted to tankers.

Their cargo bays below the floors of these aircraft received new fuel bladders that hold jet fuel used during the air-to-air refueling process. Finally, when transporting passengers, both of these tanker aircrafts use military seats that are not the comfortable seats found in civilian airliners even though the US government pays three times as much for the seats. Hubert would log thousands of hours as a passenger onboard both the KC-135 and the KC-10 aircraft traveling between overseas deployments.

Alternatively, a shorter take-off roll is able because take-off can be at a lighter weight before refueling once airborne. Aerial refueling is a means to reduce fuel consumption on long distance flights greater than 3,000 nautical miles. Potential refueling fuel savings range in the thirty-five to forty percent for long haul flights. The two main refueling systems are probe-and-drogue, which is simpler to adapt to existing aircraft, and the flying boom, which offers greater fuel transfer capacity, but requires a dedicated operator station. The training gained during this initial phase of Hubert's career would help him in Iceland, Spain, and every assignment after that as he progressed in his military career. Where understanding the fighter and tanker aircraft basics would add to creating new weapon systems or new programs vital to national defense.

"You might as well finish a master's degree now since I am used for you not being with us," said Darlene. On a few occasions, Hubert had an opportunity to support Air National Guard (ANG) Ground Tactical and Control System (GTACS) units doing exercises in New Mexico, Mississippi, Gila Bend, Arizona, and other deployed locations that also provide Hubert with added experience. While taking classes, Tawny would sit with her daddy in the table while he did his homework with a marker and do her homework. As a little girl, Darlene and Hubert had read to her and she had hundreds of books. Now she could use them to highlight them as she did her homework with her daddy. Tawny's room was full of books and every night either Darlene or Hubert read her a book. Over time, Tawny would prefer to read or outside with her daddy or mommy than spend time in front of a television. In time, she would have an extra room that would become her library and playroom where she and her playmates would receive the freedom to do anything she wishes in order to stimulate her mind freely.

Then when daddy finished his homework, he would either go outside and play with her or go into her bedroom and play dolls. Outside playing meant going to the park and the swings or taking long walks. Going to the back yard meant daddy-pushing Tawny in her bike. More than once, he fell asleep but Tawny did not mind. Tawny simply wanted her daddy with her in her room. She knew that he had to work for her and was always studying trying to become better. She simply colored her daddy's fingernails and his face with her play makeup. She did this because she wanted her daddy to be pretty as she talked to her dolls. Normally, Hubert ran in the morning and took a shower except when he had an early controlling mission.

The following morning Hubert had an early mission and reported to the squadron. He noticed that he fellow officers were looking at him funny until someone said, "I like your pink nails". It was then that he noticed that his fingernails were pink and when he went into the bathroom, he noticed that his face still had makeup. He simply smiled and new that Tawny had gotten mad with daddy when he fell asleep. It would not be the last time that she would color his nails and face when daddy was too tired while playing with her.

Nevertheless, daddy never said he was too tired to play with Tawny. He always played as long as he could until fatigue won. Tawny knew that once her daddy walked in the door that she only had to wait for him to take off his military uniform and that then he would play with her. Then if he had to do school work, he would tell her after they played first. At that point, she would sit next to him with her books and yellow markers as she did her homework with her daddy. As daddy took time occasionally to check her progress, gave her a kiss, or made sure she had a snack, and a drink.

As a second lieutenant, Hubert quickly advanced as a controller and Technical Training School instructor. He also decided to finish a master's degree. In sixteen months, he would actually finish two master's degrees. Darlene had decided to return to college and started taking night classes. He received a master's in public administration and a master's in business administration. During this period, on a few occasions when Darlene had classes and Hubert had night missions, Tawny got a chance to go with daddy to work. While daddy was controlling missions, she took the white markers her daddy gave her to work on the plotting boards and a headset to hear her daddy's missions. Before the mission, her daddy had shown her how the marker displays looked on the board and during the mission, there were plenty of extra technicians available to help her until her daddy completed his tactical air-to-air and air-to-air refueling missions.

With the headset on her tiny head, she could hear the four F-15 Eagles talking to each other and her father and he controlled the fighter aircraft against a different four-ship F-16 Falcons element. All fighting simulated Dissimilar Aerial Combat Tactics (DACT) profiles during real airborne air-to-air missions. As the two Weapons Controller (WCs) yelled at each other passing shots on different radios simulated shots to each other. As Tawny listened on her headset and seeing on her own controller console as a technician explained what her daddy was doing in a different console next to her. Two years later, when in Europe, Tawny would laugh because a 'WC' would be a water closet or a bathroom. She would laugh each time when she would make jokes about her daddy being a 'WC' when they went to the 'WC'.

In addition, when walking on the North Atlantic Treaty Organization (NATO) E-3A Airborne Warning and Control System (AWACS) aircraft during elementary school field trips, Tawny would explain to her friends the controller consoles. After all, she learned about the controller consoles back in Arizona as a little girl when she was a little girl and now she was a big girl in the second grade. Now she was a big girl and saw the consoles in Spain that her daddy had explained to her in detail. Darlene and Hubert believed in talking to their daughter as a normal person and not as a child. In addition, she knew what her daddy was doing each time he flew in the US E-3B/C AWACS consoles because she talked to her daddy each time after he flew. She was proud of him and her beautiful mommy that everyone always talked about in school. Especially since both were always involved in her, school activities and regularly volunteered as teachers assistants.

As part of Hubert's aircraft control training, the most difficult was the controlling German F-104 Starfighterseventy-degree stern mission that most unit controllers avoided. Since the F-104 Starfighter does not have onboard radar to assist the fighter pilots, they depend on the Weapons Controllers (WCs) to assist them conduct their intercepts. The mission profile consisted of controlling two German F-104 Starfighter aircraft and accomplishing a sixty-degree stern. The objective was to turn the both aircraftwhen they had thirty miles separation and on opposite headings. The German pilot trainee would be in the intercept aircraft and the American Instructor Pilot (IP) would be flying the target aircraft.

Since the F-104 at altitude took twenty to thirty miles to turn back on the final headings, most controllers were not able to meet the final attack criteria. Especially since the German F-104 Starfighter was more of a flying rocket that took forever to turn at higher altitudes that required the controller to plan for wide turns in the thinner higher altitudes, which was hard to guess. Especially for new aircraft Weapons Controller (WCs) or even experienced WCs due to the speeds that the controlling German F-104 Starfighter were flying.

The objective was for the intercept fighter aircraft that was traveling at . 98 Mach to have the target cross his nose with five miles separation, then push up his speed to 1. 04 Mach, take the targets heading, and take a simulated missile shot. With practice, Hubert would eventually be one of the few controllers that were able to accomplish this difficult mission profile. Since the Sells Airspace was large, Hubert was able to manage the F-104 Starfighter placement effectively, which allowed the final geometry to give the fighter's the needed seventy-degree rear placement. At those speeds, the WC had to see the German F-104 Starfighter element not only flying at 98 Mach and 1. 04 Mach, but also had to see in their minds the exact time when to turn the interceptor on its final turn. Otherwise, the interceptor would overfly its target, which in a combat environment would be deadly.

Only two unit controllers would be able to control the F-104s in this type of geometry missions. A disciple that would come handy once Hubert became a member of the NATO E-3A AWACS Component where being a manual controller is important. Hubert was the only American that was able to control aircraft at the level that European aircraft controllers were able to control. This would make the US look good in the eyes of the NATO allies where the US represents all other nations. However, within the US ranks, it made most Americans mad since they were not able to meet the higher levels of control that Hubert easily met.

As training requirements, Hubert was also able to fly in the back seat of the aircraft he controlled. The modern Air Force F-15 Eagles and F-16 Falcons were not like the older F-104s or the F-4s when it came to turn radius. Even at higher airspeeds, these aircraft and their US Navy counterparts could easily turn within a mile or easily turn within a few thousand feet. Hubert would fly in both the F-15 and F-16 aircraft many times and experience the G-Force turn radius that would make him a better aircraft controller.

His first flight was on an F-15 Eagle where he flew on a 2v2 or two versus two F-15 Eagle aircraft, which was two F-15s flying against two F-4 Phantom aircrafts in Dissimilar Air Combat Tactics (DACT). One the first intercept, Hubert got a tally on the converting F-4 Phantomand called out the target to his pilot. The next thing Hubert remembers was going straight up, multiple turns, and successfully converting behind the F-4 for a simulated fox-two that was a simulated infrared radar (IR) missile shot from behind. It seemed that within seconds after Hubert reported the visual of the F-4 converting on them to his pilot that his pilot reversed tactical advantage and converted on the attackingaircraft.

This would also be the last time that Hubert would decide to call out tallies since he had no control of the aircraft that allowed him to position his head versus his head flying in all directions as the fighter aircraft tool countless turns. When Hubert got home, Darlene would laugh since it would be days before the coloring of his face would get color again versus being very white. Hubert also learned that his first flight should not have been a DACT mission. By the time he flew on another DACT mission, he gradually established G-tolerance that was acceleration forces taken as fighter aircraft took quick turns in the air. Before Hubert was able to sustain the upper limits of eight or nine Gs, he knew that he had to build his resistance to those levels without blacking out. In time, he would even learn to fly fighter aircraft since he would log almost two hundred hours flying in Arizona, Iceland, Spain, and other areas in fighter aircraft.

"Do you want to go to the Air Force Ball" asked Hubert. This would be the first time that Darlene and Hubert would meet Brigadier General Gordon. Two years later, Hubert would work for Major General Gordon in Torrejon Spain who would be his boss as the 16th Air Force Commander. For now, Brigadier General Gordon was the 56th Fighter Wing Commander at Luke Air Force Base and he was hosting the annual Air Force Ball.

Unlike the Air Force Ball at Medina Base, by now, Darlene had matured more now that she was twenty-one and was a mommy. A year of Business College had also helped her grow and given her more confidence that one gets with age and time. However, as Hubert had always known, with each year Darlene would blossom into a stunning beauty although in his eyes she had always been his beauty queen. On this night, Darlene would truly look as a Beauty Queen when she walked in into the Medina Base Ball Room.

Although many historical events were unfolding, Hubert and Darlene had many social functions to attend. Darlene had always been one who could ware colorful dresses that complemented her blond hair and dark tan. She had a way of being able to speak her mind and although some did not like it, that never stopped her. Darlene believed that since over the years many had made that clear, she was not military, and that if Hubert could not make it based on his own merits, that he did not deserve anypromotion. Hubert had the same feelings and over the years would tell his bosses that Darlene could be herself since his career should be based on his record and his performance and not Darlene and his record as a couple. After all, all his bosses made it clear and kept saying that if the military wanted Hubert to have a family that they would issue one to him.

Hubert put an ad in the base and local newspaper searching for a baby sitter for Tawny. However, since Darlene was a new mommy, she would interview dozens of baby sitters and each had something wrong. Eventually, Hubert decided that the only way that he and Darlene would go to the Air Force Ball or any formal function was if a family member would take care of Tawny. Therefore, he asked his oldest sister, Lupe in Tucson, which was 115 miles south of Glendale, Arizona if she would take care of Tawny. At the time, Lupe did not have any children but had been trying for over ten years to have children. Hubert's sister said yes so Hubert took a day of leave the day prior to the Air Force Ball, which was on a Saturday, he and Darlene drove Tawny to Tucson and dropped Tawny at his sister's house.

As would be the custom for every Air Force Ball, Hubert would always purchase Darlene a new Air Force dress. Darlene would never wear the same twice the same dress twice to a formal function. For this Air Force Ball, the gown was a long blue gown and as always, Hubert wore his black military tuxedo with military medals during the winter months. During the summer or warmer months, the white coat was the normal military tuxedo coat with military medals. As was the custom, once Darlene and Hubert arrived at the Ball, they went through the receiving line and met General and Mrs. Gordon followed by taking their pictures by the Ball photographer. Darlene and Hubert was a stunning couple and over the years always invited to social functions mainly because of how they looked together.

Around three hundred military members with their partners attended the annual Luke Air Force Ball. Darlene ate the steak meal and Hubert ate the chicken meal followed with coffee and cake. The Air Force Band played the customary music and Hubert and Darlene as usual danced the night away. Hubert and Darlene had a unique dancing style that many thought of them as professional dancers. The truth was that Darlene had learned to dance from her father Alfred and Hubert followed Darlene well on the dance floor. Since Darlene and Hubert had become a good disco dancing couple, once Darlene mixed the Fred Astaire and Ginger Rogers dancing style on the dance floor, everyone thought they were professional dancers. In fact, Darlene and Hubert were in their early stages of making up their own style of dancing. In the meantime, the couples would meet a few times on the dance floor and chat as they danced.

As Hubert and Darlene walked through the receiving line, Darlene would make an impression on the 56th Fighter Wing Commander. Years later, he, and his wife would recall their conversation during this first meeting in Spain. Hubert and Darlene would always look good in the dance floor as a good-looking couple that represented the traits of a good officer and typical military family. This would be the first time that Colonel and then the new Brigadier General Gordon would start asking for Hubert as his controller during his air-to-air missions.

After the Air Force Ball, Hubert and Darlene drove to Tucson early Sunday morning to pick-up Tawny and returned to Glendale. This would be the typical routine anytime Darlene and Hubert went out on a date or an official Air Force or unit function. Darlene would only let family baby sit Tawny until she was eleven years old. It did not matter to Hubert because Tawny was important to him as well and Darlene being happy was a plus.

In was also during this period that Professional Air Traffic Controllers (ATC) Association (PATCO) went on strike. On August 3, 1981, almost 13,000 Air Traffic Controllers (ATC) went on strike after months of negotiations with the federal government. During the contract talks, Robert Poli, president of the PATCO, explained the union's three major demands as a $10,000 across the board raise, a thirty-two hour workweek down from forty, and a better retirement package. While the press and hearings in Congress focused almost exclusively on the demand for a pay raise, certain commentators recognized that the air controllers' walkout not solely, or even primarily, an economic issue.

In case the message was still unclear, President Ronald Reagan declared a lifetime ban on the rehiring of the strikers by the Federal Aviation Administration (FAA). It was forty-eight hours after the walkout that President Reagan fired the 11,350 Air Traffic Controllers (ATC). Almost seventy percent of the workforce, fired, did not return to work. Initially, Hubert and his fellow controllers had provided fight follow service to the wing aircraft from the air base to the working airspaces. On one mission, an F-16 Falcon had engine problems and the pilot had to bailout. Unfortunately, the pilot has his wallet in his top pocket and during the ejection, phase his lungs collapsed and he died.

After a few weeks, Hubert deploy to Albuquerque Center in New Mexico to provide a manning assistance to the Federal Aviation Administration (FAA). Hubert would deploy to Albuquerque for a hundred and twenty days and serve as an en-route controller after receiving certification by the FAA. Many active duty controllers received new tasks to augment their civilian counterparts during this US FAA firing crisis. The civilian Air Traffic Controllers (ATC) found out that like the military, they too were not able to strike in America and therefore had most rights that other employees had to improve their economic conditions.

The Air Traffic Controllers (ATC) too were at the mercy of whatever the political system was willing to pay them based on their manning levels and how expensive it was to maintain them and not any benefit that they provided America. Albuquerque Center normally controlled 5,000,000 aircraft per year. Although because of the strike the number of aircraft flying had diminished, there were still plenty of aircraft to prove air route information as they transited from the east to California. This would also prove to be an excellent training opportunity for Hubert since he was a new Weapons Controller (WC). At the same time, it was a time-period where the US airspace was under complete turmoil because of the PATCO controller demands.

This stopped most flying throughout the US except aircraft flying using Visual Flying Rules (VFR). Under VFR rules, the pilot is responsible for flight separation and can only fly in clear weather. Initially Hubert had been one of the controllers who volunteered and provided flight follow service to the Luke AFB, Arizona aircraft. Most of the 607[th]TCTS Weapons Controller (WCs)thought that it was below them to conduct this type of controlling.

In Hubert's point of view, any type of control service was important. Especially flights follow service where safety of flight was crucial. Everything was simply a matter of perspective. He took every opportunity he could to fly in fighter aircraft so that he could learn the fighter pilot perspectives. Once Hubert was on the base newspaper, then all the other unit controllers wanted to be flights follow controllers. Countless aircraft were flying to the ranges located over the Southern Arizona airspace just west of Tucson in the Sells Airspace.

Normally the fighter aircraft would allow him to control a few close control mission profiles until they were a joker fuel, which meant that they had to return to the airbase due to fuel. Since the airspace Notice-to-Airman (NOTAM) airspace, the unit controllers are able to control the military aircraft once the aircraft entered the Sells airspace. In this case, Hubert regularly went out on the guard or Ground Control Intercepts (GCI) common frequencies and told all military aircraft that he was available for flight follow or any type of control that they might require. In most cases, the elements gave him one or two intercepts under his control for practice.

"Babe I just received orders to go to Iceland for a remote" said Hubert. Darlene new that a remote meant that he would be gone for a year and that she and Tawny would not be able to go with him. After a brief discussion, Hubert and Darlene agreed that while he was gone that they should move back to Florida to be close to family. They would take vacation time to go to Bradenton, Florida to look for an apartment. With every move, Hubert and Darlene would use most of their savings since the Air Force would always not pay for half of their family move.

Once the furniture was packed, Darlene and Tawny went to Bradenton to get the apartment set up. As it turned out, by the time Darlene and Tawny arrived in Bradenton, Florida, the furniture had also arrived two days later. The eighteen-wheeler drove straight through to Florida after Darlene spoke to him in Glendale. Once he arrived in Bradenton, he found a helper to assist him to unload and set the apartment the way Darlene wished. On this move, Darlene felt blessed that the mover was a considerate individual who helped her move into her apartment even though he did not have too.

Once he realized that Hubert was going to Iceland, he went out of his way to make sure that his family received their furniture and settled in before he departed for Iceland. Then Darlene's brother Rickey would also assist her during the move to include hooking up the washer and dryer. Overall, this move would be the easiest move that Darlene would have out of the thirteen moves that Hubert would have in his military career. This did not count the nineteen years that Hubert deployed overseas on his own.

It did not change the fact that many of the costs related to this and Hubert and Darlene would pay all future moves. On an average, for each move, they would pay $5-10,000 out of pocket for costs that the Air Force would not pay depending on location. The state side moves would be less expensive than the overseas moves. Each time taking away the savings saved during each assignment to pay for the next mandatory military move.

Hubert would follow Darlene and Tawny to Florida a month later since he did not have sufficient vacation time before he departed Arizona for Florida and then depart for Iceland. Besides, he still had to work until just before his report date. He knew that for one year, his family would be alone and he had to make sure Darlene and Tawny were in a safe location. He decided to get a condominium for his family near the beach so that Darlene and Tawny would be close to her mom and dad's home and still enjoy the Florida lifestyle.

He would also give Darlene the checkbook and give himself an allowance. An allowance that Darlene would force him to live on in order to successfully save month throughout the year. This would force him to teach nighttime college classes in order to have extra spending monies, which he did not mind once he arrived in Iceland. During the year, Darlene would save thousands of dollars by keeping the checkbook.

"Please do not leave me," cried Darlene. As Hubert drove off in his mustang on his way to Norfolk AFB, Virginia where he was dropping off his car for shipping to Iceland, he could see Darlene holding Tawny in her arms. Over the years, Hubert would drive I-75 and I-95 many times, as he traveled in the east coast traveling overseas or supporting a temporary commitment. Working around the Washington D. C. beltway or the Suffolk, Virginia area where the Tactical Air Command (TAC), later changed to the Air Combat Command (ACC) was located or the Joint Forces Command (JFCOM) agencies were located. Once Hubert became a Captain, he would spend months and years in both areas supporting once command or another as a staff officer or a Joint Staff Officer (JSO).

Learning how corrupt the US Defense and contracting environments were and how he would decline lucrative job offers not only as a junior officer but also once he retired as a Senior Officer. However, on this trip, it was Hubert's first driving trip and one that he would be thinking of Darlene and Tawny most of the time. He wondered if he made the right decision and separated from the Air Force and run for the US Congress as Senator Goldwater had offered.

He also wondered if turning down a job offer to enter the banking industry once he recently earned his Master in Business Administration (MBA) to stay in the Air Force was a wise decision. After finishing his second master degree in fifteen months, a banker called Hubert, took him out to lunch, and tried to recruit him as a banker. Hubert declined the job offer saying that he loved the Air Force after his legal immigrant Mexican mother raised him as an idealist American. This was the beginning of a yearlong assignment in Iceland and the longest separation for the Contreras family at this point. This would be the first of three remote assignments for Hubert over the years during his military career.

932ND AIRBORNE WARNING & CONTROL (AW&C), KEFLAVIK AB ICELAND

"Don't leave me," yelled Darlene as Hubert started to drive away on his way to Virginia to drop off his Mustang car at the Bayonne, New Jerseyport. Then Hubert would catch his flight to Iceland. Hubert tried to see Tawny and Darlene waving as long as he could as he drove away. Hubert kept waiving back as Darlene as long as he could but later he would realize that she was not waving back but yelling, "Don't leave me" as he sat in the C-141 Starlifter in the Norfolk AFB, Virginia flight line. There he would leave his car at the port and take a C-141 to Keflavik, Iceland. This would be the first trip that Hubert would travel to the Bayonne, New Jerseyport by himself and later travel with his family on two other trips to pick up vehicles as he traveled to European assignments. Six months later, Hubert would return on leave when he took a two-week vacation back in Bradenton, Florida. This way, he hoped the year would not look as long for him and his family.

"It's so dark and gloomy here" thought Hubert to himself as he walked out of the C-141 aircraft. When he arrived in Iceland, it was early and seemed as if it was dusk but he quickly learned that during the winter this would be all the light he would see. At the time, the 932nd Airborne Warning and Control (AW&C) squadron was the only Air Force unit designated as a Naval Air Station (NAS). The primary mission of Naval Air Station Keflavik is to maintain and operate facilities and provide services and material to support operations of aviation activities and units of the operating forces of the Navy and other activities and units, as designated by the Chief of Naval Operations (CNO).

Once Hubert arrived in Virginia, he caught a military C-141 Starlifter aircraft to Keflavik, Iceland. It was November 1982 and in Iceland it was already the winter. As a First Lieutenant, Hubert went to a remote radar site next to a Navy Installation. After his assignment to Luke AFB, Arizona, he went to a remote assignment in the 932nd Airborne Warning and Control (AW&C) Squadron, Keflavik Naval Air Station, Iceland. Once Hubert drove from Arizona to Bradenton, Florida, Hubert did not have much time to settle in before he had to leave for Virginia. As he did during each short visit with his family, he did as much as he could during the limited time that he had with Darlene, Tawny and the rest of his family.

The 932nd AW&C was under the command of a Lieutenant Colonel Freeman who was a Weapons Controller (WC) that later changed to Airborne Battle Manger (ABM) even though he was one of a few officers allowed to crossed trained into the finance career field. Lieutenant Colonel Freeman brought his wife Bobby to Iceland. He and another First Lieutenant were the only two officers that brought their wives to Iceland although both paid all their travel expenses and all their living expenses.

The second in command was Major Raymond Parson who was also a Weapons Controller (WC). Both Lieutenant Colonel Freeman and Major Parson were exceptional Officers and good mentors who selected Hubert over Senior Officers based on experience and not rank. Major Parson selected Hubert as his Training Officer, making him one of the number three Officers in the unit and in his absence.

The US Air Force has about 2,000 active-duty flyers stationed with the 85th Group at Naval Air Station (NAS) Keflavik. F-4 Phantom in the 1980s assigned to Iceland later replaced by the F-15 Eagle fighter aircraft in the 1990s rotating every 90 days to Iceland that carried out the Air Defense mission. Using four ground-based radars, occasionally Airborne Warning, and Control Systems (AWACS) aircraft, the 85th Group's 932nd Airborne Warning and Control Squadron (AWACS) provided air surveillance of Iceland and the North Atlantic. Over time, the two radars north of Iceland received closure notices from the US military. The resignation of the E-3C AWACS flying units changed to Air Control Squadrons (ACS) later during the decade. In Iceland, two E-3C AWACS aircraft were part of the 932nd ACS and supported by the 552nd Wing at Tinker AFB, Oklahoma.

From 3 November 1982 to 2 November 1983, Hubert received an assignment to the 932nd Aircraft Control and Warning Squadron (AC&W), Rockville Naval Installation, Iceland. During this period, Hubert served as a Weapons Director (WD), Battle Commander (BC), and Unit Training Officer referred to as the Director of Training (DOT). Hubert would continue filling positions that Senior Officers would normally fill causing friction among his peers and fellow Senior Officers. Although Hubert would discuss the issue with his bosses, each time the Operations Officer or Unit Commander would make it clear to him that it was in the best interest of the unit and the US Air Force. Unlike most officers that took three to four months to reach the Mission Ready (MR) status as a WD, Hubert would earn the MR status within weeks even though that period could have been a week if the Stan/Eval officer decided on waiting.

Hubert's aggressive personality let to his selection as the Training Officer and as the first Battle Commander (BC) in Iceland as a First Lieutenant versus the Director of Operations (DO) a Major and the Commander who was a Lieutenant Colonel. This allowed the DO and the Commander more flexibility to work on issues that are more important by having an additional officer to fill the Battle Commander (BC) duties, which had to be, filled 24/7. Each officer completing a twelve-hour shift in the dark room also called the operations room filled the BC. Eventually, Hubert convinced the DO that the Chief of Stan/Eval should also become a BC receiving approval. That provided the operations four Battle Commanders (BCs) to cover the 24/7 operations. Since Hubert had new Officers in upgrade training and he was the alternate Stan/Eval officer, he maintained a busy schedule and seemed to live inside the operations room.

"Why do not you take control of these aircraft," mentioned Hubert to the Mission Ready (MR) controller who was instructing him. The Instructor Weapons Controller (IWC) did not want to take control of the aircraft since there were six aircraft conducting multiple mission profiles in separate airspace. Hubertas an aircraft controller started directing the sixF-4 Phantoms while the Instructor Weapons Controller (IWC)searching for the qualified skilled Instructor Weapons Controller (IWC), Lieutenant Kimberly Oaks (Lieutenant Oaks) that was found making pottery. Throughout the period that the technician was searching for Lieutenant Oaks, Hubert continued skillfully controlling the six aircraft without hesitation.

By the time Lieutenant Oaks arrived, Hubert had already completed four mission setups without any hesitation. Later on, Hubert would learn that in Strategic Air Command (SAC) environment, the skilled rating allowed aircraft controllers to control more than three aircraft. Since Hubert came from a

Tactical Control Command (TAC) environment, Hubert was used to controlling whatever number of aircraft flew into the airspace. Unlike SAC where different levels of training a controller received in order to control more aircraft, in TAC the controller took control of all the aircraft that were in a controller's frequency at any given time. In the tactical environment, levels of control were not required in order for a controller to be qualified as an aircraft controller.

Lieutenant Oaks would force Hubert to wait another month to schedule six aircraft so that she can formally schedule a mission as a check ride for him. Hubert received the 'skilled' rating in record time while assigned to the 932nd Aircraft Control and Warning Squadron (AC&W), which meant that Lieutenant Oaks thought she had competition that she did not like. Hubert made it clear that in his view, she could have all the glory because it did not matter to him because he would only be in Iceland for a year and then leave. He was there only to do his duty as an officer. As a Senior Director (SD), Hubert was responsible for a crew and rating half of the enlisted members assigned to Iceland. Already, Hubert on his own received the initial qualification on every officer and enlisted crew position within the operations center. He felt that in order to manage his enlisted members that he should be qualified in their crew positions to understand their tasks. Besides, the additional training killed time and being remote, time meant nothing and staying busy was always important to Hubert.

"Sir I do not think it's a good idea for me to be the Chief of Training since I am a Lieutenant and we have four Captains," said Hubert to his Director of Operations (DO). The DO had already made up his mind that Hubert would not only be the new Chief of Training, but also his new Assistant Director of Operations (ADO) in his absence. Mainly because Hubert was the best aircraft controller in the unit, which in his view was a prerequisite for the Chief of Training and the Director of Operations (DO) positions. This new job did not sit well with the three Captains who each felt that they should be the Chief of Training. In some ways, Hubert agreed with them but knew that the DO was the boss and that officers followed orders.

One of the benefits of serving as the Director of Training (DOT) or Chief of Training was the ability to fly with the local missions with the fighter squadrons. Hubert knew that he probably received the selection as the Chief of Training because he had just been a Technical School Instructor and the 932nd AC&W training program needed to a new structure. Since becoming a new Weapons Controller (WC), Hubert believed that the best way to understand what fighter aircrews needed in the air was to fly as many sorties (missions) with fighter pilots to learn different techniques as possible. On this flight, Hubert had the experience to fly a four-versus-four F-4 Phantoms Air Combat Tactics (ACT) mission that was difficult to execute in Iceland mainly because of the limited number of aircraft that were available.

Part of the Iceland mission called for F-4 Phantoms to maintain a five-minute alert status fully loaded with missiles. This further limited the availability of aircraft for training missions. However, in the Strategic Air Command (SAC) since unit controllers required the 'skilled' rating, this meant that complex controlling and multiple aircraft where a minimum of different elements controlled at once were required for such a rating. Hubert was lucky to fly in such a mission where he was no only able to hear the controller on the primary frequency. He was also able to hear the four aircraft that were part of his elements coordinate their multiple attacks. At the same time, Hubert had the two single targets on opposite vectors under his control in different airspaces. This meant that he had to separate 2v1 or two versus one F-4 engagements in two airspaces at the same time under his control. His instructor never saw such a mission and was impressed but scared at the same time since he knew that he was not qualified.

Hubert simply reacted to what was natural as he did in the tactical control environment. On one attack, the pilot even allowed him to fly the aircraft to the ten-mile point. At the tem mile point, the controller must make a mandatory call or the 'ten miles' call that is a safety call telling all aircraft to go to their assigned altitude blocks. Normally, one four ship or four aircraft flying together as an element are assigned even numbered altitudes and the other four ship are assigned odd numbered altitudes. At the ten-mile call, all aircraft know that they must fly an assigned altitude block altitude to assure safety of flight. All fighter aircraft make sure they fly the appropriate assigned altitude blocks when the Weapons Controller (WC) makes the 'ten mile' call, which assures safety of flight during the simulated dogfight or combat maneuvers. In this case, since Hubert was still flying the aircraft, he expected the pilot to take control of the aircraft since he knew that he not really flying an exact altitude due to the rough weather.

A few seconds later when Hubert Heard the pilot say, "I have the aircraft," Hubert was relieved. This meant that the pilot had a visual on his wingman, which was a good thing. It also meant that he was able to joint up with his wingman as an element. At that point, the two F-4s including the aircraft that Hubert is flying in starts a left turn to the right as an element. Since our element has the tactical advantage over the second element, the other element is on defense. Therefore, the dogfight starts and the Air Combat Tactics (ACT) profile commences with the 2V2 or the two versus two aircraft mission profile. On this set-up, the dogfight continues until the knock-it-off or a termination call by one of the pilots flying in the dogfight receives a radio call on the radio and either the Weapons Controller (WC) or one of the pilots makes a call on the primary frequency.

"I can't believe the car is buried in the snow again," thought Hubert to himself. Initially Hubert took his Mustang to Iceland with the intension of keeping it for the entire year. After the first few months when each day the winds filled the engine full of snow, he knew that having a small car in a remote radar station not a smart decision. After a few months Hubert decided to sell his mustang and purchase the 'bomb' that was an old 1959 Ford station wagon. Fully loaded with studded winter tires that helped the vehicle to never be stuck anywhere during the winter. Mainly because the Ford station wagon was too heavy to be stuck during the winter. Another benefit of the vehicle was that, it had extra summer tires.

"We need you to go to Reykjavik and work with the civil air control sector to create new airspace around the naval air station," mentioned the Director of Operation (DO). Since the radar had much clutter within forty nautical miles and the cross Atlantic air routes ran east-west starting at 120 nautical miles, Hubert proposed that the new routes and the proposed boundaries become the new airspace. In an effort to provide multiple working airspaces, Hubert divided the airspace by making a five-mile boundary each side of the inbound arrival air routes that were destined to Reykjavik. Over the years, the US had proposed changing the airspace multiple times, but each time the Reykjavik Federal Aviation Administration (FAA) officials had denied the American request mainly because the airspace changes had been too complex. The Reykjavik FAA officials would approve Hubert knowing this had created a simple new airspace structure that he believed, which approved the new airspace in minimal time.

The departure routes divided the airspace, which made the airspace logical and each area containing the same amount of airspace between the boundaries. The inner boundary was the moving-target-indicator (MTI) radar ring where controllers were not able to see aircraft due to the radar clutter and the outer boundary was five miles south of the international air route. This would provide sufficient working airspace for training missions with full support of the civil air control facility. In the end, creating the new airspace took just under a month to get approval instead of the normal six months to a year. This new training airspace would become a permanent part of the US Air Force organizational structure until the year 2006 when the wing closure by the U. S military. Hubert would keep the original slides that he created to use on future tasks since in Iceland he did not need them. The new airspace was now part of new lesson plans and new FAA agreement plans.

"Sir, we have Union of Soviet Socialist Republics (USSR) Russian BEAR Bombers in the system," said the Senior Director (SD) technical. Hubert knew that this meant that two BEAR Bombers were on their way to Cuba and that they normally flew on a southerly vector on the east side of Iceland. Hubert serving as the Senior Director or as the Battle Director who scrambled on a BEAR bomber aircraft and intercepted by the F-4 Phantoms aircraft, call sign Slowgin. The Tu-95 BEAR (Tupolev) was perhaps the most successful bomber produced by the Soviet aviation, enjoying long service in a variety of roles and configurations.

It was the only bomber deployed by any country to use turbo-prop engines, which provided extraordinarily long endurance at speeds only slightly less than comparable turbojet-powered heavy bombers. At random, the Tu-95 BEAR Bombers flew flights from northern Russia in the Northern Sea between the United Kingdom and Iceland gap and then south past Greenland. Along the way, the Iceland forces would intercept the BEAR Bombers and identify their aircraft tail numbers before the continued their flights towards the northeast United States (US).

As the Battle Director (BD) on duty, Hubert knew that he would have to scramble to armed F-4s Phantom aircraft and a KC-135 Stratotanker aircraft to conduct an intercept on the BEAR Bombers. The F-4s had both AIM-9 and AIM-7 missiles loaded on their wings as well as having thirty millimeters (mm) cannon guns. The AIM-9 Sidewinder is a heat-seeking, short-range, air-to-air missile and the AIM-7 Sparrow is a medium-range semi-active radar homing air-to-air missile. Within a year, he would repeat this routine and account for 278 BEAR intercepts or 139 actual intercepts, which was a record up to this point within the Icelandic airspace. He would have to scramble the USE-3C AWACS aircraft to assist in this mission as well.

"Sir you can recommend her for an evaluation but I won't since I do not think she should be a controller" he heard himself tellingMajor Parson the Director of Operations (DO) who had always been a good boss. Yet, he knew that Starlet allowed getting qualified since she was going to the radar station on the east side of Iceland. Later she would be the only controller who had positioned two F-4s Slowgins (call sign) whom were on Tanker in between two Union of Soviet Socialist Republics (USSR) BEAR Bombers. Hubert would think to himself that he was glad that he did not recommend her for a check ride. He only hoped that this event had not taken place. Hubert was sure that the Union of Soviet Socialist Republics (USSRs) not impressed with the US fighter control capabilities. During one exercise, the USSR would use six of its AWACS aircraft in an effort to control its exercise to the level that the US used one ground radar unit or one of its new E-3C AWACS aircraft.

"We have two BEARs in the systems," yelled the Movement and Identification (M&I) technician. This would be a repeat event that Hubert would see often during the next two decades while living or deployed overseas. Although the USSR regularly copied the US weapon systems and purchased every US magazine, they were not able to duplicate the USE-3C AWACS system or any of its new radar systems. After this event was over, Major Parson who was an excellent artist, painted two BEAR Bombers and two F-4s Slowgins on the wall as one entered the Operations. A major simulated Air Defense scenario conducted and as the Battle Manager on duty, Hubert knew he had two minutes to scramble the alert F-4s Slowgins (call sign). Even though he had the Keflavik M&I technician confirm that the two reported tracks from the Hofn Radar site, the two tracks in the system were reported as live tracks. At the two-minute point, Hubert knew that he had no choice but to hit the scramble button. At the same time, he called Hofn and spoke with Starlet who was the acting Commander.

Over the months, as either the Senior Director (SD) or Battle Commander (BC), Hubert would be involved in conducting BEAR intercepts over-and-over. With each mission, the timely decision was vital to mission success and making errors would be part of the events of the day. At this point, Hubert had been in the Operations for over three days non-stop due to the weather. Since the females were living on Keflavik, each time the weather was bad, they were always stuck on base, which meant that Hubert would have to work two or three shifts in a row or more. By now, the six-month point had passed and Hubert applied for leave so that he could return to Florida and visit his family. First, he put his name on the list to see if he could get a flight back to the US and then once he was anywhere in the Continental US he would purchase a roundtrip ticket from Sarasota, Florida.

This had been the first time that he had be separated from Tawny now that she was older and starting to understand what family separations were all about. Upon returning to Bradenton, Florida to visit, his family at the six-month point Hubert was glad to be home. After all, home was where Darlene and Tawny lived. It would break Hubert's heart when Tawny would start crying when she did not recognize her daddy at the airport because he did not have his mustache. Hubert had just taken an official promotion picture and in the Air Force, Officers normally do not have mustaches. It would be another six months before Hubert would return to move his family to Spain. This still meant that the Contreras family would be apart for almost one year except for the three weeks that he returned during his short visit in the middle of his Iceland tour. Being with his family was being home, going to Leto Beach, and going to the bowling alley visiting friends that had been proud of Hubert becoming an Air Force Officer.

"Sorry that I missed the class," said Hubert to his college class. Hubert had passed time by teaching college level classes at the radar site. His Timex watch had the latest technology of the day with a PM and AM dial to distinguish the time of day. By mistake while making an annual time zone change, he had mixed the dial to reflect the opposite of the actual time zone. Although he had relied on the on-duty SD technician to wake him up just before going on duty, teaching college classes not part of his official duties. Because of the bad weather, his replacement, Lieutenant Oaks was stuck on Keflavik, Naval Air Station (NAS) so Hubert had worked three shifts in a row for the second time in a week. During the week, he had only been out of the operations for one twelve hour shift where all he did was sleep in his room and return to the operations center.

"Sir, you won't believe it, Lieutenant Oaks was on the bus," said TSgt Orillia. Finally, after days of sleeping in the Battle Staff cab on a cot, Lieutenant Oaks relieved Hubert. Lieutenant Oaks had used the weather as an excuse five times during the past month and had not reported to work. Strangely, the other two female Officers did not seem to have any problems coming to work on time in spite of the Iceland winter weather. Then, the other two female officers did not use their gender as an excuse to get special treatment or as a weapon. It did help the Lieutenant Oaks was also an attractive female while the other two females were average looking. What was clear, Hubert had little respect for Lieutenant Oaks since she had to use her gender to advance her career at every opportunity as he had seen so often at Luke. This meant that Hubert would finally get to sleep in his bed and not on the cot for the first time in seven months. Soon the Unit Commander would find out that Hubert worked in construction and had built homes. He would ask him to create the blue prints and built new female rooms in the RORO.

Hubert would donate the car to the Remote Officers Radar Operations (RORO) station that would drive it for a few years before it gave out. In the RORO, an Icelandic boat built with everyone's name with a countdown by month when each Officer would depart. The ROTA station had been self-help with two pool tables and served as cooking building for all the Officers. Officers would normally leave extra cans of food so when they got off a late shift they could warm up a bowl of soup and eat it with crackers or have a hot dog with the soup. That is until the new Unit Commander decided that he wanted the female Officers to live on the radar site and the Officers build four bedrooms in the RORO. Once he found out that Hubert used to work in construction and built homes, he knew who the project officer would be for this self-help unit project.

The RORO included new Icelandic furniture purchased in downtown Reykjavik. Unfortunately, in time, some of the furniture started falling apart mainly because some of the glue on the wood did not dry before moving to the radar site and the RORO. The RORO was next door to the mail Officers living barracks and across the street from the Chow Hall. It was also not far from the Radar Operations and the Commanders Administrative Building. This was important because on cold windy days the only thing that would save you when the winds took you would be the ropes between the buildings. When walking between streets where there were not ropes, the only thing individuals could do was fall down and hope that when you got to the end of your sliding that you would reach one of the ropes or poles to grab. Standing was never an option when the Icelandic winds took you on its random trips.

The Rockville Chow Hall known for having the best food in Iceland was another place where many of the military members would hang out. Military members would take the base would take the bus for diner regularly especially on special days were being served. Besides, the Rockville Chow Hall also known for having a Pac-Man machine that took all your quarters with plenty of individuals lined up to put their money in the machine. The Rockville pottery and recording room were also favorite places as was the theater. During the year, Hubert would record dozens of tapes consisting of rock, country, and many other classic types of music.

Although had movies once a week and the movies were never new movies. Nevertheless, at least the movies were inexpensive, it gave everyone something to do, and the popcorn was cheap after the normal twelve-hour shifts. The Iceland movies came with its special humming winds that normally came from the surrounding waters of the Atlantic sea. Not that anyone minded working long days since almost everyone was away from family and wanted to stay busy to kill time since time meant nothing in the dark winters and the bright summers in Iceland. Although many military members had trouble handling the long nights and the long days in Iceland, staying busy was the best way to deal with the long night or the long day dilemma. Especially since time seems to mean nothing when one is apart from family for long periods in remote and austere locations.

The base gym was at the end of the site next to the water. Year round, one could hear the winds and the waves but after a while, their sounds seem to fade. Although there was supposed to be some heating in the gym, due to the cold temperature in Iceland, it seemed that the gym was always cold inside. However, compared to the outside, it was in some ways not as cold. Basketball seemed to be the only sport that filled the gym and the time of day did not matter since everyone worked different shifts. It was only a matter of getting enough individuals to agree to meet at the gym at anyone time to play a game of basketball. Since it was always dark in the winter, the day shift treated time the same way as the night shift. Meals were always available four times per day so meals were never an issue.

The two weeks of self-help construction would payoff in more ways than everyone thought after all. As a result, the Unit Commander would ask the male Officers to convert the RORO, which was the Officers recreation building into a female barracks to move the female Officers on the radar installation. The Officers built four rooms within two weeks as a self-help project, which meant now every Officer would pull their scheduled shift. After sleeping for the first eight hours of his time off, Hubert wrote Darlene and Tawny a letter after taking a shower. The time off also gave him time to record Tawny and Darlene a letter including signing Tawny the songs that he wrote for her when she was a baby. Each time he wrote to Tawny he would draw a picture of himself with a face that included a mustache so that she would remember her daddy.

During that era, it was normal for Hubert to go weeks without receiving letters for days or weeks from Darlene and then all of a sudden receiving a dozen letters all at once. He was sure that Darlene experienced the same occurrence with his letters. It would be another fifteen years before technology would improve so that Hubert and Darlene would be able to talk to each other more often. In the meantime, Hubert purchased calling cards and put as many points as he could afford when he was in the US each month so that he would have the card available overseas. At the same time, the radar site had the only 1940s style telephone operations in Iceland and Keflavik Naval Station. As the Assistant Director of Operations (ADO) and Director of Training (DOT), the Technical Sargent (TSgt) worked for Hubert, which made it easier for him to get short calls back to the US can call his wife Darlene. However, Hubert made sure that he gave this option to every military member assigned or deployed to Iceland once he spoke to his supervisor and commander.

After discussing the issue with his supervisor, Major Parson and the Unit Commander, all agreed that during the evening hours when the telephone usage was normally down, military personnel would be able to call their families three times per week. During these moral calls, each member received permission to talk for no longer than five minutes. What was strange was not getting a line in Iceland by once the Iceland Operator called a US Base Operator; she would have problems with them who would set shorter time limits. Many times Hubert would have to call bases hundreds of miles from Bradenton, Florida and call collect because the local MacDill AFB Operator would not allow a local phone patch more than once per week. It did not matter that he was away from his family thousands of miles for a year at a time. The base commander policy was that even on weekend or during night time when the lines were not in use moral calls received more than once a week.

"Sir, we have an unknown track in the system," said the Senior Director (SD) technician. This policy remained for Hubert's entire military career for over thirty-one years even though he received deployments for over twenty-three of those years mostly overseas in hostile areas. This policy remained in spite of the busy work schedule where everyone worked seven days per week twelve hour shifts. Many times during the winter months, the three female Officers assigned to the unit would be unable to take the two-mile trip from Keflavik, Naval Air Station (NAS), Iceland, to the radar site. This meant that Hubert would take back-to-back shifts and on call the remainder time. Over the winter, he slept in the dark battle staff room where he slept on a cot. Whenever needed, the SD technician would wake him up to conduct what became another mission. As the months passed by, since the Iceland winter nights were always dark, he never truly knew if it was day or night. Since Hubert stayed busy, the long nights never bothered him, as it seemed to bother many of his coworkers.

Within twenty seconds, Hubert knew that the scramble aircraft would find no BEAR Bombers on this day. He quickly went to the surveillance section and directed the technicians conduct another search in the area where Hofn reported the BEAR Bombers and found no radar contacts. As the Battle Commander (BC)on duty, Hubert quickly called the Wing

Commander and tried to cancel the scramble. After a short discussion with the Wing Commander, he was instructed the unit to conduct training intercept events. The Hofn Battle Commander (BC) for the second time in two-months received notice on the radio to take a flight that would be bring her to Hofn to pick her up for the mission debriefs. At the mission-debrief once after all events completed, everyone knew that the events that had occurred served as an excellent training opportunity.

However, everyone also knew that the Hofn Battle Commander(BC) was an accident waiting to happen but that this event would be another none-event because she was an attractive blond-haired female. After the mission debrief, Starlet actions resulted in a downgrade and returned to basic controller training. Hubert reminded the Director of Operations (DO) that he recommended her for an evaluation. As the Director of Training (DOT), Hubert would not recommend Starlet for a check ride as was the normal process in the unit per the training regulations that he approved. Only because she was not able to control the minimum required aircraft and able to accomplish simple sterns required by the Air Force Regulations.

Two major mishaps spoke for themselves so the corrective action was to have Starlet return to Hofn as the Commander since the Hofn Commander did not have to control aircraft. She still served as a Battle Commander (BC) but was required to have a strong Battle Commander Technician (BCT) to keep her out of trouble. Hubert trained the enlisted BCTs that received approval to supervise Starla in the Hofn Operations Center. Being an attractive blonde-haired person just happened to be a coincidence in this case as was always the case in the Air Force that always seemed to be unfair in the current decade.

"Hi sweetie, daddy loves you," said Hubert to Tawny. He was lucky that the Icelandic operators were located in the radar site and he could make short calls to his family once a week. He had also written to his family regularly over the months normally writing to both his girls daily. On one occasion, since it was Christmas, Hubert created Santa's Flight Plan (FP) and mailed it to his little girl. He used a real Flight Plan and added hundreds of cities that went around the world ending in Bradenton in his daughters address. He worked on the Flight Plan over a week each night shift for hours until he completed the Flight Plan since at the time the technology of the consisted typing every character manually. It also included her daddy's letter when he had departed for Iceland that included a picture that he drew of himself waving from the C-141 aircraft and a second picture with him waving from his controller console.

"Hubert I need you to host the TAOC for this exercise," said the Director of Operations. This would be the first time that a US Marine Tactical Air Operations Center (TAOC). This would also be a training opportunity for Hubert to control off a different radar system. He had just finished helping install the first US Navy data link system referred to as the MULTOTS. The US Navy as a port-based simulator had developed the MULTOTS. The local naval leadership hoped to give the US Air Force its first data link system that would become operational. Hubert and his team would make MULTOTS operational, thanks to a lot of hard work. It was because of the use of such data link systems that within ten years the US military would soon lead the world in this area. Soon within the next ten to fifteen years, the White House situation room would be able to see the air battle from anywhere in the world real-time thanks to US data link capabilities.

Within a few months, BEAR intercepts controlled while the data link picture relayed from the E-3C AWACS aircraft to the Keflavik Command and Control (C2) dark room. During the exercise that included the TAOC data link picture, the Iceland data link picture had started what a decade later would be a typical Air Defense scenario with operational data link during each mission. Nevertheless, in the early 1980s, having data link available in an operations dark room was not a common occurrence. No one had been able to make any data link operational with a ground unit until Hubert and his team successfully worked all the technical issues that MULTOTS offered. Not only did the Keflavik operations personnel cheer when the MULTOTS data link picture came through from the US AWACS aircraft, but the generals at the Tactical Air Command (TAC), and the Pentagon also cheered.

"Sir, I not responsible for the initial COMSEC equipment," said Lieutenant Myer to Hubert. Installing the MULTOTS system had been a difficult task for Hubert and the action Officer that he had given the task to accomplish. Lieutenant Oaks had received a Commendation Medal for her initial efforts in installing the system. Hubert had seen the same type of event when he was enlisted at MacDill AFB, Florida when TSgt Peavey was award a Meritorious Service Medal (MSM) for what was an Outstanding Records Branch only to find out that he had not accomplished records receives for over four years.

Hubert's first six months at MacDill had been working seven days a week fourteen hours per day for what he called fixing TSgt Peavey's Meritorious Service Medal (MSM). He did learn the Records business well in the first six months in Consolidated Base Personnel Office (CBPO) that served him well. Unfortunately, Lieutenant Myer did not accomplish a Communications Security (COMSEC) inventory when he accepted the MULTOTS project from Lieutenant Oaks. Whenever an officer takes over as project officer of a technical project, the first requirement is that he or she accomplish an inventory to ensure that one know what they are accountable for before starting the project.

After conducting an investigation and providing the facts to the unit Operations Officer and Unit Commander, they directed his to take the final administrative actions against Lieutenant Myer. Months later, countless COMSEC security deviations found during an annual inspection. As the Deputy

Director of Operations, Hubert was received the task to take administrative actions against a fellow lieutenant. Even though Lieutenant Oaks was responsible for the security violations, Lieutenant Myer career would end. Hubert's investigation found that Lieutenant Myer had not accomplished an audit when he took over the task. Therefore, it was his fault for not accomplishing the task although Lieutenant Oaks accomplished all the security violations. Over the years, taking such difficult investigations would be a task that Hubert would accomplish.

"What do you think about going to Madrid," asked Hubert. Darlene at first was excited about going to Spain. Nevertheless, she knew that this would take her overseas for at least three years and away from family. Hubert received his first choice for a follow-on assignment since he had volunteered for a remote assignment in Iceland. The year had been rewarding but difficult since he missed Tawny and Darlene dearly. He was glad that the year was over and that he would reunite with his family. After a year in Iceland, it was time to rejoin Hubert family for a short vacation in Florida.

Just before leaving the radar station, thepromotionresults came out and Hubertreceived a notification of selection Captain. Although thepromotion rates to Captain were high, Hubert had just served with one First Lieutenantnot promoted. However, for now, it was a good feeling knowing that Hubertreceived apromotion to Captain even though he was in a career field that had the lowest promotion rate in the Air Force. Within the Weapons Controller (WC) career field, it was common that officers not receive the selection to Captain or every other rank on a regular basis. By the time Hubert would meet the Lieutenant Colonel Promotion Board, he would have a four percent probability of making the Lieutenant Colonel rank.

Even though the First Lieutenant was in a critical career field as Hubert was, he would eventually make Captain since his next assignment would be the USE-3C AWACS Wing. However, he would never receive a promotion to Major. He would enter the Reserves and easily receive promotions to Lieutenant Colonel. Hubert would maintain contact with him since those individuals that receive a remote location tend to be close friends. At least that is what Hubert thought. One such officer would change Hubert's mind later in his career once assigned in Alaska and a former friend worried about his promotion opportunities over his friendship.

The flight from Keflavik, Iceland to Norfolk AFB, Virginia on a C-141 was relatively smooth for a military flight. Unfortunately, the flight arrived late in Norfolk AFB, which meant Hubert had to stay at a hotel until the following morning when he would be able to take the first flight to Sarasota, Florida. Since Hubert was paying out of pocket for all the expenses, this would be the norm over the years. Each move would average around $5,000 or more out-of-pocket costs that would add up over time with thirteen military moves.

CHAPTER 3

CAPTAIN

For now, the Iceland tour had finally ended and Hubert was returning to the US to pick-up his family and then takes a new assignment to Madrid, Spain. This would be an opportunity to take a short family vacation in Bradenton, Florida with family and asked him mother to travel from Arizona to be there when he arrived. After decades, he would finally find out that although he believed that she was afraid of flying, she in fact was not afraid but enjoyed taking the train to New Olean's, Louisiana and then the bus the rest of the way to Florida. Hubert was returning to Florida to pick-up Darlene and Tawny while enjoying his short vacation together before flying to Spain traveling through JFK in New York City, New York.

For now, Hubert arrived in Sarasota on a Saturday and started a two-week vacation before driving be New Jersey to drop off their Camaro for shipment to Rota, Spain. Unlike the trip to Iceland, this time, Darlene and Tawny would drive north with Hubert on this trip. Once in Bayonne, New Jersey, Hubert and family dropped their Camaro at port and took a taxi to JFK airport to catch their flight to Madrid, Spain. On this trip, the timing worked just as planned without any problems. On the day of arrival at Barajas International Airport, Madrid, Hubert and family would arrive as a new Captain. Spain would be a new experience for Darlene and Tawny living overseas and for now, not realizing that this trip would be the start of a decade of living in Europe. Where Tawny would grow up learning more in here first seven years of school that her entire life in the US education system once returning to America.

JOINT AIR C2 CENTER (JACCC), 16TH AF,TORREJON AB, SPAIN

Hubert had just pinned on Captain the day Darlene, Tawny, and he arrived to Spain. This was the first time the Contreras family traveled outside the US as a family and they were excited to live in Madrid, Spain. From the late 1950's to the early 1990's, The US Air Force maintained a presence in the Southern Mediterranean to counter the Soviet Threat to Western Europe. The tip of the sword was Torrejon Air Base (AB), Spainout-side of Madrid, Spain. Torrejon began its life as a support base for Strategic Air Commands (SAC) reflex missions in the late 1950s to mid-1960s. It provided ground support, tanker support, and Air Defense for SAC's rotational alert forces, as well as supporting the Spanish Air Defense System.

From 16 November 1983 to 15 November 1986, Hubert arrived in Madrid, Spain with Darlene and Tawny after spending a vacation in Bradenton Florida. He received an assignment to the Joint Air Command and Control Center (JACCC) later redesignated to the 7116th Tactical Control Flight (TCS), Headquarters 16th Air Force, Torrejon Air Base (AB), Spain. Again, Hubert would become Mission Ready (MR) in less than a month and quickly became the Chief of the Training Branch. He quickly implemented the Spanish Air Force Sector Operations Center (SOC)/Combat Operations Center (COS) Program at the Ala and Alerta de Control, which is Spain's Air Defense Center. Hubert received an offer to remain at 16th Air Force as a full time Staff Officer but declined mainly because he did not like how his new supervisor was administering his section. Like most Lieutenant Colonels, he too was more concerned in making promotion to Colonel and not what was best for the Air Force and 16th Air Force.

Hubert also created a training program that allowed USWeapons Controller (WCs) (WDs) to control US aircraft deployed to Spain and the local F-16s Falcons using Spain's SOC/COS equipment. This allowed Spain to become certified and received approval for Spanish Weapons Controller (WDs) to control US F-16 Falcons in English. These two controlling programs became the busiest controlling facilities in Europe. In spite of not being one of the brown nosers in this political unit, Hubert received a by-name selection as a Command Briefer and at the Status and Forces Negotiation Team due to his Spanish skills and maturity. Hubert's accomplishments earned him the Air Force Commendation Medal, Third Oak Leaf Cluster, awarded by Major General, J. R. Bailey, 16th Air Force, Commander. Hubert received the nomination for the Meritorious Service Medal but his supervisor downgraded the medal because Hubert did not extend in Spain as he had requested.

Later in 1966, with the arrival of the 401st Tactical Fighter Wing (TFW) and its F-100s, Flashbacks, at Torrejon Air Base (AB) became United States Air Forces in Europe (USAFE's) primary nuclear and non-nuclear contingency operations wing. The F-100s provided rotational and rapid response forces to other European and Middle Eastern locations with the primarily units in Incirlik, Turkey and Aviano Air Base (AB), Italy. The North American F-100 Super Sabre was a supersonic jet fighter aircraft that served with the USAF from 1954 to 1971 and with the Air National Guard (ANG) until 1979. The first of the Century Series collection of USAF jet fighters, it was the first USAF fighter capable of supersonic speed in level flight.

North American Aviation as higher performance follow-on to the F-86 air superiority fighter originally designed the F-100. These locations served as the primary training or tactical nuclear alert locations. Initially, the US Air Force replaced the

F-100s with F-4 Phantoms and then during Hubert's era with new F-16B two seat Falcons. This allowed him to fly throughout Spain and the Mediterranean in the back seat of the F-16. During many squadron parties, Tawny was also able to sit in the F-16 cockpit and have her picture taken inside and outside the F-16 Falcon with her friends growing up.

Hubert would work for Major General Gordon who had been the Wing Commander back at Luke Air Force Base, Arizona. Hubert recalled that they had met on the dance floor as couples more than once. Darlene and Hubert had met him and his wife during the Air Force Ball and Hubert had controlled him many times as a Weapons Director (WD) while assigned to the 607th Tactical Control Training School (TCTS) at Luke. Now Major General Gordon was his Commander here at Torrejon Air Base (AB) Spain. During the assignment to Spain, the F-16 Falcon served as the 401st primary fighter aircraft.

On the day that Hubert's family and Hubert arrived in Torrejon Air Base (AB), Hubert became a new Captain assigned to 16th Air Force and Spain's Ala Alerta de Control (Air Defense Center). As the Chief of Training, one of Hubert duties included creating a controller course for the Spanish Air Force to be able to control US aircraft. What Hubert did not realize at the time, it would become the beginning of a new lifestyle, mainly because he would be deployed seventy percent of the time or more regardless of where assigned.

As part of the US foreign assistance program, Spain served as the test site for Americas' future strategic Air Defense program. Spain given a new Air Defense system called Combate Grande. Combate Grande consisted of radar and ground communications stations referred to as Ground/Air Task Oriented Radar (Gator) units. These units were tactically located throughout Spain and the Majorca Island off the coast of Spain. Using a dual Regional Air Operations Center (RAOC) and the Sector Air Operations Center (SAOC) control system at the Ala de Alerta de Control, Spain with the assistance of the

US tested a new strategic Air Defense system implemented in the United States (US) during the following decade.

This assignment was an exciting assignment primarily since Hubert assigned to a Numbered Air Force (NAF) staff position and liaison to Spain's Air Defense Center. Like most assignments, Hubert reported to work and the first week consisted of in-processing appointments throughout the air base. It was nearing the holiday season and with the family still living in base billeting when Darlene got sick. Hubert was at work when the electricity was lost in the billeting building and Tawny had to walk outside in search of help for her mommy. Feeling her way in the dark, Tawny knocked on doors until finally someone opened the door. Although she was only six years old, she knew that her mommy was sick and that it was up to her to find someone to help her get better.

It was the Harris family and Alicia asked the little girl what was wrong. Tawny mentioned that her mommy was sick and Alicia called her husband Bob to come and help. The Harris family consisted of Alicia, Essi her five years old daughter, and Bob who flew F-16 Falcons in the 963rd Fighter Squadron, call sign Squids. The Harris' asked where Hubert worked but Darlene did not know since they had just arrived at Torrejon. At the time, Alicia was pregnant and later would have a boy named Jonathan. The Harris' took Darlene to the hospital and fed Tawny until Hubert came from work. Darlene did not know where Hubert worked and only knew that he was an aircraft controller. Besides, she was too sick and was not thinking straight to think that he just down the road from Billeting at 16th Air Force.

Alicia would be the Air Force wife who would help Darlene learns how to be an Air Force wife. This would be the first time that Darlene would see firsthand the way Officer's wife acted and how many wore their husband's ranks. The Harris and Contreras family moved into the Royal Oaks family housing which was twenty miles from Torrejon. Only the senior military members received base housing at the Torrejon Air Base housing facilities. This included the 16th Air Force Commander and his Deputy Commander. All other military members assigned to Torrejon lived at Royal Oaks near the Moralejas, which was about five miles from downtown Madrid City and Plaza Mayor. From the Royal Oaks, one could see the Madrid City skyline and the direct view to the city.

Royal Oaks built next to the Spanish Airport but once the airfield was build, Franco had decided to make it into Madrid's new international airport. The old American base of Torrejon would serve as first and final base location for the Americans. The Royal Oaks was also near the Madrid golf course and the Moralejas where the Spanish wealthy lived. The Moralejas golf course was often in the news used for international golf games. Each time Darlene and Hubert drove to Torrejon Air Base using the back road, they had to drive through the Moralejas and passed by many homes of the wealthy including Jack Lemon, Mrs. Peron from Argentina, and many other famous world citizens.

"Hubert, you have to get to Tawny's school right away. They just found a bomb at her school. " Although Royal Oaks had some security, it was an open family facility. Many times Tawny and her kindergarten classmates had real bomb evacuations. Spanish terrorist wanted the American's out of their country. An empty bag left in front of the Contreras family driveway around fifty feet from the end of their house. At first, the security Police thought it might be a bomb but after they shot the bag with a rifle, it not. However, everyone tried to live a normal life without letting the bomb scares take away from the experience of living in a beautiful country.

In spite of the threats, every day after work when Hubert was home, he would take Tawny for a walk around Royal Oaks after work. At the opposite side of the Royal Oaks was a small Taska (family bar) where Hubert and Tawny would stop and get a drink and snack. This would be where Tawny would learn how to play computer card games. In Spain, it was normal of children to come to bars with their parents. While parents had a class of wine, children had a coke, as both shared cheese and bread together. Later, Darlene would get Tawny a puppy and on her own she would take her puppy on a walk. Franticly, Darlene would go after Tawny as she walked her puppy. As Darlene found both a few minutes later, she first yelled at Tawny but then she was glad that Tawny was all right.

"Do you think it's time to change our furniture?" Darlene had asked. It had been six years since they purchased the living room set and had survived Tawny's baby days. By this time, they replaced the bright red velvet living room set that they had purchased when Darlene and Hubert first got married. Darlene cutout a picture of a living room set and took it to a local furniture store. At the furniture store, she asked if they could take their old furniture and create something similar to the picture. When Darlene and Hubert received the three pieces of living room furniture back, they were surprised at how beautiful it was. They could not believe that it was their original velvet furniture purchased with the monies from their first income tax return.

The old furniture had high sidearm and back and the new furniture was low cut and not fluffy as the old velvet arms and back. The furniture would survive five moves until Darlene and Hubert moved to Arizona where they would give it to their young movers as startup furniture. Except for the back of the sofa, the furniture remained in good condition after all the moves. The furniture was still in the original white color that the Spanish furniture maker had re-created the furniture back in Spain. Hubert would soon learn that in Europe, if one has a picture of any item, in any country they are able to make an exact copy of the original item.

At the JACCC, Hubert worked for his old Commander, Lieutenant Colonel Russ from his first assignment in Arizona. The Operations Officer was Lieutenant Colonel Ernest Somoza;

a Texmex married to an Irish American and had two daughters. Initially, the unit's first problem became deciding what to call everyone mainly because most of the unit's first name was 'Jose' and everyone in the unit were Officers. One had to be careful when walking into an office or answering a telephone and saying that a call was for 'Jose' since the unit had too many individuals with the Jose name assigned to JACCC. This issue required a unit meeting to decide how to handle how to call each other at work. Eventually, this name agreement came in handy during social gatherings.

The Assistant Operations Officer was Joe Lopez who was a Texmex and was married to Danish American. The Stan/Eval (evaluator) was Captain Jon Swann and was from Ohio the only bachelor in the unit. Caption Joe Alvarez, Hubert's Deputy Chief of Trainings, was a Mexican American married to a Mexican. Captain Joe Vazquez was married to a German and Joe Martinez a Puerto Rican was also married to a Puerto Rican. Joe Vazquez was the Commanders' pet because he liked his wife that reminded him of his daughter that was in college, Alvarez was "Al" because we had too many Joe's in the unit, Somoza was Joe because he was the Operations Officers, and Lopez was Jose, Martinez was Marty. Jon and Hubert did not have 'Joe' as a first name so we did not have to worry about our first name.

There are many problems in units where individuals are concerned with their careers. Hubert and Jon became good friends mainly because they were the only two Officers that did not play the politics. Many times, individuals playing political games think that in order to advance one's career, this requires back stabbing games in order to advance one's career. These Officers were the result of the unit senior leadership whopromoted such an organizational culture. The strange outcome of such a unit is that socially, these types of individuals are one hundred percent different as if they have a different personality. In the social environment, all were friendly and actually enjoyable to be around with all the time as if each had a 'Jackal and Hide' personality.

"Sir, I'd like to go to the altitude chamber so that I can fly with the local squadrons?" asked Hubert. Lieutenant Colonel Russ supported Hubert's request to deploy to Germany and go to the altitude chamber so that he would be able to fly in fighter aircraft on training missions. Both Officers felt that the best way to understand as controllers how to control aircraft in air-to-air and air-to-ground missions was to fly in fighters aircraft. At Torrejon Air Base (AB), Hubert flew over eighty sorties while in Spain, Italy, and Turkey flying in Dissimilar Air Combat Tactical/Air Combat Tactical (DACT/ACT) sorties, Low Level missions, air refueling missions, Air Combat Maneuvering Instrumentation (ACMI) sorties, and Tactical Range sorties.

Unlike Hubert who loved flying on fighter aircraft, Jon did not like flying on fighter aircraft. However, he did attempt to fly on one operational F-16 Falcon flight. In normal fashion, Jon attended the required altitude chamber training in Germany. Upon his return to Spain and Torrejon AB Spain, he went to one of the three flying squadrons and put himself on the flying schedule to fly a local sortie (mission). He attended the Mission Planning (MP) the day prior and the following day he reported to the squadron for his 1. 3-hour sortie at 6:00 AM in the morning. Hubert tried to fly with one of the three fighter squadrons once a month if not more.

The sortie started in normal fashion as the aircraft taxied onto the runway. Once airborne, Jon was in number two of a two-ship of F-16s going to Training Area 104A just east of Torrejon AB. Each aircraft had a separate frequency and controller with Pegaso control, which was a US Weapons Director (WD), later redesignated to Airborne Battle Manager (ABM). Jon's F-16 was the wingman so after the initial mandatory warm-ups, Soligen-2 flew to the west side of 104A and Soligen-1 stayed in the east side of 104A. Once the Pegaso Weapons Controller (WC) told the Soligen Flight that they had twenty-five miles separation, Pegaso declared, 'Fights-On' and both F-16 aircraft turned inbound towards each other.

At this point, the first Air Combat Tactical (ACT) mission started. At the merge, the aircraft conducted ACT maneuvers until one F-16 aircraft simulated killing the other F-16 aircraft, which could prove the kill using his aircraft tapes. This simulated process repeated three times until the aircraft reached joker and the aircraft returned to base (RTB). Throughout the flight, Jon was cold mike, which meant the pilot in the front seat could not hear him vomiting. Jon did this on purpose because he did not want the pilot to hear him. Eventually, the Instructor Pilot (IP) decided to end the flight early and RTB early. During the flight, the IP had overall responsibility for safety-of-flight.

Once Jon landed, Jon did not attend the mission debrief and decided to drive back home. Throughout his drive back home, Jon had to pull over every ten minutes to vomit. Even though Jon lived twenty minutes from the base, it took him over two hours to get home. The following morning, he made it clear to the Unit Commander the he would never fly again in any time of fighter aircraft. Jon made it clear that he not a pilot and that since he did not get flight pay, which he would refuse to fly again for the rest of his military career. His co-workers gave him a hard time at work for a few days. Hubert was the exception except he could not help smiling whenever he looked at Jon mainly because he could not forget how he explained how long it took him to get home after his one F-16 flight.

Hubert would be qualified as an instructor and assigned as the Chief of Training and as the alternate Standardization and Evaluation (Stan/Eval) Officer. Hubert was responsible for training USWeapons Controller (WCs) that came from all over Europe and US based guardsmen. Hubert had also created the controller certification program to qualify Spanish controllers. The Major Command in Germany eventually approved the program. That allowed the Spanish controllers to control US fighter aircraft. The Spanish Officers like all of the European

Officers all went to a military academy, which eventually gave them a college degree.

Unlike the US Air Force where enlisted members are able to become Officers, few European nations have such a program available. Most officers came from affluent families with a small percentage coming from the college levels until recent decades. In most European nations, officers were required to take technical degrees as part of their commissioning requirements. In addition, most European nations had a dual commissioning program. One where the officer chose to take the promotion path and the other where the office chose to take the technical or operational path. Not only allowing the officer to choose which promotion path, but also improving moral within the military force.

Hubert's training program received the outstanding rating by the Major Command (MAJCOM) inspection General's visit. He received a commendable mention certificate because of his training program that he qualified hundreds of controllers. He had also been a primary controller when the Spanish Federal Aviation Administration (FAA) went on strike. Hubert controlled aircraft throughout Spanish and surrounding airspace. Hubert had become qualified as a command briefer in Spanish and English. This meant that in addition to all of his normal duties and deployment commitments, Hubert had to make sure that he was available to present the Command Briefing when scheduled by the 16th Air Force Commander.

Hubert would always say that as long as one is the best at his or her primary duty, then they do not have to play politics and brown nose. Although Hubert's direct bosses did not help his career, Commanders at the next levels made sure that his Commander would not write poor performance reports because they knew that he was the top Officer in the unit. They also knew that Hubert was the old school type of Officer, as they would often say. A 'Promote' meant that his Commander would use his contributions and achievements to help theirpromotions and not help Hubert. Hubert would receive eachpromotion based on his own accomplishments.

For example, after Hubert and Marty selection to attend Weapons Schools, which helps Officer'spromotions, Hubert was too important to attend. Hubert's Commander said that he could not let Hubert go to Weapons School because he was too important and Marty not doing anything important. Therefore, Marty attended Weapons School even though Hubert was the unit's top controller. Hubert had just received a special award from the Spanish Air Force for being a top controller in Spain's history. The Spanish Air Force had initiated the award on their own and not at the request of the Air Force individuals as other had done in the past.

"I think we need coffee before we go home," said the group after a long night of taska hoping in Madrid, Spain. Taska's were little bars that were located in manufactured caves where locals and tourists would go drink sangria, eat the specialty of the house, and sang to organ music. Each visit to a Taska was a new adventure mainly because the group never knew what the night would bring. The only thing that was constant was where the group would meet, normally at the Plaza Mallor, but then nothing else was normal because every visit to the Taska's were random.

"Singing in the rain," sang Darlene and the US Ambassador. After one visit by the US Ambassador to Spain, Hubert, Darlene, and a few friends went tasca hopping in downtown Madrid, Spain. Tasca's were little bars with some being in caves around Plaza Mallor. Each Tasca had a specialty snack and singing and drinking was the custom. The USAmbassador to Spain and new friends had a great time singing and drinking until four the following morning. On this night, it was three couples out for the night enjoying the Madrid nightlife and having a great time. As was the custom, one would drink coffee con leche (coffee and milk) and a cognac before taking the metro or a taxi back to their Royal Oaks neighborhood.

"Would you like to meet King Juan Carlos?" asked Colonel Carasco in Spanish. King Juan Carlos I of Spain was visiting the Ala de Alerta y Control and the Americans had to leave with the exception of Hubert. Hubert was busy working in his small office in theAla de Alerta y Control when one of the Spanish Majors walked in and asked him to come out to the hallway for a private conversation. As a matter of protocol, only members that worked in the Spanish Air Defense Center, on this trip expected to meet the King of Spain now that the Regional/ Sector Air Operations Center (RAOC/SAOC) was officially becoming an activated by the Joint Air Command and Control Center (JACCC). Hubert returned to his office and asked the other Americans to go to the main Sixteen Air Force building until he called them to return.

He would only tell them that it was a request from the Spanish Commander. Hubert as the JACCC Chief of Training played a key role in training the Spanish controllers in addition to hundreds of deployed US Air Weapons Controller (WCs), later redesignated as rated Airborne Weapons Directors. Hubert was glad that on this day that he wore his blues since on days that he was either planning on flying with the local squadrons he wore his flight suit. Hubert was surprised that all the other Americans had to leave the Spanish Air Defense Center during King Juan Carlos I of Spain visit to the Ala de Alerta y Control. After all, the US taxpayers including every American asked to leave the Ala de Alerta y Control, paid for these facilities. Except for the deployed Air Force members, the JACCC contributed to training the Spanish Officers assigned to the Ala de Alerta y Control.

"Sir I would like to attend FWIC and SOS" said Hubert to his Commander. Hubert deployed outside of Madrid much of his time in Spain. He would deploy to Italy, Turkey, and Germany supporting the local flying wing and doing headquarters duties. Twice Hubert the major command selected him to attend Staff Officers School (SOS) and once to Fighter Weapons Instructor

Class (FWIC), which was beneficial forpromotion and his Commander, Lieutenant Colonel Millard had not allowed him. Instead, Lieutenant Colonel Millard let one of his coworkers go in his place since according to the Commander, "they weren't doing anything important" in their jobs.

"I get to go to SOS after all," mentioned Hubert. After selection by the US Air Force Europe (USAFE) to attend Staff Officers School (SOS) and the Fighter Weapons Instructor Class (FWIC) and each time told that he was too important to go, Hubert did not expect to attend either course. Hubert had to attend the summer class in Montgomery, Alabama, which meant Darlene and Tawny could go to Florida and visit family. This allowed Hubert to drop Darlene and Tawny in Bradenton before flying to Montgomery, Alabama. Darlene and Tawny would also go to Georgia and visit family during this trip before returning to Spain.

This time, the flight from Madrid to Florida took the Contreras family through JFK in New York City, New York. The Contreras family route took them through New York City, New York because of Hubert's return flight from Montgomery, Alabama after he completed his SOS training. Each time Hubert went to a school for supported a deployment in the US, he would have to purchase his family's airline tickets. Although they did not have to return to the US, Hubert thought that since his flight was partially paid, this gave his family an opportunity to visit family in the US even if only for a short period.

While Hubert was in Florida, Darlene had a chance to take Tawny and visit her sister at Fort Benning, Georgia for a week. Bobby, her husband was in the Abrams M-1 Battalion Headquarters as the Battalion Sargent Major as an E-8, Sargent Major. Years earlier, Darlene and Hubert visited Bobby, Janis, and family in Kentucky, Georgia when stationed in Fort Knox, Kentucky when Bobby worked on the M-60 and M-60A1-A3 Patton tanks. The 105-millimeter (mm) Gun Full Tracked

Combat Tank, M-60, is a first-generation Main Battle Tank (MBT).

The M-1 Abram tank named after General Creighton Abrams, former Army Chief of Staff and Commander of US military forces in Vietnam from 1968 to 1972. It was during this visit that Darlene and Tawny had the opportunity to go down a raft with her family. Darlene would have an opportunity to visit Bobby's unit with her sister and family during her visit to Fort Benning, Georgia that was hosting a family picnic. Four main versions of the M-1 Abrams deployed, the M-1, M-1A1, M-1A2, and the M-1A3, incorporating improved armament, protection and electronics. These improvements, as well as periodic upgrades to older tanks have allowed this long-serving vehicle to remain in front-line service.

The M-1 is a well-armed, heavily armored, and highly mobile tank designed for modern armored ground warfare. Notable features of the tank include the use of a powerful gas turbine engine (fueled with JP-8 jet fuel), the adoption of sophisticated composite armor, and separate ammunition storage in a blowout compartment for crew safety. With a weight of close to sixty-eight tons (almost sixty-two metric tons), it is one of the heaviest Main Battle Tanks currently in service in the US Army.

It was during the Fort Benning, Georgia family picnic at the Battalion Headquarters parade grounds that Bobby introduced Darlene to his Battalion Commander and Colonel. As always, there were plenty of family games and food for the family and kids. Once the Colonel heard that Darlene's husband was an Air Force Captain who flew in the AWACS, he insisted that Darlene drive their M-1 tank. Reluctantly, Darlene got into the driver's seat as Bobby explained that if you turn the M-1 peddle to the right, the tank would turn left, and if you turn to peddle to the left, the tank would turn to the right. Darlene found that accelerating the M-1 tank not an issue since it felt like a sports car with its quick acceleration. Stopping on the other hand was a different issue.

Since Darlene was only five feet four inches high and only weighted a hundred and ten pounds, even putting all her weight against the M-1 breaks would only slow down the tank. Eventually, Bobby had to jump down and over step Darlene to stop the M-1 tank. Darlene still had a great time driving the US Army M-1 Abram tank. After Hubert completed SOS, he drove the M-1 Abram simulator. Hubert decided that he did not have Darlene's good looks to warrant driving the M-1 Abram. Soon Hubert and his family would fly back together to Madrid, Spain. Once they arrived at Barajas International Air Port, Hubert, Darlene, and Tawny took a taxi to Royal Oaks and life was back to normal for an Air Force family stationed overseas.

"Since you wanted to go to SOS, this deployment doesn't count towards your commitments," said Millard as he agreed to allow Hubert to attend this class. Colonel Dame, the 16th Air Force Director of Operations (DO) made Hubert's Commander sent him to SOS. Millard had accused him of going to the DO to complain so that he could attend which not true. Same on his own had made the decision that Hubert deserved this class and that he would attend this school back in the US

Hubert had been completely surprised when told that he would attend SOS from the start. He had been disappointed too many times at Luke and now in Spain. Hubert was considering becoming a lazy officer so that he could attend Air Force schools to improve his promotion opportunities. Either that or change his surname to Dixon. Especially since excelling and working hard only seemed to be get him punishment by his commanders for being 'too important' and his coworkers receiving all the schools that he kept being selected by the Major Command (MAJCOM).

"I can't believe that Millard doesn't think that this trip counts towards Hubert's commitments," thought Hubert to himself as he read the message from Spain. Although this class was only 90-days long, he felt that he not punished for attending. It was the early 1980s and email or other modern communication methods were not available in the military. When he read the message that reflected his next four deployments, he called Darlene and suggested that she visit with her mom another five months. He knew that he would not be in Madrid for at least five months once he returned to Spain.

Spending time with Tawny was always important to Hubert. On weekends, he would take Tawny and her friends to the Torrejon AB Theater to see the matinée. It did not matter what the matinée movie was playing in the theater. It was a custom that Hubert started where he would pick-up Alicia children, Essi and Jonathan first, followed by Katy and Kevin who were Kim's children. Both of their daddies deployed to Incirlik and Hubert stayed home. Later, many Torrejon Officers would become better fathers when they saw how Hubert spent time with Tawny and their children. Although Kim was a friend, later she would change because she would be jealous of Darlene's looks even though Darlene thought she was an average person.

Overseas, military families become one big family mainly because they have to depend on each other. Once a few couples feel comfortable with each other, when one husband is home and the two other officers receive deployment orders, the husband home takes care of all three families. Hubert started this process with the Harris and Kim's family and within the first six months, it seems that dozens of families in the Royal Oaks started doing the same type of behaviors.

Hubert never took monies from parents mainly because this gave Tawny plenty of playmates. After picking the children up at their homes, Hubert would normally take the back road to the base mainly because it was a scenic drive. He would stop at a small store, purchase them a coke, and snack for the road. Then at the movies, everyone one had to get their favorite snack before going to the front of the theater. Tawny normally had to get popcorn and a drink that she shared with her daddy. After the movies, he would ask for a group consensus on where to stop and have lunch. Either on base or somewhere on the way back to Royal Oaks.

"Daddy can we go to the park?" asked Tawny on this occasion as Hubert returned from Italy. First, they went by the Prado Museum and then to the park near the museum. The Retiro Park was a favorite place to visit during the weekend. In the center of the park, one could find a rose garden (Rosaleda) and a boating lake, around which there was always a large variety of shows and street theatre during the weekends. Retiro and was opened to the public by decree of the First Spanish Republic in 1868. Since that time, civilians were able to visit the park and enjoy what was once the royal family's private park. Except now, one could purchase snacks or rent a boat on the lake with their loved ones.

Hubert made many trips to Decimomannu Air Base (AB), Italy. His first trip was commercial, which meant that Hubert would travel through Rome and then fly to Cagliari, Sardinia. Traveling commercial meant that all of his military identifications went in his luggage mainly because of terrorist threat. Even though regulations clearly stated that Hubert was required to travel with his identification with him, since Hubert could travel as a Spaniard due to his skin color and Spanish skills, he chose to be safe and disregard the regulations. It had not been that long since his fellow Navy member killed while traveling on a commercial flight. Once he arrived in Decimomannu Air Base (AB), his controller duties remained the same.

Once Hubert arrived at the Cagliari Airport from his flight from Rome, he went to the local rental desk to pick up his vehicle. On this trip, Hubert was supporting the 614th Fighter Squadron, which has staying in Cagliari at a hotel that had opened a hotel normally closed for the winter except for the basement disco. Decimomannu Air Base (AB) was north to northwest of Cagliari and depending of the local traffic it would take around half an hour to get to the Italian Air Force (IAF) ACMI range on a two-lane road. Decimomannu AB itself was a typical Air Base that supported fighter aircraft and logistics aircraft bringing equipment or personnel to Decimomannuto participate in an Air Combat Maneuvering Instrumentation (ACMI) exercise.

Hubert would provide the initial big picture on the ACMI system, which is a three dimensional system. Pods are loads on each fighter aircraft and the ACMI displays the pods as near real-time aircraft. However, when Hubert first arrived he determined that the radar did not seem right and requested a pace flight be flown by the IAF. The following day one of the 614th F-16s flew a profiled flight reporting at designated points on the radio to Hubert to verify that the radar was correct. Hubert determined that the radar was ninety degrees off even though the radar used for over a decade to control civil aircraft by the local civil aviation facility.

On day one, Hubert's first duty was to get Range Training Officer (RTO) qualified, which in Hubert's view was simply another aircraft control method. Once a member became RTO qualified, a permanent party RTO was always on position with the deployed RTO during live flying. Even though the ACMI was in Italy, the facility was a US facility used to train US fighter aircrews. Hubert was the first deployed non-fighter pilot to get RTO qualified. This was the early-1980s when the Torrejon Wing Commander recommended him based on his controlling expertise and based on Hubert's performance. This led to the use of USWeapons Controllers (WCs) becoming RTOs throughout the US Air Force in the future.

The only difference was that the pods loaded on the aircraft provided radar returns displayed on the computer screens versus the radar screens that Hubert used to control his missions. Unlike other non-US controllers, Hubert always controlled his aircraft in the X-mode versus the virtual mode, which forced the aircraft displayed as an 'X' in the screen versus as real aircraft. The advantage of the ACMI was that aircrews could display fighters as they appear in flight to include seeing missiles deployed. Once the missile hits its target, if target killed, a simulated kill box appears around the target. In the X-mode, the target once killed would turn red to signify killed and flashes.

"That's a Bullshit call," said the F-15 pilot. On this deployment, the Torrejon Air Base F-16s Falcons were conducting air-to-air Dissimilar Air Combat Training (DACT) against the F-15s from the Soesterberg Fighter Wing (FW) and the Italian Air Force (IAF). Many times non-when Torrejon aircrews suggested that Hubert made calls that were not realistic, first he would always tell them that he always used the X-Mode that surprised them and each time the Torrejon aircrews would always come to his support. The pilot leading the mission debrief, told the aircrew member challenging his controlling capabilities that once controlled by Hubert that they would change their minds.

"How about a toga" said one of the Lieutenants? The Americans had been at the hotel almost two weeks working long days and needed to relax. Dressing in toga attire seemed logical and without thinking, all the Officers took off their cloths except their underwear and tee shirts, went to the beds and their bed sheets became their toga. Then it was a matter of everyone getting a beer, forming a line and heading downstairs to the disco floor. Since the Americans were hotel guests, they entered free as the locals went wild. The only sad memory would be that the Lieutenant that made the toga suggestion would die while Hubert was controlling him back in Torrejon when he blacked out while self-medicating.

"How are we going to get this wicker furniture to the car?" asked Darlene. Another favorite location that Tawny and Darlene both enjoyed going to for shopping on weekends was located at the Plaza Mallor on Saturdays when Hubert was home. The Rastro was by Plaza Mallor where Tawny and her daddy regularly went to purchase old American coins and stamps. After going through all the coin and stamp racks throughout the Plaza Mallor with Tawny, Hubert would go to the opposite end where the tables with white sheets were always available. There, Tawny would have hot chocolate and Hubert would have his café con leche as each ate some churros. The Rastro was always a favorite place to go shopping for wicker and jewelry. Hubert would have to carry a wicker love seat through crowded sidewalks and back to the Plaza Mallor parking lot.

Since it was a Saturday and the wicker stores was north of Plaza Mallor well over a mile, at first Hubert wasn't sure how the wicker sofa, wicker table, and wicker chair would fit in their small Ford Fiesta. Then Darlene mentioned how the group was going to carry the furniture to the car parked under the garage in the Plaza Mallor. Hubert led the way as he put the wicker couch on his back and told Darlene who carried the wicker table to follow close as Tawny held her hand. Alicia came on this trip so she volunteered to carry the wicker couch as Essi held her hand. Alicia was still pregnant and Bob not in Madrid and deployed to Incirlik, Turkey.

As the Pegaso Training Officer, Hubert would train many Weapons Controllers (WCs) from the Germany Ground Tactical Control Systems (GTACS) units who did not receive enough control activity in Germany. One such officer was a former officer Tom Stevens who Hubert trained while assigned at Luke AFB, Arizona. Unfortunately, Hubert could not recall Tom since he had trained two WCs every sixty day. Tom had never forgotten Hubert referring to him as the best instructor at Luke and his first Air Force mentor.

At Torrejon Air Base, Tom continued to gain more respect for his former mentor. Hubert was able to monitor new controllers and control a mission at the same time safely. He would always make sure that his aircrew knew of the "limited control" that he was providing. However, that meant when Hubert was controlling that it was like having an additional wingman flying in the air. He had flown so many times in different fighter aircraft and in his mind could see the geometry in radar blimps as long as the pilots talked to each other and to him as the controller.

It time, the Torrejon pilots also knew that if they talked to each other and to their controller on the ground that they would receive good Ground Control Intercept (GCI) information. Tom and all the Germany controllers were learning invaluable controlling experience that would make them better officers. In three years, Hubert would train hundreds if not thousands of Germany Weapons Controllers (WCs). Unfortunately, like Tom, he would train so many officers that he would never be able to remember all of them since every month two new officers would come to Torrejon for missions.

"Daddy can we go see the parade," asked Tawny. Every Saturday, Hubert and Tawny would go into Madrid and explore the city although their other favorite place was the Puerta Del Sol. Puerta Del Sol on weekends had booths that sold stamps, coins, and knick-knacks for shopping. It also had pastries, hot chocolate for Tawny and coffee for daddy. However, on their last visit they heard beautiful harp music and went to see what it was thinking that it was a parade. The parade turned out to be a Communist Party rally with marchers carrying bright red banners and marching bands playing beautiful music. Fooling the crowds to think that it was a wonderful parade only to find out that it was a parade of hatred and taking control of Spain and controlling its people.

"GCI destroyed," said the NATEVAL (NATO Evaluation) team chief. Since the Pegaso Ground Control Intercept (GCI) controllers had assisted in destroying one hundred percent of the simulated targets attacking Incirlik, he felt that the Wing's aircraft should conduct autonomous operations on the third and final day of the evaluation. Hubert and a few of his co-workers, or Pegaso (call sign) controllers had been too effective in identifying on raw radar the inbound simulated enemy aircraft that had been Turkish F-4 Phantoms and US Navy F-18 Hornets. After a trip to Turkey when Hubert and his crew had received much phrase for receiving the first Excellent rating, he returned to a series of parties. The Air Force during that period seldom gave Excellent ratings on formal inspections. The 401st Wing had done a great job and Hubert played an important role as the primary controller using the old airport radar to control the wing's aircraft in base defense missions.

"We just missed the bomb at the Rib House," thought Hubert and Darlene as they heard the news in the radio as they were driving back to Royal Oaks. The Squids had just held their victory party at the local Rib House, which was just outside the Torrejon Air Base main gate. Lucky for the American's the bomb exploded during the normal time that Europeans eat and the normal time that Americans eat dinner. American's are used to eating dinner around five in the afternoon and Europeans normally start their dinner after nine in the evening. The bomb exploded at nine in the evening as the American party had just departed the restaurant.

"Should we attend this function?" asked Darlene. Hubert reached for the bottle of sangria as he walked to the table where Darlene and the Harris' were sitting. Parties in Torrejon always had a theme. Hubert and Darlene always invited to US and Spanish formal and informal functions had a busy social life. In the summer, it was the caddy shack theme at the golf course. Anofficer dressed in a gorilla suit would come and give out the cold drinks.

Since everyone had too much to drink, the players seldom made it past nine holes before the darkness forced the party into the clubhouse. After trying to golf, everyone came into the clubhouse to each and dance. Hubert brought Tawny Barbie pool where he found out that the snicker bar actually did not float on water like the caddy shack movie. Like all the unit parties, everyone would have a good time and behave throughout the night. After party, Hubert would return to Decimomannu Air Base (AB), Italy with the 613[th]Fighter Squadron.

"Hubert I'd like for you to support US in Decimomannu Air Base (AB)," said 'Bear'. 'Bear' was the call sign for Lieutenant Colonel Thompson the Commander for the 613th Fighter SquadronSquids. Again, on this trip, Hubert would control fighters using the Air Combat Maneuvering Instrumentation (ACMI) and the AN/TPS-43 radar systems. The F-16 Falcons would be fighting against the Italian F-104s Starfighter's and the deployed Bitburg's F-15 Eagles. To prove a point, Hubert would use both the ACMI system the AN/TPS-43 radar during this deployment. He would prove to the F-15 pilots from Bitburg Air Force Base (AFB) that manual radar with an experienced controller could provide the same level of control that the ACMI provide when the Range Training Officer (RTO) cheats using the ACMI equipment.

The AN/TPS-43 is transportable 3-dimensional air search radar produced in the US originally by Westinghouse Defense and Electronic Division, purchased by Northrop-Grumman. It completed development in 1963 and entered US service in 1968. The entire system can be broken down and packed into two M34 trucks for road transport. The TPS-43E2 was redesignated the ANTPS/-75, which is the current transportable air control and warning (AC&W) radar used by the USAF. The AN/TPS-43 allowed a Weapons Controller like Hubert that took the time to train himself to become literally a 3-dimensional aircraft controller of the twenty-century before the technology became available.

The AN/TPS-75 is transportable 3-dimensional air search radar produced in the United States. It was originallydesignated the TPS-43E2. Although the antenna is a radically new design from the TPS-43, the radar van itself, which houses the transmitter, receiver processors, and displays, is very similar to the older TPS-43E2. Other than the antenna design, from a controller's viewpoint, the radar provided the same function within the same political culture. Where becoming such a controller meant passing up promotion since the Air Force culture promoted staff officers and not operational officers that were proficient in their primary specialty.

Hubert arrived with the rest of the 613th Fighter Squadronmaintenance aircrew and staff aircrew onboard the Cargo C-130 Hercules. Once Hubert got off the C-130 aircraft, Hubert received two sets of keys, one for his hotel room and a key for his rental car. Then Hubert received a folder with the schedule and all the normal training material that normally came with week one of the mock air war. Decimomannu Air Base (AB) would be two months of weeklyfourteen to sixteen hour days for Hubert since air Weapons Controller (WC) does because they do not have crew rest restrictions. Only Air Traffic Controller (ATC) has the same crew rest restrictions that aircrew aviators have in the military. At the same time, pilots normally flew once or maybe twice a day making their day the Mission Planning(MP) plus the 1. 0 to 1. 3 that it takes to fly the sortie (mission). It was during this trip that Hubert would fly in a C-130 loaded with three coffins of soldiers killed in a classified operation.

The Lockheed C-130 Hercules is a four-engine turboprop military transport aircraft designed and built originally by Lockheed, now Lockheed Martin. Capable of using unprepared runways for takeoffs and landings, the C-130 originally designed as a troop, medical evaluation, and cargo transport aircraft. The versatile airframe has found uses in a variety of other roles, including as a gunship (AC-130), for airborne assault, search and rescue, scientific research support, weather reconnaissance, aerial refueling, maritime patrol and aerial firefighting. It is the main tactical airlifter for many military forces worldwide. Over forty models and variants of the Hercules serve with more than sixty nations.

Later, during Hubert's last flying assignment, he would fly in the EC-130E, used for the Close Air Control (CAS) mission conducted during Vietnam. The EC-130E Airborne Battlefield Command and Control Center(ABCCC) aircraft were airborne aircraft on a basic C-130E platform. It mission was to provide tactical airborne command post capabilities to air commanders and ground commanders in low air threat environments. This EC-130E ABCCC has since been retired in order to assist the F-22 raptor program activation. During Operation Desert Storm, the ABCCC played an important role.

"Spike Zero One, Break right, bandit southwest inside three miles" said Hubert. This call meant that for the number one aircraft that Hubert was controlling, he had a bandit aircraft that was converting on his six o'clock. During the mission debrief, the F-15 fighter pilot called Hubert's call a bullshit call. This debrief was done in a room full of all the F-16 pilots, they all defended Hubert including 'Bear'. To prove a point, Hubert said that the following day that he would use the AN/TPS-43 radar. The AN/TPS-43 radar uses raw radar and Hubert made it clear that as long as the pilots talk to his controller, that nothing can be better during the air battle. In addition, theWeapons Controller (WC)has the option to lower the expansion down to as low as twelve miles, which gives the WC detailed radar returns. An experienced WC can see fighters within hundreds or thousands of feet turning, as long as the fighter pilot continues telling him what maneuvers his is in the process of executing or going to take.

The following day during a four versus four mission (4 F-16s versus 4 F-15s), Hubert used the AN/TPS-43 radar to control this mission. The pilot that said that Hubert's call was bullshit was one of the F-15 pilots. During one of three set-ups where the fighters fight the mock war where a fights on is called to knock it off, Hubert made multiple narrow escapes. In one case, Hubert made the following call, "Snake Two One, brake right, bandit inbound inside half a mile". This call was made to wing man number two, telling him that he had a bandit converting on his six o'clock within a half mile closing on him most likely with guns. Such a call would most likely save his live. The F-15 pilot was astonished that Hubert was able to make such a call. Hubert made it clear that with the loss of raw radar, that the US was giving away a great capability. The right controller with the right experience, with the right aircrews would be deadly, and effective.

On this trip Bob Harris was one of the pilots, which made the trip more enjoyable for Hubert. Each night after a long day, Hubert would join Bob and a group of pilots on a trip to one of the towns for diner. Diner was always an adventure in cases when you wanted to try new foods. In one case, Hubert thought he was trying a house meat that turned out to be horsemeat. Other than being a bit tough, it tasted ok, thought Hubert. The hot and spicy mushrooms were always Excellent at the restaurant that they went to on a regular basis. Moreover, as was always the custom, once the meal received its customary praise and the staff rewarded, the group of aviators had to sing their customary military songs in unison as they drank the local beers toasting to the days dogfight victories. After all, this was an era forever gone from American military history for soon drinking and having fun would become illegal in the Air Force due to a new political social change policy.

"We just missed getting shot at the airport," said Darlene to Hubert on the telephone. She and Tawny had just returned from Madrid's Barajas International Airport after returning from a trip in Florida to visit family. The Spanish 'Basce' terrorist group strafed the TWA counter with machine guns demanding the US forces depart Spain. Hubert, Darlene, and Tawny had just walked away a few minutes earlier from the TWA terminal when they heard the loud sound of the machine guns and civilians yelling. Living under terrorism had been part of the European experience taken seriously not only by military members but also by family members and the local citizens. If not, their lives were in danger because ignoring terrorist was dangerous.

Upon returning from Decimomannu Air Base (AB), Italy, the wing had a party. As was the custom, anytime the wing had a party, a theme was a requirement. Since it was near Halloween, everyone came in costume at the Torrejon ABOfficers Club. The Torrejon ABOfficers Club had been the center of the social life during the 1950s, build to cater to Madrid and Americas' top politicians. In the 1980s, Torrejon had become a major fighter pilot air base for both the US and the Spanish Air Force. The party started with for Officers carrying a black coffin into the ballroom and laying it down in the front of the ballroom dance floor.

"What is going on," Thought Hubert to himself as the doors opened and he saw a coffin entering with four men in dark costumes. Halloween called for costumes with Elvira coming out of a rented coffin brought in by four members in costume. In the Elvira attire, she came out as everyone yelled and clapped and the party started. Nevertheless, the formal functions with everyone dressed in military tuxedos and wife's wearing the latest European fashions were the most fun. For each formal function, Darlene would go downtown and to Corte Eglez and one of the fashion stores where the dresses locked behind windowed doors received special attention by patrons one at a time. Each time, Darlene, Tawny, and Hubert would take their time making sure they picked the right dress for each function. Hubert and Darlene did not realize that this era was the end of the old Air Force.

One of the Officer's wives was a body builder and once the coffin was on the floor, she slowly opened the coffin door and stepped out. With her punk style her colored in purple; she was just what the party needed to start in the right manner. It would be a long night of dancing, eating, and fun. Like all of the wing parties, after a deployment, everyone behaved but everyone had a good time with the friends and loved ones making lifetime memories. The new Air Force would have new rules and having fun would become illegal.

"Momma, daddy is making me mad," said Tawny with her hands on her side. Hubert and Darlene had made a bedroom for Tawny into a playroom where she could do anything she wanted. She and her friends could even color on the walls. Hubert had purchased an entire set of small furniture to include a refrigerator, stove, table, sink, and an entire Barbie set to include the pool set. In this room, Hubert would regularly play with Tawny as he did in Arizona and Florida. Where Hubert would many times make Tawny mad and she would go to Darlene telling her mommy that her daddy not behaving.

"Hubert, the Squid's just asked for you by name to return to Incirlik to support them for their ORI," said Colonel Same. Although Hubert was assignment was in Torrejon Air Base (AB), Spain, up to that point, most of his time in Spain had been on the road supporting the local flying squadrons in Italy, Greece, Turkey, and the 16th Air Force requirements in Germany and Great Britain. Considering that he had just completed a remote assignment where Hubert had left his family for an entire year, he felt as if he continued to be away from his family. The only difference, at Torrejon he was able to visit Darlene and Tawny for a few weeks before asked to volunteer again. Of course, when a bossed askedHubertto deploy, that meant that they told him to deploy or were asking him to volunteer.

Again, Hubert found himself controlling from a 1940s Air Traffic Control (ATC) shelter with a twenty miles search radar serving as the primary radar and the Identification Friend or Foe (IFF) which was forty miles serving as the secondary radar. The primary Ultra/Very High Frequency (UHF/VHF) radios did not have an adjustable knob since the technology was still decades away. Instead, Hubert had a miniature screwdriver that serves as his primary radio tuning devise during flying operations. Turkish and US Navy fighter aircraft served as the Red-Air or simulated enemy aircraft while the Squids served as the friendly aircraft or Blue-Air defending the airbase defense flying Close Air Patrol (CAP) profiles. This required multiple sets of F-16 Falcons elements flying in orbits over Incirlik Air Base (AB) and Hubert would commit them whenever he detected Red-Air targets attacking Incirlik.

Since Hubert was using a 1940s Air Traffic Control (ATC) radar with primary radar that only had a twenty-mile capability, this meant that the commits would be short-range commits. Especially since the area around Incirlik AB was mountainous and aircraft could easily use the mountains to hide them while inbound. The trick was the fighters were not supposed to engage within five miles of the airbase for safety reasons. At that point, Hubert as the aircraft controller would call the "knock it off" call on the radio including making calls on emergency radios and all fighter aircraft would accomplish vertical climbs away from the airbase. Hubert controlling skills were so effective on the first two days of the three-day evaluation that the evaluation team scripted Hubert's ATC shelter as a kill by a ground commando team.

Again, since Hubert had seen this evaluation tactic at another similar deployment that he had recently supported, since he was a 16th Air Force (16th AF) staff member. Hubert made a call and requested the NATO E-3A AWACS from Konya Air Base (AB) that always keeps an NATO E-3A Airborne Warning and Control Systems (AWACS) fly a sortie on day three to support the Squids. On day 3 of the exercise, it was a complete success as were the previous two days earning the Squids the "Excellent" rating and a rating seldom given by the NATEVAL team. Even though the military took mil-air travel throughout Europe, it was normal to have a layover in cities throughout major cities in Europe. When Hubert and his team departed Incirlik, Turkey in-route to Madrid, Spain, they had a day layover in Athens, Greece. Since the Air Force Base at Athens did not have any rooms available, they were force to take a hotel near the beach and report the following day at 2:00PM for their flight to Madrid, Spain.

During the evening, the group went out to dinner in Athens and when they ordered their meals, they received one menu. However, when they received their bill the group felt the amount was much too high so they asked to see the menu. At that point, they received a different menu where the prices were different and much higher. As tourists, the group had no choice but to pay the overpriced amounts even though the group knew the waiter ripped them off. The following morning, the group had time to go to the Athens beach prior to going to the base operations to take their flight back to Madrid, Spain.

"Do you have the checkbook," asked Darlene. Even though Hubert deployed to Incirlik for two-months, it was normal for his Commander to expect him and his co-workers to return to work the following day. Compensation time off was something that Officers received from this Commander since he was coming up forpromotion. Darlene called Hubert asking if she could have the checkbook but did not tell Hubert the reason why she needed the checkbook. An hour later, she called Hubert asking him if he could take a week of leave time and gave him the days she needed him to take off from work. Hubert said he would since he had plenty of leave time saved. Darlene mentioned that she would explain everything once he arrived at home.

"Alicia and a group of ladies are going to the Canaries so can I go?" asked Darlene. This was the first time Darlene did something on her own. In a way, Hubert was proud of Darlene for it proved that she was independent and he knew that she deserved to vacation with Alicia who was her close friend. All this group of women wanted to do was go to the Canaries, rest without their children, and not bothered by their husbands or any men. They flew into the Canaries for five days and would ask for adjoining rooms where they would open the doors, purchase food, fruit, drinks, and just enjoy themselves at the pool or beach.

In the meantime, since Bob deployed to the US, Hubert would baby sit Tawny, Essi, and a newborn baby Jonathan that would get a cold on his second day. On day four, Bob returned from his deployment and took Essi and Jonathan although Hubert mentioned that he did not have to take time off to take his kids during the day. Unlike Hubert's unit, Bob's unit gave members compensation time off so Bob received a week off when he returned from his month long deployment. Initially, Bob believed that Hubert was on comp-time off and not on leave. Especially, since Hubert had just returned from Incirlik and a deployment for two-months.

"General Gordon's check ride is coming up and he wants you as his controller," said Colonel Same to Hubert. As a matter of practice, Hubert attended face-to-face briefings with fighter aircrews daily on mission that he controlled and on missions that he trained students. It did not matter if Hubert was at Torrejon or deployed to Incirlik or Turkey, he believed in doing the face-to-face briefings with aircrews. In this case, this meant that Hubert would have to meet General Gordon the following morning at the 614th Fighter Squadron the following morning at 5:00 AM for the pre-brief for a two versus two F-15 Eagles Air Combat Training (ACT) mission.

General Gordon served as the primary pilot for the first element and took the lead role to brief the entire mission. General Gordon briefed that if they had fuel leftover for a forth setup, that the two elements would accomplish a guns only setup. The initial mission would take place in the training airspace southeast of Madrid, Spain with General Gordon's element always orbiting to the north and the second orbit always orbiting to the south after the knock-it-off. The knock-it-off call is normally either a normal termination or safety call to end the air-to-air mission either by any aircrew or by the aircraft controller.

The missions started in normal fashion with Hubert starting with General Gordon and his wingman on his frequency. Once the four aircraft on the same frequency accomplished the initial warm-up maneuvers, Hubert transferred the second element to the second controller who would provide individual control. Once the two elements had were on opposite vectors, had more than thirty miles of separation, and both controllers verified that their elements were ready for 'fights on call', both controllers on their frequency called the 'fights on call'. Important information during this type of setups includes providing the aircrews the distances between the merging elements when opposing single aircraft are attacking each other.

In this case, knowing how far the other element is fighting from them is important so that the pilot can continue fighting his opponent freely without fear of crashing to another aircraft. Then once his simulates killing his opponent, he pilot needs a quick vector to his wingman as soon as possible to help him kill that opponent. This procedure continued, for three setups with General Gordon's element winning all three setups. On the last, what Hubert found amazing was that General Gordon at his age also won the guns only setup with the assistance of his controller that provided timely information. After the four aircraft landed, the mission debrief held at the squadron with the simulated kills being verified when the aircraft tapes. Every controller call heard on the recorded F-16 Falcon tapes.

"Guys the Wing is surging and the Spaniards are only giving US one console because they are having an exercise," said the Captain Lopez. During a surge, the three F-16 flying squadrons launch their fighters as quickly as possible as if being attacked. In this case, the Pegaso Weapons Controller (WC) selected was Hubert that the Commander volunteered. Hubert kept the local fighters safely in the airspaces throughout Spain providing area monitor on one frequency. Aircrews ordered to conduct their primary aircrew coordination on the alternate frequency. To make matters worse, the Pegaso Weapons Controller (WC) had to conduct air-to-refueling operations over water and live-fire operations all on the same frequency.

In this case, Hubert made it easy, in minimal time he would vector the fighter to their Tanker and then back to their airspace. For aircraft working the live-fire, Hubert would give them a snap vector to the target keeping both nose to nose until around ten miles when he would bring the target into an orbit so that the shooter could start firing at the target. The nose-to-nose call means that the fighter nose pointed directly at the nose of the target's aircraft, which gives the pilot having the information the offensive advantage. The goal was to get the fighters behind the target to be able to simulate shooting at the target.

Hubert was doing well keeping the frequency relatively quite as possible since he was used to brevity when all of a sudden he heard, "Pegaso, I think I lost my wingman". Hubert said, "Aircrew that made last transmission, please repeat your last transmission". For a few minutes, Hubert did not hear anything since the lead pilot went down to search for his wingman. In the meantime, to be on the safe side, Hubert scrambled the Spanish Search and Rescue (SAR) helicopter from Zaragoza, Spain. By the time the lead pilot climbed back to altitude, the SAR helicopter was just taking off from Zaragoza and he could see his Identification Friend or Foe (IFF) code on his screen.

Hubert quickly verified with the lead pilot that his wingman had crashed. By that time, Hubert had already deployed the adjacent flight flying in the next airspace to orbit above him to relay radio calls, which worked well both ways. In the meantime, the Spanish Senior Director (SD) provided Hubert an additional frequency that allowed him to transfer the dozens of other fighters that were in the other airspaces working to ensure that safety maintained. By Hubert then transferred the monitor duties to another unit controller until he finished the SAR mission, which not complete until he reviewed the voice recordings and accomplished a script verified by the wing. Once he completed this task, the first comment that Captain Lopez made to Hubert was, "How did you mess up?"

Although the young Lieutenant that died that day died because he self-medicating and he passed out when he was accomplishing Basic Flight Maneuvers (BFM) and he should have known better, he was still a close friend of Hubert. He had been the Officer in Cagliari that suggested that everyone go to the Disco in Toga attire. In spite of occasions when Air Force Officer learn to live with people dying in service for their nation since individuals do things they love doing for their country. Without asking Hubert's top performance as a controller, he and Darlene did not pay for a single drink the entire night. That was something that the other Mexican American Officers that Hubert worked with could never understand. While they were too busy brown nosing, Hubert was busy becoming the best Officer, the best Training Officer, and the best aircraft controller that he could be in the US Air Force.

"I'd like for you to serve on the forces and status negotiations team this week at the Spanish Embassy," said General Gordon to Hubert. He had just returned from Turkey after another long deployment where Hubert received a by name request to deploy to Incirlik Turkey and support an Operational Readiness Inspection (ORI). One of Hubert's last duties as a 16th Air Force Staff, Hubert selection as a member of the forces and status negotiations team where the US would have to pay for its military presence Spain. Unfortunately, in Hubert's view, Spain's asking price for the US to keep its military presence was much too high due to ongoing military and foreign aid cuts in the mid-1980.

After decades of neglect where the base facilities were not improved, the US Air Force finally decided to spend monies to build a new Base Theater, Base Exchange, new Bowling Alley, and other facilities. Hubert recommendations of stopping improvements and paying the penalties prior to base closure at Torrejon Air Base went to a file by Officers seekingfuture promotions. In Hubert's case, other than a one-line entry in an annual Performance Report and knowing that he represented the United States properly, he received no other benefits from representing the US during this important Spanish and US Forces and Status Negotiation Team that closed Torrejon AB and eventually resulted in all US Forces departing Spain. Due to contractual obligations, the US is obligated to make sure, that when turning in to its hosts any facilities, they must be in the best working conditions possible. However, within years of Torrejon Air Base closure, many former facilities were in neglect with over growing grass and in need of repairs.

Hubert was not sure why Darlene came over to see him at work because she rarely visited him at work. Darlene asked for the checkbook since she needed to get a few groceries. As she walked into the Ala Alerta de Control's primary build, Hubert met her as was about to give her the checkbook when Colonel Carasco was entering with a fellow General. Carasco asked Darlene to join them at a luncheon where Hubert and a few of his coworkers would receive an award of the Spanish Controller Badge. In Spain like all European nations, aircraft controllers are certified aircraft controllers. The Spanish Controller Badge had an official number awarded by Spain and assigned in their Federal Aviation Administration (FAA) allowing controllers to control aircraft in Spanish airspace. Although Darlene went reluctantly, she was not happy since she only wanted to buy a few groceries.

Colonel Carasco asked Darlene to come with him and the General who was the Spanish Air Force Chief of Staff in their limousine to the Pavillon. Darlene smiled and declined saying that she would drive her Camaro and meet the party there. Darlene's charm and her natural beauty always allowed her to get away with politely declining official protocol related formalities. Especially since Darlene did not realize that, she was a beautiful woman and thought of herself as average even though every time she walked into a room all the male eyes looked at her. The Pavillon was the Spanish Officer's club and until that day, Darlene was the second female to enter the special luncheon room. The other female had been the Queen of Spain, Queen Sofía.

At the luncheon, sitting across from her had been a young junior Spanish Naval Officer. Although Darlene kept ignoring him as he tried to make small talk, Darlene thought that the General and the various Colonels were more important. The luncheon would last for over five hours, as the Spanish Naval Officer would keep asking Darlene questions. At first, Darlene would talk about Hubert for she was proud of how he had worked so hard to become an Officer working two jobs and going to college fulltime. Then Darlene would talk about Tawny and family that all seemed to interest the Spanish Naval Officer. Later on, Darlene would find out that it was Prince Felipe.

Prince Felipe had the staff bring her yellow roses and a plate with the Ala Alerta de Control Emblem. Prince Felipe would reach over the table and formally present Darlene the roses and the plate. As was the custom, each time she went to the bathroom, the entire room of Officer's and dignitaries stood up. Eventually Darlene asked them not to stand up or they would be standing up all the time. Throughout the meal, the group discussed many topics. The Spanish General asked Darlene if she liked Spanish men and Darlene replied that she loved her Spanish man.

When discussing religion, Darlene mentioned that Hubert grew up as a Catholic and Mormon, while she believed in a different religion. When the Naval lieutenant, Prince Felipe asked Darlene her religion, she replied, "I'm southern Baptist. " Although Hubert knew who the lieutenant was, he did not stop Darlene from being the person she was. After all, Darlene's wit had been one of the things that had attracted him to her. Years later, Hubert was convinced that Prince Felipe would marry a civilian that had a personality like Darlene that left an impression on this young Officer on this day.

NATO EW & CONTROL FORCE (NAEW&C FORCE), GK AB, GE.

After Spain, Hubert received an assigned to the North Atlantic Treaty Organization (NATO) Early Warning and Control Force (NAEW&C Force). Aircraft from the NATO NAEW&C Force provide airspace surveillance support as part of the NATO E-3A Component, which is NATO's Flagship Fleet in NATO Air Base (AB), Geilenkirchen, Germany. The E-3A Component is the world's only integrated, multi-national flying unit, providing rapid deployability, airborne surveillance, command, control, and communication for NATO operations. Fourteen of NATO's nations contribute to the E-3A program and more than 3,000 military and civilian personnel call the Geilenkirchen area home.

The E-3's radar and other sensors provide deep-look surveillance, warning, interception control, and airborne battle management. The NATO E-3A Component is one of two operational elements of the NATO Airborne Early Warning & Control Force. It is NATO's first multinational operational flying unit, making it unique in military history. The Component's mission is to provide aircraft and trained aircrews to deliver a surveillance and/or control platform whenever directed by the NATO Airborne Early Warning & Control Force Commander on behalf of the NATO commander, the Supreme Allied Commander, Europe (SACEUR).

The Component consists of five main functional areas: the Operations Wing, Logistics Wing, Training Wing, Information Technology Wing and Headquarters as well as other normal staff functions. A colonel from a variety of NATO nations commands each of these major units. The position of the Component commander alternates between a German and American Brigadier General. Overall integrated operating of the Component consists of 2900 multinational military and civilian personnel. This figure includes military and civilian personnel in support functions, such as base civil engineering, national support units and morale and welfare activities.

When Hubert was in Geilenkirchen (GK) and the NATO Component there were eighteen E-3A AWACS aircraft. Currently seventeen E-3A aircraft are part of theNATO Component since one was lost. Normally only a number of the E-3As are at NATO Air Base Geilenkirchen at any given time. The remainder deploys to the Component's Forward Operating Bases (FOBs) in Aktion, Greece; Trapani, Italy; and Konya, Turkey and its Forward Operating Location (FOLs) at Ørland, Norway or other allied airfields. Each of the forward operating facilities is located on a national installation, although the Component has approximately twenty personnel at each site. They are NATO personnel assigned to the Component, but all are from the respective host nations. Thirty multinational aircrews from sixteen of NATO's twenty-eight nations are currently in the Component's three operational E-3A squadrons. When Hubert was in GK, only sixteen nations were members of the Component's three operational E-3A squadrons. The Training Wing has a flying squadron as well, the Aircrew Training Squadron.

From 4 December 1986 to 30 December 1989, Hubert was assigned to the North Atlantic Treaty Organization (NATO) and Allied Command Europe as the Chief Weapons Section, Deputy Chief Mission Flight, Chief, Standardization/Evaluation (Stan/Eval) Fighter Allocator (FA), flying Squadron-Two, E3A Component, Geilenkirchen, Germany. The Fighter Allocator (FA) position is the same position as the Senior Director (SD) in the US AWACS program. Initially, Hubert managed thirty international weapons directors (WDs) and the component Stan/Eval or training programs that significantly enhanced the readiness posture of the NATOs Air Defense capabilities in Europe and throughout the five NATO regions. In addition, like all NATO E-3A aviators, Hubert deployed throughout the five NATO regions, to the US, and Canada to support countless major Maritime, Combined, or Composite Exercises.

Hubert was responsible for creating new unit and component directives, support plans, joint training, and Stan/Eval program plans contributing to NATO AWACS receiving an Operational Rating. All of these accomplishments were done while supporting a heavy deployment commitment. At the time, as a rater in Europe, Hubert's primary mode of communication was the mail system especially while writing performance reports for his subordinates that he took a primary interest.

The NATO AWACS had Forward Operation Bases (FOBs) in addition to the Main Operating Base (MOB) located in Geilenkirchen Air Base (AB) also referred to as GK. The MOB at Geilenkirchen (GK) had eighteen NATO E-3A aircraft assigned to Geilenkirchen, Germany. The US provided sixty-five percent of the total staff or aircrews assigned in GK. The remaining aircrew members received work force from the remaining NATO nations. The nations included Norway, Denmark, Denmark, Germany, Italy, Turkey, Greece, Portugal, Netherlands, etc. During Hubert's time in Germany, the NATO Component was responsible for making the NATO E-3A Component Operational at the end of his tour. At the completion of a NATO Evaluation (NATEVAL), E-3 NATO aircraft deployed throughout Europe conducting an evaluated composite exercise.

The Squadron-Two Canadian Commander, Lieutenant Colonel Smith came from London, Ontario. This would be Hubert's best Commander during his military career mainly because he would allow Hubert to implement any program or idea that would benefit the unit. Lieutenant Colonel Smith flew C-130 Hercules aircraft in the Canadian Air Force (CAF). The Director of Operations (DO) was an Italian F-104, Starfighter Fighter Pilot. Captain Paulo Vitosi reported to the NATO Component for training and by the time he finished the academics portion of the training, he received apromotion to Major. In order to become the Squadron-Two DO, Vitosi received anotherpromotion to Lieutenant Colonel.

Unfortunately, Lieutenant Colonel Vitosi did not have the experience of a Lieutenant Colonel. He arrived in Geilenkirchen, Germany as a Captain and received temporary promotions from Italy to Lieutenant Colonel so that he would receive key positions since the US would pay for those slots. Like all E-3C AWACS flying units, Squadron-Two had a mission and flight assistant director of operations (ADO-M and ADO-F). Next, Squadron-Two had a Chief of Training, Chief of Stan/Eval, the Chief of Resource Management (RM), Chief of Safety, and Chief of Weapons. Finally, Squadron-Two had the Chief of Current Operations, which was the largest division in the unit.

On 5 April 1985, Hubert official duty title became NE3A Stan Eval Weapons Controller (WC) and awarded the Air Force Specialty Code (AFSC) G1745G. A rare accomplishment never achieved and a first accomplishment done in the Air Force Element (AFELM) NATO E-3A AWACS Component in the E-3C AWACS North Atlantic Fleet. The normal progression for E-3C AWACS aircrew members calls for members to first get qualified as instructors, normally after a year or two after being qualified in their primary aircrew position. The top five percent selected become evaluators. Hubert arrived in Geilenkirchen Air Base (AB), Germany in November 1984 and arrived in NATO Flying Squadron-Two in early January 1985. By the end of February 1985, he had completed Instructor Training and selected to become an evaluator.

Hubert was in the training squadron until he became qualified as a Weapons Director (SD) and a Senior Director (SD). Since Hubert was an experienced Weapons Controller (WC), it took him less than two-month to get qualified versus the year that it takes most trainees. The majority of the training consisted of learning the E-3C AWACS switches and not learning controlling, which Hubert already knew. Here Hubert met many new and future friends like Captain Margie Marrow and Raymond and his wife Carol. Margie would become a friend of Darlene and proved herself as an Excellent Officer. Carol would be there for Darlene when Tawny became diabetic when Hubert took an E-3C AWACS aircrew to Denmark to support the Baltops Exercise.

Darlene normally did not like military women mainly because in her view, they received special treatment and did not earn their rank. She had seen too many military women in the pool while Hubert was working twelve to fourteen hour shifts seven days a week. Margie was not that type of female officer and earned every promotion she received. Darlene could see that from the first time she met Margie in Squadron-Two and not the Base Pool. Like Hubert she preferred to work at learning how the NATO Operations or the NATO politics and not who she should meet within NATO to help her career.

The previous group of Americans and NATO allies had just stood up NATO E-3A AWACS component. Hubert's American group received the task of making the component operational and war ready. Geilenkirchen AB served as the Main Operation Base (MOB) and NATO E-3A AWACS had four Forward Operating Bases/Locations (FOB/Ls) throughout Europe, one in Orland, Norway, one in Trapani, Sardinia, one in Aktion, Greece, and the final FOB in Konya, Turkey. Hubert would travel to each of the FOBs at least three times for thirty days to pull alert as part of his duties as a requirement for the NATO Component to be rated Operational. Later, Iceland became an FOB and Hubert would create all the training material mainly since he had served a tour in Iceland.

Since he had just departed Iceland, Spain, and been an instructor in for the Tactical Air Command (TAC) back in the US, he quickly became Combat Ready (CR) as an aircrew member and selected as the first US selected as the Chief of Squadron Weapons on 1 November 1985. Up to now, no American received the top qualification since in NATO the custom was to select your best operators or best controllers for key positions versus selecting by the date of rank or by an Officers grade. Hubert retained his instructor and evaluator flying duties that did not interfere anytime that he flew as an NATO E-3A AWACS aircrew member.

Not only had Hubert become the Chief of Squadron Weapons in less than a year after arriving in NATO AWACS, but also he had completed the NATO E-3A AWACSBasic Training, instructor training, and become an evaluator. A task that normally took two or more years for the normal E-3C AWACS aviator to complete, took Hubert less than a year to complete. This quick rise in Squadron-Two had caused many problems for Hubert within the US chain-of-command and his senior peers. Many had gone to the Squadron-One US leadership to complaint once Hubert received his selection to key positions over them.

In Hubert's case, he was a junior American and junior ranking Officer when compared to his fellow allies. He was responsible for thirty controllers from fifteen nations. When he arrived, he saw that the American's were too busy talking about each other in front of the allies and he put a stop to that behavior. As the best controller in the unit, European respected him since he was the best aircraft controller in the flying squadron. However, as an E-3C AWACS flying member, normally the USE-3C AWACS flyers thought that they were better aviators and talked about how they did work tasks back at Tinker AFB. The European did not care much for the Tinkerites and they knew that Hubert not one of them because of his controller skills.

Overall, American's were better at controlling dissimilar aircraft in large dogfights and the European controllers were better in the close control environment. Since Hubert had spent so many years controlling both, he was able to accomplish both types of environments with ease. He quickly became an instructor and evaluator in nine months versus the normal two to three years to get qualified. Due to Hubert's E-3C AWACS aircrew qualification, he became the units Squadron-Two Chief Standardization and Evaluation (Stan/Eval) and the Wing Representative Stan/Eval Representative. Many American E-3C AWACS aircrew members would not be happy with this selection since they had been in the AWACS systems six to ten years and Hubert had been in AWACS only a year.

Even though Hubert was new into E-3C AWACS and NATO Component, his first task received a request to join a group of Joint NATO Evaluators to travel throughout Europe and train flying and ground personnel on how to better use the E-3B/C Airborne Warning and Control Systems (AWACS). The goal was to travel to all the major European Fighter Wings and Air Defense installations and present them the latest NATO Component training doctrine while retaining their latest training information to bring back to GK to update the Components training manuals. The first trip was to the 15 em Wing, Belgium Air Force, where F-16s Falcons were first stationed in Europe. The Belgium Air Force was the first to purchase the US F-16s, put on alert in military history. Each flying squadron visited received the NATO training material.

In spite of all these travels, Hubert still had to maintain his squadron duties and flying currency duties. Each month, as the Team Chief, Hubert scheduled a trip to one of these units, completed a deployment, and scheduled time with family making every month a full month. As much as possible, he would volunteer to fly night sorties (missions) so that once he landed he would go to Tawny's school and volunteer at her school. Her he would read to the children books or any tasks the teacher directed him. Then after spending three or four hours at Tawny's school, he would go home and go to sleep. Spending time with Tawny was always important to Hubert and Darlene, as was her education.

Even during the week, he would always work into his schedule time to volunteer at Tawny's school. He would simply tell his squadron members where to find him. While other squadron members went to the gym or other locations, squadron members knew that Hubert was always at Tawny's school. Darlene and Hubert were both heavily involved in Tawny education throughout her live regardless of where was assigned. Furthermore, both were heavily involved with Tawny participation in local sports where Hubert supported peewee, basketball, track, bowling, and other sports.

In addition, the NATO Component Team took the time to learn as much as possible about the 15 em Wing and requested data to take back to Geilenkirchen to use to update their training documents. This process repeated at every unit the team visited throughout Europe. After the long day of training, the NATO Component Stan/Eval Team made time to go to the local pubs to taste their beers. Although locals claimed that there were thirty-eight different types of local beers, the NATO Component Stan/Eval Team not able to taste all of the beers but they made a good effort in trying to taste as many as they could.

The next site that the NATO Component Stan/Eval Team visited was Chièvres Air Base Belgium, Air Defense, which was north of the 15 em Wing. Being an Air Defense site in this case was easier mainly because one of our Stan/Eval members came from this unit. Therefore, Hubert was able to prearrange receiving all the required training material. However, this trip did allow the all the remaining team to receive additional training of the capabilities that Chièvres Air Base offered. After each trip, as the team leader, Hubert was required to accomplish a trip report and submit it to the NATO Component Commander.

The next trip was to Reims, France that also included the deployment of an E-3A AWACS aircraft in support of a major exercise. The initial phase consisted of the NATO Component Stan/Eval Team visiting the Reims Air Force and providing them a detailed E-3C AWACS presentation. Since the NATO

Component, Stan/Eval Team included deploying to Reims with an E-3A aircraft to support the French Air Force as their Red-Air or simulated enemy aircraft Control. The US Air Force was flying from Bitburg AFB, Germany and each day a C-130 would take all the aircrew that flew in the exercise at Reims to Germany for the pre-briefs and debriefs. This exercise had an air-to-surface and air-to-air battle, which made the exercise extremely complex.

The air-to-air battle occurred in northern French airspace below 20,000 feet. The French were so impressed with the NATO aircrew that they decided to purchase four French E-3F E-3B/C Airborne Warning and Control Systems (AWACS) aircrafts. These visits continued for over six months during weekly visits by the NATO Component Stan/Eval Team. These visits provided Hubert detailed information on key European installations. Detailed information that Hubertlearned about specific installations that he would use to update or create new NATO AWACS Components Alert Plans depending on the region.

Upon completing this dual inspection and training road show, Hubert reported into his Canadian Commander's office. Unsure as to why he was being called mainly because he had been out of town for months, Hubert was slightly tense but felt comfortable since he liked Colonel Smith who was an Excellent Commander. To Hubert's surprise, the news was in two parts, first that the British Air Force would be joining NATO Squadron-Two in an effort to gain training once the British Air Force purchased a E-3D AWACS aircraft. However, this would take away most of the important positions that formerly filled by the Americans and as usual the senior US representative said nothing.

Next, Hubert received a task to create the Iceland Alert Procedures for the NATO AWACS since NATO Squadron-Two would be the lead unit in Keflavik, Iceland in its first E-3C AWACS Alert mission. Luckily, Hubert kept many of his Iceland training material, which made it easier to develop the Iceland training guide. Since he created the new Icelandic airspace, creating the aircrew training aids proved to be easier than normal since he had the overhead power point slides that he used in Iceland that he used when he trained the wing aircrews. As usual, without formally receiving a task, he volunteered to create the newNATO E-3A AWACS Iceland Alert Procedures and the new NATO E-3A AWACS Alert Plan that the NATO Component aircrews would use. The Iceland deployment would be an additional deployment added to the long list of overseas FOB deployments.

This would end Hubert's first two years at the NATO Component and start an era where he would start supporting exercises throughout Europe and North America. This would be the beginning where Hubert would start taking Darlene on deployments with him as much as possible. Especially now that Tawny was getting older, so that he could spend time with Darlene. The list of exercises for 1987 alone would include Aiming First, Fein Angle, Spring Exercise (USSR Fleet) Ocean Safari, French Exercise, and six deployments of the Tactical Leadership Program (TLP) throughout central Europe. It seemed that Hubert would deploy and support every key exercise that the NATO E-3A Component received. Considering the limited amount of time that Hubert had been in the Component, everyone was surprised. Especially since it required that one, know so much information. However, since Hubert had already been in Europe five years, he was not the normal American.

One of the first deployments that Hubert supported was to Prevessa, Greece in support of a Maritime exercise. The Blue-Air was part of an Aircraft Carrier Task Group (TG) floating off the Caribbean Sea in Naval Air Station (NAS) Sigonella, Sardinia, Italy. Hubert's Orange-Air included the Italian F-104s and US F-111 bombers stationed at Royal Air Force (RAF) Alconbury. Initially, the US TG had its E-2 Hawkeye early warning aircraft airborne that maintained its typical pattern, which made it easy to identify using its normal identity friend or foe (IFF). In addition, the aircraft used its normal mode one used by the US Navy for identification of its forces while over water.

Boeing initially proposed a purpose-built aircraft, but tests indicated that it would not outperform the already-operational 707, so the USAF selected the latter. To increase endurance, this design was to power the aircraft by eight General Electric TF34s, or carrying its radar in a rotating dome mounted at the top of a forward-swept tail, above the fuselage. Boeing received the official selection ahead of McDonnell Douglas's DC-8-based proposal on July 1970. Initial orders for two aircraft, designated EC-137D as test beds to evaluate the two competing radars. As the test-beds did not need the same 14-hour endurance demanded of the production aircraft, the EC-137s retained the Pratt and Whitney JT3D commercial engines, and a later reduction in endurance requirement led to retaining the normal engines in production.

The first EC-137 made its maiden flight on 9 February 1972, with the fly-off between the two radars taking place during March-July that year. Favorable test results saw the selection of Westinghouse's radar for the production aircraft. Hughes's radar initially thought to be a certain winner, mainly because of its design was also going into the new F-15 Eagle's radar program. The Westinghouse radar used a pipelined Fast Fourier Transform (FFT) to digitally-resolve 128 Doppler frequencies, while Hughes's radars used analog filters based on the design for the F-15 fighter. Westinghouse's engineering team won this competition by having a programmable 18-bit computer whose software, which was modifiable before each mission, and for multiplexing a Beyond-The Horizon (BTH) mode that could complement the Pulse-Doppler radar mode. This proved to be beneficial especially when the BTH mode detects ships at sea when the radar beam is point below the horizon.

On 26 January 1973,the USAF gave approval for full-scale development of the AWACS system. The actual build-up of the North Atlantic Treaty Organization (NATO) E-3A Component started in January 1980; in October 1980, it received the status of a NATO International Military Headquarters by the NATO Defense Planning Committee (DPC). Flying operations began in February 1982 after delivery of the first E-3A aircraft. The NATO Component received the official status, activated on 28 June 1982, and reached "Full Operational Capability" by the end of 1988. Hubert played an important role during the final phase of the NATO Component official status phase. During a phase where the NATO Component was executing endless exercises that it had to prove during exercises that its aviators and the component as a whole was able to go to war.

Especially since the NATO E-3A,Airborne Warning and Control System (AWACS) during exercises always were practicing what it would do in wartime. Before the AWACS system became operational, the US had the Connie that provided the same function. Therefore, its IFF was on stand-by, which means the US aircraft and ships could only see a radar dot on its radars. In addition, as a matter of practice, we flew random patterns and not the normal orbit that the E-3B/C AWACS aircraft normally fly's. Many of the initial American aviators came from the RC-121CWarning Star (Connie), which the AWACS aircraft replaced. Therefore, the NATO Component had its most experienced aviators training the NATO Component.

The thinking being that this would make it more difficult for anyone to locate the E-3B/C AWACS aircraft since it does not act as if it normally would. At times, employment of tactical deception is appropriate. For example, if there is a Tanker airborne, the E-3B/C AWACS may fly above or below at a sufficient altitude to ensure there is no radar threat to both aircraft so that other aircraft only see one radar return. Then when the E-3B/C AWACS aircrew wants to commit, it goes on its random vector.

In this mission, once Hubert saw on his E-3B/C NATO AWACS console using the maritime radar that the E-2 Hawkeye landed on the US Carrier and the US Carrier turned into the winds, he committed the F-111s on the TG. TheE-3A NATO AWACS had ten consoles while the USE-3B/C AWACS has an additional four consoles. Hubert had two sets of four F-111s bombers flying at five thousand feet, five miles apart. At fifty miles, he noticed that the Aircraft carrier was starting a turn to the north suggesting that it was turning into the winds and told the F-111s to break their attack. For every mission, all aviators and NATO aircrews know the local winds and the winds of the areas of where they will be working based on times and sea states. Knowing such data is vital during mission execution.

Once Hubert confirmed that the carrier returned to its normal path to the northeast, Hubert vectored the F-111s to a re-attack and eventually the F-111s over flew the flat deck of the USS JFK working in the Mediterranean. The next time Hubert would work with the USS JFK would be during Operations Desert Shield and Desert Storm. On this mission, all eight F-111 pilots were impressed with Magic control, which is the NATO E-3A AWACS mission call-sign. They truly believed that NATO E-3A AWACS could provide magic information after Hubert finished providing them air-to-air close control as their primary Weapons Director (WD). This was also the exercise when one of the F-111 pilots reported seeing a Russian submarine floating on the surface. Clearly, the submarine was embarrassed that a fighter aircraft visually spotted him since normally only Naval Subsurface aircraft with the use of special equipment after working hard maybe locate a submarine.

The USS John F. Kennedy was the last conventionally powered aircraft carrier built by the US Navy. Originally scheduled to become the fourth KITTY HAWK class carrier, the JFK received so many modifications during construction that she formed her own class. Named in honor of the 35th president of the United States, John F. Kennedy who was assassinated on November 22, 1963 in Dallas, Texas, the USS John F. Kennedy was the first ship in the Navy to bear the name. Transferred to the Naval Reserve Force in 1995, the USS John F. Kennedy returned to the active fleet in October 2000.

The Navy initially wanted to decommission the USS John F. Kennedy in mid-2005 because the carrier was in bad shape and was in need of expensive repairs that just did not seem to be cost-effective. However, the Congress decided to keep the USS John F. Kennedy in service to have twelve active aircraft carriers. The John F. Kennedy was subsequently berthed at the Mayport Naval Station for several months. Her flight deck was not certified for aircraft operations and the Navy was just waiting to decommission the ship. In late 2006, the decision was finally made to retire the USS John F. Kennedy. The USS John F. Kennedy made a final voyage up the east coast for a final port visit to Boston, Massachusetts, in early March 2007. The decommissioning ceremony for the John F. Kennedy was on March 23, 2007, at Mayport, Florida. The official decommissioning date for the USS John F. Kennedy was August 1, 2007.

As the Chief of Weapons, Hubert loaded himself on the first aircrew to deploy to Iceland, which made the deployment a total success. Once the aircrew arrived in Iceland, the NATO E-3A aircrew and maintenance stayed in the same building as the US AWACS aircrew. For this deployment, the Deployment Commander (Detco) did not take maintenance personnel since the US would provide the required maintenance technicians in Iceland. At this point of Hubert's career, he was only required to worry about planning about the Weapons Personnel that consisted of the Senior Directors (SDs) and the Weapons Directors (WDs). This enhanced the aircrews bonding and training opportunities in between flights even though each aircrew flew its own E-3B/C AWACSaircraft when scrambled or supporting an exercise.

During the first deployment, it just happened to occur during the normal Union of Soviet Socialist Republics (USSR) summer rotation to Cuba, always had an exercise in the North Sea called "Spring-Exercise". During this Spin-up and/or deployment to Cuba, the USSR Fleet would simulate attacking Iceland. In this case, USSR BEAR Bombers attacked Iceland from both sides of Iceland forcing the scramble of both the NATO E-3A AWACS and the US E-3C AWACS. The NATO E-3A received a scramble order first since it was the primary alert on this day to the east side of Iceland. An hour later, the US E-3C AWACS was scrambled when the NATO E-3A as it was flying east bound picked up multiple unknown tracks east and north of Iceland.

At the time, the US had a Strategic Air Defense (SAD) system throughout North America that provided low, medium, and high altitude coverage. The North Radar Air Defense (NORAD) system included a communication system with the call-sign 'Offutt Green Pine' followed by specific numbers for each unit. At specific times, regular daily checks are appropriate every day. Since Hubert was a Battle Manager (BM) and a Senior Director (SD) when in Iceland, he understood how this system worked. Hubert was able to add this information into the NATO Iceland Alert Procedures Plan. On this day, the Norwegian Radar system first reported the Union of Soviet Socialist Republics (USSR) fleet starting its 'Spring Exercise' and in route to Iceland.

On this deployment, at all times, the NATO E-3A and US E-3C aircrafts were in pre-flighted and ready for scramble status. During Mission Planning (MP), part of the alert process requires that the technicians and part of the aircrew pre-flight their aircraft for flight and the remainder of the aircrew load their flight bags on the aircraft. This way, once scrambled, individuals can expedite getting on the aircraft and becoming airborne in minimum time without having to worry about loading these items. In Iceland, a primary and secondary E-3C AWACS alert crew was always alert. The primary E-4 AWACS alert crew was on a twenty-minute alert status and the secondary crew was on an hour alert status. Within the next 72-hours, the 'Offutt Green Pine' system started reporting the Union of Soviet Socialist Republics (USSR) fleet east of Iceland in route to the Atlantic, the northeast US, and Cuba. It was at this point that USSR BEAR Bombers were airborne and inside the Icelandic Identification Zone (IIDZ).

The east unknown tracks was a two ship target flying in a ten mile formation heading southeast. The north unknown target, was heading southwest and was a two ship target flying in a ten-mile formation. This meant that both targets met the BEAR Bomber profile, which meant the NATO AWACS had to commit to the nearest target of the eastern target and the US E-4C target would have to be scrambled and commit on the northern target, which is what occurred. At the same time, Hubert scrambled two F-4Fs Phantom Fighters followed with a KC-135 Stratotanker heading east. Later, a second set of two F-4Fs Phantom Fighters received a scramble order followed with a second KC-135 Stratotanker heading northeast. This meant that both Icelandic Tankers were airborne and additional F-4Fs received an alert order. All F-4Fs were fully loaded with a full complement of air-to-air missiles.

The first element of F-4Fs, call-sign Slowgin-01 Flight (01/02) contacted Magic, which is the call-sign of the NATO E-3A AWACS mission back end. The second element of F-4Fs, call-sign Slowgin-11 Flight (11/12) contacted the Darkstar, which is the call-sign of the US E-3C AWACS mission back end. Eventually, with the help of the E-3C AWACS Weapons Directors (WDs), the F-4Fs converted behind the BEAR Bombers, identified the type of BEARs, and passed the tail numbers to the WDs who passed the information back to the Senior Director (SD) 932nd at Keflavik, Iceland on the radio. The standard tactic is for the

F-4Fs to convert on the rear BEAR flying on the ten-mile trail formation. Fighters never attack the front element unless it simultaneously attacked by a wingman. The F-4Fs tailed the BEARs until they simulated attacking Keflavik and returned to Union of Soviet Socialist Republic (USSR). At that point, both E-3C AWACS aircraft landed.

During a scramble, the NATO Aircraft Commander (AC) who was also the Squadron-Two Operations Officer, Paulo Vitosi, decided to go sightseeing. One hundred miles northwest of Iceland, there is a volcano. The AC left our normal flying altitude of 31,000 feet was in a decent to 10,000 when he hit an air pocket. At that point, the AC lost control of the E-3C AWACS aircraft. At the point where the E-3 inverted, with the help of the co-pilot, both pilots were able to regain control of the aircraft around 7,000 and returned to altitude. Not everyone talked about this event except to tell the AC that he almost killed the entire crew.

"That felt like a roller coaster ride" thought Hubert as the NATO E-3A landed at RAF Waddington. Upon returning to Geilenkirchen, Germany Hubert was only home for ten days before redeploying to England. For Ocean Safari, Hubert created a deployment list for two aircrews to deploy to Cambridge in Great Britain. The crew deployed to Royal Air Force (RAF) Waddington in Lincolnshire, Great Britain. The primary runway at RAF Waddington had a dip at the center of the runway, which at a top speed made the E-3A aircraft feel as if it was a roller coaster ride. This would also be the first of many times that Hubert would see the RAF Flying Wing, which was the Avro Vulcan also known as the Strategic Bomber.

The last time that Avro Vulcan flew in an operational mission was during Operation Black Buck in the Falklands War during the conflict between Britain and Argentina in 1982. Although the Avro Vulcan flew with nuclear weapons, it was capable of conventional bombing missions. Therefore, it was extremely exciting to see the Avro Vulcan on the runway each time Hubert flew into RAF Waddington. Since Hubert was a history buff, he had studies the Falklands War more than one and knew the Avro Vulcan flying profile well.

Once the NATO crew arrived at RAF Waddington, they quickly stayed at the RAF Waddington Officer's Club Quarter and Non-Commissioned Officer's Quarters. Unlike in the culture, in NATO, the custom was to first relax and then work. Therefore, the NATO crew including the Americans first left their bags in their rooms and quickly met downstairs for their visit into downtown Lincolnshire. Lincolnshire like most cities in Europe was full of history and available to Hubert and the visiting NATO crewmembers. After sightseeing all day, the group agreed on having dinner at one of the many Indian Cuisine Restaurants.

The following day, it was back to work and discussing who to attack the American Task Group (TG). In this case, Hubert as the senior American would provide the key inputs on how, when, and where to attack the TG in the Atlantic Ocean over the course of the exercise. Mission Planning (MP) in NATO like the US was a serious event since in the end it contributed to a military force that would train the force into a Combat Ready (CR) unit. As was the case in most major exercises, the US Navy would send its Exercise Mission Planners to all exercise planning and the end-of-exercise debrief in Lincolnshire. Normally a weapons and surveillance representative that would be able to discuss both areas during these exercise meetings.

From there, the NATO E-3A aircraft would fly in support of the Ocean Safari Exercise. The NATO AWACS Component was supporting the British Air Force playing the Orange-Air attacking the US Navy consisting of two Task Force (TF) Aircraft Carriers. The two carriers were the USSJohn Fitzgerald Kennedy (JFK) Aircraft Carrier and the USS Yorktown Aircraft Carrier. Throughout the exercise, the goal of the Orange-Air was to attack the US Aircraft Carriers. Since the US Navy had the E-2 Hawkeye, this made this Orange-Air goal more difficult. Therefore, employing the proper tactics was crucial in attacking the US Aircraft Carriers and their Task Force that had its own awesome air power.

USS Yorktown (CV-5) was an aircraft carrier commissioned in the US Navy from 1937 until sunk at the Battle of Midway in June 1942. The USS Yorktown named after the Battle of Yorktown in 1781 and the lead ship of the Yorktown Class, designed after lessons learned from operations with the large converted battle cruiser Lexington class and the smaller purpose-built Ranger. She represented the epitome of U. S. pre-war carrier design. The Newport News Shipbuilding and Dry-dock Company laid down the Yorktown on 21 May 1934 at Newport News, Virginia. The Yorktown launched on 4 April 1936, sponsored by Eleanor Roosevelt and commissioned at the Naval Operation Base (NOB), Norfolk, Virginia, on 30 September 1937, Captain Ernest D. McWhorter in command.

After fitting out, the aircraft carrier trained in Hampton Roads, Virginia and in the southern drill grounds off the Virginia capes into January 1938, conducting carrier qualifications for her newly embarked air group. That drill became a US Navy standard for all operational deployments and all US Navy exercise deployments. Therefore, having the USS Yorktown participating in Ocean Safari was truly an honor not only for the Americans, but also for all the NATO aircrews. Having the USS JFK who represented a great president in Europe only added more honor to protecting these two US aircraft carriers. However, Hubert was a member of a NATO AWACS aircrew and his job was to make sure that the US Navy did their best to protect all their ships including both aircraft carriers during war. He would make sure that the Navy aviators and surface warfighters did their job as best as they were trained.

For this exercise, the NATO AWACS went all the way to the east coast of the US along with its British Victor Tankers and started monitoring the US Navy start their Spin-up Exercises. US Navy forces always conduct Spin-up exercises when they go operational in order to be prepared once they enter an operational environment. If as was the case in this exercise where they are part of a two Aircraft Carriers, the two carriers on the water float on a trail formation with the distance varying as dictated by the Task Force (TF) Commander. The remaining ships float side by side to protect themselves in order to protect themselves as they would in a group formation. As a whole group, the TF employs different tactics as a single element as directed by the TF Commander. In the Air Force, the same concept applies except the concept applies in the air versus the surface or sub-surface as it does for a Naval Force.

On day two of week two, of Exercise Ocean Safari, Hubert's NATO E-3A with Tanker in tow flew nearly all the way close to the continental US and found the US carriers floating southeast of Iceland heading due west towards England. As the Senior Director (SD), Hubert's job consisted of attacking the Aircraft Carriers Task Force and developing the attack plan. Once Hubert noticed that the E-2 Hawkeyes landed and that the US Navy no longer had any airborne early warning aircraft in the air, Hubert scrambled BritishBlackburn Buccaneer attack fighters. Normally, all the Buccaneers were physical stationed at RAF Mildenhall and deployed to exercise locations. After refueling with a British Victor Tanker, he committed the Orange strike package on the US Navy Task Force. Hubert kept the British fighters well outside the Aircraft Carriers surface radar coverage area and circled around from the northeast at two hundred feet.

In the meantime, south of where the US Navy Task Force (TF) was floating east bound, Hubert's NATO AWACS was on an east to west international air route. Hubert had the NATO E-3A Aircraft Commander (AC)squawk stand-by, which means that he put the aircraft transponder on standby and the E-3A transponder, was off and its Information Friend-of-Foe (IFF) codes used by the civilian ATC facilities to identify aircraft were not transmitting. The E-3A aircraft each time flew east on the jet route at Flight Level 300 (FL300) and once it was outside the US Navy TF radar range, it took a southerly heading away from the TF maintaining an orbit parallel to the US Navy route. Once Hubert saw that the E-2 Hawkeyes landed, that was when he gave the orders on Satcom to scramble sixteen British Buccaneer attack fighters.

Since the attack heading was a 300 degree inbound attack heading, the US Aircraft Carriers never expected the Orange-Air to come from the north or northeast since Britain was located to the east. This meant the British Buccaneer attack fighters would enter each separate US Aircraft Carrier from the 300-degree heading at their maximum speed at two hundred feet and simulate dropping bombs. The attack time for the British Buccaneer attack fighters was not 2:00 AM in the morning, with all sixteen aircraft flying at initially at two hundred feet. At the final attack, Hubert had two sets of eight British Buccaneer attack fighters, each successfully attacking a different US Carrier at two hundred feet. Post attack, the first set of British Buccaneer attack fighters climbed to six thousand feet and the second set climbed to eight thousand feet until the NATO E-3A had positive control of both sets of elements and continued climbing the British Buccaneers. By the time the British Buccaneer attack fighters attacked the US Carriers, theUS Navy did not have sufficient time to turn into the wind and scramble any defense fighters to protect them.

At the final exercise debrief, Hubert made it clear that the NATO E-3A AWACS with its Maritime radar can see when its E-2 Hawkeye is airborne. Hubert made it clear that any AWACS aircraft with Maritime radar that had the right controller can be deadly. Especially if he or she uses smart tactical deception as he did on this mission. The NATO E-3A AWACS can also see with its Maritime radar when the Aircraft Carrier will turn into the wind to launch its aircraft. This gives the NATO E-3A AWACS the tactical advantage and the US Navy should have known better. Being in the middle of the Atlantic south of Iceland gave them a false sense of security that during the Ocean Safari Exercise they would learn not to repeat in combat. Hubert made sure that he made this point clear at the mission debrief at the end of the exercise.

Upon returning to Geilenkirchen, Germany, the next deployment was in support of the Tactical Leadership Program (TLP). While assigned in Spain, Hubert attended the US Aggressor School in Great Britain. As a Lieutenant, Hubert had completed the Fighters Weapons Instructor School (WIS) at Tyndall, AFB, related to this program. This was part of the European Tactical Leadership Program (TLP). Later, these programs would lead to the development of the US Air Force Fighter Weapons Instructor Program (FWIP). When assigned to NATO E-3A AWACS, Hubert would support the TLP School each quarter as it held a class in a different European nation. Eventually, Hubert would convince the NATO Component to deploy an NATO E-3A aircraft and aircrew in support of the TLP School, which included a Weapons Director (WD) NATO Component student each graduating class.

During the TLP, the NATO E-3A AWACS, would fly as the Red-Air, while European Air Defense System would serve as the Blue-Air. Each controlling agency would control their perspective strike package in hopes of winning either the ground or the air battle. Normally, the Red-Air was the attackers or air-to-air mission while the Blue-Air accomplished the surface or air-to-ground mission. While airborne, each controlling agency controlled their assets on different frequencies and provided close control. The NATO AWACS aircrew deployed to the TLP location and attended all the TLP briefings and/or presentation. The European Air Defense accomplished all the TLP briefings and/or presentation via the telephone.

It was after a Tactical Leadership Program (TLP) night mission that Hubert asked Darlene to join him for breakfast at the Geilenkirchen Air Base (AB) Officer's Club. Being at a NATO AB with sixteen nations often required that one display proper protocol wisely. However, Hubert believed that he was in the military and that his family was free to be they wanted. After all, Darlene had often heard that if the military wanted Hubert to have a family they would have issued one to him. However, she regularly was asked to help military members and military families as Hubert's wife that was taken for granted because she was an officers wife in the same manner when she was an non-commissioned officers (NCOs) wife.

Soon Darlene would standup a first ever Diabetic Program at Geilenkirchen AB, which was badly needed. In Spain Darlene had raised thousands of dollars for a Spanish orphanage and hundreds of toys during the holidays for orphans and the Ways and Means representative. At this point, she had dealt with her first family suicide when a family member could not handle the heavy deployment rates. The day prior, she had dropped Hubert at Squadron-Two after dropping Tawny at school for his flight. At the time both did not know that, the following morning would be a foggy day. Hubert started his Mission Planning (MP) in the squadron basement in normal fashion and then proceeded to the main floor for the main briefing at the scheduled time. The TLP mission was a twelve-hour flight in Northern Germany.

After the mission, the NATO E3A AWACS aircraft had to accomplish low approaches although none waspre-planned. At the time, after an hour of accomplishing low approaches with Geilenkirchen Radar Control (RAPCON), which meant that each was flown at two hundred feet above the fog on Runway 18. Runway 18 was the runway used where the E-3A AWACS flew a route north of Geilenkirchen AB. Hubert received selection to sit in seat five, which is directly behind the Aircraft Commander (AC). The seat five individual serves as an observer during the transition phase of flight. During each transition, Hubert noticed white flocks of birds flying south in a "V" shape. The birds were normally flying in two groups separated by around two hundred feet laterally and fifty feet vertically.

Within an hour, it became evident that the fog would not burn up fast enough so two buses went to the alternate German AB to pick up the NATO E-3A crew. In the meantime, family members received notification of the delays back in the squadron. Upon landing at the German AB, Hubert and the Mission crew took the first bus back to Squadron-Two, which took about an hour due to the fog. The ride up to Geilenkirchen AB was hilly on a two-lane road. By the time Hubert arrived at Squadron-Two, it was lunchtime and like most of the crew, he was able to take a short nap. Once he arrived in the squadron, he simply took his aircrew bags, put them in his vehicle, and departed Squadron-Two for the Officers Club.

He decided to take Darlene to the Officers Club for lunch even though she insisted that he go home and go to bed. Darlene as unusual was wearing a dress with matching accessories for she would never go out in public in jeans. Many times while traveling on commercial flights, the pilots had offered her private tours of the cockpit and she always declined because, she was happy being a proud mommy and happy wife. Most of the time Hubert was not able to travel with his family due to his military commitments, which meant Darlene and Tawny had to travel by themselves. The only exceptions was during permanent moves and each move cost them five to ten thousand dollars out of pocket since the government did not pay for many of the moving costs or costs at the new location.

Once she entered the Officers Club, as usual, everyone stopped to look at her. She always looked so elegant and beautiful even though she did not believe that she was a natural beauty. For lunch, she decided to have a steak well done but the German Chef refused to cook it well done. The German Chef insisted that it should be rare and as a 'Five Star' Chef that he knew best. The German Chef insisted that it should be rare and as a 'Five Star' Chef that he knew best even though Darlene tried nicely to have him cook the stake the way she wanted. Then he stated that Americans only knew about hamburgers and hotdogs. At that point, Darlene told him that anytime he wanted to learn about American cooking that she would gladly show him how to cook American foods. A few minutes later, he slammed a burned stake on her plate. Darlene looked at Hubert and asked him to pay the bill as she walked out as she smiled at the German Chef and said "Chus" (good-bye).

Hubert had to travel to Fleet Command (Flottenkommando), in Gluckburg, Germany to visit the maritime headquarters in northern Germany. At first, the town looked like a Cinderella's fairytale town from one of Tawny's book. Hubert was the NATO Component Maritime Subject Matter Expert. Hubert still did not like the 'expert' title since he felt that no one was truly an expert but only someone that tried to stay informed in a subject area or as was the case in this task, someone that stayed informed as a maritime Subject Matter Expert (SME). Therefore, Hubert became the NATO Component Maritime SME and represented NATO throughout Europe as its Maritime SME even though many preferred the 'expert' title.

Part of this task was to create annual exercises in the Northern Sea or in the sea north of the Netherland where the ferry between the Dutch and Great Britain regularly had its route taking vehicles. In the past, accidents had occurred and one of the goals of the NATO E-3A AWACS Component was to see how the AWACS would assist civilians in case of emergencies. Hubert drove to Glücksburg since it was in Germany and Geilenkirchen was in northern Germany. Later, he would wish that he had brought Darlene and Tawny on this trip due to the beauty of the town of Glücksburg. He knew that he would have enjoyed Glücksburg better if he his family were with him on this trip.

Glücksburg is a small town in the district Schkeswig-Flensburg, in Schkeswig-Holstein, Germany. Glücksburg is located on the south side of the Flensburg Fjord, an inlet of the Baltic Sea, approximately ten kilometers (km) northeast of Flensburg. The town was originally the home of the family Schleswig-Holstein-Sonderburg-Glücksburg (or simply Glücksburg), since 1863 the royal family of Denmark and since 1905 of Norway. A branch of the family was the former royal family of Greece, which includes Prince Philip, Duke of Edinburgh, and therefore includes the lineage of the current Commonwealth monarchy.

Glücksburg is home to a German Navy base and the Maritime Headquarters where Hubert had to travel to and develop the NATO AWACS Maritime Search and Rescue (SAR) Procedures for the German Fleet Command and the NATO AWACS Component. Among the facilities at the base is the transmitter, call-sign DHJ58. DHJ58, situated at 54° 50' north, and 9° 32' east, ceased its transmissions on long wave frequency 68. 9 kHz in 2002 and in 2004, its long wave antenna. The communications capabilities from the Fleet Command regularly used in SAR operations.

On one mission, although the NATO E-3A AWACSreceived no task for a down civilian aircraft, after a citation was lost southeast of Glücksburg, since there was a NATO E-3A AWACS flying in the area at the time, a data reduction done, which is a playback of the recorded data link of the mission and the aircraft was located. Within twenty-four hours, the down citation aircraft was located although by then the pilot was no longer alive. Hubert suggested that a data reduction since a NATO E-3A flew in Germany each day. During the data reduction, the mission crew was able to isolate the citation aircraft and tell the rescuers the area to concentrate their search.

Hubert returned to Geilenkirchen it time to take leave and take a Dutch Bus Tour with Darlene and Tawny to England. Although Tawny was still in second grade, she was a well-behaved female. Darlene would always take a bag of coloring books and crayons with plenty of books to read. The Dutch Tour Bus took the ferry in Antwerp, Belgium to Birmingham,

England. At each stop, the Dutch would interpret in English the local stories so that the Contreras family would also enjoy the tour history. This had been the second tour with a Dutch tour and each time it had been the same of nice people.

At the Beefeaters Restaurant, everyone was surprised at how Tawny was well behaved. Later, they would tell Darlene that their children would never sit at a restaurant and behave like Tawny. Especially when the group requested Darlene get up as, be the traditional server in King Arthur's era, yelling for their meals or drinks. The trip ended with the bus driver giving Tawny a small bear as a personal gift. Visiting castles throughout southern England, visiting museums, and visiting the queen's main castle in London. Upon returning to Geilenkirchen, Hubert deployed to Trapani, Italy in Sardinia to support a normal Forward Operating Base (FOB) deployment and not support an exercise.

During a follow-up deployment to Trapani Air Base (AB), Sardinia, the level of control consisted from one-versus-one; intercept missions in local training areas near Sardinia to supporting major exercises in the Mediterranean Sea, which were normally Maritime Exercises. Hubert and his Weapons Directors (WDs) controlled the Italian F-104 Starfighter's that Hubert learned to control while assigned at Luke AFB Arizona. Hubert was one of the few American's that could easily control the F-104s since the 77A airspace just north of Sigonella was known as a difficult airspace for any Weapons Controller (WC) especially an America.

The 77A triangle airspace was almost an impossible air geometry airspace to control in since controllers had to maintain 2-½ nautical miles boundaries and not bust the 77A airspace. Normally, most controllers were not able to stay in the 77A airspace including the Italians, except Hubert. Hubert had learned in Arizona that the F-104 required a vectored right away from the post merge because it took so long for the aircraft to turn. Any delays in directing the F-104 pilot to turn, guaranteed an airspace violation. In those cases, depending on the mission circumstances, the controller had to report the violation to the local Federal Aviation Administration (FAA) agency.

One of our servers in the Chow Hall or Mess Hall was a conscript that was serving in the Italian Air Force for two years. The conscript was a medical doctor drafted into the Italian mandatory service. When Hubert asked why he not working in a hospital or a related area, he mentioned that in the Italian military, they never used common sense. The Hubert replied that the US military was the same. It seems that military or governments agencies never use common sense. Especially in this case since this soldier was a heart surgeon who for the next two years was losing proficiency. One would think the Italian military could use him better in one of its hospitals even as a medic if they did not want him to be a practicing doctor since he was a conscript who refused to be a career officer.

It was while in Trapani AB, Italy in Sardinia while conducting an exercise that Hubert's crew decided to go to diner after a long flight. A NATO aircrew custom was that once arriving in the local area, to confiscate an item in the local area, hijack it during the current deployment, and not caught by the local magistrate. Then on the following deployment, the same crew would return the item and put a plaque on the item with the name of the crew and dates confiscated. In this case, the crew went to Jolla de Col for dinner and noticed a large town sign as it was entering the town.

The crew got the idea of taking the town's sign on its way out if it had the right tools in the crew van, which it did. The sign removed successfully and returned on the following trip to the local mayor with a case of German wine with the proper explanation. Followed with a dinner with the mayor at the same restaurant who had not yet replaced the sign per the note left at the time the sign taken, signed anonymous. At the time the sign taken, the crew knew it would return within a month.

Upon returning to Trapani AB, Hubert made sure that the same Weapons Director (WD) crew was loaded on the crew so that they would participate in the diner when the sign received its official return to the town of Jolla de Col. The crew purchased a box of German wine as a bonus gift to give the town of Jolla de Col. After the exercise, it was time to return to Germany and fly local sorties (missions).

It seemed that most of the time that Hubert was in Germany that physically he seemed to live throughout Europe and not to Germany. On the other hand, Darlene and Tawny lived in Obspringen, Germany where Hubert visited his family and took short trips in between deployments. During his time in Geilenkirchen, Germany he spent as much time as he could with his family but still had responsibilities in Squadron-Two and as an aviator. Then there was the next deployment somewhere in Europe or North America to Mission Plan for his crew, his Weapons Team, or for the next quarter of flight evaluations. For now, Hubert had to plan on his next trip to Orland, Norway.

In Orland, Norway, the NATO AWACS Component, maintains a twenty-six foot boat, and a small wooden cabin for the E-3A AWACS aircrews to relax when they were not flying. In order for the NATO aircrew to use the twenty-six foot boat, individuals simply had certified on the boat in the Norwegian Faeroes at least one time. Then they are able to take the boat as many times as they like. The wooden cabin is ten miles south of the NATO AWACS Orland Facility. The wooden cabin is two levels and is able to sleep ten individuals. The Component permanent staff maintains plenty of wood at the cabin year round so that visiting aircrews can stay warm when visiting the wooden cabin since there is no electricity. The wooden cabin is located in private land next to a lake, which freezes in the winter.

During 'Spring Exercise', Hubert created a crew that he planned to deploy to Iceland as the first Alert crew. First, the crew deployed to Norway to their detachment for a month deployment and tracked the Union of Soviet Socialist Republics (USSR) fleet returning to homeport. This way, this NATO crew had recent experience of the USSR fleet and BEAR employment tactics prior to deploying to Iceland. For two weeks, the NATO E-3A AWACS aircrew worked with US Navy and British Nimrods trying to identify the USSR fleet while it transited east in the North Sea. The US Navy and British Nimrods had failed to identify the USSR fleet and their ship numbers mainly because of their constant movement in the North Sea.

On that deployment to Orland, Hubert was controlling two Norwegian F-16 Falcons identifying the Union of Soviet Socialist Republics (USSR) fleet ship numbers when one of the pilots reported what he thought was a submarine. Hubert was providing radar information using the E-3C AWACS maritime radar system to assist the F-16 pilots. At first, the F-16 Falcon lead pilot reported his contact as a submarine, which during Ocean Safari Hubert had seen as a Senior Director (SD) and as a Weapons Director (WD). Hubert asked that the lead F-16 pilot to confirm that it was a submarine. Upon the F-16 Falcons returning to the surface contact, the pilot confirmed that it was a dead whale floating on the North Sea.

Later, many other NATO Weapons Directors (WDs) would claim credit for the mission that Hubert controlled in the North Sea. Although British Nimrods and other US Navy P-3 aircraft had been trying to identify the Union of Soviet Socialist Republics (USSR) ships, they failed using their maritime technology. Due to this Norwegian over flight and identification of their ship numbers, upon landing back in Orland, the next day the crew received notification that they could return to Geilenkirchen, Germany a week early. Normally the crew would stay for the entire month but in this case, since this crew scheduled to deploy to Iceland, an early return was appropriate. Nevertheless, this experience would be beneficial here in the Iceland Alert Operation.

During 1988, the level of exercise support would increase for Hubert as a crewmember, as an Instructor, and as aFlight Examiner. The year would end with Hubert supporting thirteen major exercises and sixteen other exercises throughout Europe and North America. The year would begin with two French Exercises, followed with the Arrow Head Exercise, the 'Tactical POL' one of NATO AWACS first exercise in Poland, a Maritime Float Exercise, two TLP Exercises, a Bright Stardust Exercise, a Maple Flag Exercise in Canada, and the annual Spring Exercise in Norway in April. Upon returning from Norway, Hubert quickly turned around and supported the Tactical Air Meet, the French Deployment Meet, the first ever Bloodhound Test Flight in England, and deployed to Florida so support the Copper Flag Exercise.

During the Tactical Evaluation (TACEVAL) exercise when the NATO component became Mission Ready (MR), Hubert's crew was the only crew to receive a Superior rating. This had been the first time in recent history that any crew had received a rating other than Satisfactory. Just before the execution of the evaluation, Hubert had deployed to Norway. As the Chief of Weapons, he had established the crew set up for the evaluation that had aircrews in England, Iceland, Norway, Italy, Greece, and Turkey. Great Britain joined the NATO E-3A Component during this period and agreed to provide the NATO E-3A Component two complete E-3A aircrews distributed throughout the component. In this manner, Great Britain received free training not only in the E-3A aircraft, but also on every aspect of the AWACS management, operations, flying, and training at no cost.

In cases where Great Britain needed key positions, they simply gave their officers on the spot temporarypromotions. The NATO E-3A Component allowed Great Britain to take any position they wanted taking away countless of key positions mainly from the Americans while the senior US leaders said nothing. Mainly because under the US promotion system the temporary grade system are not used other than during a World War. This forced American officers to compete for what was already a limited pool of few good jobs. However, what made the NATO E-3A Component different was that receiving these jobs went to officers based on competency and not based on politics, which was the norm under the US promotion system. Only those officers that were good in their primary duties as aviators, aircraft controllers, and officers would lead to the selection of the few top jobs.

This would be a new dilemma for most US Officers especially for those assigned from Tinker AFB, Oklahoma. This made Hubert a very unpopular American among the US Officers since the allied Officers all like him and Darlene. Most considered Hubert a Spaniard or European and not an American although he made it clear that he was one-hundred percent American. Once Hubert became the Squadron-Two Chief of Weapons, the tension among his US peers increased especially since most out ranked him. However, in the NATO E-3A Component, rank meant nothing as did that held the position since everyone knew that receiving a position required experience and competency.

As the Chief of Weapons, Hubert was responsible for scheduling personnel in all four Forward Operation Bases (FOBs), normally five to six exercises per month, two or more employees always in upgrade training, and two or more employees always or more employees always on vacation. The main difference in NATO was the meetings were at a minimum unlike the US military. Hubert's idea of a meeting was putting a note on a sticky note sheet. In the NATO Component, taking a vacation was always a challenge since some nations paid their employees with vacation time. For example, the Belgium Air Force members received fifty-six days per year and weekends did not count as vacation days. The scheduling job alone could be a fulltime job but if fact had to be done like most Air Force jobs part-time.

As the Chief of Weapons, Hubert set three standards for his thirty International Officers and Senior Non-Commissioned Officers (SNCO); (1) first, he set high goals for with a measurable timeline, (2) second, delegation, because he believed a good manager delegated as much as possible, and (3) third, accountability, because he believed holding every person accountable for their actions. Especially since most were in their forties or older and not in their mostly in their twenties like the Americans. By now, Hubert was mature enough as an Officer to understand that he did not like the use of the 'expert' and 'leader' words. The 'expert' word in his word tended to be overused in the professional world suggesting that someone could become somehow almost like a robot. In Hubert's view, the military like the business world also overused the 'expert' term without first ensuring that the individual receiving the label truly deserved the label. The only phrase that he accepted was the Subject Matter Expert (SME) since the SME term suggested that one could specialize in a specific area or areas.

In Hubert's view, he thought that at best, one could only hope that, as a professional one should try to be consistent so that when one has a bad day that on that day, one's actions is still safe on position. As for the word 'leader', Hubert thought that unless one had someone to follow you, then you could not be a leader only because you had the 'leader' label, which was commonly give in the professional world. Another word overused in Hubert's view is the manager versus the leader term. Individuals forget that in order for someone to be a leader, they require at least one individual must follow them. The military or civilian work culture where individuals order subordinates to accomplish a task based on his or her position or rank does not automatically make one a leader but only a titleholder who can direct or influence someone to take an action.

Understanding the difference is important. The military like all large organizations automatically gives the leader, manager, and expert title freely without first ensuring that the individual filling the position first meets the proper criteria. Before long, Hubert's division was the best in NATO AWACS and the NATO Component. It did not take Hubert long to believe this since he saw firsthand what good or poor leadership was in the military. However, it was crucial that the officer at the top serve as a role model and set high standards for those under them as Hubert made it a point in every job that he took within the military environment. That is why many Senior Officers had issues with Hubert and so many junior officers, Non-Commissioned Officers (NCOs), and junior enlisted members looked up to him as a leader and mentor.

Hubert returned the day before the evaluation start date and saw that some of the crews changed and given an all-American Weapons Controller (WC) team. Since the evaluation called for a war like control environment, the team's performance recognized as outstanding. Their first mission had been in the Mediterranean Sea working with the Spanish Ala de Alerta y Control (Spanish Air Defense Center). Since he knew all the frequencies and control procedures that the Spanish controllers used, when they were being jammed, he went out on the radios in Spanish and directed counter measure and change of frequencies. The exercise jammers were not able to affect his crew since they stayed one-step ahead of the simulated enemy.

The second mission was in southern Italy. Controlling the Maritime forces that consisted of a US naval fleet task group, his crews were able to control the surface and air tracks with easy. On the third day, they successfully controlled US Navy aircraft simulation attacking Turkey and landed in Konya, Turkey at the NATO Air Base (AB). Only the NATO E-3A aircraft landed at the Konya AB installation since it was the NATO Component Forward Operating Base (FOB). The following day they successfully controlled Turkish fighters against the US fleet. For this exercise, Exercise Bright Stardust, the Turkish fighters were the simulated enemy aircraft.

Since Hubert had spent months in all of these countries as a Weapons Controller (WC) and headquarters' staff Officer, know his simulated enemy's capabilities gave him the advantage over those tasked to defeat. On his last trip to Izmir and Incirlik, Turkey, he had controlled Turkish and American aircraft using what every control facility allowed to use. In one case, he had controlled off 1940s radar when he used a small screwdriver to tune his 1940s radio. In this exercise, the wing that he was supporting received the only excellent rating that they had received up to that point in time. After three days of simulating killing all attacking aircraft by friendly fighters, the Tactical Evaluation (TACEVAL) evaluators simulated that the control facility Hubert was working in destroyed by ground missile fire.

Tawny was always the center of Darlene and Hubert's life and they always made time for her no matter which Hubert as assigned. Hubert taught Sunday school when not deployed with Tawny. Finding Sunday school teachers to fill in when not in Geilenkirchen was always a challenge since the congregation was more concerned with volunteering for the chorus than teaching their children about the Bible. Especially since the Base Child Care gave free care for Church Service. In Germany Hubert volunteered to run the children's Sunday school so that Tawny and he could teach the five year olds and younger together. Each week Tawny would pick the story in the bible and then she and Hubert would practice at home who would teach what to the class. The church had different magnet Prompts that they used to teach their weekly lesson.

It was early May 1988 when Hubert had to go to an advance NATO Electromagnetic Jamming class in Oberammergau Germany and visited the Neuschwanstein castle. Since this was a joint school, Darlene and Tawny were able to stay with Hubert in the Officer's quarters. On the weekend, they visited Munich where Hubert repeated World War II storied that he had heard from his father. Hubert asked to teach a class on the NATO E-3A AWACS systems and at the end of each day, they would go into town for shopping and dinner. During the day when Hubert was in class, Darlene and Tawny walked in the beautiful town of Oberammergau and did some shopping and exploring around the local area. Since the course in Oberammergau was a two-week course, it gave Hubert and his family a chance to visit the local area.

On weekends Hubert, Darlene, and Tawny traveled to Munich and the Neuschwanstein Castle where they were like all foreign tourists. Munich was the city that Hubert had heard from his father as a young teen when he was in WW-II. The Neuschwanstein Castle was a 19th-century Romanesque Revival Palace above the village of Hohenschwaugau near Füssen southwest Bavaria, Germany. The palace commissioned by Ludwig II of Bavaria as a retreat and homage to Richard Wagner. Contrary to common belief, Ludwig paid for the palace out of his personal fortune and extensive borrowing, not with Bavarian public funds. Walt Disney used the Neuschwanstein Castle as his model when creating his castle in Florida. As usual, upon returning to Geilenkirchen, Hubert had to deploy again, this time back to Italy. However, he was glad that he had spent some time with his family before deploying again.

"Great job, Paulo," said Hubert. Both had just completed their annual check ride in Sicily as both controlled F-104s in the 77A airspace. This airspace known as a difficult airspace for any Weapons Controller (WC) but seem to be more difficult for Americas. Paulo had busted airspace twice but still passed his check ride since the Flight Examiner knew that controlling in triangle airspace was almost impossible air geometry wise. The Flight Examiner knew that the 77A Airspace was the most difficult airspace to keep F-104s aircraft in this tiny triangle although he was surprised when Hubert did not bust the airspace. On the other hand, Hubert came within the normal 2-½ nautical miles boundaries but never busted the 77A airspace. He had learned well as a new Second Lieutenant while controlling student German 104s while assigned at Luke AFB in Arizona. Although the 77A airspace was in Trapani, Italy Hubert and his NATO E-3A aircraft was deploying to Prevessa, Greece on this deployment so after this mission they landed there.

"OK guys, Paulo and I will pay for the beer until the piles cans reach the ceiling," said Hubert to his NATO crew. As was the custom, those that successfully passed their check rides would normally buy a round of drinks. Since the aircrew landed in Prevessa, Greece and the beer not expensive, Paulo and Hubert would buy the drinks until the cans reached the ceiling. In Paulo's case, the US paid him a bonus for serving in the NATO E-3A AWACS program in Geilenkirchen, Germany. Hubert knew that his monthly pay was well over his so buying drinks for a while would not hurt either individual financially. Even though Paulo was a Captain, the US was paying him as a US Air Force Colonel receives, pays wise and would continue receiving that pay for two years upon returning to Italy.

"So what do you think about Konya," asked Brigadier GeneralJay D. Blume, Jr. Hubert and his crew were at breakfast as was the custom before any flight. Being a member of NATO E-3A AWACS had some benefits and having free meals for every flight was necessary for NATO aircrews. The NATO AWACS Component Commander had visited the Konya Air Base and was asking the aircrew for their thoughts about the ground support and the Konya AB leadership. Later, the General would ask Hubert why he did not make any comments. Hubert mentioned that if the General wanted his honest opinion that he would say what he felt was the truth. He had seen the Turkish Base Commander taking advantage of the funding, support equipment, and did not think that he was an honest individual.

The general entered the Air Force in 1963 as an honor graduate through the Reserve Officer Training Corps program. He attended undergraduate pilot training at Williams Air Force

Base, Arizona, and earned his wings in 1965. General Blume commanded a fighter squadron, fighter wing, the NATO Airborne Early Warning Force Component and a technical training center before assuming his current duties. A command pilot, he has logged more than 4,900 flying hours, principally in fighter-type aircraft, including 303 combat missions over Southeast Asia in the F-100, Super Saber. He commanded all NATO AWACS support throughout the European Southern Region during Operations Desert Shield and Desert Storm. Major General Blume retired on 1 February 1966.

First, he asked if General Blume if he wanted more of what he had already heard or what how Hubert truly believed. When he mentioned to the General about Colonel Atatürk not being a very honest individual who misused funding, misused support equipment, and regularly took to his house equipment purchased for the component, he mentioned that he had felt the same. Under Colonel Atatürk, large televisions purchased for the AWACS aircrews purchased by NATO disappeared and old black and white televisions appeared that the Turkish Air Force used. This behavior continued until this visit by General Blume that these types of covert behaviors stopped at Konya AB.

"Viper 1, snap 0-2-0, target nose on 0-2-0, two thousand feet at ten miles opposite heading," snapped Hubert to two F-15 Eagles from Bitburg AFB, Germany. As General Blume watched Hubert control multiple fighters, he was impressed with the aggressive and best controlling that he had ever seen. Hubert was having a great day controlling where everything he did was the best that he had ever controlled. Bitburg AFB was having a sortie generation day and their aircraft were flying training missions throughout Germany.

"You need to make me look as pretty as possible," mentioned Darlene to the hairdresser. She did not realize that General Blume's wife was on the other side of the patrician. Darlene had mentioned that she wanted to look her best to make the stuffy Officer's wife envious. Mrs. Blume would tell her at the receiving line that evening that she enjoyed her comments at the beauty salon and agreed that the Officer's wives were in deed stuffy. The previous weekend, Hubert hadtaken her to Monchengladbach to purchase her a formal dress. The dress that he picked out was pink but he knew that she would look beautiful in the dress. Only Darlene had the looks for such a colorful dress. Darlene had her older sister, husband Robert, and his sister visiting from Florida were at this formal function, which made it much better. Robert had his US Army formal dress and everyone thought he was an Admiral. As for Robert's sister, she too had a great time on the dance floor when her slip fell and no one missed a step in the dance floor.

In spite of the late night, the following morning the Contreras family went to church AB. The church was an all denomination church where the only thing that mattered was that everyone was a Christian. Hubert would set the easel for the Bible stories in the center of the room with two tables on each side. Each table would have fruit and toys that Tawny and Hubert would purchase at the market in the Netherlands for the children each week. Instead of tables, Hubert had the preacher used mats from the base gym and asked the parents to have the children bring a pillow to the class. Each time that the children answered a question when asked during the story telling, the children received a snack. It did not matter what the children said for what matter was learning about the Bible. The children loved giving Hubert and Tawny hugs each time when they arrived in class and before their parents picked them up or anytime they saw them on the base.

Hubert also volunteered to serve as the peewee, basketball, track, and bowling coach so that he could spend time with Tawny. Tawny loved to run since she would see her daddy run all the time. She also like bowling since her mommy was a great bowler. The bowling alley was in the Netherlands and each year Darlene and Hubert would go to the Bowling Alley to see the Super Bowl. The hardest part of seeing the Super Bowl in the Netherlands Bowling Alley was starting the game at 3:00 AM due to the time difference in the US, with a nine-hour time difference. Darlene had purchased the bowling ball from the Sears catalog and Tawny was the only girl that had her own ball. It was a shiny white ball and Hubert was surprised that it was so light.

Hubert made sure that all the children played during the game, which made many parents mad. Nevertheless, Hubert would explain that since the children were still young he was teaching them teamwork and the importance of winning. The idea was in making sure that all the children learned about running and learning to control their tiny bodies. Learning the importance of hitting the ball and running to the base was equally as important as having fun for the children. Unfortunately, many of the parents all had different ideas of what Hubert, as the primary coach should teach their children. However, since all of the Officers worked for Hubert, they were afraid to challenge him on the field, which in this case benefited their children.

Darlene had used the Sears Catalog since Spain when she started purchasing Tawny her school clothing. Everything had to match, from her shoes, to her purse. Then there were all her toys and the new television. In Germany, the only television was the European television so Hubert had to make sure the new television was US, European, and had a Video Home System (VHS) connection so that the connection cords attached to the television. This was family or could mail VHS tapes from the US recorded months earlier. When the Contreras family returned to the US after their Europe assignment, they did not know any of the television stars since most of their VHS tapes were years old.

Hubert found a house in Obspringen, Germany and the Contreras family was one of two families that lived in Obspringen. Obspringen was twenty-five miles from

Geilenkirchen (GK) where Hubert worked and where Tawny went to school. When Hubert not flying, Tawny would drive to GK with her daddy and the route took them through Heinsburg. Many times, in Heinsburg, a Hubert had to stop at a light to turn right and take the road to GK. At the light, an old German woman in her eighties would open the Camaro door and ask Tawny to get into the back of the car in German. Then she would get into the front seat and she and Hubert would talk all the way into GK until she reached GK and got off at the same store.

Tawny also severed as Darlene's navigator mainly because she knew how to read a map. Since the house where they lived was in Obspringen, Germany four miles from the Netherland border, it called the tri-border town. To the southeast was Maastricht, Belgium, which meant it was each to turn around if you were not careful. Especially since there was, a road that the Americans referred to as the International road that by-passed the base from the Marine Base in the Netherlands to Germany where one could go to purchase groceries. Tawny was able to navigate the complex roads using the European maps even though she was only in second grade. Nevertheless, like in Spain, Tawny not only knew how to read maps, she also knew how the gas coupons worked and was in charge of paying for gas whenever Darlene needed to refill in Europe.

For now, all Hubert wanted to do is spend time with Tawny. Hubert regularly volunteered to go with Tawny on her school field trips. This was one of many ways that he spent quality time with her during field trips. Tawny's teacher would always make sure that Tawny and Hubert were in the same group. This meant that he had to take his annual leave. On one trip, Tawny and her class went to Amsterdam, in the Netherlands and visited where the Pilgrims came just prior to going to America. Hubert like the rest of Tawny's class learned that the American Pilgrims left the United Kingdom and came to the Netherlands starting 1607 before going to the New World. After living in the Netherlands, the Pilgrims decided that the Dutch were too liberal and took their ships to the new world.

Although the Speedwell and the Mayflower received the final approval to cross the ocean, only the Mayflower came to America in 1620. Like most Americans, Hubert and most of the class knew nothing about the Speedwell boat and the role that it played in the American history. The Speedwell took on water and diverted to Dartmouth, Devon, which meant the Mayflower, would be the only ship going to the new world. Like most Americans, it took this field trip for Hubert to learn this minor fact about his own US history. Of the 121 passengers that were on the initial list, 102 individuals received the final approval to board the Mayflower with the consolidated supplies. It was during the Pilgrims migration to Amsterdam that was part of the American history learned not in American history books but during this Amsterdam, Netherlands field trip.

That is when the Pilgrims decided to go to the new world. It was during this trip that Hubert and Tawny's class tried the Dutch Panican's, which is like the French crepes but better. Each volunteer parent given a dozen children and Hubert was no exception, except that Tawny was in his group. One young boy named David was so full of energy that Hubert had to stay on top of him. Especially, when they were in the busy streets of Rotterdam and had to keep the group together. Dave always had a different idea and wanted to go so where else, which forced Hubert to yell at him more than once. Besides, David truly was a good young boy who was simply full of life and just needed to learn a little discipline. It was not long after the Rotterdam field trip that Hubert deployed again.

"I have to go to Cold Lake in Canada," mentioned Hubert. The Maple Flag Exercise was in Cold Lake, Alberta. Canadian Forced Base Cold Lake, referred to as CFB Cold Lake, is a Canadian Forced Base located within the City of Cold Lake, Alberta. The International Air Transport Association (IATA) indicator is 'YOD' and the International Civil Aviation Organization (ICAO) indicator is 'CYOD'. The IATA or ICAO are used by the NATO E-3A AWACS flight or mission aircrews while Mission Planning(MP) or during flight and loaded into the aircraft systems to operate their mission or aircraft systems. On this trip, Hubert would deploy with the NATO E-3A AWACS aircraft while a second aircrew would fly commercial to Cold Lake and the Maple Flag Exercise.

Cold Lake is an Air Force Base (AFB) administered by the Royal Canadian Air Force (RCAF). It is one of two AFBs in Canada using the CF-18 Hornet fighter/interceptor aircraft. Its primary lodger unit assigned at Cold Lake is the 4th Wing. Over the years, since Hubert was the Chief of Weapons, to be fair, he would rotate flying commercial versus flying on the NATO E-3A AWACS aircraft to Cold Lake Canada. Regardless of where Hubert deployed to, he still was responsible for creating rosters to support every deployment that his E-3C AWACS squadron had. Hubert's portion consisted of loading the Weapons Directors (WDs) and Senior Director (SDs) aircrew positions, both positions that he was qualified to fill in the NATO E-3A aircraft.

Flying commercial to Cold Lake included stopping for two days in Edmonton, Canada after flying through Amsterdam in the Netherlands. This would allow the crew sufficient time to become acclimated to the new local time zone. During that time-period, the crew visited the Mall of the America, which at that time was the largest Mall in North America. Years later, when Darlene, Tawny, and Hubert departed Alaska and drove to Arizona, they stopped in Edmonton and Hubert showed Darlene and Tawny the Mall of the America. Over the years, Darlene and Tawny had heard of the mall many times of this mall and Hubert wanted them to visit the mall first hand. Especially the roller coaster ride and the other rides in the center of the mall because he knew Darlene loved roller coaster rides.

Once the crew arrived at Edmonton,Canada, they rented vans and stayed at a Holiday Inn that became the same Holiday Inn for all Maple Flag Exercises. On this first trip, it was during the winter so the days were long and the nights were short. Once the crew rested in Edmonton, they drove to Cold Lake and arrived at the same hotel that the lead NATO E-3A AWACS crew were staying. The following Monday, both crews went to the 4th Wing Base Theater for the Maple Flag In-Brief and the exercise began. Like any Flag exercise, all exercise participants must attend the In Brief in order to fly or participate in any manner in the exercise.

Just like any flag exercise, there was a morning and afternoon go, each lasting approximately four hours each. Unlike the Red Flag airspace, the Maple Flag airspace is much larger but smaller than the exercise air space in Alaska. Where the Red Flag airspace has civil jet routes overhead that puts limitations on the overall training, there are no civil air routes in Northern Canada. This allows the military to maximize its training and the only limitation is ones imagination. In one scenario, Hubert put four US F-15 Eagles under the NATO E-3As wings as AWACS self-protection. Once the Red-Air attacked the NATO E-3A aircraft, all Red-Air were surprised when out of nowhere the F-15s came after them and simulated killing them. Hubert had many other surprises during the Maple Flag Exercise that became permanent Lesson Leaned.

During most Maple Flag Exercises, the NATO E-3A received a task to support an Air Show somewhere in Canada. The same aircraft used in the Maple Flag Exercise receives tasking orders for the Air Show except that not some of mission aircrew. All of the Flight Crew is used and only a third of the Weapons and two of the Surveillance Crew receives orders for the Air Show. The Air Show received its official task on the weekend, which meant that the crew supporting the Air Show would not receive any rest during the deployment. The first year, the Air Show was in Edmonton, which meant that the flight from Cold

Lake to Edmonton was short. On the following deployment six months later, the Air Show was in London, Ontario. This meant that the NATO E-3A flight to the Air Show was over five hours just to get from Cold Lake to London, Ontario.

For the London Air Show, the crew required a four-day weekend in order to support the Air Show. Once the aircrew arrived in London, the crew stayed at a five star hotel and received the VIP treatment. At the Edmonton Air Show, the NATO AWACS crew stayed at its normal Holiday Inn hotel, which was very nice. The Aircraft Commander (AC) on the crew was the Squadron-Two Commander, Lieutenant Colonel Smith who was born in London, Ontario. Therefore, the media treated the entire crew as local heroes. Everything in the hotel including all the meals at any time was completely free to the entire NATO E-3A crew during the entire London Ontario, Air Show.

During each day of the Air Show, the NATO E-3A Aircraft accomplished a low fly-by at 2,000 feet on the main runway. On the first day, during the first fly-by, Lieutenant Colonel Smith flying as the AC or main pilot, while going around the airport flew a bit too fast and overflew the main runway. Therefore, once he turned towards straight to the main runway, he had to turn the aircraft right to get back to the center of the runway. Since the NATO E-3A aircraft was flying too fast, by the time the aircraft was finally in the middle of the runway, the NATO E-3A Roto-dome directly pointed at the crowd. It was because of the NATO E-3A aircraft over speed that this occurred and not due to planning but due to the crowd that loved the aircraft flying so low with the Roto-dome displaying at them a perfect picture opportunity.

At this point, since Hubert was flying as aircrew, an instructor, and as an evaluator, he was flying both the AM and PM goes each day. This was his typical schedule during all flag exercises. This was also one of the few times that Hubert used the E-3 bunks because of a migraine headache and a stiff neck.

Since he was not a drinker, Hubert preferred to work hard versus take time off and get drunk like many of his co-workers. His work philosophy was always to 'be the example' versus 'setting the example'. Each deployment to Canada was for a month in order to make the deployment cost effective for the NATO AWACS Component. Hubert's Officers all truly admired him not only for his skills, but also for his professionalism and his family values. Many Officers were jealous of Hubert and felt that they could not measure up to him personally. After the London Ontario, Air Show, the crew returned to Cold Lake for another two weeks before returning to Germany.

"You're my new Assistant Flight Commander," said Colonel Smith. The second part of the Commander's news was the Hubert would become the new NATO E3A Deputy Flight Commander for Flying Squadron-Two effective 17 June 1986. Within a year and a half from the time Hubert arriving in NATO E-3A AWACS and Flying Squadron-Two, not only had he been qualified to the highest aircrew positions possible, he had been selected to a leadership position normally held by the top three Officers in the unit or Field Grade Officers and Hubert was only a senior Captain. Again, many senior US Officers complained to the Senior US Air Force Officer assigned in Squadron-One. Years later, Hubert's final Commander, Colonel Coxe would be one of these Officers. He would make Colonel even though he lacked operational experience and never saw combat making promotion because he attended Professional Military Education (PME) Schools.

Hubert was not home for long before he had to deploy again. This time there was another deployment to North America. Instead of going to Canada, the deployment was to Florida and the Copper Flag Exercise. Hubert had gone to Tyndall AFB, Florida to attend the Basic Weapons Controller (WC) School when he first became an Officer. During that time-period, Darlene had visited him for a week so he thought that since it was the summer, that it would be idea for Darlene to go to

Florida and visit family and gone to Tyndall and visit him at Copper Flag.

"Do you want to go to Tyndall with me?" asked Hubert. Hubert was going to Tyndall AFB, Florida and support the Copper Flag Exercise. NATO E-3A Airborne Warning and Control Systems (AWACS) was going to take an E-3C AWACS aircraft to the US and support Canadian F-18 Hornets during the William Tell Exercise in the airspace over water south of Tyndall AFB, Florida. The USE-3C AWACS would be supporting the local wing F-15 Falcons. The William Tell Exercise was a two-week exercise. The flight over to the US took the normal flight from Geilenkirchen through the United Kingdom, South of Iceland, through Maine, and directly to Florida.

The first operations stops were in Mildenhall, Britain in-route to Tyndall to refuel. Throughout the flight down to the US, the Mission Crew provided E-3C AWACS Monitor to the Flight Crew. The E-3C AWACS Monitor calls for the Mission Crew Commander (MCC), the Senior Director (SD), or a Weapons Direct (WD) to give the E-3C AWACS pilots traffic advisory of airline traffic on the jet routes. In addition, once flying on international routes, a different WD went out on UHF/VHF (Ultra/Very High Frequency) Guard and asked civilian airliners if they wanted air traffic advisory calls and/or information. The NATO E-3A AWACS Mission Crew provides many civilian airliners requested E-3C AWACS assistance. This practice was a normal practice that Hubert had started as part of his mission training in addition to simulation over live training when flying a deployer or redeployer sortie (mission).

The second leg of the deployment flight was the ops stop in Maine to refuel and to get aircrew rest. At the same time, the crew purchased lobsters for the planned party at the end of weekend one. During the flight to Tyndall, the crew had lobster races in the hallways between the bunks in the rear of the aircraft. Another prank that the Mission Crew did on our Turkish Pilot that our Aircraft Commander who was the unit

Operations Officer suggested was that most of the mission crew ran to the back of the aircraft and then all run to the front of the aircraft. This would change the weight of the aircraft forcing the Turkish Pilot to correct the E-3 aircraft yawn, which would require constant corrections if the crew kept running back and forth.

At all times the crew kept front curtain closed. This forced the co-pilot to keep trimming the aircraft autopilot. The maneuver worked three times until the laughter gave the joke away. On the third day, the NATO E-3A AWACS aircraft landed in Tyndall, AFB Florida. By this time, the maintenance personnel had pre-deployed and were waiting to recover the aircraft and crew in cutoffs and colorful shirts. When the Base Commander received notice of the NATO attire, he ordered his staff to have the NATO aircraft part at the end of the apron away from the base operations. The apron was located at the end of the Base Operations but at the far end of the flight line.

"Round, round, round, round, I get around" could be heard in the loud stereo speaks. A favorite saying that Hubert would say was "The AWACS is a big toy for big boys and girls". When the aircraft door open, Beach Boys music played and the cold beer was ready for everyone. Cold water bottle was also available but to Hubert's knowledge, no one took water. The Base Commander clearly mad told Hubert that the behavior not acceptable. Hubert mentioned that the Aircraft Commander (AC) was the Squadron Operations Officer and that he would mention his concerns to him, which he did. The same procedures continued for the entire four weeks that the NATO AWACS crew received a deployment to Tyndall, AFB Florida and the Copper Flag Exercise.

This would be the start of the following two weeks and the Copper Flag Exercise. The NATO crew believes in working hard and playing even harder. It also believes in taking care of its maintenance and security personnel in the same manner as aviators. Although Hubert flew to Florida with the rest of the aircrew onboard the E-3C AWACS aircraft, Darlene and tawny flew to Florida to Bradenton to visit family first, then Hubert went and picked her up once he arrived in Tyndall and had complete the initial briefings. After flying three days to get to Florida and two long days of nearly working fourteen hour each day with non-stop briefs and Mission Planning (MP), Hubert drove to Bradenton. He picked up Darlene and returned to Panama City in time to enter crew rest with a few minutes to spare.

The following morning he had to fly as an evaluator then a second mission as a Senior Director (SD). The nice thing about exercise missions (sorties); they were only four-hour sorties (missions) each. However, each required two hours of pre-briefs and then the post-briefs making each day a long day. Each day, a morning, and afternoon push the routine as part of the Copper Flag Exercise. Each push included a pre-brief, the exercise, and the mission debrief. Airborne jammers flew in each push that forced all aviators to work their internal systems to the maximum capabilities. For every push, a nation executed the plan and executes the entire mission to include controlling the presentations. The entire process normally consisted of six to eight hours from start to finish per push. Every push normally had approximately forty or more aircraft flying or two formations that consisted of the Blue-Air and the Red-Air attacking them were normally eight to twelve aircraft.

The Blue-Air was under a Package Commander during each Push. The Red-Air used enemy tactics that the Blue-Air had to counter as part of their tactics. The Red-Air was under one Package Commander during each Push. Normally, the NATO Squadron-Two Weapons Controller (WC)aircrews out controlled the Americans because they were more aggressive than the American's were mainly because Hubert had instilled this attitude in his NATO Weapons team. The American Weapons Controllers (WCs) used the Air Defense system consoles and controlled from the System for Automatic

Program Generation (SAGE) Radar consoles that Hubert used in deployed in Europe. Since becoming the Chief of Weapons, Hubert had instilled jamming concepts into his training program. This exercise included jamming, which received allot of attention extensively throughout Eastern and Western Europe.

Although the F-106 Delta Dart received the acknowledgement as the classic interceptor, only 340 were built, far fewer than the number of F-102s. Soviet ICBMs had replaced nuclear bombers as the main strategic threat. The F-106 was the best interceptor in the fleet until the F-15 began replacing it in the 1970s, but even then, the Six continued to find work almost to the end of the Cold War. The final alert tour for the F-106 was with the New Jersey Air National Guard (ANG) on July 7, 1988. The data link capabilities of the F-106 and the lessons learned during this era led to the development of the drones or Unmanned Airborne Vehicles (UAVs) used in the twenty-first century.

Since Hubert took the lead to introduce jamming practices on his own, his Squadron-Two aircrews were well prepared and excelled during all the exercises. After each exercise, our NATO Aircraft Commander (AC) who was also the Squadron-Two Operations Officer, Paulo Vitosi, always took the crew sightseeing. Each time he would declare Visual Flight Rules (VFR) so that he would not have to talk to the Federal Aviation Administration (FAA). Each time the AC would fly the NATO E-3A AWACS aircraft over water, 1,000 feet from the Florida beach and go 'babe sightseeing' as he did with his F-106 back home. Then he would let the crew take turns run up to the flight deck and take a 'babe check'. Although NATO AWACS had females within its ranks, the male Officers were still chauvinist especially the males from the Mediterranean nations. None of the NATO nations had female members assigned as aviators and the only females were administrative or worked in the base hospital.

As the senior Air Force Officer, Hubert regularly cautioned the NATO Officers that they had to be sensitive to the American females especially those not assigned to the NATO Component. Hubert in a way was glad that the Squadron-Two only had two females and both were Americans. Margie was one of them and the second was Maggie who like Margie was equally competent, which made Hubert's job easier. Both did not use their gender to get ahead and wanted to receive promotion based on performance and not their gender as was becoming the standard in the US Air Force. Both became close friends of Darlene and Hubert that were always welcomed to their home without an invitation. Unlike most of the NATO crew and maintenance that had to stay in a normal motel, the Danish paid as Dignitaries by their governments. This allowed them to stay at a condominium suite on the Tyndall Beach when four of the Danes decided to share a suite.

As a result, the crew had a party suite during the trip that most of the crew used especially on their way to the Beach bars. Hubert and Darlene decided not to use this suite mainly because of the stories Hubert Heard from the other crewmembers. Besides, Hubert and Darlene were too busy going dancing as much as possible. Darlene would also drop Hubert off at Tyndall since Hubert rented a vehicle for her when she arrived in Panama City. Hubert felt that the crew vehicles were for the crew and he did not want to take one of their vehicles even though he was a senior crewmember. After he landed, he would hear how Paulo Vitosi, the Squadron Operations Officer and Darlene would drag on the main road, which was Highway 90 and the road to Tyndall AFB. Paulo as the Italian was always the instigator and Darlene not one to give into a challenge.

After a long week of work, everyone was ready for the weekend party at the Tyndall, AFB Park. The party started with the Canadians bringing two pickup beds full of Canadian beer with ice. The Eagle Drivers (F-15 Pilots) brought food and kegs of beer. The NATO crews brought the lobsters, schnitzels, and dozens of boxes of German wines. The music varied since everyone simply dropped his or her tapes in a pile and anyone picked a tape to play at random. No one seemed to care what music played at any given time. At any given time, you could see anyone's hands flying in the winds symbolized a mocked air war that occurred during week one. Family and children invited so plenty of soft drinks were available and no one misbehaved. At the end of the day, the party was a huge success that everyone spoke of the entire following week by everyone including family.

The following morning Hubert had to go on base to mission plan for the first morning mission of the Copper Flag Exercise. The Intelligence Officer asked Darlene to go with her to the Tyndall Beach tanning, which worked out well. Since Hubert had to mission plan for two pushes, that meant that Hubert would be on base for at least six hours or more, that gave Darlene plenty of time to sunning at the Panama Beach. Especially since Hubert could go to the base with the rest of the crew, so Darlene could keep her car and take Carol. Later, Carol Morehouse would become a Colonel and her husband would become the E-3C AWACS Wing Commander. Hubert never liked Carol's husband who would start the demise of the AWACS Wing. Like manypromotable staff Officers and Air Force pilots, Major Morehouseeventually received promotion to General with the assistance of his scratch golfing abilities.

Officers like Hubert were never home to play golf. They always received deployment orders to the latest hostile areas or the latest major exercises serving the nation's wars. Officers like Hubert also never seemed to have good Air Force bosses that took care of them by writing good Officer Performance Reports (OPRs) or making sure that the allowed them to go to military Professional Military Education (PME) schools. Officers like Hubert were always too important and had to deploy to the latest hot spot or the unit would fail and they would not be able to get the needed success to promote their careers properly as they selfishly planned. Once Hubert became a Senior Officer, he chose to be different and take care of his troops and made promotion in spite of the Air Force promotion system that was in place.

Carol would ask Darlene to baby sit her daughter mainly because she knew how she raised Tawny. However, this was not possible because Hubert did not like her husband and the way he was administering the wing. Hubert decided to take an early assignment to Alaska against the advice of his squadron Commander. It was Carol's husband, which put E-3C AWACS Wing in the worse position in its history. It was also the reason Hubert left Tinker AFB before becoming dysfunctional. The remaining year of 1988 would not slow down for Hubert, as he would continue deploying throughout Europe. It seemed that Hubert spent more time with his family at US deployments where Darlene visited him at the deployed site. Especially when during some weekends, he saw Tawny and family. After the Copper Flag Exercise, Hubert requested a week of leave so that he could return with his family using commercial travel that he would have to pay out of pocket. The unit agreed as long as he returned in time to support another deployment, which Hubert agreed to without any problem.

After returning from the Copper Flag Exercise in Florida, he quickly turned around and supported the Fan Exercise, the Team Work Exercise in the Mediterranean, and Display Determination. Next Hubert deployed in support of Exercise Team Elder, Exercise Salty Hammer, the FOST Exercise, the Joint Star Exercise, the Bright Start Exercise, and the Helicopter Exercise. Finally, he had to support the Exercise Interpol, the Electro-Spectrum-Magnetic (ESM) Test Flight, the Fire Air Force (FAF) Exercise, two Tactical Leadership Programs (TLPs), and the Tactical Air Force (TAF) Live Exercise. Many of these exercises were major exercises that required Hubert to deploy for two or more weeks outside of Geilenkirchen, Germany, to one of the NATO Forward Operating Base (FOB), or to an exercise location. He felt lucky that on his last trip that he was able to spent time with his family part of the time even though he had been busy supporting the exercise most of each day.

"Daddy, our class is going camping in the Netherlands and is looking for volunteers," said Tawny. For Hubert and his family, 1988 seemed like a blur since he was always coming and going somewhere. At the end of 1988, Hubert supported twenty-nine exercises and had deployed to Canada, the US, and every NATO Component FOB multiple times. He still had time to go with Tawny on some of her school field trips in spite of his busy work schedule. In Europe, the government augments its citizens and helps them pay for all recreation activities to include the camping grounds. Since the Americans were living on the economy and paying the local taxes, they were entitled to use all the same facilities as the European citizens. The next day, Hubert asked for leave and took five days of leave but was only able to get three days because of an ongoing wing inspection. In this case, the three days were sufficient to support the most important days of Tawny's camping trip in the Netherlands.

The following week, Hubert and Tawny made all the preparations for the camping trip. Tawny took her daddy camping equipment and knew that he would be joining her as soon as he could. Tawny and her class started their camping in the Netherlands with the initial group of volunteers and Hubert joined them two days later. It seemed that during every day that there was an over cast. However, that did not stop the campers from having fun and from going exploring in the wilderness. During the camping, each morning, the children took walks on the trails and learned about the local wild life and the different types of birds. Hubert enjoyed walking in the misty Dutch overcast in the windy woods with a group of children teaching them many of the survival techniques that he learned at Survival School. As the clouds seemed liked layers of stripes in the sky until the lower layer dropped its mist of water on the top layer of pine trees and mist touched the ground.

On the last day, all the parents invited to a large picnic with their children. Darlene joined Hubert and Tawny on the final picnic where Tawny told her mommy all the different adventures that she experienced during her camping. Hubert suggested to the volunteers that the children prepare the final meal for their parents with their help. The children prepared and served the cool aid, cooked the pancakes, prepared and cooked the scrambled eggs for their parents. All the children feeling proud of themselves as Dutch campers, with faces full of smiles. After returning from the camping trip, Hubert had to start preparing for the Display Determination Exercise.

For the Display Determination Exercise, the USS Forrestal (CV-59), served as the primary Task Group (TG) Commander. From 28 September to 10 October, the USS Forrestal Aircraft Carrier participated in the third and final NATO exercise of the deployment. During this phase, the NATO E-3A aircrews were the Orange-Air regularly attacking the US Forces throughout the Mediterranean who were the Blue-Forces. The operation, involving ships, all types of aircraft, and personnel from eight NATO countries, designed to practice rapid reinforcement and resupply of the southern European region in times of tension or war. The USS Forrestal Aircraft Carrier arrived in Rota Spain on 11 October for the last overseas port stop of the deployment.

As part of the Orange-Air, the NATO E-3A AWACS controlled, FB-111, deployed from the 19th and 20th Fight Wing (FW) stationed at Royal Air Force (RAF), Upper Heyford. In addition, F-16 Falcons stationed in Aviano, Air Force Base (AFB) Italy and F16s deployed to Incirlik, Turkey participated in the exercise along with aircraft from participating nations. The USS Forrestal Aircraft Carrier was in charge of the 6th Fleet, and served as the single major impactor on readiness in DisplayDetermination Exercise lacked the readily available aircraft parts. The long supply lines to CONUS (Continental US) and the limited availability of high priority items such as computers and main rotor blades affected the daily maintenance efforts. While the replenishment pipeline scrambled for new procurements, planned and executed an aggressive maintenance program. Skilled liaison with the host air station, functional wing, and type commander ensured all alternatives exhausted in providing in theater aircraft repair.

For this exercise, the NATO AWACS Component deployed aircraft to Trapani, Turkey, Prevessa, Greece, and Konya, Turkey. All NATO E-3A AWACS aircrews participated in the Display Determination Exercise from their three Mediterranean Forward Operating Bases (FOBs) simultaneously. Hubert and his crew deployed to Prevessa, Greece where they stayed at their normal facilities. Normally, the AWACS aircrew billeted in the second floor in an effort to ensure that their crew rest not violated when the crew is flying night sorties (missions). In the bottom floor, the maintenance personnel billeted with the front rooms normally kept open near the front of the building due to the noise level.

This Display Determination Exercise was a three prong simulated war exercising NATOs logistics capabilities, it ability to assess it operations real-time, or abilities to augment its forces during contingency operations. In the Display Determination Exercise, its Blue and Red forces play its normal offensive or defensive roles. Each trying to either get the upper hand while Blue logistics supplies arrive to its objected targets protected by Blue-Air and the Red-Air forces tried to stop the Blue Forces. As the Orange-Air, Hubert and his aircrew developed tactics to stop the Blue-Forces from achieving their objectives.

It was after one of the Display Determination Exercise missions that the crew was winding down and watching television in the common area that the US Navy Commander, our Tactical Director (TD) named Mike challenged Raymond Bell (Jimbo), the Canadian Surveillance Controller (SC) to a Weed (whiskey) drinking contest. The Tactical Director (TD) position is the same position as the Mission Crew Commander

(MCC) in the US AWACS program. The crew had just landed after a successful flight and felt good about doing a great job stopping the US Navy Forces and the rest of the Blue-Air. Unlike the US military culture, in NATO, Officers normally used first names during informal settings and used surnames in formal settings. Prior to going to the common area, the crew had dinner at the Chow Hall and then went to the FOB Bar next to the Television room for a few beers.

Hubert told both Officers that they were crazy since in a few hours the crew was going into crew rest and he did not think it was a good idea to drink up to the time that they would enter crew rest. Nevertheless, Jimbo being a Canadian would never decline a challenge, especially when a US Navy squid was the challenger. Before long, the whiskey bottle was empty and Mike went to his room for his second bottle. Again, Hubert cautioned both of the Officers in vain. Finally, there was no more 'weed' to be had, the Officers started drinking beer until crew rest started, and there was a tie. At that point, Mike went to his bedroom and Jimbo stayed in the television area. Before long, Jimbo's body went limb and before Hubert could catch it, his head hit the tile floor more than once. Since Jimbo was a tall and heavy Canadian, with the help of two Officers, Jimbo put in one of the first floor empty rooms and everything seemed well.

The next morning when the housekeepers arrived and Hubert and the crew heard the housekeepers screaming. Hubert quickly ran down stairs and found the housekeepers outside Jimbo's room. As he walked in the room, he smelled nothing but vomits so he walked outside and told the housekeepers that they should not worry because the Officer would clean his own mess. This seemed to make them happy and for now, all was well. At that point, Hubert returned into the room and woke Jimbo. Luckily, it was still four hours before show time so Jimbo had plenty of time to wake-up, clean his mess, and get ready for the exercise flight. Hubert made it clear to Jimbo it was his responsibility to clean his own mess reminding him that more than once he told him not to take the challenge.

Before going to the Chow Hall, Hubert went into the room and made sure that it was clean so the Jimbo would not be in trouble. An hour and a half later, Jimbo came into the Chow Hall. Then he saw Jimbo taste his soup and quickly get up and go into the bathroom. For the next week, Jimbo could not eat anything solid. Eventually, Jimbo could eat his soup and not get sick as long as he ate the soup with crackers. Mike not much better off physically. Then the crew went on its normal flight and both Officers accomplished their aircrew duties as expected.

The typical Display Determination mission supported from Prevessa, Greece took place took off the coast of Eastern Italy in the Adriatic Sea. Eventually, this training would prove vital during the Balkans War. Hubert's aircrew would support the F-16s Falcons aircrews from Aviano, AFB Italy and the FB-111s Aardvark aircraft deployed for Britain conducting air-to-air or medium-range interceptor and tactical strike aircraft filling the roles of strategic bomber, reconnaissance, and electronic warfare missions. At the same time, US Navy, Italian, and other participating Navy Forces participated in the exercise conducting a simulated air-to-ground surface war.

Back home in the US President George H. W. Bush had just become the new President of the US and Hubert's new Commander-in-Chief (CINC). Overall, President Bush would be a good CINC although he would soon take the US military into war in the Middle East. Unfortunately, for President Bush, he would have a hard role to follow becoming president post President Reagan who had been president for the last eight years. President Reagan had been very popular with all of the military and had made countless improvements within the military. To everyone's surprise in the military, President Bush would only be president for one term.

After the Display Determination Exercise, Hubert and his NATO AWACS crew returned to Geilenkirchen, Germany, as was the custom and met by their family in the Squadron-Two. Since everyone put their bags in the bus once everyone got off the NATO E-3A aircraft, it did not take much time to meet their families. Unlike the US Air Force, custom of going into the squadron and signing off various logs, in NATO, the custom was to go to the bus and go home. It was optional if a member wanted to go inside the squadron to drop any personal items once they arrived from a deployment. Hubert normally put his bags and flight gear in his car trunk and went home. Since he delegated important work before he deployed and he maintained communications with his deputy while deployed, he trusted his deputy to be responsible. This rule worked well for Hubert until years later when he trusted a close friend, Tony in Alaska.

Next, Hubert and his crew had to deploy to Trapani, Italy to support the Bright Star Exercise. For this exercise, NATO AWACS deployed two NATO E-3A AWACS aircraft to Trapani. Bright Star Exercise was a series of biennial combined and joint training exercises led by American and Egyptian forces in Egypt. These exercises began in 1980. They designed to strengthen ties between the American and Egyptian militaries and demonstrate and enhance the ability of the Americans to reinforce their allies in the Middle East in the event of war. These deployments usually centered at the large Cairo West Air Base (AB). Other allied nations joining Bright Star Exercises in Egypt have included the United Kingdom, France, Germany, Italy, Greece, the Netherlands, Jordan, Kuwait, and the United Arab Emirates.

While taxing, two NATO E-3A AWACS aircraft were required to fly and participate in the exercise. Hubert was in aircraft number two as the Senior Director (SD) when his NATO E-3A AWACS aircraft was on the active taxiway when all of a sudden, aircraft number one, which was in from stopped. Within NATO, the three squadrons always competed against each other. In this case, Squadron-One took a jet and crew to the exercise and did Squadron-Two. For this mission, Squadron-One was the first aircraft to take-off, followed by the Squadron-Two aircraft.

A standard procedure within the AWACS community is for the Tactical Director (TD) or the Fighter Allocator (FA) to have the Communications Systems Operator (CSO) to tie the nets, which allows the Mission Crew to hear the Flight Deck communications during take-off. It was during this phase when the Aircraft Commander (AC) in our aircraft told the AC in the NATO E-3A AWACS aircraft in front of us that his rear wheels were smoking. Within seconds of the aircraft stopping, aircraft number one's rear doors opened and the emergency slides popped with the crewmembers sliding out. About the same time, their AC was on their intercom telling them not to worry because their aircraft had just received new rear brakes and it was common for the wheels to smoke.

Unfortunately, the entire Mission Crew was outside the aircraft. In this case, NATO E-3A AWACS aircraft two went around NATO E-3A AWACS aircraft one and started the exercise until three hours later when their aircraft was ready again for flying. That NATO crew purchased a lot of free beer that evening after the exercise. They were lucky to be in Trapani where the beer was cheap until they returned to Germany and Geilenkirchen where the German prices were not cheap. It was months before the Squadron-One mission crew would live down that Trapani overreaction.

Hubert and his NATO E-3A AWACS aircraft flew the first mission, which served as the Air Traffic Control (ATC) facility in the air for the exercise. Later, the NATO E-3A AWACS aircraft conducted the typical biennial combined and joint training exercise. The role of the US logistics was to reinforce their Middle East allies at the large Cairo West AB while the simulated enemy made it difficult for the friendly arriving forces. In this scenario, the NATO E-3A AWACS mission crew received a special task to provide the thread warning to the Blue-Air and the Ground Air simultaneously. Hubert and his NATO AWACS crew returned home for a few weeks to Geilenkirchen and take a vacation to Italy with Tawny and Darlene.

This would be the first time the family would drive through Switzerland and the beautiful Alps mountains. Stopping to east their tasty cheeses and breads. Hubert would stay away from the major highways in order to see the old Italy. They would drive to the Italian Riviera near Pisa and stay at a five star hotel on the beach where Darlene would be sunburned badly. This would be a great two-week vacation where Hubert and his family would truly enjoy themselves. Like most European hotels, Hubert made sure that meals were included with the room. This did not mean that they would eat the meals in the hotel but when they were in, they were available as an option.

It was then that Hubert thought that it might be a good idea for the family to drive to Florencia since Darlene was hurting too much to go to the beach. That proved to be a bad idea since once in Florencia, Darlene was in too much pain to enjoy the beautiful churches and the beautiful city of Florencia. After a late lunch, Hubert decided to return to Pisa and their hotel and relax at their hotel until Darlene was feeling better. The following day, the family took a walk where Hubert saw Arizona silver and turquoise jewelry that he purchased for Darlene. He never thought that he would find Arizona Indian turquoise jewelry in Italy. The Leaning Tower of Pisa would be better in person than in pictures as were many other scenes in Europe. Especially when seeing the sights with family versus seeing the sights with fellow military members during another deployment somewhere else in the world.

Hubert would not be home for long before receiving another task to deploy again. For Exercise Joint Star, Hubert and his NATO AWACS aircrew deployed to Konya, Turkey to their

Forward Operating Base (FOB). From Konya, NATO AWACS would support the US Air Force F-16s Falcons deployed to Incirlik, Turkey and conducting an Operational Readiness Inspection (ORI) and US Navy F-14 Tomcats on an US Aircraft Carrier. The primary role of the F-16 assigned to Incirlik is to conduct a tactical nuclear alert mission. Turkish F-4 Phantoms were the attacking aircraft flying as the Red-Air. The exercise started initially in the Greek versus Turkey scenario with the NATO AWACS supporting the Greek Air Force.

During the initial flights, the Tactical Director (TD), a Turkish Officer directed the crew to carry the Greek tracks as hostile. Hubert quickly objected since the Greek were also NATO allies. Quickly the Surveillance Controller (SC), Hubert as the Senior Director (SD) and Flight Examiner on the aircraft, and the TD discussed the issue on net two. Eventually, the TD agreed to carry the tracks as unknown in order to not create an international issue as Hubert mentioned would occur would happen once the tracks went through the data links to both nations. In this case, Hubert's tactfulness was the right thing to do to prevent an international situation from occurring since the other Americans were planning to ignore the situation. Hubert never understood why he seemed to always to take the leadership role even though there were plenty of senior Americans in Squadron-Two and assigned to his crew. They were never willing to put their careers on the line and play it safe even when they knew that something was wrong.

On a different mission during this deployment where Hubert was controlling US Navy F-14 Tomcats, when Hubert asked the F-14 lead pilot if he wanted to conduct a data-link (dolly) attack mission. Since the Turkish Air Force was conducting jamming, this was the ideal control profile. The F-14 pilot agreed and quickly agreed with Hubert to 'follow dolly' Using the NATO E-3A AWACS data link computer, Hubert was able to direct the F-14 aircraft to the primary target by simply hooking the target and committing the target. The all that was required by the controller was entering additional instructions to the computer. Hubert was able to commit the F-14s element successfully to its target without having to say a single word on multiple missions. During this deployment, Hubert was able to train his NATO E-3A crew the Link 4C or in the TADIL-C system that he learned to use as a 407L instructor in Arizona.

Link 4C or in the TADIL-C is a fighter-to-fighter data link, which intended to complement Link 4A although the two links do not communicate directly with each other. Link 4C uses F-series messages and provides some measure of ECM resistance. Link 4C fitted to the F-14 only and the F-14 cannot communicate on Link 4A and 4C simultaneously. Up to four fighters may participate in a single Link 4C net. Later, the Joint Tactical Information Distribution Systems (JTIDS) [later called fighter-JTIDS] became more capable than the old Link 4C or in the TADIL-C role in fighter-to-fighter operations with message standards defined in STANAG 5504 while standard operating procedures laid down in ADatP-4. Decades later, JTIDS would become common in the military and even the White House would have a Data Link picture to another war zone environment real-time thanks to the lessons learned during this era.

"Wow, who is that walking in the doors," asked the French visitor. Darlene had just gone through the receiving line when he noticed her. The day prior, Darlene had gone to the base hairdresser to get her hair done and mentioned that she wanted her hair done special. "I want my hair done so those bitches will be jealous," mentioned Darlene to her hairdresser. She did not notice that General Blume's wife was sitting next to her. At the formal Receiving Line Mrs. Blume would tell Darlene that she was delighted with her comments while she was getting her hair done. Mrs. Blume mentioned to Darlene that she was one of those bitches and that she looked marvelous with a big smile. At first Darlene's face turned red because she was not sure what she said because she knew that she tended to be too honest. Hubert always blamed it on her youth since she was a strong willed person and that is what he liked best about her when he met her.

The week prior, Hubert had taken Darlene to Monchengladbach, Germany to her favorite dress shop and picked out her formal dress. Every time Hubert took Darlene to Monchengladbach to select he dress, she knew that her dress would be behind a locked window and be a one of a kind dress. Darlene's dress was a flowery black and white dress, with layers of silk that only Darlene could ware to an Air Force Ball. This year, Hubert would pick Darlene's dress for this Air Force Ball. Hubert wore his Air Force tuxedo with all his military medals. Darlene's sister Janice and her husband Bobby who was an US Army Senior Non-Commissioned Officer (SNCO) and his sister Christine also came to the Air Force Ball. Christine never attended a formal function in her life and was surprised that Hubert and Darlene wanted her to attend. During the dancing, Christine's slip fell in the middle of the dance floor as no one seemed to care since everyone was having too much fun. What was amazing, she did not miss a dance step during the waltz as she grabbed the slip as everyone laughed and kept dancing. Both made it clear that she was family and that she would be welcomed.

Once the young officers noticed that Hubert and Darlene were at the formal gathering, they knew that tonight would be a fun night. Darlene had a reputation for making everyone at ease and for wanting to have a good time at any of the formal gatherings. Except that, she had always expected formalities to finish and the party to get started. Hubert on the other hand had always been more quite, which made this couple perfect. They countered each other's personality differences. Even the British Officers asked Darlene to join them for shots. They knew that Hubert was too square and would not join. Nevertheless, Darlene on the other hand, she would join then without any problem because she wanted to have fun although she was a formal woman.

This Air Force ball was different since Darlene's sister Janice and brother-in-law Bobby had joined them. Many thought that Bobby was an admiral since he had his formal US Army tuxedo with wide white stripes that represented three years of service. By then, Bobby had served almost twenty years in the US Army. This was the first time that Darlene and Hubert had family with them at a formal function, which made it more fun for both of them. Bobby received a formal posting in Trier, Germany as the Battalion First Sargent of the M-1 Tanks throughout Europe. This would be the last Air Force Ball before departing Europe and returning to the US.

"Babe I just received a Definitely Promote to major" mentioned Hubert to Darlene. That meant that they could expect another assignment. After discussing the next career move, they decided that Tinker AFB, Oklahoma was their next permanent change of station (PCS). Hubert had avoided Tinker AFB for over ten years but thought that at this point since he had would most likely get promoted and receive an assignment to Tinker AFB would not hurt his career. The Tinker AFB political climate expected Officers to play politics and brown nose in order to receivepromotion. Hubert decided early in his career that he would receive all his promotions based on merit and not because he had a sponsor or play politics. He also decided that his wife did not have to play the political games to help his career as was common in the military culture.

His efforts earned him the Joint Service Commendation Medal awarded by General John R. Calvin, US Army, Supreme Allied Commander upon arriving at Tinker AFB, Oklahoma. For the third assignment out of four, he received a recommendation for a Meritorious Service Medal (MSM) but his timing would be bad and the MSM downgraded. Although his accomplishments warranted the MSM, each time he received a nomination for the MSM award, which was during every rank, his rank each time he was nominated for a MSM award his current rank was deemed too low until he was a Major. Therefore, Hubert lost four MSM nominations during his career in a row. Hubert was starting to believe that performance did not matter in the military for Hispanics. He had seen many non-Hispanics receive MSM that had his rank that had done little in their job and only played politics to earn the award.

"Babe how are we getting to Brussels," asked Darlene. The Contreras family was taking a military van from Geilenkirchen Air Base (AB) to the airport in Brussels, Belgium. Darlene blushed deeply as Senator Edward Kennedy, D-Massachusetts, fell over the row of chairs as he walked passed her and unable to take his eyes off her. Darlene was smartly dressed with a matching suit caring for Tawny at the Brussels airport. Although Hubert was near, Tawny wanted mamma to hold her as Kennedy's bodyguard asked Darlene whom she was. Darlene proudly said, "I'm a no body, just a mommy". Darlene then reached down and proudly picked up Tawny.

965ᵀᴴ AWACS, TINKER AFB, OK

"Where are you going this time," asked Darlene. Darlene knew that Hubert could not tell her where he was going. She also knew that he could not tell her when he might return. These trips would vary from a yearlong and with luck; the trips would only be between four and six months. Unknown to the Contreras family, Hubert like baseball player that trains all his life for the World Series or the super bowl, he was finally going use years of training in one war zone to another. It would also be the beginning of many sleepless nights. In time, he would learn to deal with the nightmares in his own way. Like many soldiers when asked about what they had seen in combat, he would talk around the subject but never tell the events that had haunted him many nights.

From 3 December 1989 to 20 May 1992, Hubert would be assigned to the 965th Airborne Warning and Control Squadron (AWACS), 552nd Air Control Wing (ACW), as a Flight Commander, as an Instructor Mission Crew Commander (IMCC), Chief of Mobility, Chief of Current Operations, and Deputy Assistant Operations Officer-Mission (ADO-M). During different periods, he would manage different groups of employees. Initially, Hubert started as an Instructor Mission Crew Commander (IMCC), then an a Flight Commander responsible for seventy-five individuals, then the Chief of Current Operations responsible for sixty employees each time gaining more responsibility in the unit. During this period, Hubert would manage over 650 personnel from twelve different specialties significantly enhancing their readiness posture.

Initially, he managed 280 mission employees until the squadron merged the maintenance personnel with the operations personnel during a test period. All tested under Hubert's oversight even though he was junior Field Grade Officer in the squadron. He would play a key role in ensuring successful accomplishments of highly visible missions in the Caribbean and South America during counterdrug operations. Hubert's consummate technical skills ensured successful accomplishments of Operations Desert Shield and Desert Storm. Hubert never dreamed during his first trip to the Middle East that he would deploy fourteen times to Iraq after this trip.

"What, you are in Mission Crew Commander (MCC) training as a Captain," asked Hubert's fellow Captains. Upon arrival to Tinker AFB, he started training in the 552nd Training Squadron where Hubert started Mission Crew Commander (MCC) training. Hubert reported to the 552nd Tactical Training Squadron (TTS) located in Tinker AFB Air Force Base (AFB), Oklahoma on 13 December 1989 as an "AWACS Student". Although he was a Captain and assigned to a Mission Crew

Commander (MCC) aircrew position that was a field grade position which was major and above position, he was allowed to start Mission Crew Commander (MCC) training since he had a definitely Promote recommendation to major.

As a Flight Commander, Hubert was responsible for seventy-five individuals from twelve specialties. The Flight Commander Responsibilities consisted mainly of supervisor duties that at times were difficult since writing annual performance reports was difficult since the only way to communicate with fellow subordinates was the mail system. One Captain worked for Hubert for two years and he never met him until both received the same assignment to Alaska during the next posting. During most of the time both were in Oklahoma, Hubert and the Captain communicated using the Air Force mail system to pass information to each other so that Hubert could write the Captain's annual performance report(s).

As the Chief of Current Operations, his management of sixty-five personnel in flight and mission scheduling, mobility, life support, exercise planning, and ground support significantly contributed to the combat readiness of the squadron with the unit able to support National Command Authority (NCA) commitments. One of the reasons that Hubert returned from Saudi Arabia during Operation Desert Shield was because of his Chief of Current Operations responsibilities. The Squadron Commander wanted him to return to Oklahoma and ensure the squadron deployed the required-Aircraft and aircrews to Saudi prior to Operation Desert Storm and still allow Hubert to return prior to the start of hostilities, which he did.

In the end, Hubert would be one of the few 965th AWACS members to support Operations Desert Shield, Desert Storm, and Desert Calm earning the Combat Stars. He received countless awards in the Squadron, Wing, and the Air Division to include Aircrew of the Year for 1990 and 1991 earning him the Meritorious Service Medal awarded by Colonel John M. Loh, General, USAF, Commander, and Air Combat Command

(ACC) that Hubert received once he arrived in Alaska. However, this would mean that most of the time assigned to Oklahoma would be on the road and little time spent with his family. Hubert would spend less than sixty days each year during the assignment to the 965th AWACS and be deployed overseas most of the days assigned to the 552nd ACW.

From 7 August 1990 to 28 September 1991, Hubert would fly crucial command, control, and surveillance missions in Europe, Iceland, and the Middle East, under hazardous conditions. His efforts earned him the Aerial Medal after flying the first twenty combat and combat support sorties (mission) over Iraq. Additional sorties would go towards an Aerial Achievement Medal that the 552[d] Air Control Wing (ACW) would fail to submit due to the heavy deployment rate that Hubert maintained during his time at Tinker AFB, Oklahoma. Repeated efforts to receive the award that should have been automatic seemed a problem for the Tinker AFB wing awards point of contact office. Brigadier General David Oakes, the 552[d] ACW Commander awarded Hubert the Aerial Medal.

Hubert had worked twice for General Oakes including his tour at Tinker AFB, Oklahoma where he was his Wing Commander. Brigadier General David Oakes was the commander of the 552[d] Air Control Wing (ACW), Air Combat Command (ACC), Tinker Air Force Base, Oklahoma. He is responsible for the worldwide operations of the E-3, EC-135, Airborne Command and Control EC-130 aircraft and the 3rd Combat Communications Group. Hubert had first met General Oaks in Europe while working as a member of the 16th Air Force staff. General Oakes retired on 31 August 1994.

After NATO AWACS, the Contreras family assigned to Tinker AFB, Oklahoma. The 552nd Air Control Wing (ACW) flies the E-3B and E-3C Sentry Airborne Warning and Control Squadron (AWACS) aircraft and is part of the Air Force's Air Combat Command Air Expeditionary Force. The 552nd ACW encompasses three groups: the 552nd Operations Group, the

552nd Maintenance Group, and the 552nd Communications Group. In the Operations Group (OG) during that period, there are seven squadrons: the 963rd Airborne Air Control Squadron (AACS), 964th AACS, 965th AACS, 966th AACS, and the 552nd Training Squadron. During the mid-1980s, the 970th AACS Reserve Wing activated and Hubert would assist this unit and the parent Reserve wing become operational.

The wing was formerly located at McClellan AFB, California, and before the delivery of the E-3B/C Airborne Warning and Control Systems (AWACS) in 1977, was the home of the RC-121C Warning Star (Connie). An RC-121C Connie is on static display near the Wing's headquarters building. Some of Hubert's coworkers had flown in the RC-121C and had been involved in creating the wings proud history. Many of the older USE-3C AWACS aircrew members were RC-121C aviators that Hubert flew with in Geilenkirchen, Germany. Over the years, Hubert Heard 'Connie' war stories of the and how they accomplished the RC-121C start-up for the NATO Component.

It was during this trip that Hubert would support a commitment to the Balkans while deployed to Tinker, Air Force Base (AFB). In 1995, NATO intervention in the civil war in Yugoslavia featured airpower in Operation Deliberate Force, which brought the Serbs to peace negotiations within a few weeks. Operation Allied Force in the Balkans in 1999 was completely airpower. No ground forces received engagement orders, however, US and NATO air forces received employment orders for the first time making this campaign a total air campaign. This would earn Hubert another few Campaign Medals while supporting this operation. The force's operational tempo was higher than it had been in the Cold War, and almost fifty percent of the active duty fighter forces continuously deployed overseas.

Since it was the holidays, Hubert would not start training until 12 February 1990. Before long, Hubert would deploy to Panama and support his first war, followed with the Counterdrug (CD)

War in Latin America, and finishing the year in Saudi Arabia flying south of Iraq as the first E-3C AWACS aircrew before the year was over. It seemed that during Hubert's career, he routinely received notification to deploy in minimal time. Only on a few occasions, did he have more than a few weeks or days to prepare his family for a long deployment. During 1990, Hubert would also deploy to Site-2 (Classified Site) three times, which at the time was still a classified location in the Middle East.

Hubert was the only Captain in a crew and Field Grade position that it made many of his peers mad since Hubert not a "Tinkerite". Hubert was an outsider since he came from the NATO AWACS Component and not the Tinker AFBAWACS Wing. However, he would insist that he start training as soon as possible since he had arrived at Tinker AFB with a guaranteed training slot. The Air Force Military Personnel Center (AFMPC) has assured him a training slot once Hubert had received a 'Definitely Promote' to Major. Brigadier General Blume the NATO Component Commander had assured AFMPC that Hubert was the NATO E-3A AWACS 'number one' Captain Selectee. Once Hubert started training, he excelled during the academic and flying phase.

Upon arriving in Oklahoma, Hubert and Darlene found a home in Choctaw, Oklahoma mainly because of the school district. There were many differences after living overseas for over ten years that Hubert, Darlene, and Tawny had to adjust once they returned to the US such as the poor education system. As it turned out, the only subject that Tawny would learn overall would be English and Math since the US curriculum was decades behind the Department of Defense (DOD) and European educational system. In Middle School, Tawny would do Excellent but stopped learning in 7th grade. If it were not for Hubert and Darlene staying on top of education, she would have dropped out of school.

"We have a new mission in Central and South America," said Lieutenant Colonel Johnston. Hubert quickly went through training and became qualified in minimal time. This meant that he would have to become Mission Ready (MR) as soon as possible. Once he arrived at the 965th Airborne Air Control Squadron (AACS), he became MR in three days versus the normal thirty to forty days. Hubert had always been aggressive in getting MR in all systems that he worked in. Hubert took an initial flight with a unit instructor and a second flight with an evaluator that qualified him as MR in minimal time. During the same time, he completed the required certification in the five worldwide regions that the E-3C AWACS deployed to meaning that he knew that regions and procedures that aircrews needed to operate in each region. In this case, since Hubert had lived in each region over the past decade, completing the certifications were easy to complete and in many cases, Hubert was able to provide the training office newer information to update their lesson plans, which the wing leadership noted.

The years would start with the wing standing up a new Counterdrug (CD) Mission only to divert to Saudi Arabia and eventually going to war. By mid-year 1990, most E-3C AWACS aircrew members had already flown their annual flight hours. Nevertheless, Hubert not surprised to hear that the Air Combat Command (ACC) had waivered the 552[d]flying hours and all aviators new hours was 'zero'. Within days, Hubert would support the Cornet Sentry Exercise, Agate Path Exercise, Combined Endeavor Exercise, Deploy back to the Middle East, return to Puerto Rico twice and support two Counterdrug (CD) deployments, and have to return before the end of the year to support the Joint Electronic Interference (JEMI) Test. By the end of the year, Hubert would return to Saudi Arabia.

Upon completing training at the 552nd TTS, Hubert assigned to the 965th Airborne Air Control Squadron (AACS). Hubert completed Mission Crew Commander (MCC) training after only 4 flights and in only six weeks including the first month of mostly academics. This only made his peers more irritated with Hubert once they heard that he was Mission Capable (MC), which meant that he was basic qualified as an E-3C AWACS aircrew. This also meant that on 11 May 1990, Hubert was officially a "Mission Crew Commander" and a G1711, which meant he was qualified as a MC USE-3C AWACS aviator in record time in the same fashion that he had excelled in NATO AWACS.

Upon arriving at the 965th AACS, Hubert's first Commander was Lieutenant Colonel Johnston who would be one of Hubert's best Commanders in the US Air Force. Lieutenant Colonel Johnston would not base his selection of what positions Hubert would fill on his rank but on his experience and the needs of the unit. Although the 965th had forty-five Field Grade Officers in the Lieutenant Colonel grade and Hubert was only a Captain who had a line number to Major, Lieutenant Colonel Johnston selected him to fill the Chief of Current Operations position. Initially, Hubert received the task just prior to starting the Counterdrug Operations in the Caribbean, Latin American, and East Pacific.

Lieutenant Colonel Carter was the Director of Operations (DO) who like Lieutenant Colonel Johnston was an E-3C AWACS pilot. The unit Vice-Commander was an Airborne Battle Manager who entered the Air Force during the Vietnam War. Finally, the 965th had two ADOs, one for the mission crew and one for the flight crew. The Assistant Director of Operations (ADO) positions were in the rank of Lieutenant Colonel or had a line number to Lieutenant Colonel. Then the unit had a Training Officer, a Stan/Eval Officer, the Recourse Manager (RM), Chief of Safety, Chief of Weapons, and the Chief of Current Operations, which was the largest division.

Within days of being qualified, Hubert found himself loaded on the crew list to support the Panama invasion as the Mission Crew Commander (MCC). The crew reported three in the morning and took off towards Panama and after airborne for five hours took fuel from a KC-135 Stratotanker. Hubert had accomplished air-to-air refueling missions many times but mostly as the Senior Director (SD). As the MCC, other than the few air-to-air refueling missions that Hubert did during the Mission Crew Commander (MCC) training, this would be the first combat related refueling mission. However, Hubert had controlled hundreds or thousands of air-to-air refueling missions as a Weapons Director (WD) or Senior Director (SD).

Once the E-3C Airborne Warning and Control Systems (AWACS) arrived southeast of Panama, Hubert found out that the US was very confused over the primary and backup Satcom radios. Hubert was lucky that he had been the Officer that was responsible for establishing the Satcom nets earlier in Panama, as the AFFOR staff so knew all the procedures. Later he knew why he added to this crew as the Mission Crew Commander (MCC) considering that he was a new aircrew member and a brand new MCC. For the next few days, the E-3C AWACS crews would serve as the airborne air traffic control (ATC) facility mainly because the Panamanian military consisted of a ground Army and a law enforcement threat. This was the first operation where the B-2 Bombers used.

This operation would also be the only time that an E-3C AWACS would conduct three air-to-air refueling missions. Normally, the E-3C only accomplishes two air-to-air refueling that allows the E-3B/C Airborne Warning and Control Systems (AWACS) and aircrew the maximum hours and crew duty. In the Panama Operation, due to aircraft problems and weather issues, Hubert's crew and aircraft was required to stay longer than normal once asked. The Aircraft Commander (AC) and Mission Crew Commander (MCC) both agreed that they were able to stay the additional time airborne to complete the mission until relieved by another E-3C AWACS aircraft. In the end, the on-station aircraft flew 26. 3 hours non-stop, which is a record. The E-3C AWACS aircraft was never an issue but the humans onboard and the lack of water or toil facilities were the main issues.

Regardless of the system or its complexity, Hubert always seemed to apply himself to learning any new system in minimal time including becoming a trainer and evaluator in months versus the normal year or years that other members took. Many times, other members assumed that he been assigned to each system that Hubert worked for years and then became irritated with Hubert once they learned that he had only been in the unit and the system for six months or less than a year. Hubert was on one of the first aircrews to deploy to Puerto Rico in support of the Air Forces new Counterdrug (CD) mission, which later called Counternarco-terrorism operations.

Upon returning from Puerto Rico, Hubert received a new task to deploy to Panama to setup a new Counterdrug (CD) Air Force Forces (AFFOR) Command in Panama. Already, Hubert had become the Wing CD expert and since Hubert was fluent in Spanish, he was the ideal candidate to deploy. While assigned to Tinker AFB Air Force Base (AFB), Oklahoma one of Hubert initial duties was to open the new AFFOR Battle Staff (BS) and E-3C AWACS communications detachment at Howard Air Base (AB), Panama.

Howard AB was the bastion of US air power in Central and South America. In its heyday, it was the center for counterdrug operations, military and humanitarian airlift, contingencies, joint-nation exercises, and search and rescue. During the CD operations, Howard would come alive once again until President Carter transferred Panama back to the Panamanians in 1999. However, to many military members, what would not make sense would be the US spending millions of tax dollars to fix all the American military buildings only to see the Panamanians let the weeds destroy what were once beautiful military installations. At least when Hubert made all his improvements, Howard AB was still years before President Carter came to office and quickly changed the military and the US in four years. Even though Carter had been a former Annapolis Naval Academy Graduate, he fooled many Americans when he nearly destroyed the US military during his watch and Hubert lived through another Democratic President.

Howard Air Base (AB) would become the future E-3C AWACS detachment but for now, it needed a communications delay detachment between the Naval Detachment located in Puerto Rico and the E-3C AWACS detachment. US Navy Ships in the Caribbean or the East Pacific, and the US and Host Nation (HN) ground radars deployed in Latin America were the initial uses of this network. Since Hubert had former US Embassy experience while assigned in Spain, was fluent in Spain, had both ground and E-3C AWACS experience, he was the ideal candidate to open the new detachment for the 24th Wing, Howard Air Base (AB) AFFOR BS.

Carved out of a jungle a five hundred yards from the Pacific Ocean, it opened in 1942. It was name after Major Charles H. Howard, who flew in Panama in the late 1920s. Howard Air Base was once the busy hub of Air Force operations in Latin America, boasting fighters, cargo planes, Tankers, airborne warning and control system planes, executive jets, and search and rescue helicopters. It was also home for a host of Army and Navy aircraft. This would remain the standard until the 1990s when the US Air Force entered the counterdrug war and started deploying to Howard Air Base (AB) Panama.

Its military people tracked drug traffickers out of South America. In addition, its cargo planes provided airlift for US Southern Command (USSOUTHCOM) contingencies, exercises, disaster relief and conducted search and rescue in the vast region. Yet, only the C-27 Spartan transports and executive jets belonged to the wing. The others were Guard and Reserve or active duty planes that rotated into the base. The Air Force deployed the E-3B/C AWACS aircrafts with the KC-135 Stratotanker to support their counterdrug operations followed with fighters to conduct interceptor duties. All operations that would no longer commence once Howard AB and Panama would close once President Jimmy Carter transferred Panama to the Panamanians control.

Hubert flew into Panama from Oklahoma City via Houston, Texas on Continental Airlines. Once Hubert arrived in Panama, on his own he took a taxi to the Marriot, downtown, which was by the waterfront and near a local steak restaurant that many of the visiting military members regularly went for diner. The following morning, Hubert took a taxi to the 24th Wing, Howard Air Base (AB) where eventually he found the building where told to report. The 24th Wing, the 24th Wing, Howard Air Base (AB), which was a logistics wing, offered an area to the Air Force above its Finance Office that included a large conference room.

The first month consisted of setting up different types of radios and control scopes to be able to see the data link pictures from different units. As the E-3B/C Airborne Warning and Control Systems (AWACS) liaison, Command, Control, Communications, and Intelligence (C3I) Officer, Hubert was responsible for making sure that all systems worked properly and for their installation. Once installed, he created the training procedures needed to communicating with all the units throughout the Latin American theater for each unit but platform. Each morning Hubert was required to conduct tests with each unit in the net on all three Satcoms.

After work, Hubert and his US Army coworker decided to go to the local steak house by the Marriot for diner. While sitting at their table in the patio just after ordering their diner they noticed four men sit next to them followed by two groups of men that sat at tables on opposite sides. Something just did not seem right then all of a sudden, Police vehicles started to surround the restaurant parking lot on both sides of the patio that had high hedges. Without warning, the men on the two tables pulled weapons and yelled to the men in the middle to raise their hands. At the same time, the Police on the outside of the restaurant fired warning shots.

At that point, the two men pulled their weapons and started shooting at the Police. All Hubert could think was to tell his Army friend to run to the bathroom, which were just five or ten feet from their table to get away from the gun battle. By then the men in the middle had pulled their weapons and a gunfire war had commenced ending when the four men in the center table were all shot. To this day, Hubert does not recall having dinner at the restaurant. Since the hotel was just a block from the hotel, after the gun battle, he believes the he and his co-worker went to the hotel and ate at their. Both officers did not bother to file an incident report since the day prior knowing that by pure luck somehow they were not hurt as bullets flew around them.

Instead, Hubert returned to work as if nothing had occurred. Creating the permanent party manning plan was also part of Hubert's responsibility once the Deployed Commander (Detco) found out the he was a prior Air Force Personnel employee. Hubert had created hundreds of work force documents when he was a Non-Commissioned Officer (NCO) and worked as a Personnel Systems Manager (PSM) and Manning Control Specialist (MCS). Hubert worked with the labor and the Military Personnel Flight personnel and created the manning document for the new permanent party, which meant the Air Force-Force (AFFOR) would become a remote assignment. Permanent party personnel for one year to eighteen months depending of individuals are by themselves of with their family's fills remote assignments.

Eventually the hundred and twenty days in Panama ended and Hubert returned to Tinker AFB only to deploy to Puerto Rico the following week. He would have deployed sooner but since Hubert had not flown in a hundred and twenty days, he needed a flight with an instructor before he could deploy again. This meant thatHubert would fly a local E-3B/C Airborne

Warning and Control Systems (AWACS) a single flight in the US prior to deploying again. Although Hubert had not been, long in the unit, his Commander, Lieutenant Colonel Johnston recommended him for Instructor Mission Crew Commander (IMCC) upgrade mainly because of his expertise, maturity, and his aggressiveness. The fact the he was still a Captain and had not been in the unit did not go well with many in the unit and at assigned at Tinker AFB much longer.

This meant that he would be able to fill additional unit tasks including staff positions. Hubert returned to Tinker AFB for two weeks long enough to get prequalified Mission Ready (MR). Due to the type of flying done in the Counterdrug (CD) Operations, most of the Mission Crew is not able to remain MR. Therefore, once the aircrew returns to Tinker AFB they have to fly local missions in order to return to MR status. In this case, Hubert had to fly a local E-3B/C AWACS mission in order to get back to MR status. Hubert would return to the 552^{d}Technical Training School (TTS) in order to become IMCC qualified. Here too, he would become instructor qualified in minimal time receiving proficiency advancement and a quick check ride.

"Daddy can you take US to see Skit Row?" asked Tawny. Skit Row was visiting Oklahoma City and giving a concert and Tawny want her daddy to take her and her school friend to see her favorite band. Hubert would first take them to dinner and then to the concert. Hubert made sure that he fought through the crowd to get his girls almost to the front of the stage. The concert hall was full of fans so Tawny asked her daddy if he would put her on his shoulders.

Before long, both girls would take turns on his shoulders so they could see 'Skit Row'. It would take Hubert over a week to get over two teens jumping and yelling their heads as they cheered at their favorite band, Skit Row. Later daddy would ask Tawny, as they were standing, "They have the prettiest blond hair, and do not you wish you had that pretty long shinny hair?" That would make Tawny so mad but later she would smile as she told momma. Especially since all her friends would be so jealous of her and her friend because they went to the concert, were able to see Skit Row, and have a clear view.

"I have to deploy to Rosy," said Hubert. Still flying as an Mission Crew Commander (MCC) or Instructor Mission Crew Commander (IMCC) which was a field grade position (Major and Lieutenant Colonel) as a Captain who was a Major select, Hubert had to support the first E-3B/C AWACS Counterdrug operations in Roosevelt Roads (Rosy) Naval Air Station, Puerto Rico. Opening a new counterdrug detachment served as an Excellent training opportunity since it was a new Air Force mission. Hubert did not realize that this mission would be a primary mission for his remaining Air Force career along with countless deployments to the Middle East. As he had done in NATO AWACS, during every flight, he made sure that he accomplished some type of training anytime that there was a slow period in flight. Now that he was the Mission Crew Commander (MCC) and in control of the crew, he was able to challenge the crew to learn as much as possible and work closely with the Flight Crew. Soon, many of the practice sessions in flight would come in handy during wartime operations in the Middle East.

Upon Hubert's return from his first deployment in Panama, Lieutenant Colonel Johnston assigned him as the Chief of Current Operations responsible for scheduling, mobility, flight operations, Operations Readiness Center (ORC), and maintenance of nine E-3B/C AWACS aircraft. He replaced one of his former bosses in NATO AWACS, Major Jackson as the Chief of Current of Operations that had just transferred to the 552ᵈ TTS. Shortly after returning from Howard Air Base (AB) Panama, Hubert asked to be part of the Airborne Warning and Control Systems (AWACS) Staff for the new Counternarcotics (CD) Detachment. Prior to any deployment, all personnel go into the training simulator and practice the typical profile that the crew will experience in that Base Theater. In this case, the crew practices three different Counterdrug profiles. Hubert served as an instructor on two of the profiles and took to Mission Crew Commander (MCC) seat on the third and final profile.

The following morning, the crew reported to the squadron at 3:00 AM in the morning. Hubert always reported half an hour early to make sure that his Operations Readiness Center (ORC) had all the required documentation ready and that the aircraft was Mission Ready (MR). A few minutes later the Aircraft Commander (AC) reported to the ORC and one-by-one the remaining forty-four aircrew, maintenance, and security personnel reported to the squadron. On this deployment, since the unit was standing up a detachment, the unit was taking its maintenance and security personnel. The idea being that a detachment would serve as a stand-alone squadron at any location. A sister squadron was deploying two E-3B/C AWACS aircraft and aircrews but the 965th AACS was the lead squadron.

Once all the crew arrived and the initial briefing conducted, the buses took the personnel to the two aircraft. Within less than an hour, all four aircraft were airborne thirty minutes apart and on their way to Roosevelt Roads (Rosy), Puerto Rico. Once the E-3B/ Airborne Warning and Control Systems (AWACS) aircraft and personnel landed at Rosy and were all bedded down throughout Rosy, the first task was to standup the E-3B/C AWACS Operations Center. The E-3B/C AWACS personnel had done this task so often that it took little time mainly because the main task required setting up the needed military and civilian telephone lines.

Both Ultra/Very High Frequencies (UHV/VHF) and Satcom radios used to communicate to any airborne E-3B/C AWACS and Tinker AFB Command Post. In normal fashion, priority given to billet a crew at the Officer's Club billeting, this served as the primary and secondary alert aircrews at Rosy. The maintenance personnel billeted on Rosy with the remaining AWACS personnel billeted off base at local hotels. Each aircrew leader received a brick tuned into the AWACS Coordination Control Center (AWACS-CCC). The AWACS-CCC under the oversight of the Deployment Commander (Detco) was responsible for scrambling the E-3B/C AWACS aircraft whenever an unknown target was found flying anywhere in Latin America, in the Caribbean, in the East Pacific, or an unknown surface target found floating in the Caribbean or the East Pacific.

After setting up the detachment in Puerto Rico, his first duty was to fly with Major Barrera since Hubert was an Instructor Mission Crew Commander (IMCC). This did not go well with Major Barrera since Hubert was still a Captain. Major Barrera had been mad when Hubert who received notice by the Deployment Commander (Detco) to fly with her on her first Counterdrug (CD) mission in Puerto Rico. She took it personally since he was only a Captain and she was a major. Since this was the first E-3B/C AWACS sortie flying in the Caribbean, Hubert made sure that Major Barrera provided a detailed pre-brief to the crew mainly because during their pre-mission preparation. Initially, she intended to give the normal Tinker AFBE-3B/C AWACSflying presentation, which Hubert told her not appropriate since this not a training mission and the crew was not flying within the US airspace.

This did not go well with Major Barrera but she complied since Hubert was the IMCC and also the Detachment E-3B/C AWACS Staff MCC, which was a position that she had applied for and denied. On the other hand, Hubert hadasks for neither position, and Lieutenant Colonel Johnston had recommended him for both positions based on his qualifications and aggressive training accomplishments since arriving at Tinker AFB. Major Barrera was one of many Officers that were mad at Hubert for she too had asked for the Chief of Current Operations Position and denied. Another officer assigned to Tinker AFB and received a line number to major but not allowed to become a Mission Crew Commander (MCC), Captain Roland had also been hostile towards Hubert was on Barrera's crew as her Senior Director (SD).

The Commander gave it to Hubert based on the ongoing critical operations that the unit was going through in the Counterdrug Operations (CD), soon the war in the Middle East, and knew that Hubert had extensive knowledge in this area. He also knew that Hubert had just returned from Europe after ten years and no other Officer in the unit knew more about Europe than he did in spite of only being a Captain. He also knew that Hubert had been an enlisted member for over six years that meant that he had more overall experience than any other Officer had in the unit, which in his view, made him indispensable. Overall, Hubert had as much time in the Air Force as he did and Lieutenant Colonel Johnson new that rank had nothing to do with maturity and experience.

Once airborne, the flight went normal with the E-3B/C Airborne Warning and Control Systems (AWACS) aircraft initially flying deep into the Caribbean. At first the E-3B/C AWACS Mission Crew worked with the Joint Interagency Task Force-South (JIATF-S),which is a US Navy detachment in the Key West and US Navy ships working in the Caribbean on High Frequency (HF) and Satcom radios. On this mission, the E-3B/C AWACS Surveillance Controller (SC) was able to establish an Ultra High Frequency (UHF) data link TADIL-A network and the normal HF. This meant that the data link quality was exceptionally better than normal due to the UHF data linknetwork.

Within minutes, the E-3B/C AWACS Surveillance Controller (SC) and his section also established multiple data links and the first US Air Force (USAF) Counterdrug (CD) Mission from Rosy started. Since the E-3B/C AWACS was within the JIATF-South UHF range, the SC maintained the TADIL-A data link with JIATF-S, the HF TADIL-A with the various US Navy ships working throughout the Caribbean,and the AFFOR/CD located at the 24th Wing, Howard Air Base (AB). TheE-3B/C AWACS Surveillance Controller (SC) is able to maintain a good working data link with all the participants using the aircraft systems simultaneously. During these mission three targets, meeting the CD criteria identified by the E-3B/C AWACSUS Navy assets intercepted them. Later, the Senior Director (SD) added control of a US Navy and US customs P-3 aircraft and allocated each aircraft to each of his Weapons Directors (WDs).

Two unknown targets later busted in the US near Texas and one unknown target busted near Southern Florida. After fourteen hours, the E-3B/C AWACS aircraft returned to Rosy and the aircrew returned to the E-3B/C AWACS rotation. Hubert on the other hand as staff had the flexibility to choose when he wanted to fly. The only E-3B/C AWACS policy was that a staff member would fly with each new crew on its first flight in-theater. This meant that the Operations Officer or Hubert as the staff Mission Crew Commander (MCC) took turns flying with each new crew once they arrived in Panama even if they had flown during past deployments. This procedure was an AWACS standard worldwide in order to promote safety of flight regardless of the level of experience of the aircrew.

Hubert's official duties included his normal Chief of Current Operations duties, which included making sure that he had four E-3B/C AWACS aircraft working jets that were fully Operational Ready (OR) or Mission Capable (MC) and able to fly 24/7. Back at Tinker AFB, Oklahoma, unlike only having the four aircraft available, a typical unit had nine E-3B/C AWACS aircraft assigned to each flying squadron. In cases when there were maintenance issues, it was Hubert's responsibilities to work with the Maintenance Officer and work out the issue to include getting the needed parts from Tinker AFB or any other location to include getting the parts through customs, regardless of the location. It was during this period that Hubert gained valuable experience in the maintenance and parts areas since the USE-3B/C AWACS aircraft are old and a maintenance challenge.

Hubert also chose to fly as the lead Mission Crew Commander (MCC) to maintain currency and his own proficiency as an aircrew. As a MCC, Hubert always challenged his crew while flying anytime they had a slow mission. In addition, Hubert always had the Senior Director (SD) run simulation for his Weapon Directors (WDs) while airborne. At the same time, Hubert would generate pop-up targets to keep both the SD and WDs alert. As an experience SD and WD, Hubert made sure that his weapons section learned as many controlling techniques as possible. While assigned to Iceland, Hubert Has also been qualified in the surveillance areas and ensured that he challenged the surveillance aircrews as well. Hubert felt that knowing how everyone did his or her job in the system that he was responsible was the best way to understand any system.

In addition, during flight, he asked that each technician teach him how to wake-up and power down his or her system in an effort to help him learn his or her crew position. Although the Mission Crew Commander (MCC) position required that he learn parts of each crew position, Hubert wanted to know more information about every crew position and he felt that by having every crew teaching him how they did their jobs that he would benefit from that knowledge. By knowing, which circuit breakers to pull or which cables were important or not, such he felt knowing such detailed crucial information was important to the MCC. This type of attitude that he would instill in his crew that would earn his crews at Tinker AFB both years the Aircrew of the Year awards from the 965th AWACS.

In flight, Hubert would always give his crew a training objective even on operational mission (sorties). He would challenge the Flight Deck aircrew by doing non-standard profiles that he learned while flying in NATO AWACS. More than once some of his crewmembers challenged him including going to the Operations Group (OG) Commander when one of his Sergeants did not like the techniques that Hubert used. For example, once Hubert asked the Pilot to depart the normal altitude of FL300 and fly down to 20,000 feet. At the time, the mission crew had a target on the radar and scope. Hubert challenged the Surveillance Controller (SC) and the Airborne Surveillance Technicians (ASTs) not to lose contact of the target.

A technique that the SC can use is change the main beam to the horizon in an effort to maintain contact with a target as the E-3B/C AWACS changes altitude or the weather changes. This also means that the ASTs have to work harder at tracking the targets. Real-time, during the decent, the target was never lost. This technique is a viable option when the E-3B/C AWACS aircraft is a target during a real-time mission. During Operations Desert Shield and Desert Storm, many of Hubert's aircrew would recall this training and appreciate that he accomplished the training in the Caribbean where their lives was not in danger.

When the mission debriefed with the Operations Group (OG) Commander after the Sergeant complaint, Hubert proved his point and this experience proved important when a MIG aircraft came after an E-3C AWACS aircraft during Operation Desert Storm and the crew had to execute an evasive maneuver. This peacetime training saved a combat aircrew of twenty-six members in wartime only because Hubert was creative and some of the crew remembered the training that they had in the Caribbean during the early days of the Counterdrug (CD) mission. Eventually, Hubert flew twenty-four Combat missions logging 346. 4 hours onboard the E-3B/C AWACS on countless combat support missions in the Middle East.

On a different mission when Hubert was flying as the Mission Crew Commander (MCC) in the Caribbean, while tracking an unknown target north bound from Cartagena and started positioning the E-3 for its primary mission. In the meantime, the crew picked up a weak Ultra High Frequency (UHF) Emergency call from a Colombian Ship that had last power and was floating on the water south of Colombia. Hubert instructed the Surveillance Controller (SC) to turn on the Maritime Radar and locate the ship, which quickly identified within a few minutes. The ship was one hundred miles west of Panama floating.

Once the ship information received from the Ship Captain after repeated calls mainly because the radio was so weak, the information relayed to the E-3C AWACS detachment to pass the US Coast Guard and requested a tow. Hubert made sure that the Ship Captain knew that the US Coast Guard was on its way to rescue them in addition with a tow. In addition, the E-3C AWACS aircraft stayed within range to ensure that it maintained communications with the surface ships in case they rescueship-required assistance.

In the meantime, the unknown target continued south on its normal path towards southern Florida. While the E-3C AWACS crew was accomplishing the rescue mission, they had tracked the unknown target as long as they could and knew that the target had taken a route towards Florida and not the USmainland. Once the rescue mission was complete, Hubert reprioritized the mission crew and redirected the E-3 on its new mission. By the time the E-3B/C AWACS crew reacquired the unknown target, the aircraft was south of the Dominica Republic. At that point, Hubert scrambled a US Customs interceptor who later confirmed that it was a viable Counterdrug (CD) target.

During the intercept, a CD target intercepted from behind so that the CD target does not see the interceptor if possible. CD aircraft can vary from citations to larger aircraft mainly because South American terrorist had an unlimited amount of funds from North American drug users. For example, one Colombian terrorist group makes five Billion dollars each year from drug users in the US and Canada. Colombian terrorist have unlimited drug monies that in 2003, the US confiscated Union of Soviet Socialist Republics (USSR) submarine purchased by the Colombian Revolutionary Armed Forces of Colombia-People's Army (FARC-EP or FARC). Once captured by the US as part of its counterdrug effort, the submarine became part of the Colombian Navy.

In this case, the aircraft intercepted was a DC-3 aircraft that is able to carry tons of illegal cocaine drugs in its cargo bays. Eventually, this unknown target transferred to the US Navy and the US Coast Guard that were able to bring the interceptor to an end game. That ended when local law enforcement north of Key West busted the aircraft pilot and the vehicle driver that met the pilot at a remote landing strip. Later in the week, Hubert and his crew read about the results of the bust in the Miami News Paper and received a formal confirmation from the JIATF-South Counterdrug (CD) Office.

In the meantime, the E-3B/C AWACS aircraft that Hubert was flying in was experiencing compressor stalls on engine three. While discussing the issue with the Deployments Commander (Detco) on Satcom, the Detco had suggested that the crew remain airborne since the E-3B/C AWACS still had three good engines. After discussing the situation with the Aircraft Commander (AC), Hubert and the AC both agreed to return-to-base (RTB). At that point, they had been airborne for over twelve hours, they had completed the main mission, and since compressor stalls was a potential emergency issue, there was no reason to remain airborne.

Hubert as the Mission Crew Commander (MCC) would take the heat once they landed from the Deployment Commander (Detco) since the AC was also a Captain. However, Hubert was the senior Captain as a Major select and as the MCC, which was a Field Grade position. While serving as the 552nd Air Control Wing (ACW) Detachment Commander (Detco) the 24th Wing, Howard Air Base (AB) Panama responsible for four E-3B/C AWACS aircraft and two KC-135 Stratotanker Aircraft. Hubert was in the process of a crew rotation with an inbound

E-3 AWACS from Tinker AFB, Oklahoma declared an inflight emergency(IFE).

The Aircraft Commander (AC) declared an inflight emergency (IFE) when the pilot's window cracked and started a decent below Flight Level 200 (FL200). At the same time, another E-3B/C AWACS aircraft was operational in the Caribbean and a third E-3B/C AWACS aircraft was operational in Latin America with a KC-135 Stratotanker conducting an air-to-air refueling. At this point, Hubert had the E-3B/C AWACS aircraft airborne and a KC-135 Stratotanker. Two of the E-3 AWACSs were still operational while one of the E-3 AWACSs and the KC-135 Stratotanker were inbound to Panama. At the same time, the weather was changing rapidly as a black wall approached Howard AB ten to twenty miles south of Panama.

Initially, the inbound E-3B/C AWACS aircraft had been on a Flight Plan under the Federal Aviation Administration (FAA) control. However, since the E-3B/C AWACS aircraft has its own mission crew and its own radar, once the window cracked, the Aircraft Commander (AC) cancelled the Flight Plan and declared Due Regard, which allows the AC to go autonomous. Once under Due Regard, the E-3B/C AWACS aircraft was able to decent to Flight Level (FL 200). According to International Civil Aviation Organization (ICAO) rules, 'Due Regard' is a call that a crew makes while flying in international airspace where they declare that they are responsible for safe separation of all traffic. Although the E-3B/C AWACS aircraft was still pressurized, the AC and Mission Crew Commander (MCC) discussed the situation with the Panama Detco (Hubert) on the Satcom and decided that flying to the 24th Wing, Howard Air Base (AB) at FL200 was the appropriate decision. The final decision always falls on the AC flying the aircraft.

The typical over land E-3B/C AWACS profile consisted of entering Latin America between Colombia and Ecuador heading due west at Flight Level 300 (FL300). Just after take-off, the E-3B/C AWACS aircraft and a US Tanker aircraft accomplished an air-to-air refueling mission where the E-3B/C AWACS aircraft filled up of JP-4 or JP-5 jet fuel normally about 65,000 pounds. Mainly because the E-3B/C AWACS aircraft is not able to fill-up to its maximum capability during takeoff because of the short runway at the 24th Wing, Howard Air Base (AB) Panama.

To make matters worse, the Howard Command Post (CP) called Hubert and declared that the Tropical Storm upgraded to a Hurricane. While the emergency E-3 AWACS was talking to the Tinker AFB CP to advise them that they had declared an Inflight Emergency (IFE), the Tinker AFB Wing Commander (Ramon-24) and their Home Station Commander (Falcon-1) decided to some up on Satcom and tried to control their E-3 AWACS that was now in our area of control (decentralized control). At that point, Hubert instructed the radio operator, to direct Ramon-24 and Falcon-1 to stay off the radio since our station their E-3 AWACS had chopped to our control and that Hubert would call them after the mission from my trailer.

In the meantime, Hubert was on the telephone talking to the Howard AB Weather Officer and had just returned from the flight line where he was supervising the tie down of the unit equipment and the aircraft. While returning to the operations, he noticed that to the east and south of Howard AB over water about two miles there was a black wall of weather coming towards to base. Upon entering the Communications room, Hubert quickly took control of the situation by first directing all aircraft to return-to-base (RTB). Next, he called the Tinker AFB Command Post, call sign Raymond-24 and directed them to stay off the Satcom Nets. He also instructed them that once this operation was over that he would call the Wing Commander and lead Squadron Commander in a telephone patch through Raymond-24.

The KC-135 Stratotanker would be the first aircraft to arrive at Howard AB well ahead of the weather mainly because the Tanker had the stronger engines and could travel at faster airspeeds. The second aircraft to land was the aircraft working over land but first the E-3C AWACS had to drop most of the fuel that it had just taken during the airborne air-to-air refueling mission. This aircraft landed using Runway 18 or from the south at Howard Air Base and was able to when the black wall of weather was less than a quarter of a mile from the base. The aircraft that was working in the Caribbean used Runway 36 and landed just as the weather was just starting to approach the base from the south.

This meant that while on the taxiway and on its way to the ramp, that the heavy rains started to hit the base. At the end of the day, the hurricane turned just south of Panama and since Howard Air Base was to the south of Panama. For a few hours, it experienced extremely heavy rains that included much destruction to many of its pine trees and some of its buildings. In the meantime, the aircraft that Hubert and the maintenance crew tied down with chains seemed to be holding. However, many of the sheet metal buildings received substantial damage.

Unlike the initial mission when the E-3B/C AWACS entered from the north and conducted autonomous counterdrug operations, by now, the US ground radars throughout Colombia, Ecuador, or Peru talking and working closely with the E-3B/C AWACS aircrews. In addition, the E-3B/C AWACS aircraft stayed clear of any civilian terminal airspace in an effort to retain safety of flight between themselves and civilian aircraft. Any unknown targets or tracks reported to the applicable host nation through the Host Nation (HN) Riders (HNR) representing each country flying on-board the E-3B/C AWACS aircraft. Hubert developed the AWACS HNR program and knew all the specifics about the program and the use of the HNRs.

Six hours after the Mission Crew Commander (MCC) declared that the E-3B/C AWACS was operational. A second Tanker aircraft returned from the 24th Wing, Howard Air Base (AB) and the E-3B/C AWACS aircraft took additional JP-5 fuel.

Normally the AWACS aircraft receives between 65,000 to 70,000 pounds of JP-5 fuel because it allows the AWACS aircraft to remain airborne for the scheduled twelve-hour on-station flight. All of these operations were under the oversight of the Mission Crew Commander (MCC) and the Aircraft Commander (AC) working as one team. The MCC is responsible for executing the mission while the AC is responsible for safety of flight.

During one deployment, Peru and Ecuador were at war and Hubert's E-3B/C AWACS directed to monitor the entire air battle covertly. The Alto-Cenepa War in 1995 called a limited war that the underdog Ecuador military would win to a superior military force Peru. Peru used the most modern and most powerful military force in Latin America and lost to a small Ecuadorian force. Peru had the more modern former Union of Soviet Socialist Republics (USSR) Mikoyan and the Gurevich MIG - French Mirage I, F-1s, and modern helicopters. Ecuador was still flying the old US A-37s, Jaguars (most modern), and old helicopters like the Boeing Ch-47 Chinook Helicopters. Yet, the Ecuador Air Force used better tactics and defeated a superior Air Force that should have easily defeated an inferior Air Force in minimal time.

The Ecuadorian leadership led to Ecuador's win in the Alto-Cenepa War. Ecuador won because they had a radar network in the war area, which gave them a tactical advantage in the combat area whereas the Peruvian radars were fifty percent in operational. The Ecuadorians keeping their Jaguars in reserves proved to be another wise decision that gave them the advantage that eventually won the Alto-Cenepa War. All under the eyes of Hubert's as the MCC reporting to the US using data link and Satcom radios who protected the sensitive information. This would be another expeditionary medal Hubert and his E-3B/C AWACS crew.

As the staff MCC, one of Hubert duties was to fly with any new crews on their first sortie (mission) as an Instructor Mission Crew Commander (IMCC). After setting up the operations area and arranging for billeting within Rosy, four E-3B/C AWACS aircraft supported 24/7 missions initially in the Caribbean. In addition to using it search radar, the E-3B/C AWACS maritime radar searched for ships that were possibly doing illegal operations. Working closely with host nations and US Navy and Coast Guard assets, the E-3B/C AWACS crews reported airborne and surface tracks intercepted and boarded. These potential aircraft and ships searched for possible transportation of illegal drugs and monies with the information provided by the US E-3B/C AWACS aircrews.

It was during one of these missions that Hubert would fly with a fellow MCC, Major Barrera who resented having a Captain Mission Crew Commander (MCC) fly with her since Hubert was still a Captain. Later, as a Lieutenant Colonel, she would have a negative impact on an assignment when she was the Branch Chief for Airborne Battle Managers (ABMs) assignments at the Air Force Personnel Center (AFPC). It was the Deployments Commanders' (Detco) policy that as the deployed Mission Crew Commander (MCC) that he fly with all new crews.

The Deployment Commander (Detco) who was a Lieutenant Colonel and fellow Mission Crew Commander (MCC) and we took turns flying with any new crews. Another duty of the staff Mission Crew Commander (MCC) was to serve as Duty Not Involving/Including Flying (DNIF) back up for any MCCs who could not fly. Occasionally flying as the primary crew Mission Crew Commander (MCC) occurred, which was something that Hubert truly enjoyed. During this period, it seemed that most of his flying consisted of flying as an instructor, which meant sharing the MCC duties and receiving little primary mission time as an MCC. When one flies as an Instructor Mission Crew Commander (IMCC), one does not get to sit in the MCC seat in your primary crew duty position.

These deployments were three weeks at Rosy and one week back home at Tinker AFB. Since Hubert was a new Mission

Crew Commander (MCC) in the squadron, Hubert deployed each month from May through June 1999 and scheduled to return in August 1999. On the first sortie (mission) over land, Hubert Commander selected Hubert crew to fly the first mission over land in support of the Counterdrug (CD) mission. For the first time, a USE-3B/C AWACS aircraft would over fly land by flying in Colombia. The mission profile called that our aircraft meet a KC-135 Stratotanker and take 60,000 to 70,000 pounds of full before flying inside Colombia. These missions were communications out procedures and initially flew under the Tanker taking fuel when both aircraft flew over land. After our aircraft was full of fuel, the Tanker came off to the right and the E-3B/C AWACS continued flying north. Normally after a refueling, the Tanker is the first aircraft to climb and since the E-3B/C AWACS pilot has a visual on the KC-135 Stratotanker, the E-3B/C AWACS aircraft is the second aircraft to climb post-refueling.

This first mission was quiet with all the airborne tracks detected being data linked to US control facilities in Colombia and back in Puerto Rico. Eventually, the level of support of the Counterdrug (CD) mission varied depending of E-3B/C AWACS availability. Other operational theaters such as the Middle East would lower the ability of the E-3B/C AWACS Wing to support this important mission. It was in early August while Hubert's crew was on alert to return to Rosy that his crew received orders to divert to support Operation Desert Shield when Iraq was unprovoked and attacked Kuwait. The only difference was that normally where he is unable to tell his family where he is going to deploy to with his AWACS crew. This time all he had to do was turn on the television and no one had to guess where the US military would soon be fighting a war. In normal fashion, the US Navy and the US AWACS Force are the leading edge of America's National Power.

For the previous two-months, Hubert haddeployed three weeks out of every month until August 1999. Hubert crew scheduled to return to Roosevelt Roads, Puerto Rico when put on alert for a possible Southwest Asia deployment. Upon seeing in the news that Iraq had attacked Kuwait, it did not take much to know why our crew was on alert to deploy along with three other crews. Two aircrews had been ready to redeploy to Puerto Rico. What was clear about the upcoming operation was that everything associated with it was the result of controlled confusion. As the Mission Crew Commander (MCC), it was Hubert responsibility to keep Hubert crew ready and prepared for deployment. Nevertheless, what each aircrew member did not realize that like them, other than waiting for a call to deploy, they knew as much as Hubert did about the operation.

This operation started when the E-3B/C AWACS aircrew received the call to deploy. As was normal, Hubert contacted three other individuals on the alert roster that we had prepared before going to crew rest. Then these three individuals call the following person on the roster until they called Hubert to advise him that all members alerted. Now the entire aircrew had an hour and a half to report at the squadron with bags ready to deploy. All accomplished using the telephone or the new cell phone that some of the crew had that was still new technology. Hubert did not have one of the new large cell phones that looked like a military brick since he had just returned from Germany.

Not many E-3B/C AWACS aircrew members had cell phones since they were still expensive and only available for use in the US but not in the military. Hubert normally purchased a calling card that he kept thousands of minutes on the card so that he could call Darlene and Tawny from anywhere overseas. Usually, the minutes did not last long depending from where one called overseas. Especially in the Middle East where the calling card minutes are used much faster than many areas on the world, which meant the thousands of minutes that Hubert, had saved would not last for long. It still did not matter to Hubert since he had purchased more than one card and over the months, he kept purchasing minutes on both cards anytime he had extra monies knowing that eventually he would use the telephone calling cards.

In the meantime, Hubert returned and had to work some issues as part of his squadron duties. In October 1995, the first E-3B/C AWACS aircraft (tail number 80-0137) received the Block 30/35 upgrade rolled out at Tinker AFB Air Force Base. The Block 30/35 comprised the single largest upgrade to the E-3B/C AWACS aircraft ever accomplished. Block 30/35 affected four major subsystems aboard the E-3B/C AWACS aircraft including integration of Joint Tactical Information Distribution Systems (JTIDS), Global Position System, Electronic Support Measures System, and Data Analysis Program Group. Since the 965th E-3B/C AWACS was the lead squadron for the Block 30/35 upgrade program, this meant the Hubert and his staff would be busy no matter where he was deployed to.

During the spring of 1999, the wing began to see the results of the Radar System Improvement Program (RSIP); the first E-3B/C AWACSE-3B/C AWACS aircraft to go through RSIP rolled out of the hangar. RSIP is a joint US/NATO development program involving a major hardware and software intensive modification to the existing radar system. Installation of RSIP enhances the operational capability of the E-3 radar electronic counter-countermeasures, and dramatically improves system reliability, maintainability, and availability. He would have to work extra hours on the telephone or on email when not at home.

Upon entering the squadron, Hubert was first surprised by the level of confusion within the unit. Initially it seemed that everyone was running around like chickens with their heads cut off. As Hubert spoke the Flight Operations Officer, the lead mission planner mentioned that the wing had special mission planners who would accomplish the crew Mission Planning (MP). He also mentioned that since there were too many Distinguished Visitors (DVs), that a MP Cell (MPC) would accomplish the Mission Planning for our crew. Since this MP process had been a normal expectation in the Counterdrug (CD) missions, Hubert asked his crew to report to the main planning conference room using the PA (Public Address) System.

At that point, Hubert put his crew on crew rest. Once everyone signed into the roster as they entered the conference room and took a seat, Hubert, the Aircraft Commander (AC), and the Senior Non-Commissioned Officer (SNCO) all went to the front of the room. At that point, each went over their pre-deployment slides followed by the specialized briefings. Then the crew was put on a 24/7 alert status and signed the alert roster. This meant that each member tied to a telephone or to his or her homes or both. The following morning, Raymond-24 (Tinker AFB Command Post) called Hubert and advised him that he and his crew were scrambled and to report to the squadron with bags.

The crew all reported the following morning in less than thirty minutes from the time Hubert started the recall. No one knew how long they would be deploy for or when they would return home. Families were used to this type of deployments. This was a typical deployment for AWACS aircrew members. While the AWACS aircrews that were always on the road or deployed and never at home with their families doing the mission of the nation. Although all the indicators were there such as the highest alcoholism rates, the highest family abuse rates, etc. , AWACS leaders chose to ignore these symptoms. On the other hand, each time Hubert identified many of these issues, squadron and wing leaders labeled him as a troublemaker.

Over the years, the AWACS leadership continued to disregard the needs of its aircrews that eventually led to the decline of the Wing Training Standards that led to the rebuild of the AWACS Wing. Even the shoot-down of a helicopter and the loss of an E-3B/C AWACS aircraft received no attention by the E-3 AWACS leadership that only priority seemed to be their nextpromotion. Even after decades when AWACS aircrews received the lowestpromotion rates in the US Air Force except the Senior Officers. This in stipe of being the first warfighters involved in every major war in recent US military history along with the US Navy Aircraft Carrier Forces. The main difference, the US Navy took care of promoting its Carrier Force warfighters whereas the US Air Force did not.

"Darlene what should we do? Our husband's pay was just decreased because he is deployed to Saudi," said the women from Hubert's flight. Hubert was the Fox Flight Commander and sixty-five percent of his flight was enlisted members. When the crews deployed, the finance office stopped their rations allowance. In many cases it was only about $150 dollars, for enlisted families it meant making it paycheck to pay check or not having enough money for groceries. Darlene started making potluck dinners that she would take for families in need. Before leaving home, the hardest thing that he had ever done to this point of his life was giving his wife and daughter a kiss, hug, and saying goodbye.

It seemed that over the years, that it did not matter where Darlene met husbands or wives, they would always stop her for help. Regardless if the individuals asking for assistance came from the enlisted of Officer Ranks, they trusted Darlene and knew that she would go to Hubert and get them the help they need for themselves or their families. They would also tell Darlene that even though Hubert was a 'hard ass,' he was the best boss and best Officer that they had ever worked for in their military careers. Many times, this feeling by unit members would cause Hubert problems with the squadron members that most had loyalty to Hubert versus the unit senior leaders. However, Hubert did not let the issues with the Senior Officers interfere helping unit members or their families.

Finally, it was time to continue processing for the deployment. When the crew arrived at the squadron, there was a truck where each individual dropped off their bags with our personal items and flying equipment. All three of US had gone through this routine many times but this time we each knew that it would be a major war. Cable News Network (CNN) was reporting a war from afar but we were going to the real thing and for most of US eventually the E-3B/C AWACS aircrews would all be combat veterans. A title that Hubert is sure none of US wanted but was necessary and in the end, they were airmen.

Once Hubert's crew reported into the squadron and signed in, there was no time for thinking about anything except getting ready to launch on time. In spite of the confusion by the other squadron members who had done dozens of Mission Planning (MP) tasks, the crew started our mission briefs. This briefing was as if any other mission-planning brief except the final destination was Riyadh, Saudi Arabia. Once the general briefings were complete, the crew broke up and the specialized briefings started. This allowed the Flight Engineer and the technicians to go to the aircraft and start aircraft pre-flight. At the same time, two Air Surveillance Technicians (ASTs) went to the Chow Hall to start preparing the meals for deployment and making sure that the coffee and water jugs would be ready once the bus went to the base operations for the weather briefing.

As the specialized briefings continued, this allowed all the administrative issues to be completed and within the allotted time, all the crewmembers met at the scheduled time. Next, the bus took the crew to the base operations building where half of the crew went into the base weather shop and the remaining crewmembers went into Sally Ann's for breakfast. Sally Ann's had been a Tinker AFB Flight Line favorite place to eat especially if you like a greasy burger with fries. As the pilots, the MCC, and the Weapons Controller (WCs) given the local, US, European, and Middle East weather, the remaining crewmembers started their early meal.

Hubert knew that once the E-3 AWACS is airborne that the Communications Systems Operators (CSO) would have to get weather updates but for now, this weather update from the

Tinker AFB Weather Shop would have to do. Especially since this trip would start in Oklahoma and land in Saudi Arabia. Hubert not sure how many hours it would take but scheduled to take around eighteen hours with two KC-135 Stratotanker air-to-air refueling missions conducted in-route for each E-3B/C AWACS aircraft. For this deployment, initially four E-3B/C Airborne Warning and Control System (AWACS) Aircraft deployed to Saudi Arabia.

There were forty aircrew seats in each aircraft, which meant that one hundred and twenty individuals would be on the first rotation. While the two aircraft were on the taxiway, the aircraft had to stop on final and drop a member because the total aircrew count was one hundred and twenty one. Hubert's aircrew was from the 965th Airborne Air Control Squadron (AACS) and went down the taxiway as the second aircraft. Somehow, during Mission Planning (MP), an extra aircrew member received orders to deploy by mistake.

Initially, for some unknown reason, the aircraft came to a stop and the Aircraft Commander (AC) said that the flight engineer (FE) had just reconfirmed a body count and we had forty-one aircrew members on board the aircraft. After the AC and Hubert as the Mission Crew Commander (MCC) discussed the options with Falcon-1, the crew decided that a pilot not needed since the rest of the mission aircrew members were the minimum we could accomplish for augmented missions such as this one. An augmented sortie (mission) calls for one extra pilot and an extra navigator. If the E-3B/C AWACS Wing had more Flight Engineers, it would load and extra FE as well.

Normally, Hubert would take an extra FE but the wing did not have enough FE's qualified. Falcon-1, is the Squadron Commander who helped decide who the unit would deploy with just prior off. One would think that the best Air Force in the world would be better prepared to go to war but this is an indication of the havoc that the E-3B/C AWACS Wing and warfighters go through initially when they go to war when they are not prepared. It is common for the AC and the Mission Crew Commander (MCC) to call the Squadron Commander (or Detco) or the Squadron Operations Officer (Falcon-2) in the absence of the Commander to discuss options whenever they are having problems anytime they are airborne on Satcom radios.

This procedure is followed anywhere worldwide. Another communications method used in the US is by using an Ultra High Frequency (UHF) telephone patch from the E-3B/C AWACS aircraft to the E-3B/C AWACS Squadron and communicating to Falcon-1 or Falcon-2. The E-3B/C AWACS Mission Crew member is able to have the Communication Operator role-in up to four radios in his or her console. The E-3B/C AWACS Flight Crew is able to have the Communications Systems Operator (CSO) role in a radio into one of their communication port stations. This allows the mission crew to hear all of the flight crew communications in the cockpit. The Mission Crew Commander (MCC) calls this procedure as 'tying the nets'.

The systems wake-up went as expected and we proceeded to our first mission objective, which was to take on fuel east of Maine. Since the four E-3s were spaced by thirty minutes, we knew that we had to go on the KC-135 Stratotanker aircraft and accomplish our first refueling mission. All four E-3s took on 65,000 pound of JP-5 fuel. Then we proceeded east over the Atlantic Ocean. Our next refueling mission would be in the Gibraltar straits. As both E-3B/C AWACS aircraft traveled over the ocean for practice, Hubert went out on Ultra/Very High Frequency (UHF/VHF) radio and let the airliners know that if they wanted traffic advisory calls that we were available willing.

Throughout the night, Hubert and his Weapons Directors (WDs) spoke with airline pilots who gladly received flight follow service from the 'friendly any face'. The 'Any face', code word is used to represent the AWACS platform. As the MCC, Hubert had always been aggressive in training Hubert crews.

Providing air traffic advisory service was not a mission that the E-3B/C AWACS did on training flights. However, in Hubert view, Hubert weapon's controllers could get some practice. We had already done hours of simulation training with the E-3s sim-over-live capability. With experience sim-drivers, the sim-over-live capability seemed as good as any live mission data. Before we knew it, we had traveled across the Atlantic Ocean and had arrived at the Gibraltar straits for our second air-to-air refueling.

This meant that we were on our last flying leg to Riyadh. The last time Hubert had seen air-to-air refueling missions in the Gibraltar straits was when Hubert assigned at Torrejon Air Base (AB) in Spain. Knowing all the procedures and frequencies made the Mission Planning(MP) easy and the air-to-air refueling execution executed well. As we entered flew north of the Red Sea, we had made contact with the air traffic control (ATC) controllers and were cleared hot so we could continue our flight to Riyadh. A few hours later, we landed Riyadh. At this point, we had flown 17. 3 hours but we knew that our day would not end. Just as we had left confusion at Tinker AFB Air Force Base in Oklahoma, we arrived to confusion.

Except Hubert knew that in Riyadh, we had an American E-3B/C AWACS detachment that he could use in the Mission Planning(MP) process to assist him. Initially our crew went to the Marriot, Riyadh and stayed there for two days. When we landed Hubert sawMajor Kenny Minor who had been one of Hubert first bosses as a second lieutenant was in the Saudi Arabian Mission Training Mission, which was established when Saudi Arabia purchase a Royal Saudi Air Force (RSAF) E-3B/C AWACS aircraft. Hubertsaw Kenny and informally started getting local flying information. We went into a secured area and he showed Hubert their mission kits, which contained all the local procedures needed for Mission Planning.

Shortly after meeting with Kenny and his staff, we departed to the Hotel Marriott where our crew stayed for the next two days. Initially all the crews had to stay at hotels that had rooms available. The only restriction for billeting was that each crew would be at the same hotel if possible. Other than a short nap, most of the crew slept little during these two days since the crew was either Mission Planning(MP) or flying. Hubert did not realize that the seating plan, the communications plan, and many other procedures, and tactics that he would create his crew during this phase would become the AWACS Combat Crew Standard.

"Guys, Major Johnson is taking over duties as the crew Mission Crew Commander," said Hubert to his crew. When we departed Oklahoma, Hubert's Commander had already told him that his crew would be the first crew to fly once we arrived in Riyadh. Expecting to allow to mission plan as soon as possible, Hubert spoke with Hubert Commander asking him our show time for Mission Planning (MP). He said that the Flight Operations center should have the show times. The routine for arriving aircrews called for crews arriving at the Riyadh Air Force installation, to go into the mission briefing room where they were given weather and intelligence briefings. However, what was missing was any mission data. Having talked to Kenny the day before, Hubert knew they had mission cases that had the local flying data used during the Mission Planning process.

Because our crew did not mission plan and the Mission Planning data not given to our crew during the Mission Planning briefings, Hubert asked Kenny if we could borrow their mission flying kits. There were two boxes with one containing the data needed by the flight deck and one for the mission crew. As we proceeded to our aircraft, Hubert directed his Surveillance Control (SC) Officer and Senior Director (SD) to open the mission kits and review the flight books as best as they could. At the same time, he directed the rest of the crew to review sections of the books and try to get smart as quick as possible.

They followed Hubert directions and Hubert started creating a mission communications sheet (communications-sheet) so that we could accomplish our mission. The communications-sheet was the primary execution tool for any Command and Control (C2) mission. However, we still needed the air tasking order (ATO) which would tell US what American and RSAF aircraft scheduled to flying during the first Operation Desert Shield mission. In weeks that followed, the crew received the name change for the contingency operation. Up to that point, the crews had heard two different names for the ongoing operation.

The Royal Saudi Air Force (RSAF) established in 1950 during the reign of Abd al Aziz. Its early air operations had been under control of the Army. In its initial years, chiefly the British, who provided aircraft, advisers, helped train Saudi pilots, and maintenance personnel in the kingdom and in Britain, influenced the Saudi air force. The US influence, emanating from the air base at Dhahran leased by the United States from 1952 to 1962, was also pivotal to the early development of the Saudi Air Force. Some US aircraft transferred to the RSAF from units operating at Dhahran and the United States Military Training Mission at Dhahran trained Saudi pilots and maintenance personnel.

Saudi Arabia's E-3B/C AWACS fleet is part of the Peace Sentinel program that began in 1981. It included the five E-3B/C AWACS aircraft and eight KE-3 refueling Tanker aircraft, along with spare parts, trainers, and support equipment. The first Saudi E-3s delivered in June 1986, with deliveries of the remaining E-3s and Tankers completed by September 1987 (RSAF AWACS). Hubert thought to himself how lucky we were to have local American E-3A AWACS unit with trainers that he could talk about his upcomingCommand and Control (C2)flight data. Someone like Kenny that Hubert worked with in Arizona that he trusted as a friend and former supervisor.

The advantage that Hubert had was that the previous year Hubert assigned to NATO E-3A AWACS and had Hubert flight kits with some of the data we needed. Kenny's mission kits had the remainder of the information we needed. As we started Mission Planning(MP) as we started to taxi down to the end of the main runway, suddenly our aircraft came to a complete stop. As our four Boeing 707 engines were burning fuel just short of the main runway, about ten minutes later maintenance Sargent came up the aircraft lower lobe, which contained many of the aircraft mission systems. The Sargent gave Hubert the ATO and passed on a few notes that applied to the first Operation Desert Shield contingency sortie (mission). Once we confirmed that the soldier was off our aircraft, we became airborne.

Once we landed, we returned to the Riyadh RSAF Mission Planning room and started debriefing the E-3B/C AWACS Staff. We knew that sixteen hours from the time we landed that we had a show time for the following mission. The mission debrief lasted over two and a half hours and the staff advised US that we would be changing hotels. In order to have all the crew in one hotel, all the crews received hotel rooms at the Hotel Al Yumama in downtown Riyadh. Since the E-3B/C AWACS aircrews were throughout Riyadh, this would take a few days to accomplish.

Many portions of the Hotel Al Yumama closed and many rooms in the hotel were not in livable conditions. In some cases, the rooms had an inch of sand on the floors and although there was a pool, not maintained. According to regulations, the E-3B/C AWACS aircrew rotation fly's three sorties (missions) in a row and then the crew receive twenty-four hours to crew rest. Headquarters Tactical Air Command (TAC) had already waved the sixteen hours flying time minimum requirement so that the Aircraft Commander (AC) and mission crew Commander (MCC) normally tried to stay within the sixteen-hour criteria. However, at times when our replacement E-3B/C

AWACS had maintenance delays or had radar problems, the on-station aircraft stayed airborne. In addition, the aircrew that was in crew rest normally augmented the day staff once members received given eight hours of sleep.

In between flights, it was common for aircrew members to play harts in the common areas. It was a way that members would relax instead of seeing television. A benefit to living in the Hotel Al Yumama was that the aircrews were able to order snacks from the hotel and sign for them in addition to the regular meals held at the regular times. Every day, the deployed staff would hold staff meetings where they would report the latest intelligence information. However, it took over thirty days for the US to move the satellites in order to receive any real-time information. During the time, the E-3B/C AWACS and the Rivet Joint (RJ), RC-135 data link was the only intelligence information that the national authorities received.

The RJ or the RC-135 is a family of large reconnaissance aircraft used by the USAF to support theater and national level intelligence consumers with near real-time on-scene collection, analysis and dissemination capabilities. Based on the C-135 Stratolifter airframe, various types of RC-135s have been in service since 1961. Many variants modifications numerous times, resulted in a large variety of designations, configurations, and program names. The aircraft is an extensively modified C-135 with onboard sensors, which enable the crew to detect, identify, and geolocate signals throughout the electromagnetic spectrum. The crew can then forward information in a variety of formats to a wide range of consumers via the onboard secure communications suite.

In cases when aircraft diverted to Dhahran when there was landing restrictions in Riyadh, this flight not counted as one of the three missions flown in a row. The crew still conducted a mission debrief and the AC and Mission Crew Commander (MCC) called E-3B/C AWACS operations to give them an informal telephone debrief using the appropriated aircrew checklist. Because the sortie flown the following day normally was a few flight hours from Riyadh, so the mission crew technically could crew rest on the aircraft. According to the flying instructions, aircrew members receive eight hours of uninterrupted sleep within a twelve-hour period.

While coming across the Atlantic Ocean, Lieutenant Colonel Johnson, Hubert's Commander had mentioned to Hubert that his crew would be flying the first E-3B/C AWACS mission once the US contingent arrived in Riyadh. Hubert passed on to his crew to try to get as much rest as possible. Although everyone was already sleeping on the floor or in their seats, with minimum crew rest, the crew was ready to fly once they arrived in Riyadh. Hubert made sure his crew knew that they would be the first aircrew to fly once they landed. He made sure that everyone tried to get as much sleep as possible during the 17. 3 hours flight from Oklahoma to Saudi Arabia. Especially after having to control to air-to-air KC-135 Stratotanker refueling, this meant that he had to stay alert and could not get any crew rest.

"Brian, you're the bus driver," mentioned the crew Senior NCO. The Unit Commander had decided that the soldier that had the least rank would serve as the bus driver for each crew. Airman First Class (A1C) Brian Van Leer would be the bus drive for Hubert's crew. A1C Van Leer had never driven a bus and on his first day driving the bus, he ran into a post as he entered the runway. Hubert made it clear to A1C Van Leer, that he not responsible for any damage since he did not receive any training. A1C Van Leerwould be the crew driver for months in addition to serving as an Airborne Surveillance Technician (AST) onboard the E-3B/C AWACS aircraft.

It was at the Hotel Al Yumama that the deployed aircrew and maintenance staff had a chance to talk to the local employees or other hotel guests about the ongoing operation. Kuwait refugees who escaped from Kuwait and staying in our hotel were telling our aircrew firsthand what had happened in Kuwait. It was difficult to understand how humans could be so cruel to their fellow citizens what seems related to religious beliefs. The refugees staying in the hotel spoke of the Iraqi rapes and other events and the E-3B/C AWACS aircrew seemed more focused in wanting to accomplish the given mission better.

"Do you want to play another hand of harts," asked Raymond. He had been one of the original groups that arrived in Riyadh in early August. In 1990, fellow Arab Gulf states refused to endorse Iraqi leader Saddam Hussein's plan to cut production and raise the price of oil, leaving him frustrated and paranoid. Iraq had incurred a mountain of debt during its war with Iran that had lasted for most of the previous decade, and the Iraqi President felt that his Arab brothers were conspiring against him by refusing to raise oil prices. Therefore, after weeks of massing troops along the Iraq-Kuwait border and accusing Kuwait of various crimes, Hussein sent seven divisions of the Iraqi Army into Kuwait in the early morning hours of 2 August 1990.

In 1969, Saddam Hussein came to power in Iraq. In early January 1990, Saddam Hussein sent troops into his neighbor, Kuwait in a dispute. The United Nations (UN) stood against him, giving Iraq unit 15 January 1991 to withdraw and avoid military conflict. In the meantime, on 1 August, Iraq had pulled out of talks with Kuwait on Iraqi grievances over land, money, and oil in their view giving Iraq justification to attack Kuwait on 2 August 1990. On August 3, Kuwait forces mount a futile final resistance. Iraqi troops push to within a few miles of the Saudi Arabian border.

On 4 August, Iraq announces a new military government for the Iraqi-occupied Kuwait. European Community imposes a trade embargo on Iraq. On 6 August, UN Security Council orders worldwide embargo on trade with Iraq. On 7 August, President Bush orders deployment of US combat troops and warplanes to Saudi Arabia. On 8 August, Iraq declares Kuwait is part of Iraq. Due to the time change, four US AWACS aircraft fly non-stop for Tinker Air Force Base (AFB), Oklahoma after refueling twice and land in Riyadh, Saudi Arabia. Hubert's crew receives orders to fly the first mission once it lands after flying 17. 3 hours from Oklahoma.

During Hubert's first E-3 AWACS flight, that was the first US AWACS mission (sortie) in country. The best way to reflect on what occurred was that the crew received little preparation to fly in a new theater. Luckily, E-3B/C AWACS members receive normal training in each theater prior to deployment and it turned out that this was the only training that these initial aircrews received that replaced real-world flying experiences. Although Hubertas the Mission Crew Commander (MCC) received advice, each time he asked the staff advised him that they would accomplish the Mission Planning (MP). Instead, the MP received no emphasis and not done. Instead, upon reporting, the crew received the normal weather and take-off information.

This group had deployed to Saudi with four E-3B/C AWACS aircraft. When the crew showed up for the first mission, the crew had to wait for the Air Tasking Order (ATO) at the end of the runway until a young airman brought this ATO document through the front wheel door of the aircraft and the aircraft became airborne. The ATO had arrived late from Dhahran, Saudi Arabia and without this document, Hubert and his weapons controllers would not have the list of aircraft flying during this mission in addition to the classified details. Normally, during Mission Planning, Hubert would direct the Senior Direct (SD) and his Weapons Teams to break down the ATO and list the various mission by time, call sign, and other mission details required. In this case, Hubert as the Mission Crew Commander (MCC) directed his SD to have his Weapons Teams conduct that task while going to the first tanker, which was not optimum for the first mission in theater. However, this was not the first time that Hubert reacted to a real-timemission where something had gone wrong operational wise within the AWACS community.

Lieutenant Colonel Farrel, the squadron Vice Commander flew with Hubert as the second Mission Crew Commander (MCC) under the premise that he would serve as an instructor. Hubert'sE-3 AWACSaircraft air aborted the first aircraft when they experience smoke in the lower lobe. Then they air E-3 AWACS aborted a second E-3 AWACS aircraft when they got behind the airborne KC-135 Stratotanker, refueled and the radar would not transfer post refueling returning to Riyadh to change aircraft. Finally, the fourth E-3 AWACS aircraft available got airborne, went to theKC-135 Stratotanker and refueled and finally had a mission capable aircraft and went on station.

After flying 14. 7 hours, the relieve E-3 AWACS aircrew was not able to go on-station when their aircraft mission systems would not wake-up. Hubert stayed on-station to the last minute by accomplishing an emergency power down. Since the crew had not properly mission planned Hubert's communications plan would serve them well. Iraqi fighter aircraft were airborne throughout southern Iraq and Kuwaiti airspace and Hubert only had four US F-15s that were on Combat Air Patrol (CAP) missions. Hubert decided to direct the four F-15s fly as two sets of two F-15s in order to give his E-3B/C AWACS and RJ conducting intelligence gathering more protection. During this mission, a Saudi F-5 aircraft had entered Iraqi airspace by mistake and when he entered the E-3B/C AWACS radar coverage, this aircraft not squawking any modes or codes, which was the primary identification method.

To make matters worse, the F-5 Eagle was nose-on to the E-3B/C AWACS and flying supersonic. Nose-on means the aircraft nose, pointed directly in front of the other aircraft, or is pointed nose-to-nose. Hubert's training quickly kicked in and he directed an engagement of four F-14 Tomcats running two sets of F-14 Tomcat two-ship fighters on a pincer maneuver.

A few minutes earlier, the E-3B/C AWACS was controlling four USF-15 Eagles but had just sent the aircraft to the KC-135 Stratotanker. In a pincer, the target positions between the target and the friendly fighters hook the target in the middle. Once the Saudi F-5s started getting raw on his aircraft warning systems, he quickly started squawking friendly modes and codes and went on the Ultra/Very High Frequency (UHF/VHF) guard radio advising the E-3 AWACSaircrews that he was friendly.

After a few weeks in Saudi Arabia, Hubert received a special request to Mission Plan (MP) for a special mission in the Red Sea to provide relief for the US Navy currently Task Force. Again, like flying the first E-3 AWACS flight in Operation Desert Shield, he was surprised with so many Lieutenant Colonels deployed in Riyadh with him he expected that one of them would have received this task instead of him based on rank and experience. He took his crew to the RSAF building, conducted the typical MP, returned to the hotel, and put his aircrew into crew rest for their flight. The drive from the RSAF building to the Hotel Al Yumama in downtown Riyadh was over thirty minutes depending of the traffic.

The following morning at three in the morning, the crew reported to the RSAF building for their flight and their initial pre-flight briefing. By this time, the AWACS detachment had been in Riyadh for over a month and in addition to the weather and the intelligence briefings, nothing had changed to their morning MP slides. This meant that Hubert would conduct a maritime mission with the US Navy without their crypto, which would be extremely difficult due to their operational security (OPSEC) procedures once they are operational. The only thought that went through Hubert's mind was that the admiral knew that an US AWACS was supposed to provide them some relief.

Once everyone had signed in and read the aircrew read file, Hubert and the Aircraft Commander conducted the initial mission briefing. While the crew conducted their specialized briefings, Airman First Class (A1C) BrianVan Leertook the technicians and the Flight Engineer to their AWACS aircraft to prepare the E-3 for takeoff. Approximately twenty minutes later, A1C Brian Van leer returned and picked up the remainder of the crew and took them to the AWACS aircraft. Once everyone loaded their bags on the aircraft, Hubert conducted roll call and thee E-3 took off for the tanker to take on 65,000 pounds of fuel before continuing to the Red Sea and the unknown.

Hubert was glad that once airborne that this time their E-3 AWACS aircraft did not give them maintenance problems. Once taking the required fuel, they continued due west and flew to the Red Sea under control of the Saudi Arabian Air Traffic Control (ATC). Just prior to entering the Red Sea, Hubert declared "Due Regard" and went operational, which meant that he was under his own control and was responsible for his own separation from all civilian and military air traffic. Well before entering the Red Sea, Hubert and his US E-3 AWACS aircrew already had their system operational and had their data link and radar operational. Unfortunately, Hubert and his crew were not able to talk to the US Navy since they did not have any of the crypto and the US Navy only talks on secure NETs when it is operational. Especially, with non-US Navy assets even US AWACS aircraft.

The US Navy aircraft also had their information-friend-or-foe (IFF) on, which told them which types of aircraft were flying to include many of the US Navy aircraft flying in the Red Sea. US Navy aircraft use modes one, two, three, and four that provide the E-3 AWACS aircrew more than enough identification information. The mode one tell the controller the type of profile or aircraft, the mode two and four using special crypto equipment tells the controller that it is a friendly military, and the mode three is used by civil ATC. Hubert was surprised at the number of US Navy aircraft flying when they arrived in the Red Sea. At this point, their E-2 Hawkeyes had been flying 24/7 for weeks and need some downtime for maintenance badly.

Hubert simulcast on ultra-high frequency (UHF) and the very high frequency (VHF) guard, and since he had just returned from the NATO E-3A AWACS, he had the Alpha Whisky (AW) Net, which is the Anti-Warfare Net and the Alpha Sierra, which is the Anti-Surface Net frequencies. Each US E-3B/C AWACS contacts their participants on the Alpha Sierra (AS), which is the Anti-Surveillance Net or the Alpha Whisky (AW) Net, which is the Anti-Warfare Net. Eventually, the Admiral on the Aircraft Carrier could tell from Hubert's voice that he was an American that knew the US Navy's procedures and started talking to him on the AW Net.

At that point, Hubert directed his CSO (Communications Systems Officer) to set up secure communications with the surface RO (Radio Operator) using the "I set" line of a common crypto. Within fifteen minutes, secure communications was established and message PLADS were passed in order for the deployed AWACS detachment to receive the Operations Tasks Communications and the Operations Tasks Orders (OPTASKSCOMS and OPORDS) documents required to work with the US Navy. This is how the US AWACS commenced their working operations with the US Navy.

The confusion did not decrease during this first maritime missionas if it did not stop during the first AWACS flight in Saudi Arabia. On occasion, the E-3B/C AWACS radar system would pick up slow moving targets on the ground. Lieutenant Colonel Farrel thinking that this slow and low moving target was a thread to the E-3B/C AWACS and once he explained that it was not an aircraft, he asked that he, his Senior Director (SD), and his Surveillance Control (SC) Officer take off their heat sets. Unfortunately, for Hubert, Lieutenant Colonel Farrel would not listen to what he was saying. He kept going through flashbacks from Vietnam and at times Hubert had considered instructing two of his officers taking him back to the aircraft and tying him down since he was getting in the way and detrimental to the safe execution of the mission.

Lieutenant Colonel Farrel yellowed, "If you can't get your heads into this war, when we land I will send you home. " Hubert replied, "If that car on the ground is a thread to the AWACS, I will give him a medal. " Lieutenant Colonel Farrel would later tell Hubert that he had flashbacks from Vietnam and apologized. After over seventeen hours of being on station, Hubert decided that it was time to get this crew on the ground when he saw all three of his E-3B/C AWACS pilots with rubber heads due to fatigue. Their replacement E-3B/C AWACS was having radar problems and not able to be on station to replace them as scheduled.

"What should I do? If Hubert's husband doesn't enter his application by the end of the month he won't be able to apply to pilot training again," said the Captain's wife to Darlene. As always, she would hear herself saying, "Do not worry, Hubert always calls me, and I'll talk to him about what to do. " Hubert had always purchased international calling cards that he could rechargeto maintain contact with his family. Half of the time, they discussed issues pertaining to his flight personnel that needed help. Eventually Darlene and the Captain's wife would get the required signatures and submit the application in time to the Air Force Military Personnel Center (AFMPC).

Captain Cox would become a pilot and another couple would be grateful to Darlene for her concern and assistance in submitting the application even though her husband was in a war zone. Military members have to be careful when discussing any flying activities and have to be aware of their surroundings all times. At one point, Hubert had to remind our crew about Operations Security (OPSEC) when Hubert called Darlene and she knew when Hubert was flying next. It seemed that the Tinker AFB wives new a lot about when their husbands were going to fly next from their partners. As for getting to learn and see Riyadh, first hand, even though Hubert lived there well over a year not possible until Hubert third deployment during future operations where our goal was to maintain peace in the region.

Once the crews got into a flying routine, members had time to play cards and read books. The hotel lobby had many chairs where individuals could rest and talk to fellow flyer. A primary concern was hotel security when the Deployed Commander (Detco) decided not to issue weapons at the hotel since we were living in the city. Eventually, an soldier was posted just outside the front hotel door with bottled water and instructed that if they saw something that did not seem right or a vehicle that was going to ram the hotel to run inside and yell bomb so that everyone could run away from the lobby. Many of the AWACS personnel felt that having such a security procedure in place was not sufficient since it would not protect them. Especially since they all had, their weapons available, which remained locked in the RSAF armory and as aviator, AWACS were the only flyers not allowed to fly with weapons.

When Hubert discussed his concerns with his squadron Vice Commander, Lieutenant Colonel Farrel, it was made clear that he was to keep mouth shot and that as the Mission Crew Commander (MCC) he was there only as a witness. Hubert instructed his crew reprimanded for missing the last minute meeting that they should talk to the Commander but added that if they had real concerns to call their mothers who in turn could talk to their congressional representatives. Eventually, the E-3B/C AWACS detachment moved outside of Riyadh called Escon Village. Not everything was negative during this period. During one mission when Hubert's crew was in the process of flying, his bus driver was late picking up the crew.

Normally, the driver was part of the surveillance team given a large bus with no training to drive. In Hubert's case, he selected Airman First Class (A1C) BrianVan Leer who was a single aviator around twenty years of age. A1C Van Leer was a good aviator who showedpromise with good mentoring. Hubert had first met A1C Van Leer at 552ᵈ TTS when he was going through MCC upgrade training. A1C Van Leer like Hubert was going through initial E-3B/C AWACSsurveillance upgrade training. Once Hubertheard that he was going to the 965ᵗʰ as he was, he took him under his wings and became his mentor. At the 965ᵗʰ, Hubert made sure that A1C Van Leer received his first Flight under Hubert's crew as one of his Airborne Surveillance Technicians (ASTs). Later, A1C Van Leer would follow Hubert to Alaska and he knew that he could always go to Hubert for advice in confidence and as a mentor. On the road, both men would go out to meals as equals knowing that depending on who was around, there was a certain protocol.

On this flight, A1C Van Leer drove the flight engineer and the technicians to the E-3B/C AWACS aircraft to start the pre-flight checks for the aircraft as the remaining of the crew received their pre-flight briefings and picked up the meals and water. Normally it took the driver twenty to thirty minutes to return to the RSAF building but for some unknown reason A1C Van Leer was running late. As it turned out, the US Secretary of Defense (SECDEF) who was at his aircraft saw a blue US bus, he asked A1C Van Leer to take him to base operations. At first, A1C Van Leer explained that he could not since he was on a tight time-line since he was returning to pick-up the rest of the E-3 AWACS crew. Then after thinking for a bit and realizing that the SECDEF was his ultimate boss he changed his mind.

On 9 August, Iraq closed its borders to foreigners, trapping thousands of Americans and other Westerners in Iraq and Kuwait. On 10 August, twelve of twenty Arab League states voted to send all-Arab military force to join the Americans in defense of Saudi Arabia. Iraqi President Saddam Hussein urged Arabs to sweep "emirs of oil" from power in Gulf States. On 13 August, Iraqi troops in Kuwait round up American and British visitors from two hotels in Kuwait for transport to Iraq. On 20 August, Iraq announces that it has moved Western hostages to vital military installations to use as human shields. On 25

August, UN Security Council passes resolution that would allow military action to enforce economic embargo of Iraq.

A1C Van Leer recognized the SECDEF and smartly gave him a ride. When he arrived late and mentioned why, Hubert knew that even A1C Van Leer would not create such a story. This was just part of the chaos that occurred in a war zone. Over the years, A1C Van Leer had done many dumb things that Hubert had overlooked due to his age and maturity. In Rosy and Panama, he had displayed poor judgment but each time he let him learn from his repeated mistakes. This time and the recent bus damage were not A1C Van Leer's fault. Living at a downtown hotel also allowed the crew to meet Kuwaiti refugees who each told the crew of their experiences as the Iraqi Army marched in to their country. As the E-3B/C AWACS aircrew spoke to the Kuwait casualties of first hand experiences made one feel that each mission was contributing to achieving national objectives. However, the horror stories at times made one wonder how evil humanity truly is in today's modern society. Especially when one landed and saw on Cable News Network (CNN) the opposite lies reported. Hubert would return to Choctaw, Oklahoma to turn off CNN.

During this period, Tawny had become ill and since Hubert prepared his crew for combat, Hubert asked Hubert Commander if Hubert could return to Tinker AFB. At the time, the Tinker AFB Hospital had wanted Darlene's permission to accomplish exploratory surgery on Tawny since she was gravely ill. In the end, although Tawny's records had a red stamp that stated that she was allergic to penicillin, during routine dental work she was administered penicillin. Darlene moved into the hospital and refused to give her permission unless they had a better medical explanation for any surgery. With time once the penicillin went through Tawny's system, she was well.

At that point, Hubert's crew been noted as the best aircrew in Saudi so Hubert asked to return to Tinker AFB to deal with his daughter's medical condition. While sitting at the hotel lobby, his Unit Commander walked up to him and told him to report to the base operations because there was a flight back to Tinker AFB in two hours. Hubert quickly packed his bags and started his flight back home. The flight took him through Rota, Spain and then directly to the east coast in America. Once the aircrew rested, they continued to Oklahoma and the rest of the way to Tinker AFB, Oklahoma. Within two days, he was in the Tinker AFB flight line and left his bags at the base operations.

Upon Hubert's return to Tinker AFB Air Force Base (AFB), Oklahoma, Hubert received notification he was the Chief of Current Operations and assigned to the 965th Airborne Air Control Squadron (AACS) on 13 December 1990. Hubert would work for the same Lieutenant Colonel that Hubert worked with in Saudi and during Hubert first deployment in Puerto Rico. This meant that Hubert had to worry for the various ground and flying divisions within Hubert squadron and oversight of approximately 650 Air Force members. This was an era when maintenance merged with operations under the Unit Commander. Hubert still expected to support the regular deployment schedule, support E-3B/C AWACS operations, and support any Spanish operation since he was bilingual.

"You're not god," said Darlene to the female doctor. From there he walked to the base hospital to see how Tawny and Darlene were doing. It not until the day Hubert arrived at Tinker AFB that the hospital finally determined that Tawny received penicillin by mistake and that was the cause for her medical condition. Darlene had stayed with Tawny 24/7 at the Tinker AFB hospital and refused to allow them to accomplish exploratory surgery as the doctor had planned. During the entire week, not once had they noticed that in her records that Tawny was allergic to penicillin even though penicillin stamps in red on front of her medical records.

It would be a few days before Hubert had to return to his squadron once Tawny and Darlene were back at home. At that point, the Exercise Officer advised Hubert had been loaded on a crew to deploy to Nellis AFB to support a Desert Flag (DF 91-1) event. At that point, the Air Force thought that the Saudi war would be a long-term event so the aircrews were in training. Since Hubert had just returned from Saudi, he was a valuable instructor. Hubert would support Desert Flag 91-1 and 91-2 before redeploying back to Saudi Arabia and Operation Desert Storm.

Unlike most Nellis exercises, this Desert Flag 91-1 and 91-2 was different mainly because all the aircrews and the support personnel knew that they were preparing for a real war. Although warfighters know that all training may result in eventually fighting our nations wars, this time, the war was about to start. In Saudi, each day, the aircrews were accomplishing the same type of exercises similar to the Desert Flags except they were in Saudi Arabian airspace, over the Red Sea, or over the Persian Sea. Since Hubert had just returned, he had just completed those real-time missions (sorties) or real-time training while assigned to NATO AWACS.

During Operation Desert Shield, Lieutenant Colonel Johnson Hubert's Commander mentioned to Hubert that he was needed him back in Tinker AFB more than in Riyadh. Hubert's Commander also mentioned that since his crew was doing well, he should return to Oklahoma and take care of his daughter. He had already decided to select Hubert and his crew as the Aircrew of the Year. Johnson stated that Hubert was the best person to have back home to prepare and deploy crews before hostilities. Lieutenant Colonel Johnson made it clear that Hubert would return if war broke out. In January 1991 when the President gave the order to commence Operation Desert Storm, Hubert returned to Riyadh.

During 1991, Hubert would deploy to Saudi Arabia and fly over Iraq during two deployments in addition to supporting a busy schedule in the US that kept him away from home most of the year. At this point, Hubert had deployed in support of operations in Iraq three deployments in minimal time. During

1991, Hubert would also deploy to Site-2 (Classified Site) three times, which at the time was a classified location in the Middle East. Hostilities commenced in January 1991, resulting in a decisive victory for the Coalition Forces, which drove Iraqi forces out of Kuwait with minimal Coalition deaths. By the end of Operation Desert Shield, the following Troop Strengths existed between Iraq and the US Forces as listed in Table 1, Titled,Opposing Forces in the Gulf:

A United Nations (U. N.) ultimatum, Security Council Resolution 678, followed on November 29, 1990. It stipulated that if Iraqi dictator Saddam Hussein did not remove his troops from Kuwait by January 15, 1991 a US-led Coalition authorized to drive the Iraqi military out. Early in the morning of January 17, Baghdad time, the US-led Coalition launched air attacks against Iraqi targets. The main battles were aerial and ground combat within Iraq, Kuwait, and bordering areas of Saudi Arabia. On February 24, Coalition ground forces begin their attack. The war did not expand outside the immediate Iraq, Kuwait, Saudi Arabian border region, although Iraq fired missiles on Israeli cities.

OPERATION DESERT STORM

On 13 December, Ambassador Nathaniel Howell and four other diplomats from US Embassy in Kuwait join Americans leaving Iraq as the thousands of captive Westerners go home. On 8 January 1991, US Secretary of State James Baker meets with French, German, and Italian officials to maintain cohesion of anti-Iraq alliance. On 9 January, James Baker and Iraqi Foreign Minister Tariq Aziz meet in Geneva but fail to defuse a crisis. UN Secretary General Javier Perez de Cuellar says he will go to Baghdad for one last try at persuading the Iraqis to pull out of Kuwait. On 16 January, less than nineteen hours after time ran out on an UN-mandated deadline for Iraq to withdraw from Kuwait, allied warplanes streak north on a moonless night from Saudi Arabia and make raids on Baghdad.

"Ok guys, try to get as much crew rest as you can," said Hubert to his E-3C AWACS crew. He knew that the near future would consist of many unknowns since they would be flying in hostile airspace. The invasion force of 120,000 troops and 2,000 tanks quickly overwhelmed Iraq's neighbor to the south, allowing Hussein to declare, in less than a week, that Kuwait was his nation's nineteenth province. The United Nations responded quickly, passing a series of resolutions that condemned the invasion, called for an immediate withdrawal of Iraqi troops from Kuwait, imposed a financial and trade embargo on Iraq, and declared the annexation void.

"Babe, I'm not sure when I'll be calling you again," mentioned Hubert on the telephone to Darlene. At the request of the Kuwait and Saudi Arabian government, the US military deployed forces to oust Saddam Hussein's Army from Kuwait. In Hubert case, this would be the starting point of fifteen years as an Officer supporting countless versions of missions through the Middle East including Operation Desert Storm, Operation Desert Calm, Operation Iraqi Freedom, and Operation Uphold Democracy. By the time the US Air Force approved the Expeditionary Medal to award for the Iraqi operation, Hubert would earn the basic medal with four clusters. This meant that he had deployed to Iraq five times since each award earns a military member theExpeditionary Medal awarded for that operation.

"Guys, according to Intel, they expect three E-3B/C AWACS aircraft to be destroyed by Iraqi forces," mentioned Hubert to his crew during Mission Planning (MP) for their first combat support mission, Operation Desert Storm had begun and the Coalition Forces had trained for was for over six months that proved to be part of a well-executed war plan. During the initial operations, the Iraqi Air Force not seen until January 17, 2001.

This day was a busy for the USE-3B/C AWACS and Coalition fighter aircraft. The average sortie (mission) flew between fourteen to seventeen hours depending on the day's activities.

The fourteen-plus hour sortie required a minimum of two air-to-air refueling missions and the seventeen-hour sortie required three air-to-air refueling missions (sorties). Two US orbits were manned 24/7 inside Iraqi airspace and the Saudi Royal Air Force (RSAF) maintained a backup orbit south of the US orbits. The US orbits separation was approximately 150 nautical miles apart, one E-3B/C AWACS flying to the east in Iraq and one air-to-air refueling mission to the west near Kuwait. The E-3B/C AWACS Weapons Directors (WDs) assisted Coalition Aircraft in destroying the Iraqi Air Force (IAF) with no loss of friendly aircraft from assists deployed from Saudi Arabia or surrounding southern areas. This would be the greatest display of air and ground power in military history.

At other locations in Saudi Arabia, at 12:50 AM, F-15Es Strike Eagle Fighter Bombers took off from the largest US Air Base in Central Saudi Arabia. At the same time, from press dispatches the US Navy initiated its initial "wave of cruise missiles" from US battleships in the Persian Gulf. Hundreds of other types of aircraft took off and started their attack coordinated all on different strategic Iraqi Command and Control (C2) targets all at the same time. Special attacks in the Baghdad area included the military command center located just outside the Iraqi capital. This would be the first time that the F-117A Stealth nearly invisible single-seat, stealth jet received orders in the original raid on Baghdad with its range and armaments, which are classified.

The US Navy supersonic F-14 Tomcat fighter with its variable sweep wing that can track up to twenty-four targets simultaneously also attacked Baghdad. The Tomcat carries a crew of two and can travel up to twice the speed of sound. B-52 flew non-stop air assault from outside the Middle East fighting conducting bombing missions. Early priority targets included communications centers, radar and missile bases, air bases, headquarters, chemical weapons plants and nuclear facilities. In addition, US Navy ships launched high tech guided cruise missiles while the US Air Force and the US Navy fired "smart" bombs. All under the control of US Airborne Warning and Control System (AWACS) aircraft that consists of a Boeing 707 jet that monitors the air space with its big exterior radar dome. The AWACS aircrew guides fighters and bombers to their targets using the pulse Doppler radar, Over the Horizon Radar, or Maritime Radar simultaneously based on controller proficiency and experience.

In a different mission, a Combined Mission was flown where assets from different nations are tasked in this case aircraft from the US, Great Britain, and Saudi Arabia. Limited Iraqi military response reports were received or observed throughout Iraq. Preliminary reports indicated that nearly all the attacking aircraft returned to base safely without any damage. There were no early reports of allied casualties. At the same time, reports received noted the Iraqi Air Force destroyed. US reported inside the Iraqi capital reported, "Wave of explosions" rocking the Baghdad area. No specific targeting of Iraqi President Saddam Hussein in the attacks was part of the US plan. At his point, President Bush announced on television, "The liberation of Kuwait has begun," in a nationally televised speech from the White House a few hours after the air assault was launched. The inclusion of cruise missiles in the attack were launched to force the Iraqi anti-aircraft defenses to turn on their radars and be spotted and successful destroyed by their attackers.

At the same time, the ground war was about to start after the Iraqi Command and Control (2) structure was destroyed. Sadly, it the Iraqi forces turned on their weapons or trucks to get warm in the cold desert, which meant that they would send out a heat source that would also send out an infrared target source that would be targets by multiple systems. The A-10 known by its nickname "Warthog" or simply "Hog" proved to be a deadly aircraft in Iraq. As a secondary mission, it provides airborne forward air control (FAC), guiding other aircraft against ground targets. A-10s used primarily in this role are designated OA-10. The A-10 aircraft will be in the USAF until 2028 or later.

During one mission alone, a single A-10 Warhog destroyed one hundred Iraqi tanks. After controlling multiple Close Air Support mission, Hubert received a Video Home System (VHS) tape of one of the A-10 missions that to this day he has never replayed. He has always felt that he did his duty fighting a war that civilian politicians had sent the military to fight. Another war fought by warfighters directed by politicians who had never served for their nation. Another war fought by warfighters directed by politicians who had never felt that they should serve in uniform for their country. Even worse, they also felt that their children should not serve for their country. America was becoming a new nation run by a small elite society.

In the meantime, On Baghdad radio, Saddam said in a radio message, "The 17th of January the hypocrites struck. The great showdown has begun. " He said, "With the perseverance of the believers, the dawn of victory nears as this great showdown begins. " In the meantime, Armed Forces of the southern Soviet Union were on high alert according to Tass as quoted by Chief of the Army General Staff Mikhail Moiseyev who said, "We are watching closely the development of the situation in the Middle East. " He also stated that the "fighting in the gulf was a tragedy for the people of the Iraq and the entire Arab East. " In the meantime, Saddam started launching scuds into Israel and Saudi Arabia as the US Patriot weapons systems started destroying most of the in-bound scud missiles.

During the initial operations, on January 17, 2001, eight Iraqi MIG-29 Fulcrums and one, F-1 Mirage aircraft destroyed. Two days later, January 19, Coalition fighter aircraft destroyed two more F-29s and two MIG-25s Foxbats. On January 24, Coalition forces destroyed two additional F-1s. Then the E-3B/C AWACS crews experienced a busy period when on the 26th and 28th three MIG-23 Floggers and then eight additional MIG-23 Floggers destroyed. This would be the end of Iraqi fighters destroyed during January 2001. From Turkey, Coalition E-3B/C AWACS and Coalition fighter aircraft destroyed two F-1 Mirages on January 18 followed by one MIG-23 Flogger on 22 January 2001. The Coalition air forces noted little Iraqi offensive actionsduring the air-to-air combat missions.

"I'm glad that we over estimated our enemy," mentioned Hubert. The following month starting, slow until January 5 when two SU-22 Fitters and two MIG-21 Fishbed aircraft destroyed. The next two days an Iraqi helicopter and then three additional Fitter aircraft destroyed. This would be the end of aircraft destroy during February until the 15th when an Iraqi helicopter destroyed. It would be until March 20 when one SU-22 Fitter destroyed. Two days later, the last Iraqi aircraft, a SU-22 destroyed. During mid-February, the Coalition Forces in Turkey destroyed two Iraqi helicopters. It seemed that by this time, few Iraqi aircraft remained with most destroyed on the ground by Coalition bombing efforts.

"Would you like copies of the pictures," asked the Riyadh AAFES sales representative. The war had just ended and already individuals could purchase war pictures of burnt Iraqi convoys and dead bodies. The pictures make Hubert realize that he was lucky to be fighting this war in the air and not on the ground as many of his fellow Coalition soldiers. Some of the pictures only showed burnt hands melted into the steering wheel of the truck that someone had been driving. Hubert thought to himself that he was glad that he would not have to relive first hand those memories for years to come. He also knew that he did not want to purchase any pictures that reflected the realities of war.

"It seems like a long dream," mentioned Hubert to his crew. On February 27, Kuwait City declared liberation, and with allied forces having driven well into Iraq, President Bush and his advisers decided to halt the war. A cease-fire took effect at 8:00 the following morning in accordance with the United Nations (UN) Official Document System (ODS). At this point, those E-3B/C AWACS aircrews knew they would stay behind and start another phase of another military operation due to a political decision. During ELF-1, the E-3B/C AWACS aircrews had remained in Saudi Arabia for ten years. Initially, the aircrews started in Saudi Arabia then transferred to Qatar once the Saudi citizens tired of having the Americans in their territory for decades.

"Crew we are still counting our sorties as Combat Support or O-2 missions for Operation Desert Calm," mentioned Hubert at the pre-mission briefing. During Operation Desert Calm, aircrews were reporting that the Iraqi Air Force (IAF) was flying Red Cross helicopter missions against their citizens in and around Basra. Unfortunately, due to Rules of Engagement (ROE), the US had allowed Iraqi helicopters to fly humanitarian missions. The negotiators did not put into the cease-fire that the helicopters not allowed to fly without weapons onboard. This error would cause many civilians Iraqi lives since the Iraqi military had to maintain control of its citizens in the normal fashion that had been part of their culture for hundreds of years. Military force had always been the manner that had successfully kept the Sunnis in their place in the Iraqi society.

"Sir we have two bogies flying low and slow over Basra," said the Airborne Surveillance Control (SC) Officer (ASO). Hubert had already been monitoring the Iraqi helicopters near Basra. On a separate internal net, he had directed the Senior Director (SD) to vector two US F-15s Eagles to accomplish a visual identification (VIS ID) mission. Flying over Kuwait during night mission, one could see an orange flow from miles away throughout Kuwait from the burning oil fields. Coalition fighter Combat Air Patrol (CAP) aircraft would intercept the Iraqi helicopters fully loaded with missiles and return to Bagdad after they used their weapons against their owncitizens. All the E-3 AWACS aircrew were able to do was report the Iraqi massacre results after each flight.

Since all the Coalition, aircrews were accomplishing flight-follow duties on the scheduled Iraqi missions in the Basra area. All the E-3B/C AWACS and Coalition fighter crews could do was monitor the enemy helicopters machine guns and rockets explode on the ground. What was frustrating, Hubert knew that the following day that Cable News Network (CNN) would report of another massacre in Iraq as US aircrew watched. Each time, it would seem that CNN was more interested in selling the US into going to war than telling Americans the truth. This dishonest reporting would convince Hubert to not sign up for CNN cable news.

"Sir, Airman Napier took pictures from seat five," said the communications technician. The E-3B/C AWACS crew knew that they could not take pictures inside the aircraft without first receiving approval. "What do you think we should do," asked the Aircraft Commander (AC). The AC tended to be stricter that Hubert so he honored his requests to confiscate the camera. Hubert replied that he would confiscate the camera and discuss the matter at the post-mission debrief. This mission was a night sortie (mission), the dark sky's was orange, and many AWACS aircrew wanted to remember the moment in time in history. When they flew over the orange skies of Kuwait and they flew over the orange skies and not the black skies that CNN reported on television.

One could see what seemed as an endless field of burning fires throughout Kuwait. On their consoles, it seemed like a different world, since the USE-3B/C AWACS computer generated symbols that each represented an aircraft and ground targets. Months' later E-3B/C AWACS members would complain about joint pains since the aircraft filters would not filter out this type of synthetic pollution. Especially, since the E-3B/C AWACS, aircraft was flying over the Kuwaiti burning oilfields during every flight.

Operation Desert Storm known for its ground war, executed during the initial one hundred days. During that period, the Iraqi Air Defense, Command, Control, Communications, Intelligence (C3I), and the entire Iraqi industrial base destroyed by the US and Coalition bombing air strike. In this effort, the USE-3B/C AWACS aircraft served as Air Traffic Control (ATC) facilities controlling the B-52s, B-1 Bomber, B-2 Bomber, and all the various Reconnaissance aircraft flying throughout Saudi Arabia while the US Navy launched its missiles from the Red Sea and the Persian Sea as part of this effort. Then the air-to-air operations commenced leading to the first two MIGs 29s, Fulcrum's aircraft killed on 17 January 1991.

The US Airborne Warning and Control Systems (AWACS) E-3B and E-3C aircraft air battle accomplished in two phases, the first fought from Saudi Arabia and the second phase fought from Incirlik, Turkey. In Saudi, the US Air Force (USAF) and the Royal Saudi Air Force (RSAF) flew its E-3C AWACS aircraft from Riyadh, Air Base (AB) and Jedi AB. Jedi AB selected as an alternate Air Base mainly because intelligence data suggested that the US Air Force would lose four aircraft during war. By disbursing the E-3B/C AWACS aircraft fleet, this would minimize losing aircraft by not having them all at one location. The RSAF E-3A aircraft were all at Riyadh, AB since that was their Main Operating Base (MOB) and supported by US contractors. At the end of Operation Desert Storm, Hubert would know the day and type of every Iraqi shoot down.

During Operation, Desert Storm,the E-3 AWACS flown from Riyadh, AB and Jedi, AB. The US flew all the forward orbits while the RSAF flew all the back-up orbits to the south and well inside Saudi Arabian airspace. On 17 January 1991, the USE-3C AWACSreceived credit with killing two MIGs 29s, Fulcrum's in during one air-to-air mission Iranian airspace. On 17 January 1991, the USE-3B/C AWACSreceived credit with killing two MIGs 29s in Iranian airspace. The second orbit was also busy shooting down Iraqi fighters. On 17 January 1991, the

USE-3B/C AWACSreceived credit with killing two MIGs 29s in Iranian airspace.

On 17 January 1991, the USE-3B/C AWACSreceived credit with killing two MIGs 29s in Iranian airspace. On 17 January 1991, the USE-3C AWACSreceived credit with killing an F-1, Mirage in Iranian airspace. During the third week of January, eight enemy aircraft killed in Iranian airspace. On 18 January 1991, the USE-3C AWACSreceived credit with killing two MIG 29s in Iranian airspace. On 19 January 1991, the USE-3B/C AWACSreceived credit with killing two MIG 29s in Iranian airspace in a different mission. On 20 January 1991, the USE-3C AWACSreceived credit with killing two MIG 29s in Iranian airspace in a different mission. On 18 January 1991, the USE-3B/C AWACSreceived credit with killing two MIG 25s, Foxbats in Iranian airspace.

During the January operations, on one of the missions, a US F-15 fighter pilot was engaged on a MIG 29 and directed by the CAOC to knock-it-off in order for the Saudi Prince to engage and get the kill. The US fighter pilot not pleased but he followed orders. On more than one occasion, the Iraqi MIG 29s that had better missiles and the tactical advantage did not get a kill because they broke lock once engaged by Coalition air forces. Since the Iraqi pilots trained by the USSR, each time they received raw radar, they broke lock, and ran. At that point, the Iraqi aircraft engaged eventuallykilled. The US was fortunate that the USSR Air Force had trained the Iraqi Air Force. Where the Iraqi culture provided a poorly trained military force used to hiring Westerners as their caretakers for everything in their lives making them near hired slaves.

During the last week of January, thirteen enemy aircraft destroyed. On 24 January 1991, the USE-3B/C AWACSreceived credit with killing two F-1 in Iranian airspace. On 26 January 1991, the USE-3C AWACSreceived credit with killing three MIG 23s in Iranian airspace. On 28 January 1991, the USE-3C AWACSreceived credit with killing four MIG 23s in Iranian airspace. On 28 January 1991, the USE-3B/C AWACSreceived credit with killing four MIG 23s in Iranian airspace in a separate mission. Overall, the month of January was a busy month for the Coalition Forces. Throughout this phase, the US AWACS aircrews also supported the air-to-ground forces. The EC-130E Airborne Battlefield Command and Control Center(ABCCC) aircraft daily conducted Close Air Support (CAS) and other ground mission (sorties) throughout Iraq. The E-3B/C AWACS Monitor provided threat warning service for the ABCCC to ensure that no enemy aircraft attacked them when airborne. This service continued throughout the entire Iraqi war.

During February, nine enemy aircraft destroyed. On 5 February 1991, the USE-3B/C AWACSreceived credit with killing two SU 22s in Iranian airspace. On 5 February 1991, the US E-3C AWACS received credit with killing two MIG 21s Fishbed's in Iranian airspace in a separate mission. On 6 February 1991, the USE-3B/C AWACSreceived credit with killing one Helicopter in Iranian airspace. On 7 February 1991, the USE-3B/C AWACSreceived credit with killing three SU 22s in Iranian airspace. On 5 February 1991, the USE-3B/C AWACSreceived credit with killing three Helicopters in Iranian airspace. The ABCCC aircraft did not fly out of Turkish Air Bases (ABs) since the major Iraqi Abs were farther south in Iraq and not near the Turkish borders.

Towards the end of the air-to-air war, Iraqi fighter aircraft and Iraqi airline pilots tried to fly to Iran. In some cases, the US allowed the aircraft to proceed depending on the type of aircraft. Each situation was evaluated real-time on the Satcom radio, which was possible since the USE-3B/C AWACS has SIGINT capabilities and the Rivet Joint (RJ) aircraft was airborne 24/7 that also had SIGINT capabilities that gave the US full intelligence information of the type of aircraft was defecting to Iraq. The Rivet Joint (RJ) aircraft, the E-3B/C AWACS aircraft, and the ABCCC all shared many SIGINT systems on data link therefore extending the range of the overall coverage within the battle area.

The air-to-air battle during Operation Desert Storm ended on 22March1991 when the final SU22 killed by a US fighter aircraft. On 20 March 1991, the USE-3B/C AWACSreceived credit with killing one SU 22 in Iranian airspace. The final kill during Operation Desert Storm occurred on 22 March 1991 and received credit to the US when one SU 22 killed in Iranian airspace. In early April 1991 when the Cease Fire received approval, with only Helicopters allowed to fly. In this area, the US and General H. Norman Schwarzkopf, US Army, Commander in Chief, US Central Command (USCENTCOM), Commander of Operation Desert Storm made a serious mistake by not making sure that he insisted that only Red Cross helicopters fly in Iraq. This would be a major strategic mistake for the US government since Iraqi military helicopterskill thousands of Iraqi civilians daily and Cable News Network (CNN) failed to report the real news again. It is amazing how Washington politicians can so easily hide news as the liberal media tell Americans what they want to hear while the US military stays quite or goes to jail.

Instead, the Iraqi Air Force flew armed helicopters to control the Shiites in Basra and other major cities as USE-3B/C AWACS aircrews and US fighters intercepted the Iraqi Helicopters and were not able to do nothing. At nighttime, US aircrews could see the Iraqi Helicopters rockets freely killing civilians as reported by CNN once the aircrews landed and debriefed intelligence. Westerners will never learn or understand the Iraqi and Muslim culture. In Iraq, the Roman Empire failed to change the culture, as did the British Empire, as will the US Empire. Two thousand years of hatred is hard to change with three tribes all hating each other at different levels for good reasons. Especially when one considers that in the region, the Bible and its history came from this area.

OPERATION PROVEN FORCE

The first USE-3B/C AWACS aircraft deployed from Saudi Arabia to Incirlik, Turkey to set-up the US detachment. From Turkey, USE-3B/C AWACS aircraft while airborne communicated to aircraft working in northern Saudi Arabian airspace using Satcom communications. During these sorties (missions), the initial coordination achieved its objective that led to the wartime E-3 AWACS Plan, which flew orbits in the Iraqi airspace from the north and in the southern orbits. This allowed attacking strike packages to hit their targets 24/7 throughout Iraq. At the same time, AWACS Weapons Directors (WDs) provide B-52 and other Bomber aircraft threat warning on a dedicated frequency. At the same time, other Weapons Directors (WDs) are responsible for multiple Tanker cells flying in Tanker orbits.

Operation Proven Force was flown from Incirlik, Turkey by USE-3B/C AWACS aircrews flying E-3B and E-3C aircrafts and Konya, Turkey by NATO E-3A AWACS aircrews flying E-As aircrafts. The NATO E-3A AWACS aircrews consist of fourteen nations of which sixty-five percent of the aircrews are Americans. Two orbits were flown in northern Turkey and then in northern Iraq by these aircrew. On 18 January 1991, the USE-3B/C AWACSreceived credit with killing two F-1 Mirages in Iranian airspace. On 20 January 1991, the USE-3B/C AWACSreceived credit with killing a MIG 23 in Iranian airspace. In Mid-February 1991, the USE-3B/C AWACSreceived credit with killing two Helicopters in Iranian airspace. This was the total air-to-air kills received credit to the north for Operation Proven Force flown from Incirlik. Data for the NATO E-3A AWACS aircrews not reported to the USE-3B/C AWACS detachment.

In early April 1991, the US and Iraq formally signed the Cease Fire. At this point, in Hubert's view, The US made a serious mistake by allowing the Iraqi Air Force (IAF) fly its Helicopters without ensuring that it not fly its armed Helicopters as it did. The US assumed that the Iraqis would fly humanitarian flights but instead flew flights from Bagdad into southern cities like Basra where thousands of massacred civilians by the Iraqi Air Force (IAF) HIP and Hine Helicopters. During each Iraqi flight, the Coalition Forces intercepted the IAF, escorted them to their final targets, and reported the final targets with the help of the US AWACS aircrafts. Unfortunately, Coalition fighters and the US AWACS aircraft were under strict orders to conduct the flight follow operations and not interfere with theIraqi Air Force (IAF).

In the meantime, aircrews and E-3B/C AWACS aircraft kept deploying and redeploying from Saudi Arabia and Tinker AFB, Oklahoma. Since all E-3 aircraft have maintenance phases, at specific number of flying hours, each aircraft returned to Tinker AFB and entered for different levels of maintenance programs. During these maintenance phases, aircrews deploy back to Tinker AFB along with the E-3 aircraft. However, most of the E-3B/C AWACS aircrews deploy to and from Saudi Arabia using Commercial travel or Charter Aircraft due to the limited number or E-3B/C AWACS aircraft. All of this planning is part of the AWACS Deployment Commander (Detco) responsibilities, in addition to all the local flying duties.

After Hubert returned from Saudi Arabia, he cancelled his Cable News Network (CNN) connection because of all the lies that CNN reported while deployed. In Hubert's view, he felt that CNN reported nothing by lies for resulted in the US military going to war. Many of the hotel guests suggested that the Kuwaiti and Saudi Arabia governments hired an advertising agency to convince Americans of false Iraqi allegations to go to war. The E-3 AWACS aircrews were hearing the stories from the Kuwaiti civilians in their hotel first hand and not the CNN propaganda. After returning from a warzone, it was not hard to imagine that any nation would do anything in order to win back its country. Especially if oil was at stake even though Hubert knew that Americans would benefit little in the end.

"Sir how are we getting back to Tinker AFB," asked the Senior Surveillance Technician (SST). Hubert not sure but knew where to start his search for flights. He went to the RSAFBase Operations front desk and asked if they had any Tanker aircraft scheduled back to the US or Europe. Hubert knew that once he and his aircrew were in the US that he could arrange to get back to Oklahoma. In the RSAF Weather shop, he found an Aircraft Commander (AC) that was going to Norfolk AFB, Virginia with enough open seats. Hubert had gone shopping for an aircraft with enough seats available to take him and his crew back to the US to get everyone to their home stations.

The AC agreed to take them as passengers (PAX) and gave Hubert a copy of the flight manifest. At that point, the stragglers mentioned to Hubert that they had been there for weeks waiting for travel and that no one would help them get back to their home stations. At first, the E-3B/C AWACS Deployment Commander (Detco) would not release him saying that if he let Hubert and his crew departed that he would lose control. The Deployment Commander (Detco) wanted Hubert and his crew to wait and take the next crews charter flight the following week, which made so sense to Hubert since that meant that it would delay all the departures for all the crews. That would result in all the AWACS crew rotations delaying by a week, which made absolutely no sense to Hubert. Clearly, the Detco was not a good manager and had spent too much time working in staff duties during his career.

REDEPLOYING AFTER WAR

"Babe I am not sure when we will get home," mentioned Hubert. The E-3B/C AWACS Staff had forgotten to put his aircrew on the rotator list. Hubert and his crew had no option to take the charter flight on the following week. This meant that another crew would have to wait an additional week before departing for the US and would delay his departure. After a long discussion with the Deployment Commander (Detco), he had convinced him that he would try to make flight arrangements on his own. "What control do you have once we leave regardless of which aircraft we leave on," said Hubert. The Detco mentioned that he was against this option since in his view he would lose control.

Eventually, Hubert won the logic discussion with the Detco and he and his crew departed for the US and Tinker AFB, Oklahoma. Once Hubert had approval for his crew to depart, he could not believe that the Personnel Flight was so non-caring but not surprised when he found other military members had been waiting for flights back to the US for weeks. He noticed other air force maintenance and support soldier who were trying to return to the US and added their names on the list. He mentioned to these passengers of opportunity that if anyone asked who they were to reply that they were part of the E-3B/C AWACS crew.

The list included Officers, Non-Commissioned Officers (NCOs), and junior enlisted members from multiple support career fields. Hubert did notice that all of the personnel were Captains and below in rank like him, although Hubert was a major select, which in the Air Force is a 'Captain'. At this point, Hubert had been a 'major select' for over a year and still had to wait an additional seven months before he would become a major. Hubert found a typewriter and started adding their names, ranks, and social securities of his crew on the manifest. After all, Hubert had started in the Personnel Specialty when Hubert was a Non-Commissioned Officer (NCO).

"Sir the Chow HallNCO wants US to pay for our meals," mentioned the junior enlisted member. Hubert knew that many of his aircrew did not have enough money to pay for their meals. Many had taken pay cuts months earlier and were glad that they were returning home so that their paychecks would return to normal. Hubert had never been afraid to make decisions and never afraid to challenge anyone that made a decision that did not make sense. Especially after coming back from war where most were just glad to be alive and did not expect our own military to give US a hard time.

After the meals, the bus took the crew to the local billeting office where Hubert made sure everyone had rooms. Again, Hubert hadto work billeting for all the personnel with some of the junior enlisted members having to share rooms. At first, the local billeting office wanted the enlisted members to pay for their rooms but eventually Hubert was able to convince the Officer-in-Charge (OIC)to let the enlisted not pay. In the end, only the officers were required to pay for their rooms so he directed them to use their government credit cards and file them on their final travel as a legal expense.

Not all military personnel that served during Operation Desert Storm had received their rations or quarters pay during the entire time they were in combat, which meant they had taken about a forty percent pay cut. For those that had families, this caused a serious financial burden. Since Officers receive more pay than enlisted, they tended to handle the financial burden better than the enlisted member's did. At home, Darlenedid her best helping families as best she could and on the road, Hubert did what he could. Even though he was at war, since his crew had a bus assigned to them, he would go down town every two weeks and have a crew dinner. For the junior enlisted, he and his Aircraft Commander (AC), also a Captain, both shared paying for their meals.

Therefore, during the stopover in Mildenhall, Air Base United Kingdom, Hubert asked that only the officers pay for their reimbursed rooms once they filed their final travel vouchers. Mainly because they might be able to afford the room and the enlisted members could not. Hubert's logic made sense to the billeting Officer who agreed. The following morning the crew bus picked everyone and took him or her to the Chow Hall for a meal prior to the final flight to Norfolk AFB, Virginia. Unfortunately, due to head winds, Hubert and his crew missed their connection flight to Oklahoma City, Oklahoma due to the winds. At this point, Hubert thought, what else could go wrong to himself. "Who is the Officer-in-Charge (OIC) of the show hall," asked Hubert. Hubert mentioned that everyone on the bus was all on Operation Desert Storm travel orders and that they were all entitled to meals since they lost their rations pay that all received prior to leaving Home Base and the deployment into the warzone. Hubert also mentioned to the Non-Commissioned Officer (NCO) and Officer-in-Charge (OIC) that everyone on the bus was a member of the AWACS unit. In Hubert's view, everyone was part of his crew and he did not care that the aviators were not truly AWACS aircrew since all were in the US Air Force.

All Hubert knew was that he would get them home and for now, they were his responsibility to feed them and make sure that they had a place to sleep. After all, after being at war, they deserved better treatment than the staff ignoring these enlisted members because of their ranks or crew positions. Every job in the military allowed the Coalition Forces to win the war and not just the air or ground power. In Hubert's view, the cook was equally important as the fighter pilot for each did their duty and their part in winning the war for the US and the Coalition Forces. Hubert made sure that each knew that they were equally as important and he personally thanked each one of them before departing for their home station.

"Where are the maintenance and administration members," asked Hubert. At that point, Hubert noticed that all the AWACS aircrew waited inside the Chow Hall so he told them to go ahead and get their meals. He had just noticed that only the E-3B/C AWACS and KC-135 Stratotanker aircrew had entered the Chow Hall and the remainder of his Passengers (PAX) had stayed on the military bus. He went outside and reminded again that the remaining members that he had directed them to say that they were all E-3B/C AWACS and directed everyone to go have a meal. Hubert was old school and believed that until he made sure that his men and women were taken care of first, he could not eat.

The Boeing KC-135 StratotankerBoeing 367-80 prototypes build since its first model was build. The KC-135 was the US Air Force's first jet-powered refueling tanker and replaced the KC-97 Stratotanker. The Stratotanker, initially tasked to refuel strategic bombers, but used extensively in the Vietnam War and later conflicts such as Operation Desert Strom to extend the range and endurance of US tactical fighters and bombers. Like in Vietnam, Hubert and his crew would return to Tinker AFB, Oklahoma in a KC-135 Stratotanker. After his Detco and his staff made a mistake with the charter, flight schedules during the confusion at the end of the war and left them behind. Hubert improvised as he did so many times before.

He did not have to be a Lieutenant Colonel to think like one or have simple common sense. Hubert walked over to the bus and told the group that he thought that he madeit clear in Saudi that they were all part of his crew. He instructed them all to go inside and have whatever they wanted to eat. Hubert again made sure they understood that all that was required was their signature on the sign in roster. Eventually the Colonel in charge of the Chow Hall agreed that each individual only had to sign their names and social security number for their meals. Apparently, either the NCO in charge or the OIC had just spoken with the Wing Commander who agreed that the AWACS crew deserved a meal without having to pay out of pocket. As at Mildenhall, United Kingdom, once the crew arrived at Norfolk AFB, Virginia, Hubert noticed that the remaining enlisted that joined his crew were still in the bus. Again, Hubert mentioned to the group that they could eat anything and as much as they wanted and only had to sign their names. Each enlisted member was completely surprised that an officer truly cared for him or her since none had seen such behaviors often in the military. After walking into the dining hall and getting their meals, Hubert made it a point to sit with them. That would be the last time that this group of twenty enlisted members would not feel that they were not part of Hubert's AWACS crew.

As Hubert would remind them, "we are all in the same US Air Force team". He also asked everyone for a copy of his or her deployment orders. While the aircrew and Passengers (PAX) ate breakfast, he went to the Norfolk AFB, AFB base operations and asked for the TMO Officer of the day. Before departing Saudi Arabia, Hubert made sure that he received a copy of everyone's deployment orders and made plenty of copies of each individual deployment order. He did not want to have problems with any administrative personnel at a deployed location arguing that he needed to make copies of deployment orders. Because they were transit personnel, reminding them that they were all part of the same US Air Force only.

"We have a head wind and we probably won't make it to Norfolk AFB on the scheduled time," mentioned the Tanker Aircraft Commander (AC). Hubert also gave them a list of names and phone numbers for the Passengers (PAX) that had joined his crew. Initially, Hubert wanted to make sure that the stragglers were taken care of first. He was surprised that these individuals had been in Riyadh for weeks waiting to return to their home stations.

Hubert did not expect this trip to work out almost as smooth as it did going to Saudi when he flew the E-3B/C AWACS aircraft to Saudi Arabia. Hubert's crew would fly together to Oklahoma City and others would travel throughout the US to their home stations. Hubert knew that he and his crew only had six hours from the time of arrival to the scheduled departure time at the Norfolk AFB airport. He was not sure what would happen until they arrived late at Norfolk AFB. He asked that the Norfolk AFB TMO Officer of the day meet them upon arrival.

"Sir, can I help you," asked the lieutenant. By the time, the crew finished their meal; the Norfolk AFBTraffic Management Office(TMO) Officer was able to make travel arrangements once they arrived in the US for the entire crew. Since Hubert had divided everyone's deployment orders in groups in order to expedite making travel arrangements based on the final destination. When Hubert returned to the Chow Hall with airline tickets for everyone, the entire crew yelled in sequence with a cheer. Hubert knew from experience that at each point that the group stopped that he would need to give a copy of their deployment order to the administrative personnel.

He also knew that he would need a copy of each individual to the TMO Officer to arrange travel for each member. The travel order had a change number that one uses to charge the airline ticket to for each member. At first, the TMO Officer had arranged for a flight the following morning for Hubert's crew. However, when Hubert finally went to for a meal, he found a C-141 Aircraft Commander (AC) that was flying to Beale AFB, California that had just returned from Saudi Arabia. Hubert asked the AC if there was any way that he could do an ops-stop, which means that the C-141 would fly to Tinker AFB in-route to California. Hubert knew that Beale AFB was in California and knew he had nothing to lose by asking the AC.

The Lockheed C-141 Starlifter was a military strategic airlifter in service with the Air Mobility Command (AMC) of the United States Air Force (USAF). The aircraft also served with AMC-gained airlift wings and air mobility wings of the Air Force Reserve Command (AFRC) and the Air National Guard (ANG) and, in later years, one air mobility wing of the Air Education and Training Command (AETC) dedicated to C-141, C-5, C-17 and KC-135 training. This would be the first military aircraft that Hubert would fly in during his military career while traveling to Iceland and his remote assignment.

"By any chance are you guys going near Tinker AFB," asked Hubert. The C-141 Aircraft Commander (AC) mentioned that they were going to Beale AFB in California and that he just received permission from his command post to make an ops-stop at Tinker AFB. Upon arrival, all the Passengers (PAX) had plenty of time to make their scheduled flight times for their next flight. However, the TMO Officer advised the E-3B/C AWACS crew that they would have to wait for a morning flight at the local airport. That meant that Hubert and his crew would be departing Norfolk AFB in less than an hour and fly directly to Tinker AFB, Oklahoma. "Babe I do not have much time," mentioned Hubert.

Hubert called Darlene and asked her to call the Tinker AFB Command Post and have them notify all the families of their arrival time. The AC said he would call his Commander and get back to me in a few minutes. Five minutes later when the AC explained to his Commander that the E-3B/C AWACS aircrew had returned from war, Hubert and his crew had a direct flight to Tinker AFB within two hours. Prior to departing Mildenhall, Hubert prepared the phone list and was ready to fax the list to Raymond-24 once he had a firm final plan when he knew he and his crew would arrive in Oklahoma. Hubert called the Tinker AFBCommand Post to tell their flight information and requested that all the family members receive a call to notify them of their arrival times.

"Babe I lost my wedding band in Saudi," mentioned Hubert. Without hesitation, Darlene would not let Hubert touch her or kiss her in spite of him spending months in a war zone. He mentioned how he had been swimming in the pool in Saudi Arabia and his wedding band slipped off his finger. For over an hour, he and his friends looked in the pool without any luck. Darlene made it clear that they would first go to the Base Exchange (BX) and purchase a new Gold Wedding Band. Therefore, Hubert, Tawny, and Darlene drove to the BX and purchased a new wedding band. This time, Hubert made sure that new wedding band fit tighter than the previous wedding band.

"OK guys, you know that when we get home that we are all going to be BQ," mentioned Hubert to his crew. Basic Qualification (BQ) was the normal rating that E-3B/C AWACS aircrews received when they returned from any contingency. As was the case with all contingency operations, everyone arrived to a period in time when they would return to their loved ones left back home. After the latest nine-month deployment, he expected to stay home for a while before deploying again. Most aircrews returned form was expecting to take time with family or friends as promised only to find out that nothing changed, as the operations tempo remained the same.

Since aircrew members were not able to fly and accomplish the normal training events to maintain Combat Ready (CR), this would require additional flying missions to log the required events. This meant that Hubert would have numerous training requirements that he needed to accomplish and catch up fill the administrative duties that he had as the Chief of Current Operations. Hubert did not understand why the E-3B/C AWACS Wing had training events that were required to stay CR and that in spite of returning from war. All the E-3B/C AWACSaircrews were Basic Qualified (BQ) upon returning from any oversea contingency deployment.

Especially, since each year the new Wing Chief of Training Major David Peterson kept decreasing the training requirementssubstantially each year. In Hubert's view, over time, the new AWACS Training Program was an accident waiting to happen created by the new deficientAWACS Training standards. Hubert declined promotion opportunities and instead chose to depart Tinker AFBand not to work within such a political culture. Besides, no one would ever think that at this point that the US would be at war year after year, as the US would keep electing presidents that would keep America in war.

CHAPTER 4

MAJOR

After the crews returned from Operation Desert Storm and war, the E-3B/C AWACS 552ᵈ Airborne Warning and Control Wing (AWC&W) found it again go through a major reorganization. In October 1991, the 552ᵈ AWC&W had been the redesignated to the 552ᵈ Air Control Wing (ACW) then in May 1992; the wing resignation occurred to the 28ᵗʰ Air Division (AD), which had been on 1 October 1983. Although Hubert had not been back at Tinker AFB for long, he had returned long enough to serve as the 28ᵗʰ AD Battle Staff (BS) working in the Tinker AFB Command Post. Only to have the 552ᵈ AWC&W designated on 1 April 1985 redesignated 552ᵈ ACW on 1 October 1991.

All of these reorganizations kept the aircrews not only guessing what to call themselves, by also guessed whatpromotion the 'promotables' were working on and who was on that short list. This also kept wasting millions in tax dollars as all the AWACS regulations received a rewrite with each unit and wing change that became the Friday O-Club joke. Although Hubert saw his name on the list to be on the wing as a Chief of the Counterdrug (CD) Branch, he decided to leave Tinker AFB at the two-year point and take a Permanent Change of Station (PCS). Tinker AFB was a mandatory five-year assignment since it was AWACS, which was a national asset. No one believed Hubert would be able to depart Tinker

AFBwithin two and a half years except Hubert. Many took bets that he would not be able to achieve this goal.

After being at war for nearly a straight year, the AWACS Wingpromised the AWACS aircrews' time to rest. A week after returning to Oklahoma, the AWACS aircrew received notification that their annual hours had been waivered for the year. Especially since everyone had already flown his or her annual hours by the end of May. This meant that everyone restarted his or her flying hours for the year. As was expected by the entire AWACS aircrew members, everything in the military is waver able. Since Hubert had started in Personnel Office, he knew the Personnel regulations well and understood that the regulations stated that the five-year rule clearly stated 'five years in the AWACS' and not five-years at Tinker AFB.

Since Hubert was going to another US E-3 flying unit and he had already flown for five-year straight, this meant that he was qualified to move at the two-year point for an overseas assignment if he volunteered. Therefore, once Darlene said she was ready to move again since it was her turn to select a location, Hubert made the call to Headquarters Air Force Military Personnel Center (AFMPC) and within two-week's he had his new assignment to Alaska. At that point, a fellow Senior Officer, Lieutenant Colonel Dave Johnson who Hubert knew from Geilenkirchen (GK) had also decided to leave Tinker AFB at the two-year point.

Dave was a member of Squadron-One and Hubert had flown with him when he had given check rides to some of his Senior Director (SDs) on his crews. Dave and Hubert had also met many times at GK social functions since GK only had 650 Americans assigned to the NATO AWACS Component. Within the Americans, it had been the custom to use first names and use surnames around foreign Officers. NATO Squadron-One had a hundred and fifty Americans and an American Commander. NATO Squadron-Two and NATO Squadron-Three had about a hundred Americans each assigned with the Squadron-

Two Commander being Canadian and the NATO Squadron-Three Commander being German. The NATO Component Commander changed every three years from American and German.

965TH AACS, TINKER AFB, OK.

Initially, Hubert's Commander, the 552d Operations Group (OG) and 552d Wing Commander all asked to talk to him. The wing leadership making it clear that he was on the fast track, would be a flying squadron Commander, and wouldpromote him to Lieutenant Colonel with a 'Definitely Promote' if he stayed at Tinker AFB. Hubert kindly declined stating that he planned to retire at the twenty-years on active duty point and that Darlene wished to live in Alaska. Since all three Officers knew who Darlene was, this comment did not require further explanation. Hubert was at the Panama Officer's Club having lunch when the 552d Operations Group (OG) spoke with him trying to convince him to cancel his assignment to Alaska.

Hubert mentioned that in his view, Senator Stevens, R-Alaska had more power than any Air Force General had and did not believe the E-3B/C AWACS unit would close because of the Union of Soviet Socialist Republics (USSR) Bomber threat. After all, The E-3B/C AWACS was the only aircraft that was able to see deep into Union of Soviet Socialist Republics (USSR) airspace now that the US Congress took away Americas' Strategic Air Defense capabilities in the Mid-1980s when Carter took office. Then Clinton finished by taking away the Fighter Interceptor Squadrons (FISs) when he took office. Now anyone aircraft can fly below Americas' Strategic Radars without being seen unless there is an E-3B/C AWACS or Navy E-2 Hawkeye airborne, which is not that often due to other worldwide commitments.

In gest, Hubert bet a future beer knowing that he would win the bet. Upon his return to Tinker AFB, he met with his Commander and the 552ᵈ Commander and mentioned that he was going to Alaska to retire. At Tinker AFB, Dave too had seen the same problems and after fighting the same type of issues, Dave could see that it was a fight that he could not win. However, Dave was not willing to put his career on the line and chose to say nothing like most US officers. Therefore, like Hubert He too would chose to depart Tinker AFB, move to Alaska, and fly with the Elmendorf AFB AWACS squadron. Therefore, Hubert and Dave have a bet on who would arrive in Alaska first. In the meantime, unlike Dave, he did identify problems and chose not to stay quite.

Hubert won the bet by a few months when Dave thought that the AWACS squadron in Alaska would close. Dave followed Hubert to Alaska six months later. Upon returning to Tinker AFB, Hubert had to support a deployment to Panama to open the first AWACS operations as part of the Air Force Forces Command (AFFOR) Battle staff (BS). As part of the AFFOR BS, Hubert duties included creating a new AWACS operations instruction for US Southern Command (USSOUTHCOM) and the local 24ᵗʰ Wing. Having worked on the new AWACS detachment in Puerto Rico and counterdrug operations experience as an AWACS Mission Crew Commander (MCC) made Hubert the ideal choice to fill this new position.

In the meantime, Hubert continued working as the Assistant Operations Commander-Mission assigned in the 965ᵗʰ AACS. In this position, one of his jobs was to work with the wing training and weapons shops in upgrading the wings training curriculums after learning all the lessons learned in Iraq. In Hubert's view, the Chief of Training was creating a poorly trained E-3B/C AWACS force by lowering the training standards each year by lowering the training standards ten to twenty percent per year. Hubert was very vocal to the wing leadership, as were many Senior Officers. Nevertheless, the Operations Group and

Wing Leadership did not seem to listen. They seemed to worry more about politics and their nextpromotion. Each time any experience Mission Crew Commander (MCC) flew with any E-3B/C AWACS mission aircrew.

They could see the results of the new training program, which concerned them and the recent training programs reductions did not matter to the senior leadership. It was an accident waiting to happen as soon as the right circumstances with the right inexperienced aircrew flew together in the right contingency. Even as a Captain, Hubert could see this outcome and felt helpless because in a bureaucratic organization. Where individuals in power made crucial decisions in a political climate that put lives in danger just to advance individual careers. However, Hubert knew that he did not have the rank to make the needed real changes created by the AWACS and Air Force politicalpromotion climate that he learned to hate as an Officer. After all, as a new officer his Colonel told Hubert that he too idealist and that he would never advance past the rank of Captain.

One would think that all of this would be impossible for a Captain in such a large wing with so many Senior Officers. Part of the responsibilities included monitoring any E-3B/C AWACS flights supporting the counterdrug operation. The normal duties were twelve hours tours, seven days per week, or as required when an E-3B/C AWACS was airborne. As the sole Mission Crew Commander (MCC) on the AFFOR BS, there was no one else who could cover his duties when Hubert was not on position. Overall, this deployment went fast primarily since Hubert lived in the operations area. Always working on one task or another, after a while all looking the same just a different day.

During 1991, the year would be a year when Hubert would support less exercises but support more operational contingencies. He would start the year in Saudi Arabia flying over Iraq and return to support two Desert Flag Exercises, only to return to Saudi Arabia to support Operation Desert Shield, and Operation Desert Calm. Again, Hubert would have to return to Tinker AFB to conduct the JEMI Test, this time administered from March, AFB in California. A week later, Hubert returned to Saudi and another deployment of Operation Desert Shield only to return to support a Counternarcotics (CD) deployment, and a Fleet Exercise at the end of the year. Overall, most of the year spent flying the skies of Iraq and Kuwait with a few months in the warm skies of the Caribbean.

Hubert deployed for two-months to Roosevelt Roads (ROSY), Puerto Rico to set-up a new operation in support of the Commander-in-Chief (CINC) Task Group 4. 1 (TG-4. 1) in support of the Counterdrug (CD) Mission. TG-4. 1 was the US Navy working in the Caribbean. Since Hubert had developed the Air Force (AF) Force (AFFOR) Satcom procedures for the Task Group (TG) in the East-Pacific, creating new procedures were extremely easy for him to create. In less than six hours, Hubert had created a new TG-4. 1 Command and Control (C2) and a new Counternarcotics (CD) AWACS Procedures Plan added to the CD Operations Plan used for all CD Operations.

He did not realize that this would make him not only the Squadron expert, but also the Wing, and Air Division expert in counterdrugs. Hubert always hated the 'expert' label since he believed that everyone had good and bad days and the goal was to try to have good days as much as possible. Even on a bad day when everything was going wrong due to things that one could not control. However, in the military, every Senior Officer as was the leader label that went with every Senior Officer automatically regardless of how poor the officer performance is overused. Like most large bureaucratic organizations, the expert term is freely over used and every officer receives it even when unearned.

It was during this trip since Hubert was part of the Detachment Staff; Hubert received a request to support the Fleet Exercise 1-91 and 2-91. NATO E-3A AWACS deployed two aircraft to Roosevelt, Naval Air Station (NAS) for these exercises and stayed off base. Since the US had, four E-3B/C AWACS aircrews on base supporting the Counterdrug (CD) mission, two E-3B/C AWACS aircrafts diverted to support Fleet Exercise 1-91 and 2-91. Officially, Fleet Exercise started on 12 December 1991 with the first week consisting of spin-up training. However, Hubert first had some personnel issues to deal with caused by the new NATO aircrews.

On a, the NATO staff arranged for their crews to stay at hotels new the local beaches near San Juan. Since the exercise events would normally only last four to six hours, crew rest would not be an issue so Hubert as the Mission Staff Officer did not see any planning issues. However, on day four the hotel manager called him to complaint that the NATO crew during one of their parties had destroyed the bathroom washroom. Normally when aircrews stay off base, a Deployment Commander (Detco) takes special steps to make sure that the aircrews do not violated crew duty restrictions. Especially when staying at a resort near a popular beach in a tropical island filled with many tourists.

Due to over drinking, many of the aircrew members became careless and started breaking the surroundings in the suite that they were renting. What concerned Hubert was that the party was well into the crew duty day and the NATO E-3A AWACS Deployment Commander (Detco) not aware of the behavior of his personnel. Since Hubert was in NATO in a past assignment, he knew that many of the aircrew members tended to force the issue of not following or violating the twelve-hour rule of not drinking prior to starting crew duty. Although he did not mention this to the Detco, as the staff MCC, he took it as a personal action to make sure that the NATO aircrew met the flying directives.

The staff should not deal with such matters during a major exercise this issue. However, Hubert agreed to let the Deployment Commander (Detco) not deal with the situation since the aircrew was a NATO crew. Once Hubert became aware of the incident, he simply took care of the situation. There wereold friends on the NATO crew that were, not that it mattered. He saw no reason to wake-up the Rosy Detco in the middle of the night to advise him of the situation mainly because the issue was resolved.

The following morning, as far as Hubert knew, a different NATO aircrew reported to support a mission as part of the Fleet Exercise and two USE-3B/C AWACS aircrews reported in the main-Briefing room. Both aircrews received their normal pre-mission exercise briefing, intelligence briefing, and then each crew broke up and gave their individual briefs. The day prior, the crews had already completed their specialized Mission Planning (MP). The exercise airspace was west of Puerto Rico over was with the NATO E-3A AWACS serving as the Red-Air or Enemy assets and the USE-3B/C AWACS serving as the Blue-Airor Friendly assets.

Two opposing US aircraft carriers with associated ships assigned in the exercise surface area received orders to participate as opposing forces. In addition, US, US Customs, and British Navy ships were supporting their respective forces as were sub-surface forces (submarines) all assigned per the normal Operations Tasks Communications and the Operations Tasks Orders (OPTASKSCOMS and OPORDS) documents. Each E-3B/C AWACS contacted their participants on the Alpha Sierra (AS), which is the Anti-Surveillance Net or the Alpha Whisky (AW) Net, which is the Anti-Warfare Net. Red Forces started the exercise each day from the south and the Blue Forces started the exercise each day from the north. All aircraft and surface ships were required to stay five miles within the exercise area.

Possibly the most difficult mission to control from any E-3B/C AWACS is the Vector Assist Tactic (VASTAC) provided to B-52 Stratofortresses during maritime mission's. The intent of the VASTAC mission of to provide an initial attack vector to the B-52 and amplifying target information. The VASTAC attack also provides a post-attack to the B-52 aircrew once it comes off the target. During the Fleet Exercise, Hubert was the only US controller able to provide the VASTAC control mainly because he had conducted such control while assigned to NATO AWACS. Actually, only personnel assigned to the US Navy understand the VASTAC control requirements and all the technical requirements.

During one attack, formations of fighters were attacking the fleet at low level when Hubert noticed the southern aircraft carrier turn into the winds. Such a maneuver suggested that the carrier was in the process of launching fighters. Hubert quickly passed that information to the attacking fighter formation, which broke the attack once he advised the flight lead that he had contact of multiple fighters airborne from the Red-Air aircraft carrier. As soon as the Red-Air aircraft landed, Hubert re-engaged the Blue-Air attacking fighters on the aircraft carrier who then completed their attack. During the mission debrief, Hubert made it clear that the E-3B/C AWACS using its maritime radar can easily provide such control.

After the Fleet Exercise, Hubert remained in Puerto Rico for an additional month supporting the Detachment staff as the Mission Crew Commander (MCC) and flying Counterdrug (CD) Missions in the Caribbean. Since the TG 4. 1 was relatively new in the Caribbean, Hubert was one of the few MCCs with the in-theater experience, which meant that he had to fly more often than normal since he had to fly with every crew more than once to ensure training properly administered. During this era, airborne track started appearing from Colombia more often in the Caribbean mainly because it was the shortest route to North America and its drug customer base. Because of the effectiveness of the CD operations in the Caribbean, the terrorists would transfer many of their aircraft to the East Pacific.

On 2 November 1991, Hubert had to become the Assistant Operations Officer-Mission (ADO-M) for the 965th Airborne Air Control Squadron (AACS). Hubert accomplished the ADO-M duties in spite of being deployment normally two or three weeks every month. Upon returning to Tinker AFB, within a week Hubert was returning to Saudi Arabia for his third deployment to Saudi in support of Operation Desert Calm, Hubert finally pinned-on Major. As one of the few individuals who had supported all three operations (Shield, Storm, and Calm) in Saudi, the flights were over Iraqi airspace. The oil fields over Kuwait were still burning and on night sorties (missions), all that one could see was the orange skies.

Although some of the aircrew wanted to take pictures of the burning oil fields, by regulation, taking pictures not allowed. On one mission, a crewmember was caught taking pictures and the Aircraft Commander (AC) and Hubert both agreed that the aircrew would have to take the film away from the aircrew member and turn it in to the staff. In one case, while airborne, Hubert Heard a camera click, asked the member for the film, and gave the film to the Aircraft Commander (AC). Hubert decided to give the aircrew member a verbal reprimand since he was a junior aviator and in Hubert view, his actions did not warrant any higher punishment. An in taking a picture of burning oilfields during a flight that one could see on Cable News Network (CNN) daily not a major issue.

During Operation Desert Calm sorties (missions), the missions were primarily surveillance missions. In accordance with rules of engagement (ROE), Coalition Forces did not commit to take offensive actions against Iraqi helicopters that were still conducting offensive missions over Basra. Our crews would fly our missions where we intercepted the Iraqi helicopters with our fighter aircraft and simply escorted them in and out of the area. The next day we would learn from Intelligence Personnel or CNN that many civilians killed and there was little that we could do in accordance with ROE.

On one of these missions while over flying just south of Bagdad, the HAWK radar taken by the Iraqi military locked the E-3B/C AWACS the Hubert was in command. The HAWK is a medium range, surface-to-air guided missile that provides Air Defensecoverage against low-to-medium-altitude aircraft. It is a mobile, all-weather day, and night system. The missile is highly lethal, reliable, and effective against electronic countermeasures. Kuwaiti air-defense units equipped with US HAWK antiaircraft missiles downed about twenty-two Iraqi aircraft and one combat helicopter during the invasion of 2 August 1990.

The system later posed a possible threat to the US-led Coalition because Iraqi forces captured both HAWK and the M-220 Tube-launched, optically tracked, Wire-guided missile (TOW) missiles in Kuwait. As the MCC, Hubert quickly re-positions the AWACS, RJ, fighter CAPs, and other airborne assets under our control to stay outside the Hawk battery range. Iraq forces had taken the HAWK from Kuwait during their invasion. Upon reporting our actions to the CAOC, they directed US to disregard this threat stating that it was the F-14 Tomcat radar. Hubert tactfully replied to the Combined Air Operations Center (CAOC) that Hubert wanted to compliment the F-14 pilot for staying stationary for over ten minutes and instructed them that our assessment was different.

When our aircraft landed, the Combined Air Operations Center (CAOC) director on duty was there to meet the crew during the mission debrief at the RSAF building. As Hubert made it clear to the Colonel, it was Hubert responsibility as the Mission Crew Commander (MCC) to deploy airborne assets based on our assessment of any potential threats. Hubert would rather be safe than sorry. Hubert Wing DO agreed with Hubert actions, as did the rest of the crew and staff. However, Hubert did not make a friend in the Colonel who felt that his orders be executed without question as the command and control facility.

One of the unspoken rules of E-3B/C AWACS crews was that crews redeployed to Tinker AFB based on the rule that the first aircraft that arrives on station departs first. During this deployment, we had departed Tinker AFB with another E-3B/C AWACS who became airborne an hour after our departure. We had an ops-stop in England where we crew rested. Normally, this called for crews to accomplish a refueling over water just off the Maine Coast. On the second leg of the deployer mission, crews took additional fuel during a second refueling mission in the Mediterranean. During this phase, both deployer aircraft normally tried to arrive in Riyadh first since they knew that this would allow their crew to depart a week before the second aircraft.

At the end of the deployment, the Aircraft Commander (AC) tried to have her crew leave before our crew since her husband was the squadron Commander of her unit. As the MCC, Hubert made it clear to the staff that if her crew departed before his crew, that he would file a formal complaint since this not the normal process. Eventually, Hubert's crew was able to depart on time. However, by some administrative oversight, the staff forgot to arrange for the normal charter flight. After a heated discussion with the Deployments Commander (Detco), he agreed to allow Hubert to try to find other arrangements instead of waiting for the charter flight the following week. If we took the charter for the following week, this meant that all crews would delay by one week. Living in Riyadh even for one additional day seemed like an eternity.

Hubert's next stop was to go to the Riyadh base operations to find a US aircraft that was going to the US that had space for passengers (PAX). After talking with various Aircraft Commander (ACs), Hubert found a KC-135 Stratotanker aircraft going to Norfolk AFB, Virginia the following day that had not PAX. The AC gave Hubert a copy of his manifest to add our crew to the Tankers manifest. Hubert found a typewriter and added the names of our crew. As the MCC, Hubert always had a list of our flight orders on him. Hubert found other E-3B/C AWACS and non-AWACS maintenance and administrative members who were looking for transportation back to the US who were having problems finding flights.

Hubert asked them all for a copy of their deployment orders and added them to the manifest. Hubert instructed the ground personnel that if anyone asked that they were to say that they were E-3B/C AWACS crew and gave them a show time for our flight. Hubert returned to the E-3B/C AWACS Detachment and told the Deployment Commander (Detco) of our flight. Initially, again he was reluctant stating that he would lose control of the crews if he allowed our crew to leave the following crew. Hubert stated that it not logical since he lost control of all crews once they departed Riyadh. He agreed and allowed our crew to depart the following day on the KC-135 Stratotanker.

The first leg of the redeployer to England was non-eventful. Upon landing in England, Hubert found the Mobility Officer that with copies of our orders made follow-up flying arrangements once we landed at Norfolk AFB on civilian flights. The next morning we all reported on time and went to the Chow Hall for breakfast. Initially, Hubert had problems with the Chow Hall staff that wanted US to pay for our meals. Hubert spoke with the Senior Non-Commissioned Officer (NCO) and Major in charge of the Chow Hall and Hubert stated that we were on combat orders and that following those rules that our meals were supposed to be free. After Hubert said that Hubert would file an Inspector General (IG) complaint if we paid, they both agreed that all we had to do was sign our names and social security numbers on the meal sign-in sheet.

Hubert also noted that the non-AWACS members were still on the bus and he went to the bus and told them to have breakfast. At this point, Hubert advised that someone would meet the KC-135 Stratotanker once we arrived with airline tickets to our final destination. Hubert reminded the non-AWACS members that Hubert had instructed them in Saudi

Arabia that if anyone asked that they were E-3B/C AWACS and if anyone had a problem to come and discuss it with me. When we arrived in Norfolk AFB, they all thanked Hubert saying that they had never met an Officer such as Hubert who took care of everyone. Hubert reminded them that we were all part of Team US and thanked them for their recent efforts in war. Without their help, then not all flyers could accomplish our duties as a single team.

During our flight to Norfolk AFB, we had head winds that delayed our arrival in Norfolk AFB by two hours. This meant that our crew would miss our connecting flight to Oklahoma City, Oklahoma. The good consequence was that the non-AWACS members were all going all over the west coast and were able to make their show times. Not wanting to delay our arrival back home, Hubert went to base operations in search of any aircraft going west. Hubert found a C-141 Transport aircraft that was flying to Beale AFB, California and once the Aircraft Commander (AC) found out that we were returning from Saudi, he agreed to make an Ops-Stop at Tinker AFB. This gave time for Hubert to call Raymond-24 and fax them the list of phone number of family members to call to let them know their arrival times back in Oklahoma.

The C-141 Starlifter fulfills the vast spectrum of airlift requirements through its ability to airlift combat forces over long distances, deliver those forces and their equipment by air, land or airdrop, resupply forces, and transport the sick and wounded from the hostile area to advanced medical facilities. A few hours later, the E-3B/C AWACS crew loaded our bags in the C-141 and started our final flight to Tinker AFB. At the end of this redeployment from Saudi Arabia to Oklahoma, the total flight time had almost been the same as if we had taken our own aircraft. The C-141 took our crew directly to Tinker AFB where our families were waiting for US or those who were single had their cars parked.

Hubert had not been home long and due to his unit duties worked long days. In addition to flying two or three times per week, this kept him busy but he always made time for Darlene and Tawny. On Fridays he always made time to take Darlene to the Officers Club for Happy Hour and on Saturday's it was time to go dancing at one of two country dance places either in the local area. The Tinker AFB Officer's Club on Friday night was always full mainly because everyone was ready to relax after a long week of hard work. For married couples, it meant that they could spent time together and for singles it was an opportunity to meet someone else. Happy Hour always had free snacks for club members, which most Officers normally were.

In Dell City, Oklahoma, there was a Country and Western Dancing Place where Hubert and Darlene went to every Saturday until they heard of a club in Oklahoma City named the 'Club Rodeo' on Meridian Avenue with a large circular dance floor. Club Rodeo would be Darlene and Hubert's regular dance place whenever Hubert was in town now that Tawny was older and she was able to have friends spend the weekend with her. She refused to let Darlene get her a baby sitter because now that she was in Junior High, she was too old for one. Therefore, Darlene allowed a friend stay the night with Tawny and she would regularly call her nearly hourly.

Choctaw, Oklahoma was a great place to live for a family. Choctaw was a tiny town with a small old fashion restaurant where a family could take their time to eat their meal and then read their newspaper. Followed with a conversation with their neighbors or one of the old timers who would tell you one of the stories of the good old days of how Choctaw used to be. Then go by the local Braums and get an ice cream before returning home. In Oklahoma, Braums known for their great ice cream and their old fashion hamburgers or cheeseburgers throughout Oklahoma was a common restaurant that Darlene and Hubert looked forward to eating. Braums also offers any dairy products that you can find at the grocery store but at cheaper prices and better quality.

During the week of 18 July 1991, Hubert received the task as the lead for the Joint Electromagnetic Interference (JEMI) Test Project Manager (PM). Pre-Operation Desert Storm, Hubert had served as the PM for the JEMI test that created the pre-war jamming plan for the war. This test had taken place of the southeastern part of the US and the jamming had taken out most of the radars in that part of the US Now it was time to see the results of the jamming. This second test would take place off the coast of California over water near San Diego. Again, US Navy, Air Force, and Coast Guard assets would jam each other and see their effects on the Federal Aviation and their internal systems. At the end of the JEMI test, the engineers determined that it would take a hundred years to analyze all the recorded data taken from the E-3B/C AWACS aircraft.

For the next few months, Hubert went through a period where he received regular commitments to support multiple exercises. Initially, Hubert requested that task to support the Green Flag 91-5 and Green Flag 91-6 exercises located in Nellis AFB, Nevada in August and September 1991. He hoped to take some time off to take Darlene skiing as he had planned but each time it seemed another deployment seemed to get in the way. During November and December, Hubert returned to Puerto Rico to support the Counterdrug (CD) mission.

"Ok Darlene, it's your turn to pick an assignment," said Hubert. Darlene asked what the options were and he made it clear that he did not want to take the assignment to Langley AFB, Virginia. Taking the Air Combat Command slot was better forpromotion but he mentioned that going to Alaska for the last assignment might be good. Darlene and Hubert had always selected their assignments together and based on where they wanted to live versus what was good forpromotion. Many past bosses had always mentioned that hispromotion potential was unlikely unless he took key jobs. Yet, Hubert had always believed that if he did his best at whatever job he was doing thatpromotions would follow. At least he would enjoy what he was doing.

At this point Hubert had been assigned to Tinker AFB for over two years of which Hubert had been home less than three months. Hubert decided that Hubert would volunteer for an assignment to Alaska. The Wing Director of Operations (DO) and Hubert's squadron Commander both called him in to discuss this assignment hoping that he would stay in Tinker AFB. Hubert explained to both of them that Hubert planned to retire once Hubert had the two-year time-in-grade requirement, as a major and that living in Alaska would be something that Hubert would enjoy doing. They both explained that Hubert had a Promising career at Tinker AFB and would eventually become a squadron Commander.

However, Hubert received apromise of the Chief of the Counterdrug Division at the 552nd Air Control Wing (ACW) and now it seemed to be on hold. For some reason, Hubert's timing always seemed to be bad when it came to wing jobs. Every time he received a wing job, each time they seemed to be on hold at the last moment for some unknown reason. Hubert decided that if the Wing Commander could not keep his work as a Colonel, then hit was not worth much as an Officer much less as a leader. Therefore, Hubert decided that he did not want to work for that type of Officer or leader regardless of what future Hubert would Receive at Tinker AFB. Promotion had never been a priority for Hubert in the military. Trying to do what was right and doing a good job during every assignment was always his goal.

At the time, the E-3B/C AWACS squadron at Elmendorf AFB, Alaska was received notification that the unit scheduled for closure and the Wing Leadership both felt that Hubert would probably not be in E-3B/C AWACS for too long once Hubert arrived in Alaska. Hubert explained to both of them that Hubert had no problem working in the Elmendorf Air

Defense unit since Hubert had been qualified in that system. Hubert made a bet with the Wing Director of Operations (DO) that the E-3B/C AWACS unit would not close and later in Panama, Hubert collected on that bet when Hubert saw the DO during a deployment.

"Dad, I took those classes five years ago," said Tawny. Living overseas and going to a Department of Defense (DOD) school, had given her an excellent education. After kindergarten, she had always gone to a DoD school and had loved school, Even though she was in the Honor Society, she was getting bored with school since her classes were repeating what she had learned in the past. Hubert knew that it was time to return overseas and leave Oklahoma after two years of living there. Besides, since arriving at Tinker AFB, he deployed nine months of every year and he was getting tired of living off a mobility bag where all his belongings were packed.

Just prior to departing Tinker AFB, Hubert made an appointment with the wing leadership and mentioned that in his view that due to the lack of training that the wing was going to have an accident. Each year, the wing lowered its training standards by ten or twenty percent, which meant the all-new aircrew members, were being trained too much lower standards. Hubert used the airborne surveillance technician (AST) crew position as an example and noted that once the AST was required to build sectors and needed to know detailed information pertaining to the radar. Now ASTs only had to track radar targets, which in Hubert's view even monkeys could accomplish the tasks trained by the Wing Training and the TTS Instructors.

On 14 April 1994, while deployed in Turkey, two USAF F-15s controlled by a 552nd Air Control Wing (ACW) E-3B/C AWACS aircraft and aircrew accidentally shot down two US Army Black Hawk helicopters while they passed through the northern Iraq no-fly zone. The F-15s had mistaken the two aircraft for Soviet built HIND helicopters. This friendly fire incident led to the deaths of 26 people and galvanized national interest in E-3B/C AWACS activities. This unfortunate accident also provided the genesis for a massive recertification process for all 1,300 Airborne Warning and Control (AW&C) members within the US AWACS community. Sadly, to most senior Airborne Battle Mangers (ABMs), it was an "I told you so," situation that could have been avoided. Unfortunately, the military is toopromotion oriented and warfighters do not receive Promotions over staff Officers who run the Air Force and the military.

A senior member of the mission crew received a court-martial for dereliction of duty for this incident, but some individuals received acquittal. In Hubert's view, his former boss sold out the mission crew who received a court-martial in an effort for apromotion. The helicopter victims all received purple hearts, when the medal expanded eligibility to include friendly-fire wounds or death. The lack of experience played a major role in this event as did the lack of training that the 552nd refused to admit since then it would have to admit that its leadership played a crucial role and that the wing and training leadership failed. Most E-3B/C AWACS aircrew members were not surprised when they heard of the accidental shoot down regardless of where they assigned in the world.

962ND AACS, ELMENDORF AFB, AK.

After Tinker AFB, the Contreras family received an assignment in the 962nd Airborne Air Control Squadron (AACS) located in Elmendorf Air Force Base (AFB), Alaska. Initially upon arrival to Alaska, Hubert received the task as the Chief of Mission Standardization and Evaluations (Stan/Eval)-Mission. Elmendorf AFB, which is adjacent to Anchorage, is the largest Air Force installation in Alaska and home of the Headquarters, Alaskan Command (ALCOM), Alaskan NORAD Region (ANR), Eleventh Air Force and the 3rd Wing. Construction on Elmendorf Field began on 8 June 1940, as a major and permanent military airfield near Anchorage.

From 22 April 1992 to 9 May 1999, Hubert received an assignment to Alaska as a member of the 962nd Airborne Warning and Control Squadron (AWACS) as a Chief of Standardization and Evaluations (Stan/Eval)-Mission, Flight Commander, and Chief of Stan/Eval. After the 962nd AWACS, Hubert received an assignment to the 3rd Operations Support Squadron (OSS) as the Wing Command and Control Systems (WCCS) Program Manager (PM) and Assistant Director of Operation (ADO). During this assignment, he would complete at least six deployments to Panama in support of the counterdrug operations.

Upon arriving at the 962nd AWACS squadron, Hubert finally received his first Meritorious Service Medal (MSM) award for his accomplishments at Tinker Air Force Base (AFB), Oklahoma. After five nominated and only receiving the MSM once, Hubert felt betrayed by the Air Force but still honored with his achievements and sacrifices that, he and his family had endured during his time in Oklahoma. Especially when he just learned that, his Air Medal was downgraded because Tinker AFB had submitted the award too late to an Air Achievement Medal. Unlike many other aviators, he deployed too much like many aviators to make sure that the suspense dates to submit the Air Achievement Medal award were not submitted on time by the administrative personnel. This in spite that all of his flights were in Iraqi and were combat or combat support sorties (missions). To make matters worse, the Air Achievement Medal award would use the generic wording used for the Air Achievement Medal that would not even mention the Iraqi War where all the sorties were flown. Hubert knew that it was time to retire from the new Air Force where its new leaders did not care about taking care of its people or doing what was right.

His efforts during the counterdrug operations resulted in over 181 arrests and the confiscation of twenty-three aircraft, thirteen boats, and over sixteen,500 kilos of drugs, all valued at over $1. 7 Billion dollars. His efforts as Chief of Stan/Eval would include technical and managerial expertise in preparing the unit and OSS for the Pacific Air Forces (PACAF) Major Command Operations Readiness Inspection (ORI), Phase I and Phase II inspections. He received excellent ratings during all inspections for the E-3B/C AWACS unit and the OSS. His achievements earned him the Meritorious Service Medal, First Oak Leaf Cluster awarded by Colonel Wayne R. Heskew, USAF, 3rd Wing Commander upon arriving in Arizona.

In order to understand how Elmendorf became an Air Force Base (AFB), it is important that one understand that the first Air Corps personnel arrived on 12 August 1940 in Alaska. Following World War II, Elmendorf assumed an increasing role in the defense of North America as the uncertain wartime relations between the United States and the Soviet Union deteriorated into the Cold War. Even during Hubert's time in Alaska, the E-3B/C AWACS aircrews regularly were scrambled to intercept Russian BEAR Bombers flying near the Alaskan airspace. The 11th Air Force redesigned as the Alaskan Air Command (AAC) on 18 December 1945. The Alaskan Command established 1 January 1947, also headquartered at Elmendorf AFB, was a unified command under the Joint Chiefs of Staff based on lessons learned during World War II when a lack of unity of command hampered operations to drive the Japanese from the western Aleutian Islands of Attu and Kiska.

Colonel Stromp was Hubert's first Commander that had come from Tinker AFB, Oklahoma. Aviators referred to Colonel Stromp as one of the "Tinkerites" or better known as the "brown nosers" especially since Stromp did not receive apromotion to Colonel. Therefore, the older E-3B/C AWACS aviators tended no not have much respect for Colonel Stromp regardless of his rank. Colonel Stromp tended to wear her husband's rank and equally disliked by all the wives. The Director of Operations was Lieutenant Colonel Clark that also came from Tinker AFB.

Carter like Hubert had been an Assistant Operations Officer (ADO) at the 965th AACS. The only difference was that Hubert had just pinned on Major and Carter had been a Lieutenant Colonel for years. No one knew much about Carter's wife. Since the 962nd was a small unit and due to the harsh winters, the role of the wives played an important role.

Initially, this assignment was one of the most rewarding assignments. Since the unit scheduled for closure, manning levels were at thirty to forty percent, which meant that everyone had to work as one team in order to be able to accomplish all mission requirements. In the Mission Crew Commander (MCC) area, we had three individuals who were all majors in the unit at this point, which meant that one deployed, one was either flying or take time off, and the third MCC was in charge of the mission crew within the unit. It would be months before the assignment pipeline restart once the Alaska congressional representative changed the Air Force's plans of closing the 962nd AACS.

With three Majors as 17XXs in the unit, one would always be deployed to Panama, one would normally stay in the unit, and the third would try to take time off complete the required mandatory training. It was during this era that the Air Force converted the 17XX Air Force Specialty Codes (AFSCs) to 13B. Each deployment was for a month plus travel, which made each deployment nearly thirty-six days. This meant the every three months, Hubert found himself deployed in Panama if not more. In all the years that Hubert was in the military, he had missed most of the holidays and all of his birthdays, which Hubert celebrated belated.

Since Hubert was already a Mission Ready (MR) Mission Crew Commander (MCC), he received a buddy-ride to become qualified in Alaska. A buddy-ride is a qualified MCC rides with a fellow MCC, which qualifies the member as a MR E-3B/C AWACS aircrew. The fellow E-3B/C AWACS aircrew must be either an instructor or an evaluator aircrew member. Once

Darlene and Hubert found a house and they settled into his house, Hubert was loaded on a crew list to deploy to 24th Wing, Howard Air Base (AB) Panama. It seemed that during all of Hubert's assignments, that unlike all other military members who normally receive six months to a year to become MR, he always received the same rating in ten through twenty-five percent of the time. Therefore, each time leading to his none stop coming and going from one worldwide location to another. Alaska was a new record and well below the ten through twenty-five percent record.

General Barry Richard McCaffrey attended the Phillips Academy. He is a graduate of the US Military Academy Class of 1964, and earned an M. A. in Civil Government from the America University in 1970. He also attended the National Security and Executive Education programs at Harvard University. His postgraduate military education includes the National Defense University, the US Army War College, the Command and General Staff College, and the Defense Language Institute's program in Vietnamese.

Hubert's exposure to General McCaffrey occurred during the regular Howard Counterdrug meetings, which he attended as the 552nd AWACS Deployment Commander (Detco). During these weekly meeting's he requested local intelligence support. Hubert normally did not sit back and ignore problems that affected operations, his personnel, or his unit. That is why many of his senior raters had told him that he would never be promoted above Captain yet his troops respected him as an officer and a leader. Hubert's viewpoint was that no one attacked his employees without first going to him. It was his responsibility to correct his subordinates and no one else. Especially since every employee if they made a mistake deserved the chance to correct their mistake at least once without retribution as long as he or she learned from a mistake.

During this era, General Barry Mccaffrey served as the USSOUTHCOM Commander. General Mccaffrey would become Americas' first Drug Czar and an Officer that did not impress Hubert. Mainly because General Mccaffrey used his staff to create his colorful staff meeting slides. In Hubert's view, his staff was not there to assist any E-3B/C 552ᵈAWACSCommander also referred as the AWACS Deployment Commander (Detco). Since Hubert had built the briefing room that General Mccaffrey used for his staff meeting when he stood up the Counterdrug AFFOR Battlestaff, Hubert was aware of the entire Howard Air Force Base (AFB) operation. Howard Air Base (AB) had just been redesigned to an AFB by the Air Force and his the US South Air Force (SOUTHAF) that he was assigned to although he was accomplishing a six month deployment supporting the AWACS Wing at Tinker AFB, Oklahoma as the (AF) Standardization and Evaluations (Stan/ Eval) AWACS Flight Examiner.

For example, of the twenty-four intelligence personnel individuals assigned in Panama, Hubert could not depend on anyone of them for dedicated support. The intelligence support that General Mccaffrey's staff provided at best was clearly outdated on how to support aviators or at best misinformed. The information provided to Hubert'sE-3B/C AWACS Staff was clearly useless, mainly because General Mccaffrey's staff did not understand the E-3B/C AWACS employment tactics. At times, Hubert wondered if General Mccaffrey staff truly understood the terrorists' employment tactics. Considering that under his watch, the previous E-3B/C AWACS Detcos had aone hundred percent failure rate. That failure rate changes when Hubert became the E-3B/C AWACS Detco during multiple deployments.

As a deployed AWACS Commander, he and other commanders felt that the intelligence support was inadequate. During this era, Hubert was also a member of the 12th Air Force Counterdrug (CD) staff and the 12th Air Force (Stan/ Eval) Flight Examiner. Using his 12th AF position, he was able to get support for all Air Force flying units that enhance all the local operations and increased the CD success within Latin America. General McCaffrey's staff had little to do with the success achieved by the US Air Force in Hubert's view although USSOUTHCOM took the credit. However, in Hubert's view, this did not matter since it was a team effort and it was "Team US," which achieved the drug busts.

During this deployment as an E-3B/C AWACSDeployment Commander (Detco) when Hubert was also a 12th Air Force Counternarcotics Officer, he called 12th Air Force and had his office deploy and pay for a Non-Commissioned Officer (NCO) intelligence specialist. During one of General Mccaffrey's staff meetings, Hubert made this point clear to the General. However, after the E-3B/C AWACS Detco failed achieving any drug busts until Hubert became the E-3B/C AWACS Detco, having a successful Detco kept the General from saying anything to Hubert who tended to be vocal.

General Mccaffrey would depart USSOUTHCOM and General Wesley K. Clark, Sr. would be the new Commander. Like General Mccaffrey, General Clark would also not impress Hubert, convincing him that like in the US Air Force, all modern US Army or all military Generals were simply staff Officers and no longer warfighters. In addition to working with General Clark in Miami, Hubert supported the General at various Human Rights Conferences. It was at these conferences that convinced Hubert that General Clark was a true politician and not a soldier's General. Although, like all general's General Clark was accustomed to accomplishing many tasks all at one time. Over fifteen years, Hubert would work at USSOUTHCOM supporting many SOUTHCOM Commanders. Unlike General Mccaffrey that did not impress Hubert, General Clark would prove to be one of the better US Army generals.

Wesley Kanne Clark, Sr. , born on December 23, 1944 is a retired general of the US Army. Graduating as valedictorian of the class of 1966 at West Point, Clark received the award of a Rhodes Scholarship to the University of Oxford where he obtained a degree in Philosophy, and later graduated from the Command and General Staff College with a master's degree in military science. General Clark received the US Southern Command (USSOUTHCOM) post despite these rumors. Congress approved his promotion to full general in June 1996, and General John M. Shalikashvili signed the order. Clark said he was not the original nominee, but the first officer chosen "hadn't been accepted for some reason."

In Hubert's viewpoint as a senior Air Force Officer, he was impressed with General Clark operational knowledge but unfortunately, unlike other USSOUTHCOM commanders that he would work over the decades, General Clark would spend little time in country and more time working on his political career. In many ways, General Clark was like the new Air Force generals and missed his former Air Force generals that had all retired and no longer on active duty. However, in fairness to General Clark, Hubert had only been in contact with the general a few dozen times during his time in Miami as a member of the USSOUTHAF staff or while supporting the US Bogotá MILGP Staff.

The Human Rights Conference received the task at a major hotel in Miami with military and civilian leaders from Latin America serving as the representatives. Two twelve-hour shifts received formal scheduling with Hubert working on the day shift. During his second day, Hubert noticed a Chief Master Sargent (Chief) sleeping on the couch in the day room where the day shirt would take breaks. Hubert spoke with the Chief when he saw that he was awake later in the morning and asked him why he was sleeping in the couch. He mentioned that since he was in the Reserves, that he had to pay for his own hotel and that he could not afford a room due to the high cost in Miami, Florida.

Hubert told the Chief that since he had two double beds in his room and he was working the day shift, to take his key and sleep in the empty double bed. Once he got off the day shift, he would go to the hotel and get an extra key. Since they were on opposite shifts, this way both would have the room to sleep. Hubert continued working with his Human Rights Conference group, led by an Argentinean General. Hubert's primary role was to serve as the group's interpreter and create the team's slides for each meeting. At the final presentation, General Clark and Lieutenant General Randall Mark Schmidt presented the closing remarks. It was during this conference that Hubert first met General Clark. Prior to working with him at the new US Southern Command (USSOUTHCOM) headquarters, built in Miami. Even though Hubert on paper received a permanent assignment to Tucson, Arizona, it seemed that physically he lived in Miami, Florida and Latin America.

As a young Airman First Class (A1C) assigned to the Consolidated Base Personnel Office (CBPO), Hubert had met many Generals at MacDill AFB, Florida while he in-processed them into the base. As an A1C responsible for the In-Processing Branch at MacDill AFB, Hubert would assemble the entire team that would normally in process all personnel into a new installation except Generals. For Generals, Hubert would take the in-process team to the Generals' office and one at a time accomplished the in-process requirements. During those initial two years assigned to the CBPO, Hubert in-processed dozens of Generals assigned to the Readiness Command.

It was also the first time that Hubert saw an executive Officer working for a General who was a major. The executive Officer was responsible for providing the General his coffee and his newspaper first thing in the morning. It was at that moment that Hubert determined that anyone could become a US Air Force Officer. Especially an Air Force pilot and a General's executive Officer. It was also the exact moment that Hubert decided that he would never become a pilot or an executive Officer for a General. He felt that if that is what it took to receivepromotion, that he rather not received apromotion in the US Air Force.

The 24th Wing Commander was a C-24 Douglas Aircraft Commander (AC) who supported Hubert as a Detco and later as a 12th Air Force Stan/Eval Officer. The 24th Commander would also request that Hubert deploy to the 24th Wing for six months on a Stan/Eval SAV assist that the 12th Air Force commander approved. Colonel Winhead, the 552nd AWACS Deputy Wing Commander who had been one of Hubert's past supervisors also worked with Hubert during this era. During this era, the 24th Wing Commander was in Panama the entire period that Hubert deployed to Panama until the 24th Wing, Howard Air Base (AB) closure.

"You have to deploy already?" asked Darlene. Darlene mentioned to Hubert that they should have stayed in Oklahoma since Hubert deployed just as much here in Alaska as in Oklahoma. What made it difficult, for the past six months before Hubert arrived, the unit slated for closure until Senator Stevens, and Republican-Alaska changed the Air Forces mind. It made no sense to the Senator to close the AWACS, which was the only unit in the military that would see the Union of Soviet Socialist Republics (USSR) BEAR Bombers just a few hundred miles east from Alaska with its radar. Hubert had mentioned that same logic to his Tinker AFB Wing Commander when he tried to talk him out of coming to Alaska.

During this era, Hubert deployed to Panama four different times. Each time, he was the Detachment Commander (Detco) for sixty days and flew as an Instructor Mission Crew Commander (IMCC) or MCC while supporting the Counterdrug (CD) operations. During the first two deployments, Hubert was responsible for standing up the CD operations and then establishing the wartime maintenance capabilities. Since he had served as the Air Force (AF) Force Battle Staff AFFOR (BS) BS, this gave Hubert many insights and advantages over other Detco's that followed him.

During 1992, in addition to deploying to Panama, Hubert received the task to support Amalgam Chief 92-1 and 92-1,

Cope-Thunder 92-1, 92-2, 92-3, and 92-4, Aloha Hornet 92-1 in Hawaii, the 9th Operational Readiness Inspection (ORI), and four deployments to Panama beginning in February, June, September, and December 1992. Amalgam Chief would be one of the first exercises where the Predator received the task during an OJCS/J3 sponsored exercise. The Cope-Thunder received the task in Alaska in the largest airspace anywhere in the world. During 1992, Hubert would also deploy to Site-2 (Classified Site) two times, which at the time was still a classified location in the Middle East, which meant that he would be home but a few weeks overall.

This type was a typical schedule for an AWACS aircrew member that would eventually lead to the AWACS Wing closure. Due mainly because of poor leadership who refused to tell the national authorities that the AWACS received higher headquarters tasks year after year. Nevertheless, as long as the senior leadership continued to receivepromotions, the wing leadership never said 'no' and the remaining E-3B/C AWACS Officers continued to have the lowestpromotion rates in the USAF in spite of executing the primary mission of the military. Even supply Officers or security Police had much higherpromotion rates than E-3B/C AWACS aircrew Officers who most retired as majors if lucky.

"You'll never believe who wants to have dinner with us tonight," said Hubert. Captain James an old acquaintance from Geilenkirchen Germany and Tinker AFB, Oklahoma wanted to go out to dinner with Hubert and Darlene. Hubert was surprised that he insisted to this dinner. Captain James was visiting from Virginia where he James worked at the new Air Combat Command (ACC). He would tell Darlene and Hubert that he divorced his wife of over twenty years and married a wife that looked like his wife. Darlene and Hubert were surprised since she was his High School sweet heart and they had two boys. Captain James apologized to Darlene for his behavior in Geilenkirchen noting that he tended to be too structured.

"I have to return to Hawaii," said Hubert. The year prior, Hubert had deployed in February in order to be home so that he could be home during the months that he thought the snow would be worse. The two years prior, the worse snowfall of the year had been in January and February 1992. The first year Hubert deployed to Panama and the second year Hubert deployed to Hawaii to support Aloha Hornet 92-1. It was the middle of the winter and only a week after returning from Panama that Hubert told Darlene that he had to take an E-3B/C AWACS aircraft and aircrew to Hawaii for a Naval exercise. Unfortunately, the Hawaii trips were too short to have Darlene join him.

Before Hubert departed to Hawaii, Darlene called him at the squadron and told him that Tawny had a problem at school. A teacher wanted her to punish her for not turning a paper in on time that she had turned in on time. There was another student named Tammy Contreras that had not turned in her homework and he gave her Tawny's homework credit. Two students' recalled Tawny turning in her homework, yet the teacher refused to admit his mistake. What made this matter worse was that the school Vice Principle supported the teacher, which made matters worse. It seemed that modern educators had lost all common sense and Darlene had no choice but call Hubert to take care of the situation.

At first, Darlene went to school and she clearly was too mad to handle the situation. When Darlene called Hubert at work, without hesitation, he dropped everything at work and drove to Bartlett High School, which was just off the south gate of Elmendorf AFB. Once he arrived at school, he walked into the Vice Principals office who took the teachers position. Hubert made it clear that since both men were not making any sense, that if they both wanted to handle this matter in court that it was up to them to make this decision at that point. They could see from Hubert's face that he was serious and they decided to drop the issue and not give Tawny detention. Then Hubert returned to the base to continue his Mission Planning (MP) for Hawaii.

Like the year before, Hubert hadpromised to be home during the winter and had made sure that he was home during the worse months of the winter. However, once he left, the worse snowfall of the year would occur two days after Hubert departed Anchorage. Again, Hubert would hear on the telephone, "you are never here when it snows". Darlene would be up 24/7 in order to keep the snow clear until the plows came into the local streets. The first year Darlene had to use a shovel until Hubert purchase a snow blower. Although that helped, it still was hard work when the snow pile reached higher than the house. In this case, on the first day Darlene would open the garage and see the snow all the way to the top of the garage when she started opened the garage door and started clearing the snow. Tawny would help her and bring her coffee 24/7 day and night until the city plows came through.

The Aloha Hornet 92-1 in Hawaii was a maritime exercise with the US Navy. On one mission, Hubert challenged the Mission Crew to conduct an emergency power down overhead the airport with the Aircraft Commander (AC) conducting a control landing overhead spinning into a landing pattern. Within five minutes, the mission systems powered down, which is the minimum time that the systems powered down safely. At this point, the mission radar had been already been powered down, which is the main system. On one occasion, Hubert had only the crew leader's mission plan and allowed the remaining crewmember to go down town for dinner.

While the crew that went to dinner, they were dancing. Unknown to one of the female Officers, they kept filling her drink with rum and got her drunk. Later in the night, the group wanted to continue dancing at a different location, decided to leave the drunken female Officer in the military van, and took a picture of her. The data link picture sent to one of the wives back in Alaska that eventually given to the Commanders wife. In the meantime, the friend who requested if he would join him at the restaurant to take her back to the base called Hubert.

The Aloha Hornet 92-1 in Hawaii exercise supported the F-15s Falcons from Kadena, Okinawa and US Navy F-18s deployed to Hawaii. This operation also called for air-to-air refueling missions using KC-10 Extender tankers. US Navy ships were working south of Hawaii and Japanese Naval ships were supporting the exercise. The exercise play area was south of Hawaii, which meant that the E-3B/C AWACS aircrew had a lot of flexibility as to where it wanted to orbit. Normally, Hubert chose to orbit north of the play area although he was able to declare "due regard" and fly anywhere he wanted without the control of the Air Traffic Center (ATC) rules. In Hawaii, Hubert and his Weapons Controller (WCs) also had to Mission Plan (MP) to control KC-10 Extender Tankers versus the normal KC-135 Stratotanker. The KC-10 is a three-engine KC-10 aircraft airline that does the transferring of fuel in the air to aircraft including the E-3B/C AWACS and multiple fighter aircraft. One KC-10 provided much more fuel than the KC-135 so this exercise would be easier for the Weapons Team during the exercise when aircraft had to return for re-attack.

The McDonnell Douglas KC-10 Extender is the military adaptation of the three-engine KC-10 airliner for the USAF. The KC-10 incorporates military-specific equipment for its primary roles of transport and aerial refueling. The KC-10 developed to supplement the KC-135 Stratotanker following experiences in Southeast Asia and the Middle East. The KC-10 was the second McDonnell Douglas transport aircraft selected by the Air Force following the C-9. Sixty KC-10s, produced for the USAF and two similar tankers, build for the Royal Netherlands Air Force under the designation KDC-10.

The KC-10 Extender, used mainly in the Pacific by the Air Force, in Europe, or during contingencies was not the main Air Force tanker. Like the KC-135, which was the main Air Force tanker, both tankers served as transport aircraft in route to deployment locations. The KC-10 plays a key role in the mobilization of US military assets, taking part in overseas operations far from home. These aircraft participated in the 1986 bombing of Libya and 1999 NATO bombing of Yugoslavia, and more recently, Operations Enduring Freedom, Iraqi Freedom, and Noble Eagle. However, the KC-10 was most notable for its participation in the Gulf War. The KC-10 proved vital the airlift and aerial refueling effort and will serve in the Air Force until 2043.

The fighters used the normal Dissimilar Air Control Tactics (DACT) air-to-air tactics with Blue forces attacking Red forces. Normally the Blue-Air tactics consisted of attacking the Red surface targets early in the morning just prior to sunrise. Since the E-3B/C AWACS has the maritime radar, it is able to identify when the aircraft carrier will launch aircraft, which assists attacking aircraft during its attack. This exercise not exception and Hubert's Mission Crew provided timely inputs that assisted the Blue-Air. After the mission that was typical of most of theAloha Hornet 92-1 missions, Hubert tried to let, as many of his crew not mission plan after the first few missions.

Mainly because by then most members had seen enough to know, what the exercise required. However, Hubert made sure that a crewmember from every crew position was present to mission plan. This way every possible option or every section received the proper planning and preparation for the next mission. Then once the Mission Planning (MP) crew completed the next day MP, the crew would normally meet somewhere for a crew dinner. That was the case on this day when one of his Captains called him at the MP room to advise him that a female officer was a crew van left by her fellow friends. Without knowing the details, Hubert became aware that she was drunk and Hubert told the Captain to keep it quiet for now.

Hubert drove and picked both Officers and the Captain took the drunken female Officer to her room alone with the hotel-staff who was a female employee. The next morning Hubert gave the riot act to the crew for using bad judgment on leaving a drunk female in an empty van and put in danger. That is not how a professional should treat a friend and also told them that sending a picture back to Alaska was stupid at best or malicious. Especially, since all the wives called Darlene to ask her what was going on. They knew that Hubert always kept in contact with her no matter where deployed. They also knew that she would also find out what truly occurred. Then Hubert's Commander called him to find out what was going on and he told him what actually happened.

During the first Mission Planning (MP) session, Hubert made sure that everyone was ready to participate in the exercise and put his or her mistake and guilt behind. He also made sure that those involved apologized to the female Captain who in his view they put her in danger. In spite of this, the exercise was a success until the final day when the mission radar broke. Once the Hubert was as the Mission Crew Commander (MCC) was able to confirm that the radar was broke, he got on the Satcom radio and told the 962nd Airborne Air Control Squadron (AACS) Commander that he would have to redeploy to Tinker AFB to either fix the aircraft or change aircraft. A week later, Hubert and his aircrew departed Tinker AFB with a new E-3B/C AWACS aircraft and returned to Alaska.

In addition, to the 962nd AACS AWACSaircrews deploying to Panama every two or three months, and the crews regularly deployed to other areas in the Pacific. For example, Hubert took E-3B/C AWACS aircrafts and aircrews to Nellis AFB Nevada for Flag Exercises. On more than one occasion, he had to take an aircraft to Hawaii to support an exercise. In addition, the 962nd AACS and Hubert had to support real-world operations missions in Korea whenever there was tension in Korean Demilitarized Zone (DMZ). Finally, many other commitments had higher priorities commitment wise where E-3B/C AWACS aircraft received tasks. For example, Hubert deployed to Fuchu, Japan in support of a 5th Air Force exercise in the Japanese Combined Air Operations Center (CAOC) as each commitment adds additional months away from home.

Prior to Hubert's fifth deployment to 24th Wing, Howard Air Base (AB) Panama, Hubert became an AWACS Flight Commander on 1 October 1992. The 962nd AACS was responsible for creating the 24th Wing, Howard Air Base (AB) E-3B/C AWACS alert facilities and alert procedures. Since Hubert was the first Mission Crew Commander (MCC) to deploy to Howard, it would be his responsibility to achieve this responsibility in one month. Upon arriving, Hubert had an advantage since he had served as AFFOR Battle Staff as a new Captain and new the Air Base layout well. Serving as part of the AWACS Staff in this case made sense, which is something that rarely makes sense in the military. Perhaps that is why the AWACS Counterdrug Standup operations were such a successful unit from day one.

In this case, Hubert simply took out his Tinker AFB Alert checklist that he had used while pulling alert at the Tinker AFB Alert Facilities and plagiarized that list to create the new 24th Wing, Howard Air Base (AB) AWACS Procedures. Then it was a matter of working with the local wing standardization and evaluations (Stan/Eval) branch and the local training branch to ensure that he met their local flying regulations. Finally, he met with the Tanker Deployment Commander (Detco) and included the Tankers inputs in the AWACS checklist since the KC-135 Stratotanker is a vital participant in the AWACSAlert checklist.

Now it was all a matter of a practice scramble. The next day, Hubert coordinated with the staff to have a surprise scramble. Hubert requested that he advised of the time start time so that he would also be surprised and executed within the next 72-hours. Fourteen hours later, the scramble bricks could be heard saying, "scramble, scramble, scramble. " Within twenty-six minutes, the E-3B/C AWACS aircrew and aircraft was airborne and operational using 'due regard' (operational) followed by the KC-135 Stratotanker thirty minutes later a fragged (scheduled). This became a high standard for the Alaskan E-3B/C AWACS squadron and a challenge for the Tinker AFB aircrews to beat. Especially, since normally it takes thirty minutes to wake the radar up. There are procedures to accomplish a fast radar wake-up, used in this case.

"I need you to be the Joint Commander at Nellis," said his Commander. This exercise would be the first major Flag exercise executed just after the end of Operation Desert Storm and named Exercise Green Flag. This would be the first time that the Alaskan E-3B/C AWACS unit tasked to lead E-3B/C AWACS Detachment at Nellis AFB Nevada. The 552nd Air Control Wing (ACW) did not have a problem with their selection of the 962nd AACS Detachment Commander (Detco) since they knew Hubert.

The Wing Operations Officer and Wing Commander had both tried to talk him out of leaving Tinker AFB especially after only two years. In two and a half years at Tinker AFB, Hubert had been Aircrew of the Year both years during Operation Desert Shield and Operation Desert Storm. However, he always felt that the credit was due to his aircrews, their hard work, and his training objectives that he made sure that he used during every AWACS flight. Hubert had told them both that he not impressed with the leadership at Tinker AFB and that since he planned to retire at the twenty year point, that he wanted to go to Alaska. Again, both Officers tried to convince Hubert to stay in Oklahoma.

At this point, the 962nd AACS had its two aircraft but still working on building four E-3B/C AWACS aircrews. The 962nd AACS was able to deploy two aircrews to Nellis to support the exercise in addition to being able to deploy its E-3B/C AWACS aircraft to 24th Wing, Howard Air Base (AB) Panama. Since

Hubert was able to deploy the aircrew, staff, and the required maintenance personnel, this made this deployment initially easier to plan for as the Detco. Security personnel not tasked for this deployment since Nellis was an Air Force base with the aircraft and personnel departing for Nellis early Friday morning.

Elmendorf AFB and Eielson, AFB Alaska are the home of Cope-Thunder (redesignated: Red Flag-Alaska) exercise, a realistic, ten-day Air Combat Training (ACT) exercise held up to four times a year. Each Cope-Thunder exercise is a multi-service, multi-platform coordinated; combat operations exercise and corresponds to the designed operational capability of participating units. In other words, exercises often involve several units whose military mission may differ significantly from that of other participating units. Cope-Thunder Exercise planners consider those factors when designing exercises so participants get the maximum training possible without placement that create an unfair advantage during simulated combat scenarios.

It was during the Cope-Thunder Exercises that Hubert noticed that the E-3 flight crews were making too many mental errors while flying transition. At the same time, crews were being committed to support tasks at Tinker AFB, Oklahoma and Panama. Unfortunately, one of the reasons Hubert never worried about promotion was that many military members who are concerned with promotions tend to use their squadron and their employees as a stepping-stone to their next promotion. That is why he took formal academic training to know the difference between leadership and management concepts even though within the military culture these concepts were difficult to implement. As a leader, one has to know when to say the unit tasking's have amounted to an over tasked condition. As a manager, normally one has tasks to achieve and setting goals to achieve the tasks are simple as long as one is goal oriented.

As the Chief of Stan/Eval, he ordered his Flight Examiners to keep an eye on the crews that the over task condition created by the Unit Commander was created mainly to help his upcomingpromotion and not safety-of-flight. Captain Elmer, one of Hubert's Stan/Eval Officers went to the Unit Commander and told him what Hubert was doing so Hubert requested a meeting with the Unit Commander and all his flight evaluators. After the meeting, Hubert thought to himself that he should have done this sooner. However, nothing changed since this Unit Commander was more concerned with doing whatever it took to receive his next promotion to Colonel and not the welfare of his unit personnel.

Therefore, Hubert knew that he could not stay in this unit under this Commander and continue working in a hostile work environment. He had worked too many times in units where he was the only officer identifying serious problems and this unit had twenty-six other officers that were also responsible for the unit. Since he was the only office worried about the unit problems, he was the problem. Hubert spoke with the Commander and requested a move to anywhere in the base. It did not matter what job he received since he was qualified to serve at the Air Defense unit or at many of the Wing level positions.

"Daddy, I want to visit Peepaw," mentioned Tawny. Alfred had just had his heart attack back in Florida and Darlene, Tawny, and Hubert all agreed that each would go back to Florida alone to spend time with Darlene's daddy. Tawny would be the first one to fly back to Bradenton, Florida and visit Peepaw for two weeks once school vacation started. Once she arrived in Florida, first she was sad that Peepaw was not his old self, full of life.

Even those that lived next door did not visit him regularly in spite that Peepaw paid for all of their living expenses during their most of their lives except the recent five years. Tawny would tell her grandfather, that she would live in his garage to be able to see him every day. This trip would be the last time Tawny would see her Peepaw alive.

In front of the squadron Commander, at the meeting Hubert made it clear that all evaluators worked for the Commander and per the regulations, their primary duty was to keep the flight activities safe. Therefore, his instructions were per the regulations and that in the future if anyone had an issue to come to him. Although the Commander did not tell him, it was Captain Elmer, based on his conversation with the Commander. Hubert made it clear of his concerns and of his responsibilities in accordance with the flight regulations.

In 1993, starting in January, Hubert started supporting exercises with Artic Cover 93-1, then deployed to Panama to another Counterdrug (CD) Mission. Upon returning from Panama, Hubert would do a quick turn to Las Vegas as the AWACS Deployment Commander (Detco), supporting the Green Flag Exercise, accomplished three Cope-Thunder Exercise (i. e. , 93-1, 93-2, and 93-3). After the Cope-Thunder Exercise, Hubert returned to Panama, followed by two Amalgam Warrior exercises, (i. e. , 93-1 and 93-2). Hubert then finished the year in October by supporting Polar Thrust 93-1 and Distant Frontier 93-1, followed by another deployment to Panama.

On 20 January 1993, President Bill Clinton had just become the new President and would be Hubert's Commander-in-Chief (CINC) for the next eight years. President Clinton would spend the first four years tearing down the military until after making countless mistakes, which cost many military lives that changed him as the military CINC. His second term, President Clinton would become a better CINC. During one visit to Elmendorf AFB, many military members would lose their careers because they would refuse to attend a mandatory gathering with President Clinton at the Elmendorf AFB flight line. Hubert would make sure that his flight member attended telling them "How often do they have the privilege to see a US

President. Besides, military members do not have the choice to like or dislike their Commander-in-Chief. "Hubert would plan and execute multiple operations for President Clinton in Colombia and other areas around the world after receiving by name requests.

"How about joining me in Vegas" asked Hubert. Hubert decided to have Darlene and Tawny join him in Las Vegas so he purchased them airline tickets on Alaskan Airlines. Hubert was able to pick his girls at the Vegas airport and take them to the motel. Since he already had a room in Las Vegas, this meant that all he had to do was rent them a vehicle so that they could get around when he was at work on base. Both knew that Hubert would work long days. He had asked for two double beds, which allowed Darlene and Tawny to each have a bed when they arrived in Las Vegas. The motel was just off the highway that led to Nellis AFB and had a pool. Since it was the summer, this worked out well for Darlene and Tawny.

Darlene and Tawny had their favorite places to eat in Las Vegas, as did Hubert. The motel also had a restaurant that offered three meals each day, which made it easier on days when Hubert was running late at work. The Maxim Hotel was Darlene's and Tawny's favorite casino on Sundays since it had the best seafood in Las Vegas. The Old Town has the best Mexican Food in Las Vegas and their Sunday buffet Excellent. Nevertheless, the new light show in down town Las Vegas was the favorite place to visit. Then there was always the Burger King on base that was ok for a quick meal.

The Green Flag progressed like all other flags with the exception that this exercise was much larger than most past exercises. Tinker AFB had deployed two E-3B/C AWACS aircraft and aircrews that were under Hubert's Command. Especially since the US E-3 AWACS fleet were getting old and they were a maintenance challenge to keep flying. With the aircraft, build starting in the 1970s and having millions of mission systems, keeping a working E-3B/C AWACS aircraft airborne is always the hardest challenge of any Detco. The Green Flag Exercise was no difference except that the turnaround was much less since each aircraft flew four-hour sorties (missions) each day with two sorties scheduled each day.

The Nellis play area is south of Nellis AFB where all the aircraft fly and normally join up into two sets of formations. Each formation normally employs a Blue-Air tactic, which means the aircraft are in four ships separated each by altitude and mileage so that if attached that can engage the attacking aircraft. Each aircraft package had distance between its elements to maintain safety and to make the enemy work harder when engaging them. The Blue-Air accomplishes these maneuvers in the east side of the Nellis range.

In the meantime, the Red-Air sets up in two sets of formations. Normally consists of four aircraft each and employs Red-Air tactics while trying to kill the Blue-Air while attempting to complete its mission or mission objectives. The Red-Air accomplishes this initial maneuver in the west side of the range. The E-3B/C AWACSaircraft and the Rivet Joint (RJ) aircraftmaintained an orbit outside north of the range and on the air route maintaining an orbit as directed by the Mission Crew Commander (MCC). Depending on the flow of the Blue and Red-Air, the MCC controls the position of the AWACS aircraft in order to maximize the surveillance systems and be able to provide threat warning information.

Maintenance was truly a challenge for Green Flag. On one occasion, Hubert approved to have a battery from the 962nd AACS E-3B/C AWACS aircraft transferred to the 965th AACS E-3B/C AWACS aircraft. This meant that the 962nd AACS would have some down time noted by the Pacific Air Force (PACAF) during the time the aircraft was airborne. The 962nd AACS Commander called Hubert from Elmendorf AFB Alaska yelling at him on the telephone asking him why he had approved that maintenance procedure. Hubert replied, "Sir, I thought we were in the United States Air Force and I am here as the Air Force E-3B/C AWACS Deployment Commander (Detco) and not the PACAF Detco, if I am the PACAF Detco, please replace me. " The Lieutenant Colonel was the typical Tinker AFB Officer that played politics to become an "Air Force Promotable".

Hubert was proof that one was able to receive a promotion and not have to play politics, just work hard, and do what was right for the Air Force. For this Green Flag Exercise this would not be the last issue that Hubert would have to deal with. After the first week of the exercise, Hubert and the Detco received notification to go into the main auditorium and briefed by intelligence that the local blacks were rioting. The Wing Commander recommended that all personnel staying at hotels off base down town redeploy to their home stations. At that point, the local news and Cable News Network (CNN) were already reporting the news on television.

After discussion this information with the Commander in Alaska, Hubert decided to redeploy most of the personnel back to Alaska with the exception of the Weapons Directors (WDs) who were able to find hotels in the local area. The Tinker AFB aircrews were already on base so Hubert continued as the Deployment Commander (Detco) with two aircraft and aircrews using the Alaska maintenance personnel. The Tinker AFB crew surprised Hubert with a plaque on the final day. In spite of this final distraction, Green Flag proved to be a success for the 962nd AACS E-3B/C AWACS Squadron and PACAF.

Upon returning from the Green Flag, Hubert had to become the new squadron Chief of Standardization and Evaluations (Stan/Eval) on 1 June 1993. The unit was having many problems with its aviators and the Operations Officer was concerned while the Unit Commander was more concerned with the unit image since he was up forpromotion to Colonel the following year. It seemed as if these deployments all seemed the same after a while in Hubert's mind. Traveling from Anchorage to Panama always started on Alaskan Airlines to Seattle in the

US, which was the AWACS crew favorite leg of the travel to Panama. Then the crew would take the flight on Continental from Seattle to Houston with a layover for four hours then the flight to Panama.

The return flight was the reverse routing. The meals were the only thing to look forward to each day. In Houston, there were the large dozen shrimps and a large cold beer. In Seattle, there were the seafood nachos and the local cold beer. Occasionally, Hubert would meet some nice individuals on the flights to talk with during the return flights. For example, he spoke to a Cable News Network (CNN) camera operator on the flight from Houston to Seattle and invited him to try the seafood nachos and local beer with him before the flight to Anchorage.

He spoke of how he had divorced his first wife when he went through mid-life crisis and married a younger wife. Now he had another young child and wish that he stayed with his first wife when Hubert told him that he was still married to Darlene going on twenty years. He mentioned that if he had not divorced, he too would have been married twenty years. Hubert felt sorry for the individual for he had held similar discussions with other military men in the past that had done the same mistake when they when through mid-life crisis. He never understood how any man could give up his family so easily only because of mid-life crisis, which he considered a selfish male act.

After this deployment, the 962nd AACS finally received the work force that it had on its books. However, by this time, the unit officially received a new Squadron Commander who was up forpromotion. Hubert Hoped that for once, he would work for a Commander that would not worry about his next promotion but he knew that Air Force culture was not conducive with that type of behavior. This meant that in his view, whatever the Wing Leadership wanted of him and his flying squadron, he would never say no if it would make him look better and help hispromotion opportunity. This meant that the unit would be support every local exercise in addition to every exercise that the F-15 Falcon's deployed to since they would be the first wing to deploy with a fleet of E-3B/C AWACS aircraft.

Years earlier, the Air Force tried to deploy fighter aircraft and the E-3B/C AWACS aircraft as a composite wing but was unable due to operational requirements at the 552[d] Air Control Wing (ACW) at Tinker AFB, Oklahoma. Now the 3rd Wing in Alaska was the first wing to deploy as a Composite Wing with fighter and AWACS aircraft to exercises to Hawaii and Green Flag Exercises in Nevada. A first deployment of its kind, within the US Air Force and this meant that in addition to the deployments to Panama, the E-3B/C AWACS aircrews and aircraft were overtasked. Even with eight crews assigned to the unit and two crews as staff, the unit received enough tasks to its limit.

Hubert would return to Alaska and have to support to Operational Readiness Inspections (ORIs) followed by three Cope-Thunder 94-2, 94-3, and 94-4 Exercises. Next, Hubert would support the Snowbird 94-1 Exercise and return to Panama and the Counterdrug (CD) Mission. Hubert became concerned once he became the Chief of Stan/Eval and was responsible for maintaining ensuring that all the aircrew were qualified in the unit. However, with so many Field Grade Officers in the grade of Major and Lieutenant Colonel and with so few Promotable jobs to fill within the unit, many Officers started acting strangely even though many had known each other for decades. The 932nd had eight positions known aspromotable and the unit had approximately twelve Field Grade Officers.

It was during this period that Hubert lost respect of many close friends. Many close friends that he had known for ten or more years. This alone made this from one of the best assignments to the worse assignment professionally up to that point in his career. Hubert never believed that close friends would behave in such a manner only to get ahead and receive apromotion. He was glad that two close friends were junior and that they did not have to worry aboutpromotion. Otherwise, Hubert would have been completely distraught by this group of Officers.

The year of 1994 would begin with Hubert returning from Panama escorting one of his Non-Commissioned Officers (NCOs) whose son died while deployed to Panama. Like most years for aviators assigned to an operational squadron, Hubert would next take a crew and aircraft to support a Weapons School Mission Employment exercise back in the US at Nellis AFB in Nevada. Without any warning, Hubert received notification to support the Haiti Humanitarian Operation from Tinker AFB, Oklahoma.

Hubert's longtime friend from Iceland had been in charge and had been telling the Commander that he had been implementing changes that Hubert had implemented. Tony was up forpromotion to Lieutenant Colonel as was Hubert with a group of five fellow Majors. Hubert had mentioned to all six Officers that he not in competition with them since he was retiring. Hubert never expected his friend to take credit for his programs once he returned. Upon returning, Hubert asked for the new position so that he could be the Flight Commander as he wished. Hubert was distraught that his friend of twelve years would be so unethical only because he was worried aboutpromotion even though he made it clear that he was retiring.

Even after all their political games, three officers in the wing that had "Definitely Promote" to Lieutenant Colonel did not get apromotion, which was a first in the USAF. Within the 962nd AACS Officers, only Hubert received apromotion to Lieutenant Colonel even though he wanted to retire from the Air Force. Hubert waspromoted with a "promote" based on his military records that revealed his accomplishment and was Promoted without the help of the unit or the wing leadership. Hubert's request to retire received a disapproval from the Pacific Air Command (PACAF) major command and three of the passed over officers forced to retire early even though they asked to remain on active duty. Hubert had twenty years on active duty with no commitments owed to the USAF.

"You are never home when I need you," said Darlene. Hubert was in Panama on a Counternarcotics deployment. Mount Spur, which is seventy miles from Anchorage, Alaska, had erupted and the volcano ashes had made a mess of the city. Over two inches of ashes were throughout the city. It seemed that each time that a crisis occurred in the Contreras family that he was always deployed in one country or another. Darlene had learned to take care of the family crisis on her own over the years. Mainly since Hubert was always deployed somewhere in the world and never home when she needed him home to fix mechanical problems that broke.

"I'm going to Bradenton to visit you daddy," mentioned Hubert to Darlene. It was during this assignment that Hubert decided that it was time to retire from the Air Force. The last family member to visit Alfred in Florida would be Hubert. After this deployment, Hubert was required to return through Miami, Florida and stop at USSOUTHCOM. After his week in Miami where he worked with the Counterdrug Branch and updated their AWACS and Panama Procedures, Hubert had a ten days of leave approved. This allowed him to rent a vehicle and drive to Bradenton and visit family. His main goal was to spend time with his father-in-law, Alfred who had just had a heart attack. Although Hubert had a job interview and offered a job once, he returned to Alaska, his main goal was to spend as much time as he could with Alfred. Hubert and Alfred played canasta card games nearly day and night non-stop as both men also drank coffee non-stop.

What Hubert did not realize at the time that it would take him over eleven years before he would actually be able to retire from the Air Force? His experience at the 962nd AACS as the Chief of Stan/Eval had made him feel that unit that would lose its first E-3B/C AWACS aircraft. The Commander surrounded himself with Officers and NCOs who told him what he wanted to hear in the name of mission accomplishment. Hubert and a few of his NCOs were the exception and they would pay the price by receiving poor performance reports and not receiving the normal award given to members considering what the contributed for the unit.

"You have to go to survival school," said the Commander. Hubert could not believe that he had to complete winter survival school again even though he had completed the training in Tacoma, Washington, prior to starting AWACS Training as a requirement only because he had a Commander that had no common sense. Having the training documented in his records did not make any difference to his Commander mainly because he was too worried about makingpromotion and did not want to upset the Wing Leadership in his mind. Hubert did not know that the Commander would also attend the same winter survival course in northern Alaska.

Winter Survival is a two-week course with the first week consisting of academics. Week 2, consists of a field event where the individual has to survive on his own by building his or her own igloo and survive for a week in the wilderness in the wildlife with a team of four. If the temperature is minus sixty degrees, individuals cannot go in the field because it is too cold. During week, one the temperature was below sixty degrees but dropped to below fifty during week two. Hubert's first mistake was to wear his flight suit but he wore his flight suit since that would be the uniform he would be wearing if shot down in a survival situation.

His Commander wore fatigues, which in Hubert's view not the proper uniform. The difference being, once you build your igloo, you have to take off you clothing and get into your sleeping bag in order to get warm. In the meantime, your clothing stays outside your sleeping bag. The next morning, your clothing is like ice but you still have to put it on. You put in on with a few choice words and many colorful yells. The

Colonel was in charge of the second team. Each team had to compete with each other.

During the night, Hubert and his team snuck up to the Colonel's team and scared the heck out of them. They made animal noises but eventually the laughter gave them away. Since this was training, both teams walked to an open fire under a tent for a mission debrief. The team inputs included that the other team was extremely easy to locate mainly because of their lack of blending their igloo's into the environment and the noise that they made when talking to each other. The group made the point that they were not on a camping trip. The hardest part of living in a winter environment was waking up in the morning at a specific time. Especially since alarms never work in fifty below degree environments.

Obviously, this did not sit well with my Commander since he was ultimately responsible for the team. This was an indication of this Officer's leadership style that Hubert should have taken notice of. Darlene had warned me on the first time that she met him at the Elmendorf AFB Officers Club when we gave him a ride home when he drank too much. Darlene told me to be careful of him because he could not be trusted. Darlene was never wrong of her initial judgments when she met someone. Hubert only wished that he had listened to her more often for each time she gave him her first assessments on someone, she was always right.

"Skip, I just got you an Aircraft Commander (AC) slot at Tinker AFB," said Hubert to Captain "Skip" Rogers. As the flight Commander, Hubert was responsible for advancing his flight member's careers. Although Skip was his neighbor, he also knew that he was ready to enter AC training. By this time, Skip had become Darlene's adopted son and had come to dinner many times. Ship had also invited Hubert and Darlene to parties at his house. Since Skip's house was just across the circle, going to parties and having fun not an issue. If they had too much to drink, all they had to do was walk across the circle.

Except for the snow that was normally piles in the middle during the winter, getting home was always an easy task.

"I have to deploy again," said Hubert. Many times Hubert not able to tell Darlene where he was deploying to as was the case when he deployed to support the Haiti Humanitarian Operation. In September 1994, Hubert flew eight missions over Haiti in support of Operation Uphold Democracy from forward operating locations and Tinker AFB, Oklahoma. Initially, the crew-received notice that they were going to the US, bring warm clothing for forty-five days, and nothing else. Once Hubert arrived at the deployed location, as he normally did, he made sure that his crew had a room and started crew rest knowing the report time for their first flight.

Hubert and his crew were staying at the Holiday Inn near Tinker AFB in Del City. For this trip, they rented two vans for the aircrew and two vans for the maintenance crew. Once Hubert made sure that the maintenance crew had a room, he went into crew rest himself in preparation for his next flight. By this time, normally, he had been up two or three days so falling asleep was never a problem and he quickly fell asleep. He would always call this type of flying, "controlled fatigue" since your body never adjusts to the lack of quality sleep. Mainly because one flies, different time shifts where you fly one day during the day, then in the afternoon, and then followed by a late night flight all ending twelve hours or more depending on the mission requirements. This operation, directed by President Bill Clinton, ousted military leaders to return the duly elected leader, Jean-Bertrand Aristide, into power. However, the rebels had other ideas that President Clinton or any American leader.

It was during this deployment that Lieutenant Colonel Margie Marrow Hubert and Darlene's friend from Geilenkirchen, Germany visited Alaska with an aircrew and E-3B/C AWACS aircraft while supporting a local Cope Thunder Exercise. This would be an excellent opportunity for Darlene, Tawny, and Margie to have dinner and talk about Germany and

Geilenkirchen. This gave Darlene, Tawny, and Margie and opportunity to talk about old times in Germany. After all, they were old friends and had been at many unit parties and unit picnics together in the past. Margie was in Alaska for two weeks and Darlene had her over to the house a few times for dinner since they were good friends. As always, Hubert deployed to Panama.

"Good morning, I love you," mentioned Hubert on the telephone to Darlene regardless of the time. Once one of the two alarms woke Hubert up, he took a shower, took a quick jog and dressed. Normally, the first thing Hubert did was call Darlene back in Alaska if possible. Today was a good day and Hubert was able to get a line through to Alaska and then get an off-line to Darlene. Sometimes he would go to breakfast and always report early to Mission Planning (MP). Hubert as a habit always reported thirty minutes early to make sure that the aircraft was Mission Ready (MR) or Mission Capable (MC). He also made sure that all the administrative documents were also ready, signed off all the required documents, and reviewed all the required flying documents that were part of every aviator.

Once the aircrew arrived and signed in, Hubert led the mission brief and then the specialized briefs continued. Once all the specialized briefs were complete, all the crew met at the bus and traveled together to the aircraft. By then, the technician and the Flight Engineer (FE) were there because they had already departed the unit thirty minutes prior to start preparing the aircraft for take-off. Soon everyone loaded their bags on the aircraft and the crew completes the aircraft for take-off. Once the Aircraft Commander (AC) and the Mission Crew Commander (MCC) complete their crew roll call, the E-3B/C AWACS aircraft becomes airborne. Once airborne, Hubert initiates the mission systems wake-up.

First, the Flight Engineer (FE) tells the Mission Crew Commander (MCC) that it is OK to power up. In turn, Hubert clears all the mission technicians to power up their systems.

The communications, computer, and radar technicians turn on their systems and eventually conduct their systems checks. Once their checks are complete, Hubert clears them to transfer their systems to the Weapons and Surveillance teams. The Weapons and Surveillance teams then turn on their systems and combine all the three systems to use it as a system-of-system to communicate to external agencies and external aircraft or external ships. Overall, this effort displayed good teamwork.

This deployment consisted of a series of scrambles initially into the East Pacific and then diverting to the Caribbean. Anytime an unknown target received attention, reported by the Caribbean Air Defense system, or the Air Force (AFFOR) Battle Staff, the Joint Interagency Task Force-South (JIATF-S) initiated the E-3B/C AWACS scramble. The E-3B/C AWACS aircrew was allowed an hour to become airborne. Normally, the E-3B/C AWACS aircrew became airborne in less than forty-five minutes in spite of being physically throughout 24th Wing, Howard Air Base (AB). Hubert's aircrew had the record when his crew became airborne in twenty-three minutes from the time they were scrambled.

The unknown target consisted of airborne and surface contacts. The largest airborne target was a DC-3 aircraft, or smaller jet aircraft. The largest surface target was a Russian submarine, which is now part of the Colombian Navy. The confiscated ships varied in size and type. The cash confiscated was always US currency preferred by the cartels and then by the terrorist groups that replaced them. The only difference was that the cartels tended to help their local towns in an effort to convince them that they were not bad while the terrorist groups were deadly to the local habitants and all Colombians equally.

"It's your turn to visit your daddy," mentioned Hubert. After Hubert returned from Panama, since Tawny and Hubert had already visited Alfred in Florida, it was Darlene's turn to go to Bradenton and visit her father. This would also be the last time that Darlene would see her father alive before dying of complications pertaining to his heart. Darlene, Tawny, and Hubert would all agree that all three, wanted to not return to Florida and see Alfred sickly. Seeing him alive would be their last memory. Darlene would go with her daddy shopping where he would purchase her a dress and shoes that she would cherish for the rest of her life. Darlene would finally talk to her father of the issues she had when she was young and every issue settled between father and daughter.

Like the Panama Operation, the Haiti Humanitarian Operations also proved to be mainly an operation where the E-3B/C AWACS served as an Air Traffic Control Facility. Mainly since C-130 cargo and C-141 cargo aircraft were delivering humanitarian supplies to Haiti, non-stop. Hubert maintained a figure eight orbit over Haiti but at times ran random orbits when there was no air traffic in the area. In these cases, the E-3B/C AWACS conducted long legs normally flew one hundred miles straight lines before turning back to the original origin.

At the forty-five coordinate point on the map, another 962nd AACS aircraft relieved Hubert's aircraft and returned to Alaska. The aircraft was on the schedule to return to Tinker AFB, Oklahoma for a maintenance phase. Otherwise, the aircraft would have remained in Alaska and the crew would have returned to Oklahoma using commercial air travel. Upon landing from this mission, Hubert would be home for only a few days before he would be required to deploy to Arizona to support another exercise.

During the Snowbird 94-1 exercise, Hubert deployed as the Deployment Commander (Detco) with two E-3B/C AWACS aircraft, maintenance, and aircrews to Davis-Monthan AFB, Arizona. This was the first time F-15s Eagles from the local 3rd Wing at Elmendorf AFB and deployed to Davis-Monthan AFB with their wing AWACS deployed together. This was also the first time that the F-15 3rd Wing deployed with its own E-3B/C

AWACS aircraft and aircrew as a joint team in support of an exercise.

The unit preparing for Operation Snowbird was in the process of a pending Operational Readiness Inspection (ORI). "Snowbird" received the task at Davis-Monthan AFB, Arizona. Snowbird designed to give pilots favorable weather locations for clear weather flying opportunities and was to provide its pilots with proficiency for real combat conditions. This exercise allowed wings from the northern Air Force bases to deploy to good weather locations and maximize their training under good weather conditions.

The E-3B/C AWACS Weapons Directors (WDs) controlled the air-to-air missions in the southern Arizona airspace called the 'sells' airspace. The A-10 Warhog's from the Davis-Monthan, AFB wing aircraft, conducted air-to-ground missions. The 'Sells airspace' is the southern one third of Arizona under the control of the US Air Force. This exercise was a busy exercise with little time to rest since Hubert was the Detco. Before long, the exercise ended and the crews and aircrafts returned to Alaska. The local wing also used its EC-130E Airborne Battlefield Command and Control Center(ABCCC) aircraft during the Snowbird Exercise.

"Boss, Newsburg in going to Tinker AFB for Sim training," said Master Sergeant Clark. Hubert had not gotten along with the squadron Commander, Lieutenant Colonel Newsburg. As the Chief of Stan/Eval, he had seen a Commander who worried more about his squadron image than doing what Hubert felt was best for the unit and the Air Force. He had mentioned to Lieutenant Colonel Newsbury that he felt that the unit was taking too many deviations to flying regulations. Hubert felt that eventually this unit would be the first E-3B/C AWACS squadron to lose an aircraft.

"Babe I just resigned as the Chief of Stan/Eval and asked to be reassigned," mentioned Hubert. He had followed the chain-of-command by going to his Director of Operations, Squadron Commander, Operations Group Commander, and

Wing Commander to emphasize his concerns of the lack of compliance within his unit. In the end, the General told him that when he was a major that he had worked with a major that was better than he was and learned to accept it. Hubert never truly understood what this comment meant since he knew that he most likely had ended his career by going against his Commander. Nevertheless, he knew that it was his responsibility to tell the chain-of-command that his unit had serious leadership problems.

On 17 July 1994, Hubert became the 3rd Operations Support Squadron (OSS) Wing, Wing Command Control Systems (WCCS) Program Manager (PM). The WCCS systems was a new US Air Force (USAF) automated logistics and management system that allowed the Wing Commander and all the unit flying commanders to manage their flying activities. The WCCS system accomplished the Command and Control (C2) function before there was the real-time technology available that allowed units to manage all their logistics and flying data. While working the WCCS program, the 3rd OSS Commander selected Hubert for more responsibility within the wing and the 3rd OSS.

"Well at least I won't be part of a mishap investigation," mentioned Hubert. Darlene had always known that he would do whatever he felt was right regardless of the consequences to his career. In this case, this career change would lead to a new posting in the Third Operations Support Squadron (OSS). Within a few weeks, Hubert would start filling in as the Assistant Director of Operations (ADO) and on the same week, he received notification that he was a Lieutenant Colonel. The same week, Hubert received notification that he had been assignment to Davis-Monthan AFB, Arizona. Within two-months he would be out processed and on his way to a new assignment.

"I'd like to go to Tucson to be close to your mom," said Darlene. After departing Alaska, the Contreras family was in

Davis-Monthan AFB, in Tucson, Arizona. By this time, Darlene, Tawny, and Hubert had traveled the world and except for their visits to Tucson and Bradenton, Florida, Darlene felt it was time for her to be closer to Hubert's mother. Hubert's mother Olga had always had a problem with Darlene since did not speak Spanish. Olga blamed Darlene for Hubert's decision to make the military a career. Even though Hubert had explained to his mother many times that, he had made a career of the Air Force well before Hubert met and married Darlene. After all, he was in the Air Force two years before he met Darlene and married her.

"Sir, there is nothing we can do, we only post house openings here at the Housing Office," said the Elmendorf Housing Officer. Perhaps one of the main problems of serving in the military is the cost that each move brings that the government does not cover. This time the house owner, Jackie had refused to return the $700 deposit. The she alleged Hubert replace the damaged houseplants. The Contreras family had moved into the house in the winter and all the plants were less than five feet of Alaskan snow. Although they had taken the house with a vehicle in the driveway that was broken and in the side of the house there had been a winters of trash piled up. After two-months of looking for a house, the housing office forced the Contreras family to take the house before they would have to move out of the base billeting.

After departing Alaska, Jackie refused to take the certified letter requesting a court date. Out of principle, Hubert was determine to not let another house renter take advantage of a military member only because the military member would most likely not return to go to court. The US Post Office confirmed that she had refused to accept the letter. In the end, this would be another occasion where in addition to the normal out-of-pocket costs, this deposit was lost. It was too expensive to return to Alaska to go to small claims court and Jackie knew this. That is why she rented to military member as her husband had mentioned when he came by the house when he spoke to Hubert. She did not care that she stole the $700 deposit from the Contreras family and the Elmendorf Housing Office knew that she did this every time she rented her house.

12ᵀᴴ AF, DAVIS-MONTHAN AFB, AZ.

Each time, the hardest decision for Darlene and Hubert to return to the Continental United States after a tour overseas involved Tawny's future. Alaska had been a disappointment education wise when the state legislation made the wrong decision and used it vast oil revenues and gave every citizen a thousand dollars every years as a tax dividends. Yet, its curriculum was five years out of date and none of the parents seemed to be concerned as long as they kept receiving their annual dividends from the states. After Europe, Hubert's research told him that the Oklahoma education system was a second rate. Now Hubert research told him that the Arizona education system was a third world system.

"How about driving to Tucson," said Hubert? Initially, Darlene and Tawny did not like the idea of traveling in the family Voyager Van for fourteen days. The initial 364 miles from Anchorage to Fairbanks, Alaska, had been a familiar drive for the Contreras family. Once the Contreras family entered the Canadian border, the 1,522-mile long road from Fairbanks, Alaska to Dawson Creek, British Colombia started with 500 miles of unpaved roads. The first two hundred miles had been full of mole-holes, as Hubert would compare them to his skiing days. The Contreras family had just driven Alaskan/Canadian (ALCAN) highway in our Dodge Van during a two-week period.

"Sweetie there goes another flock of deer's crossing the road," said Hubert. Along the way, we had seen the most beautiful scenery and for the first thousand miles of driving, we saw wildlife crossing in front of US countless times. Since it was the end of July, there was snow only on mountaintops but the turquoise colored lakes were on both sides of the two-lane highway. For the first seven hundred miles once we entered Canada, the roads were still dirt roads and we would not see a normal highway until just before arriving at Watson Lake, British Colombia. Driving to Edmonton, Albert would be faster since the next 365 miles would be on a paved road. Since Hubert had been at Edmonton many times when assigned to NATO AWACS, we stayed there for three days and saw what at that point the largest shopping mall in North America was at Edmonton.

"I need to fly every day this week to accomplish check rides," mentioned Hubert. Cold Lake was about an hour drive from Edmonton and the home of the Canadian Wing-4, which had two operational CF-18 Squadrons and two training squadrons, including Phase IV of NATO Flying Training in Canada (NFTC). During his last deployment, he had flown each day during the exercise. He had flown as a Senior Director (SD), Weapons Controller (WC), instructor, and Stan/Eval Officer. He had many good memories about his deployments to Cold Lake.

"It is so beautiful up here in the north," mentioned Darlene. The Contreras family had seen what seemed as endless wild life and turquoise colored lakes. During this long drive, Hubert had decided to retire within two years from the Air Force. Darlene and he had plenty of time during their fourteen days of travel on the Alcan Highway. On one of the daily travels, they came upon a road marker that said Lake Watson and shortly that another sign that said Watson Lake. The only difference was that one road was north and the other was on an easterly direction.

By mistake, they had traveled north for a while before realizing that they had taken the wrong road when they did not reach the next town on the map. They had decided that he would retire on his first opportunity when he arrived in Tucson, Arizona. Hubert never dreamed that instead, he would live in the same house for over eleven years before retiring. However, he never dreamed that he would never live in his house for more than a month. At least not until he retired from the military and for a year straight until he became fully disabled a decade later from his military injuries.

"Wow, there is a roller coaster in here daddy," said Tawny. Darlene and Tawny had heard about Edmonton shopping mall during squadron gatherings when the Contreras family lived in Germany. The Contreras family stayed at the Holiday Inn, which had been the first hotel that Hubert's crew had stayed during his first trip to participate in the Maple Flag Exercise in Cold Lake. Then the Contreras family would drive to Los Angles (LA), California to pick up Tawny's car at the port, which was 1,903 miles from Edmonton. This still left another 490 miles from LA to Tucson, Arizona. Within two weeks, the Contreras family drove 4,280 miles from Anchorage, Alaska to Tucson, Arizona with a slight detour to Edmonton, Alberta, Las Vegas, Nevada, and Los Angeles, California.

"I remember taking Hubert's first tour to the Boneyard at Davis-Monthan when Hubert was in a young boy," said,Hubert. He had also taken his last flight on a C-130 Hercules cargo aircraft that at the time was the oldest C-130 in the Air Force. The C-130 had been the same type of aircraft that he had seen during the elementary school tour to the local Air Base. Tucson was Hubert's hometown where as a young man second grade; his had made a field trip to the Boneyard and later renamed as the Aerospace Maintenance and Regeneration Center (AMARC). Hubert would always recall his first field trip when he was in second grade at Menlo-Park Elementary to the Boneyard.

Over the years, Hubert had visited the local Air Base well before he returned as a military member. In April 1946, the 4105th Army Air Force Unit established at Davis-Monthan Air

Force Base (AFB), Tucson, Arizona. The primary responsibility was to provide a storage location for the large number of aircraft no longer required by the Army Air Force following the end of the Second World War. In 1947, the US Air Force created as a separate service. Thisprompted a re-organization and name change. The support of active flying units added to the center's responsibilities. During 1948, the unit changes its name to the 3040th Aircraft Storage Depot.

In the coming years the unit saw many name changes but its basic mission remained the same. The bone yard is the US military aircraft storage. AMARC is a joint service facility managed by the US Air Force Material Command located in the town of Tucson, Arizona. Often referred to as 'The Boneyard', AMARC is an aerospace storage and maintenance facility adjoining Davis-Monthan AFB, Arizona, which provides a service to all branches of the US military, which included the USAir Force, USNavy, USMarines, the Coast Guard and the USArmy, as well as other national agencies.

"I can't remember how many different types of aircraft that I have seen here in the Boneyard over the years," mentioned Hubert. Currently controlling over 4,200 aircraft as well as many other types of military equipment, AMARC works very hard in Promoting itself as not just a 'Boneyard' and takes every opportunity in explaining how it operates its cost effective, tax saving operations. Many of the stored-aircraft returned to an operational status in a short period and there is a continual process of anti-corrosion and re-preservation work, which keeps the aircraft in a stable condition during their stay. The reason the Boneyard reference exists is due to other work that AMARC carries out, that of reclamation of spare parts and the eventual disposal of spent airframes.

"Why are all those airplanes being dismantled daddy," asked Tawny. The AMARC Center divided into two distinct areas. The Reclamation Insurance Type (RIT) area located to the east side of Kolb Road that has aircraft in various states of completeness. The junkyard appearance belies the fact that these aircraft controlled by a process of careful part reclamation, both to a schedule and to ad-hoc (reactive and nonstandardized) requests. On careful examination, many of these re-sealed aircraft remained sealed to protect their remaining components from the dirt and heat. Every aircraft fully able to return to flying status by maintenance personnel upon prepared for flight on request by proper authorities.

During this tour, Hubert would staff one hundred new F-16 Falcons purchased by the USAF and then parked in the AMARC facilities. There are many times that aircraft from the RIT area leave AMARC to become instructional aircraft, targets on Army or Air Force ranges, museum exhibits or display pieces, although most end up smelted down into ingots by nearby metal processors. AMARC has also been heavily involved in the elimination of B-52 Stratofortresses under the Strategic Arms Reduction Treaty (START). AMARC is also responsible for the elimination of 445th Ground Launch Cruise Missiles (GLCM) and their launchers under the Intermediate-Range Nuclear Forces (INF) Treaty. Hubert recalled when in Spain traveling to GLCM sites during his 16th Air Force Site Inspection Tour.

"I'll be working in the drug shop," mentioned Hubert. On 17 June 1995, Hubert was in the 612[th]Combat Operations Squadron (COS), Counternarcotics Branch as the Counternarcotics Operations Officer. The Counterdrug Branch was still in the old 12th Air Force building since a new building was still under construction. Hubert's office was next to the 12th Air Force Director of Operations (DO), who was Colonel Hue Smith. Colonel Smith would be one of the best bosses that Hubert would work for including his supervisor who was an F-16 Falcon Pilot.

This position required that Hubert maintain flying status and augment the 12th Air Force Stan/Eval branch as their E-3 AWACSFlight Examiner. The Contreras family had heard of the drug shop while in Oklahoma when he worked in the Counternarcotics Branch just before serving as the E-3B/C AWACS squadron Assistant Operations Officer-Mission (ADO-M). Hubert arrived as a Major at Davis-Monthan, AFB who was a Lieutenant Colonel selectee, which everyone referred to as a major. Like Tinker AFB, Oklahoma, it would be a year and a half before Hubert would pin-on the Lieutenant Colonel rank. Hubert would take so long to become a Lieutenant Colonel, mainly because his year group was the largest year group in the history of the Air Force.

This was the first of two times that Hubertwould work in this position. However, Hubert fully understood the job requirements including knowing the government employees who he had worked with for years since he had worked with them while working in Panama as AFFOR BS Staff. Being responsible for all Counternarco-terrorism Operations throughout Central/South America and Mexico, his duties included planning joint operations including the US Customs assets and all law enforcement agencies. During 1985, his team was extremely successful with $4. 3 Billion dollars in drug busts and confiscation of drugs and equipment that included ships and illegal aircraft. This allowed Hubert to move from one Counterdrug (CD) position to another based on the branch needs.

Once Hubert planned and executed multiple CD operations at 24th Wing, Howard Air Base (AB), Hubert created a new Stan/Eval program for the 24th Wing, Howard Air Base (AB) Logistics Wing. Upon completion of the new logistics Stan/Eval program, Hubert started augmenting the 12th Air Force Stan/Eval branch more and more during their flight inspections, which kept him on the road most of the month due to the dual commitments of two divisions. Hubert was a vital member on the 12th Air Force Staff and added to the Commanders on call list.

"The Counterdrug shop is part of the 12th Air Force Staff," mentioned Hubert. Hubert was in the Battle Management (BM) Division when Hubert pinned-on Lieutenant Colonel. On 15 December 1995, Hubert was the Chief of Battle Management when the 12th Air Force picked up the Strategic Command (Stratcom) mission. The 12th Air Force command comprised of seven active-duty wings in the western and mid-western US with 396 aircraft and more than 32,600 active-duty military and civilian personnel. Hubert ensured the operational readiness of 12th Air Force-gained units of the Air Force Reserve (AFR) and Air National Guard (ANG), featuring an additional 17,700 people and more than 214 aircraft.

Among many duties, Hubert received a task to staff the closure of the SR-71, Blackbird aircraft program, which included sending aircraft to museums one of which was the local Pima Air museum. The Lockheed SR-71, Blackbird was an advanced, long-range, Mach three plus strategic reconnaissance aircraft. As a Weapons Controller (WC), many times Hubert recalled seeing the SR-71 on console at Luke AFB flying at Mach 3+ where it took the entire state of Arizona to turn around. The Lockheed Skunk Works by Clarence "Kelly" Johnson developed the SR-71 as a black project from the Lockheed A-12 reconnaissance aircraft in the 1960s.

"I remember seeing the aircraft on console," mentioned Hubert to the little boy in the Pima Museum as he relayed the story. Hubert also recalled a refueling mission over water in Norway when the SR-71 came off Tanker just prior to his NATO E-3A AWACS aircraft going on Tanker and seeing the SR-71 speeding up. Each ten seconds on Hubert's NATO E-3A AWACS console, the SR-71 flew over twenty miles. It would take Hubert over a month to accomplish all the staff work to retire the SR-71 Blackbird from the active Air Force. The Tucson Pima Air Museum has a list of every A-12 and SR-71 squadron ever built.

The 12th Air Force Commander wears different hats including serving as the 12th Air Force Commander (12th AF/CC), and the US Air Force Commander (USSOUTHAF/CC). At the same time, 12th AF supports many commands as part of its mission. Hubert oversaw Air Force assets provided to US Southern Command (USSOUTHCOM) in Central and South America as Commander of the air component to that unified command and serves as the USSOUTHAF of Component Joint Task Force 224 (JTF-224), the battle management arm of US Strategic Command (STRACOM). Hubert's duties as the Chief of JTF-224 included supporting US STRACOM in the Pacific and Offutt AFB, Nebraska.

The origins of 12th Air Force starts with a series of meetings conducted in mid-1942 when Allied planners were developing a strategy for the invasion of North Africa, called "Operation Torch". Because this extensive operation would require a new organization to provide enough work Force and equipment, plans for the activation of 12th Air Force were prepared simultaneously with the invasion strategy. Operation Torch was the British-American invasion of French North Africa in WW-II during the North African Campaign that started on 8 November 1942. The Soviet Union had pressed the US and Britain to start operations in Europe and open a second front to reduce the pressure of German forces on the Soviet troops.

Hubert's uncle, Jesus was a Senior Master Sergeant when Operation Torch started and would earn a fieldpromotion to second lieutenant. A year later, Jesus would lose his commission once he arrived in Europe when a new Officer gave him a hard time when he had his young brother over his shoulder after a night on the town. After five invasions, Jose did not have much of a temper for new Officers in theater that wanted to prove themselves. Especially when they saw a junior,Mexican American Officer who he wanted to put in his place. While the American commanders favored Operation Sledgehammer, landing in Occupied Europe as soon as possible, the British commanders believed that such a course would end in disaster.

An attack on French North Africa received approval instead, which would clear the Axis Powers from North Africa, improve naval control of the Mediterranean Sea and prepare for an invasion of Southern Europe in 1943. American President Franklin D. Roosevelt suspected the African operation would rule out an invasion of Europe in 1943 but agreed to support British Prime Minister Winston Churchill. Jesus would fight his way through Africa until he met his foolish seventeen-year-old brother Jose who changed his birth certificate to join the US Army before the WW-II ended.

"Babe, you need to sit down, Elmendorf just lost an AWACS," said Hubert to Darlene. By this time, they had discussed losing an aircraft was a possibility. Hubert had been on the telephone line talking to the maintenance Officer when his assistant mentioned that he was on another line talking to Elmendorf when they mentioned that he had to terminate the discussion because they had lost an E-3B/C AWACS aircraft. Hubert quickly the Elmendorf squadron and transferred to the base command center when he asked about a member on the crew. At that point, he knew that Marlin and many of his friends had perished on that mishap.

On 22 September 1995, Major Marlon Thomas was the Mission Crew Commander (MCC) on Yukla 27, which at the last moment established with an all-volunteer aircrew to fly out . 02 hours at the end of the Fiscal Year. Marlon and many of Hubert's friends volunteered to fly on a US Air Force E-3 Sentry AWACS aircraft. Call Sign Yukla 27, serial number 77-0354, that crashed shortly after take-off near Elmendorf AFB, Alaska. The Aircraft Commander (AC), Captain Skip Rogers worked for Hubert and was his next-door neighbor in Anchorage. Hubert had recommended Skip for AC upgrade.

As the Chief of Stan/Eval, before departing the 962nd AACS, Hubert had voiced his concerns to the Unit Commander and the Wing Leadership that firing the two civilians that kept the Canadian Geese clears around the flight live was a wise decision. The plane lost power to both port side engines after these engines ingested several Canadian Geese during takeoff. The Geese flew out of the exact location that he forecasted and the safety investigation never highlighted this fact. The aircraft went down about two miles (three kilometers) northeast of the runway, killing all twenty-four crewmembers on board the E-3B AWACS aircraft.

Hubert knew all but three of these crewmembers some for over sixteen years. Hubert and Marlon had been assigned together at three units together and on sergeant had been assigned to all the units with Hubert except Arizona. The Unit Commander eventually made Colonel, thanks to the beautiful televised burial of the Yukla 27 aircrew followed by family members hiring lawyers blaming the Unit Commander. During 1994, the US Air Force lost sixteen aircraft because Air Force Commanders chose to fly out their hour's program similar as the Unit Commander in Alaska according to 1994 Air Force Safety records.

"Hey bud, would you be interested in a job at DM," asked Hubert. The previous week, Hubert had called Marlin to see if he was interested in taking an assignment to Davis-Monthan. Marlin mentioned that he just received a 3rd OSS job and was in good standing for the upcomingpromotion board. Hubert was glad that his friend was doing well in Elmendorf. He never expected that he would be on board this aircraft. The E-3B/C AWACS flight flown in Elmendorf at a last minute was an add-on fight. As was the custom within the Air Force, squadron Commanders normally ended the fiscal year without any annual hours on their books.

In this case, this E-3B AWACS squadron had . 02 hours on their books and the fatal mishap aircraft had flown the required flight time. According to safety statistics, every year the Air

Force loses sixteen aircraft due to the flying hours program where commanders want to finish their year with zero hours.

On 1 March 1995, Hubert became the Chief, Command and Control (C2) Integration. Since the Air Force was experiencing manning shortages within the Airborne Battle Manager (ABM) career field, Hubert supported one ABM contingency every eighteen months including deploying to the Middle East. Being a field grade Officer, which consists of the Major and Lieutenant Colonel Ranks, there was also a shortage of experienced ABMs, which meant Hubert twice served as the Deployed E-3B/C AWACS Commander at the 24th Wing, Howard Air Base (AB) Panama.

During countless deployments to Panama and Colombia as a Counternarcotics Operations Officer, Hubert duties included flying as the headquarters E-3B/C AWACS (E-3B/C AWACS aircraft) flying Flight Examiner. At this point, during two deployments as the E-3B/C AWACS Deployed Commander in Panama, Hubert was responsible for four E-3B/C AWACS aircraft and over 180 deployed operations and maintenance personnel. As a Major, Hubert supported the Counterdrug (CD) mission at Howard AFB as the E-3B/C AWACS Deployed Commander. The Counterdrug (CD) mission was the primary mission for the Air Force E-3B/C AWACS Wing.

Aircrews were on alert and scrambled when US Navy ships in the East Pacific or in the Mediterranean reported unknown air targets. Once airborne, the E-3B/C AWACS aircrews would remain airborne and search the seas using their maritime radars or working with US Navy Maritime P-3 aircraft. Working with Host Nation (HN) interceptors or US Fighter Alert Aircraft, the airborne targets intercepted, identified, forced to land, and their drugs were confiscated. Unfortunately, over the upcoming decades, these procedures would be lost as US democratic politicians would start forces draw down and training dollar funds needed to complete operational commitments.

Hubert, his enlisted, and his Officer Aircrew rooms were near the base Officer's club. Each member had a brick assigned and assigned to a vehicle with four individuals. Any time anyone wanted to go anywhere on the base, the group assigned to each vehicle had to agree to go together. For example, if an individual wanted to go to see a movie. This way if the group were scrambled, they would all four members had to go together. However, one never knew when you would be scrambled since it could happen 24/7.

For example, it was normal to be woken with your brick blaring with the works, "scramble, scramble, scramble, report to the E-3. " Then within minutes the entire crew would be dressed and in their vehicles and driving towards the flight line and the E-3B/C AWACS aircraft that was already pre-flighted. A pre-flighted E-3B/C AWACS aircraft only requires that its engines start and the aircraft is ready for take-off. In addition, many of the mission systems are also pre-flighted. Once the aircrew arrives at the aircraft, the maintenance personnel are already on position and once the aircrew loads their bags on the aircraft, the takes-off in minimal time. At the same time, the KC-135 Stratotanker aircraft that is also on alert takes off in minimal time. The E-3B/C AWACS needs fuel shortly after getting airborne mainly because the runway at the 24th Wing, Howard Air Base (AB) is too short.

This allows the E-3B/C AWACS mission crew to wake-up their mission system to make sure that they have a good working system. Once the mission crew confirms that the mission system is working, the Mission Crew Commander (MCC) working with the Senior Director (SD) or the Weapons Director (WD) joins behind the Tanker aircraft. Once the E-3B/C AWACS is behind the Tanker, the Mission Crew Commander (MCC) transfers the E-3B/C AWACS radar to the radar technician to make sure that it does not transmit. Otherwise, both aircraft would brow-up, until after the E-3B/C AWACS accomplishes the air-to-air refueling mission and takes at least 65,000 pounds of JP-4/5 fuel. After the refueling, the MCC makes sure to purge the radar before it is transferring back to the mission crew, and normal operations are commences. This clears any fumes from the radar that would lead to an explosion of the E-3 AWAC aircraft.

At this point, the Mission Crew Commander (MCC) quickly searches for radar only unknown targets. In this case, the E-3B/C AWACS was scrambles south of Panama and the unknown target flew due west from Colombia or Ecuador. Drug aircraft normally fly from Latin America directly to the island of San Cristobal deep in the Pacific Ocean using it as a navigation aid. Once the drug aircraft find San Cristobal, the pilot turns right and fly's north towards Mexico. On this mission, Hubert was the Mission Crew Commander (MCC) and once the radar was operational, he was the operator that picked up the radar contact.

As the MCC, Hubert directed the SD to scramble the alert F-16s from 24th Wing, Howard Air Base (AB). Once Ticker-One and Ticker-Two were on radar and on radio contact, both aircraft went on Tanker to refuel. Throughout that time, Hubert had the WD vector the Tanker with chicks on tow (fighters) towards their unknown target. Post refueling, Ticker-One as an element vectored towards the unknown target that at that point was due west of Panama by the E-3B/C AWACS Weapons Director (WD).

Eventually, the F-16s had to return to the 24th Wing, Howard Air Base (AB) mainly because they ran out of crew duty day. E-3B/C AWACS aircrews have a standing waiver that gives them a maximum of sixteen-hour crew duty days where all other aircrews only have twelve-hour crew duty days. This Tanker returned to Panama and a second Tanker refueled the E-3B/C AWACS aircraft as the mission continued north to Mexico. At one point, weather became an issue. Whereas the unknown target flew through the weather that included thunder, the E-3B/C AWACS flew around the weather taking the E-3B/C AWACS further into the Pacific.

Just South of Acapulco, Mexico, Host Nation (HN) Law Enforcement airborne assets joined the operation. Initially, the aircraft was on an intercept vector to the E-3B/C AWACS aircraft until Hubert went out on UHF and VHF guard frequencies and transmitted in Spanish, "aircraft approaching friendly any face, maintain twenty-five miles separation due to radiation hazards". Within seconds, the aircraft took a one hundred and eighty degree heading vector correction. At that point, Hubert provided information to the aircraft on the unknown target. Within minutes, the unknown target landed near a lake and the pilot seen running toward a hill.

At the same time, an eighteen-wheeler vehicle seen driving towards the unknown target aircraft and started loading drugs. Then the Host Nation (HN) aircraft continued monitoring the vehicle to a building that had a silver roof where eventually law enforcement and local military personnel busted nearly a dozen individuals. As a result, Hubert's E-3B/C AWACS aircrews received credit with nearly a Billion dollars in drug busts, confiscation of aircraft, ships, and millions in US currency. As the Deployed Commander (Detco) or the Mission Crew Commander (MCC), under Hubert's command, he accomplished one hundred percent of all the US Air Force drug busts for the years that Hubert deployed to Panama.

Hubert and the E-3B/C AWACS aircraft continued towards the US since they did not have enough fuel to return to Panama. Since the US has permission to fly through Mexico on Counterdrug (CD) mission, Hubert coordinated real-time with the appropriate agency and landed in San Antonio at the military base. They received an order to land next to Air Force-One since President Bush Senior was visiting Texas. The E-3B/C AWACS aircraft seemed small next to the Air Force-One thought Hubert when he walked off the AWACS.

Being in the US even if the first day was sleeping and the following day only allowed everyone to go downtown San Antonio to the River Walk to have diner. It also gave everyone a chance to call home since it was more affordable to call from Texas than from Panama. Besides, AWACS crewmembers always thought that crew rest was controlled exhaustion since one always flew different schedules, which meant getting naps whenever one was tired even on position in the AWACS. In this case, Hubert called the Tinker AFB Command Post, Call Sign, Raymond-24 and asked that he receive a phone patch with the 552nd Operations Group (OG) Commander. After talking to the OG Commander, Hubert received thirty-six hours crew rest for his crew.

After the crew rested the required forty-eight hours, they returned to Panama flying the normal Caribbean route. Once in the 24th Wing, Howard Air Base (AB), the aircrew received a copy of the Miami Daily where they saw the results of their mission efforts reported in an article. The article displayed the drugs and monies confiscated. This type of feedback was new for the E-3B/C AWACS aircrews since normally they received feedback once they returned to their home station. However, with cable new becoming the norm in America, since Hubert and his crew was staying at a hotel during their stay in Houston, Texas, they had access to the cable news where their mission results was reported.

"Do you want to go down to the piano bar tonight," asked Hubert. Darlene was in Panama for a month to spend time with Hubert since it was the only way that she could see him. This had been her second month long visit to Panama but this time Hubert was staying at a local hotel. "I had to local Police following me everywhere when I went shopping today," mentioned Darlene. This had made her uncomfortable when the local Panamanian Police walking with machine guns would not let Darlene shop without following her throughout the store. The previous visit she had lived in a small one-room trailer at the Naval Installation near the 24th Wing, Howard Air Base (AB). During this deployment, the staff had to move into a local hotel when scorpions in a trailer floor caved in and a scorpion bit a sergeant.

It was during this deployment that Hubert first worked for the future first American Drug Czar who at the time was the Southern Command Commander. During the regularly weekly meetings, the General would have his staff and detachment Commanders provides their units status. As the E-3B/C AWACS Commander, Hubert had experienced problems getting Intelligence support for the Southern Command (SOUTHCOM) division. When Hubert brought out this shortfall during the staff meeting, the SOUTHCOM Commander not pleased that Hubert had suggested that his staff not supporting the deployed units.

Nothing changed in the near future and since Hubert was in the Counterdrug (CD) Division responsible for supporting the E-3B/C AWACS Panama Operations, he called Davis-Monthan AFB, Arizona and had an Intelligence Senior Airman (SrA) deployed as the E-3B/C AWACS Intelligence representative. In addition, Hubert briefed all HubertE-3B/C AWACS crews that it was the responsibility of the Mission Crew Command (MCC) and the Aircraft Commander (AC) for Mission Planning (MP) all sorties (missions). SOUTHCOM staff only provided the material needed as part of the planning process. The Mission Crew Commander (MCC) working close with the AC were the individuals who made sure that the AWACS aircraft was in the proper location that allowed the mission systems to detect the unknown target with the illegal drugs or targets conducting illegal drug operations over land.

The E-3B/C AWACSDetachment Commanders' (Detco) responsibilities included employing the AWACS aircraft and achieving mission objectives. For the Counterdrug (CD) mission, AWACS crews assisted ground military and Police agencies for South and Central American nations. A normal mission profile allows for tactical deception as a key factor. Normally, AWACS aircraft have a three-hour flight window in case they have maintenance problems and still fly a scheduled Air Tasking Order (ATO) mission. During this phase, as the AWACS Detco, Hubert directed that the operations staff plan for maintenance slips for scheduled missions. He decided to implement some tactical deception tactics into his plan since he believed that the local intelligence branch supported by SOUTHCOM and General Mccaffrey was not doing a good job.

"I want our crews to report four hours after their scheduled take-off time," said Hubert to the Operations Officer and scheduler. Without telling anyone other than the Deployed E-3B/C AWACS Staff to ensure Operations Security (OPSEC), aircrews reported two hours later than the ATO scheduled times. The staff knew than there were E-3B/C AWACS information leaks within the civilian Air Traffic Control (ATC) centers and other agencies supporting flight operations. According to the Civilian ATC center, the aircraft were supposed to launch on time.

On random days, Hubert inserted the two-hour maintenance slip, and the E-3B/C AWACS aircraft became airborne two hours early or late. This meant that the aircraft had this additional time at the end of the scheduled land time or two hours before they were supposed to be airborne. The aircrew show time was never was controlled by Hubert to ensure that the crew rest rules were never violated. During Hubert's command, the crews detected illegal aircraft airborne when the E-3B/C AWACS aircrafts were not supposed to be airborne. Countless missions resulted in $398. 2 million in drug busts and confiscation of aircraft and ships in the Pacific and Caribbean during this deployment. General Mccaffrey's intelligence officers soon started listening to Hubert's tactical deception tactics ideas, which he gladly shared.

"Would you mind flying again with me," asked Major Gills. Although she was Mission Ready (MR) in accordance with the Kedena AFB, Okinawa AWACS and Pacific Command (PACAF) flying directives, she did not have operational experience and did not feel safe flying over North American airspace. Years later, she would be the Colonel that Hubert would work for at 12th Air Force Theater Air Control Group (TAG). She would also be the Colonel who took advantage of Hubert's operational experience by asking him to volunteer for what seemed like an endless string of deployments.

As a Mission Crew Commander (MCC), or an Instructor Mission Crew Commander (IMCC), and Deployment Commander (Detco), Hubert flew every two weeks for currency and always flew with the crews on their first sortie (mission) in theater. In theater meant flying somewhere within Latin America or in one of the tasked nations. During these missions as an E-3B/C AWACS instructor MCC, he made sure that the MCCs knew the allowed latitude of deployed E-3B/C AWACS aircraft over land following international and agreed national laws. Crews received an order to report their aircraft position to the host nation. As an MCC, a technique used in reporting the E-3B/C AWACS position was to report the E-3B/C AWACS aircraft position using a plus or minus one hundred miles factor.

"I need you to keep the crew at the hotel until the rain stops," said Hubert on the cell phone to the Aircraft Commander (AC) at the hotel. The Wing Commander had just briefed all the Detachment Commanders (Detco's) that the Panama streets were all flooded and that American's should not drive inside Panama. Hubert had his E-3B/C AWACS Staff conduct a recall and directed them to stay at the hotel. He had an E-3B/C AWACS crew that was going to fly this morning but had the flexibility to delay its take-off by four hours without losing the flight planned take-off flight plan within the Air Traffic System. All of the staff in charge acknowledged that they receive information pertaining to any delays.

"Airman Van Leer, get in my office," said Hubert. A1C Brian Van Leer could see that Hubert was mad at him. He had known Hubert since he was a new Airman and had followed him during three assignments. A1C Van Leer had been Hubert's bus driver in Saudi Arabia during Operation Desert Shield and Operation Desert Storm when he first learned how to drive a bus in the busy streets of Riyadh, Saudi Arabia. On this day, A1C Van Leer had driven a van full of flyers to the 24th Wing, Howard Air Base (AB) for their flight even though he received notice not to drive to the base. In spite that there were other Senior Non-Commissioned Officers (SNCOs) in the van and Officers in the van with A1C Van Leer that allowed him to drive to the 24th Wing, Howard Air Base (AB).

Hubert made it clear to A1C Van Leer that it did not matter that he made it to the base, what mattered is that he endangered everyone including himself in the van because he violated an direct order. Hubert told A1C Van Leer that he was no longer a teen and had to start acting as young man and take responsibility if he wants to go further in the Air Force. For now, Hubert made it clear that the event was close but for him not to repeat it again but learn from his mistake. Especially, since there was a van full passengers that were equally at fault.

It was during this trip that Hubert was able to get his teeth fixed in Colombia. It was well before the Air Force provided dental coverage for family members. Actually, even for Hubert, other than getting his teeth cleaned once a year, the Air Force never gave him or his family dental coverage and all dental expenditures were out of pocket. Even when Hubert eventually had his teeth fixed, he had to wait to deploy to Colombia where he could afford to pay for braces and the dental care. For Darlene, he went further when he went into $25,000 debt to fix her teeth. Again, the Air Force did not cover the cost of the needed dental coverage even though Hubert had the Military dental coverage, which he paid for over the years the annual dental fees.

Crews received an order to stay outside any civilian Terminal Control Airspace (TCA) and the radars that surrounded airports since raw radar as a primary control identification source. The airport control facilities controlled the TCA airspace and could see any aircraft within their radar coverage. It was vital that the E-3B/C AWACS aircraft not overfly aircraft control facilities in order that they not see the E-3B/C AWACS aircraft on raw radar. During night operations, the E-3B/C AWACS aircraft flew with its external lights off. Since the E-3B/C AWACS aircraft had its own radar, it was able to maintain safe separation from other aircraft.

All travel was from home station was done using commercial airlines with the exception of the aircrews that flew the E-3B/C AWACS aircraft from Elmendorf Air Force Base (AFB) or Tinker Air Force Base (AFB) to Howard Air Base (AB) and back. This meant that on the last day prior to returning home, the crew stayed at a hotel, mainly near the airport so that they could take the hotel shuttle to the airport. This also allowed the E-3B/C AWACS Staff not to worry about having to commit their limited administrative staff to drive departing staff to take them to the airport as they during the initial phase of the 24thWing, Howard Air Base (AB) operation. However, at times there were issues that arose for departing crews.

For example, during one of Hubert's crews, the hotel manager alleged that one of his crewmembers broke a beer bottle in the hotel bar. Since Hubert was at the airport at that point, he not able to investigate that matter properly until later once he arrived in Alaska. In the meantime, back at the 24thWing, Howard Air Base (AB), the Deployment Commander (Detco) over reacted and believed the hotel manager without first finding the facts. Once Hubert talked to his crew and the hotel manager, it turned out that another hotel visitor who was a visiting British Officer. Hubert demanded an apology in writing from the hotel manager be sent to the Detco who would then forwarded to his Unit Commander informing his of the false allegation pertaining to the Alaskan crew. On future trips to the 24th Wing, Howard Air Base (AB), Hubert refused to stay at that Hotel even though the Hotel manager offered many special benefits to his crew.

COUNTERDRUG LESSONS LEARNED

Using these techniques, the E-3B/C AWACS crews started reporting countless drug busts. During 1995, as a Counternarcotics Operations Officer, the 12th Air Force Counterdrug (CD) Division played a crucial role in $4. 3 Billion in drug busts and confiscation of aircraft and ships used to deliver the drugs. During 1996, as the AWACSDeployed Commander (Detco), the AWACS aircrews accounted for one hundred percent of all the USAWACS drug busts in Central and South America. Although these monies seemed impressive, they accounted for a small percentage of the total drug operations in North America.

Unless the US and Canada does more in preventing the drug use demand, the illegal drug operations will continue its highly successful operations mainly due to its profits. In addition, unless the US secured the southern borders, the drug problems will only get worse as drugs and weapons continue to enter America. Furthermore, as world terrorism grows, this treat will continue to flow through the southern borders mainly because they are not secure onlypolitically according to Washington bureaucrats. Only air assets like the E-3 AWACS and troops on the ground can stop this flow and not the fictional fence that can easily be avoided. The fence can be avoided by either going underground or by climbing over the fence.

In Panama, the Counternarco-terrorism (CD) Mission at least slowed down the flow of illegal drugs in the US and Canada even though it was only superficial or symbolic. However, once closed, that symbolic flow no longer exists. In the end, until the US and Canada gets serious about the drug usage and the demand for illegal drugs slows down in North America, nothing will change. Until the Southern border in the US secures its southern border, not only is Americas' security further in jeopardy, but the drug war will only escalate.

As the illegal aliens issue becomes the main issue in America and overcomes the drug issue, many citizens will discuss legalizing illegal drugs. Already, could see new terrorist groups gaining control of Latin America. Especially since Washington keeps selecting inexperienced politicians to lead its Drug Enforcement Agencies (DEA) that tend to be politically corrupted by politicians and their political agendas and not drug prevention. Individuals experienced in Counternarcotics similar to Hubert could apply for employment 24/7 to every vacant government position and still never be hired.

CHAPTER 5

LIEUTENANT COLONEL

"I guess I might as well retire since I'll never be home when I pin-on any rank," thought Hubert to himself. As a Captain, he had pinned-on Major while deployed to the Middle East and now as a major who would become a Lieutenant Colonel. He was in Panama for one hundred and twenty days as the deployed AWACS Commander (Detco) when he pinned-on his new rank as his did when he pinned-on Major. Darlene had just returned to the US after a short visit for a month to spend time with Hubert. Darlene had visited Hubert twice in Panama since this was the only manner that she could spend more than a few weeks with her husband. Although he worked his normal longs days that average sixteen plus hours per day, seven days a week, at least once he got off work they could spend time together as they had a quick dinner.

As the 12th Air Force Deputy Stan/Eval Division, Hubert's duties included inspecting all the ground radar and flying units west of the Mississippi. The area of responsibility included the Caribbean area (including Puerto Rico), Panama, and any deployed units throughout Central and South America. The Commander of 12th Air Force, Davis-Monthan Air Force Base (AFB), Arizona, also serves as Commander of US Southern Command Air Forces (USSOUTHAF), and Air Force component Commander, US Strategic Command. Therefore, he was responsible for inspecting all flying and ground units within each applicable command. Hubert created a detailed annual schedule that included each unit to include the required number of Staff Assistance Visits (SAVs) based on his team inspections to ensure that each unit was ready for a formal 12th Air Force Stan/Eval inspection. Since the Chief of Stan/Eval would stay deployed overseas, this management of the entire inspection program would fall on Hubert even though he too would have a heavy overseas deployment commitment. Luckily, the new Email system made this process easier to accomplish in addition to the military autovon telephone system.

12TH AIR FORCE, DAVIS-MONTHAN AFB, AZ.

From 1 June 1995 to 22 February 1999, Hubert served as the Counternarcotics Operations Officer, Chief Battle Management, Chief Command and Control (C2), and Assistant Chief, Standardization and Evaluations (Stan/Eval), Headquarters 12th Air Force, Davis-Monthan Air Force Base (AFB), Arizona. He received a new task as the Team Chief for Operations GREEN CLOVER and LAZERSTRIKE, contributing to a record year with drug busts valued at $42. 3 Billion dollars in Central and South America. He participated in every instruction rewrite for airborne and ground C2 assets within a three-year period and staffed the Ground Based Radar and AWACS FY98-03 CINCSOUTH Integrated Priority List and Program. The entire time, Hubert managed his duties as Chief, Stan/Eval using the new Email system purchased by the Air Force.

Twice deployed as the E-3B/C AWACS Commander to Panama where he commanded 140 aircrew and maintenance personnel, plus over $800 million dollars in assets. As the AWACS Commander, Hubert raised the launch rate from seventy-two percent to ninety-six percent while generating eighty sorties (missions). His aircrews achieved all the 1996 and 1997 United States Air Force drug busts in Latin America, totaling $924 million dollars. As the Assistant Chief, Stan/

Eval Division, he flawlessly managed twenty-three flight and ground examiners while conducting sixty-five Formal and Staff Assistance Visits (SAVs) throughout the western US, the Caribbean, and Panama. His efforts earned him the Meritorious Service Medal, Second Oak Leaf Cluster once he arrived at the Joint Interoperability Test Command (JITC), awarded by Lieutenant General Lansford E. Trapp, the new 12th Air Force Commander.

Hubert had been an examiner in every system that he had been qualified since entering the Air Force, which meant that few Officers, had his qualification. Unlike all the other officers considered, Hubert had be a flight and ground examiner since he was a lieutenant and qualified in every crew position and every rank since, which no other officer could match. As a new Captain, Hubert quickly became a Flight Examiner, which is also a qualification seldom achieved by new Officers. Especially how Hubert became a Flight Examiner in NATO E-3A and US AWACS E-3B and E-3C in less than a year, which no other officer had ever achieved. However, at this point, the Airborne Battle Manager (ABM) career field was still a non-rated career field and historically only rated Officers had served as the Deputy Chief of Stan/Eval Division. He was responsible for every compliance evaluation of every flying and ground unit west of the Mississippi, Puerto Rico, and Panama.

After returning home for less than a month, from 6 March to 8 May 1998, Hubert received a task to for a multi-command Air Combat Command (ACC) Air Mobility Command (AMC) Stan/Eval Staff Assistance Visit (SAV) at the 24th Wing, Howard Air Force Base (AFB), Panama. During this era, Howard received a new designation from an Air Base to an AFB once the E-3B/C AWACS, the KC-135 Stratotanker, the F-15 Eagles, or the F-16s Falcons started the counterdrug operations. As the Team Chief for the first ever Central and South American Theater Command and Control Risk Management Review (RMR), Hubert identified critical deficiencies caused by the ongoing Howard AFB closure. Hubert's efforts earned him the Air Force Achievement Medal awarded by Colonel David J. Scott, the 24th Wing, Operations Group

During this deployment, Hubert and his team travelled throughout Latin America onboard every aircraft assigned or deployed to the 24th Wing, Operations Group. As the lead Stan/Eval Flight Examiner, Hubert flew to Equator and Colombia onboard the C-27 Cargo and the C-130 Cargo aircrafts conducting no-notice Stan/Eval Flight Evaluation (SEFE) evaluations to ensure that the aircrews were in compliance of the AMC and ACC flying directives. At the same time, since Hubert was an Air Battle Manager (ABM), since each deployed location had US radar, he conducted a no-notice RMR review. Every aspect of the 24th Wing, Operations Group activities including the Base Hospital activities were evaluated to ensure that Howard Air Force Base (AFB) would be ready to close on time without any issues. Although Hubert and his team were at Howard AFB for three months during this RMR activity, they worked seven days a week normally working fourteen or more hours per day in order to complete the required tasks given by three Major Commands and the Department of State (DOS).

During this trip to Panama, that Hubert received notice that Major Redman died in an aircraft accident while accomplishing an airborne evaluation in the Northern US. Major Redman was serving as the 12th Air Force F-15 Falcon Stan/Eval Flight Evaluator when his oxygen compressor malfunctioned and he blacked out and crashed into a mountain. Although he was an experienced aviator and his wingman kept calling him on the radio, Major Redman disoriented just prior to crashing into the mountain never knew what happened before dying. Not only was Hubert shocked with Redman's loss, Darlene who became a close friend also cried for his loss and for what it would mean to his young wife and children.

The 12th Air Force Commander called Darlene at home asking that she go to Mrs. Redman's home since she was asking for her. Redman had often talked about Darlene to his wife mainly because she had reminded her of her mother who was a general's wife and old military. Darlene in normal tradition would first cook one of her Mexican specialties before going over to her house. Upon entering, the women would hug each other for a long time where Darlene would tell Mrs. Redman of how Major Redman always talked of how he loved her and his family.

Then Darlene would meet her mother and father who was a retired USAF general. Both would also say how Redman also often talked about Darlene. Darlene would stop them and tell them that today was not about them but about Mrs. Redman and both would say, that is what Redman would expect her to say since he often talked of how he liked her and how they both always talked about family. Mrs. Redman would thank Darlene for making her marriage stronger while Redman was alive. In normal fashion, she influenced another military member. Regardless of the position that Hubert was holding, she always helped anyone who need assistance regardless if she was the commander's wife or a wife of a senior Air Force officer. Darlene had been responsible for the lives of many families that worked for her husband who was always deployed out of country with their husbands.

Again, Hubert wasn't home for long when he deployed again to Panama, "OK guys, get in the bus. " Hubert had just overheard locals talking in Spanish discussing starting a fight with the Americans. President Bush (Sr.) had just visited Panama and the rioters had taken their aggression to the airport looking for American visitors. The new AWACS aircrew had a High Mobility Multipurpose Wheeled Vehicle (HMMWV) escort with an M-60 Machine Gun in front and back of the bus. They also had two Air Force Security Police Airmen with M-16 rifles in each bus to protect the newly arrivedE-3B/C AWACS crew but Hubert knew that the quickest they entered the buses and departed the airport that it would be in the best interest of all visitors. Many Panamanians were still mad at the Americans for Operation Just Cause in late 1989. Hubert had participated in this operation while assigned to Tinker AFB Air Force Base (AFB), Oklahoma as part of the first E-3B/C AWACS aircrews. He made sure that he kept this information to himself and made sure that anyone in his crew did the same for the sake of themselves and the entire group of Americans.

While sitting on the bus, Hubert recalled, "We need you on the Mission Planning team," Hubert's Commander told him. Operation Just Cause had been a last minute operation with planning that normally took weeks or months accomplished within days. After Hubert completed the planning, he would be loaded to one of the aircrews that would support this operation. By the fall of 1989, the Noriega regime was barely clinging to power. Tensions increased when Noriega voided the election results and the Noriega's Dignity Battalions (DIGBATs) physically beat the opposition leaders. In December 1989, the regime's paranoia made daily existence unsafe for US forces and other US citizens. On 15 December 1989, the National Assembly of Panama declared that a state of war existed with the US and adopted measures to confront foreign aggression.

"Bogy dope," yelled the F-117 Nighthawk on the radio recalled Hubert. Operation Just Cause had been his first major operation as a new member of the USE-3B/C AWACS Wing. He recalled the air battle had been one of complete ciaos with F-117 asking for vectors to the US Tankers as they were running low on fuel. Although illegal, the USE-3B/C AWACS crews had used the Ultra High Frequency (UHF) guard frequency to locate scheduled aircraft. In one case, he recalled the Tanker and scheduled receivers flying away from each other with over one hundred and fifty nautical miles apart from each other.

The high casualties and use of resources usually associated with all-out urban warfare did not occur. The United States suffered 23 KIA and 324 wounded in action (WIA), with estimated enemy casualties around 450 WIA. There were an estimated 200 to 300 Panamanian civilian fatalities. Noriega's Dignity Battalions and others killed inadvertently by US troops. The US troops involved in Operation Just Cause achieved their primary objectives quickly, and troop withdrawal began on 27December. Noreiga eventually surrendered to US authorities voluntarily. He is now serving a forty year sentence in Florida for drug trafficking.

"Hubert, you will be the one integrating the GTACS evaluators into the flying program for the Air Force" he recalled his boss, Taco (Colonel Bell) who was the 12th Air Force Division Chief, telling him. The Ground Theater Air Control System (GTACS) or ground radar Stan/Eval function had just transferred from the 612th Combat Operations Squadron (COS) to the headquarters 12th Air Force. Although 12th Air Force was only responsible for the GTACS units west of the Mississippi and a few units in the Mid-West, the Air Force had not inspected all the US GTACS units in over fourteen years. Hubert and his team would take the lead in bringing these units back within the prescribed regulations but at a cost of making many enemies for himself.

On 1 August 1995, Hubert became the Deputy Chief, Standardization/Evaluation, 12th Air Force. During all the inspections, Hubert served as the Team Deputy or Team Chief. The Stan/Eval job consisted of over sixty flying squadrons compliance inspections. Each inspection consisted of taking a team and the team inspecting the unit in two parts. The first part was to help the unit prepare for the formal inspection. At this point, the team reviewed each program for errors with corrections given to the unit with suspense to correct them. Flight Stan/Eval Flight Evaluations (SEFE) check rides were also administer in order to ensure all aviators were flying with the proper aircrew aids, the aviators knew their flying regulations and were in compliance with the regulations, and were good aviators on position.

The second phase was the formal flying inspection. During this phase, the Stan/Eval team accomplished the process as the first phase but went into more detail. Here the flight evaluations were overall percentages of the overall unit staffing levels. A pass or fail grade received to each flying unit and the unit or individual sections could receive ratings such as "Excellent" or "Outstanding". Bad unit grades could lead to a downgrade or unit closure if a unit failed a Stan/Eval or compliance inspection.

Most flying squadron and ground radars unit inspections last one complete week. The only exception was the E-3B/C AWACS unit and the Rivet Joint (RJ) unit because of their size. Both require more time and more Flight Examiners to complete their inspection. The mid-1990s was a period when small computers were starting to be part of the Air Force as most of American organizations. The 12[th]Stan/Eval team started deploying with their computer, which allowed the team to provide the local unit a draft of the final inspection report. The final inspection report is not final until the 12[th]Air Force Commander reviewed the report and signed the report.

All inspections regardless if it is a flying or a radar unit must have a regulation library inspected. The regulations must be in accordance with the major command directives and posted properly according to Air Force Directives per the Technical Orders (TOs). Then there are half a dozen flying programs that must follow major command directives and follow Air Force Directives that also inspected by the Stan/Eval team for compliance. This is the administrative portion of the inspection. In addition, every aircrew member tested from a test made up from a test that comes from a random master major command bank. Then twenty percent of the aircrew receives no-notice flight check rides while flying in their primary aircraft. The 12[th]Air Force Flight Examiner fly's as the wingman or in the case of the larger aircraft like the E-3B/C AWACS or the Rivet Joint (RJ), flies as an Evaluator.

The 185th Fighter Wing (FW), in Sioux City, Iowa (IA) and its 174th Fighter Squadron (FS) F-16 C/D Falcons was the first inspection that Hubert accomplished as Stan/Eval Team Chief. Sluggo was the co-team chief and this trip was the official handover trip to Hubert from Sluggo who was retiring. Four days into the evaluation, Sluggo had to depart when Sluggo's father got sick and went into the hospital. At that point, Sluggo gave the 185th FW Commander the impression that the inspection was going well, which was a violation of the 12th Air Force Stan/Eval protocol that unit grading be discussed until the final day.

Unfortunately, the second week did not go well for the unit. At that point, the overall grade resulted in the unit receiving a grade of "satisfactory". However, the unit expected a higher rating even though individual sections received "Excellent" ratings. During the informal debrief done just prior to the final out brief, the 185th FW Commander became extremely hostile because he thought the unit would receive an Excellent rating. However, Hubert explained to the Colonel that he had the option of disagreeing with the teams ratings once he received the report in writing.

Furthermore, within six months, all open items would be looked again by the 12th Air Force team in person who had to close them. The team goal is not to make them look bad but to help them. Hubert reminded them that a satisfactory rating says that the unit is doing everything correctly and is able to go to war. In recent years, many units had lost sight of the inflated ratings that many inspectors gave unlike the 12th Air Force Stan/Eval. In other words, the unit is Combat Ready (CR) and that the 12th Air Force Commander would be one hundred percent happy with the grade. Hubert's duty not display the anger the Wing Commander showed him in the informal out brief.

After a while, every inspection seems like the other. The weeks become months and the months become years.

Nevertheless, their importance remain more important since this is the only way that the 12th Air Force Commander is able to know how his flying and radar units are doing and if they are ready for war or contingencies. Especially, since many Commanders tend to fudge their daily status reports in an effort to make their units seem better than they are and play thepromotion game. This is an area that Hubert was never good at since he believed in integrity and honesty and received notice as a young Captain that he was too idealist. Once Hubert became an Officer, Colonel Rush his first Commander told him would retire as a Captain because he was too idealist. Hubert replied that he did not mind because he "did not care in what was best for best for his career and cared more for what was best for the Air Force".

One of many units was the Ninth Operations Group (OG) at Beale Air Force Base (AFB), California. The 9th OG consisted of the Ninth Reconnaissance Wing (RW), with its 3,000 personnel, and 3rd Flying Squadrons, the 1st Reconnaissance Squadron (RS), the 9th Reconnaissance Squadron, the 5th Reconnaissance Squadron (RS), and 12th Reconnaissance Squadron (RS). During this era, Beale was flying U-2 Dragon Lady Dragon Lady aircraft, which is a single-engine, very high-altitude reconnaissance aircraft operated by the United States Air Force (USAF) and previously flown by the Central Intelligence Agency (CIA). The U-2 Dragon Lady aircraft provides day and night, very high-altitude flying at 70,000 feet (21,000 meters), all-weather intelligence gathering capabilities. The U-2 Dragon Lady aircraft used for electronic sensor research and development, satellite calibration, and satellite data validation.

The team flew into Sacramento, California, picked up their rentals, and drove to Beale, AFB and settled into in their rooms on base. Next, the team reported to the Ninth Operations Group (OG) Stan/Eval building where the Officer-in-Charge (OIC) was waiting for them to show the team their working area. At that point, Lieutenant Colonel Michael, call sign 'Action',

Jackson set-up the team's computer where each team member would load their daily inspection results. Unfortunately, the computer technology was still new when Hubert by mistake unplugged the computer without saving the days inputs resulting in losing the days report. This meant that all the team had to recreate their daily inputs and Hubert had to buy the first beer at the club even though Hubert not much of a drinker.

Another interesting aspect of the U-2 Dragon Lady Stan/Eval Formal Inspection was flying in the U-2 Dragon Lady aircraft and accomplishing the Flight-Line Chaser Inspection. The U-2 Dragon Lady flight accomplished in the 'guppy' is the only two seat U-2 Dragon Lady aircraft in the USAir Force. Unlike the typical your normal two seat aircraft where the back seat is directly behind the front seat, in the U-2, the back seat was offset to the right so that the instructor could either instructor or take control of the aircraft if needed during flight. During the formal 12th Air Force inspection, the Stan/Eval Flight Examiner flew in the guppy as part of the formal inspection.

The second portion of the U-2 Dragon Lady Stan/Eval Formal Inspection is the Flight-Line Chaser Inspection. Initially, since the U-2 Dragon Lady was a glider, once the aircraft was landing an Air Force truck with a military member on the truck bed would grab the wing and keep the aircraft straight. This would allow aircrews to accomplish tough-and-goes, which is part of the transition training for aircrews. Once the U-2 Dragon Lady aircraft transferred to Beale, AFB California the Air Force decided to purchase soaped-up Camaros to take over the Flight-Line Chaser Inspection role.

Here, Hubert and his team road in the right seat of the Camaro with the pilots as they drove to the end of the runways and waited for the U-2 Dragon Lady to approach them. Once the aircraft started its decent, the Camaro started speeding down the runway until it reached the same speed of the U-2 Dragon Lady aircraft. At that point, the pilot in the Camaro grabbed the right wing of the U-2, and kept the aircraft level throughout the length of runway until the U-2 Dragon Lady reached the opposite end of the runway. At that point, the U-2 Dragon Lady took off again for another transition and touch-and-go approach.

The day spent at the Wing Base Theater giving the wing personnel their inspection Stan/Eval grade. Nevertheless, first the team met at the Operations Group (OG) to go over the report and clean up the working area. The 12th Air Force team always left the working area the same way that if received it from their hosts. Prior to the final presentation, the team packed their bags and paid their billeting bills in preparation to depart for Sacramento to take their flight back to Tucson. Then an hour prior to the formal presentation at the Wing Base Theater, Hubert and the Colonel went to the 9th OG Commanders office and conducted informal Stan/Eval out brief. This 12th Air Force Stan/Eval out brief went well mainly because the overall rating was "Excellent".

Throughout his assignment at Davis-Monthan AFB, ArizonaHubert returned to Tinker AFB, Oklahoma initially to remain qualified as an E-3 AWACS Evaluator Mission Crew Commander (EMCC), which allowed him to remain qualified as a Number Air Force (NAF) Flight Examiner, and as the E-3B/C AWACSFlight Examiner.

This gave Hubert and Stan/Eval eight more individuals plus twenty-nine more inspections per year. This also meant that after ten year of neglect, Hubert would have to inspect units not been inspected for ten or more years. At first, the 612th COS Commander, a former co-worker that Hubert knew from Tinker AFB was mad with Hubert. Nevertheless, Hubert knew that the GTACS culture was in need of adult leadership, true Stan/Eval compliance, and not token unit inspections. He was surprised that the Air Combat Command (ACC) had allowed the GTACS community to get to such a dysfunctional status. However, once he found out that Lieutenant Colonel David Peterson was in ACC/DOY, which was the office responsible, he knew why. Timmy had been the officer back in Tinker AFB after Operation Desert Storm that allowed the AWACS community Training Standards to its lowest levels in order to receive his Colonel rank in normal "Air Force promotion tradition".

While visiting a Tactical Air Control Systems (TACS) unit in Washington, the 12th Air Force team found that the unit had not been using the Air Combat Command (ACC) Training and Stan/Eval Operating Instructions (OIs). This meant that the entire unit program was in violation of the major command directives. Since the unit controllers were controlling live aircraft dropping live bombs, this was a serious issue. Hubert gave the Unit Commanders the option of either it downgrading a unit, which meant the unit, would close or he would have the 12th Air Force Commander close their unit.

Hubert's closure of two GTACS units for non-compliance of Stan/Eval and Training Air Force Instructions (AFIs) upset higher headquarters and made him extremely unpopular at the Air Combat Command (ACC). ACC needed the TACS units in the deployment cycle. Hubert also had to create a new TACS training manual since the training manual he found was also ten year old. The last time the manual was when Hubert was in GTACS and the Air Force had a different control system no longer used by the Air Force. Later, Hubert went to Hill AFB, Utah as an Inspector General (IG) Investigation Officer (IO) when a Captain officially filed a complaint that the unit had created its own training program and gave all good-looking females preferential treatment. Especially, a short blond-haired enlisted female that most of the officers seem to cater to in the unit that arrived months after the Captain and seemed to get all the missions she wanted ahead of male trainees.

Hubert's IG investigation found thirteen allegations substantiated by eleven recorded witnesses including the top two allegations of both genders. Yet, nothing happened to the Unit Commander since he had been the former 12th Air Force

Commander Executive Officer. Nothing happened to the Operations Officer, or the Training Officer, or the Stan/Eval Officer, which made Hubert wonder why he wasted nearly four months in his 12th AF IG investigation. The only benefit was the items added to the ACC Major Command Lessons Learned bank, which received new information. This would be Hubert's first experienced the military and government Inspector General (IG) program and how politics easily override the IG IO data or factual investigation.

The Inspector General's (IGs) Process was nothing more than a political game played to tell the public that everything was fair regardless of the truth in most cases.

It was easy to identify an old time general from the new generation military general. Just look at their chest and any military member could easily see the difference. New military generals had what was referred to as the "I was there ribbons" and normally three rows of ribbons. Lieutenant General James F. Record was commander, 12th Air Force and U. S. Southern Command Air Forces, Davis-Monthan Air Force Base, Arizona. The command is comprised of eight active-duty wings in the Western and Midwestern United States and Panama with more than 450 aircraft and 35,000 active-duty military and civilian personnel. One of Hubert's jobs at the Deputy Chief of Stan/Eval Division, consisted of conducting compliance inspections of every flying and ground units within 12th Air Force.

General Record also ensured the operational readiness of 12th Air Force-gained units of the Air Force Reserve and Air National Guard, featuring an additional 21,000 people and more than 360 aircraft. His duties also involve overseeing US Air Force assets provided to US Southern Command (USSOUTHCOM) in Central and South America as commander of the air component to that unified command. He also serves as the Air Force commander of Component Task Force 224 (TF-224), the Battle Management (BM) arm of US Strategic Command. During his assignments at 12th Air Force, Hubert was the Chief of TF-224 and Chief of BM. In Hubert's view, General Record would be the last general that Hubert would have the honor on active duty to work for that would be a "generals, general" that took care of their troops and not their careers or next promotion.

Lieutenant General Record was old school and refused to play by the new rules and Hubert was old school. Once the new 12th Air Force Commander arrived, he removed all the chairs from the conference room stating that by removing the chairs that this would minimize the meetings. In fact, the meeting times doubled mainly because the General like hearing himself talk. Then he repeated himself and wasted dozens of Officer's valuable time because he could. Hubert would never meet another good Air Force General during his active duty time since all clearly came from the staff ranks. The last good Officer that Hubert would work for in the Air Force was Colonel Hue Smith. Colonel Smith was Lieutenant General Record's Director of Operations.

His efforts in this job would make him competitive for ColonelPromotion and selected to the Commander's list the flowing year. He was also on the school's list but by this time, he no longer wanted to pursue that career path. He knew that not taking a school slot at the Air War College (AWC) was going to lesson his chances atpromotion. However, he had never worried aboutpromotion during his entire military career. It was at this point that Hubert's accomplishments would no longer matter when it pertained to his annual Officer Performance Reports (OPRs). Especially since none of his achievement seemed to make it to any of his annual performance reports. Mainly because all of his home station supervisors were responsible for minor duties while he was serving as a Commander or Operations Officer or more important roles in hostile environments. Hubert would earn dozens of Air Force and Department of Defense Medals and all omitted in every future OPR and promotion recommendation.

The 1990s started with President Clinton in 1993 changing the military in the same manner as President Carter did during 1977. The 2000s would start with President George W. Bush with what many military member feeling as he had to return to Iraq to finish a war that his father did not finish in Iraq. However, the new military would be a military where senior generals had to reorganize the old military to what many thought was only to promote their friends. Prior to the endless reorganizations that the Air Force commenced during the 1990s and 2000s in an effort to promote more Colonels to General, most units had commanders and Operations Officers.

Today, there from have a dozen to a dozens of reserved parking slots in most units including countless titles making Air Force tradition a lost art. Air Force tradition is only a buzzword used in the military in modern times. The new 12th Air Force Commander Lansford E. Trapp would replace Lieutenant General Record. Unlike General Record, General Trapp would be more of a politician, and typical of the modern military general. Like General Trapp, Hubert would have no problem with General Trapp at his staff meetings. Although General Trapp was similar to General Record and more of a staff officer, at least he was a fair officer who would listen to the facts and make smart decisions not based on an officer's rank.

While at Davis-Monthan AFB, he met Lieutenant Colonel Bob Meriwether as a co-worked that had been the KC-135 Stratotanker pilot, which refueled him in-route to Saudi Arabia. It was during a conversation about refueling operations that the two Officers discussed the Gibraltar Straits air-refueling mission and found something in common. Hubert had been the Mission Crew Commander (MCC) on the E-3B/C AWACS aircraft and Bob had been the Pilot on the KC-135 Stratotanker. It showed both Officers how small the Air Force truly was when it came to conducting worldwide operations.

"Are you sure you don't want to take the Commanders job?" Darlene said, hoping that Hubert would change his mind. In the end, she knew that she would do whatever he wanted. He was tired of moving his family and wanted to stay in one place for more than two or three years. He never thought that staying in Tucson would mean that for the upcoming future that he would be gone on deployments for six to nine months each year. After all, Lieutenant Colonel's normally stay home since they have already paid their dues. In his case, his bosses would tell him that they needed his experience in one hostile area or countless war zones. Especially since, each time he did well that would help their careers. The only reward that Hubert received for the endless deployments was the twenty medals that he received and could ware in his uniform during this period.

The Tinker AFB formal consisted of inspecting the 552nd Air Control Group (ACG), which had the 552nd Technical Training School (TTS), the 960th Airborne Air Control Squadron (AACS), the 963rd AACS, the 964th AACS, and the 965th AACS. The 552nd TTS was the academic school for the E-3B/C AWACS Wing and the 960th AACS was the flying school for the E-3B/C AWACS Wing. The 963rd AACS, the 964th AACS, and the 965th AACS are the three E-3B/C AWACS operational flying squadrons responsible for deploying worldwide.

During a Numbered Air Force (NAF) Standardization and Evaluation (Stan/Eval) inspection, all flying programs inspected for flying regulations compliance. In addition, at random, aircrew members are given no-notice check rides to ensure that they too are in compliance with the flying regulations and able to accomplish their primary duty as an aviator. During Hubert's era, 12th Air Force was the only NAF that was accomplishing compliance inspections in the US Air Force. All other NAFs were accomplishing paper inspections.

The 12th Air Force Stan/Eval team deployed for two weeks to Tinker AFB, Oklahoma nearly all of its flight evaluators due to the size of the E-3B/C AWACS Wing. Hubert served as the Deputy Team Chief for the Tinker AFB Stan/Eval Formal. The first phase consisted of examining all of the squadron branches to include all of their publications in detail. Each day, the 12th Air Force Stan/Eval team met in their team room, discussed the day's progress, and updated the draft report. The normal team process was to update the unit's grade reports as you go so that each evaluator accomplishes the grading in the report while the information is fresh in their mind. Then later all that is required is the normal editing by all team members.

The second phase consisted of the flying phase. Normally, at least half of the 12th Air Force Stan/Eval team was still evaluating different sections so only half of the team schedule allowed them to give Stan/Eval Flight Examinations (SEFE) check rides. The only exception was Hubert since he was a qualified E-3B/C AWACS flight examines and could give E-3B/C AWACS check rides. Hubert accomplished both types of check rides while at Tinker AFB in addition to accomplishing evaluation different programs. Normally Hubert evaluated the programs associated to the Operations Readiness Center (ORC) since he had been the Chief of Current Operations and knew all the programs well. The ORC is the center responsible for launching and recovering the E-3B/C AWACS aircraft on each daily sortie (mission).

At the end of week two, the team makes sure the each section has the proper grade. Then the 12th Air Force Stan/Eval team decides as a team on an overall Wing grade. On the final day, the 12th Air Force Stan/Eval team and the 552nd Air Control Wing (ACW) personnel met for the final out brief at the Wing Base Theater and out briefed the entire wing. Prior to going to the Wing Base Theater, the Colonel and Hubert go to the Wing Headquarters and meet with the Wing Leadership for the informal debrief. Here the Wing Leadership receives a copy of their draft report and the 12th Air Force Stan/Eval Chief goes over the report with the Wing Commander. Once the informal meeting is complete, the group goes to the Wing Base Theater. Here a formal presentation to the Wing personnel presented with each section receiving its grade and finishing the presentation with the final grade.

As part of his regular monthly training, Hubert added a week to his schedule to the 513th Air Control Group (ACG). Each time, he visited a different 513th ACG section helping them develop their programs. During different visits, Hubert brought 12th Air Force Staff Assist Visit (SAV) Teams each time either to develop a program or to provide a pre-inspection. Eventually, the 12th Air Force Staff Assist Visit (SAV) administered a 513th ACG SAV to the entire wing. Upon returning a month later, all open discrepancies closed by the visiting 12th Air Force Staff Assist (SAV) team. During this period, Hubert traveled to Tinker AFB fourteen trips including two six-week trips to assist the 513th ACG become operational in the first year alone.

On 11 September 2001, Hubert and the 12th Air Force Stan/Eval team were inspecting the 513th Air Control Group (ACG) when the terrorist attacks on the World Trade Center and the Pentagon. The 513th was one of the first units tasked by the North American Aerospace Defense Command (NORAD) to protect the airspace over North America as part of Operation Noble Eagle (ONE). Within hours, E-3B/C AWACS was patrolling the skies over North America in homeland defense. Hubert recalled how as a lieutenant the US and NORAD had a Strategic Air Defense System with Fighter Intercept Squadrons (FISs) throughout the US that was able to protect America against a terrorist attacks.

On 20 January 2001, President George W. Bush would become Hubert's last Commander in-Chief(CINC) for his last eight years on active duty. Hubert would meet President Bush in Santiago, Chile while supporting him at the APEX 2004 Conference after receiving a by name request. He would also plan and execute an operation for President Bush in Colombia at the request of President elect Uribe. He worked closely with the US Secret Service on protecting President Bush and numerous dignitaries from throughout the Pacific area. Hubert would also work on the Joint Staff in Washington and meet the President while visiting the White House on multiple visits.

This also meant that the F-15s would have to get within the guns parameter or less than 4,000 feet range if the president or the vice president per the rules of engagement gave the orders. After 9/11, the 12th Air Force Stan/Eval team like all US travelers would be stuck at the Oklahoma City (OKC) Airport. The OKC airport like all US airports was in complete confusion. The team even tried to rent a van to drive back to Tucson but there were none available in the state of Oklahoma. After a week in OKC, the team finally returned to Tucson. Hubert not impressed with the new security that he saw in the US airports after having live overseas for nineteen years.

In July 1996, the Air Force Reserve activated the 513th Air Control Group (ACG). The 513th ACG worked in conjunction with the 552nd Air Control Wing (ACW) and the host reserve unit at Tinker AFB and the 507th Air Refueling Wing (ARW) in Oklahoma City, Oklahoma. This activation would have a significant impact on the wing's ability to support its mission and improve quality of life for the members of the wing, by reducing the number of Temporary Duty Days (TDYs) the members would endure each year. The 513th's mission would parallel that of the 552nd ACW. The 552nd ACW would maintain actual "ownership" of the E-3B/C AWACS aircrafts, but would allow the reservists to assist in the maintenance of the aircraft and fly actual missions with the E-3 AWACSs.

Hubert was instrumental in helping the 513th ACG create all of the Wing's training and Stan/Eval programs. Then Hubert assisted the wing during all the initial deployments as a Mission Crew Commander (MCC), as an instructor, and as an evaluator mainly due to a lack of qualified aircrew members. Hubert volunteered to deploy with the 513th ACG overseas to major deployments as part of his deployment commitments. Within the USAF, for Airborne Battle Managers (ABMs), due to a shortfall of ABMs, all 13B Airborne Battle Manager's (ABMs) on staff must deploy at least once during each three-year tour to assist active unit's operational units.

Both times serving as the Deployed Commander (Detco). Starting in Europe and the finishing Panama and then on the second contingency spending the entire time in Latin America as the Detco. Hubert used the 513th or the 552nd needs to fill this ABM major command deployment fill. During his assignment to 12th Air Force, Hubert supported two six months contingencies as a rated 13B ABM on flying status. Instead of waiting for the Air Combat Command (ACC) to task him to wherever they wanted to send him, Hubert took the lead and selected the location based on where needed most.

During this era, over twenty percent of Hubert's time deployed overall at the 513th helping the Reserve AWACS Wing earns the operational status. Hubert would drive his van to Oklahoma City and have Darlene join him whenever she could since Tawny was in college. This allowed Darlene and Hubert to spent time together since they separated three weeks of every month or more. Normally, Hubert would leave on Sunday for an inspection and return on Friday or early Saturday. He maintained this routine for five years.

In March 1999, the commander of the European Command requested that the 552d Air Control Wing adjust forces in the European theater in support of Operation Allied Force, NATO's response to the crisis in Kosovo. Again, in April, the wing received a request for additional crews and aircraft in support of Operation Allied Force. Since Hubert was in Geilenkirchen supporting an exercise, before the US took action on this request, he flew three sorties (missions) with the NATO E-3A AWACS during the exercise down time. This provided the NATO E-3A AWACS aircrafts the needed US prospective until the USE-3B/C AWACS aircrafts arrives in-theater in support of the Kosovo operation. Hubert was able to take the information that he had used during Mission Planning (MP) for his flights with the NATO AWACS Component back to the US and the 552[d] ACW.

The 513th Air Control Group (ACG) (Associate) mission is to provide theater and Air Force commanders with trained aircrews and maintenance personnel and systems for airborne surveillance, warning and control of US and allied military aviation assets similar to the active duty AWACS. Hubert deployed with the 513th ACG in May 1997 as the lead E-3B/C AWACS unit in support of Exercise Central Enterprise, designed to test the integrated Air Defense system throughout Western Europe. Besides the United States, a French E-3F AWACS and Coalition NATO E-3As AWACS provided Airborne Early Warning (AEW) support.

The consolidated joint forces focused their training over the central and northern regions of Germany and the North Atlantic against simulated outside Coalition aggressors. The two-week exercise allowed the composite force to hone air-to-air, theater missile defense and employment skills. The multinational event provided extensive theater data link training, surveillance training and large force exercise training. Since Hubert arrived in NATO AWACS, his experience provided many insights to the 513th ACG E-3B/C AWACS aircrew as the deployed Detachment Commander (Detco).

Immediately after the conclusion of Central Enterprise, the 513th ACG took part in Exercise Baltops 1997. This weeklong Joint Chiefs of Staff (JCS) exercise supported a multinational fleet in the Baltic Sea Baltops 1997 a naval support exercise, emphasizing theater/naval data link training with some weapons activity training for fleet defense. The exercise focused primarily in the Baltic Sea, east of the Danish mainland. This was the first time a USE-3B/C AWACS had worked in the Baltic Sea and flown deep into Eastern Europe. Again, Hubert's experience proved vital during the Mission Planning (MP) phase since assigned in Europe for over ten years and knew all the wartime procedures prior to the deployment allowing the crew to start the needed training ahead of the deployment.

"We want you to take a squadron at Tinker AFB," said Colonel Belton. This was Hubert's dream assignment of getting an E-3B/C AWACS squadron at Tinker AFB, Oklahoma. Nevertheless, by now he had started his doctoral degree and decided that becoming a Doctor in Management and Organizational Leadership would be best in the end of his military career. He was proud of a second chance as a Commander since normally once you declined command the first time, members knew that they had ended their Air Force career. He never thought that he would be denied retirement two more times and stop loss an additional time that would delay his retirement by six years. Unfortunately, due to the non-ending deployments he would not be able to complete the doctoral program at this point going to classes taking traditional classes.

"Babe I thought that you knew this Colonel well," mentioned Darlene. By this time in his career, instead of being home as was the custom, an endless string of Colonel's would keep him deployed in order to advance their careers. This also meant that he would spend nine months of every year deployed mostly overseas in hostile and dangerous areas. This would also be the part of his career where he would lose past friendspromoted to Colonel and forgotten about their past friendship. It was as if these Colonels' had memory loss or knew that Hubert was qualified to take any operation or job knowing that they would be accomplished well.

JOINT INTEROPERABILITY TEST COMMAND (JITC)

"Babe I should be able to put in Hubert's retirement papers at the end of the month," mentioned Hubert. After declining command, Hubert Hoped to retire but three weeks before he would be able to request for a retirement and be able to retire as a Lieutenant Colonel. Luckily, Hubert had made many loyal employees throughout his career that felt that they owed him a favor. His assignment manager at Palace Scope, Mark had worked for him at Tinker AFB and called him to tell him that he would be getting an assignment within the next two weeks. Palace Scope took care of all the assignments for the Airborne Battle Managers (ABMs) throughout the Air Force. Mark maintained his loyalty to Hubert as a past boss and would take many personnel risks help Hubert. Joint Interoperability Test Command (JITC) had a position that was not going to receive a work Force fill due to the shortage of ABMs in the Air Force but Mark made the exception and put Hubert's name in the position since he was a volunteer.

"Sir it does not make sense for me to take a job as a Mission Crew Commander (MCC) at Tinker AFB when I could have been a Commander," said Hubert to his Colonel. The senior Palace Scope manager who had remembered Hubert when he was a Mission Crew Commander (MCC) on staff in Puerto Rico was going to force him to go to Tinker AFB, Oklahoma even though she knew that he had just declined a Tinker AFB command position. Hubert mentioned to Mark that he intended to put his retirement papers on the first of the following month. Mark made it clear that Lieutenant Colonel Barrera would force him to either accept the assignment or retire as a Major. On 12 February 1999, Hubert arrived at the Joint Interoperability Test Command (JITC) as the Deputy, Air and Missile Defense Division. JITC was under the Defense Information Systems Agency (DISA). Throughout his assignment at JITC, Hubert remained qualified as a 12th Air Force AWACS Flight Examinerand Stan/Evalaugmentee.

Hubert worked for two Air Force Colonel's with a Communications background while assigned to JITC. His first Commander was an alcoholic that worked his way through the ranks that from day one did not like Hubert mainly because of Hubert's ethnic background and because Hubert would not brown nose. This Commander made every effort to hurt Hubert's career even though he was not aware that Hubert had already decided to end hispromotion opportunities prior to taking the JITC assignment when he declined two Commander position's and the Air War College (AWC) position that would have given him a better opportunity forpromotion.

The first requirement after arriving at JITC was to attend the Joint Command, Control, Communications, Computers, & Intelligence (C4I) School at the U. S. Joint Forces Command (USJFCOM) School, which is located in the Technology Corridor at Suffolk, Virginia. The month long course, which meant that Hubert and his classmates, would provide their military experiences during class activities to graduate. He stayed on base and had a rental vehicle, which made this trip relatively easy compared to his military operational deployments.

The class stayed at the Sheraton downtown, which made the long days seem better after walking all day. Part of the course curriculum was to take a week and visit all the US government agencies including a private tour of the White House. One of his classmates had been a tour guide at the White House, which made the tour more informative than normal since she gave the tour. This would also be the first time that Hubert would visit the Central Intelligence Agency (CIA), the Drug Enforcement Agency (DEA), and other key agencies that would be beneficial since in a few months he would be working with both agencies regularly.

Upon graduating, Hubert returned to Fort Huachuca and continued with his duties as the Deputy, Air and Missile Defense Division. He was surprised at how the civilian government service wasted so much money in expensive oak desk when he walked into his new office. Even the new oak desk in Panama could not compare to the old oak desk in his office at JITC, which was twice the size that in the Air Force not even a General would warrant. Soon he would start his bi-monthly trips to Washington beltway to represent JITC or support Joint Theater Air and Missile Defense Organization (JTAMDO) or Ballistic Missile Defense Organization (BMDO) as their C4I liaison and subject matter expert.

During one of his regular trips, Hubert met his old friend Captain James who worked at the Air Combat Command (ACC). Hubert and Captain James both represented their respective commands on different Working Groups during the upcoming months. This gave them the opportunity to have lunch during which Captain James mentioned that he wished that he had never divorced his first wife, which he considered his biggest mistake. He was ashamed that he destroyed his family only because of his ego. Over the years, Hubert would see this type of mistake many times where individuals would reach their mid-life crisis age and destroy their families for no reason other than selfish ego.

Each week, Hubert would take a flight from Tucson to the Reagan Airport in Washington and stay at a hotel near Crystal City. Hubert normally left for Washington on Sunday or early Monday depending on the first scheduled meeting. From there he would take the Metro to the Pentagon or other meeting locations. He would try to take a flight back to Tucson at mid-day on Friday so that he would arrive in time to take Darlene dancing at the Cactus Moon, a country and western dancing location near the Davis-Monthan AFB, Arizona.

Within sixty days after arriving at JITC and attending meetings at JTAMDO, the JTAMDO director agreed to give JITC $120,000 per year so that Hubert could come to Washington and represent JTAMDO at meetings as their representative throughout Washington. The JTAMDO organization was located in Crystal City and held many of its meetings in surrounding buildings or the Pentagon. BMDO would follow the same format within the next month after attending meetings at the Pentagon where the BMDO organization was located or throughout the beltway as JTAMDO. The highly classified meetings were always at the Pentagon or other US agencies such as the CIA.

"We need to prepare the budget requests for end-of-year monies," mentioned Hubert to his financial manager. This planning would lead to the TADIL (Tactical Digital Information Link) Branch being able to make over $140,000 in improvements. Hubert had a $1. 3 million budget to work with and was able to make the improvements plus $220,000 in additional improvements without having to ask European Command (EUCOM) for extra monies. For the first time in over ten years, all the servers would receive new computers and testing equipment.

Hubert was able to hire two new engineers without asking for more monies. Other administrative upgrades would allow the branch to use new software and hardware in their daily operations. His new management changes allowed more deserving and senior government employees to get the positions that were in the best interest of the government and not their bosses. Hubert bosses were not happy that he was so successful since it made all the other officers look bad. After all, he expected to spend all the allocated monies and not use the funds wisely as a good manager. His JITC Commander would hold this success against him during the Hubert's upcomingpromotion recommendation where he would hold it against him.

"You need to go to Korea for this planning conference," said Hubert's Commander. On 1 February 2001, Hubert took over the duties as the Chief of TADIL testing that was in dire need of many fixes. Hubert was responsible for certifying all the US data link systems for the Department of Defense (DOD). This planning conference was important since it would identify weaknesses in the primary US data link systems. However, it would also make many enemies since Hubert tended to take the high road and support the interest of the Warfighter

(US military) and not interests that were politically correct. Although Hubert could receive permanent government service (GS) jobs and high paying contractor jobs, he declined the offers and highlighted serious data link deficiencies that protected the warfighter.

"Rich how did the testing go in Korea," asked Hubert. His TADIL Testing team had just certified the new Korean Air Defense Center to conform to US data link standards. The testing of data link systems throughout the Pacific and Europe had meant that Hubert and his team would deploy for weeks at a time throughout the world. Hubert did his best in scheduling his overseas trips around his trips to Washington District of Colombia (D. C.) and the Pentagon. Each trip to Washington had different trip objectives. Each trip consisted of testing objectives, some supported missile testing while others supported different systems testing.

Since Hubert lived in Tucson, traveling to Washington was easy since he took his flight to the beltway from the Tucson International Airport. Normally, twice a month or more, Darlene would drop Hubert off at the airport on early on Sunday or early on Monday and he would return on Friday or Saturday after his last meeting at the end of the week. Hubert's meetings held at the Pentagon or at surrounding areas like Crystal City supported the Joint Theater Air Missile Defense Organization (JTAMDO). Hubert supported the JTAMDO and the Ballistic Missile Defense Organization (BMDO) in addition to his parent organizations, the Joint Interoperability Test Command (JITC) and the Defense Information Systems Agency (DISA).

For example, Hubert saw one of his Commanders give to one of his competitor privileged information that gave them advantage over other companies on specific projects. It just so happened that he was retiring and that company hired him as a contractor. Strangely, the majority of the senior Government Service (GS) and Contractors working at JITC were all former Commanders. All given waivers by DISA even though the government has a regulation that says there must be a five-year waiting period before hiring someone holding such a senior position. Then one wonders why the US acquisition system is so corrupted. Hubert too could advance but declined when he made it clear that he was at JITC representing the warfighters and not his career.

In this area, Hubert worked every new military and US government system through 2025. However, what Hubert saw was how military and civilian government employees sold themselves in order topromote their future careers and not protect taxpayers or America that left him to lose trust of the Federal Government leadership. It was because of this tour that Hubert decided to retire instead of continuing in the military and pursuing a doctoral degree. Hubert did not realize that the US Air Force would not allow him to retire for another five years once he declined to retire and declined Command that would have given him higherpromotions.

"Sir during our testing in Korea we found seventy friendly unknown targets that had been converted to hostile tracks by the gateways," mentioned Hubert to the General. The General replied that this was simply a software problem that the computer would correct. "Sir, in Hubert's command and control job, seeing red hostile targets on console brings out Hubert's fangs. Not knowing that the hostile targets are friendly due to a gateway problem will cost lives someday," stressed Hubert. He tried as best he could to stress that this was a hardware problem that could cost lives in a war zone. Months later he would resign from his job and ask that he allowed retire or return to flying. In the resignation letter Hubert emphasized that the two primary systems that had these problems that would someday cost lives. Years later, one of these systems would cause a friendly aircraft shoot down in Kuwait as he predicted.

"I have to return to D. C. again, I have meetings at the Pentagon and Crystal City," said Hubert to his division chief.

Earlier in the year, Hubert supported JTAMDO and BMDO and was as their primary liaison Officer (LNO). They each had given this command $120,000 per year for travel and billeting for another year of support. Nevertheless, after a while Hubert received a request to take other tasks so he transferred the JTAMDO and BMDO duties to his deputy, Major Barth. For example, as a Joint Staff Officer (JSO), he received a request to be a member of joint staff working group (WG) with a selective team of seventeen members.

"I want you to join the I-JWCA Working Group," said the JTAMDO Deputy Director to Hubert. The JTAMDO Deputy Director knew his expertise first hand since he had been Hubert's former supervisor and 552nd ACW Wing Vice-Commander in Oklahoma. The Interoperability Joint Warfighting Capabilities Assessment (I-JWCA) Working Groups primary goal had been to take each service one hundred top systems that they hoped to develop within the next five years and combine the lists down to one list of 100 military systems for the Department of Defense. Other working groups include the requirements working groups for the new F-22 Raptor, the newX-32Joint Strike Fighter (JSF), or the newX-35JSF.

The X-32/X-35 meetings normally were at the Rosslyn buildings, as were the National Missile Defense (NMD) meetings. During the JSF selection, as a requirement Team Member, Hubert could easily see that Lockheed Martin would win the JSF contract since Boeing clearly did had not do a very good job bidding for the JSF contract. Over the next six months, Hubert would return to Rosslyn and attend various meetings that would lead to the development of the Joint Strike Fighter (JSF) new Command and Control (C2) systems.

During the Boeing and Lockheed Martin presentations, in Hubert's view, Lockheed Martin presented a better weapons system and better overall program. Some would suggest that the aircraft looks contributed to a non-selection, which was not true. Later, he received selection to be a member of the JSF selection team that would recommend, which aircraft received the final selection as the aircraft of the future. This would require additional work since it required additional analysis of the future systems that warfighters would need.

"How many missiles does the US Army have in its inventory?" As the sole compliance Officer in the room, Hubert asked only one question to the group. Another task that required spending time in Washington was the National Missile Defense (NMD) program. Regularly, Hubert had multiple tasks simultaneously that included the 'Chief' title and only one in the Air Force system. As the Chief of NMD, during a different meeting to Washington, Hubert served attended a meeting after a live missile fire accomplished at the Pacific Missile Range. For this live-fire, missiles for US Navy Ships and a US Army Patriot Missile System were able to shoot down a missile entering from space. During the analysis, the Patriot proudly announced that it successfully shoot down the missile during the reentry phase using multiple missiles.

At first, everyone was uncertain with the meaning to my question. Nevertheless, once Hubert clarified my meaning and noted that for this so-called successful live-fire only five Patriot Missiles (actual number classified) to shoot one Intercontinental Ballistic Missile (ICBM) missile, then the US Army must have an unlimited number of missiles to shoot against its enemies. As an experienced aircraft controller, Hubert suggested that the Patriot Command and Control (C2) Battle Staff (BS) required improvement in an effort to minimize the number of missiles used to shoot down one target. In my view, shooting at debris made no sense. Clearly, Raytheon had engineers in charge and missile operators informed in C2 concepts were not part of the decision process during the employment phase.

Although Hubert makes few friends at these meetings, his comments were part of the official final report and he was not sure if he would ever receive another invitation to another similar meeting. Hubert found out that knowing too much and being too honest as a Joint Staff Officer (JSO) was not good for one's career. Many in the Beltway expected him to agree with all the Senior Officers and not highlight any issues or systems problems. Hubert felt that if that was the case, why he should waste his time traveling from the west coast if they only needed a body. He could simply call in, have someone on the phone where he could put his telephone on mute, go about his normal business, and technically have a JITC representative on the telephone during these meetings.

On a different and more crucial occasion, as the Chief of TADIL Testing, Hubert identified numerous critical deficiencies associated with the Patriot system to his JFCOM counterpart. Part of the review process includes the Joint Analysis Review Panel (JARP) where the JITC has an important role under the oversight of the Chief of TADIL Testing. For each system, there are three systems ratings given to systems errors, white (low), yellow (medium), and red (high). In this case, both Officers as Senior Officers in the military expected their respected service to commit either to each fixing each critical error or by stating that each system error as not being feasible due to the US not having the technology or the fix is too expensive.

Both options are viable options available to each service. Instead, Hubert and his counterpart received orders to drop their concerns even though both made it clear that these noted systems deficiencies could be deadly in the tactical environment. Years, later, the exact conditions noted in this situation occurred and a US Patriot shot down a British fighter with the loss of life of two British Officers. It did not matter that Hubert and a fellow Navy Commander from the Joint Forces Command (JFCOM) both ended their careers when they both noted the same issue with the TADIL problems within the military systems. Loss of life was only a matter of time and the right circumstances occurring as they did in Kuwait.

"How about having a router in the sky?" asked Hubert to the group around the table. After this discussion, an Advanced

Concept Technology Demonstration / Demonstrator (ACTD) package would submit. This new system would result in the new Joint Range Extension (JRE) or Beyond Line-Of Sight (BLOS) TADIL J (link sixteen) system that served as a router using satellites as relays versus ground relays. He would take one of his engineers to Nellis Air Force Base, Nevada while he served as the operations expert where the new system was first tested. He recalled seeing a gateway with wires going everywhere that this group would make the JRE equipment part of the US data link operations.

"Ok guys, we need to make sure that we are ready for this deployment to Ukraine and then Romania," said Hubert to his crew of twelve contractors. He was responsible for the Partnership for Peace (PfP) testing and evaluation of systems. President Clinton had decided to give the former WARSAW Pact nations some of the US technologies in hopes of helping them become independent nations. Hubert's team was the primary team in given these Eastern European nations five different types of US technology. His efforts led to the only feedback during this assignment. His boss called him into his Officer and mentioned, "You are making US look bad" due to all your program savings.

"I do not need the additional $1. 3 million that Hubert's predecessor requested," stated Hubert. He had made program savings that led to savings that allowed him to accomplish the tasks that used as justification for the additional monies. He was able to hire one additional full-time systems engineer, upgrade all the servers, and purchase badly needed testing equipment. He also purchased the airline tickets for the next planning conference overseas by committing the one-year monies prior to the end of the fiscal year. He was also able to purchase new desktops and other administrative equipment.

"It is not Hubert's fault that I flew as her instructor when I was a Captain and she was a Major," thought Hubert to himself. Lieutenant Colonel Barrera had always been mad when Hubert received notice by the deployment Commander to fly with her on her first Counterdrug (CD) mission in Puerto Rico. She took it personally since he was only a Captain and she was a major. Hubert asked Mark if there were any openings at Fort Huachuca, Arizona and he said there was a slot that he planned not to fill but would put his name in the open slot. Once Hubert received the assignment listing he quickly accepted it before Lieutenant Colonel Barrera would be able to take any action to terminate the assignment.

"Base we do not have to move from Tucson," said Hubert. He was in the Joint Interoperability Test Command (JITC), which was a joint billet. The JITC was the place for "one-stop systems test" with its one-of-a-kind array of hardware, software, and staffing, along with its state-of-the-art technological flexibility. The command can interface with all its on-site capabilities and network with any other testing or operational facility worldwide (JITC, 2006). During this period, 13B Airborne Battle Manager (ABM) career field became a rated career field like the pilots and navigators. A few years prior, the Air Force had changed the 17XX Air Force Specialty Code (AFSC) to 13Bs AFSC and the career field name and number changed to the Airborne Battle Manager (ABM) versus the Weapons Controller (WC) career field once the majority of their members were aviators.

42ND ABCCC & 12TH AIR FORCE, DAVIS-MONTHAN AFB, AZ.

"I love doing well for the Warfighters in the beltway but I am tired of the JITC politics," mentioned Hubert. At the two-year point at JITC, Hubert decided that he not enjoying himself and it was time to either return to flying or retire. Hubert called his scope manager Major Ballard who had worked for him when she was a Captain. Hubert mentioned that he was going to put in his retirement papers but suggested that if there were any open slots at Davis-Monthan AFB in Tucson, Arizona that he would be willing to take a final assignment. At the time, he was not aware that it would have to take three more assignments before the Air Force would allow him to retire. He would have to return to flying duties and accomplish two more staff tours. Not that it would matter since most of the time Hubert received orders and stayed deployed overseas. During this period, he was denied retirement once again and stopped-loss twice more. The Air Force used these two methods as their best staffing methods since the Washington politicians refused to implement the draft.

From 29 January 2001 to 30 September 2002, Hubert received an assignment to the 42nd Airborne Command and Control Squadron (ACCS), 355th Operations Group (OG), 355th Wing, Davis-Monthan AFB, Arizona. During this period, he would work as the Assistant Operations Officer-Mission (ADO-M) and Chief, Mission Support Division. In this capacity, he was directly responsible for testing, evaluating, training, and implementing every command and control system onboard the $29 million Airborne Battlefield Command and Control Center (ABCCC) weapons system. Under his oversight, Hubert would lead to a seventy-five percent increase in operational capacity.

Hubert would also serve as the 12th Air Force E-3B/C AWACS Stan/Eval Flight Examiner during two formal inspections at Tinker AFB, Oklahoma. His efforts would earn him the Meritorious Service Medal (MSM); Third Oak Leaf Cluster awarded to him by Colonel Paul G. Schafer, the 355thWing Commander once he arrived at his new assignment at 12th AF. At that point, he also received two other medals that he earned in Colombia, the Joint Commendation Medal (JCOM) and the Joint Service Achievement Medal (JSAM).

The following day Ballard called Hubert and said that she could put in a slot assigned to the 42nd Airborne Air Control Squadron (AACS) as a Defense Airborne Battlestaff / Battlestaff

Operations Officer (DABS/BSOO). On 29 January 2002, Hubert officially assigned to the 42nd AACS as the Assistance Director of Operations (ADO). Throughout his assignment at JITC, Hubert Has remained qualified as an AWACS Flight Examinerto augment the 12th Air Force Stan/Eval in the same manner as he would during the first year prior to starting the DABS/BSOO upgrade course. He received a request to return to Tinker AFB, Oklahoma and assist their formal inspection.

"What is a DABS/BSOO babe," asked Darlene. The BSOO was a rated Airborne Battle Manager (ABM) and directed battle staff operations by supervising execution of air tasking orders, directing immediate and pre-planned close air support fighters, and coordinating rescue of downed aircrews. In simulation and during Flag Exercises at Nellis AFB, Nevada Hubert had done many downed aircrew exercises and new how to execute the Downed Aircrew Procedure Checklist well. The DABS/BSOO selects targets and determines appropriate ordinance. The DABS/BSOO monitors fighter and tactical air-control-party status and limitations. The BSOO supervises the spectrum of employment of tactical air-to-ground air power when the battle staff functions as an extension of the Tactical Air Control Center (TACC).

"At least I will end Hubert's career at DM as a flyer for two years," thought Hubert. Unknown to him at this point, the Air Force was considering closing down the unit in the near future. The 42nd AACS had been the home of the EC-130E Airborne Battlefield Command and Control Center (ABCCC) consisted of seven aircraft used as an Airborne Battlefield Command and Control Center. The EC-130E is a modified C-130 "Hercules"; aircraft designed to carry the USC-48 ABCCC Capsules (ABCCC III). These one-of-a kind aircraft include the addition of external antennae to accommodate the vast number of radios in the capsule, heat exchanger pods for additional air conditioning, an aerial refueling system, and special mounted rails for uploading and downloading the USC-48 capsule.

"I cannot believe that I will end Hubert's career flying in the first aircraft that I saw on Hubert's field trip to the base," said Hubert to Darlene. The ABCCC has distinctive air conditioner intakes fore of the engines ("Mickey Mouse ears"), two HF radio probes-towards the tips of both wings, and three mushroom-shaped antennas on the top of the aircraft and numerous antennas on the belly of the aircraft. Provide a highly trained military force of Mission Ready (MR) crewmembers and specially equipped EC-130E aircraft to support worldwide combat operations. Mission roles include airborne extensions of the Air Operations Center (AOC) and Airborne Air Support Operations Center (ASOC) for command and control of Offensive Air Support (OAS) operations. It also serves as the airborne on-scene command for special operations such as airdrops or evacuations.

"Babe when I report to DM I have to go with Stan/Eval to Tinker AFB," mentioned Hubert. The first day as a new member of the 42nd AACS unit, Hubert deployed to Tinker AFB Air Force Base as the 12th Air Force Stan/Eval team Chief at the 960th AACS (Reserve) and 963rd AACS E-3B/C AWACS flying units. Three weeks later, he would return to inspect his new wing and squadron as the E-3B/C AWACSFlight Examiner. Then Hubert would enter training in the EC-130E as part of the Battle Staff (BS) aircrew. This was the only time that an individual was duel qualified in two aircraft. Hubert remained qualified as the E-3B/C AWACSFlight Examiner for another year until the deployments to South America made it impossible for him to support this commitment.

A month later, Hubert reported to his unit as a member of the 12th Air Force Stan/Eval inspection team that was conducting a regular schedule Stan/Eval on his new parent wing, the 355th Wing. Due to these inspections, he started DABS/BSOO training two-months later. After getting DABS/ BSOO Mission Ready (MR), on 1 November 2002, he received the task as the Chief Mission Support Division. After returning from Tinker AFB, Oklahoma Hubert spoke with the Unit Commander and asked if a Major David Valier that worked for him at 12th Air Force Stan/Eval could replace him as the unit Assistance Director of Operations-Mission (ADO-M). David was coming up forpromotion and this opportunity would help hispromotion opportunities. The Unit Commander agreed that David was qualified for the position and was a good officer to fill the position of Assistance Director of Operations-Mission.

"I'd for you to take Major's Contreras' slot to Colombia," said the Commander. A deployment commitment came for a Major to deploy to Colombia with Hubert's surname. His fellow ABM, call sign Potts whom he had known for a while was the 42nd AACS squadron Commander. Potts took it upon himself to volunteer him since he did not have small children and did not see any problems in volunteering him to take the deployment during the holidays. After all, this Commander was up forpromotion and in his eyes; the only thing that mattered to him was looking good to the Wing Commander. Over the years Hubert referred this as the 'Colonel Symptom' where Senior Officers were willing to do anything to reach the Colonel rank and sacrificing their employee lives did not matter as long as their careers benefited.

"You mean that you are going to miss, Thanksgiving and Christmas this year," asked Darlene. Hubert did not have a choice on when and where he was going to receive deployment orders. After over ten years of flying over Colombia in an E-3B/C AWACS aircraft, this would be the first time that he would land in Bogotá. He reported to the Military Group (MILGP) that was in the US Country Team under Ambassador Anne Peterson. As the Operations and Plans Officer, he had various duties including serving as the Colombian Joint Intelligence Center's (JICs) Liaison Officer (LNO) and eventually assigned as the Executive Officer (XO).

As the Plan Colombia Operations and Plans Officer from 8 December through 8 March 2002, Hubert conducted this duty in a hostile and imminent danger area in support of the counter narcotics operations created by President Bill Clinton. In addition, he served as the primary liaison to the United States Southern Command (USSOUTHCOM) Counterdrug Intelligence Center (JIC) located at Tres-Esquinas. In this capacity, Hubert traveled as required to Tres-Esquinas and produced accurate and timely daily situation reports on the Joint Task Force-South (JTF-S) Headquarters.

This would be the first time that Hubert would work closely with Colombian Officers. Hubert would find out that Colombian Officers like the European Officers, all went to a military academy in order to become an officer. Unlike the European Officer where some came from humble beginnings, most to all of the Colombian and Latin American Officers came from affluent families. Colombia did not have any program where enlisted members were able to work their way through the ranks and become officers as was possible in the US Air Force on US military. Furthermore, in order for any promotion in Colombia or any of the Latin American nations, employees receive school slots to many schools in the same manner as US military personnel are expected. In the US, the military pays all costs associated for these school slots while in Colombia and Latin America the individual pays for all the costs associated with attending any school that would help them get a promotion.

That is why Latin American Officers apply for US schools because selection to these schools also means that the US pays for all costs associated with attending including temporary living costs for the individual to pay for their meals. During Hubert's deployments to Colombia, he would meet countless officers that attended more US Professional Military Education (PME) schools than most of his E-3B/C AWACS peers put together. Some attended two or three schools while the US officer attended none because no slots were available due to the US Schools giving out too many slots foreign countries or

US military members received negative attendance notices to attend due to operational requirements. Hubert twice received negative attendance notices after selection for PME schools due to operational requirements.

Hubert's staff duties within the US Embassy kept him busy. He was also the main liaison for the MILGP and the Colombian military at the C. A. N. (Colombian Departamento Administrativo Nacional de Estadistica de Colombia) on any intelligence or operations issues. Additionally, he generated the weekly MILGP Commander Situation Report to USSOUTHCOM on Plan Colombia and Security Assistance engagement operations and flawlessly maintained the status of all outstanding Ambassador Tasking's or Suspense Actions in a timely manner. These efforts earned Hubert the Joint Service Achievement Medal awarded by Colonel Keen, US Army, and the US Military Group (MILGP) Commander.

On this first deployment, Hubert would report to Bogotá, Colombia and work with a group of permanent party US Army and USAir Force Officer assigned to the US Embassy in Bogotá, Colombia. During most of the four to five years that Hubert would deploy to Colombia, most of the same Officers remained in Bogotá and the US Embassy Staff. The MILGP Commander was a Special Forces Colonel in his forties and an extremely professional Officer. During Hubert's last deployment, the MILGP Commander would receive a line-number to Brigadier General. In addition, the MILGP was responsible for Process Action Teams (PAT) deployed throughout Colombia. PATs were similar to Mobile Training Teams (MTTs).

Next in line in the MILGP was a US Army PERSCO (Personnel Company) Administrative Officer who was a Lieutenant Colonel. This Officer tended to be quite and a competent professional who taught Hubert the Embassy processes. As the Operations, Plans Officer, and XO (Executive Officer), Hubert was the number three Officers in the MILGP although a deployed Officer. The remaining Officers were responsible for multiple programs such as travel, finance, or other areas and worked in the C. A. N. , which is equivalent to the US Pentagon. During Hubert's first deployment, he would learn how the US Embassy and the MILGP works.

The C. A. N. was approximately five miles from the US Embassy with Embassy Armed vehicles running regularly during the day as taxis. In the C. A. N. , the US has an Air Force Flight under the command of an Air Force Colonel. The senior Officer was an aviator and a fighter pilot serving as the Air Force Commander (AFC). His deputy was a Major who was an Airborne Battle Manager (ABM) who was the Director of Operations (DO). The DO was responsible for the Counterdrug Operations Control Center (CDOCC), manned by over twenty deployed personnel. In addition, the DO was responsible for Mobile Training Teams (MTTs) deployed throughout Colombia. During different deployments, Hubert would serve as the AFC, DO, Chief of the CDOCC, and Commander of all the MTT Teams throughout Colombia.

The MILGP Logistics Officer was from Puerto Rico and reminder Hubert of all the Puerto Ricans that he worked with in Spain. The best was to describe the Logistics Officer is to compare his to a weasel whose main concern in life was his nextpromotion. This Officer would have done well in the E-3B/C AWACS community where backstabbing is a way of life. This was why Hubert had only spent a little over two years as a permanent member of the Tinker AFBAWACS Wing in Oklahoma. He knew that he did not have the personality that Tinker AFB required to survive ethics wise or lack of ethics wise.

"Do you need Viagra since you are in your mid-40s", asked Hubert apartment cohort. Officers assigned to the MILGP lived in three or four bedroom apartments in northern Bogotá. Individuals would normally take the rooms of those that had recently departed for their home stations. "No I do not need Viagra, I'm not Puerto Rican, I'm a Mexican," replied

Hubert to his thirty year old roommate. He was surprised that someone so young would ask him such a personal question but automatically replied with his normal humor. Living in an apartment with single Officers at times was strange. Especially during the holidays like Christmas and New Year's, when Hubert wished he could be back in Arizona with his family. Then, over the years, he had rarely been home during the holidays.

"Sir I need to go to Tres Esquinas (TQ) and the JIC to fully understand their needs," remarked Hubert. He quickly updated the Counternarcotics reports by going to Tres Esquinas and meeting with the primary Officers assigned to the Colombian JIC. During this period, the US was transferring control of the TPS-43 radars under Colombian control. Hubert's expertise worked well since he had worked with the TPS-43 radar systems throughout the world. His E-3B/C AWACS operational expertise also provided real world experience in employing and planning of the new US and Colombian Counterdrug employment plans.

The main issue at TQ was the electric power availability, which was only available during the daytime and for the radar and operational equipment during the nighttime. In addition, no one fished in the TQ River due to the deadly Parana that was actively in control of the river. All the fish, which was a favorite meal for all Colombians, arrived from Bogotá. Tres Esquinas was also where Hubert first learned how to create legally cocaine as part of his duties as a Counternarcotics officer. He was shocked at some of the ingredients that included acid used to create the cocaine paste. It was no surprised as how eventually all cocaine users would eventually have flashbacks or have some kind of effects of the cocaine use later.

As the US Embassy Operations Officer, Hubert had many duties. Each week on Friday, he had to author the weekly Ambassador's USSOUTHCOM Military Counternarcotics Update Report with all the drug busts throughout Colombia.

This report had the detailed results from each town and city and each Colombian installation to include any US involvement or support. In addition, there were the regular staff meetings with the various Embassy staff agencies each responsible for providing Ambassador Ann W. Peterson a weekly status of their programs.

Anne Woods Patterson, born in 1949 is an American diplomat and career Foreign Service Officer (FSO). She currently serves as the US Ambassador to Egypt. She previously served as acting US Ambassador to the United Nations in 2005 and as US Ambassador to Pakistan from July 2007 to October 2010. Patterson was born in Fort Smith, Arkansas. She attended The Hockaday School in Dallas, Texas. She received her Bachelor of Arts degree from Wellesley College and attended graduate school at the University of North Carolina at Chapel Hill for one year. Patterson is married to David R. Patterson, a retired Foreign Service officer and the couple has two children.

Hubert provided the Military Group's (MILGPs) weekly update presentation. Finally, Hubert was responsible for coordinating with the Colombian Intelligence and Law Enforcement agencies located in the C. A. N. (Colombian Departamento Administrativo Nacional de Estadistica de Colombia). In this area, Hubert took regular trips to the C. A. N. , daily as required. After ninety days, Hubert returned home. This would be the shortest trip to Colombia for Hubert after the initial deployment years prior. It all seemed like decades ago since so much had happened since Hubert deployed in support of the latest deployment.

"I want you to you were the Mission Assistant Operations Officer but I need you to take the Systems Integration Division," replied Hubert's Commander. Upon Hubert's return from Colombia, a fellow Lieutenant Colonel Slammer was the Assistant Flight Commander responsible for administrative oversight of all the DABS/BSOOs in the rank of Lieutenant Colonel within the Flight. Lieutenant ColonelSlammer had just pinned on the rank and thought that he be the Systems Integration Division Chief. Lieutenant ColonelSlammer did not like the idea that Hubert was already an Assistant Operations Officer and Slammer was only a Deputy Flight Commander. Especially since Hubert was not competing forpromotion since he declined Command. A senior Captain normally fills the Deputy Flight Commander position.

To make matters worse, the largest division in the unit was in need of a chief since the Lieutenant Colonel that was in charge of the division had retired. Lieutenant Colonel Potts, the Unit Commander decided that Hubert had the best qualifications to fill this position and asked him to take over as the division chief. Since the Airborne Battlefield Command-and-Control Center (ABCCC) mission systems were going through a major systems upgrade, the Commander selected Hubert as the Chief of the Systems Integration Division. Furthermore, Lieutenant ColonelSlammer had never supervised enlisted members while Hubert had supervised members his entire career. Hubert had also been a Commander multiple times for ground and flying units.

Lieutenant ColonelSlammer was a navigator while Hubert was an Airborne Battle Manager (ABM) and engineer with the proper experience and qualifications. In the Air Force, normally,promotions were for pilots and navigators and not based on qualifications so this was a rare occasion. Lieutenant Colonel Slammer was upset that Potts selected Hubert as the Division Chief and a few years later he get his revenge even though Hubert had no input in the selection. Hubert was in Colombia when the Commander decided that would Hubert would be the new Chief of the Systems Integration Division. In spite of Lieutenant Colonel Slammer's behavior, Hubert invited him to both of his retirement parties.

"Babe I'm going back to 12th Air Force since the 42nd ACCS is closing," said Hubert. In May 2002, the Air Force announced its Fiscal Year 2003(FY03) force structure changes, which included the transfer of EC-130E Airborne Battlefield Command-and-Control Center (ABCCC) aircraft missions to other platforms. In a political move, the Unit Commander volunteered to close the unit to support the future funding of the F-22 programs that was still coming on line in the US Air Force (USAF). The Unit Commander was willing to lose his unit in order to gain a promotion to Colonel. It did not matter to him if the US Air Force lost a vital Warfighting capability. Hubert noticed that his close friend Gina Giles was his close ally at the 12th Air Force assisting him with this unit closure at the Air Combat Command (ACC).

This would be a major mistake for the USAF mainly because the ABCCC was the only platform that accomplished the Close Air Support (CAS) mission for the Warfighters. Upon returning from Colombia, Hubert worked with the E-8 JSTARS Wing Training personnel to transfer the CAS training program. With the loss of the EC-130s and the ABCCC, this meant that either the E-3B/C Airborne Warning and Control Systems (AWACS) or the E-8 Joint Surveillance Target Attack Radar Systems (E-8 JSTARS) would have to take over the CAS mission. In the end, the E-8 JSTARS received the limited CAS mission. Picking up the ABCCC mission was the E-8 JSTARS aircraft wing assigned to a base in Georgia. At Davis-Monthan Air Force Base, the 355th Wing lost six ABCCC EC-130E aircraft, along with 506 military and six civilian positions.

The 42nd Airborne Command and Control Squadron (ACCS) inactivated on 30 September 2002, after thirty-four years of existence. A mission that the 42nd ACCS had picked up from the Air National Guard (ANG) after Vietnam that created the need for the CAS mission when it determined someone needed to control CAS aircraft on immediate requests to save lives in wartime. Hubert was just glad that the ABCCC was still active during Operation Desert Storm even though needed in Afghanistan when he arrived as the Chief of Command and

Control. An observation that he regularly noted in his after action reports since he was responsible for the E-8 STARS.

Since the unit was closing, Hubert was in the 12th Air Force Counterdrug branch effective in the middle of the year. However, Potts again volunteered Hubert to take another deployment to Colombia since we had spoken about his previous deployment and mentioned that the Colonel Skymer had asked for Hubert on the telephone to return to Bogotá and become his Director of Operations (DO). The Colonel mentioned that his DO was going to a Joint Professional Military Education (PME) course in the US and needed someone that he could trust to serve as his DO. Hubert went home and after talking to Darlene accepted, the six-month deployment extended to nearly seven months. This meant that he would be away from home for over a year with the exception of the week that he had been back at home.

Just prior to closing the 42nd AACS, Hubert received a reassigned to the 612th Combat Operations Squadron (COS) as a Counterdrug Operations Officer. Hubert would be back in the 612th COS for less than a week when he received notification that he would return to Colombia. Again, Hubert received notification that he would fill a crucial position that only he was qualified. The Colombian Air Force Mission Commander had called asking that Hubert return to fill the US Military Group (MILGP) Air Force Mission Operations Officer position. This had been the first time that a deployed Officer filled a permanent position at the Colombian MILGP.

"Babe I am going back to Colombia but this time it is for six months," mentioned Hubert to Darlene. This would be the first time that a deployed Officer would serve as the Colombian Air Force Mission Operations Officer. At this point, Hubert had completed a deployment for 98 days, 127 days, 181 days, 180 days, and countless other short states side deployments. He had made four short trips to Tinker AFB, Oklahoma for two or three weeks for 12th Air Force Stan/Eval inspections. His short trips to Tinker AFB, Oklahoma did not count since they were trips to maintain E-3 AWACS aircrew qualification. To make matters worse, Hubert had spent less than two-months back home of the past few years. On one deployment, Hubert received a few hours to process out from the base and his gear was FedEx overseas after he departed for a six-month deployment.

In spite of this, both Deployed Commander (Detco) had written Letters of Evaluation (LOEs) showing all of his deployed accomplishments to that Hubert would use the for his annual evaluation reports. Even though Hubert gave the LOE to his Unit Commander, they did not use the LOEs inputs that showed that he served as an Operations Officer or Unit Commander of an Operational unit in a Combat Unit versus working in an administrative unit that in their minds would have made seem less of an Officer. What was more important, were the specific daily achievements that he achieve as part of his leadership duties as a Lieutenant Colonel. However, Hubert had experienced this typical occurrence throughout his Air Force career.

During every deployment, Hubert received an LOE and not one input used his Commander in the last eleven years even though during this period he deployed to Colombia, Chile, Qatar, Balkans, Iraq, and Afghanistan. During this period, he served in a hostile and combat environment as a project Officer for the President of the United States, as an Operations Officer, Commander, Negotiator, and Commander of a Mobile Training Team (MTT) with twenty-one Teams throughout Colombia among other senior duties. During this period, Hubert due to his injuries sustained in Iraq became disabled and earning twenty-eight medals in hostile or combat areas.

"I'm getting tired of living out of a suit case," remarked Hubert. In the last five years, he had deployed more than any officer in three different organizations had. Upon his return to Bogotá, he became the Air Force Mission Director of Operations (DO). He had hoped to simply be one of the workers and get a break of serving as a formal boss. This job meant that he was responsible for a 24/7 Counternarco-terrorism Center or the Counterdrug Operations Control Center (CDOCC), planning and flying of all US aircraft throughout Colombia, working close with the Colombian military and the US embassy personnel as part of the MILGP Country Team.

During the short time home, he had just enough time to find Tawny a small apartment near the University of Arizona (UofA) as he and Darlene hadpromised her for her senior year. Since Tawny had started at the UofA, he hoped that Darlene would join him in Bogotá for a month. At this point, he had not seen her for almost a year except for the short time back home and thought it would be nice for her to come for a short visit. Tawny was old enough and knew that school would keep her busy. Besides, he made sure her apartment was safe and installed a new air conditioner and freezer full of food. Throughout these activities, Darlene supervised Hubert as he did the labor on Tawny's new apartment.

"I'm glad you came," mentioned Hubert to Darlene. It had been two-months since Darlene had seen Hubert when she arrived in Bogotá. On this trip, she would join Hubert as the only American couple invited to a reception filled by the Ambassadors to Colombia. Darlene had always been good for Hubert at these types of events. This had not been the first time that Darlene and Hubert received invitations to similar events by their Colombian hosts. When she walked in the main ballroom, all the women asked who she was. This night would be filled with allot of small talk where she spoke her mind as Hubert smiled at her as he could not take his eyes off her.

As a surprise, Hubert had a manicurist come to the apartment for Darlene. In Bogotá, you can order anything from MacDonald's, to Italian Food, to Oriental food to a manicurist to get your nails done. All one had to do is pay for the taxi both ways plus her regular fee. All that is required is that the front door attendant received notification that the manicurist is coming and a time. In this case, Hubert waited for a Saturday so he could be there to take case for paying so that Darlene would not have to worry about translating in Spanish. Afterwards, Darlene and Hubert went to the Bogotá Hotrock Café in Bogotá for the first time for lunch where they became regular customers.

Although Darlene had come for a visit, Hubert worked the normal long days that he did when she not around. His workday would start each day at five in the morning with his driverpromptly waiting in front of his Bogotá apartment. If he had a good day where there were no problems, he would return to the apartment by 6:30 each evening. He would call Darlene from the C. A. N. to give her time to get dress once he knew what time he was getting off work. Their favorite place became the Bogotá Hotrock Café in Bogotá. Where Darlene and Hubert could hear their favorite music each night when Hubert got off work late at night.

"Babe I want you to have lunch with me today at the US Embassy," mentioned Hubert. He would send his driver to pick her up at the apartment and lake a lunch break at the Embassy with his bride. Like a proud husband, he would take her by his arm and show her off to all the Colombian's and fellow American's. On weekends, he would take her to the leather shop and have pants and jackets made for her. Then we were off to the shoe store to have leather shoes hand made for their next visit to the Bogotá Hotrock Café. Hubert also had four leather pants and coats made for Darlene had made in black, blue, and brown. All tailored to fit Darlene like a glove.

"Los mismo para tomar," (the same to drink) asked the waiter. For this month, Hubert and Darlene had become regulars at the Bogotá Hotrock Café. The waiters knew what this couple normally drank and that they would receive a good tip. As soon as Darlene and Hubert entered the Bogotá Hotrock Café, theypromptly received their regular table unless they wished to go to the bar. They knew after diner that we would move to the bar for a few more cocktails. Since the Bogotá Hotrock Café was only four blocks from the apartment, this allowed US to walk hand-to-hand as we talked about our day and the future. Hubert also knew the route to take since the primary road had been an unknown target of local terrorists who had blown up a few of the restaurants in the area.

Each time Darlene visited Hubert, she would stay not more than a month. As all visits, this visit ended it seemed too fast like all the others but in this case Hubert was glad. Each day at 5:00 AM and 5:00 PM, the CDOCC driver would take one of four routes to pick up either the day or night Air Force Mission Staff. Since Hubert was the Air Force Mission Operations Officer, he worked the Day Shift, which worked the twelve day time hours. The reason the CDOCC driver varied the routes was so that terrorist would have a harder time planning a direct attack on the US Embassy Vehicle full of Americans.

Three days after Darlene departed Colombia, as normal, the CDOCC driver picked Hubert as his apartment. In this case, Hubert was the first member to pick up and the driver started his route to pick up the second member. The driver turned towards Septima or Seventh Street, which is a major road in Bogotá with four lanes on each side of the road. Septima runs north south in Bogotá and the driver was on a small side road driving towards Septima. Upon reaching Septima, the driver took a right turn and started heading towards the US Embassy.

It was at that point that across the street some bombs destroyed a high riser building. The building was an eight-story apartment building with a dance floor on the top floor. Initially, Hubert and the driver were busy talking and did not realize what had happened. All they knew was that the armored Embassy vehicle was flew up in the air thirty meters according to the witnesses. At that point, since the vehicle, the driver, and Hubert all seemed well, they all continued with their normal day. Later Hubert and the driver went to the hospital for a checkup and received news that the x-rays looked normal.

Months and years later, Magnetic Resonance Imaging's (MRIs) and other medical conditions would prove otherwise.

"You need to develop a plan to transfer the US radars to Colombia," mentioned the MILGP Commander. Hubert had deployed many times to the radar sites during the last decade and knew each capability well. However, it was also a sad feeling knowing that American's would no longer operate these radar sites and that he would be the American Officer that would be responsible for their closure. Even though the closure meant that, the sites would remain and that American's would not operate the sites. After weeks of staffing the requirements, Hubert transferred the radar at Leticia, Tres Esquinas, and two other units to Colombia. All ground radars that Hubert had worked with for over ten years.

"Mam all five C-130 aircraft are no longer able to fly," mentioned Hubert to the Ambassador. The US had transferred ownership to the Colombian Air Force five C-130 Hercules Cargo aircraft and within a year, the aircraft grounded due to maintenance problems. It was Hubert's duty to bring American contractors or military maintenance members to fix the aircraft so that they were Mission Ready (MR). It was also Hubert's responsibility to develop a training program so that the Colombians would be able to maintain the aircraft. After six months of hard work, Hubert and his team achieve this goal and the aircraft were fully Mission Ready (MR).

"I need you to lead the negotiations team as the operations rep," mentioned the MILGP Commander. Hubert would go with the Air Force Mission representative and negotiation with Colombian representatives with the US monies and instead upgrade its intelligence, fix its C-130 fleet, upgrade their Air Defense System (ADS), and upgrade its Command and Control (C2) systems. In the end, with Hubert's expertise, the US convinced Colombia that it was in their best interest to follow their recommendations. Especially since Hubert would be in Colombia to assist them in implementing the fixes during the same period and Hubert was able to achieve every recommendation during this deployment. At the end of the deployment, Hubert would be mentally and physically worn-out, as he would tell the Air Force Mission Commander when his USSOUTHCOM told they could not find a replacement.

Although this trip had started with the first week when Hubert worked nearly full time in support of the Colombian President elect Uribe's inauguration and many bombs going off around the apartment. It had been a deployment where Darlene had visited three months after Hubert had left the US and home. Hubert had fixed the Colombian C-130 Hercules Cargo fleet and many other programs. He had also been able to play a crucial role as a member of the status and forces negotiation team where the Colombian military purchased military systems that it needed and not fighter aircraft like most fighter pilot Commanders normally desire.

What he found amazing was that not one of his accomplishments would ever be part of his military annual performance reports since none of his commanders would use his inputs. Even though he would take Letters of Evaluation (LOEs) signed by Colonels showing that he was a Commander or the Operations Officer responsible for dozens or hundreds of employees in a hostile environment. He kept telling himself that it did not matter since doing his job, as an officer was what mattered. For now, he had to worry about not going to jail and accomplishing the next operation since the local Colonel went on leave to Canada. Especially, after none of the US Embassy Central Intelligence Agency (CIA), the Drug Enforcement Agency (DEA), and the US Department of Justice, Alcohol, Tobacco, and Firearms (ATF) agents refused to execute the POTUS operation requested by President Bush without a written amnesty.

Hubert had scheduled the trip in the middle of the deployment so that it would break up the time away from home and the normal feeling of loneliness that each trip brought. He would often wonder if it was a wise decision after the operation was over and seeing the stress, that Darlene had gone through by herself. Knowing that it was another part of being a military wife. Nevertheless, one that he should have not asked her to live through. Nevertheless, he was glad to depart Colombia and each time in hopes of not returning mainly because it meant that he would not leave his family. On inauguration day, three bombs would go off just down the road from where Darlene was staying in the apartment by herself. Like most mornings, Hubert left at five in the morning to prepare for Operation OSCUDO (Operation Shield).

Uribe ran as an independent liberal candidate, having unofficially separated from his former party. His election platform centered on confronting Colombia's main guerrilla movement, the FARC. Other relevant propositions included slashing the national administration's expenses, fighting corruption and a national referendum to resolve several of the country's political and economic concerns. During this era, Hubert deployed to Colombia nearly the entire time prior to Uribe taking office and throughout Uribe's time in office.

The Colombia's government under president Andrés Pastrana was undergoing peace negotiations with the largest guerrilla group, the Colombian Revolutionary Armed Forces of Colombia-People's Army (FARC-EP or FARC). However, after four years of peace negotiations without cease-fires, disapproval of Colombia's main parties grew. Violence was rampant. The FARC had taken control, as they claimed, of some one hundred municipalities of Colombia out 1093 at that moment; kidnappings were common and were among the highest in the world, as well as the assassination and crime rate. The United Self-Defense Forces of Colombia (A. U. C.) was also gaining influence and expanding its massacres, and illicit drugs production, competing with FARC and the National Liberation Army (ELN) and other narco-traffickers.

President Andrés Pastrana Arango's presidency made history for his negotiations with the two left-wing guerrilla groups Colombian Revolutionary Armed Forces of Colombia-People's Army (FARC-EP or FARC) and the National Liberation Army (ELN), culminating in the grant of a demilitarized safe haven to the guerrillas the size of Switzerland, and second for his breaking off said negotiations. President Pastrana is remembered for a growing degree of unpopularity in polls as his term progressed. Some critics accused him of possibly accepting unspecified bribes from leading FARC and ELN members, but no concrete evidence of that was presented during his presidency. His administration proposed and initially oversaw the implementation of the Plan Colombia aid package and anti-drug strategy. He was also heavily criticized for all the seemingly pleasure trips he took around the world during his term. Hubert would learn firsthand how a liberal, a socialist, and an inexperienced president could nearly destroy his country single handedly. Hubert never dreamed that in his lifetime that America would have a Pastrana as a US president.

Until at least 2001, polls showed that at most two percent of the electorate contemplated voting for Uribe and that the Liberal Party's Horacio Serpa would probably win. Nevertheless, public mood shifted in his favor after the peace process with the guerrillas degenerated. The administration of President Andrés Pastrana had failed for four years to secure a ceasefire, and Álvaro Uribe became the candidate who may provide a viable security program. Former General Harold Bedoya, a candidate with a superficially similar program, remained marginalized.

Uribe received the office of President of Colombia in the first round of the 26 May 2002 elections with fifty-three percent of the popular vote. His running mate was Francisco Santos, a member of the Santos family, who has a long-lasting tradition as members of the Colombian Liberal Party and as owners of Colombian daily newspaper El Tiempo. Santos was also one of the founders of the anti-kidnapping NGO Fundaciónpaion Pais Libre, created shortly after his own experience as a hostage of drug lord Pable Escobar.

612^(TH) COMBAT PLANS SQUADRON (CPS), DM, AFB, AZ.

After returning from a six-month deployment from Colombia, Hubert found his personnel items in a box in his formal office. He received a call on his answer machine to report to his new job at the 612th Combat Plans Squadron (CPS). Hubert had just returned from two back-to-back deployments with 130 days and then a six-month deployment from Colombia when Darlene called him in Phoenix and mentioned that the General had called him. Hubert had been working on his Doctoral degree in Management during his last trip to Bogotá, Colombia. Hubert was in the second week of Hubert's residency and the last day of class. Up to this point, Hubert had expected a call any day to tell him that he would have to return to the Middle East. Hubert was surprised that the 12th Air Force Commander wanted to ask Hubert to volunteer to return to Colombia. Anytime a General asks an Officer to volunteer, it is the same as telling an Officer to say "yes".

From 1 June 2002 to 26 November 2002, Hubert deployed to Bogotá, Colombia a hostile file area to support a counterdrug operation. In the absence of the Chief and Deputy Chief of the Air Force Mission, Hubert would be the only deployed Officer to serve as the Action Officer as the Country Team for Operation ESCUDO (Operation Shield). At the Country Team Action Officer, his primary role would include planning and flawlessly executing the operation that consisted of a short-notice Airborne Early Warning (AEW) support for the Colombian Presidential Inauguration. Upon completion of this operation, Hubert would complete other important tasks including the forces and status negotiations with Colombia and numerous key flying and radar tasks throughout the region. His distinctive accomplishments earned him the Joint Service Commendation Medal awarded by Brigadier General R. A. Hunk, US Marine Corps, and Chief of Staff, US Southern Command (USSOUTHCOM).

By the time, Hubert arrived in Bogotá, Colombia and the US Embassy. Initially Hubert stayed at one of the local hotels until the Officer he was replacing departed a week later. Then Hubert took the apartment the departing Officer was living in once he departed. The US Military Group (MILGP), Bogotá, has two detachments. One in the US Embassy and one in the C. A. N. (Colombian Departamento Administrativo Nacional de Estadistica de Colombia), which had an Air Force Mission and the Counterdrug Operations Coordination Center (CDOCC).

The Colombian mission varied depending on the slot the deployed member received the task in support of as a member of the US country team and the Counternarcotics-terrorism War. Although Hubert was supposed to fill operations level slots, he kept receiving volunteer notifications to fill key leadership slots, which not normal for a deployed Officer. The Colombian terrorist groups consist of three major terrorist groups, the Colombian Revolutionary Armed Forces of Colombia-People's Army (FARC-EP or FARC) terrorist group and two Colombian paramilitary terrorist groups the National Liberation Army (ELN) and the United Self-Defense Forces of Colombia (A. U. C.). The FARC was the largest group in the 1990s with over 17,000 members many recruited from the Colombian military who were former conscripts. The ELN and A. U. C terrorist groups started as groups hired by the large farmers or the drug cartels to protect them and to counter against the FARC hostage adductions.

On this trip, Hubert, initially assigned as the Chief, Counterdrug Operations Coordination Center (CDOCC) became the Air Force Director of Operations (DOT). Within two weeks, Hubert became the Air Force Mission Operations Officer under the Colombian Military C. A. N. Every trip regardless of the location seemed to vary. It seemed that Hubert would reports to a location expecting to work at a lower level job and each time receives a higher-level position. Normally, each time, selected to fill the unit's top two positions especially at hostile locations. Mainly because of Hubert's experience and ability to make timely decisions and his lack of not be afraid of making hard decisions, which is something that few Air Force Officer make. This is something that Hubert Has done his entire military career.

"Do you think the Air Force will support this mission?" asked Ambassador Patterson. Hubert would reply, "In the Air Force when the POTUS requests, Officers follow orders". After meeting with Ambassador Anne W. Patterson, they shared their views on the upcoming mission. Hubert then met with the Military Group (MILGP) Commander Colonel Keen who made it clears of the importance of his mission that would be under his oversight and control. In 1999, the US Clinton administration unveiled "Plan Colombia", a massive military and social support program, valued at US $1. 3 Billion aimed at destroying the FARC and the Ejército de Liberacion Nacional (ELN-National Liberation Army) as well as offering alternatives to coca-farmers and intensifying the war on drugs.

The Bush administration, which inherited "Plan Colombia" endorsed the plan and, with some modifications, put it into operation. Its first effects became apparent the following year when military forces retook part of the former "liberated zone" after the breakdown of the agreement FARC and the Government. The new hard line adopted by the Colombian Government bolstered in May 2002 when the right-winger Alvaro Uribe, who favors all-out war against the left-wing guerrillas, won a comfortable victory at the presidential election, illustrating the will for peace of the Colombian people. In 2002, the US government provided Colombia with $415 million in military aid and, in a new development, lifted restrictions preventing the Colombian security forces from using the funding to combat illegal armed groups.

"Do you want a doctoral degree?" said the email from the University of Phoenix (UofP). Hubert was working in the CDOCC in the middle of the night when a pop-up message from the UofP appeared. Without thinking, he clicked on the email and answered the questions. The following day he received a follow-up email and answered additional questions. At that point, Hubert called Darlene to get her inputs and she said for him "to go for it". Hubert received notice that he needed to get the UofP a copy of his college transcript so the following day he called the Golden Gate University and had the university mail a transcript. Next, he received notice that he needed to write a ten-page paper on why he wanted a doctoral degree.

Since Hubert only had two days to write the paper, he worked on the paper after work so he not too sure on the overall quality. He emailed the paper to the UofP and mailed a hard copy as well to the address given and then it was a matter of waiting. A week later, Hubert received notice that he was accepted and given the dates for the first residency that would be two weeks long. By then Hubert had all the program details. Now it was a matter of working on a student long that he would be paying for the rest of his adult life. Hubert did not realize that he would accomplish many of his doctoral academics from Bogotá, Colombia in the future. Each trip would provide different challenges since Hubert received tasks outside Bogotá when he came to Colombia. However, eventually, he would become Doctor Contreras even though he would earn the degree while deployed from Colombia, Chile, Iraq, Afghanistan, Qatar, Kuwait, and many other nations in the Middle East.

"Hubert, what do you think the odds are that the US will support our President's request to support this operation?"

asked Colonel Carasco, Hubert's counterpart and operations Officer in the Colombian Centro de Comando e Control de Operações Aéreas de Fuersas Aéreas Colombiana (CCOFA). He replied, in the American military when the POTUS (President of the United States) requests that the Department of Defense support a mission, that request is an order. What he could not tell the Colonel was that during the initial planning stages of this Colombian request; US agency representatives had declined to support this request unless the President gave them immunity if case something went wrong.

This list of agency representatives included the Central Intelligence Agency (CIA), Bureau of Alcohol, Tobacco, Firearms and Explosives, US Department of Justice, Alcohol, Tobacco, and Firearms (ATF), and Drug Enforcement Administration, US Department of Justice (DEA) representatives. They all shared their concerns when their CIA friends who were in Peru when the civilian aircraft carrying American missionaries was shot down, ended because of this event. They did not have immunity and their careers ended abruptly. Therefore, none of the US agencies accepted President Bush's request to support the Colombian President-elect Uribe mission unless they received immunity. Hubert was the only one to accept the mission noting that the military never declines a POTUS request since a "Presidents request is like an order".

This deployment would not call for the protection of the US president but President elect Alvaro Uribe sworn in for a second term with Colombia's capital Bogotá and the palace in the middle of the city, which made protection a difficult and dangerous challenge. Like Operation ESCUDO (Operation Shield), Bogotá was under virtual military and law enforcement occupation to prevent rebel attacks like those that nearly marred his prior swearing-in. This is the first time that the Colombian military and law enforcement worked closely as a unified team to protect their new president and the visiting distinguished visitors.

Foreign dignitaries at the event were to include the presidents Michelle Bachelet of Chile, Alan Garcia of Peru, Oscar Arias of Costa Rica, and Antonio Saca of El Salvador, as well as the vice-presidents of Venezuela and Cuba and Prince Felipe of Spain. Washington represented by Commerce Secretary Carlos Gutierrez and Treasury Secretary Henry Paulson. Military helicopters buzzed over Bogotá and soldiers in armored vehicles guarded key city avenues as Uribe, Washington's main South American ally, took the oath of office for another four years. However, while Uribe was taking oath to become president, he was not aware that Bogotá was under attack by terrorist but thanks to execution of the plan developed the week prior, all would be well during Operation ESCUDO (Operation Shield) inside the Colombia Palace.

Operation ESCUDO started with bombs going off at the Colombia military academy as diversion tactics by the Colombian Revolutionary Armed Forces of Colombia-People's Army (FARC-EP or FARC). Overall, seventeen bombs would go off during this day with fifty civilians killed by the terrorists as Hubert conducted the operations from the C. A. N. Air Defense Center after nearly two weeks of planning. As the senior planner and Officer-in-Charge (OIC), the CIA, DEA, and ATF had declined taking part of the operation unless the US gave them full immunity. US Ambassador had asked Hubert, what he felt, and his reply would be, "Mam, in the US military, when the US President asks an Officer to execute an operation or mission, he executes the mission". Military Officers do not require immunity like civilians however, he did purchase insurance in case something went wrong and he lost his career for he knew that military would not be there for him.

Since a year had passed since Hubert left home, he asked Darlene to come to Bogotá for a month. Without thinking of the timing, it happened that Darlene would arrive the day prior to the start of Operation ESCUDO. Hubert made all the travel arrangements for Darlene, which meant that she would have a stay over in Miami, Florida. To make Darlene's travel as easy as possible, Hubert made a reservation at the Miami airport hotel and directed the hotel to approve all expenses that Darlene requested be charged to Hubert's credit card automatically. Darlene only had to sign for whatever she desired during her stay anywhere at the hotel.

In an effort to make Darlene feel safe, Darlene's room was next to an Ambassador that had security outside his room, which indirectly gave her security as well. At the Miami Airport Hotel, Darlene ordered room service and relaxed until the following morning when it was time for her flight to Bogotá, Colombia. During the evening, she decided to go for a coke and noticed that the next door had a bodyguard that at first made her nervous. After she spoke to him, she felt better. Darlene's trip to Bogotá, Colombia was uneventful. When she arrived at the Bogotá airport and got off the gate, Hubert was waiting for her. Once Darlene arrived at the Bogotá airport, since Hubert was part of the US Embassy staff, he was able to go to the arrival gate to meet Darlene and escort her through customs using his US Embassy badge.

Once Hubert and Darlene were at their apartment, they decided to order Italian food for dinner. In Colombia, one is able to order any type of food including McDonalds for home delivery. Hubert also arranged to have Darlene's nails done later in the week after Operation ESCUDO was over as a surprise. However, during Operation ESCUDO, Hubert never expected the bombs to be as close to Darlene as they were. During the day, whenever Hubert had an opportunity, he tried to call Darlene on his cell phone, which he carried with him. Depending on his location, Hubert would talk to Darlene each time for a few minutes on a telephone or a Satcom iridium telephone. Hubert told Darlene on the cell phone that at the end of the day that they would go to the Bogotá Hotrock Café.

Within half a mile from the apartment, the Colombian Military Academy was located and the FARC set of the first few bombs as a tactical deception effort. A tactical deception that the Colombian military did not fall for but that shook the apartment building where Darlene was located at during Operation ESCUDO. Even shaking the apartment widows of the ninth floor apartment where Darlene and Hubert were staying in Bogotá.

Even though the MILGP had a permanent staff of Officer consisting of over thirty, Hubert had mainly because he was known and trusted by the MILGP and Air Force Mission Colonel's that had worked with him for over three years. The reason Hubert knew that he was on his own even though deployed to Bogotá, the Colonel that ran the Air Force Mission; Colonel Skymer took leave with his family the entire period of the operation. The MILGP Commander made it clear that the operation was an Air Force mission and therefore stayed away from the entire execution phase. In this case, Hubert was completely responsible for Operation ESCUDO from start to finish. It did not matter that he was not permanent party and only on temporary orders.

"Do you think we can safely support this request?" asked Ambassador Patterson who had met him during two previous deployments. He had served as her liaison to the Joint Intelligence Center and Military Group (MILGP) Operations and Plans Officer. She also met with him regularly in his current posting as the Air Force Mission Operations Officer. With his assurance that the mission received safe support, the POTUS ordered the country team to plan and executed Operation ESCUDO (Operation Shield). This operation called for the defense of Bogotá when Colombia President-elect Uribe took office as President. This would be the first of two similar missions that Hubert would support. Dozens of dignitaries would require protection against possible terrorist attack.

"Mam, we'll make sure that our participation is properly planned and executed," said Hubert to Ambassador Peterson. Uribe, a 49-year-old former governor and mayor of Colombia's second-largest city, Medellin, easily won the election. The hardline independentspromised in an acceptance speech at a Bogotá hotel to bring "Security, so (the rebels) do not kidnap the businessperson, so they do not kill the labor leader, so they do not extort the rancher, so they do not force the peasant to flee his home. " Uribe had to change many policies that President Pastrana had implemented that made it easy for the terrorist to prosper throughout Colombia.

Hubert was part of the US Country Team was tasked to support the new Colombian Government. He worked closely with countless civilian and military officials throughout Colombia. At this point, Hubert had supported two former Colombian Presidents and their Governments as part of the US Country Team as a member of the US Embassy Military Group (MILGP). After this deployment, Hubert Held every possible position that any permanent and temporary Officer could hold in Colombia including many some that only the senior Air Force Officer could hold. Hubert would also earn his tenth joint medal under a hostile environment. It is amazing what a human can endure under hostilities. However, with the help of a loved one, the hostile environment seems less hostile somehow even if only for a few moments.

After a long day, even in hostilities, Hubert knew that Darlene needed to relax as he did. The Bogotá Hotrock Café would become one of their favorite restaurants and the staff would come to know the well. Each time, within minutes of arriving at the Bogotá Hotrock Café, Hubert and Darlene would always be seated or go to the bar depending on what their preference was on any given day. Each night, Darlene and Hubert would meet friendly locals that would make every effort to speak with Darlene although she did not speak Spanish. Another favorite restaurant was a small French restaurant owned by an American who kept passports from France, the US, and Colombia. In addition to the rich French food, Hubert and Darlene enjoyed the different types of cheese and breads eaten with the Colombian breads. The owner would play the piano and allowed the couple to dance behind it to his music.

After a romantic night on the town, Hubert would return to his normal life as the Air Force Flight Commander where for now in addition to his day-to-day responsibilities, he was working on creating four major Execution Orders simultaneously. A week before the official inauguration, Colonel Skymer went on vacation back to Canada to visit his wife's family. This meant that Hubert was now dual hatted as the US Embassy Colombian Air Force Mission Flight Commander and the Operations Officer since Colonel Skymer was out of the country. It was at this point that Hubert decided that all of his junior officers and all of his enlisted members would not participate with this operation. He did not want them to put their careers in jeopardy if something went wrong.

Hubert received a request by the Military Group (MILGP) and the US Colombian Ambassador to serve as the Country Action Officer for Operation ESCUDO, the short-notice Airborne Early Warning (AEW) support of the Colombian Presidential Inauguration responsible for the planning and execution for all the required execution plans and execution orders. Hubert drafted the initial Ambassador request, worked on the initial Concept of Operations (CONOPS), the Chairman, Joint Chief of Staff (CJCS) Execution Order (EXORD), the Secretary of State Order (SECSTATE), and the Secretary of Defense (SECDEF) Orders. Luckily, there was a lot of redundancy in the EXORDS. The SECSTATE and the SECDEF orders were the political orders. The US South Command (USSOUTHCOM) and the US South Air Force (USSOUTHAF) Orders were the Military Execution Orders.

Each execution order covered legal requirements in case something went wrong during the operation except Hubert. In this case, Hubert took the recommendation of the CIA Chief and purchased Insurance on his own in case something went wrong. Hubert already knew that the staff Officer responsible for the Peruvian civilian shoot down was still in litigation although he had followed all the established procedures per law. In this effort, USSOUTHCOM deployed a Colonel select, Lieutenant Colonel Adam to assist in the creation of the USSOUTHCOM Execution Order and USSOUTHAF deployed a Lieutenant Colonel Franklin to assist in creating the USSOUTHAF Execution Order. After finding both Officers hotels and arranging US Embassy vehicles and cell telephones, Hubert arranged for the team to start the planning process. In Hubert's view, from day one, conflicts started mainly because both Officers had their self-interests in mind versus the US interests in mind. After Hubert spoke with both Officers in private, Lieutenant Colonel Franklin was willing to compromise but Lieutenant Colonel Adam continued to be a problem. Throughout the planning, as the USSOUTHCOM representative, Colonel Adam kept demanding unrealistic demands on the Colombian military met the US's requests.

As an experienced Airborne Battle Manager (ABM), Hubert had created countless Air Control Orders (ACOs) throughout the world and the Colombian airspace would need the same airspace requirement in order to protect the US, visiting, and Colombian dignitaries. In this effort, Hubert suggested that a 150 nautical mile circle be set around Bogotá as an identification area. The plan called for any aircraft entering this area: interception, identification, or forced to land if deemed not to be friendly by Colombian Air Force aircraft. At first, no one objected with this portion of the plan including Lieutenant Colonel Adam.

As a requirement as a seasoned Airborne Battle Manager (ABM) and controller that Hubert entered into the initial plan was a restricted 150 nautical mile (NMs) restricted airspace. Any aircraft entering this airspace can expect an intercept by military aircraft, identified, and diverted outside the airspace. In addition, during the ceremony, no aircraft would enter the airspace. Initially, the USSOUTHCOM and USSOUTHAF planners demanded the airspace closed the entire day. After showing how much the Colombian economy would lose, the USSOUTHCOM and USSOUTHAF planners agreed to the two and a half hours of the ceremony.

That is until Lieutenant Colonel Adam requested from the Colombian Air Force create a Notice-to-Airman (NOTAM) advising all aircrews flying into Bogotá that they would be intercepted by Colombian Air Force fighter aircraft. To make matters worse, NOTAMs normally take 72-hours or more to process through local country Federal Aviation Administration (FAA) channels. Lieutenant Colonel Adam demanded the NOTAM published within twelve hours. To Hubert it seemed as if USSOUTHCOM did not want to support this operation and sent Lieutenant Colonel Adam to put roadblocks to ensure that it did not occur.

"Sir, unless the Notice-to-Airmen (NOTAM) is published within the next twenty minutes, we will have to cancel our support," said Hubert to the Colombian Colonel. To everyone's surprise except Hubert, the NOTAM published six hours later and Hubert had a hard copy of the published NOTAM that he gave to Lieutenant Colonel Adam. It seemed as if Lieutenant Colonel Adam was making it difficult for the US not to support Colombia's request. To Hubert, it seemed as if he was acting in the same manner as the CIA and the other agencies. It seemed as if USSOUTHCOM did not understand what a POTUS request meant. It was time for Hubert to retire, he had been in the US Air Force too long when Air Force Officer decided what Presidential orders to support.

USSOUTHCOM and USSOUTHAF deployed Lieutenant Colonel's to help Hubert draft the Secretary of State (SECSTAT) and Secretary of Defense (SECDEF) execution orders for Operation ESCUDO. However, Hubert felt that these Officers were more concerned with make names for themselves and not in executing the mission or safety. Normally the CDOCC, staffed with three enlisted employees. For Operation ESCUDO,

Hubert decided that a fellow senior deployed Lieutenant Colonel and Chief of CDOCC, and himself as the Air Force Mission Commander and Operations Officer would be the two participants. The USSOUTHCOM Lieutenant Colonel and the US Southern Air Forces (USSOUTHAF) a Lieutenant Colonel's would only be observers during the execution phase.

During the planning phase, the US Southern Command (USSOUTHCOM) and USSOUTHAF planners levied almost impossible demands on the Colombian military. For example, filing a Notice for Soldier (NOTAM) normally takes days for any aviator and the Federal Aviation Administration (FAA) to properly staff, review, and publish a NOTAM mainly to ensure safety. In many cases, the visiting planners demanded NOTAMs be published by the end of the same day otherwise the US threated to not support the Colombian government's request that President Bush said the US would support. Somehow, each time, the Colombian military provided Hubert with proof that the NOTAM accomplished as requested and published.

Another issue was the closure of the Bogotá airport, which Lieutenant Colonel Adam insisted be closed the entire day. This meant that the local economy in Bogotá would lose hundreds of millions by closing the airport for a day. After heated discussions, Lieutenant Colonel Adam agreed to the closure of the Bogotá only during the time that the activity was taking place at the Palace, plus or minus thirty minutes, which meant the airport closed for approximately three hours. This information added to the published NOTAM. Although the airspace around Bogotá advertised to all flying aircraft using the air traffic notice-to-soldier (NOTAM) process, Colombian fighters within the control airspace intercepted forty tracks without incident.

From the CCOFA, attack helicopters and alert helicopters loads with Colombian Fudra (Special Forces) soldiers augmented the forces throughout Bogotá. The FARC proved that they were a well-organized war fighting force. Near the apartment where Darlene was, the power was lost for hours including the early evening hours. One unknown target included a glider that the fighter lost when the target took an abrasive turn once intercepted. The intelligence information suggested that the terrorists would fly targets that would have bombs on them. Gliders could also easily carry bombs and in this case, forced the glider to turn; it was no longer able to continue to fly its course to the Colombian Palace.

This would not be the last issue that Lieutenant Colonel Adam would highlight. As an F-15 fighter pilot, the next issue that he would suggest was a critical issue would be in the alert and airborne Close Air Patrol (CAP) procedures. In this area, Hubert had created the procedures based on the material that he brought from his Air Command and Staff (ACSC) books that he had recently completed and based on eighteen years as an experience rated ABM, as a Master Weapons Controller (WC) who's main role was to execute the Command, Control, and Communications (C3) mission.

Unlike a fighter pilot, that main mission is to fly his aircraft of responsible for an element or at best, a large package of fighters, the ABM plans and executes the entire air battle during wartime. Therefore, setting up a simple CAP profile in Hubert's view, was a simple requirement for this operation. Once Hubert Highlighted the fact that the Colombian Air Force Officer all completed the US Air Force Air War College (AWC) or ACSC staff colleges, Lieutenant Colonel Adam no longer had any issues. The Colombian Officer's had been trained in the same air employment theories by the same US military service academies. Making Lieutenant Colonel Adam seem more foolish each repeatedly biased. Other issues rose that Hubert would have to deal with and each time dealt with it as best as he could.

During the execution phase, Hubert made it clear to Lieutenant Colonel Adam and Lieutenant Colonel Franklin, if they wanted to be present in the CCOFA or CDOCC during Operation ESCUDO (Operation Shield), they were there only as observers and did not commit to interfere or say a single word. Only Lieutenant Colonel Barbachino and Hubert were the only two Americans qualified in the CDOCC systems and the only two Officers that were bilingual. Therefore, they were the only two US Officers that would work the Operation ESCUDO with no exception. Hubert ordered Lieutenant Colonel Barbachino to work the CDOCC desk and he would work the CDOCC desk and as the CCOFA liaison. This decision proved to be the right decision that made the execution phase of Operation ESCUDO (Operation Shield) flow flawlessly.

"We need to scramble the alert Blackhawk's at the airport," yelled the CCOFA offensive Weapons Controller (WC) in Spanish. The ceremonies come on the heels of several days of surging violence with the majority of the bombs going off on August 7, 2002. Mortar attacks heavily damaged an airport, and clashes between military forces and guerrilla rebels left approximately fifty civilian people dead. As reported by the local media, Bogotá had seen low and medium flying close air support (CAP) aircraft including fighter aircraft and Police and military helicopters. The Airspace Control Measures (ACMs) created by a combined American and Colombian team to protect Bogotá had worked as planned. Hubert was amazed that the Colombian military and political system could work so fast at making hard decisions at the request of the American's that had tried their best to make sure that Operation ESCUDO did not occur.

"Sir, unless the notice-to-soldier (NOTAM) is published within the next twenty minutes, we will have to cancel our support," said Hubert to the Colombian Colonel. In the Palace parking lot, a bomb would hurt two soldiers and that would be the closest a bomb would get to the new Colombian President, President Uribe and his visitors. With fighter aircraft flying overhead Bogotá and helicopters moving troops to the latest hot spot, all controlled from the CCOFA as supported by the CDOCC by Hubert and Lieutenant Colonel Barbachino his handpicked Officer.

In the Palace parking lot, a bomb would also hurt two soldiers and that would be the closest a bomb would get to the new Colombian President and his visitors. The CCOFA had Colombian controllers with Ultra/Very High Frequency (U/VHF) radios that they used to talk to the Colombian fighters and Colombian helicopters full of Fudra Special Operations soldiers assisting Law Enforcement Officers throughout the Palace streets. With fighter aircraft flying overhead Bogotá and helicopters moving troops to the latest hot spot, Hubert and Lieutenant Barbachino would provide timely inputs to the CCOFA and multiple airborne US Custom P-3s controlling Colombian fighter aircraft throughout the skies surrounding Bogotá.

"I have a contact 2-8-0 at 80 miles, heading 1-4-0, at eleven thousand feet, at 200 knots," said the Colombian fighter pilot on the radio to the US Customs P-3 controller in Spanish. Hubert had made sure that Colombian Host Nation (HN) Riders (HNRs) flew with the US Customs aircraft to serve as translators. As the 12th Air Force Counternarcotics Officer, twice Hubert had been responsible for creating the US air force HNR program and the improving the program for the Air Force in Latin America. He had also flown as a controller in Venezuela in the US Customs P-3 aircraft as a Captain and as a new Major. Therefore, Hubert was aware of P-3 employment and systems capabilities.

This allowed Hubert to react in the CCOFA much better especially considering he was bilingual in Spanish. Hubert could react to real-time information on the radio and take the appropriate Command and Control (C2) action. Each time the CCOFA received an unknown target, he could react to the information he heard as a controller and take the appropriate action on a different console and/or radio. For example, in the case where this aircraft was identified as a military aircraft and it's pilot disregarded the NOTAM, Hubert quickly told him on the radio that once he landed that he was to report to the CCOFA and answer to the C. A. N. operations officer. Later the Officer knew that he would have to answer to multiple Generals and a new Colombian President, which meant that his career was over unless his family had political connections.

Although from the CCOFA controller consoles, Hubert could maintain a good situational awareness of the air battle, from time-to-time, he and Colonel Carasco would go outside on the CCOFA balcony and look towards the mountains where the Colombian Palace was located to see how the Colombian helicopters were being employed. The Colombian Air Force with the assistance of the two US American CDOCC controllers met its objective and stopped the Colombian Revolutionary Armed Forces of Colombia-People's Army (FARC-EP or FARC) terrorists from attacking the president-elect Uribe from being becoming president of Colombia. Nevertheless, not due for lack of trying during multiple terrorist attacks throughout the city and near the Palace stopped by Colombian military and law enforcement troops.

The Colombian Air Force A-37s one could see flying low-level missions over the Bogotá Mountains making sure that no aircraft or small gliders were trying to sneak into Bogotá in between the valleys. By being able to walk out to the CCOFA balcony, Hubert and senior Colombian Officers un-expectantly were able to improve their situational awareness during Operation ESCUDO. Based on intelligence information, the Colombian military expected small aircraft to sneak through the mountains and attach their Palace that was near the mountains. Because multiple targets including the glider that faded, the post analysis suggested that the intelligence data was in fact correct and that the A-37 low-level flights served as a deterrent to the terrorists.

"Do you think we can safely support this request?" asked Ambassador Patterson who had met him during two previous deployments. He had served as her liaison to the Joint Intelligence Center and Military Group (MILGP) Operations and Plans Officer. She also met with him regularly in his current posting as the Air Force Mission Operations Officer. Hubert assurance to Ambassador Patterson that mission safety would be his top priority implemented into his plan and execution of Operation ESCUDO (Operation Shield) received approval prior to the execution phase. This operation called for the defense of Bogotá when Colombia President-elect Uribe took office as President. This would be the first of two similar missions that Hubert would support. Dozens of dignitaries would have to protect against possible terrorist attack.

"Mam, we'll make sure that our participation is properly planned and executed," said Hubert to Ambassador Peterson a week prior to Operation ESCUDO. Uribe, a 49-year-old former governor and mayor of Colombia's second-largest city, Medellin, easily won the election. The hardline independent promised in an acceptance speech at a Bogotá hotel to bring "Security, so (the rebels) do not kidnap the businessperson, so they do not kill the labor leader, so they do not extort the rancher, so they do not force the peasant to flee his home. " Although Hubert would have an opportunity to meet President Uribe, since Darlene was visiting, he would decline his invitation to spend time with his visiting wife. After all, Hubert just did his job as President Bush ordered him to support the protection of Colombian President Alvaro Uribe and his distinguished visitors.

Cable News Network (CNN) would later report, "Several explosions rocked downtown Bogotá on Wednesday, killing at least thirteen people just before Colombian President Alvaro Uribe, who has vowed to crack down on leftist rebels took office. Before the end would end, the terrorist killed fifty civilians. Earlier, three other small bombs had gone off in different locations near a military cadet academy in Bogotá, slightly wounding six people. The four blasts occurred a few blocks from Colombia's Congress building as Uribe and his wife were walking up the building's steps for his inauguration. " There were dozens of other blasts that Uribe and his wife would not notice during the inauguration but Hubert and his small US team of one, the Colombian military, and the Colombian Law Enforcement were busy stopping the terrorists throughout Bogotá as much as possible.

"Wow, you can see the entire war zone from here," said Hubert to Colonel Carasco from the top of the CCOFA building. One could walk outside and see firsthand the fighter aircraft and helicopters scrambled from the CCOFA. Hubert was assisting the Colombian military and Police forces with his Counterdrug Operations Coordination Center (CDOCC) staff, and a small team of US Air Force headquarters planners who served as US witnesses during the operations in defense of the Colombia Palace and Bogotá. For this operation, Hubert only used himself and another Lieutenant Colonel to execute the operation in the CDOCC and the two visiting staff Officers as witnesses. He had made it clear to both visitors that they were there only as witnesses and not allowed to make any comments during the tense operation where each vital second and each decision cost lives of innocent civilians.

The US deployed two US Customs airborne surveillance platforms in support of this operation, Operation ESCUDO (Operation Shield). Lieutenant General Ballesteros was the Colombian Director of Operations (DO) and Air Force Flight Deputy Commander for the Air Force Flight. Hubert's duties included being responsible for the CDOCC and the CCOFA Air Defense upgrade for this operation and worked closely on planning all the requirements needed for Operation ESCUDO with Lieutenant General Ballesteros Air Defense staff. Hubert, Lieutenant Colonel Barbachino, and the USSOUTHCOM/ USSOUTHAF deployed staff worked diligently for two weeks in planning the defense of the visiting dignitaries and Uribe's family.

From the CCOFA, attack helicopters and alert helicopters loads with Colombian Fudra (Special Forces) soldiers augmented the forces throughout Bogotá. The FARC proved that they were a well-organized war fighting force. Near the apartment where Darlene was, the power was lost for hours including the early evening hours. Since Hubert was at the C. A. N. , all he could do was occasionally call Darlene to make sure that any bombs did not injure her. On one of the days, the Embassy staff arranged to replace the outer windows with bulletproof windows without advising Hubert even though the apartment was eight floors. Darlene became scared when she heard men walking into the apartment. When Hubert talked to Darlene, she was scared and mad and Hubert called the Embassy and made it clear to the administration personnel that no one was to enter the apartment without first talking to him. He could not understand why anyone would schedule routine maintenance on such a critical week as this week.

Cable News Network (CNN) would later reported, "Several explosions rocked downtown Bogotá on Wednesday, killing at least thirteen people just before Colombian President Alvaro Uribe, who has vowed to crack down on leftist rebels, took office. Earlier, three other small bombs had gone off in different locations near a military cadet academy in Bogotá, slightly wounding six people. The four blasts occurred a few blocks from Colombia's Congress building as Uribe and his wife were walking up the building's steps for his inauguration. " Before the end of the day, the FARC killed fifty innocent civilians. From the CCOFA terrace, Hubert and Colonel Carasco throughout Operation ESCUDO (Operation Shield) would walk outside, look at the operation, look towards the palace, and see the smoke that the bombs left each time.

"Wow, you can see the entire war zone from here," said Hubert to Colonel Carasco from the top of the CCOFA building. One could walk outside and see firsthand the fighter aircraft and helicopters scrambled from the CCOFA. Hubert was assisting the Colombian military and Police forces with his Counterdrug Operations Coordination Center (CDOCC) staff, and small teams of US Air Force headquarter planners who served as US witnesses during the operations in defense of the Colombia Palace and Bogotá. The US deployed US Customs airborne surveillance platforms in support of this operation, Operation ESCUDO (Operation Shield). Lieutenant General (Lt Gen) Ballesteros was the Colombian Director of Operations (DO) and responsible for the CCOFA. His staff worked diligently for two weeks in planning the defense of the visiting dignitaries and Uribe's family. A week before the official inauguration, Colonel Skymer went on vacation back to Canada to visit his wife's family.

"If you do not come I won't talk to you until I get back home," yelled Hubert on the telephone to Darlene. He knew that deep in his heart that he did not mean this threat but after almost four years of constant deployments all over the world that Colombia was one place where she could visit him. He never stopped to think of the danger involved since he felt that the apartment was located in a safe side of Bogotá. She had arrived in Bogotá on August 7 to visit for five weeks. Later on, he would often wonder to himself if his decisions of begging Darlene visit him in such a dangerous environment had been a smart decision.

Nevertheless, he knew that unless she came for short visits to countries that were not in the Middle East that he would seldom see her. The following day President Uribe would take office the day after seventeen bombs that rocked Bogotá including three bombs near the apartment where Darlene stayed during the President Uribe event. Unfortunately, Hubert had departed that morning for the Departamento Administrativo Nacional de Estadistica de Colombia (C. A. N.) at four in the morning and did not return until nearly mid-night on the same day until the end of the event and the analysis had been completed to include the initial after-action-report.

By being able to hear the Colombian aircraft controllers in Spanish vector aircraft on unknown target real-time and then relay the details to the US P-3 real-time, both Command and Control (C2) agencies were able to support each other better throughout the operation. For example, during critical times, low flying fighters scrambled to intercept pop-up unknown targets. On one occasion, a low and slow unknown target appeared, which had to evade due to the intercept by the Colombian fighter aircraft. As a result, the glider did not get within the range of the Colombian Palace to be of any threat to any of the dignitaries. Throughout the day, many airborne unknown targets intercepted even though the airspace had a NOTAM and all aircrews knew that no one was supposed to fly inside the Bogotá airspace.

During a different Operation ESCUDO interrogation event, multiple alert Sikorshy UH-60 Blackhawks and Bell UH-1N Twin Huey loaded with Fudra soldiers (Special Forces) were scrambles to the Palace. Especially after multiple bombs went off and various attacks had taken place around the Palace during the time when the ceremony was taking place. From the roof of the Colombian Combined Air Operations Center (CAOC), many times, Hubert and other CAOC Battle Staff (BS) would walk outside and look towards the palace or the Bogotá skies' and see the execution of the operation that they were directing from within the CAOC.

What made this operation different was that as controllers and operators, Hubert and other Senior Officers were able to here both US and Colombian aircrews in English and Spanish the aircrews on the radios and see the data link pictures real-time from one system to another that not connect to another. Almost serving as a third system, Hubert was able to pass on real-time information to aircrew with Command and Control (C2) suggestions to execute during airborne operations. In the end, no one in the ceremony knew what was occurring outside but the military forces, the policy forces, and the terrorists each trying to kill each other. Perhaps President Uribe fully knew of the hostilities since his staff was keeping him informed even though Hubert was sure that his name would never be part of the Colombian Report.

Although at the end of the day the terrorists killed fifty civilians and one Colombian soldier injured near the Palace, the days military and police actions prevented the situation being worse with the help of the American team. Although Seventeen bombs went off throughout Bogotá, damage was minimal and fatalities zed mainly because of the quick response of the military forces and the smart planning done prior to Operation ESCUDO. Later, Secretary of State Powel would fly to Bogotá, but Hubert would decline to meet him. Hubert met him while on the Joint Staff and not impressed with him. General Powel impressed Hubert not as a warfighter but as a good staff Officer like most modern Generals.

It would also be a time when he would meet his assistant Ms. Condalisa Rice, which did not impress Hubert. Hubert had met Ms. Rise when on the Joint Staff and she took the time to become informedbefore making a good decision Hubert could imagine how her lack of knowledge in other theaters would also hurt warfighters in other areas. Nevertheless, thought to him that anyone could learn in time, although a hostile environment not the right environment to learn except in American politics.

Besides, in Hubert's view, Ambassador Patterson had already thanked him when she awarded him the Joint Service Commendation Medal (JSCM) for his service during this period and the previous six months and that was sufficient since he worked for her. The Colombian military would give the Air Force Colonel, Colonel Skymer an award for the US supporting Operation OSCUDO that he would accept even though he was on leave. When Hubert wrote his after action the Air Force Colonel Skymer deemed report that went to USSOUTHCOM and USSOUTHAF 'brutal' once he returned from his leave. Hubert always tended to be an honest Officer and that never played politics, which not popular in the US Air Force or good for anyone's futurepromotion.

A few weeks after Operation ESCUDO (Operation Shield), Hubert and Darlene invited to a party attended by the Officers who supported this operation. Although Hubert was not permanent party, he was the only American invited to this Embassy party. The ambassadors to Colombia including most Central and South American countries that included Japan, Mexico, France, and the Canada were invited. The party held at the Colombian Officer Club just off Calle Septima in northern Bogotá. Hubert and Darlene had attended such events many times while in Spain, NATO, and other assignments. Once Darlene and Hubert entered the Colombian Officer Club, one could see the winding steps that led to the second floor where the reception was scheduled.

Once Darlene and Hubert entered the large reception ballroom, in the center of the room was a large banquet table with foods of all types. Surrounding the walls were chairs on three walls and a podium on the fourth wall where the receiving line started. Since Ambassadors from all the Latin American, Pacific, Mexico, the European nations were present, as the sole US couple, Hubert and Darlene felt honored being invited. After going through the receiving line, as was the custom, Hubert and Darlene mingled with the Colombian Officers that he had work with for over two years. In normal fashion, Darlene spoke with all the women without any problems.

As the sole American Officer, Hubert and Darlene represented the US military in this formal social cocktail function. For this deployment, Colonel Skymer asked Hubert to bring his Air Force Blues, which he wore to this formal function. To Hubert's surprise, the Mexican Lieutenant Colonel was rude mainly because Hubert was a highly decorated Officer when compared to all the Officers in the room. They had all heard of his performance during Operation ESCUDO and other operations during other deployments and assumed that Hubert was in Colombian. To their surprise, once they learned from Darlene that she was visiting Hubert mainly because it was the only way, she could see him because he was always away from him; this is how they learned that he was on a temporary assignment.

"Colonel, if you do not let me re-deploy on time, I won't be responsible for any errors," Hubert Heard himself saying to the US American Air Force Mission Chief that did not want to release him to return to the US but knew that he deserved to return home. At this point, he had been away from home all but less than three months within the past two and a half years. Hubert knew well that mentally he was tired of working seven days a week and workdays of sixteen to twenty hours per day had taken its toll. Shortly after this operation, it was time for Hubert to return to Tucson and his home station.

"You have been somewhat moody since you got back," Darlene mentioned. By this time, he deployed to the Middle East five times and to Colombia four times without any break between each deployment. After living in hostile surrounding and seeing constant military related deaths for seven through nine months of each year for over five years, Hubert was showing combat fatigue without realizing it. His normal easy going domineer had changed to getting mad for insignificant reasons. His bosses only worried of filling another vacant slot and did not seem to care if the constant deployments had any effect on Hubert. After all, in their view, his post deployment reports filled with phrase followed each deployment. Nevertheless, the resent deployments had taken a toll on Hubert and his family.

The only good thing that Hubert had to look forward to during this period was Tawny's graduation at the University of Arizona (UofA). Just prior to departing for Colombia, Darlene and Tawny had looked for an apartment since Hubert hadpromised Tawny that during her last six months as a senior, she could have an apartment near the UofA. Although Hubert was not pleased with the apartment that they chose, he purchased a new air conditioner since the apartment had an old water cooler. Hubert also purchased her a new efficient refrigerator and other furniture to make the apartment more secure. Now it was time for Tawny to graduate as a Media Art graduate with a minor in English. As always, Hubert made sure that for important events that he was home at any cost. His family always came first since he felt that he could never replace Darlene and Tawny but could always easily replace his career.

Upon Hubert return to work back in the Counternarcotics branch, by now the section chief decided without telling Hubert that he would no longer work in his branch. Hubert had not received the first time that this had happened to him in this manner.

Later on, he would receive six additional medals related to the recent deployments. He would receive a new Expeditionary Medal recently approved by the Air Force for his deployments in the Middle East that covered the past four years. Although the Award was new, he received five awards of this new Expeditionary Medal. Hubert's duty station fired him for not working at Davis-Monthan even though it had been under the 12th Air Force Commander direction that had selected him for those duties. Although all of the items in these awards were included in a two Letters of Evaluation (LOEs), when the Chief of the Counterdrug (CD) Branch authored Hubert's annual performance report, he did not use any of his achievements included in these documents.

As he reported to his new Commander in the Combat Plans Squadron, Hubert mentioned to him that he was working on his doctoral degree and that twice a year he had mandatory in-residence requirements. Hubert had started the doctoral program wanting to retire from the Air Force but not approved, and later an Air Force stop-loss forced Hubert to stay in uniform longer than Hubert had planned. Making it to Phoenix was a challenge since Hubert Commander had lied to Hubert about taking leave to attend these mandatory in-residence classes.

During Hubert first meeting with the 612th Combat Plan Squadron (CPS) Commander, who went by the call-sign Monty, Hubert told him how important it was that Hubert takes these in-residence classes. Monty said not to worry and that he would make sure that Hubert receives time off. However, Hubert received the largest training exercise of the command as the Blue Flag Project Officer. Even though Hubert had two fellow Lieutenant Colonels who could fill in during the two-week period that Hubert needed for class, he received notice that he was too important and could only have one week. Hubert was lucky that Hubert University allowed Hubert to accomplish all the requirements within one week versus the two scheduled weeks. With the help of Hubert two fellow classmates who were in Hubert doctoral cohort team, Hubert's team were able to accomplish a class presentation, a video representation, and Hubert was able to accomplish the required four scholarly papers within the week of class.

In addition, the Commander had made it clear that since Hubert deployed for most of the 769 days during the past two and a half years, that for the upcoming Southwest Asia deployment, that Hubert would not be deploying. However, two weeks before the final deployment date, a fellow Lieutenant Colonel told Hubert that he had seen Hubert name of the deployment list. When Hubert asked the Commander if it was true, he said that Hubert was the only Airborne Battle Manager (ABM) qualified to go even thought there were two others who had not deployed during the past two years who could have gone in Hubert place.

Since by this time the Blue Flag Exercise was ongoing and it was the exercise to train those going, Hubert asked for some training, but instead those that did not deploy took the training. The Chief of Training in charge felt that since Hubert had trained her in the past and she had trainees who needed the "seat time", that she could not give Hubert any training. During the next two weeks, Hubert had to attend, countless deployment training classes so that Hubert could deploy. Before this time, Hubert not allowed to take these classes, since only those deploying took the mandatory training courses. The 612th CPS Commander felt that since Hubert was trying to retire that he did fill his obligations even though no one on the 12th Air Force Staff deployed nearly as long as he had.

Just before deploying, Hubert due to the last four deployments being in the jungles of Colombia, by this time Hubert combat boots needed replacement. Heals of the boots had come undone and as a flying officer, protocol required that the unit give members a letter of authorization to go to base supply to get replacement boots. By this time, slammer had taken over duties as Commander. Lieutenant Colonel Slammer stated that since Hubert was within nine-months of retiring, that he could not justify approving that him get replacement boots. Instead, he had to purchase the boots out-of-pocket so that he would have a pair for his upcoming deployment.

As always, Hubert believed that everything happens for a reason and deployed with a positive attitude although somewhat upset for having an unethical Commander. Hubert knew that complaining would only make things worse for him sound as if he was whining. Hubert deployed along with over one hundred and twenty members, the 612th COS team deployed on a charter aircraft to the Combined Air Operations Center (CAOC) in Qatar. The team flew from Tucson to Philadelphia, then to Ireland, and finally landing in Qatar. In Philadelphia, Hubert went to the USO and called Darlene giving the volunteer a donation. In Ireland, Hubert had to try one of the local Irish beers.

HUBERT'S TENT CITY IN IRAQ

The normal handover training period between on-station and replacement crews was two weeks. Within two days, Major Smith, Hubert' replacement took the remaining time to tour the local area. Hubert's tent was the same as the one he has in Iraq except in Qatar he had a bunk bed with both beds for himself. He used the top bed for storage and every officer kept the entry of their bed covered so that during the day the tent was always dark since everyone had different work shifts. As for Major Smith, in Hubert's view, there nothing that Major Smith could teach Hubert since Hubert knew more than the Major did. Right away, many issues were many open issues that required action. First, Hubert not able to find any continuity files that would give him any indication of the issues that were important to the CAOC other than the brief issues mentioned by Major Smith.

For the first time in US history, the AWACS man power levels had declined so low that for two years the Air Staff approved the AWACS Wing not deploy its AWACS aircraft and crews. The AWACS leadership failed to see key indicators like the increase in alcoholism, family abuse, increase in suicides, and the lack of retention to the point where it had too few Combat Ready (CR) crews. Yet, it keptpromoting all its senior leaders for their top performance. Now Americas' national asset was a fulltime training unit because all of its 'promotables' failed to 'take care of their troops'. In addition, the AWACS aircrews chose to separate from the US Air Force many giving up fifteen years of service.

After Vietnam, the Air Force culture was to take soldier and officers addicted to alcohol or drugs and rehabilitated them so that the military would not lose the millions invested in employees training. In the 1990s and 2000s, the Air Force culture changed, a few soldier rehabilitated, and Officers jailed or court martialed. This new military culture provided insecurity or mistrust of many senior military leaders. Few enlisted members trusted Officers unless it was under a political culture. However, this went well with the military work force mismanagement practices. Like most military drawdowns, the Air Force normally forced the wrong employees out and kept the employees that normally were not the top performers. The Air Force like most large organizations failed to understand that top performers are not afraid to excel under any environment even under work force drawdown conditions.

For example, both of Hubert's aircrews during Operation Desert Shield and Operation Desert Storm, Hubert's aircrew received selection as the 1990 Aircrew of the Year during and the 1991 Aircrew of the Year. Every Officer assigned to both crews decided to separate from the US Air Force at the end of their first term. Eighteen of the Officers that separated from the 965th AACS included four Air Force Academy Officers of which all were Airborne Battle Managers (ABMs). The wing leadership made no effort to keep these Officers since at the time the Air Force was trying to draw down. Nine months later, Hubert was denied retirement because too many officers were forced out or Air Force allowed too many Airborne Battle Managers (ABMs) to separate. In none-critical career fields, the Air Force had too many Air Force Officer.

"Sir you need to attend the quarterly Theater Control conference in Kuwait" mentioned Captain Estrada. The 12th Air Force team had only been in theater for about a week when this first forward deployment came about. Hubert decided to take his Airspace Manager Captain Brian and Hubert would serve as the Communications, Command, and Control (C3) Subject Matter Expert (SME). In addition, Hubert decided to take two Air Traffic Management (ATM) Officers to the conference. One was an Australian Major and one was a British Major. This would be the first trip using Mil-Air (Military Air Travel) from Qatar for Hubert. He would travel with Captain Brain, and his

British and Australian Majors that he would travel in the future to other trips based on their expertise.

Captain Brain was Hubert's Air Traffic Control (ATC) expert from the 612th Combat Plans Squadron (COS) at Davis-Monthan AFB Arizona. The process for Mil-Air was simple, Hubert asked each Officer to give him a copy of their travel order and he drove over to the Passenger Terminal (PAX) and put his or her names on the list for the following day. Normally, anytime that Hubert made the travel arrangements, for some reason the PAX managers tended to schedule Hubert and his team without any problems. He was able to get the desired dates as requested. However, when his team flew on a, they always seemed to have problems mainly because of their lower ranks.

Hubert made sure that he made a copies of their travel orders for himself knowing that he would need copies in Kuwait once he arrived at the hotel, Kuwaiti Passenger Terminal (PAX), and passible their meeting location. Hubert received notice the report time so he returned to the CAOC and told his team when and where to show. They all decided to have breakfast at the Chow Hall near the Passenger Terminal (PAX) before departing for Kuwait the following morning at 5:00 AM. This flight was a C-141 Starlifter aircraft but many times the crew took a slick C-130 Cargo aircraft throughout the Middle East since the flights were short flights. Bahrain, Kuwait, and Cairo were the only locations that Huberttook commercial flights unless there was a military flight available. Receiving commercial flights was simple since all he had to do was use his military deployment orders whenever he traveled regardless of the mode of travel.

This would be the first of many trips throughout the Middle East for this team, as they would address many hot topics in the upcoming months. Once the team arrived in Kuwait City, the team took a taxi to the Marriott Hotel in Down Town Kuwait. For some reason, after taking a walk to the local mall by the waterfront, the team found itself eating at MacDonald's, which took about forty-five minutes to walk to in the heat. Since everyone was in good shape, walking not an issue and everyone brought a bottle of water from the hotel with him. Over drinking water had been a standard practice since arriving in the Middle East.

The following morning the team agreed to meet for breakfast early. This would be the first time that Major Vinnie would join the team for breakfast. He was the US Embassy liaison assigned to the team as the host for each visit to escort the team to every meeting. Major Vinnie has a Pathfinder, which meant that taking taxis would no longer be required. The only negative benefit would be his driving habits, which would take some getting use too. He drove as if he was always in a race and always at top speed, which was 'super-fast'.

The Kuwaiti Brigadier General would be the lead for this conference. From the start of the Middle-East Theater Conference, the Kuwaiti Air Force Colonel made it clear that the US Air Force had not been cooperative. During each break, Hubert found himself on his cell phone fixing problems with his deputy Captain Estrada back in Qatar. The Kuwaiti Air Force like most International Military Officers was very formal and courteous. At that point, Hubert had served overseas for over sixteen years including serving at NATO and as a Joint Staff Officer (JSO) for seven years. Hubert knew what to expect and unlike many Americans, he was there to represent the US first, then the Coalition. During the meeting, Hubert kept a detailed list of issues andpromised to correct the issues in minimal time.

After meeting, the team met with a group of Coalition Officers from throughout the Middle East at the US Embassy. It was a Wednesday and each Wednesday at the US Embassy Kuwait, they have a Happy Hour with a cookout and the team was invited. Since alcohol is not available in Qatar, Hubert thought it would be nice to allow his team to have a few beers. Hubert normally does not drink much but did drink a beer himself and then drank diet cokes. Since it was late, Hubert asked Major Vinnie to drop the team at the hotel and then take him to the Kuwaiti Passenger Terminal (PAX) to arrange for air travel back to Qatar.

The following morning, Major Vinnie took the team to the Kuwaiti Passenger Terminal. The Passengers (PAX) Non-Commissioned Officer (NCO) insisted that the team show as soon as possible and wait at the terminal per their perceivers. Hubert could see that the aircrew show time was seven in the morning, which meant that the NCO not making any sense. At best, the team should she three hours prior and since they were traveling with carryon bags, which was too early. Nevertheless, Hubert refused to have his team to wait all night and sleep in the Passengers (PAX) terminal for no reason truly made no sense but he knew that it was the Air Force rational.

Hubert told the NCO that he had to return to the hotel and get his team and that he would return as soon as he could. In an effort not to make the NCO made, the team returned at four in the morning, three hours before the C-130 aircrew reported for their flight. They had no issue with our team showing to the so early for Passengers (PAX) terminal for their flight to Qatar three hours early. Hubert had learned to deal with stubborn NCOs many times that refused to listen to common sense.

Within five days, of the twenty-eight tasks identified at the conference and taken back to the Combined Air Operations Center (CAOC) in Qatar that needed future actions, only eight remained. Some were easy tasks and others were more difficult. One issue identified by the Kuwaiti CAOC was that their hot line with the Coalition CAOC in Qatar not operational. Months of asking the Qatar CAOC to fix this problem in their view seemed ignored by the Americans.

After returning to Qatar, Hubert found out that the problem was simply that the Qatar Combined Air Operations Center (CAOC) Combat Operations floor Officer had turned off the telephone ringer and put a pile of magazines on top of the Red

Telephone. After dusting the common dust off the magazines and turning on the ringer, the problem that existed for years no longer existed. He also had to explain to the Lieutenant Colonel in charge of the Combat Operations Cell (COC) floor that the Red Telephone was their primary source of communications during critical periods. Within the next month, the other nineteen problems eventually closed with all parties being satisfied with the results.

"Sliger, can you tell the hot line to the Kuwaiti CAOC is located?" asked Hubert. Sliger at first not sure but Hubert suggested that in his experience his best guess was that it should be at the Senior Director (SD) position. When the three Officers arrived at the SD position, the Officers asked the SD if he knew anything about the Red Line or Red Telephone and he said that he did not. However, he did look around his station and found under a stack of magazine a Red Telephone that had a 'Kuwaiti Hot Line' label. Hubert was amazed that for months dozens of officers had simply ignored the telephone ringing and did not bother picking it up to see that was on the other side of the phone line.

Hubert picked the Red Telephone and found out that it had a direct connection to the Kuwaiti Air Operations Center (AOC). The CAOC SD mentioned that he often wondered why the telephone would constantly ring but that since no one briefed him on the telephone and that since it was under a stack of magazines and full of dust, he let it ring. This was how Hubert fixed his first of many Command and Control (C2) problems as the CAOC Chief of Command and Control, which would remind him of the inexperienced military force in the Middle East.

Hubert noticed that something was wrong when Captain Estrada his communications Officer changed all the command and control frequencies throughout Iraq. The week prior, he changed these same frequencies telling Hubert that they were bad frequencies. Hubert knew that there was no such thing as bad frequencies. After an investigation, he found out that the US Army communications jammer had been jamming any frequency that their system picked up as part of the self-protection measures. The Iraqi terrorists were using any type of remote device to activate bombs around Baghdad.

After a quick trip to Bahrain where a group of communications and operations experts met including some that had come from the US Joint Spectrum Center and Central Command. Upon Hubert's return to Qatar, he and Ray established a tiger team and a list of taboo frequencies not jammed by the friendly jammers. During the year, no one truly knows how many American soldiers lives were lost because of the US Army jamming. Within two-months, a yearlong problem in the Middle East no longer existed. However, within that month, Hubert worked long hours every day and stayed on the road the entire time.

"Why are you calling me so early? Are you guys really that stupid?" Darlene said to the Davis-Monthan Non-Commissioned Officer (NCO) who was looking for Hubert. They had wakened her looking for him suggesting that he was absent without Leave (AWOL). Hubert had called her the day prior from Bagdad to tell her that he had arrived safe from Qatar. Darlene told the Air Force (AF) flyer that Hubert had deployed to the Middle East over a month and a half ago after processing out from his squadron. It was the 12th Air Force orderly room and the Military Personnel Flight (MPF) that was looking for him since his section would not tell them where he was. When Hubert called his unit to complaint, he received a reprimand. Hubert could not wait to retire from the new Air Force. In the meantime, he did not have time to worry about his squadron leadership since he was in the middle of a war zone.

"Sir we have communications problems in southern Afghanistan between the American A-10s and the US Marine Corps (USMC) Combined Air Operations Center (CAOC). Due to the high altitude of the mountains, the A-10 aircraft could not use their Very High Frequency (VHF) radios with limited range to communicate with the command and control agencies. After a short meeting with Captain DeVichenso, Hubert authorized the creation of a new air-route from southern Afghanistan to northern Afghanistan. At that time there were three routes that required a fourteen nautical miles buffer (seven miles on each side of the jet route) in order to meet international rules.

All that was required was to move the existing three routes slightly east that allowed the creation of a new north-south route on the western side of the new four-route structure. Now the A-10s were able to climb to a higher altitude and use their Ultra High Frequency (UHF) radios with their extended range to communicate to the command and control agencies. A problem that had existed for years in this Latin American Theater was cleared evaluation of the air route structure was complete. Hubert thought to himself why other officers filling his position at the Qatar Combined Air Operations Center (CAOC) had not seen such a simple solution.

Hubert's next issue was the jamming incident that identified civil traffic routing problems. Due to poor maintenance of Air Traffic Control (ATC) equipment, each day airliners reported many near misses throughout Iraqi airspace. This was Hubert's third trip to Kuwait to fix operational problems. His team included a British Major and an Australian Major who worked in the civil aviation branch at the Combined Air Operations Center (CAOC). Captain Johnson who was Hubert's ATC specialist went to the conference in Kuwait City.

On the second day of the conference, Hubert mentioned that the bi-directional routes change to uni-directional or one way and two routes replace the air route structure, this would eliminate the problem. He also suggested that the routes maintain a fifty nautical mile radius around Bagdad would insure that friendly aircraft would not enter hostile airspace. This would also eliminate any possible problems where airlines would have near misses by friendly fighters coming off close air support (CAS) missions. The weekly dozen of Hazardous Air Traffic Report (HATR) reports filed against the military each day stopped.

In the last five years, Hubert had spent less than five months at home with his family and hoped that this time; his new commander would let him stay in the US at least a few months. Of course, that was a big joke, as it would turn out. Although there were three other officers with the same Air Force Specialty Code (AFSC) that had not even deployed once overseas and he had just returned from his fourth consecutive six month in a row deployment in a row earning a second remote assignment ribbon. His new squadron commander was up for promotion to colonel, which meant that Hubert was indispensable and the only officer that could deploy for the next important deployment again.

As the 612th Combat Operations Squadron (COS), Chief of Exercises, Hubert received the task with standing up his Joint Interface Control Office (JICO) team to support an exercise in northern Chile. Unknown to him at the time, this would be the beginning of an important training relationship of this group of individuals that would eventually take them to Qatar in support of the operations in Iraq. The JICO provides data link capabilities between ground and airborne platforms so that Commanders can accomplish timely Command and Control (C2) decisions.

Once the team had, Hubert and the senior members of the team started completing the administrative requirements such as requesting the Chilean Country VISAs that normally took two weeks to receive from the nearest Chilean Embassy, which was located in Los Angeles. At the last minute, the team decided to travel to Miami, Florida and get the VISAs in route at the Chilean Embassy at Miami. Then the airlift request for the equipment and Hubert's team flew using commercial travel. The team flew through Miami to Santiago and then to the final destination Iquique where the exercise took place. From Iquique, the team would drive daily to Los Condors Air Base (AB) for the briefings and each day's exercise activities.

Once the 612th team arrived in Iquique and settled in at the local hotel, arrangements made included routing through the local military base, Los Condors Air Base (AB), Chile. The US deployed US 12th Air Force (12AF) Joint Interface Control Officer (JICO) System, General Dynamics F-16C Fighting Falcon fighters from the 188th Fighter Squadron, 150th Fighter Wing, New Mexico Air National Guard, and KC-135 Stratotanker that accomplished regular air-to-air missions. The Chilean Air Force deployed its fighters and their Israeli AWACS. The first few days consisted of the normal exercise briefings where everyone participating in the exercise briefed the exercise specifics to ensure safety throughout the exercise. Then every other day, the US and Chile swapped responsibility on executing the exercise.

Hubert executed the exercise on day three of the two-week exercise. The exercise airspace was over water off the coast of Iquique using a south and north pattern. The Chilean Air Force was using a mobile Tactical Air Control System (TACS) used in the US in the 1970s so Hubert had no problem understanding the computer symbols on the consoles or in the various panning cells. It did not matter if the planners were speaking in Spanish or English since Hubert was fluent in both languages, which was the main reason he received the exercise lead role at 12th Air Force. Especially since, he would be the primary Spanish speaker at most of the planning meetings and many of the Mission Planning (MP) sessions.

The exercise was a combination of air-to-ground and air-to-air war with the US and Chile swopping the Green (friend) and Red (enemy) roles. Each nation used its own tactics in an effort to help each other learn new lessons. This will help units learn future lessons in future wars using their weapons systems. Then each day after the exercise is executed, a thorough exercise debrief is accomplished in an effort to benefit the entire group. Each sub-section accomplished min-debriefs before the entire group meets to accomplish the final debrief. The sub-section debrief uses the aircraft tapes to debrief the actual missile shots and validate every 'kill'. The JICO data link picture can also use to provide the initial big picture when the war starts and then every phase as the war commences after each phase of the war execution similar to an Air Combat Maneuvering Instrumentation (ACMI) system where a three dimensional picture is available.

The advantage that Hubert had over most American's was that he was able to conduct the exercise both in English and in Spanish without a Translator. Although Hubert did find it a bit strange that in Latin America, males tended to be sexists when compared to the US culture. In one case, Hubert had to suggest to one of his female Intelligence Officers that she not attend one of the briefings if she could not handle the way a Brazilian Officer used material in his slides even after Hubert spoke to him.

Although the Officer toned down his slides, the Officer felt that the US males were 'wimps'. In spite of such behavior, the exercise was extremely successful for the US and Chile, once Hubert returned home he clearly did not expect to return to Chile from an exercise as soon as he did. After all, he had never been to Chile in his life and never thought that he would be in that part of the world.

DURING APEX 2004 PRESIDENT AND MRS. BUSH ARRIVING IN SANTIAGO, CHILE

"I need you to take the JICO to Chile for a Presidential support mission," mentioned Colonel Kramer. The JICO equipment provided the US with the data link picture for the APEX Presidential support mission. After creating all the required tasking orders and plans, Hubert and a small group of officers and enlisted members prepared for their trip to Chile. Hubert felt lucky that he had done similar mission in Colombia and saved the floppy disks with the files that he could use to prepare the required tasking orders and plans for this operation.

Preparation for the Chilean deployment, administrative was much easier this time for the JICO crew overall. Mainly for those that had just returned from the Los Condors exercise. On the other hand, for those added on the planning cell, this would require requesting VISAs and other requirements. Since Hubert had supported similar operations in Colombia and Europe for other presidents. In this case, it was a matter of finding the floppy disk and changing the name of the operation, changing the dates, and other administrative changes for the various execution orders. Since Hubert was deploying, he delegated this task to his deputy even though he completed most of the task.

"It's amazing what can be accomplished in two days," said Hubert to Darlene. From the time, Hubert received notice to report to his Commander's office and asked to volunteer and the time that Darlene dropped him off at the Tucson International Airport, only two days had passed. Years earlier, the normal time period between deployments had been a few weeks by lately days or hours had been the norm once Hubert became a Lieutenant Colonel. Once the team arrived at the airport, it seemed that problems for this deployment would start from day one.

"Sir, you won't believe this but I'm on the terrorist list," said Major Anderson. Major Anderson would be one of two individuals that delayed in Tucson for two days because their surnames were on the US terrorist list. In spite of having an US Official Passport (Dignitary), a US driver's license, a US military ID, a US military official travel order, and a senior military Officer validated their identification; the airline would not allow them to travel. Then once the team arrived in Miami, unknown to Hubert as the Operations Officer, Colonel Dougherty ordered

American Airlines to take off the entire luggage off because he and most of the team were staying in Miami. Since the team did not have a Chilean VISA, they would be staying in Miami for four days until the local Chilean Embassy gave them a country VISA and they were able to travel to Chile.

"Captain Jones, I need you to serve as my logistics Officer," said Hubert. While sitting at the Santiago airport waiting for the US Chilean embassy staff to pick them up, Hubert started planning the initial duties that his small staff would accomplish with the limited staff that he had available. Since Hubert was traveling to Chile in jeans and a casual shirt attire, since his luggage did not arrive in Santiago once he arrive in Chile he had to purchase a suit to attend the initial planning meetings at the Chilean Defense Ministry. Later that week Hubert would learn that a thousand professional protesters arrived in Chile before his team arrived and they took all or most of the rentals in Santiago.

DURING APEX 2004 THE TEAM SELECTED MULTIPLE DRIVING ROUTES WHILE DEPLOYED IN SANTIAGO

"Sir, there are no there are no vans available in Santiago so I need your approval to rent a bus for crew changes?" asked Captain Jones. Since the professional protestors had taken all the rentals including all the vans, Hubert had to approve the renting of a bus for pickup of the crew change since it was the only option available. Due to the road size within Santiago, selecting alternate routes became a primary mission for the entire team. Throughout the world, protesters from all over the world fly into different countries to instigate the local college students. Since hired instigators can get college students to easily riot against their country by well trained and well paid professional protestors televised by the liberal Medias.

Especially when the media failed to report over a thousand professional international protestors flew into Chile to instigate the local unsuspecting college students. One has to wonder why no one never reports the truth that the college protestors are not acting out from the start against the cause they thought they were against but the cause that the professional protesters tells them to protest. Throughout APEX 2004, world news reported how college students were against the world leaders when in fact the students were only protesting like the puppets that the professional directed them. Including the beautiful signs provided by the international professional protesters. On a positive side, these professional protesters did help the local economy by filling the local hotels and taking most of the rental vehicles even though it made Hubert's job more of a challenge.

The Ministry of Defense planning went as expected. Since Hubert had conducted a similar operation in Bogotá, Colombia, he recommended that a 150 nautical mile circle no-fly zone be set up around Santiago during the time that the APEX 2004 Dignitaries were meeting plus the time they were traveling to and from their hotels. This would minimize any threats to their lives and costs to the local businesses by only closing the air travel for the shortest amount of time. During that time, airborne fighter Close Air Patrol (CAP) would be available plus alert fighter aircraft to replace them if needed on five-minute alert. Any aircraft entering the no-fly zone received a radio notification of a pending intercept. The US deployed four E-3B/C Airborne Warning and Control System (AWACS) aircraft and the Chilean Israeli AWACS was used to cover 24/7 coverage.

DURING APEX 2004 US E-3B/C AWACS AIRCRAFTS WERE USED FLYING FROM THE SANTIAGO AIR BASE (AB)

Although Hubert was an E-3B/C AWACS Mission Crew Commander (MCC), prior to departing the US, he made it clear to the Tinker AFB, Oklahoma Wing Commander that he not in Chile as their E-3B/C AWACS planner or staff. Hubert requested that they deploy an Officer to assist him as part of the staff mainly because he would not have time to accomplish those E-3B/C AWACS duties, which was the most important aspect of this operation. Even though the E-3B/C AWACS Wing Commander was an old friend of Hubert, she declined to deploy a staff member but Hubert accomplished as many of the E-3B/C AWACS duties as time allowed until the E-3B/C AWACS aircrew and staff arrived in Santiago to support APEX 2004.

PROTECTING PRESIDENT BUSH WAS THE TOP PRIORITY WHILE DEPLOYED TO SANTIAGO DURING APEX 2004

In the meantime, Hubert worked out with the Chilean Air Force the initial location where the E-3B/C AWACS aircrew would work from and where the four E-3B/C AWACS jets would park. Then Hubert had to work with the USSS where Air Force-One and Air Force-Two would park, which was more difficult due to security issues. In this area, Hubert was lucky since one of the original members that had a country VISA was one of the security Non-Commissioned Officers (NCOs) that took care of the security requirements while Hubert worked out the aircraft locations based on aircrew requirements and safety needs.

The JICO proved to be a challenge from the start mainly because the team did not have time to deploy the shelter in a timely manner like most deployments. For this deployment, in two days, the initial planning had to complete before the planning team departed for Chile. Once the JICO team started unpacking the shelter and started the inventory, the team noted that the communications switches were missing. Without the switches, the JICO would not be able to go operational so Hubert got a stock number, with his Chilean driver went to the local malls, and went to the local equivalent Radio Shacks in search of the needed switches. Eventually Hubert found a local mall shop that has twenty switches and he purchased all twenty using his VISA card. That meant that the JICO would be operational and that he had one less problem to deal with.

That lack of problems would be short lived when the US Secret Service (USSS) arrived and Hubert had to include their requirements into the Chilean Alternate Combine Air Operations Center (CAOC). The Chilean Air Force from the start was concerned that the US not find out where their CAOC was located. Therefore, they insisted that for APEX 2004, they insisted that the Joint Interface Control Officer (JICO) system brought by the Americans use their alternate CAOC, which was located at the old airport in Santiago.

What Hubert found funny was that it took him a few seconds to scan the local area to locate the Chilean Combined Air Operations Center (CAOC). As an experience Airborne Battle Manager (ABM) and career CAOC manager of twenty-six years, Hubert could see the various antennas associated with the CAOC in the Santiago Mountain as an experience ABM and career CAOC manager of twenty-six years. It was impossible to hide the CAOC for an experience ABM who could easily find the Chilean CAOC by seen a Satcom map.

As an experienced ABM, Hubert knew every crew position well and requested that each American position have a Chilean counterpart that had Basic English skills. This capability proved to be beneficial during APEX 2004 when every second counted in making important decisions. The USSS liaison Officer with the direct communications to the gunship helicopters collocated at the alternate Combined Air Operations Center (CAOC) runway on alert could see the E-3B/C Airborne Warning and Control Systems (AWACS) data link picture of every air track that was flying inside the 150 nautical mile no-fly zone.

Dealing with power requirements was another issue that needed Hubert's attention not only with the local utility company but also with the Chilean Air Force where Hubert had to borrow a military generator. The difficult issue was having to go through the US Embassy on all funding matters by authoring Spanish commitment funding letters, which not a problem for Hubert to author. The difficult part of the duties of the Operations Officer is the requirement of accomplishing multiple tasks simultaneously from multiply locations in countries that do not have modern communication capabilities. In Chile, the cell phone was the only tool available and an on-call vehicle with a driver. It seemed once the remaining of the planning team arrived, all the planning was complete and now it was time to execute APEX 2004.

"Hi Dave, great to hear from you" said Hubert. Dave had worked for Hubert at 12th Air Force Standardizations and Evaluations (Stan/Eval) when Hubert was the Assistant Department Chief. Dave had been in Germany and called Hubert looking for a job who hired him as his Ground Tactical Air Control Systems (GTACS) Stan/Eval examiner. Then in an effort to get him Promoted to Lieutenant Colonel (Lt Col), Hubert converted his position to a flying position. Since the local wing had the EC-130E Airborne Command and Control Center (ABCCC), Hubert made Dave's position into a flying position and allowed Dave to return to flying status. In this case, Dave served as the GTACS radars Examiner and ABCCC Stan/Eval Flight Examiner. As a result, Dave received a promotion to Lieutenant Colonel after his Commander in Germany in Dave's view had not kept his promise and hurt Dave's promotion advancement opportunities.

"Did you receive all the training material that we send you?" Ask Hubert. During the planning sessions with the Chilean Defense Ministry, Hubert had been creating airspace planning guides using his Mission Crew Commander (MCC) guides that he had developed while flying at Tinker AFB, Oklahoma. As soon as he completed that planning sessions with the Chilean Defense Ministry, Hubert emailed the guides to his deputy at Davis-Monthan AFB, Arizona and requested that they review them and then forward them to the E-3B/C AWACS aircrews.

Normally E-3B/C AWACS aircrews go into the simulator and practice in the simulator the profiles that they will fly contractors simulate the targets and fighters on the radios.

Such training allows the E-3B/C AWACS aircrews to be prepared before they deploy into a real-world environment. In this case, Dave confirmed that his aircrews had not only received the training guides that Hubert created, they had used the material in the Tinker AFB simulators during different simulator profiles. For this deployment, Dave was the AWACS Deployment Commander (Detco). Hubert was glad that Dave was there since he trusted him and did not have to second-guess his judgment.

"Ok, Dave, I need all your crews including your maintenance personnel in the Combined Air Operations Center (CAOC) theater tomorrow at 10:00 AM sharp" mentioned Hubert. As was the typical expectation for any flying operation, everyone involved in flying operations is briefed on basic safety of flight factors, procedurals factors, and factors on how APEX 2004 flying operations would be executed during this two-hour briefing. This initial In Brief ensured that anyone supporting APEX 2004 had the common background and/or data needed to support this operation. Even the KC-135 Stratotanker air-to-air aircraft aircrew and maintenance personnel deployed from Iquique, Chile flew into Santiago for this in-brief presentation and discussion.

The average day for Hubert started at four in the morning and if lucky ended around ten or eleven at night daily provided the telephone did not bring another problem. As the Operations Officer, Hubert not only had to coordinate with the Chilean Defense Ministry, ensure that the US aircrews were fully briefed on every aspect of the APEX operation, stand up the JICO cell, deal with every Joint Interface Control Officer (JICO) system issue, and responsible for every administrative issue. As the riots moved throughout Santiago, the American team had to move to different hotels in an effort to ensure safety.

At the same time, certain individuals had duties at the US Chilean Embassy and the Chilean Defense Ministry so the selected hotel had to be accessible to those individuals. However, to maximize the team safety, the entire team had a room in one hotel. What Hubert did not plan for was that due to the local riots, the team would have to move three times to multiple hotels as the riots progressed in increased in size. This only created additional work for him to work on as they arose on three occasions.

Many factors complicated the management decision-making process for APEX 2004. For example, the fact the a thousand professional protestor instigators arrived in Santiago and took most of the rental vehicles meant that few rentals were available to rent by the US team. Since President Bush (POTUS) requested that, the E-3B/C AWACS support and the 12th Air Force deployed the JICO and Hubert had the right experience to execute this short notice mission. With JICO experience, with a Spanish background, and with recent POTUS planning and execution experience in Latin America, Hubert was the ideal Officer for this operation.

Only an Officer like Hubert was able to accomplish all of these tasks in a few days with little or no sleep. Even when Hubert arrived in Santiago, since the majority of the planning team staying in Miami, Hubert accomplished the majority of the APEX 2004 planning. It did not matter that again, his Commander, Colonel Coxe and then Lieutenant Colonel Murrey, did not use any of this information for Hubert's annual performance report. It only meant that Hubert would receive another Air Force Medal just before he deployed again to the Middle East and earned another five military medals.

"Tell DM to stay off line one" said Hubert. The first of two telephone lines was for the USSS since the Chilean only gave the US team only two-telephone lines. The typical profile for Air Force-One and Air Force-Two is for the two aircraft to fly in a five-mile trail formation. Even though the Combined Air

Operations Center (CAOC) acknowledged that they would stay off line one, while Air Force-One and Air Force-Two were on final arrival approach to Santiago airport, Colonel Coxe decided to call Hubert on line one to ask a routine question.

At the same time that the USSS needed to use the telephone line to make a crucial call, Colonel Coxe made a routine call to the JICO cell resulting in a communications jamming the USSS team in Santiago. Colonel Coxe is typical of the promotable Air Force Colonel that lacked operational experience but had plenty of Air Force Military Professional Education (PME) School experience and plenty of ego experience that got in the way in this operation and most other operations. Especially since the Air Force does not normally promote experienced warfighters to the senior ranks. Hubert's biggest challenge would be keeping Colonel Coxe's busy during critical phases of the operation so that he would not endanger the mission execution as was typical with such military officers. Especially senior Air Force Officers like Colonel Coxe.

"Hubert what is wrong? Why are you limping," asked Colonel Dougherty. For months, Hubert had tried to convince his Commander that the medical problems had been true. He would return to Tucson to have a knee surgery on the day after of the APEX operation. For three years, he had pulled his knee ligaments and broken bones in his knee while in Iraq while running to a bunker when an IED was inbound. A Magnetic Resonance Imaging (MRI) just before departing for Chile identified the injury even though for years his Commander kept telling Hubert he was faking his injuries.

Mainly so the he could keep him deployed overseas without Hubert seeking medical treatment. Thanks to a Romania doctor at the Tucson Veterans Administration (VA), Special Medicine Clinic who ordered dozens of tests, she was able to find many injuries that eventually led to helping Hubert receive the medical attention he needed. Especially since the Air Force, doctors only gave Hubert, pain medicines so that he would stay deployed. Regularly, Hubert returned from a deployment using crutches. Yet, it was common that he would re-deploy within weeks or even days overseas. Each time for extended deployments, this did not allow him sufficient time to seek proper medical attention.

For the last four days in Chile, he received steroid shots every twelve hours for the last two days so that he could stay on his feet and be able to work. To make matters worse the Joint Interface Control Officer (JICO) system was downstairs in the basement and the Chilean Alternate Combined Air Operations Center (CAOC) was on the other side of the building. He had to take stairs up and then down to go to the Operations Center and work with the USSS and Chilean Air Force. Once Hubert drafted a good schedule on his draft paper, he took it to Colonel Dougherty who also liked it.

"Dave I need you to review this schedule and see if the E-3B/C AWACS crews can fly it and coordinate the schedule with the Tanker LNO to make sure they can support you," mentioned Hubert to the E-3B/C AWACS Deployments Commander (Detco). The Chilean Air Force chief-of-staff General had decided to have their Israeli AWACS airborne whenever there was a foreign dignitary arriving in Santiago airport. This meant that the US E-3B/C AWACS aircraft would have to maintain an E-3B/C AWACS platform airborne 24/7 instead of the two eight-hour scheduled orbits and the Chilean taking one 8-hour orbit. With four E-3B/C AWACS aircraft available to fly continuously throughout President Bush's visit, this meant that any aircraft problems would cause problems. Chile was too far for Tinker AFB to replace an aircraft if any mechanical problems arose.

"Dave you need to call your Combined Air Operations Center (CAOC) LNO and have them convince the CAOC that this is the only way that we can complete this mission," mentioned Hubert. For this operation, Colonel Coxe and the Davis-Monthan (DM) CAOC was proving more of a problem than an asset. Hubert had plenty of problems to deal with and Davis-Monthan CAOC was getting in the way of daily operations of APEX 2004. He then had the Tanker Liaison (LNO) call Iquique and talked to his counterpart.

Hubert asked the Tanker Liaison (LNO) complete the same request of calling the DM CAOC and makes them believe that they created the E-3AWACS and KC-135 Stratotanker ATO flying schedule. This process started at 2:00 AM and was complete by 5:00 AM. Hubert had reported to work the morning twenty-four hours prior and returned to the hotel to take a short four-hour nap before returning to the Chilean Alternate CAOC for another long workday. During APEX 2005, only friendly fighter aircraft were flying in the no-fly zone and the USSS knew where President Bush was located at every moment, 24/7.

Hubert's team had to publish a daily Air Tasking Order (ATO). The US flew two 8 hour E-3B/C AWACS orbits and the Chilean E-3B/C AWACS flew one eight E-3B/C AWACS orbit each day. Although the actual eight-hour orbits were supposed to be alternated, as it turned out, the Chilean Air Force decided to fly any eight hour orbit that it felt like flying based on its aircrew availability. This complicated matters for the US Hubert explained to Colonel Coxe that the US cannot demand from a sovereign any demands. In a sovereign nation like Chile, the visiting nation or in this case the US follows whatever its hosts dictate.

Clearly, Colonel Coxe only had 'school experiences' and not 'real-world experience'. The US cannot flex its' muscles when visiting and accomplishing a support role something that a staff Officer like Colonel Coxe would never understand. In spite of Colonel Coxe, the Hubert executed the mission flawlessly by ignoring Colonel Coxe and humoring him as frustrating as it was operationally. Since Hubert was an experienced E-3B/C AWACS Commander who had worked closely with KC-135

Stratotanker, he developed a straw plan that he took to his friend that was the E-3B/C AWACS Detco.

"Dave, I need you to check my schedule and made sure you can support a 24/7 flying window with US E-3s and no Chilean AWACS support," asked Hubert. At the last minute, Hubert had his driver take him to the Santiago airport to talk to Dave to discuss having the E-3B/C AWACS fly a 24/7 orbit. Hubert also advised Dave that he needed to meet with the Tanker Liaison LNO and make sure that he had Tanker support. Hubert knew that with four E-3B/C AWACS aircraft that this option would be possible as long as the US did not have any maintenance problems. As an experienced MCC, Hubert knew that he could have the Chilean E-3B/C AWACS fly the east orbit and the US E-3B/C AWACS fly the west orbit to maintain safety of flight.

This issue started when Colonel Coxe called Hubert yelling that he wanted the Chilean Air Force demanding that they commit to a firm ATO. Hubert requested Dave to create a scheduling plan to have a US E-3B/C AWACS airborne 24/7 with Tanker support. At the same time, Hubert had his Tanker LNO call Iquique and coordinate with the E-3B/C AWACS LNO to be able to support the new flying schedule. The next day, Colonel Coxe was happy with the new ATO. In his view, he believed that he received what he asked for so he was happy. Hubert allowed him to believe what he wanted to believe since his view did not matter since he only got in the way due for lack of real-world experience. APEX 2004 did not require another Senior Officer School (SOS) perspective.

In the middle of APEX 2004, during lunch Hubert had his driver take him to a local clinic where a doctor gave him steroid shots on his knees. In addition, the doctor agreed to give him additional shots for the next three days that Hubert gave himself each twelve hours. Hubert explained that he needed to stay on his feet for the entire week almost eighteen to twenty-four hours per day. On the following day, Hubert's driver took him to his sister's house who was a nurse that gave him the shot.

Hubert gave himself the remaining two shots to his buttocks mainly because he felt that since his daughter was a diabetic that he felt comfortable giving himself the shots. Also, because he could not take the time off from APEX 2004.

This issue did not end Hubert's problems during APEX 2004. Just after arriving at his hotel and dropping at his bed without taking off his flight suit, Dave called him on his cell phone. Two of Dave's maintenance NCO's were in jail after they had used their government credit cards to pay for women of the night. Both had spent thousands of dollars, which was illegal by all standards in addition to being unethical. The following morning Hubert ordered both individuals depart Chile and return to the US especially since both no longer had a military career in the US Air Force.

"Colonel Coxe needs you to call him at DM" said Captain Anderson. Two days prior to the end of APEX 2004, just before Hubert thought that he would have time to relax and have time to prepare to return home to Tucson for his knee surgery, Colonel Coxe advised him that President Bush planned to stop in Bogotá, Colombia. The Colonel asked if Hubert felt if part of the JICO cell deployed to Colombia to support the president. Although Colonel Coxe asked Hubert to deploy to Colombia, Hubert mentioned to Colonel Coxe that he had already delayed his knew surgery three times and that he was schedules the day after he arrived. Hubert had damaged his knee during an Improvised Explosive Device (IED) explosion in Bagdad, Iraq.

Since Hubert had been in Bogotá many times including serving as the Commander and Operations Officer, he knew every aspect of the Colombian mission and told Colonel Coxe that he would deploy part of the JICO cell the following day to Bogotá once he made the appropriate arrangements. Hubert requested that Colonel Coxe have Air Force South (AFFOR), which was part of their unit call Bogotá and advise the Colombian military verbally that two Air Force members would be coming from Chile to support President Bush. This option was available per agreement between the US and Colombia

As was the custom for Hubert, he always traveled with his telephone book. Even though he asked Colonel Coxe to have the USSOUTHAF AFFOR staff call Colombia, he called the his friend running the Counterdrug Operations Center (CDOCC) in Bogotá, Colombia and asked him to tell the Military Group (MILGP) Commander and US Ambassador Ann Patterson, that he would be arriving in two days in support the POTUS mission. Additional information would be forthcoming from the USSOUTHAF AFFOR since Colonel Coxe had requested that Hubert return to Bogotá, Colombia.

Now that the coordination was complete in Bogotá, Hubert had to complete the team traveling requirements. Hubert had his driver take him to the Santiago airport where he went to the airport customs a pre-coordinated the transport of three large and three long antenna kits. Hubert knew that the American Airlines would find it strange when our team traveled with three large black luggages'. The luggages, two feet by twelve feet long had antennas, cables, and other data link equipment. Once the team arrived at the airport, from the start, the airport security quickly came over to the van and embassy driver quickly displayed his badge that made matters better. However, security followed the American team into the airport American Airline counters where Hubert requested the customs individual that he had coordinated the day prior with the customs Officer.

Since Hubert explained to the customs personnel, what the equipment was for in Spanish, the coordination want smoother. However, the airline staff not touching the crypto keying box, a classified box, was the hardest task to get through security. Mainly because the box was NOFORN (no foreign), which meant only US personnel could touch the box and only by individuals that had the appropriate clearance. That too took allot of explaining both the day prior and the travel day by

Hubert at the airport. Once the Joint Interface Control Officer (JICO) system team departed for Bogotá, Colombia, Hubert returned to the alternate Combined Air Operations Center (CAOC) to continue with APEX 2004.

612TH COMBAT PLANS SQUADRON (CPS), DAVIS-MONTHAN, AFB, AZ.

"We need you to volunteer to return to Colombia," said Hubert's Commander. After deploying to the Middle East thirteen times, Hubert never thought that in his last year that he would return to Iraq, Afghanistan, and Colombia all in one year. Except for less than two weeks, the rest of his time, Hubert deployed overseas. He would be able to take ninety days leave at the end of his retirement and sell ninety days since the days were all combat leave days. To the end, due to poor leadership, Hubert would not be able to receive four operations until after retirement for the injuries sustained in Colombia and Iraq.

Although his last year the Air Force would ground him where his Flying Status revolved due to the injuries taking away his flight pay. Still, Hubert would keep a positive attitude knowing that it not the Air Force at fault but the poor leaders in charge at 12th Air Force and the 612th Combat Plans Squadron (CPS). It had been over six years that Hubert had seen a good senior Officer, much less a good General in the Air Force. He truly missed the old Air Force, as he would say in his retirement ceremony that was not large enough for all of Hubert's friends and co-workers wishing him the best.

Hubert would be back in Colombia in three day for another Presidential support operation after returning from Colombia. He wondered why he bothered to unpack his bags. As it turned out, when Hubert called the Generals office, his executive told Hubert that there was a special mission in Colombia and the

General wanted to ask Hubert if he would volunteer. Hubert told the Colonel that Hubert was a soldier and asked when Hubert would depart and how long the Temporary Duty (TDY) would last. She mentioned that Hubert would have to leave the same day and asked if Hubert could return to Tucson to out process.

"What's going on," said Darlene. Darlene could not believe that I would depart tonight on another six-month deployment. It was noon when Hubert departed Phoenix and arrived at Davis-Monthan Air Force Base to out-process. Hubert first location was in the 12th Air Force orderly room and getting the out processing checklist. Even though every agency Hubert went to including personnel, finance, mobility, the hospital flight medicine, and the dental clinic, each specialist that Hubert spoke with said that there was no way that Hubert could out process. Hubert mentioned if they had any problems to call the 12th Air Force Commanders office (three stars General).

Within an hour and a half, Hubert out processed from the base and returned home to pack. Hubert received notice that his body armor and other equipment would Hubert FedEx to Bogotá. Hubert had to go to Miami's USSOUTHCOM to speak with the J-1 who was a Brigadier General on what he expected. Since Hubert spent so much time away from Darlene, he made every effort to convince Darlene to spent time with him. Therefore, Darlene and had to fly to Florida, which meant Hubert had to pay for Darlene's airline ticket. Paying for a roundtrip ticket was worth the cost of spending a week with Darlene before deploying for another six months.

"Well at least I will be with you for the first week in Miami before you go overseas," mentioned Darlene. The Air Force would only pay for the hotel on the first day for this long drive across the US Nevertheless, at least Hubert was able to be with Darlene for a week knowing that it would be months before he would see her again. Since Hubert had already had leave approved in Florida to visit family so, he, and Darlene departed the following morning. Hubert had only been back from a six month TDY to Bogotá and knew that the only way that Hubert could spend a week with Darlene in Miami would be great before another long deployment.

Hubert was in Miami for four days going through various classified briefings and meetings. Having been to Colombia three times already, Hubert found himself knowing more about the mission in Colombia than the headquarters experts did. He did not realize that after sixteen years and numerous deployments to Colombia, this would be his last visit to this country as a military member. After flying over 1,000 hours onboard the E-3B/C AWACS and C-130 aircraft and deploying throughout Colombia on Counternarco-terrorism deployments, this trip would be his last. As a retired Lieutenant Colonel, in 2006 Hubert received a multiple contractor's job offers but decline the offer.

Although Hubert had meetings from seven in the morning to almost six in the evening each day, Darlene and Hubert went out to dinner at a local seafood restaurant that Hubert and Darlene had gone to during other TDYs to Miami. Hubert always had time for Darlene each evening and at lunchtime no matter how tired he was after the day's meetings. Darlene and Hubert's normal order was a dozen of oysters each and a tall cold bud in an iced mug. However, as always, Hubert short visits to Miami were over and Hubert took Darlene to the airport to catch her flight to Tucson and Hubert tool a later flight to Bogotá. Hubert always took the last flight of the day to make sure Darlene left for Tucson first even if there were delays.

Upon returning to Davis-Monthan AFB Hubert received notice that he had been reassigned to the 612th Combat Plans Squadron (CPS) as the Chief of Command and Control (C2) on 28 August 2004. His time back in the US was short lived since upon his return, Hubert would receive a deployment to return to Colombia. A new training mission in Colombia received approval at USSOUTHAF. After officially receiving notification of his 12th Air Force assignment for two weeks, Hubert received his deployment orders back to Colombia. For this second six-month deployment, Hubert would out process from the base in record time and within an hour and a half versus the normal week. When he arrived in Bogotá, his body armor and other gear would be waiting for him.

Hubert would be supporting OPERATION INCA GOLD during this deployment as the Field Grade Officer responsible of a highly visible position as the Chief of Operations of Air Operations, Air Force Mission (AFM), US MILGP, which was a directed Counterdrug (CD) Operation in Bogotá, Colombia. Again, Hubert had over six other Lieutenant Colonels mainly because the MILGP Commander knew that he was able to deal with the highest Host Nation (HN) and US Government (USG) political and military problems through proper channels. This also included working with the Colombian Intelligence Directorate, which the US was in the process of delivering new US Citation aircraft and new hardware systems.

Every three-weekly meetings, Hubert meetings with the US Embassy Deputy Chief of Mission (DCM) becoming a key staff member over the CIA, DEA, and ATF representatives. Quickly became the Counterdrug Air Operations expert and "eyes and ears" on aviation issues for the DCM for the US Government (USG), US Embassy, Bogotá, Colombia and the critical link with the Country Team (CT) Intelligence Colombian counterparts. Co-drafted for the CDM CT the Airspace Tracking Order (ATO) process that stopped false start scrambles of unknown targets, which continued to be a serious problem prior to Hubert's arrival in Colombia. This provided the US Ambassador with a Flight Management Flight Service to monitor all USG aircraft, which was never possible in Colombia until Hubert created this new ATO process.

Hubert quickly identified as a seasoned public official and diplomat and the US Ambassador's first choice for sensitive

US and Colombian negotiations and dialog. During two negotiations, Hubert was the sole negotiator even though he not permanent party and was in Colombia as a deployed Officer, a first for the US Country Team. The first negotiations involved the Colombians request for hundreds of millions in foreign aid to purchase new weapons systems. In this area, Hubert forced the Colombian military to improve their Intelligence and logistics forces and/or systems versus purchasing new fighters as the Colombian Generals wanted. In the second negotiations, Hubert played the sole role in upgrading the Colombian Air Defense systems.

The Colombian Military received all of Hubert's recommendations in a positive view mainly because Hubert had worked with them for years and they knew that he was a career Air Defense expert. The third negotiations consisted for the improvement of the Colombian C-130 Hercules Cargo fleet, logistics, and intelligence systems, during these negotiations; the discussions although tense were per the US and Hubert's position. Mainly once Hubert provided historical details noting the lack of quality control by the Colombian maintenance personnel that Hubert maintained as the Air Force Mission Maintenance Liaison Officer.

The data showed that the Colombian maintenance not able to maintain their C-130 airborne per the Technical Orders (TOs) mainly because their lack of maintenance control. During this era, all four of the C-130 aircraft that the US had given the Colombians, due to maintenance problems received grounded notification. Later, Hubert would form a Mobile Training Team (MTT) that would deploy throughout Colombian to train C-130 maintenance crews and get all four aircraft back on flying status with the help of the US team and the foreign aid monies.

Next, Hubert directed the re-write of the SC21/SC38 CONOPs, which integrated the air, sea, and the intelligence, surveillance and recognizance (ISR) assets. Prior to this re-write, these assets each worked independently versus working together as a joint US team. Since Hubert was the Country Team Intelligence expert, he staffed and co-authored for the US Ambassador various key ISR documents for Colombian President Uribe, the Colombian Minister of Defense, the Colombian Armed Forces, and the Colombian Air Force Commander, all properly employed. Hubert staffed all of the key documents through the US Embassy and MILGP Staff that he authored in Spanish for the US Ambassador who only had to sign the documents.

Like all deployments, this deployment ended after six months. The only difference was that USSOUTHAF and USSOUTHCOM not able to find a replacement Officer. At this point, due to the long hours that Hubert had been working, he made it clear to Colonel Skymer that he was mentally tired. Hubert had been away from home for almost a year and if Darlene did not visit him, it would be unbearable for him. Eventually, Colonel Skymer agreed to let Hubert leave Colombia without a replacement.

Hubert returned to 12th Counterdrug shot and thought that he would be home for a while. He returned in time to take a Doctoral Residency class in Phoenix, which was a two-week class. On the final day of the Residency, Darlene called him and told him that he needed to call work. Hubert was on a break when he received Darlene's call and knew that it not good news. When he called, he received notice that he had to deploy to Colombia with a stop in Miami to meet the USSOUTHCOM/J-1 (JOINT-1), Operations General. Since the residency always ended at mid-day on week two, this would work out well. Hubert called Darlene and advised her of the deployment asking if she wanted to drive with him to Miami. Then she could fly back to Tucson so that this way they could spend some time together before another six-month deployment.

Hubert departed Phoenix for Davis-Monthan AFB to process out where initially he reported to the 12th Air Force building to get the TDY (temporary deployment) checklist. Every office that Hubert reported told him that there was no way that they could sign him off his deployment checklist. Each office Hubert told them that they could call the 12th Air Force Commander and tell him why not and then they signed the checklist. In less than two hours, Hubert completed the TDY checklist and returned to the 12th Air Force building where he received notice that they would FedEx his combat gear to Colombia.

Darlene and Hubert normally gave their vehicles to family members once they decided that they no longer wanted a vehicle. Hubert had decided to drive to Miami because he had decided to give his Van to his mother-in-law. Momma needed a car so Hubert decided to give her his Van since he was never home to drive the Van. Darlene and Hubert purchase the Van while stationed in Oklahoma when they returned from Germany.

Once he arrived to his house, Hubert packed the Van and he and Darlene got on the Road. Darlene and Hubert had driven Highway 10 dozens of times over the years and knew the route well. The only difference would be that this time they would take the new bypass to Miami first before going to Bradenton to drop the Van. It took three days to get to Miami from Tucson where Hubert reported to USSOUTHCOM/J-1. For the next three days, he met with the General and his staff where he told him about his new program and how he wanted Hubert to serve as the program manager and create the program.

Serving as a senior officer normally means that one is tasked to accomplish simultaneous tasks at the same time. Hubert received a new task to become the first Commander for the new Mobile Training Team (MTT) working closely with twelve senior Colombia Joint Staff Officers and twelve US multi-service Officers. This task required that Hubert and his teams travel initially to the US and then throughout Colombia. His teams provided a newly created Colombian Decision Making Joint Doctrine at six CACOMs, twelve Divisions and thirty-six

Brigades level Units. At the end of this deployment, Hubert received the Joint Service Achievement Medal, First Oak Leaf Cluster awarded by the Secretary of Defense.

This deployment started when Hubert first served as the first-ever Assistant Air Operations Officer (ADO-Air) position, under Lieutenant General (Lt. Gen.) Ballesteros's Comando Aero de Combate 6 (CACOM-6), at Tres Esquinas, Colombia. In the Colombian Air Force, the Lieutenant General rank is the equivalent to the US four-star General rank. Lieutenant General Ballesteros spent half of his time in Tres Esquinas and Bogotá. Hubert had worked with Lieutenant General Ballesteros while assigned to the Colombian Departamento Administrativo Nacional de Estadistica de Colombia (C. A. N.) as a member of the US Air Force Mission.

Although this was a six-month commitment, due to other real-time real-world events, after a few months, Hubert received additional requests to support other more important tasks. The Colombian Military (COMIL) TQ River Operations was always a challenge especially with the Parana's in the Amazon River. In addition, as the Comando Aero de Combate 6 (CACOM-6), Assistant Operations Officer-Air, at Tres Esquinas, one of Hubert's duties required that he schedule and monitor all air operations. Hubert was used to multi-tasking in the US Air Force. Doing the same in the Colombian Air Force and having to serve as General Ballesteros US executive officer was only an additional duty for Hubert.

Hubert initiated additional site security measures once he arrived and noticed that site security consisted of four posts, one at each end of the TQ site, which was a large unit. In the 1950s, TQ had started as a German pilot training base prior to World War-II (WW-II). That was why so many of the local youth had so many of the German features. All that ended when he and General Ballesteros were accomplishing an inspection on one of their battalions in Larandia, Colombia. Initially, an American hostage rescue situation would take Hubert away from this task. Hubert would become the Operations Officer for the Hostage Rescue Operation. Then Hubert would serve as the Commander of a Mobile Training Team (MTT) deployed throughout Colombia but administered from Bogotá. The USSOUTHCOM J-1 would be the Officer approving all the new assignments based on the new operational requirements.

After the meetings with the J-1 General in Miami, was time for Darlene to go home in Tucson and time for Hubert to fly to Bogotá. Hubert made sure that Darlene departed Miami first early in the morning and that he left hours after her. He wanted to be sure that if Darlene's flight delayed, the he would be there to see her off. Therefore, he took the last flight to Bogotá, Colombia. Once Hubert arrived in Bogotá, he took a taxi to the regular hotel that he stayed over the years. Going to the same location has some advantages. The following morning, he called the US Embassy and had an Embassy vehicle pick him up. Hubert also had all the local telephone numbers throughout Colombia since he served in every US position available in the Colombian MILGP. This too, allowed Hubert some flexibility.

From 31 January to 29 July 2003, Hubert deployed to hostile-fire areas in support of counterdrug and anti-terrorism operations. Most of the areas were at austere locations throughout Colombia. Initially served as the Assistant Air Operations Officer, Division-6, for the first ever Division-6, for the first ever Planning Assistant Team (PAT), Task-1. For this commitment, Hubert deployed to Tres-Esquinas where he lived in the US trailers. Since Tres-Esquinas as located deep in the jungles in south Colombia as a former German training Air Force training base, not only did Tres-Esquinas has a run-way, but it was also located next to an adjoining river connected to the Amazon River. Next to the river was an all ranks Club where three meals received regular serving meals during regular hours. However, due to operational requirements, Hubert received new tasks in time over-and-over during every deployment to Colombia.

At this point, Hubert received a new task as the CACOM-6 Commander as his new Division Air Operations Officer. It was as the new CACOM-6 Division Air Operations Officer that Hubert became the Operations Officer to rescue three Americans taken hostage by the Frente Armante Revolucionareo de Colombia (FARC) terrorist group. This task received most of its rescue commitments from the Colombia training base at Larandia with Hubert returning to Bogotá as required. During this period, Hubert and his team forward deployed with the rescue teams deep into the Colombian jungles on rescue missions. As the rescue aircraft, all flew using US supply helicopters during the down country missions. With all the Colombian and US rescue personnel living in a combat environment and not in hotels like in Bogotá.

Initially Hubert received the task as Lieutenant General Ballesteros's Assistant Air Operations Officer Comando Aero de Combate 6 (CACOM-6), at Tres Esquinas, Colombia. On Hubert previous trip, Ballesteros had been the Colombian J-3, which was the chief of operations for the Colombian Air Force at their version of the Pentagon called the C. A. N. (Departamento Administrativo Nacional de Estadistica de Colombia) by the Americans. At Hubert last meeting with Ballesteros, we had been working on the forces and status negotiation where the US was going to give Colombia a $414 Million grant to purchase weapons in their quest to win the war against three terrorist groups.

Hubert then went to the Bogotá airport and caught a flight in Tres Esquinas, which was deep in the jungles of Colombia. On a prior deployment, Hubert had transferred the Tres Esquinas radar to the Colombian military. Each month the General and our American team returned to Bogotá that allowed US to accomplish administrative requirements including filing requests for partial payments, which were normally hotel and rental vehicle bills. Most trips to the airport started around four or five in the morning due to all the stops that we had to accomplish. As was the case of this trip, the rest of Hubert team was at a different hotel for security reasons. However, it not very convenient when we had to go to the Embassy or and follow-on TDYs.

It was during one of these trips on February 12, 2003 that Hubert's team was to meet Ballesteros's team in Larandia. General Ballesteros traveled in his own military aircraft in Larandia to inspect the training divisions. As General Ballesteros' Assistant Air Operations Officer, Hubert was responsible for inspecting the Helicopter units consisting of the Central Intelligence Agency (CIA) augmented Bell UH-1N Twin Huey and Blackhawk's flying squadrons flown by Colombian pilots. According to treaties, as American we had to travel on American chartered-Aircraft. Hubert team consisted of a Captain who was Hubert intelligence Officer and a marine gunny that was a senior non-commissioned (NCO) Officer.

Hubert's team normally went to the Embassy and received our classified SERE briefing, which discussed procedures to follow in cases where aircraft went down in hostile territory. Hubert's team also picked up our weapons, which included a 9-Mil with three cartridges and an M-4 rifle with four cartridges. For the M-4 cartridges, Hubert's team had to load them, which included each four bullet being a tracer bullet. Hubert's team then inspected our ground communications that included a secure data box using satellite capabilities. Then Hubert's team all got into the Normal Embassy white armored vans for our trip to the airport.

However, as Hubert's team drove out of the Embassy, Hubert had a strange feeling and shortly after leaving the gate, Hubert told our driver in Spanish to take US to a local coffee stand or a pastry shop since Hubert's team had plenty of time before making our show time at Eddie Cabal. Eddie Cabal was a retired American Senior Non-Commissioned Officer (NCO) and started a charter service to support the Embassy. Having served as a cargo and air operations planner made him ideal as the individual to support air and ground support for the US Embassy and much cheaper for the US tax payers.

Our driver stopped at a local pastry shop about a mile from the Embassy and Hubert purchase Hubert team and driver pastries and coffee. It was there that Hubert decided to call Eddy's to give our seats to the normal stand-by Passengers (PAX) (passengers). Hubert went outside the pastry shop, called the transportation Officer on his cell phone, and told him that Hubert needed to stay one additional day in Bogotá and to put US on the following day's manifest. After about twenty minutes, Hubert received the confirmation of the schedule change. He then called General Ballesteros and told him that Hubert's team would meet him the following day. Hubert understood by the tone of his voice that he was asking him for his approval which he gladly approved. Then Hubert called the Embassy and told the duty officer that his team would be returning our gear later in the day and of our schedule change.

"We will reschedule the training inspection for next month," mentioned General Ballesteros to Hubert. Larandia was the training center for a new program where Compucinos who were young draftees who had just turned eighteen and received their draft notice into the Colombian military. Since over sixty percent of the Colombian territory did not have any military or Police presence, the Compucinos would return to their hometowns and help fight the terrorist groups. To make matters worse, over sixty percent of the lands in Colombia lacked electric power or other conveniences that most modern nations had. Once the Compucinos and other former military soldiers completed their mandatory two-year obligation, they returned to the unemployment ranks. Prior to American Rescue Operation, General Ballesteros truly believed Hubert would return as his Assistant Director of Operations-Air (ADO-Air) Officer.

"Let's find a place to have a coffee," said Hubert to the Embassy driver in Spanish. Hubert had a strange feeling about flying to Larandia that he could not get out of his system. He got on the cell phone and told the watch Officer to give his team seats to the stand-by passengers (PAX). Since Hubert was a Lieutenant Colonel, he could make such changes. It was then that Hubert returned inside the coffee shop and told his team that Hubert's team would be leaving the following day. They asked why and Hubert told them that he had a funny feeling not to depart today. Hubert and his team drove to the Embassy, turned in their equipment, and returned to their hotels.

It was mid-day the following day when the MILGP Commander, Colonel Keen called Hubert and asked that he attend a meeting. Hubert had worked for Colonel Keen since his first deployment to Colombia, which made this meeting easier since the Colonel knew Hubert and trusted his judgment. The meeting was to discuss a rescue mission for the charter flight that had gone down near Larandia when it had mechanical problems with one of its two engines. Hubert and his team should have taken this aircraft to Larandia.

After the meeting, Hubert called his team and met where he gave them an update on our new mission in Larandia. When the aircraft went down, it was on final approach into Larandia when it crashed and none of the passengers was hurt. That was until the Revolutionary Armed Forces of Colombia (FARC) terrorist captured them. The aircraft crashed in a hill where the FARC was holding a meeting, which allowed the FARC to surround the crash victims. Like me, Hubert knew that they had family members who loved them and knew that Hubert's team would do their best to rescue them. The Colombian escort and American pilot once on their knees, terrorist put a bullet to the back of their heads ending their lives. As for the remaining three American passengers, they became hostages.

The following day, Hubert and his team were at the hotel and repeated the same routine at the Embassy where Hubert's team picked up our weapons and communications gear. Except on this day, Hubert's team took the charter flight at

Eddy's to Larandia. Once Hubert's team arrived, his quarters, was a building where US Special Forces were living. They were there to train the Colombian soldiers in Counternarco-terrorist operations. Hubert and his gunny were given the same room and since the US Army gave, their soldier's gear that included sleeping gear, Gunny gave Hubert a blow up mattress since in the Air Force Hubert's team normally did not get such gear. It really did not matter since it was always so hot and our window was a screen. Eventually Hubert found a fan and meals ready to eat (MREs) became our Normal meal.

Larandia was the training center for a new program where Compucinos who were young draftees who had just turned eighteen when drafted into the military. Since over sixty percent of the Colombian territory did not have any military or Police presence, the Compucinos would return to their hometowns and help fight the terrorist groups. To make matters worse, over sixty percent of the lands in Colombia lacked electric power or other conveniences that most modern nations had. Once the Compucinos and other former military soldiers completed their mandatory two-year obligation, they returned to the unemployment ranks.

"The FARC will do anything to recruit fellow members," mentioned Hubert to his team. The terrorist found a good source of work force. They also use colorful recruiting methods like killing family members if any one of these former soldiers refused. After the Revolutionary Armed Forced of Colombia (FARC) and other terrorist groups set examples by killing complete families except the former soldiers, they had no trouble recruiting. After all, most of these areas lacked military and Police to protect them throughout the majority of their country.

"This building will be our billeting rooms until this mission is over," mentioned Hubert to his team as they arrived in Florencia. Once Hubert's team put their gear at our quarters, we went to the Colombian battalion headquarters. Hubert and his gunny shared a room that had two cots and two medal lockers. Gunny gave Hubert his blow up mattress since the US Army provided many types of bedding materials while the Air Force provided none. With luck, Hubert found a pillow and a sheet that he washed in the washers and dryers that the Special Forces purchased locally.

"OK guys, let's go to work," yelled Hubert to his team. Now that he was the Senior Officer, he picked up command of a US Marine and US Special Forces teams with over forty specialized soldiers. It was during the trip that he became re-weapons qualified but in the M-4 rifle and his M-9 pistol. The primary Command and Control (C2) room consisted of a few telephones, a large map of the operations area, the primary operational US satellite radio operations by US solders 24/7 and a single ultra-high frequency (UHF) radio that belonged to the Colombian military and their solders. Hubert assigned his Intel (intelligence) officer and gunny to the primary planning cell. Hubert worked from the headquarters building or the Intel planning cell.

"Sir, the American's have been split up into three groups by the FARC," mentioned the Colombian soldier in Spanish. By this time, the American prisoners were on the ground moving and with our intelligence capabilities the rescue team to follow them in hopes of rescuing them. The rescue team was able to follow the prisoners as they quickly moved them on foot, on donkeys, or perhaps on trucks deeper into the Colombian jungles. Hubert knowing the Colombian military capabilities as well as his own military capabilities allowed his team to execute the rescue mission.

"Charlie Oscar one, Charlie Oscar one, this is Larandia C2 control, over," mentioned Hubert on the Satcom radio. Having served as the Air Force Mission operations and chief of the Counterdrug Operations Coordination Center (CDOCC) and past deployments, Hubert knew that how to employ the US intelligence, reconnaissance, and surveillance (ISR) assets assigned in support of Colombian forces. He also knew that the current CDOCC Chief received a commitment to Puerto Rico during this crucial week and that those in the CDOCC did not have sufficient experience. Knowing this, initially he knew that he had to take the leadership role and direct the US intelligence aircraft that were looking for the hostages. Based on the targets from the Colombian's, he deployed the ISR aircraft in an effort to find the three US hostages.

Hubert would serve as the Operations Officer for the rescue mission and a US Army Special Operations Lieutenant Colonel staff officer received the task as the overall Officer-in-Charge (OIC). In Hubert's view, this proved to be a major mistake since this officer did not understand how the Colombian military operated, did not understand the Colombian military capabilities, and not willing to fight for the Colombian military its political wars. This caused the Colombian military many lives in support of the rescue mission. Nearly two hundred young Colombian ground soldiers killed in action while attempting to rescue three America hostages mainly because the US Intelligence providers provided poor Intelligence information. Dozens of others Colombian soldiers were hurt or crippled for life for the same reason only because the US assigned an in-experienced staff officer as the OIC of the failed Colombian rescue operation.

The terrorist found a good source of work force when the Compucinos' or former military soldiers completed their mandatory two-year obligation returned home because in Colombia there were no jobs to return to that he had not already filled. They also use colorful recruiting methods like killing family members if any one of these former soldiers refused. After the FARC and other terrorist groups set examples by killing complete families except the former soldiers, they had no trouble recruiting. After all, most of these areas lacked military and Police to protect them throughout the majority of their country. Besides, with sixty-five percent of the Colombian territory lacking military and Police protection, the FARC and the other two terrorist groups had full control of most of Colombia. Especially, thanks to the drug annual monies from North America. The FARC a long made $5 Billion every year.

Once our team put our gear at our quarters, Hubert's team went to the Colombian battalion headquarters. The primary Command and Control (C2) room consisted of a few telephones, the primary operational US satellite radio operations by US solders 24/7 and Ultra/Very High Frequency (UHF/VHF) radios that belonged to the Colombian and their solders. Hubert assigned his Intelligence (Intel) Officer and gunny in the primary planning cell and Hubert worked from the headquarters building or the Intel planning cell. Later, Hubert's Gunny would go down country with a mobile combat team and try to locate the hostages. By then the hostages were well inside the Colombian jungles and impossible to locate. Historically, if within the first 72-hours, hostages not rescued, then the rescue will not be successful as was the case in this rescue.

By this time, the American prisoners were on the ground moving and with our Intelligence capabilities the rescue team to follow them in hopes of rescuing them. The rescue team was able to follow the prisoners as they quickly moved them on foot, on donkeys, or perhaps on trucks deeper into the Colombian jungles. Hubert knowing the Colombian military capabilities as well as his own military capabilities allowed his team to execute the rescue mission. Unfortunately, the US Intelligence information given to the Colombian military was not timely, which was causing more harm than good. A know fact in the Intelligence world it that having 'late Intelligence data' is like having 'bad Intelligence data'. In this case, the late Intelligence data proved to be deadly to the Colombian military and caused many lives and many injured soldiers.

Having served as the Air Force Mission Operations and Chief of the Counterdrug Operations Coordination Center (CDOCC) and past deployments, Hubert knew that how to employ the

US Intelligence, Reconnaissance, and Surveillance (ISR) assets assigned in support of Colombian forces. He also knew that the current CDOCC chief in Puerto Rico during this crucial week and that those in charge were not experienced. Knowing this, initially this forced Hubert to take the leadership role and direct the US intelligence aircraft that were looking for the hostages. Based on the unknown targets from the Colombian's, he deployed the ISR aircraft in an effort to find the three US hostages.

As Darlene yelled at him because she had to deal with home problems on her, own again, Hubert called her as he did from countless operations in countless foreign countries. He had a hard time hearing her since he had to walk outside to call her on the phone and helicopters had returned. They were off loading body bags of dead Colombian soldiers killed in the rescue mission. Nevertheless, calling Darlene had always been his lucky charm and one or two minutes on the phone with Darlene made him happy.

"El Tiempo is reporting two of the American's were killed today when their aircraft went down," mentioned Hubert. The local newspapers also reported that the XII Police Brigade was searching for the remaining two Americans. El Tiempo also reported that the aircraft was on its way to Florencia (Caqueta) versus where the aircraft being en route to Larandia. El Tiempo also reported that local officials were searching for three remaining occupants. Darlene had never really thought of what Hubert had seen or done during his deployments until this one. He mentioned to her that early that morning he had a cup of coffee with Captain Rodriquez who was a Colombian Officer and a few hours later killed in combat.

"I don't want you to witness anything," order Hubert. The two FARC members were maybe sixteen or seventeen year olds and seemed scared out of their minds. Although he had complete faith in the professionalism of the Colombian military, Hubert did not want to take a chance that he and his

US soldiers would witness some questionable acts during the interrogation. For now, both events would be part of his daily sit-rep (situation report) to the MILGP (military group) and the US Ambassador Patterson.

"Sir, the pilot was put on his knees and shot in the back of his head along with the Colombian escort," mentioned the briefer to Hubert. He also knew that the Colombian military had paid a high price in trying to rescue them. The Colombian escort and American pilot were on their knees and a bullet to the back of their heads ended their lives. As for the remaining three American passengers, they became hostages. Although this rescue mission would fail, Marc Gonsalves, Thomas Howes and Keith Stansell had become hostages for the next five years and five months. However, for now, Hubert knew that the hostages had family members who loved them and he knew that his team and Hubert had done their best in trying to rescue them.

"Sir, you realize that the hostages could have been us if it wasn't for you," mentioned gunny to Hubert. The following day, Hubert and his team picked up their weapons and communications gear took the charter flight at Eddy's to Larandia. Once they arrived in Larandia, Hubert received his quarters, to the US Special Forces Counternarco-terrorist Operations and living quarters. They were there to train the Colombian soldiers in counterdrug operations. Hubert and his gunny received the same room and since the US Army gave, their soldier's gear that included sleeping gear, Gunny gave Hubert a blow up mattress since in the Air Force normally did not. Eventually Hubert found a fan and everyone normally ate meals ready to eat (MREs) as their primary meals.

"His body bag was one of eighteen year old that had been offloaded from the U-1 helicopter," he mentioned to her on the telephone. Later that week he visited the hospital where he saw many young Colombian soldiers with half a face, that were paralyzed, or missing other body parts as their loved ones visited them. He knew that their lives would never be the same. He also knew that in Colombia, their lives of poverty had just gotten worst. They were the poor Colombian citizens, drafted into their military, forced to serve in uniform and would depend on their poor families with little help from the Colombian military.

Since the data from the US Intelligence, Reconnaissance, and Surveillance (ISR) aircraft not releasable to the Colombians, by the time the information designed as releasable, it provided little assistance in the rescue efforts. In some cases, when the Colombian Air Force deployed the air assault assets which consisted of four US Bell UH-1N Twin Huey and four Blackhawk's flown by Colombian pilots, many times the soldiers walked into ambushes and the landing sites had been mined with plastic mines by the FARC. On one day, 18 body bags were off loaded from the UH-1N of dead Colombian soldiers. Although the Colombian military had captured two FARC members, the interrogation determined little since they were only ground soldiers with little useful information. After a month, it was evident that the terrorists had hidden the hostages deep in the Colombian jungles.

Eventually our Colombian cohorts would run out of body bags and as the senior American liaison Officer (LNO) he would be the one making the call to the MILGP asking for assistance. The MILGP logistics Officer at first was more concerned with who was going to pay for the bags. By this time, the operation had been almost a month long and living in an austere location and constant operational environment made weakened Hubert professionalism. Hubert told the MILGP logistics Commander that he could use his VISA card to pay for the badly needed body bags. After all, countless young Colombian soldiers died trying to find our three American hostages.

Hubert had seen dozens of young Colombian soldiers die in action and had gone to the local hospital and seen young wives crying over their husband that had no legs or arms.

Knowing that their government would not take care of them for in Colombia, they had no medical coverage for the veterans and knowing that the US Government (USG) had already forgotten their sacrifice for America. Hubert had lived through the same experience himself as a US veteran ever since he first entered the Air Force post-Vietnam when called a baby killer at nineteen. Only because his Mexican born mother proudly became an American raised him to love and serve his country.

"The Helicopters are returning," mentioned his Intel Officer. The Intelligence Planning Cells were next to the Helicopter Landing Pads, which made it impossible not to see the comings and goings of the Colombians soldiers supporting the American rescue mission. Many times, Hubert saw the helicopters off loaded with teens that lacked parts of a face or hip and other body parts. At the hospitals when Hubert visited the soldiers, Hubert could see their despair knowing that they knew that their lives had changed forever. As the Senior American Officer, Hubert thanked them for their sacrifice on behalf of Americans. Hubert would take them bags with cookies or fruit to thank them for their sacrifice.

After all, Colombian President Uribe had recently spoken at the United Nations stating that it was because of the North American demand for the drugs that funded the terrorist groups in his country. In America, US Senator Carl Levin, D-Michigan, suggested that Colombian had not done enough to fight the drug war. Just after the death of Colombia's Supreme Court Justice killed by a terrorist bomb and just after a Colombian, female Senator had a bomb put around her head killing her. That same week the FARC killed one of Colombia's Supreme Court Justices. Once the cartels throughout Colombia no longer existed with the help of the US, the FARC and other terrorist groups have found their source of income. The FARC alone was making over $5 Billion US dollars each year and the paramilitary groups quickly wanted their share of the drug monies.

Another task that Hubert received was to escort General Hill the new USSOUTHCOM Commander, curing his first down country Host Nation (HN) visit throughout Colombia. Since Hubert had been to most Colombian military locations, he was able to provide his perspectives to the new Commander that proved new insights. As a result, new legacy internal programs established that served as the cornerstone for future organizational growth for US and Colombian forces.

Hubert was responsible for developing a long-term strategy for the Joint Planning Assistance Team (JPAT) manning requirement fixing the oversight for over one hundred forty permanent and deployed personnel at ten locations, seven radars, and the CDOCC. In this effort, Hubert was responsible for supervising twenty joint Officers, fifteen enlisted members, and twelve civilians not including the civilian drivers.

Darlene many times got mad with Hubert since she felt that at times he was too pro-Colombian and against Americans. He tried to explain that it had nothing to do with either nation, but specific individuals in the operation who lacked leadership or military skills that made him mad and say the things that he did. As a proud US military Officer, he had been in countless battles where those with higher rank made decisions to protect their careers and not what was best for the situation and the nation.

Hubert had been proud that he never worried about his career, did his best to accomplish the mission of the day ethically and morally conscious, and based on his military training. Throughout his career, Hubert's bosses had always told him that he was too idealist. Just as Hubert hoped to get a chance to relax, he received a new task to become the Mobile Training Team (MTT) Commander. This meant that he would have to return to the US after he put the program together in Colombia and then escort the Colombian members to Fort Benning. Of course, he would have to do all the work since no one knew how to accomplish the needed staff details both for the Host Nation (HN) and the US.

On 31 January 2003 through August 2003, Hubert would create and administer the new Intelligence Mobile Training Teams (MTTs) that would deploy throughout Colombia to train the Colombian Intelligence headquarters staffs. He was the first US Air Force Field Grade Officer to serve as Force Task-One, a highly sensitive bi-national US and Colombian Planning Assistance Team (PAT) program in Colombia. During the development phase, Hubert worked with the Western Hemisphere Institute for Security Cooperation (WHINSEC) instructors as the Country-Team Operational Expert in developing every aspect of the Mobile Training Teams (MTT) program.

After this MTT team, Hubert would create a new MTT team to train all the Colombian Services in a related area that took a month to create. Then during the final presentation at the Colombian Departamento Administrativo Nacional de Estadistica de Colombia (C. A. N.), Hubert received a request by Major General Roman, the Colombian Inspector General (IG) to inspect the training units as part of his MTT training program. Each month, each MTT team would return to Bogotá for a week to prepare for the following months three MTT training trips within Colombia. The week in Bogotá ensured that the program continuity received proper attention+ throughout the course leading to its success.

Hubert built the Colombian IG criteria into the MTT program, which MG Roma and General Mora, the Colombian XO approved during a presentation at the Colombian C. A. N. in Bogotá. During this presentation, MG Mora added the Air Assault training requirement into the MTT training program, creating the final program. Hubert then created and became the primary MTT Air Assault trainer for the first presentation, which approved. Then all the MTTs teams used his Air Assault training standard to train all the Colombian units.

As the overall Mobile Training Team (MTT) Commander, Hubert had divided Colombia in half and gave Lieutenant Colonel Omar Belique was given responsibility of training half of the Colombian military installations. Although Hubert had a fellow Air Force Lieutenant Colonel, he had decided that since he would be departing two months prior to the end of the MTT training, that the US Air Force Lieutenant Colonel would replace him as the MTT Commander. In addition, the US Army Special Forces Lieutenant Colonel would take command of half of the MTT teams as part of his training as a new Lieutenant Colonel.

Just prior to the MTT received approval and was activated, the US Army Special Forces Lieutenant Colonel Belique had activated a Reserve Officer on active duty for six months. In Hubert's view, he was too green to serve in a senior role. Belique required close monitoring since the MTT team consisted entirely of Field Grade Officers and a Government Service-15 (GS-15) that was equivalent to the Colonel grade was the senior member of his team and was the most experience member of his team.

However, initially Hubert wanted Lieutenant Colonel Belique to serve as a team commander but during the training at Fort Benning, a fellow Puerto Rican friend of Omar who was also the USSOUTHCOM Deputy Counterdrug (CD) Task Lead forced Hubert to select him to share the MTT Deputy Commander duties against his better judgment. A decision that the USSOUTHCOM CD Deputy CD Task Lead would later regret in time once his Colonel had to deploy to Bogotá Colombia to stop a mutiny levied against Lieutenant Colonel Belique.

Colonel Tom Russell received complaints from every commander of every officer that was under Lieutenant Colonel Belique command including the GS-15 all asking to return to the US as soon as possible. During the MTT teams monthly week at Bogotá, Colonel Russell met with Hubert and asked him what action he recommended for Omar. This had not been the first time that Hubert had helped a fellow officer from ending their career even when they deserved it.

From the start, Lieutenant Colonel Omar Belique had not understood that their Major Commands (MAJCOMs) to be part of this MTT Process Action Team (PAT) had handpicked every Major or Lieutenant Colonel, Field Grade, US Air Force, US Army Special Forces, and US Marine team member. Therefore, all of these officers were self-starters and did not need to be micro-managed as was the custom in the US Army or at least as was the custom of US Army Officers. Part of the problem had been that Lieutenant Colonel Belique had selected to team up with a Colombian Colonel, Colonel Sanchez was a fighter pilot who had a similar selfish personality. Hubert's Colonel, Colonel Pablo Parra-Rincon was a logistics officer and within the Colombian military initially felt subservient to a pilot within his military.

As part of Hubert's leadership training, he forced Colonel Rincon to become a senior officer and an equal "Colonel" once he understood the importance that logistics played within the military. In Hubert's view, every job within the military is equally as important. During the MTT training, Hubert as a rated master aviator provided all the MTT Instructors an Operation Desert Storm example of how the ground war came to a complete stop on day one hundred when they ground forces had to wait for logistics support. As Hubert stated, "The Iraqi Army did not stop the Coalition Forces. The Coalition Forces had to wait for bullets and fuel from the loggees".

It was due to many heated discussions between Hubert and Colonel Rincon where Hubert insisted that Colonel Rincon act as a Colonel. Hubert felt the Colonel Rincon should protect their MTT teams and demand that Colonel Sanchez not think that he could schedule all the best units with the choice cities as their primary training installations. As Hubert explained it to Colonel Rincon, Colonel Sanchez and Lieutenant Colonel

Belique were both acting unethical in this case and on many other similar other issues. On a different task, Colonel Sanchez and Lieutenant Colonel Belique on their own had prepared a presentation for the Colombian Inspector General (IG), MG Roma without first having the rest of the MTT review the power point presentation as required by the US Ambassador. Luckily, Hubert had prepared a similar presentation and had followed proper US Embassy protocol.

During the Presentation to the Colombian General who knew Hubert by name based on previous deployments as the Air Force Commander and Operations Officer, he stopped Lieutenant Colonel Belique who was giving the presentation and asked what he was saying. Hubert replied, "General with all respect I understand English, Spanish, and Spanglish, but I am not sure what the Colonel is saying". Lieutenant Colonel Belique was using some kind of new language in Puerto Rican where he spoke every other word in English and Puerto Rican Spanish with a heavy Spanish accent that no one understood.

General Mora and the IG General, MG Roma selected Hubert's team to go to all the important units and conduct the IG training presentations. Eventually, Hubert reworked the entire schedule when he made an idle threat to go to USSOUTHCOM unless both major divisions receive the same training distribution of sites. In Hubert's view, as a leader, taking risks is part of the leadership role. Within three months, not only were the US officers impressed with Colonel Rincon, all of the Colombian Officers learned to respect him as well.

Hubert replied, "In the Air Force, we don't get rid of problems, we fix them". During their private meeting with Colonel Russell, he agreed to let Lieutenant Colonel Omar Belique stay in Colombia as long as he understood that he would have to make leadership changes. Hubert scheduled a private meeting, witnessed by the Air Force Lieutenant Colonel with Omar where Hubert first made it clear that he understood that Mr. Rodriquez, the GS-15 that was in his team was also equivalent to a Colonel.

Therefore, Omar for the remaining three months would now work for him for the remaining deployment. Hubert made it clear that Omar was not to say anything to his team members about them going to their unit commanders to complaint. Hubert made it clear that if he heard any complaints from anyone that he said anything to any team member that he would be out of Colombia within two days. It would take a harsh threat to get Omar's attention since up to now talking to him as a friend and fellow Lieutenant Colonel by Hubert and the other Air Force Lieutenant Colonel had accomplish little.

Mr. Rodriquez had worked in Counterdrug Operations for over twenty years and deployed in Colombia eleven times. If Lieutenant Colonel Belique were smart, he would learn to listen to Mr. Rodriquez and become a better senior officer. Hubert explained to Omar that if he ever went to the Joint Staff that he would work for many GS-15s or higher civilian officers. Hubert also reminded Omar that all military officers worked for the President of the United States and the Secretary of Defense who were both civilians that may or may not have military experience.

At the end of this conversation, Hubert made it clear to Omar that at the end of his deployment that if he did a good job that he would write a good Letter of Evaluation (LOE) that would go to his unit commander that would not include anything about his mutiny. Especially since the military does not have mutinies and Hubert reminded Omar that in war, officers with his attitude seemed to be frocked. Omar had to learn to build leaders and not destroy his team by making them feel as they were worth nothing, which was a US Army norm, at least from an Officers view.

Barranquilla Air Base (AB), which was in north Colombia was the first unit selected for Hubert's Mobile Training Team (MTT) team. Mainly because it was, an Air Base and the Asalto

Aereo (Air Assault) portion of the course that Hubert created needed validation with the students that were the experts as the actual aircrew aviators. Since Hubert had served as a Joint Staff Officer, all other portions of the course received approval and validation. This was also the first time that most of the MTT teams would be traveling using their charter aircraft since traveling on Colombian highways was extremely limited due to the terrorist threat.

Since all team members traveled with their loaded weapons, many times, this caused problems for each team depending on the location. For example, once the team arrived at the Barranquilla Air Port, even though the team was traveling in their own private charter aircraft, the Colombian civilian police would not allow the MTT members continue to the aircraft with their weapons. In Colombia, the Colombia military and the Colombia Police and an ongoing rivalry and do not work together even though one would think that due to limited forces that both should combine their forces to fight the terrorist threat.

This rivalry between the Colombian military and the Colombian Police caused a delay in the teams departing Barranquilla and arriving at the next training location in northern Colombia. The next training location would be the first time American had been in this town or this area in over fifty years. The military installation was located near the Panamanian and Colombian border in the town of Monteria. Monteria is a municipality and city located in Northern Colombia and is the capital of the Department of Cordoba.

The city is located 50 kilometers (31 miles) away from the Caribbean, by the Sinu River. The city and region are famous for their distinct cultural heritages, which include a blend of indigenous Zeun Indians, African descendants, colonial Spanish descendants, and more recently, Arab immigrants. The city is home to the Sombrero Vueltiao, a national symbol; and is the home of Porro folklore music. The city has an inland seaport connected to the Caribbean Sea by the Sinu River. As was the custom during most training sessions, the Brigada (Brigade) Commander a Brigadier General insisted that his staff and the Mobile Training Team (MTT) go to dinner at one of the local steak houses, which proved to be an experience in itself.

At the end of day for of the training where the training all was going well, at the end of the day a convoy of vehicles was waiting to take the entire class to a local steak restaurant. In route, Hubert and the rest of the team noticed a Colombian Sikorshy UH-60 Blackhawks and Bell UH-1N Twin Huey aircraft Helicopters escorting them to the restaurant. Once they arrived at the restaurant, a squad of soldiers secured the restaurant while the helicopters flew overhead to make sure that the team remained secure throughout their dinner.

In addition, each member was wearing his or her weapons, as was the standard protocol. For the Americans, each member had their 9-Mil pistol shoulder holster and their M-4 rifles in a carry-on bag. Both loaded on in the safe position as were all other weapons in the room. This occurred as members drank beer and wine during the formal dinner. At the end of this trip, the MTT team returned to Bogotá before returning on another three-week training deployment in Colombia starting in Melgar, which is southwest of Bogotá.

Like many places in Colombia, driving in Colombia was dangerous. All team members carried a fully loaded M-9 Pistols and M-4 rifles with both weapons on safe. Both weapons were always available in each member's carry-on bag. This way if needed, members would be able to use them as soon as needed. In cities to the north like Santa Maria where teams had to travel to Barranquilla where the cities were only forty miles apart, where air travel was mandatory due to the danger from terrorists. An issue that Hubert had to deal with the US Embassy at Bogotá had to do with safety, security, and common sense all at once.

As a matter of practice, a civilian at the US Embassy had decided that all US Vans would have their lights locked in to enhance safety while driving. In Hubert's view first, the Vans were all the same type, large, the same model, and with the lights on, even a blind terrorist could easily see them from long distances and easily shoot at them. The same civilian would not give into not letting his team drive in between cities with their lights off. Therefore, Hubert was able to get the lights to come off by simply putting the emergency light on slightly, which turned the headlights off. This technique worked well and kept as a secret within the military channels.

Each student received an assignment of one of three teams. Each team received a task to create a course of action (COA) and then each COA received additional testing in a simulated environment. As the picture shows, every detail for every operation, logistics, etc. , planning, and executed from start to end and defended as a team. Then the COA officially received a review by the MTT team and presented to the Commander for approval who then selected the best COA. In this case, during this training, part of the class received a special selection for a real-world operation and one of the COAs became Colombia's first ever-largest Counterdrug Operation. It just happened to be the Fort Benning Operation introduced as the initial introduction training lesson plan and modified for the local Melgar local Fudra units assigned within this area.

MELGAR AIR FORCE BASE (AFB)
OUTDOOR THEATER

The first major Colombian Counterdrug Operation received its initial planning during the training at the Melgar Air Force Base (AFB) Installation. This installation is co-located with the Colombian Fudra (Special Forces) that also attended the training. Halfway through the training, half of the trainees disappeared and a few days later CNN reported Colombia's largest Counterdrug bust in its history. Unofficially, the same exercise routing, targets, and tactical deception tactics, etc. , were part of the overall plan for this Colombia Operation. Many of the Colombian officers received selection to this MTT team because they are expected to become future Generals within their Service.

MELGAR OPEN THEATER SIMULATED GROUND AND AIRBORNE
SIMULATED CLASSROOM TRAINING

Even during tropical rains, the MTT team did not stop their training. Using toys purchased at local Bogotá Malls or downtown toy stores in an effort to make the mockup training more realistic, each officer serving as a Subject Matter Expert (SME) played a specific role during the training in order to execute a specific role during the execution on an operation. Marines, Special Operations, Aviators, and Intelligence officers from the US and Colombian were part of the Joint Intelligence Mobile Training Team (MTT) that created each lesson plan and then standardized the entire program given to all the trainees throughout Colombia and every Service. Later, the Colombian Inspector General (IG) added the additional task to Hubert's team of inspecting specific units as part of the program and given those units.

The picture above show the trainees and instructors role-playing the ground and air operation from start to finish with all aircraft assets used by the Colombian military. Operations "Strengths and Weaknesses" receive approval as three Courses-of-Action (COAs) to the Commander who selects one. Operations use Army, Navy, and Air Force assets in all operations promoting a joint environment. Hubert and his US teammate used laptops and created power point lesson plans used by all team instructors to promote training standardization.

General Mora, the Colombian Air Force Commander approved all lesson plans.

BOGOTÁ 25THBRIGADA (BRIGADE) TRAINING PICTURE

The 25th Brigade consisted of the Sikorshy UH-60 Blackhawks and Bell UH-1N Twin Huey aircraftassigned to Bogotá. These aircraft main mission was to protect the president and the Colombian leadership assigned within Bogotá and Colombia. Their secondary mission was Search Air and Rescue (SAR) operations. Hubert's team received selection to train this brigade due to their importance of their mission within Colombia. During Operation OSCUDO, one of the Courses of Action (COAs) planned where terrorists were attacking the Palace, was actually used for this important operation.

HUBERT WITH THE 25TH BRIGADE CMDR. (GEN.) PRESENTING GRADUATION CERTIFICATES

During the training, the academic portion received the appropriate attention in the middle of this classroom. Each student from the rank of senior non-commissioned officer, to lieutenant, to colonel was required to take this training throughout Colombia. Every member from ever Service attended the course training each receiving a formal training certificate from this Colombian and USSOUTHCOM approved training program.

The training at Santa Maria consisted of training the 1st Brigada (Brigade) located on the border of Colombia and Venezuela. The first Brigada is on the beach near the coast not far from Venezuela and at the time under the command of General Parra. As part of his goal, General Parra in jest asked if his personnel could create three courses of action (COAs) where his troops would attack Venezuela. In his view, eventually

Colombia would go to war against Venezuela to take back the lands that have gone back and forth between both nations. Lands that hold vast oil and gold wealth the international leaders gave to Venezuela in the 1950s under the leadership of the US.

The MTT training started in normal fashion with no issues from the start. However, mid-week, the US Army officers had problems with their US government VISA cards when their Service did not pay their monthly bills forcing Hubert to pay their hotel bill. As the senior officer, it was Hubert's responsibility to take the leadership role and determine a short term and long term fix to any team problem(s). Eventually, he was able to fix their problems when he called back to their home stations but that took over a week. In the meantime, the MTT training continued without issue and the team completed the training on schedule and flew to their next location, which was Cartagena.

During July 2003, the MTT team traveled to Cartagena, Colombian and conducted their decision-making process training at the Colombian Caribbean Naval Forces. This training used new technology that would allow the remaining training and future training not only for this MTT team but also for other MTT and other training teams within the military more effective. Lessons learned received approval from USSOUTHCOM and implemented to other Major Commands (MAJCOMs). In the meantime, the Naval Forces, Caribbean proved to be top-notch organization that created its own training disk given to the MTT team to take with them for further consideration and future use.

Like most naval installations, the Caribbean Naval Forces proved to be a highly professional facility during an ear where a Russian submarine captured purchased by the FARC became part of the Colombian Navy. As was part of the normal training, the trainees created three courses of action (COAs) given to the Caribbean Naval Forces Commander for consideration. At the

Cartagena Naval Forces facilities, a new wireless network was used for the first time, which worked error free. In addition, the Caribbean Naval Forces trainees provided their own mockup items that provided the best training to date and earned them a special award.

Hubert would end his deployment as the MTT Commander in Cartagena, Colombia. His Colombian Officers would insist on giving him a dinner on the beach. Here they would give him a clock made at the local Colombian Naval Academy with the names of the different Officers to include the US Joint Officers. Hubert would fly back to Bogotá to catch his flight back home to Tucson after another long deployment. After this deployment, he hope to stay home for a longer period and not just a few weeks as had been the norm over the past years.

After doing some deep soul, searching and reliving the events since returning to Davis-Monthan AFB, Arizona Hubert realized that he would not allow these events to change how he felt about the new Air Force. He was proud of his accomplishments and knew that he had contributed to the achievement of national objectives for over three decades. He was proud that he had served as a mentor and good boss throughout his career. He was proud that many of his former Officers had gained higher ranks and experienced successful careers.

Finally, Hubert decided not to allow the recent Officers that he had worked for affect how he felt about the Air Force that had given him many opportunities over the years. He also realized that he did not have to thank any individual for helping achieve the success that he gained while in uniform. Nevertheless, he realized that it was time to retire since the new Air Force only saw him as a number and name to put on a deployment roster without any concern for him or his family. He would invite his current bosses to his retirement festivities.

Hubert not sure what Darlene's reaction would be when he told her that finally his retirement papers had been approved.

Although Darlene had loved the Air Force all of her adult life, she knew that it was time for Hubert to retire. She knew that he not happy with the Air Force and was ready for a change. Nevertheless, the job security and constant travels would be something that she would miss. The Air Force had been a good life but she missed the old Air Force that used to be a family. Military careerist replaced a close family that no longer existed that.

Before Hubert received approval to retire, he would have to deploy one more time to the Middle East. This deployment would truly be a Middle East deployment since although he would deploy to Qatar, as the Chief of Command and Control (C2), Hubert traveled throughout the Middle East fixing C2 problems. Hubert would be responsible for all C2, air traffic control (ATC), and all communications systems for US forces deployed in every nation from the Gibraltar Straits through Afghanistan. Part of the duties as the Chief of C2 included owning all the frequencies in the Middle East consisting of over 50,000 frequencies.

"Sir, the Kuwaiti AOC Commander just called complaining that our Combined Air Operations Center (CAOC) never picks up their hot line" said Captain Sanchez. The 612th Combat Operations Squadron (COS) team from Davis-Monthan AFB, Arizona had just arrived in Qatar two days prior. Every six months, different commands took charge of the CAOC and in this case, the 612th had just taken over for the Numbered Air Force (NAF) in Germany. Hubert asked Captain Sanchez to walk with him to the Qatar CAOC floor and talk to the duty Officer.

Hubert received notice for months that since he deployed for almost three years that he would not deploy to the Middle East with the 612th Combat Support Squadron (COS) team. Two days prior, one of his friends told him that he saw his name on the deployment list. At that point, Hubert had not completed any of the deployment requirements, which normally took months to complete. Although there were three other Officers of the same, Air Force Specialty Code (AFSC) code, his Commander said he chose him mainly because he was the most qualified. These three Officers had not deployed once overseas.

In Hubert's view, he was chosen mainly because he was about to retire. Within the last six years prior to retiring, Hubert's was deployed non-volunteer, nine months of every year except his Commanders did not have the character or integrity to tell him the truth. There were three Officers with similar qualifications, AFSC, and not deployed once. All of these Officers were also Field Grade Officers and not one of them considered. However, only Hubert was trying to retire from the US Air Force and had been denied retirement three times and stop-loss four times.

Somehow, Hubert completed all the training requirements but this also meant that he did not spent much time with his family. In spite that Hubert had just returned from his second six-month deployment in a row from overseas, his Commander was ready to deploy him again. In the last deployment, Hubert had been back in the US four days when he received a request to process out and deploy within hours for six months. It also meant that Hubert had just served as the Operations Officer and as Commander of large units during his most recent deployments.

Hubert's Commander refused to use the Letters of Evaluations (LOEs) written while deployed by two Colonels during his annual performance evaluations. After all, his Commander was responsible for twenty to twenty-five employees in a state side-training unit and Hubert commanded 140 and 245 combat Special Forces or Marines soldiers in combat environments while deployed. Hubert also earned eight combat medals during this time not mentioned in any of his annual performance reports.

For this deployment in the Combined Operations Center (CAOC) Qatar, within days, Hubert received a message advising him about the quarterly Air Route Meeting in Kuwait with the

Gulf Coordination Council (GCC). In this case, Hubert took a US, British, and Australian ATC Officer to this conference. At that time, civil aircraft entered Iraq from the north and south bi-directional with controllers assigning altitudes procedurally. The US had given Iraq automated systems but since the maintenance option not part of the program, the aircraft control systems quickly became inoperable gaining dust.

A side issue that arose came from the Iranian delegate who requested an east-west route from Iran to Syria. Hubert as the senior Coalition delegate stated to the GCC delegates that this not the right conference for this new agenda and that this new issue should be addressed in the future, which was agreed to and added to the conference minutes. The main recommendation that Hubert suggested was that only two routes created to replace the current Iraqi air structures. Two one-way air routes created with one south bound and one northbound route.

All civilian aircraft separated by five miles to ensure safety of flight. Military aircraft worked under visual flying rules unless they joined the civilian control structure. To ensure that the ongoing jamming problem over Bagdad not an issue, the both routes were includes a circle around Bagdad outside 100 miles therefore outside any possible jamming range. This new Iraqi structure eliminated the near misses that Iraq had in a combat environment. The goal that was achieve was to create a new airway structure that would expedite future safe transition of Air Traffic Control (ATC) and surveillance transfer from Coalition to host nation including Iraqi civilian civil air control systems.

At the same time, military aircraft were operating with some control from military radars. However, due to the size of Iraq and the limited number of US radars, very little radar coverage was available for US military aircraft. In addition, the Airborne Warning and Control Systems (AWACS) leadership inability so say no the National Command Authorities (NCA) led to a decline in aircrew retention. The lack of sufficient

Combat Aircrews, forced the E-3B/C AWACS Wing to stop all worldwide deployments for the first time in its history for two years in an effort to rebuild its E-3B/C AWACS aircrews.

As the CAOC C2, Hubert and his staff build, the first ever plan to include the E-8 Joint Surveillance Target Attack Radar System (E-8 JSTARS) into the Air Tasking Order (ATO). In addition, Hubert created a new convoy escort communications plan and execution order for 1-Marine Expeditionary Force (1-MEF) that the E-8 JSTARS would support in Afghanistan. In the meantime, Hubert had only eight E-8 JSTARS sorties or missions to schedule and deploy per month in Iraq and Afghanistan. Hubert arranged for the new E-8 JSTARS detachment, which commanded by one of Hubert's former Captain, Major Redman. Hubert and Major Redman discussed what the best employment of the E-8 JSTARS platform was and entered the E-8 JSTARS flying schedule into the Air Tasking Order (ATO).

From the CAOC consoles, the E-8 JSTARS data link picture as well as the Tactical Air Control Systems (TACS) data link pictures one could see 24/7. Especially, considering that the limited radar limitations were in theater in the Middle East. Hubert and his staff worked closely with the E-8 JSTARS planners to ensure their inputs were included in the CAOC plans or execution orders. To make matters worse, Hubert found out that the active duty ground radars augmented by the Air National Guard (ANG) radar units and could no longer deploy because they had deployed their maximum allotted days per law. All the data link pictures maintained at the Joint Interface Control Officer (JICO) within the CAOC.

The ANG unit that the 729th Air Control Squadron (ACS), Hill AFB, Utah was replacing was located in Bagdad. However, due to the increase in enemy Improvised Explosive Devise's (IEDs) throughout the Bagdad area, Hubert agreed that once 729th ACS arrived in-country, the radar unit should be relocate 150 nautical miles southwest of Bagdad to Ballad. Hubert had damaged his knee while running to the bunker as the Improvised Explosive Device (IED) explosion was in-bound to the Bagdad military installation. While running from the explosion, he had a severe twisting injury in his knew followed by a painful pop that in time had locking swelling and pain in his knees and left hip.

It was during this trip that Hubert had to go to Bagdad that Hubert while running to a bunker injured by an IED. This IED event reminded him in many ways of the Bomb in Bogotá, Colombia but at the same time was different. In this case, it seemed that he simply reacted to the overhead siren and like all the soldiers ran to the nearest bunker. He was not sure how he felt that the IED hit next to a Senior Airman running next to him taking off his right knee perhaps saving some of his body parts. He recalled pieces of medal flying in the air and going through his knees and legs as he fell on the ground with dust flying all around him. A few months later, another soldier from the 729th ACS had a similar injury by an IED. Hubert made sure that the Airman received his Purple Heart Medal. Being injured did not stop Hubert from continuing serving in the Middle East for an additional five months before returning to the US thanks to the pain medication.

In this case, since the ANG had just completed the Iraq radar coverage, Hubert arranged for a radar unit from the 729th ACS, Hill AFB, Utah to replace this unit. Once the 729th ACS arrived in Kuwait City, Hubert arranged for a Joint Tactical Air Controller (JTAC) to join the 729th convoy to Ballad, Iraq. The JTAC controller was able to talk to airborne fighter using Ultra/ Very High Frequency (U/VHF) radios request immediate Close Air Support (CAS) when receiving hostile attacks. Once in Ballad, the radar team set up their radar and communications equipment and became operational. The team achieved the regular immediate Close Air Support (CAS) requests in spite of regular threats by enemy IEDs.

When even new units arrived in theater, either Hubert or his deputy, Captain Sanchez deployed to the location to assist in the deployment. At best, by having a staff Officer early, this individual could make sure that the local staff was aware that the new unit inbound and coordinate with the outbound unit and prepare their departure. In Afghanistan and Iraq for the ground radars, Hubert deployed since he had the ground radar experience and the timing of the radar deployments did not occur during the same period. Hubert arrived in Kabul a week before the 1-MEF arrived.

In Afghanistan, that change over did not go quite as smooth. First, the marines wanted to accomplish a maritime landing with its 1-Marine Expeditionary Force (1-MEF) and convoy their radar to Kabul. Unfortunately, the 1-MEF radar arrived with broken radar. This forced Hubert to order that the Air Force leave their radar behind until the Marine maintenance personnel fixed their radar, which the Air Combat Command (ACC) exercise staff Officer did not like since the unit scheduled to participate in an exercise at Nellis AFB, Nevada. Since Hubert was in Kabul, he saw both the US Air Force and Marine radar technicians that stayed behind, tried to fix the 1-MEFs radar, and failed until both were certain of what parts needed worked.

Eventually, the Marine Headquarters determined that the only radar parts available would have to come from their training school radar. However, that would take another three weeks before the needed parts would arrive in theater. At that point, the US radar technicians and Hubert returned to Qatar. Once Hubert confirmed that the Air Force radar fixed and would remain operational, he released the US Air Force radar. Qatar was the departing location where all personnel took returning flights back to the US stationed in the Middle East.

Upon Hubert's return to Qatar, during a teleconference, Hubert tactfully reminded a Lieutenant Colonel Montgomery at ACC that the radar in Afghanistan used in a combat theater not an exercise environment. Therefore, Hubert made it clear to Lieutenant Colonel Montgomery at ACC that he would not release the radar until he knew that the Marine radar fixed. Hubert was amazed that no one had dealt with these matters prior to his arrival since these serious issues should have been pre-planned. At that point, Hubert was so tired that at one point during the video conference, he doze off and apologized saying that he had been up for the last three days working problems with little to not sleep.

Traveling in the Middle East was always a challenge since it meant trying to find a slick C-130 Hercules Cargo aircraft that was able to transport passengers. Since Qatar was, the main operating base for the Middle East, eventually, all military aircraft flew into or out of Qatar. However, this also meant that any passengers would have to sleep in the military terminal all night waiting for their military aircraft instead of being able to report at a certain time in accordance to their local policy. This meant that after working long days fixing problems, the Combined Air Operations Center (CAOC) team reported to the Kuwaiti Passengers (PAX) Terminal and slept all night on the PAX chairs until early the next morning to catch their flight back to Qatar.

Which problem would occur next was always a guessing game. In this case, Operation Vigilant Resolve had a new problem in Fallujah with predators and Close Air Support (CAS) F-15 Eagle and F-16 Falcon fighter aircraft supporting this operation kept missing each other when coming off target. The US military had just moved into its latest hotspot, Fallujah and Hubert as the Chief of Command and Control (C2) was at the center of this critical operation. The CAS mission normally starts when the ground solder calls in for an immediate close air support because they are taking hostile fire. In this case, they provide coordinated telling the fighters where to drop their bombs.

In the meantime, the predators try to get current intelligence information that might assist the fighter and ground troops jointly. Unfortunately, no one at the CAOC took the time to create a deconfliction plan for the predator and the fighter aircraft until Hubert arrived in the Middle East, which corrected the regular near misses. Hubert worked with planners to organize complex mission profiles over congested airspace in Fallujah and other hot spots in Iraq. The Kuwaiti Air Force in Kuwait City was hosting the Quarterly Air Traffic Control (ATC) Conference. Hubert deployed with his ATC team to Kuwait and left Captain Sanchez in charge back in Qatar. Hubert instructed Captain Sanchez that he would call him on his cell phone if he needed assistance. During the week, Hubert was on his cell phone regularly working C2 issues. Hubert also identified many issues that he took back with him that required further investigation including the Kuwaiti Hot Line and forty-one other critical issues. Within less than thirty days, Hubert and his staff were able to close all of these issues.

For this trip, the US Embassy assigned one of its US Army staff Officers to the visiting Qatar Combined Air Operations Center (CAOC) team as a diplomat. Major Vinnie lived at an apartment within Kuwait City, which allowed him free access to the city. Since Major Vinnie was driving an embassy vehicle, he had a tendency of driving like a maniac in the Kuwaiti highways. However, this also meant the Major Vinnie knew his way throughout Kuwait City and that the CAOC team did not have to take a taxi to their meetings.

For this meeting, Vinnie picked Hubert and his team at their hotel in downtown Kuwait City after joining them for breakfast. The team was staying at the Marriot mainly because it offered free internet service, which was expensive and the team needed the internet to email their reports each day. Although it was still a dialup service offered to all tenets in a common area, it was still free. What surprised the team that morning were two things. First, the way Vinnie drove on the highway since he had diplomatic plates. He drove like a manic never going less than one hundred miles an hour even after Hubert asked him to slow down. Second, when Vinnie stopped to fill-up and he paid thirty-six cents a gallon for his gas. In a way it made him mad that he had just fought a war for Kuwait that was thankless as part of OPEC and forcing the US high gas prices.

After filling up his gas tank, Vinnie finally drove the team to the Kuwaiti Air Force Base where the meeting eventually held due to its center location. This allowed members from all surrounding nations to travel to Kuwait for this important meeting. As the Central Theater Air Force (CENTAF), forward representative at the quarterly Theater Coordination Board (TCB), as the Team Chief of a multi-national group of airspace and Command and Control (C2) expert. That day alone, Hubert quickly implemented twelve critical standing Kuwaiti and Combine Air Operations Center (CAOC) fixes to open tasks on his cell telephone.

In addition, an additional thirty problems identified and Hubert took them to Qatar and the CAOC to work and closed them within less than thirty days. Hubert was the expert in the theater and invited to attend the Special Coordination Meeting hosted by the International Civil Aviation Organization (ICAO), Middle East Regional Office, Cairo, Egypt, as the military representative of the Coalition Provisional Authority (CPA). Initially, Hubert was not aware that this trip would be difficult like the airspace coordination conference mainly because of the Iranian demands that he would have to defend as not part of this Special Coordination Meeting.

After returning to Qatar for two weeks to the CAOC, Hubert deployed to Bahrain to attend the 19th Gulf Cooperation Council (GCC) and US Electromagnetic Interference Conference. As the Operation Iraqi Freedom/Operation Enduring Freedom (OIF/OEF) theater Command and Control (C2) and Communications expert, Hubert provided the badly needed operations expertise. Hubert was surprised at how inexperienced the group was when it came to operational and compliance issues. Hubert was responsible for fixing the Theater-wide frequency library that consisting of over 16,000 frequencies in all three theaters.

Hubert played a crucial role in fixing the Joint Spectrum Interference Officer (JICO) data link picture throughout Iraq and Afghanistan when he conducted a point-to-point site check. His checks determined that twenty percent of the sites had been down for years. Due to the redundancy of the network, no one knew of the outage. This problem had existed for over a decade without corrective action. Mainly, because of the lack of experience in the Chief of C2 in the CAOC position at Qatar and in Saudi Arabia prior to transfer to Qatar.

In the communications area, Hubert was still dealing with the IED jamming issue in Iraq and it was at this conference that he suggested that a working group (WG) be formed consisting of either the units Operations Officers or Commanders to deal with the Jamming issue that approved by the group. Due to the importance of the issue, the WG agreed that the group should meet within two weeks. Hubert found himself forward deploying more and more as he deployed outside of Qatar and found countless C2 and communications problems throughout Iraq and Afghanistan that had gone unnoticed by other COAC Chiefs C2. Based on his replacement, he not surprised. Hubert returned to Qatar for two weeks only to return in Bahrain in two weeks.

During our first week in Qatar, Captain Sanchez, who was the Communications Officer that worked for Hubert, requested approval to change all the nets (frequencies) in Iraq due to communications jamming. This meant that nearly a hundred frequencies changed in Iraq in an effort to stop the communications jamming throughout Iraq. During week two, Captain Sanchez wanted to change all the same frequencies again suggesting stating that they were bad frequencies. Hubert made it clear to Captain Sanchez that there is no such thing as bad frequencies and that there must be another reason that required further investigation.

The following day Hubert established a team that examined the jamming problem that eventually determined that the US Army Spruce systems, which is a smart jammer was jamming all military and civilian communications systems. In this case, Hubert approved the used on the new nets for Iraq mainly because the Spruce system was already jamming them and the US military units were not able to talk with each other. At the same time, Hubert requested that the US Army program, the Spruce system not jam the frequencies allocated calling them as TABOO frequencies. Hubert also requested that the International Civil Aviation Organization (ICAO) emergency frequencies not be jammed in accordance to international rules.

The following week Hubert directed that each unit deploy either their Commander or their Operations Officer to Bahrain to the Naval Support Activity Bahrain (NSA Bahrain) US Naval Forces Central Command (COMUSNAVCENT) Communications Squadron. Hubert also arranged for the lead jamming and Defense Information Systems Agency (DISA) experts deploy from the US to Bahrain. Hubert was surprised at how inexperienced many of the Deployed Commander (Detco) and Operations Officers were during the discussions forcing him to dictate what corrective procedures would be implemented.

The flight to Bahrain was much butter since Hubert traveled using commercial aircraft. Once Hubert arrived in Bahrain, a US military bus picked up this team and took him to their hotel. The return flight would consist of taking a taxi to the airport and having one of the Combined Air Operations Center (CAOC) staff vehicles pick the team up at the airport. Therefore, traveling commercial was much easier than traveling military travel. All travel costs charged to each member military travel orders.

Hubert and all of the visiting team were staying at local hotels throughout Bahrain and took taxis to and from NSA Bahrain. Since Bahrain was hosting the formula one race, riots were taking place throughout the city. Mid-week, Hubert's taxi driver, dropped him just shy of the rioters suggesting that his hotel was just down the road and quickly road off. When the rioters noticed that Hubert was in his US military flight suit, they attacked him throwing rocks and bottles at him hitting more than once. On a few occasions, Hubert fell on the ground but quickly got on his feet and kept running until he got away and eventually found his hotel.

By the time Hubert arrived at his hotel, the knees of his flight suit were torn, his knees were full of cuts, and bleeding. Hubert decided that since the mission was too important since soldiers were dying daily throughout Iraq, he not seek medical assistance until he returned to Qatar. In his room, Hubert cleaned his knees as best as he could and wrapped them until the following day when he went to the base Shoppet and purchased Band-Aids and medication. Although Hubert reported the event to security, he failed to get a copy for future use as proof even though he had medical documentation of his visits from Qatar.

Some parts in fixing this jamming issue were easier than others. For example, according to international rules, the Ultra/Very High Frequency (UHF/VHF) guard frequencies are supposed to use only in cases of emergencies. In the case of the Spruce or similar systems, the computer system automatically picks and programs any frequency that it picks up in the frequency speck strum and jams that frequency in an effort to stop that enemy IEDs from hitting its target. Then anytime that frequency if picked up in the future, the Spruce system jams it again.

Our team first created TABOO frequencies that included the Ultra/Very High Frequency (UHF/VHF) guard frequencies that must not be jammed. The second group of frequencies consisted of the Command and Control (C2) frequencies and other friendly frequencies that should also not be jammed. Within a week, the team created a plan to fix the Spruce jamming of Coalition assets throughout Iraq. Once implemented, the jamming issue throughout Iraq minimized. Other problems like having regular aircraft near misses every week also stopped in Iraq. Hubert returned to Qatar, went to sick call and saw a doctor who gave him pain medications and crutches.

Like Iraq, the Afghanistan air route structure needed rework mainly for the US A-10s, which made it much easier since there was little civilian aircraft flying in Afghanistan airspace. Once Hubert arrived in Kabul, he quickly met with the Coalition staff and presented his airspace plan. Hubert proposed and US A-10s allowed flying below Flight Level 290. Mainly because A-10s normally only fly low-level altitudes with the exception when they are low on fuel or flying over enemy airspace. Under low fuel conditions, aircraft fly at higher altitudes since the air is thinner, which maximizes the fuel usage.

In addition, due to the mountainous terrain, Hubert proposed the highest altitude possible even though he knew it was highly unlikely that the A-10 Warhog would not climb to that altitude. The issue being that man pads can be launched from the mountainous terrain therefore FL290 is not a high altitude in Afghanistan. Within 72-hours, Hubert's airspace proposal approved allowing the US to publish a new Notice to Soldier (NOTAM) published. This allowed US A-10s to fly safely in Afghanistan.

"There's daddy," said Darlene to Tawny. Hubert was still on crutches when he arrived at Davis-Monthan AFB, Arizona on the charter flight from Qatar. It had been six months since Hubert had left on this deployment. Hubert was still suffering from previous knee and back injuries injured in Iraq during this deployment. Now that he was close to retirement, he would be able to seek proper medical attention to repair multiple injuries that he had received during the past five years in Colombia and the Middle East. Injuries that Hubert was not allowed getting proper medical attention because his Commanders kept redeploying him overseas.

While deployed to Qatar, Hubert received an Permanent Change of Assignment (PCA) to Barksdale, Louisiana and 8th Air Force (AF) as the Chief of Command and Control (C2) doing the same job that he was doing at the 612th COS. At Barksdale AFB, Hubert would take over the E-3; AWACS duties know that the eighth AF had received the E-3B/C AWACS mission from 12th AF. However, taking an assignment meant that it would give Hubert a two-year active duty commitment and he only had eighteen months left before retirement. Therefore, Hubert declined the retention but had no problem taking the assignment.

"The change-of-command ceremony planning is not going very well," said the 612th CPS Assistant Operations Officer. Although the 612th CPS was Hubert's last assignment, it was also his worse assignment because he had never worked with Officers that lacked leadership skills overall especially at the Operations and Commander Levels during his last two years. Hubert deployed almost the entire time that he a member of the 612th CPS, the unit leadership kept assigning additional duties to Hubert because they knew that soon he would retire.

Hubert had been in the military far too long to complaint and the more jobs they gave him meant that he stayed busy. To Hubert, life was all a matter of perspective. Besides, he was working on his doctoral degree. Hubert also believed that what 'goes around, comes around'. Unlike Hubert's first two tours at 12th AF, the new Air Force was Promoting staff Officers or politicians, and not warriors or leaders. Without asking Hubert, he received the responsibility to arrange and execute the change-of-command for Slammer.

As was his custom, when told that he received the task, Hubert gladly took the planning role. Although the planning have been ongoing for over two-months with little success, within a week all the ceremony's requirements had been addressed the first practice received the task. What concerned him was that he had a doctor class residency in Phoenix for two weeks and last time, his Commander forced him to miss a week. This time Slammer did not when Hubert convinced him that he had plenty of time when he returned. Especially since, he had a good deputy and the Air Force preached 'delegation of duties'. Hubert returned with plenty of time to finish the planning, setting of the final ceremony, and party.

As was the custom, Hubert was at the ceremony where the new Commander thanked him by name for his efforts in making his ceremony error free. Hubert publically thanks the employees that help him who truly deserved the thanks. What was comical to Hubert was that Slammer chose to use this change-of-command input in his annual performance report and not one entry of his accomplishments from the Middle East to include the fact that Hubert awarded four combat medals, Commanded more enlisted, and more Officers than the Commander did in the 612th CPS. However, this had been the trend and did not surprise or upset Hubert.

Hubert called eighth AF and told the Colonel, a former past Officer under his command who understood. However, one he declined getting the needed retention, Hubert finally received approval to his request to retire after three attempts and being stopped loss four times. Darlene knew that she wanted to give a party but also knew that she would have to ask Hubert if it was ok since she would need money to pay for the party. Therefore, Hubert and Darlene jointly planned his retirement party.

First, Hubert decided to hold a small retirement party at the Non-Commissioned Officers (NCO) club on the day of his retirement ceremony mainly because he started as a NCO. During his retirement ceremony, the base honor guard posted the colors or the US flag before and after his ceremony. Hubert had two Officers share the official retirement duties, his

Commander, and his oldest Air Force friend that retired as a Lieutenant Colonel, Bob that he met in Spain in the early 1980s. On retiring, normally members retiring are award a retiring medal.

Hubert received the Meritorious Service Medal (MSM) for retirement, the Air Force Commendation Medal for the Middle East deployment, the Air Force Achievement Medal for a Presidential Mission that he had supported just prior to the Middle East deployment back-to-back, the Operation Iraqi Freedom Medal, the Operation Enduring Freedom for Afghanistan, and the Medal on War Terrorism. He would end his career with forty-five medals and forty-five ribbons followed by three additional medals after retirement. After the ceremony, the party hosted at the Non-Commissioned Officer (NCO) club until the official party that Darlene and Tawny held day at the Tucson Southeast ELKs for over two hundred invitees. His oldest Air Force couple Bob and Alicia would be at the party, which would make the party special.

HUBERT'S RETIREMENT SHADOW BOX

In addition to family from both sides of the family, military members, and ELKs members invited to Hubert's retirement party. As members entered the ELKs, two large tables were set side-by-side with pictures of Hubert and Family, his retirement flag from the USS Arizona, and his Shadow Box. His Shadow Box contained all his ribbons including the forty-eight medals and forty-five ribbons, controller and flying wings, and badges that Hubert had worn on active duty including his Joint Chief of Staff (JSO) Medal. His Shadow Box also contained one of every rank that Hubert wore as an enlisted and Officer on active duty.

HUBERT'S US FLAG
FLOWN AT THE USS ARIZONA

In addition, Hubert selected the flag of that flew at the USS Arizona versus Washington or at his State Capital. Mainly because he had deployed to Hawaii as an aviator more than once and wanted to honor his follow Arizonans that died during World War II (WW-II) in service of America. The USS Arizona was a Pennsylvania-class battleship built for and by the US Navy in the mid-1910s. Named in honor of the 48th state's recent admission into the union, the ship was the second and last of the Pennsylvania class of "super-dreadnought" battleships. Although commissioned in 1916, the ship remained stateside during World War I (WW-I). Shortly after the end of the war, the USS Arizona was one of a number of American ships that briefly escorted President Woodrow Wilson to the Paris Peace Conference.

The ship deployed to Turkey in 1919 at the beginning of the Greco-Turkish War to represent American interests for several months. Several years later, the USS Arizona transferred to the Pacific Fleet and remained there for the rest of her career. During the Japanese attack on Pearl Harbor on 7 December 1941, the USS Arizona was bombed. She exploded and sank, killing 1,177 officers and crewmembers. Unlike many of the other ships sunk or damaged that day, the USS Arizona could not salvaged, though the Navy removed parts of the ship for reuse. The wreck still lies at the bottom of Pearl Harbor and the USS Arizona, dedicated on 30 May 1962 to all those who died during the attack, straddles the ship's hull.

At the party table, the letter or recommendation to Officer Training School (OTS) that Senator Barry Goldwater, R-Arizona, gave Hubert was on one of the tables and his father in-laws Alfred's Korean Plague was included. During his last ten years in the Air Force, Hubert earned twenty-four of his service combat medals mainly because he stayed in hostile areas as reflected in his shadow box. The three of the medals arrived after he retired were not in his shadow box during his retirement party. Hubert received the Iraqi Campaign Medal, the Enduring Freedom Medal, and the Global War on Terrorism Expeditionary Ribbonmonths after Hubert retired even though he received three additional medals at his retirement ceremony. He had just completed a mission for President Bush, a deployment in Iraq, and received a medal for thirty-one years plus of service in the US Air Force.

Darlene had Tom Chestnut that play music and sang entertain the party. Tom Chestnut had also played at Tawny's wedding party. Hubert also had his doctoral classmate come from Virginia with his family to his retirement party. It truly was an emotional party for Hubert especially Darlene's speech at the party. Overall, Hubert's retirement was a week of partying by Hubert, Darlene, Bob, and his wife Alicia. He would have a dance with Darlene and Tawny with pictures taken that he would receive on email. Towards the end, the open bar would need an additional hundred dollars more than once otherwise ever thing else was taken care of during the retirement party. Especially since an additional fifty non-invited members attended Hubert's party, which he and Darlene had no issue with.

Thus ended Hubert's military life after over thirty-one years, four months, and twenty-four days of service in the United States Air Force of which nearly twenty-two years deployed away from his family including nineteen years overseas. For a High School teen, that joined the US Air Force to avoid going into the US Army at the end of Vietnam. Instead, Hubert would participate in every war that the US military was involved until he retired. Learning that US politicians should serve in the military for then they would not start so many wars. Because service members also called warfighters truly, hate wars. Wars that civilian politicians so easily send warfighter to fight in order to meet their political agenda without thinking of the lives they affect.

For Hubert who played as a young boy with his brother in San Xavier River and almost drowned and for a young teen that worked two jobs all his life until the age of twenty-six she would finally retire from the Air Force. After purchasing his home in eastern Tucson, Arizona sixteen years ago from Elmendorf AFB Alaska, for the first time in his life Hubert would know how it felt to live in his house seven day a week for one full year. Unfortunately, during the year Hubert deployed with his injuries without first receiving the medical care that he required. Medical staff or Unit Commanders that routinely told Hubert that he was faking his medical conditions, to keep him deployed overseas in hostile countries. By unethical Commanders that wanted to advance their careers at his expense.

Since Hubert spent most of his life living in overseas locations, once he started living in the US, what surprised him most were all the civil rights that he lost from the time he first entered the military. This new US reminded him of all the benefits the Air Force promised him when he first entered the military and the final benefits when he retired. Like magic, each year new politicians came to Washington that never served in the military and slowly took away promised benefits that military members once had. Just like the freedoms that Hubert once had when he entered the Air Force, in the name of Terrorism that almost took his life more than once, the same Washington politicians that never put their lives on the line took away the civil liberties that all Americans once had. At retirement, Hubert lost most of the promised benefits and was shocked that he lost many of the freedoms that he fought to protect for him and his family.

Nevertheless, Hubert was happy for he was home with his family for the first time in his life, full time, which was a dream come true. Throughout this time, Darlene served twenty-nine years, four months, and twenty-seven days of the time that Hubert served in the military. Even though the Air Force and most Americans give, wives and family-members little credit for their sacrifice for their service to America, Hubert never forgot all the military members and families that she helped in nearly three decades of service to America. Throughout the time, she touched many lives in the military at times more than many military members without receiving medals as Hubert did. With little thanks from the press and most Americans except her husband and a few fellow citizens who understood, what she went through, first hand.

ABOUT THE AUTHOR

Arizona author Dr. Rene H. Contreras holds several accredited degrees; a Bachelor of Arts (BA) from Saint Leo University, Florida; Masters of Business/Public Administration (MBA/MPA) and a Doctorate of Management (DM) in Organizational Leadership from the University of Phoenix, School of Advanced Studies.

Hubert enlisted in the US Air Force (USAF) during his junior year in high school under the Delayed Entry Program in order to avoid being drafted into the US Army at the end of the Vietnam War. While enlisted, he rose to the rank of Staff Sargent working as a Personnel Systems Manager. His first assignment as an Officer was as a technical school instructor, teaching student's fighter aircraft control procedures serving in Ground, Strategic, and Airborne Radar systems as a master rated Airborne Battle Manager (ABM). Rene has been married to his girlfriend (wife) Gail a happy thirty-five years and lived with his family overseas for nearly 19 years living in Iceland, Spain, Germany, and Alaska as part of 13 military moves, which ended in 2005 after 31 years, four months, and 27 days in the USAF. After retiring from the Air Force, Rene worked as a Principle Systems Engineer and continued teaching nighttime collegelevel courses since 1982.

Refractive Thinker®: Anthology of Doctoral Learners series, Volumes 1-V is his first effort as an author in addition to his doctoral and two Master theses. Rene has published hundreds of military, engineering technical manuals, dozens of US

Embassy Manuals in Spanish (i. e. , Spain, Colombia, and Chile), and is working on a book pertaining to his military experiences on Counternarcotics (Counterdrug).

You can reach Dr. Rene H. Contreras at e-mail: ctawny01@ gmail. com or caddyvibe@yahoo. com

REFERENCES

12th Air Force, (2006). *12th Air Force US Southern Command Air Forces [SOUTHAF]*. Retrieved July 9, 2006, from http:// www. globalsecurity. org/military/agency/usaf/12a

42nd AACS, (2006). *42nd Airborne Air Control Squadron (AACS) Airborne Battlefield*

Command and Control Center (ABCCC). Retrieved July 9, 2006, from http://www. globalsecurity. org/military/systems/ aircraft/ec-130e-abccc. htm

607th TCTS, (2006). *607th Tactical control training squadron (607 TCTS)*. Retrieved July 19, 2006, from http://www. luke. af. mil/607ACS/history. asp

513th ACW, (2011). *513th Air Control Wing (ACW)*. Retrieved October 31, 2011, from http://en. wikipedia. org/wiki/ Tinker AFB_Air_Force_Base

552d ACW, (2011). *552d Air Control Wing (ACW)*. Retrieved January 15, 2012, from http://en. wikipedia. org/wiki/ Tinker AFB_Air_Force_Base

Aerial refueling, (2011). *Aerial_refueling*, Retrieved October 31, 2011, from http://en. wikipedia. org/wiki/Aerial_refueling

AMARC, (2011). *AMARC*. Retrieved July 9, 2006, from http:// www. amarcexperience. com/AMARCDescription. asp

AN/TPS-43, (2012). *AN/TPS-43*. Retrieved January 15, 2012, from http://en. wikipedia. org/wiki/AN/TPS-43

Barry_McCaffrey, (2012). *Barry_McCaffrey*, Retrieved January 16, 2012, from http://en. wikipedia. org/wiki/Barry_ McCaffrey

Boeing_E-3 Sentry, (2012). *Boeing_E-3 Sentry*, Retrieved January 14, 2012, from http://en. wikipedia. org/wiki/Boeing_E-3_ Sentry

Boeing_RC-135, (2011). *Boeing_RC-135.* Retrieved November 17, 2011, from http://en. wikipedia. org/wiki/Boeing_RC-135

Bright Star Exercise, (2011). *Bright Star Exercise.* Retrieved November 6, 2011, from

http://en. wikipedia. org/wiki/Operation_Bright_Star

C-130_Hercules, (2012). *C-130_Hercules*, Retrieved January 15, 2012, from http://en. wikipedia. org/wiki/ Lockheed_C-130_Hercules

C-141, (2006). *C-141 Starlifter.* Retrieved July 23, 2006, from http://www. af. mil/factsheets/factsheet. asp?fsID=93

CFB Cold Lake, (2011). *CFB Cold Lake.* Retrieved November 30, 2011, from http://en. wikipedia. org/wiki/CFB_Cold_Lake

cv67. htm, (2012). *cv67. htm.* Retrieved January 15, 2012, from http://navysite. de/cvn/cv67. htm

EAFB, (2006). *Elmendorf Air Force Base (EAFB).* Retrieved July 9, 2006, from http://www. globalsecurity. org/military/ facility/elmendorf. htm

FAA, (2006). *Federal Aviation Administration(FAA).* Retrieved July 24, 2006,from http://etext. lib. virginia. edu/journals/ EH/EH37/Pels. html

Fairchild_Republic_A-10_Thunderbolt_II, (2012). *Fairchild_ Republic_A-10_Thunderbolt_II*, Retrieved January 14, 2012, from http://en. wikipedia. org/wiki/Fairchild_Republic_A-10_ Thunderbolt_II factsheet. asp, (2012). *factsheet. asp.* Retrieved January 15, 2012, from http://www. af. mil/information/factsheets/factsheet. asp?id=185

First Female General in the US Air Force, (2011). *First Female General in the US Air Force.*

Retrieved October 31, 2011, from www. ada. com http://online. wsj. com/article/SB10001424052748704358004575095933914399768. html

Gadsden Purchase, (2011). *Gadsden Purchase.* Retrieved October 31, 2011, from http://en. wikipedia. org/wiki/Gadsden_Purchase

Germany Navy, (2011). *German Navy.* Retrieved November 7, 2011, from http://en. wikipedia. org/wiki/German_Navy

Glücksburg, (2011). *Glücksburg.* Retrieved November 7, 2011, from http://en. wikipedia. org/wiki/Gl%C3%BCcksburg

HAFB, (2006). *Howard Air Force Base (HAFB).* Retrieved July 9, 2006, from http://www. globalsecurity. org/military/facility/howard. htm

HAWK, (2006). *HAWK and TOW.* Retrieved July 23, 2006, from http://www. redstone. Army. mil/history/systems/HAWK. html

JITC, (2006). *Joint Interoperability Test Command (JITC).* Retrieved July 10, 2006, from http://jitc. fhu. disa. mil/testing. htm

M1 Abrams, (2011). *M1 Abrams.* Retrieved November 7, 2011, from http://en. wikipedia. org/wiki/M1_Abrams

M60 Patton, (2011). *M60 Patton.* Retrieved November 7, 2011, from http://en. wikipedia. org/wiki/M60_Patton

Operation Just Cause(OJC), (1989). *Operation Just Cause (OJC).* Retrieved September 9, 2006, from http://www. globalsecurity. org/military/ops/just_cause. htm

Operation Torch, (2011). *Operation Torch.* Retrieved November 11, 2011, from http://en. wikipedia. org/wiki/Operation_ Torch

Keflavik Naval Air Station(KNAS), (2006). *Keflavik Naval Air Station (KNAS).* Retrieved July 15, 2006, from http://www. globalsecurity. org/military/facility/keflavik. htm

Luke Air Force Base (LAFB), (2006). *Luke Air Force Base (LAFB).* Retrieved July 15, 2006, from http://www. luke. af. mil/ history/lukehistory. asp

NATO Early Warning and Control (NEW&C) Force, (2006, July). *NATO early warning and control (NEW&C) force.* Retrieved Jul 26, 2006, from http://www. e3a. nato. int/

Oaks_bio, (2012). *Oaks_bio,* Retrieved January 16, 2012 http:// www. af. mil/information/bios/bio. asp?bioID=6629

Operation Desert Shield(ODS), (2006). *Operation Desert Shield (ODS).*

Retrieved July 15, 2006, fromhttp://www. globalsecurity. org/ military/ops/desert_shield. htm

Operation Desert Shield(ODSa), (2006). *Operation Desert Shield (ODS).*

Retrieved July 15, 2006, from http://www. globalsecurity. org/military/ops/desert_shield. htm

Operation Desert Storm(ODSa), (2006). *Operation Desert Storm (ODS).*

Retrieved July 15, 2006, from http://en. wikipedia. org/wiki/ Operation_Desert_Storm

Operation Desert Storm(ODSb), (2006). *Operation Desert Storm (ODS).*

Retrieved July 15, 2006, from http://en. wikipedia. org/wiki/ Operation_Desert_Storm

Operation Desert Storm(ODSc), (2006). *Operation Desert Storm (ODS).*

RetrievedJuly15,2006,fromhttp://www.gwu.edu/~nsarchiv/NSAEBB/NSAEBB39/

Plan Colombia, (2006). *Plan Colombia.* Retrieved August 20, 2006, from http://www. scramble. nl/co. htm

Record_bio, (2012). *Record_bio,* Retrieved January 16, 2012 http://www.af.mil/information/bios/bio.asp?bioID=6858

Red Flag-Alaska, (2011). *Red Flag-Alaska.* Retrieved November 8, 2011, from http://en. wikipedia. org/wiki/Red_Flag_%E2%80%93_Alaska

RSAF, (2006). *Royal Saudi Air Force (RSAF).* Retrieved July 9, 2006, from http://www. globalsecurity. org/military/world/gulf/rsaf. htm

RSAF AWACS, (2006). *Royal Saudi Air Force (RSAF) Airborne Warning and Control System (AWACS).* Retrieved July 9, 2006, from http://www. boeing. com/news/releases/2001/q3/nr_010822a. html

SR-71, (2011). *SR-71.* Retrieved November 11, 2011, from http://en. wikipedia. org/wiki/ SR_71

Tactical Digital Information Links (TADIL), (2011). *Tactical Digital Information Links (TADIL).* Retrieved November 4, 2011, from http://www. fas. org/irp/program/disseminate/tadil. htm

TAFBa, (2006). *Tyndall Air Force Base (TAFB).* Retrieved July 9, 2006, from http://www. globalsecurity. org/military/facility/elmendorf. htm

TAFBb, (2006). *Tyndall Air Force Base (TAFB).* Retrieved July 16, 2006, from http://www. united-publishers. com/TyndallGuide/history. html

Uribe-a, (2002). *President-elect pushes law and order for Colombiaof siege*. Retrieved September 9, 2006, from http://english. people. com. cn/200205/28/eng20020528_96602. shtml

Uribe-b, (2002). *Uribe-b*. Retrieved January 16, 2012, from August 20, 2006, from http://www. turkishpress. com/news. asp?id=136710

USS_Yorktown_(CV-5), (2010). *USS_Yorktown_(CV-5)*. Retrieved January 16, 2012, from http://en. wikipedia. org/wiki/USS_Yorktown_(CV-5)

Wesley_Clark, (2012). *Wesley_Clark*, Retrieved January 16, 2012, from http://en. wikipedia. org/wiki/Wesley_Clark

Would you like to see your manuscript become a book?

If you are interested in becoming a PublishAmerica author, please submit your manuscript for possible publication to us at:

acquisitions@publishamerica.com

You may also mail in your manuscript to:

**PublishAmerica
PO Box 151
Frederick, MD 21705**

We also offer free graphics for Children's Picture Books!

---

www.publishamerica.com

CPSIA information can be obtained at www.ICGtesting.com
Printed in the USA
BVOW080504210912

301012BV00003B/62/P